QUEBEC: A HISTORY 1867-1929

QUEBEC
A HISTORY
1867-1929

Paul-André Linteau
René Durocher
Jean-Claude Robert

Translated by Robert Chodos

James Lorimer & Company, Publishers
Toronto, 1983

et j'ai hâte à il y a quelques années
l'avenir est aux sources

Gaston Miron

Originally published as *Histoire du Québec Contemporain: De la Confédération à la crise (1867-1929).*

ISBN 0-88862-604-5 paper
0-88862-605-3 cloth

Design: Don Fernley
Cover illustration: Public Archives of Canada

Canadian Cataloguing in Publication Data

Linteau, Paul-André, 1946-
Quebec: a history 1867-1929

Translation of Histoire du Québec contemporain Vol. I (1867-1929).
Bibliography: p. 564
Includes index.

1. Quebec (Province) — History — 1867-1897.*
2. Quebec (Province) — History — 1897-1936.*
I. Robert, Jean-Claude, 1943- II. Durocher, René, 1938- III. Title.

FC2911.L5513 971.4'03 C82-095029-7
F1053.L5613

This book has been published with the help of a grant from the Social Science Federation of Canada, using funds provided by the Social Sciences and Humanities Research Council of Canada.

The translation of this book was made possible by a grant from the Canada Council.

James Lorimer & Company, Publishers
Egerton Ryerson Memorial Building
35 Britain Street
Toronto, Ontario M5A 1R7

Printed and bound in Canada

CONTENTS

List of Tables *xi*

List of Maps *xiii*

List of Figures *xiv*

Preface *xv*

PART I: LAND AND POPULATION 1867-1929 1

1. The Land 4
   An American Land 4
   The Settlement of the Land 6
   The Shaping of Physical Space 10
2. Population 18
   Natural Increase 20
   Migration 28
3. Ethnic and Linguistic Groups 37
   Ethnic Composition 37
   Linguistic Evolution 49

PART II: 1867-1896 55

THE ECONOMY 57

4. The Wider Context 59
   The Empire and Canada 59

Two Interpretations of Canada's Development 67
Difficult Economic Circumstances 71
5. Internal Factors 74
An Expanding Market 74
The Transportation Network 75
The Commercial and Financial Sectors 87
Economic Policy 91
6. The Agricultural and Forest Sectors 96
Agriculture 97
Colonization 104
The Forest Industry 110
7. Industry and the City 116
Industrialization 116
Urbanization 126

SOCIETY 139

8. Social Structure 140
The Bourgeoisie 142
The Petty Bourgeoisie 148
The Working Class 149
Rural Quebecers 153
9. Living Conditions 156
Urban Life 156
Working Conditions 166
Rural Life 169
Charity 172
10. The Labour Movement 178
The Rise of the Trade Union Movement 178
The Goals of the Labour Movement 182
Labour Legislation 184
11. The Status of Women 186
Women's Inferior Status 186
A Doubly Exploited Labour Force 189
The First Stages of Organization 194
12. Two Key Institutions 195
The Churches 195
The Educational System 205

POLITICS 215

13. A Liberal State 216
The Distribution of Powers 217

The Role of the State 220
Institutions 226
Politicians 228
14. Political Development 230
The Parties 230
The Succession of Governments 240
15. The Federal Government and Quebec 254
Quebecers and Federal Institutions 254
The Political Ascendancy of Ottawa 256
Relations between Governments 257

CULTURE AND IDEOLOGY 263

16. New Themes 264
Ideologies and Socio-Economic Structures 264
Ideologies and Socio-Political Organization 268
Forms of Nationalism 274
17. Culture 281
Literature 282
Painting and Sculpture 292

PART III: 1896-1929 303

THE ECONOMY 305

18. Natural Resources and Industrialization 308
A New Industrial Front 308
The Major Sectors 309
19. Manufacturing Production 322
The Growth of the Traditional Sectors 322
A Lagging Economy? 329
20. Monopoly Capitalism and Foreign Investment 332
Competition and Concentration 332
Foreign Investment 335
21. Commerce and Communications 340
Transportation 340
Communications 348
Commerce and Credit 349
22. Quebec: An Urban Society 356
Widespread Urban Growth 356
Metropolis and Capital 359
Other Cities and Towns 369
23. The Economy of Rural Quebec 373

The Producers 373
A More Balanced Output 375
Expanding Markets 380
Farms and Farming Techniques 382
Colonization and the Forest Industry 386
24. Economic Policies 390
Quebec Government Policies 390
The Impact of Federal Policies 394

SOCIETY 398

25. Bourgeoisie and Petty Bourgeoisie 399
The Capitalist Class and the Concentration of Power 399
The Decline of the Middle Bourgeoisie 402
The Position of French Canadians 403
Bourgeois Institutions 405
The Petty Bourgeoisie 406
26. The Working Class and the Labour Movement 408
Militancy and Expansion, 1896-1914 409
Competition and Weakness, 1914-29 412
Labour Legislation 415
27. Rural Quebecers 421
Farmers' Co-operatives 422
Farmers' Organizations 425
28. Living Conditions 427
Rural Life 427
A Culture of Poverty 429
A Hesitant Government 436
29. Women and the Feminist Movement 441
Ladylike Feminism 446
The Struggle for Equality and the Right to Vote 447
30. Religion and Education 451
Religious Institutions 451
Education 460

POLITICS 476

31. New Roles for the State 477
New Directions 477
Public Finances 478
The Bureaucracy 481
Politicians 484
32. Political Parties and Movements 485

Party Structure 485
The Liberal Party: Stability and Continuity 486
The Trials of the Conservative Party 487
The Nationalist Movement 489
The Parti Ouvrier 495
The Reform Associations 497
Electoral Legislation and Practice 497
33. The Reign of the Liberals 501
Premiers in Laurier's Shadow: Marchand and Parent 501
Lomer Gouin 506
Louis-Alexandre Taschereau 511
34. Federal-Provincial Relations 515
A New Balance 515
Quebec's Struggle for Autonomy 518
French Canadians and the Federal Government 520
The Conscription Crisis 522

CULTURE AND IDEOLOGY 527

35. Ideologies 528
The Triumph of Liberalism 528
The Clerical-Nationalist Resistance 532
Ideology in the Working Class 539
36. Culture 541
Literature 541
Painting 552

General Bibliography 564
Research Tools 564
General Works 565

Bibliographies by Chapter 566

Illustration Credits 590

Index 592

TABLES

1 Population of Quebec and of the Rest of Canada, 1871-1931 19
2 Birth Rate per 1,000 Population, Quebec and Ontario, 1866-1930 20
3 General Fertility Rate, Quebec and Ontario, 1871-1931 21
4 Number of Live Births per Married Woman of French Mother Tongue by

Age and Place of Residence, Quebec, 1961 22
5 Average Annual Death Rates, Quebec, 1884-1930 23
6 Infant Mortality Rate, Quebec as a Whole and Montreal, 1871-1929 25
7 Estimated Net Emigration to the United States from Canada as a Whole and Quebec, 1840-1940 29
8 Population of Quebec by Regions, 1871, 1901, 1931 33
9 Population of Canada, Population of Quebec and French-Canadian Population, 1871-1931 38
10 Distribution of Quebec's Population by Ethnic Origin, 1851-1931 40
11 Quebecers of English, Scottish and Irish Origin as a Percentage of the Total Population, 1871, 1901, 1931 42
12 Ethnic Groups of Other than French and British Origin in Quebec, 1871, 1901, 1931 44
13 Distribution of Ethnic Groups between Montreal Island and the Rest of Quebec, 1871, 1901, 1931 48
14 Ethnic Composition of the Population of Montreal Island, 1871, 1901, 1931 48
15 Mother Tongue of Quebec's Population by Ethnic Group, 1931 50
16 Distribution of Quebec's Population by Official Languages Spoken, 1931 52
17 Economic Cycles in Quebec, 1862-1896 72
18 Chartered Banks Headquartered in Quebec, 1867-1896 90
19 Principal Wood Products, Quebec, 1870-1900 112
20 Value of Manufacturing Production in Dollars, Quebec, 1861-1901 120
21 Four Montreal Shoe-Manufacturing Enterprises, 1871 122
22 Percentage of the Population Living in Urban Areas, Quebec, Ontario and Canada, 1851-1901 128
23 Population of Major Urban Centres in Quebec, 1861-1901 130
24 Legal Status of Married Women as Defined in the Quebec Civil Code, 1866-1915 187
25 Representation of Each Sex in the Teaching Profession, 1854-1898 213
26 Clericalization of Catholic Teaching, 1853-1897 213
27 Average Annual Salaries of Quebec Teachers, 1894-1895 214
28 Quebec General Elections, 1867-1897 231
29 Premiers of Quebec, 1867-1897 241
30 Gross Value of Quebec Manufacturing Production and Value Added, 1900-1929 324
31 Average Annual Rate of Growth of Quebec Manufacturing Production, 1900-1930 326

32 Percentage of Total Gross Value of Quebec Manufacturing Production Represented by Particular Groups of Industries, 1900-1929 327
33 Foreign Investment in Canada, 1900-1930 336
34 Percentage Distribution of Foreign Investment in Canada by Country of Origin, 1900-1930 337
35 Number of Motor Vehicles Registered in Quebec and Ontario, 1906-1930 346
36 Assets of Banks Headquartered in Quebec, 1913-1929 354
37 Percentage of Population Living in Urban Areas, Quebec, Ontario and Canada, 1901-1931 356
38 Urban Population in the St. Maurice Valley and Saguenay/Lake St. John Regions, 1901-1931 358
39 Number of Cities, Towns and Villages Incorporated in Quebec, 1901-1931 359
40 Population of Major Urban Centres in Quebec, 1901-1931 370
41 Percentage Distribution by Sector of Net Production, 1922, 1926, 1929 375
42 Gross Value of Agricultural Production, 1890-1929 376
43 Percentage Distribution of Agricultural Income by Components, 1918-1929 377
44 Percentage Distribution of Farms by Size, 1901-1931 382
45 Principal Wood Products, Quebec, 1900-1930 389
46 Directorships Held by Herbert S. Holt, 1912 401
47 Students and Teachers in Quebec Schools, 1901, 1931 470
48 Catholic and Protestant Students in Selected Faculties in Quebec Universities, 1901, 1929 472
49 Current Revenues and Expenditures of the Quebec Government, 1897-1929 479
50 Percentage Distribution of Quebec Government Revenues, 1912, 1929 479
51 Percentage Distribution of Quebec Government Expenditures, 1912, 1929 480
52 Quebec Provincial General Elections, 1897-1931 502
53 Distribution between the Two Major Parties of Quebec Seats in the House of Commons, 1896-1926 522

MAPS

1 Quebec in 1931 xx
2 The Natural Regions of North America 5

3 Quebec's Changing Borders, 1867-1927 *7*

4 The Natural Regions of Quebec *9*

5 The Inhabited Regions of Quebec *12*

6 Major Railways in Late-Nineteenth-Century Quebec *77*

7 Quebec's Urban Network, 1901 *127*

8 Montreal Wards in the Late Nineteenth Century *133*

9 New Railway Lines Built in the Early Twentieth Century *341*

10 Annexations in Montreal, 1883-1918 *363*

11 Quebec City Wards, about 1914 *368*

12 Infant Mortality in the Various Wards of Montreal, 1922 *433*

FIGURES

1 Quebec's Age Pyramid, 1871, 1901, 1931 *27*

2 Percentage of Gross Value of Canadian Manufacturing Production Accounted for by Quebec and Ontario, 1900-1930 *325*

3 General Mortality Rate, Montreal and Toronto, 1897-1931 *431*

4 Infant Mortality Rate, Montreal and Toronto, 1897-1931 *431*

PREFACE

In the last twenty years, modern Quebec history has been increasingly in vogue. The infatuation with New France that was a long-standing characteristic of Quebec historiography has given way to a growing interest in more recent history — related, no doubt, to the political awakening of the 1960s.

Everyone who has explored this new field has deplored the absence of a book offering an overview of the period. Our experience as teachers and researchers has made us aware of the need for a work that would also reach the non-specialist who seeks a deeper understanding of present-day Quebec by studying its recent history.

There are syntheses available, but those published so far cover a long period, starting with New France, and the modern era is treated as something of an afterthought. Robert Rumilly's vast forty-one-volume chronicle, *Histoire de la province de Québec*, cannot take the place of a synthesis. There have been specialized studies published in the last few years, but no real overview. Filling this need is the task we have set for ourselves.

We do not conceive of history as a collection of dates or a portrait gallery. We are interested in change over time, and we have tried to understand and explain the significant phenomena and major transformations that have affected Quebec society. We have also tried to include elements of the contributions that all the social sciences can make to history, and to take different interpretations into account.

Our approach is territorial, in that our interest is in the events that have occurred within the territory of Quebec and the men and women who have lived there. We have maintained a consistent meaning for the word 'Quebecer' throughout the book. It denotes every resident of Quebec, whether his ancestors came from the northwest thousands of years ago or from France at the time of Jean Talon, whether they were Scots who crossed the Atlantic in 1780 or Irishmen fleeing the Famine or Jews trying to escape persecution in eastern Europe. We have not written a history of French Canadians, although they play a large role in this book. Nor have we written a history of Canada. Events in Canada as a whole have, of course, had considerable influence on the course of Quebec history, but we have limited ourselves to describing their effects on Quebec. Interested readers will find in the many works on Canadian history a fuller treatment of the Canadian context; in particular, the Canadian Centenary Series is a useful complement to this book.

We are interested here in modern Quebec. In our view, the modern period began with industrialization, which led to major socio-economic, political, ideological and cultural transformations. These changes began to appear in the mid-nineteenth century in Montreal and somewhat later in other centres. Confederation was also an event of some significance in that it began a new stage in the orientation of Quebec society. We have therefore taken 1867 as our point of departure, although we have not treated it as a complete break with the past. Not all events can be periodized in the same way, and we have not hesitated to go back a few years or a few decades where necessary.

While this is the first synthesis for this period, historians and social scientists in the last fifteen years have written a large number of articles, theses and books dealing with particular aspects of Quebec history. Some of these researchers have made substantial contributions to the field. The work of Jean Hamelin has been especially notable, and in his double role as scholar and guiding spirit, he has contributed more than anyone else to the growth and dynamism of research into modern Quebec. We stand on the shoulders of our predecessors, but our work is the result of our own research as well. The opportunity we have had to teach modern Quebec history to large numbers of university students has helped us acquire an overview of historical problems. We have also ventured to formulate new interpretations and explore unconventional perspectives on a number of questions.

Our attempt at a synthesis has, however, been limited by the state of Quebec historiography. Because interest in modern history in Quebec is relatively new, some fields are still undeveloped. For example, almost nothing is known about the history of Quebec City between 1870 and 1930, conditions of rural life at the time of the First World War or the state of the teaching profession at the turn of the century. It was clearly impossible for us to carry out detailed studies in all areas where information is scanty, and our synthesis reflects the current state of historical knowledge.

Despite the shortcomings of research, the history of Quebec is rich and complex, and the scope of the task led us to divide it into two volumes, of which this is the first. It deals with the period 1867-1929, covering a time of profound change during which Quebec was transformed from a rural to an industrial society. During this period, Quebec's infrastructure — railways, roads, harbours — was put in place. The telephone, electricity and the automobile were among the inventions that upset the continuity of daily life. The spread of education contributed to the development of mass media: large-circulation newspapers, magazines, catalogues and, at the end of the period, radio. The conditions under which Quebecers lived and worked in 1929 were very different from those that prevailed in 1867. We had no trouble choosing 1929 as the closing date of the first volume, as this date in some ways marks the end of an era. In the two decades after 1929, Quebec was shaken by the Great Depression and the Second World War, out of which new economic, social and political transformations developed. We will discuss these transformations in a second volume, in which the history of modern Quebec will be brought up to the present.

We have chosen to divide our subject into themes rather than treat it as a strict chronology. This method has the advantage of allowing a much more systematic and coherent examination of each dimension in the life of a society. As often as possible, we have noted the interconnections among the different themes. We have divided the period into two sub-periods — 1867-1896 and 1896-1929 — and for each of these we deal with economic, social, political, cultural and ideological history in turn. However, changes in geography and population occur at a slower pace, and we thought it preferable to deal with these subjects only once, for the entire period 1867-1929.

Because this is a work of synthesis, we have not included notes at the bottom of each page. At the end of the book, a bibliography refers the reader to the major works that have appeared on the subject-matter of each chapter. This will be only a starting point for the interested reader, who will find suggestions for further avenues to follow in the works cited. As for the illustrations, we did not include them simply to make the book more attractive. We consider old drawings, paintings and photographs pieces of evidence that help us understand an era. These illustrations cast additional light on the text and are often complementary to it.

This book truly has been the result of a collective effort. We established the initial conception and did the detailed planning of the book as a team. We then divided it into sections to be written by each author according to his areas of specialization, particular interests and availability; not all the authors participated equally in the actual writing. But the manuscript as a whole was then reread, discussed and revised collectively. The collaboration was fruitful and stimulating for all of us.

Our colleague Robert Comeau was a member of the group at the beginning and participated in the initial planning sessions, but he subsequently had to withdraw from the project and did not participate in the writing of the book. In addition, we called on two outside collaborators to deal with cultural history. François-Marc Gagnon, an art historian, wrote the parts on painting and sculpture, while Sylvain Simard wrote the sections dealing with his area of specialization, literary history.

We would like to thank our colleagues who helped us in a variety of ways, especially Normand Séguin and Fernand Harvey, who read the manuscript carefully and critically, and Jean-Paul Bernard and Marta Danylewycz, who commented on certain sections. We would also like to thank our editor, Antoine Del Busso, who assisted us at all stages of the book's production in the original French-language edition.

For this edition, the translator, Robert Chodos, deserves special thanks. The discussions we had with him proved very fruitful for all of us. We appreciated his dedication and the great care he took in his work. The editorial work of Ted Mumford and Jean Wilson was also greatly appreciated.

Paul-André Linteau
René Durocher
Jean-Claude Robert

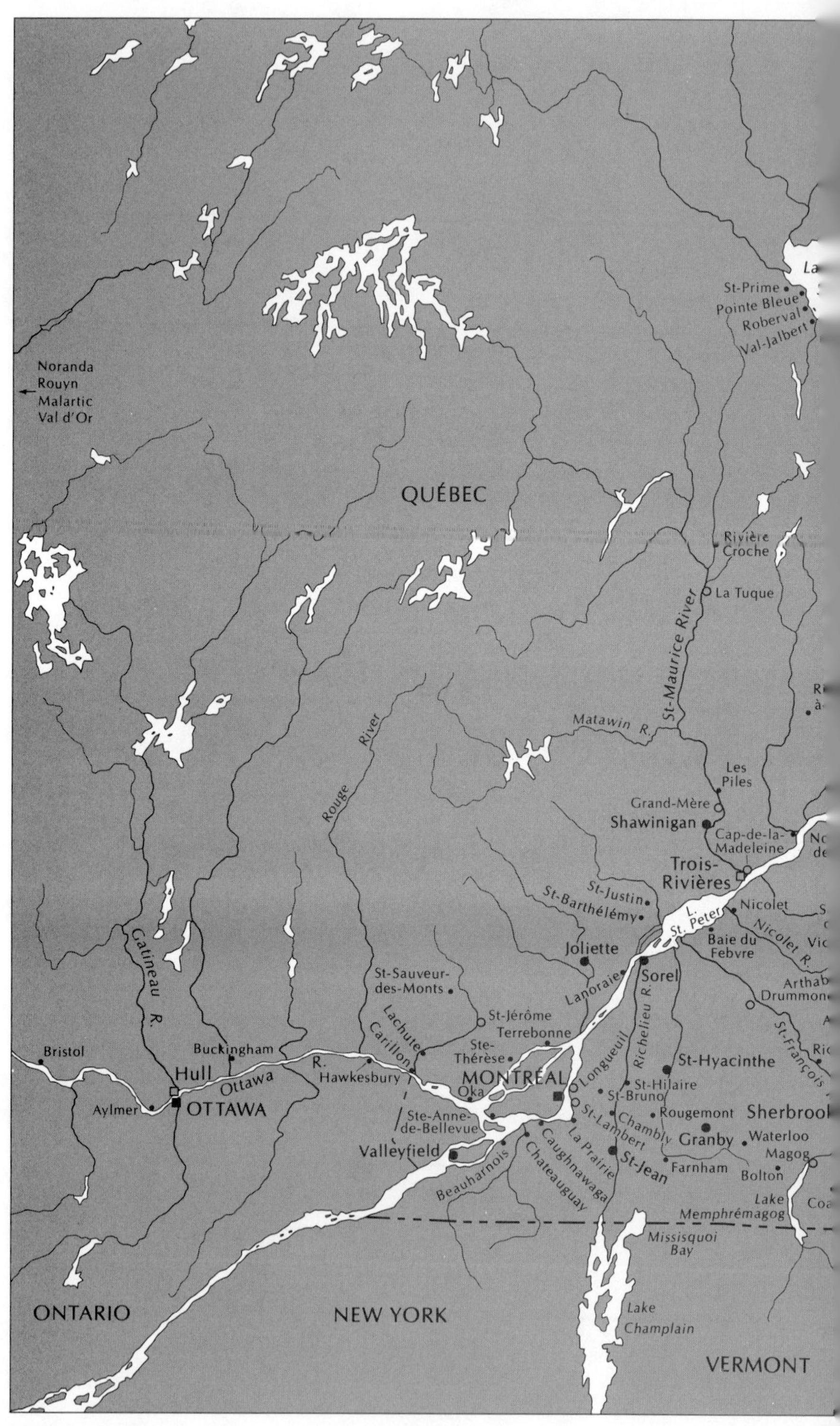

MAP 1: Quebec in 1931

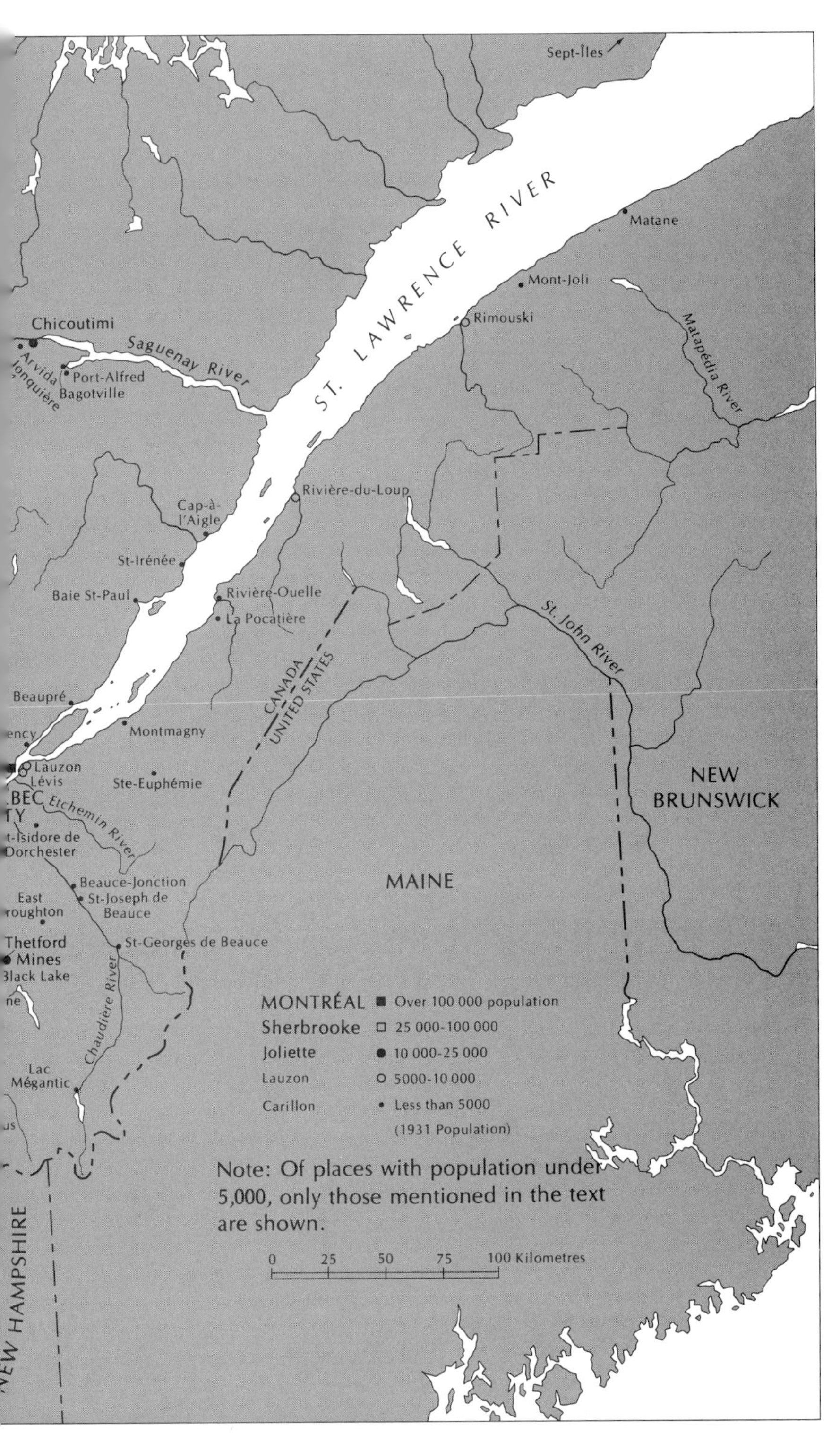
Sept-Îles
ST. LAWRENCE RIVER
Matane
Mont-Joli
Rimouski
Matapédia River
Chicoutimi
Saguenay River
Arvida
Jonquière
Port-Alfred
Bagotville
Rivière-du-Loup
Cap-à-l'Aigle
St-Irénée
Baie St-Paul
Rivière-Ouelle
La Pocatière
St. John River
CANADA
UNITED STATES
Beaupré
Montmagny
Lauzon
Lévis
Ste-Euphémie
Etchemin River
NEW BRUNSWICK
Dorchester
Beauce-Jonction
St-Joseph de Beauce
East
Thetford Mines
Black Lake
St-Georges de Beauce
MAINE
Chaudière River
Lac Mégantic
MONTRÉAL ■ Over 100 000 population
Sherbrooke □ 25 000-100 000
Joliette ● 10 000-25 000
Lauzon ○ 5000-10 000
Carillon • Less than 5000
(1931 Population)
Note: Of places with population under 5,000, only those mentioned in the text are shown.
0 25 50 75 100 Kilometres
NEW HAMPSHIRE

PART I
LAND AND POPULATION 1867-1929

LAND AND POPULATION

Land and people are the most ordinary of realities, and they can seem to be unchangeable elements in the life of a society. But behind this banality and apparent immutability, there are slow changes in the shape of physical space and the composition of the population, countless threads that in their interweaving produce effects that touch society as a whole. It is important for us to sense the feel and pace of these movements so that we can see their interrelationships more clearly. Montreal is as far from Florida as it is from the tip of the Ungava Peninsula; it is closer to New York than to Sept-Îles. This simple matter of distances suggests that it may be worth looking into the importance of geography in the evolution of Quebec.

In our survey of Quebec's physical space, we will first try to establish its relationship to the North American continent as a whole; in that context, we will then analyse the major elements in the formation of the Quebec landscape. In chapter 2, we will study the development of the population. While population changes more rapidly than physical space, it also has permanent characteristics and it is important to distinguish these from characteristics that are more variable and circumstantial. Finally, after we look at how the population of Quebec has developed, we will examine its major ethnic and linguistic components, since in Quebec these distinctions have played an especially important role. This will complete our glance at the elements that form the basis of Quebec society.

CHAPTER 1
THE LAND

Our first task in discussing the geography of Quebec is to place it in its wider context. This endeavour merits close attention because for a long time Quebec was almost exclusively interested in its differences from the rest of North America, its specific characteristics and original culture. It conceived of its past only in relation to itself, and saw its ties with the outside world as being momentary or accidental. However, the structure of its territory is dominated by the great geological building-blocks of the continent.

An American Land

Four major rock formations make up the relief system of the American continent. Three of these run roughly north-south. The easternmost is the Appalachian Chain, which rises out of the St. Lawrence River in the Gaspé peninsula; it follows the river for a distance, then continues southward as far as northern Georgia, forming a natural boundary to the coastal plain. The western face of the Appalachian Chain is the natural limit of the American central plain, which stretches to the second great north-south rock formation, the Rocky Mountains. This rock formation spans the entire American continent, from Tierra del Fuego to Alaska. The last of the great north-south relief systems is the Coast Range, located just east of the Pacific. The fourth major rock formation, the Canadian Shield, extends to the north of the central plain and forms a horseshoe-shaped curve enveloping Hudson Bay.

Along with the relief systems, the hydrographic network has played an extremely important role in North American history: from the beginning of European implantation, the rivers were the key access routes to the interior of the continent. Two great rivers dominate the network: the St. Lawrence (which drains three-fifths of the Atlantic basin) in the north and the Mississippi in the south. Both rivers rise in or near the Great Lakes, the central pivot of the hydrographic network. It is possible to go up the St. Lawrence from the Atlantic to the interior, to pass from one system to another through portages and tributaries and then to reach the Gulf of Mexico by the Mississippi. In addition to these great rivers, there are others of smaller size that have played a similar role. Notable among these is the Hudson, which crosses the Appalachians and flows into the Atlantic at New York.

Common structural characteristics define a natural region, and therefore relief and hydrography determine the major natural regions of the continent. There are seven such regions in North America: the coastal plain, the Appalachians, the central plain, the Rockies, the Coast Range, the Canadian Shield and the St. Lawrence Valley (Map 2). Quebec occupies the lower part of the St. Lawrence Valley and includes portions of the Canadian Shield in the north and the Appalachians in the south. These physical characteristics have been of fundamental importance in determining the nature of Quebec's economy and society.

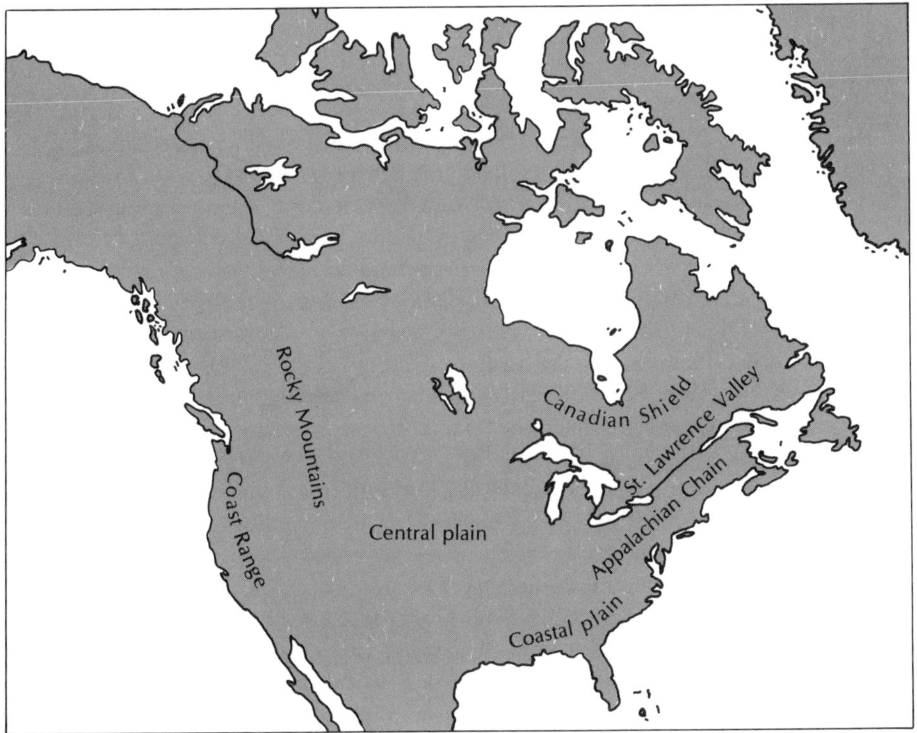

MAP 2: The Natural Regions of North America

Two geographical elements, the St. Lawrence axis and the regions of North America, have served as the bases of two different historiographic positions, the Laurentian thesis and the Faucher thesis, which we will examine in more detail later. In brief, the Laurentian thesis sees the St. Lawrence Valley as the locus of east-west lines of force that have determined the entire economic and social development of Canada. The Faucher thesis, postulating the unequal economic development of the regions of North America as a function of the state of technology and the distribution of resources, emphasizes continental influences. Up to a point, these interpretations are complementary and provide a good illustration of the twofold influence to which Quebec has been subject: while Quebec is drawn by the St. Lawrence into an east-west economic axis, it also feels the tension created by the existence of other, continental axes that pull it strongly towards the south.

The Settlement of the Land

The territory of Quebec has not been an unchanging entity but has developed in several stages. As the territory was settled, regions were formed and gradually became differentiated from one another.

Changing borders

At the time of Confederation in 1867, the entire territory of Lower Canada, as defined by the old constitution, made up the new province of Quebec (Map 3a). Briefly, this meant that Quebec at that time included only the southern portion of its present territory; neither the Abitibi region, nor New Quebec, nor Labrador (which had been annexed to Newfoundland in 1809) was part of it.

A year after Confederation, the jurisdiction of the Canadian government was extended to the territories of northern Canada that had been granted to the Hudson's Bay Company. It gradually transferred some of these lands to the provinces; in the case of Quebec, this transfer took place in two stages. In the first stage, in 1898, Quebec received the Abitibi region as far as the Eastmain River, but lost some territory in the northeast (Map 3b). The second stage, in 1912, extended Quebec's territory to Hudson Strait; the Ungava district (New Quebec) now formed an integral part of its territory (Map 3c). The only question that remained unresolved was the Labrador border; the nub of this complex problem was disagreement over definitions.

In the oldest documents, dating from 1763, the coast of Labrador was assigned to Newfoundland. The difficulty came in trying to define exactly what this coast included. The disagreement was finally taken to the Privy Council in London, which decided in 1927 that the border should follow the watershed (Map 3d). An immense territory of about 290,000 square kilometres was awarded to Newfoundland. The "coast" as it was defined thrusts deep into the interior,

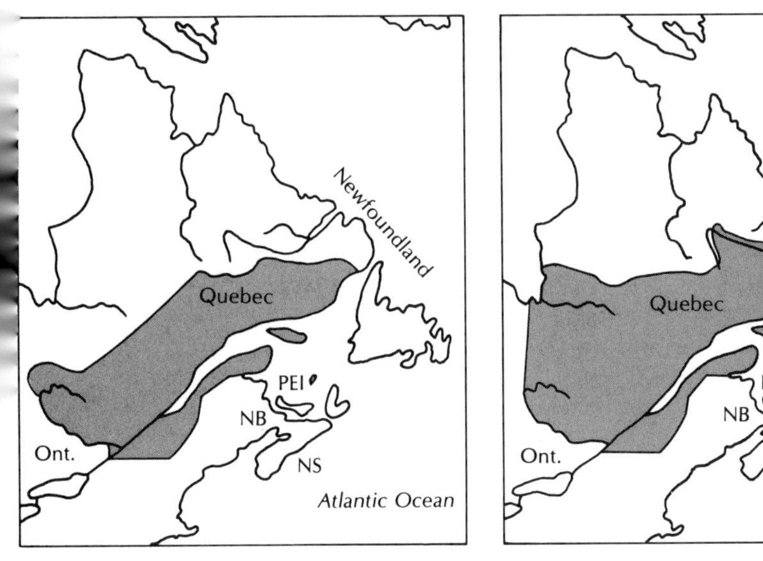

1867

1898

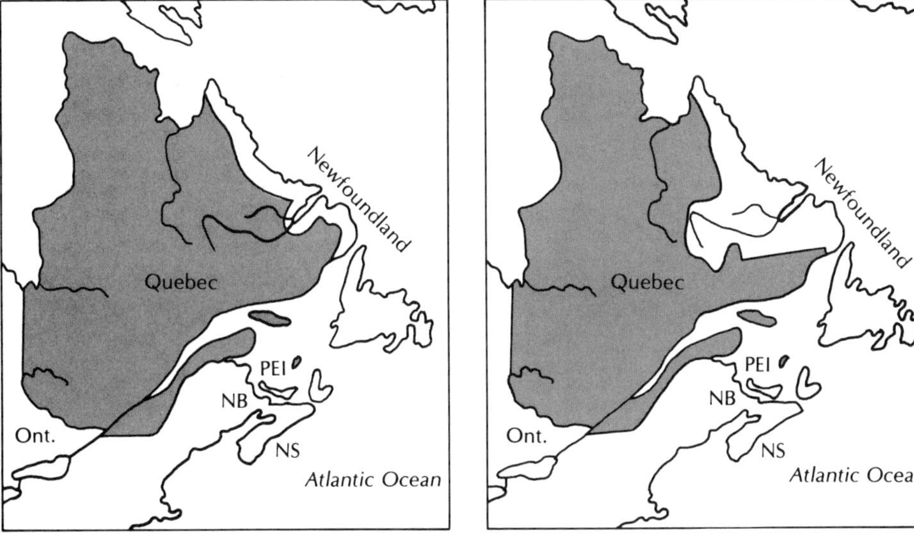

1912

1927

MAP 3: Quebec's Changing Borders, 1867-1927

extending 724 kilometres at its widest point. The Privy Council decision is still a subject of debate, and Quebec wants to reopen the case.

It should be stressed that all these additions to or subtractions from the territory of Quebec were imposed by outside governments, in London and Ottawa; in other words, Quebec has never really had direct control over the formation of its territory. In addition, it is clear that in some cases the central government hesitated seriously before allowing Quebec's borders to be extended. For example, the letters of Sir John A. Macdonald reveal that in the late 1880s he had no objection to extending Ontario's borders but in doing the same for Quebec he was afraid of creating a French barrier between Ontario and the Atlantic. He wrote: "I have no objections to the French as French or as Catholics — but the block caused by the introduction of French law and the civil code would be very great." The question of Labrador also shows the federal government's reticence about extending Quebec's borders; in 1927 it was Ottawa's responsibility to protect the interests of Quebec and Canada against the claims of Newfoundland, at that time still a separate dominion.

Nevertheless, the Quebec that emerged from these decisions was immense: 1,550,000 square kilometres, or three times the size of France. The permanently inhabited portion of this territory is much smaller — a strip of land straddling the St. Lawrence with an area about a tenth of the total.

Six natural regions

The natural regions of Quebec are determined by a very simple underlying structure, made up of three elements: the St. Lawrence, the Appalachians and the Canadian Shield. Climatic conditions correspond to these structural features; in general, the mean temperature is higher close to the St. Lawrence and lower near either of the two rock formations. The most important variable is the length of the growing season, which is measured by the number of frost-free days and affects a region's suitability for a fundamental economic activity, agriculture. Farming becomes difficult if the number of frost-free days is under 100; in Quebec, the number is below this minimum almost everywhere in the highlands of the Canadian Shield or the Appalachians. Climatic conditions are thus a constraint on practising the same kind of agriculture in these regions as in the plain.

There are six natural regions in Quebec (Map 4). The first is the *St. Lawrence Lowlands*, which extend eastward from Vaudreuil, just west of Montreal Island, and are bounded on the north by the foothills of the Canadian Shield (the Laurentians) and on the south by the Appalachians. In this region, geological structure has created conditions favourable to agriculture and transportation. The second region is the *Laurentian Highlands*, consisting of the foothills of the Canadian Shield and showing the eroded relief characteristic of one of the oldest rock formations in the world. The third region, the *Appalachian Highlands*, is

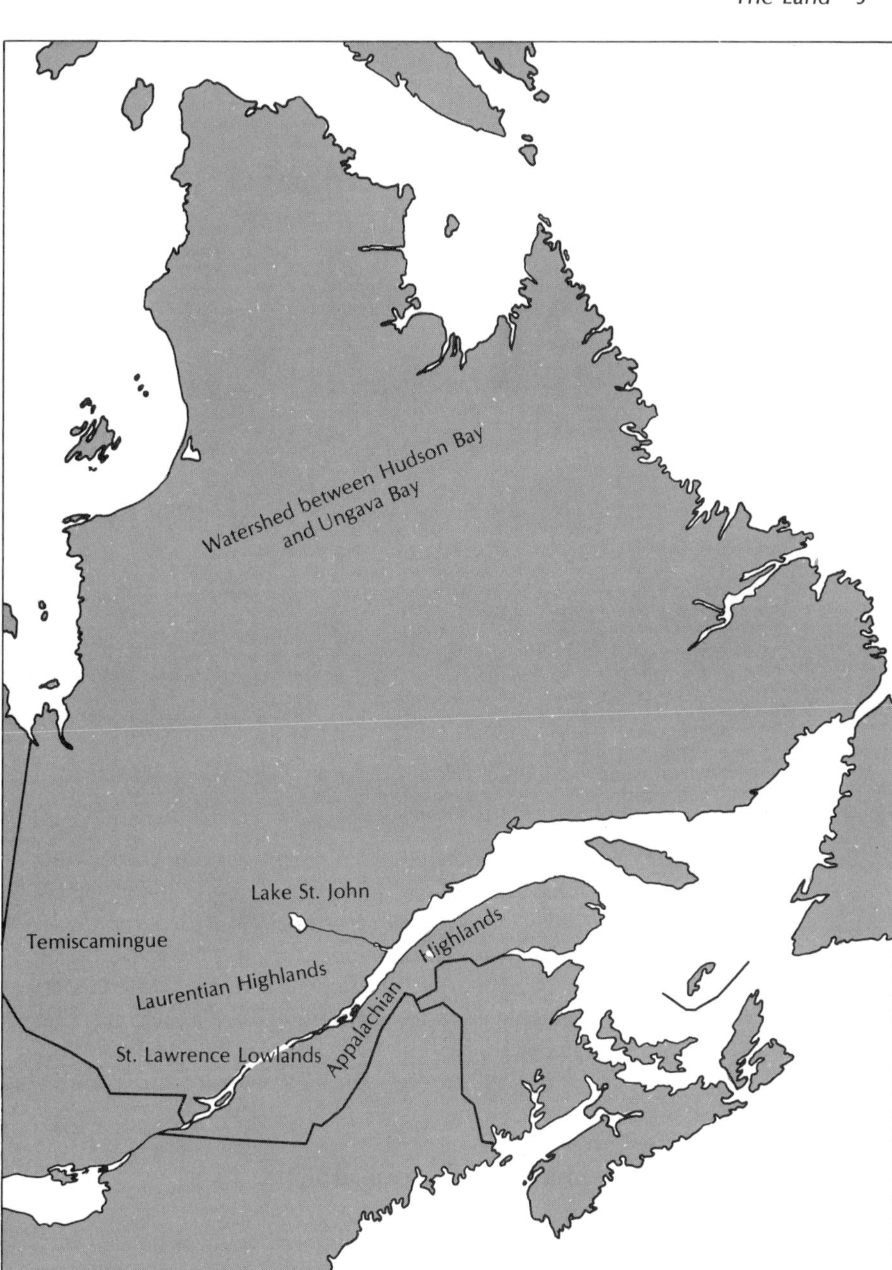

MAP 4: The Natural Regions of Quebec

An Appalachian mountain landscape: Mount Orford.

located in southern Quebec and stretches from the American border near Sherbrooke to the Gaspé; it has rougher terrain than the Laurentian Highlands. The fourth and fifth regions owe their shape to geological accidents of glacial origin; they are two deep indentations gouged out of the Canadian Shield by glaciation, the *Lake St. John* trough and the *Temiscamingue* region. Materials left by the glaciers make these suitable areas for agriculture. The last region is that part of the Canadian Shield consisting of the *watershed between Hudson Bay and Ungava Bay*; it is the largest of Quebec's regions and runs in an arc from the southwest to the north.

The Shaping of Physical Space

As an area is settled, the natural regions gradually become differentiated into distinct types of inhabited space. A natural region may contain several different inhabited regions, each with specific characteristics related to the nature and timing of its first human occupation. The dominant economic activity when a region is first settled has the most important impact; while all regions will be affected by changes in the economic base as time goes on, these effects will be felt diversely in different regions.

A typical landscape in the Montreal plain, near Saint-Barthélémy, northeast of Montreal.

Thus, all of Quebec's regions have been affected by the phenomenon of urbanization, but the actual changes produced have varied from one region to another; in some places new cities have grown up, but even in regions far from these cities urbanization has had its effects, in the form of significant changes in agriculture.

In Quebec, this process of spatial differentiation has created distinctive regions such as the Beauce, the Gaspé and the Saguenay-Lake St. John region, to name only three. Defining Quebec's regions poses a number of problems. First there is the historical dimension; what was considered a region in the nineteenth century may have become encompassed in a larger one in the twentieth. There is also a dimension related to the perceptions of a region's inhabitants, who may disagree on whether a particular parish* forms part of the region. There is also the question of sub-regions: does the Beauce, for instance, include the neighbouring Etchemin Valley? Finally, there is the influence of administrative practices, under which Quebec has been divided into ten regions which do not necessarily

*More than just a religious institution, the parish was a basis for social and spatial identification and a fundamental institution in Quebec society as a whole. See p. 102.

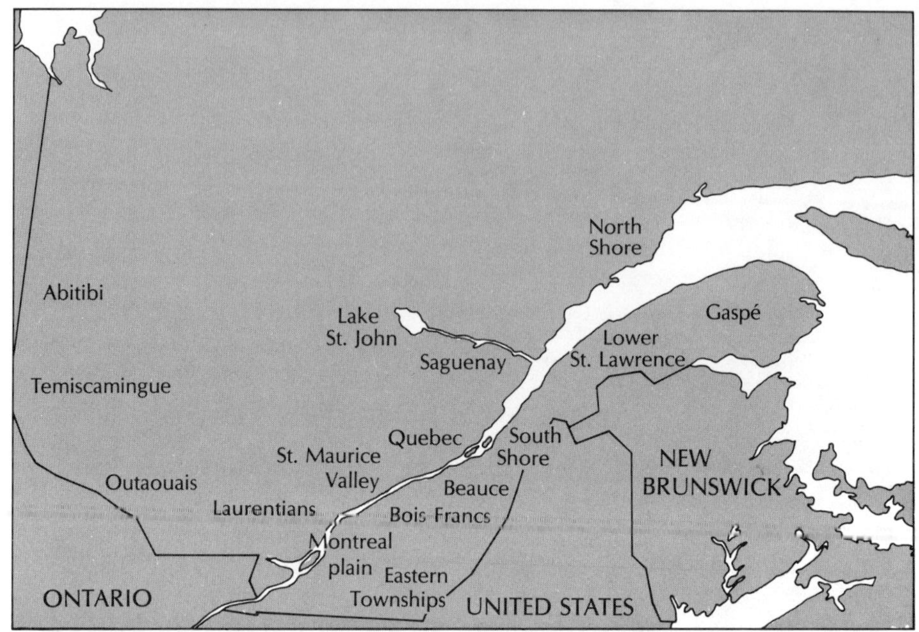

MAP 5: The Inhabited Regions of Quebec

correspond to other definitions. The Eastern Townships are a good illustration of these problems. Historically, the Eastern Townships region was limited to a few counties in the Sherbrooke area. Gradually, however, other regions such as the Bois-Francs and the zone between the Eastern Townships and the Beauce were lumped in with it. The definition of the Eastern Townships has thus been a floating one. With these problems in mind, instead of trying to define the borders of regions precisely, we will locate them approximately on Map 5. It is more important to understand how regions were formed, because the same process that underlies the formation of a region is also responsible for the extent to which it is linked to Quebec as a whole at any given time in its history.

The first major period in which Quebec's territory was settled and shaped lasted from sometime in the eighteenth century to about 1820 and bore the stamp of agriculture. The fur trade preceded this period, but since it involved only a nomadic occupation of the land and did not bring about human modification of the landscape, we will not examine it here. Agriculture presents a marked contrast to the fur trade, and is the cause of significant changes in physical space: trees are cut down, roads are built, buildings are constructed. In the first period of settlement, the lowlands of the St. Lawrence Valley were divided into seigneuries. In this way, the method of settlement and the pattern of the landscape were uniformly determined, and a homogeneous zone was created in the heart of

Quebec. How the land was divided, how it was farmed and how the seigneuries developed were the characteristic phenomena of the period. Both the division of land into seigneuries and the granting of lots within the seigneury took into account the historic basis of Quebec's network of communication — its rivers, large and small. The seigneury was generally rectangular in shape and had river frontage on one of its short sides; rows of seigneuries lined both banks of the St. Lawrence and some of its tributaries such as the Richelieu. Within the seigneury, land was granted in the form of a narrow rectangle fronting on the river on one of its short sides and stretching into the interior. This reflected the fundamental importance of access to the river, and allowed the largest possible number of censitaires (as the seigneurial tenants were called) to have riverfront lots. When the entire "range" (row) of such lots had been granted, a new range was started behind it, and so on until the limit of the seigneury was reached. To make communication possible, censitaires in these new ranges were required to build range roads co-operatively; in addition, at least one road perpendicular to the range roads was built to allow the different ranges to communicate with one another and to give the interior ranges an outlet to the river on which the seigneury fronted.

The range formed one of the basic units of Quebec society. Influenced by the shape of the lots and the desire to make communication easy, all the censitaires with river frontage built their houses at the same end of their lands, near the river bank. Thus the houses were close to one another, a lot's width apart, giving rise to Quebec's distinctive form of rural settlement, an elongated village-like agglomeration along a river that attracted the attention of more than one observer. In the interior ranges, settlement followed either the same pattern, with the houses strung out along a range road, or else a variation in which two rows of houses were built on opposite sides of the same road.

This form of settlement determined the landscape of the seigneurial area of Quebec: long, narrow lots; farmhouses and buildings built near the river or road and close to one another; a systematic network of range roads and perpendicular roads. From the end of the eighteenth century on, the landscape also began to be dotted with villages. The kind of agriculture practised in the seigneuries also left its mark, and grain cultivation led to the rapid disappearance of forests in this area.

The second important period for the formation of regions was the period of extension of agricultural settlement into the highlands. After 1820, as population pressure in the seigneuries increased, people from older settlements began to overflow into the Laurentian and Appalachian highlands. A significant complementary activity, the timber trade, encouraged this movement and influenced its nature, determining the mode of agriculture and the way of life in these new areas. This period also differed from the first in the way in which the land was occupied. Virtually no new seigneuries were created after the conquest; lands outside the seigneurial area were divided into townships and lots in these townships had to be purchased. Initially, the townships were divided into square lots and buildings

The division of the land into ranges can be seen in this aerial photo of the Joliette region. The most striking feature is the long, narrow shape of the lots; also conspicuous is the presence of wooded areas, often at the back end of the lot. In the foreground, at left, a double range is visible, with buildings on both sides of the road. A single range can be seen towards the centre of the photo.

were typically built far from the road; this kind of rural landscape can be seen in Ontario and in parts of Quebec that were settled by British colonists. In addition to these initial distinctions, other characteristics also differentiated the townships from the seigneuries: agriculture, which in the townships quickly became dominated by livestock production, and rural architecture. When the French-Canadian population began to overflow into the townships, it brought with it the patterns of land division and settlement to which it had become accustomed in the seigneuries. The transfer of the range system meant narrower lots, although not as narrow as in the seigneuries, and, most important, the characteristic arrangement of houses based on the range.

The climate and the presence of woodcutting as a complementary activity left their mark on the kind of agriculture practised in the highlands, and thus on the landscape. The shorter growing season in these regions places definite limits on the cultivation that can be carried on. We will examine the role of the forest industry in greater depth later, but it is worth noting here that its impact on agriculture was considerable, especially as a result of the interdependence that was established between the two activities.

Roughly between 1850 and 1900, occupation of the highlands was completed and settlement of the two troughs in the Canadian Shield — Temiscamingue and Saguenay-Lake St. John — was begun. Settlement in these regions had the same characteristics as in the highlands; agriculture was constrained by the climate and the forest provided a complementary activity. Finally, after 1900, an initial interest was shown in the Hudson Bay side of the Canadian Shield, leading to settlement of the Abitibi region, where agriculture was quickly subordinated to mining.

In this way, the regions of Quebec were differentiated. A single basic economic activity, agriculture, was the starting point for all the zones just defined: the seigneurial area, the townships, the highlands, the two troughs and the Abitibi. In some regions, agriculture was overshadowed by a new economic activity that would eventually replace it, and this process accentuated regional differences.

Within the large zones that we have defined, regions developed slowly and independently of one another, with agriculture being the primary source of development. To the extent that farmers became self-sufficient, regions had even less contact with one another. Linkages are created only when a given economic activity is directed and organized from a single urban centre and carried out in a number of regions. The first linkages are then established between regions and this centre; later, regions are linked to one another. In the nineteenth century, the only economic activity that could create linkages of this sort was the forest industry, which was common to several regions and directed from Quebec City. However, since it was not the dominant industry in Quebec and most of the productive population was employed in other activities, it linked regions to the centre and to one another only in a limited way.

The double movement of urbanization and industrialization, and modification

The Laurentian Mountains, near Saint-Sauveur-des-Monts.

of the structures of capitalism that are inextricably tied to it, gradually brought about greater linkages among the regions. The development of industrial capitalism leads to the integration of more sectors into the economy and the concentration of decisionmaking in a small number of centres. An important change occurred in the last third of the nineteenth century, when a new rail transportation network was laid out. In regions where agriculture or industry was tied to urban or export markets, linkages became stronger; conversely, other regions whose economic activities were not tied to these markets became increasingly marginal.

The phenomenon of linkage is related to polarization — the creation of an urban centre that controls the bulk of economic activity in many regions. Montreal rapidly assumed this role, both through the consumer market it represented and through its concentration of decisionmaking power. But while Montreal was supreme, there were also other polarizing centres, of lesser significance but by no means negligible. Next in importance was Quebec City, which polarized its surrounding regions and to a certain extent the areas of Quebec downstream from it. Finally, two cities outside Quebec were significant polarizing centres for regions within the province — Ottawa for the neighbouring Outaouais region of Quebec and Toronto for the Abitibi-Temiscamingue region, to which it was linked through the mining industry.

In sum, after Confederation a twofold evolution took place. In one development, the borders of Quebec encompassed a larger and larger territory; in the other, the different regions of Quebec, created and shaped by the history of settlement of the land, were increasingly linked to one another through economic development.

CHAPTER 2
POPULATION

Between 1760 and 1960, world population increased by a factor of three, population of European origin increased by a factor of five and population of French origin in Canada increased by a factor of eighty. This apparently phenomenal rate of increase occurred despite minimal French immigration to Canada and considerable French-Canadian emigration to the United States, and it has led many commentators to evoke the proverbial fertility of the French-Canadian people and the miracle of *survivance*.

By the time of the first post-Confederation census in 1871, the 60,000 or so French Canadians of 1760 had become a people numbering 1,082,940, or 31.1 per cent of the population of the new Dominion. An overwhelming majority of Canadians of French origin — 85.5 per cent — lived in Quebec; slightly more than 150,000 lived in the other provinces of Canada. In addition, it was estimated that by 1870 some 200,000 Quebecers, the vast majority of them French-speaking, had emigrated to the United States.

Between 1760 and 1850, the French-Canadian population doubled approximately every twenty-five years; nevertheless, some people were uneasy about French Canada's relative numerical weakness and feared its political and socio-economic consequences. In the nineteenth century French Canadians saw themselves as a majority in their territory of Lower Canada and were determined to retain this status. As a consequence, French-Canadian political leaders protested against the massive immigration from the United Kingdom that took place after 1815 and the monopolization of land by settlers of British origin.* In both these developments they feared being submerged by people from the home country, and they demanded that Britain recognize their right to a leading role in the colony's political institutions.

---

*Canadian censuses of the time used the term "British" to refer to people of English, Scottish, Welsh and Irish origin. This usage has been followed here.

The concepts of majority and minority were constant reference points in the political debates between French Canadians and the British in Lower Canada during the 1830s. After the 1837 Rebellion, Lord Durham, taking the side of the English minority, recommended in his famous report that the French Canadians be made the minority by uniting Lower Canada with Upper Canada (Ontario). Like most of his countrymen in the 1840s, the historian François-Xavier Garneau could not help being seriously disturbed by this policy and the brutal frankness with which it was expressed, and the theme of a "small, minority people" recurs often in his *Histoire du Canada*. Historians and politicians have taken up this question of numbers in every generation, and it came to be considered a determining factor in the history of the French-Canadian people. We will come back to this point in the next chapter when we look at the ethnic and linguistic structure of the population, but first we will analyse the internal and external factors that have influenced the development of Quebec's entire population, not just its French-Canadian portion.

* * *

Between 1871 and 1931, the population of Quebec grew from 1,191,516 to 2,874,662, while that of the rest of Canada grew from 2,497,741 to 7,502,124 (Table 1). Only in the last decade of this period did the population of Quebec grow more rapidly than that of Canada. Quebec represented 32.4 per cent of the population of Canada in 1871, but only 27.6 per cent in 1931. In brief, Quebec's population was growing, but other places were growing faster.

On the whole, both Quebec and the rest of Canada grew slowly in the last decades of the nineteenth century and considerably more quickly in the first three decades of the twentieth. Thus between 1871 and 1901 Quebec's population grew by only 38.2 per cent, while the rest of Canada's grew by 49.0 per cent;

TABLE 1
Population of Quebec and of the Rest of Canada, 1871-1931

	Quebec		*Rest of Canada*	
Year	*Population*	*Growth in Previous Decade (%)*	*Population*	*Growth in Previous Decade (%)*
1871	1,191,516	7.2	3,689,256	29.4
1881	1,359,027	14.1	2,965,783	18.7
1891	1,488,535	9.5	3,344,704	12.8
1901	1,648,898	10.8	3,722,417	11.3
1911	2,005,776	21.6	5,200,867	39.7
1921	2,360,510	17.7	6,427,439	23.6
1931	2,874,662	21.8	7,502,124	16.7

Source: M.C. Urquhart and K. Buckley, *Historical Statistics of Canada*, p. 14.

between 1901 and 1931 the figure for Quebec was 74.8 per cent and for the rest of Canada 101.5 per cent. Population growth or decline is a function of two variables: natural increase (births and deaths) and migratory movements (immigration and emigration). We will examine each in turn.

Natural Increase

A fertile population

Quebec enjoyed a high birth rate (number of births as a proportion of the population as a whole) during the period we are studying, as we can establish by making a comparison with the birth rate in Ontario. The best estimates that we have for the birth rates of Quebec and Ontario are the ones proposed by Jacques Henripin (Table 2).

In both provinces we can see a significant decline in the birth rate between 1866 and 1930. This decline was steeper in Ontario, especially in the last decades of the nineteenth century. The birth rate is a simple measure that gives a crude estimate of the rate at which couples in a given population procreate, but it doesn't take into account the age and sex distribution of the population, which may influence its rate of reproduction considerably. We can get around this problem at least in part by using a much more sensitive measure called the overall general fertility rate. This is obtained by calculating the annual number of births per thousand women of childbearing age, which for statistical purposes is taken to mean between the ages of fifteen and forty-nine (Table 3).

The tendency towards decline noted previously in the birth rate is confirmed

TABLE 2
Birth Rate per 1,000 Population
Quebec and Ontario, 1866-1930

Period	*Quebec*	*Ontario*
1866-76	43.2	44.8
1876-86	42.0	37.2
1886-96	39.3	31.3
1896-1906	38.3	28.8
1906-16	38.0	29.1
1916-26	36.3	26.3
1926-30	30.5	21.0

Sources: Jacques Henripin, *Trends and Factors of Fertility in Canada*, p. 370; Jacques Henripin, "Quebec and the Demographic Dilemma," in Dale C. Thomson, ed., *Quebec Society and Politics*, p. 163.

A large Quebec family in the early twentieth century.

by the overall general fertility rate. We should, however, note the tenacious resistance of Quebec's fertility rate, which decreased by only fourteen per cent between 1871 and 1921, while Ontario's decreased by twenty-nine per cent. Fertility declined slightly faster between 1871 and 1891 than in the rest of the period, as a result of difficult economic circumstances. There is a tendency to postpone marriages during times of depression, and this decreased marriage rate was probably the immediate cause of the lower fertility rate. On the whole, however, the effect of economic conditions on the demographic behaviour of

TABLE 3
General Fertility Rate, Quebec and Ontario, 1871-1931
(annual number of births per 1,000 women between the ages of 15 and 49)

Year	*Quebec*	*Ontario*
1871	180	191
1881	173	149
1891	163	121
1901	160	108
1911	161	112
1921	155	98
1931	116	79

Source: Jacques Henripin, *Trends and Factors of Fertility in Canada,* p. 21.

French Canadians does not appear to have been felt quite so rapidly, at least not before the 1920s.

These overall rates do not reveal some of the subtleties involved, such as the differences between French and English Canadians. We know in a general way that French Canadians were the more fertile group. Since we cannot analyse the development of each of Quebec's ethnic groups, we will limit our study to the case of Canadians of French mother tongue in Quebec. The demographers Jacques Henripin and Yves Péron have compiled a very interesting table relating fertility within this group to age and place of residence (Table 4).

From this table, it can be seen that Quebec women of French mother tongue, living on a farm and more than sixty-five years old in 1961 (that is, born before 1897), had an average of 8.3 children, almost as many as their ancestors in the eighteenth century! Farm women born around 1913 had an average of 7.3 children. For all Quebec women of French mother tongue born around 1913 (forty-five to forty-nine years old in 1961), the average was 4.3 children. As the authors note, this is a very high figure, since forty-eight per cent of Quebec women lived in cities of more than 100,000 population in 1961 and only twelve per cent lived on farms. To reach the averages cited in the table, there had to be many families with fifteen or twenty children. It is easy to see where the idea of the proverbial fertility of French Canadians might have come from. Henripin and Péron were led to comment: "Perhaps nowhere else in the world was the Catholic ideal of a large family realized as effectively." But pressures from the clergy don't explain everything. On the farm, children are an investment and provide cheap labour, while in cities, they represent additional costs for the family. Quebec's rural character and the low educational level of its population were circumstances that encouraged large families; nationalist propaganda for the "revenge of the cradle" was an additional factor.

TABLE 4

Number of Live Births per Married Woman of French Mother Tongue (excluding births before marriage) by Age and Place of Residence, Quebec, 1961

Age in 1961	*Total*	*Urban*	*Rural, Non-agricultural*	*Rural, Agricultural*
65+	6.40	5.90	7.25	8.32
60-64	5.59	4.95	6.59	8.18
55-59	5.06	4.33	6.06	7.82
50-54	4.58	3.82	5.51	7.52
45-49	4.31	3.56	5.46	7.27
40-44	4.34	3.66	5.59	6.86

Source: Jacques Henripin and Yves Péron, "The Demographic Transition of the Province of Quebec," in D.V. Glass and Roger Revelle, eds., *Population and Social Change.*

From cradle to grave

There are major deficiencies in Quebec mortality statistics before 1921. But we do have coherent statistics for the period 1884-1930 for Quebec as a whole that allow us to see some of the changes in mortality during that period (Table 5).

The decline in the overall death rate from 22.3 per thousand to 13.5 per thousand in forty-five years is fairly significant. In contrast to the birth rate, which declined substantially before 1891, the death rate did not start to decrease until 1901. The sharp decrease in the 1920s indicates that the belated (but nevertheless real) efforts to improve sanitary conditions in Quebec had begun to bear fruit.

The available statistical series do not allow us to compare Quebec with Ontario systematically, or to compare French with English Canadians, although we do know that the death rate for French Canadians was higher. We have statistical evidence for the period 1926-30, during which the death rate for the Quebec population as a whole was 13.5 per thousand, while the death rate for Quebecers of French origin was 14.2 per thousand.

There were also significant changes in the causes of death. In the last third of the nineteenth century, contagious diseases frequently ravaged the population, especially in Montreal. In 1885-86, for example, a smallpox epidemic killed more than 3,000 people in Montreal. Although it was known at the time that smallpox could be prevented by vaccination, French Canadians refused to be vaccinated. In 1901, the Quebec government authorized municipalities to make vaccination compulsory if they wished, but few municipalities did so. It was only two years later, after another epidemic, that the government required municipalities to institute compulsory vaccination. Only one death from smallpox was recorded after 1918, an indication that the measure was effective. Diphtheria was another disease that continued to claim lives in Quebec after methods of prevention were well known and applied successfully elsewhere.

TABLE 5
Average Annual Death Rate, Quebec, 1884-1930 (per 1,000 population)

Period	*Rate*	*Period*	*Rate*
1884-85	22.3	1906-10	18.5
1886-90	21.9	1911-15	17.4
1891-95	21.9	1916-20	18.0
1896-1900	21.6	1921-25	12.9
1901-5	18.7	1926-30	13.5

Source: Jacques Henripin and Yves Péron, "The Demographic Transition of the Province of Quebec," in D.V. Glass and Roger Revelle, eds., *Population and Social Change.*

During the 1885 smallpox epidemic, Montreal city council made vaccination compulsory. A portion of the city's French-Canadian population resisted, and the forces of law and order had to intervene to enforce the measure.

Tuberculosis — the "white plague" or "consumption" as it was called at the time — had a devastating effect on Quebec. On the average, it was the cause of 3,000 deaths annually after 1901, and during that period Montreal had the distinction of suffering the most deaths from tuberculosis of any large North American city. Methods for reducing the ravages caused by this disease were well known by the beginning of the twentieth century, as can be seen from the report of the royal commission on tuberculosis, issued in 1909. Despite the commission's precise and pertinent recommendations, it wasn't until fifteen years later that serious efforts were undertaken to fight this scourge that needlessly destroyed tens of thousands of human lives, especially among the poor who lived in the unhealthy conditions in which tuberculosis flourished. In Saint-Denis, a working-class neighbourhood of Montreal, the death rate from tuberculosis in 1921 was 202 per 100,000 population, while in St. George, a wealthier neighbourhood, it was 50 per 100,000, only a quarter as high.

Infant mortality (deaths of babies under the age of one year, excluding stillbirths), was one of the major components of mortality at the time. Between 1901 and 1929, infant mortality accounted for 12.6 -17.0 per cent of all deaths in

Quebec. The rate of infant mortality was so scandalously high that Montreal can be said to have been one of the deadliest cities in the world in the early twentieth century; more than a quarter of all children died before reaching the age of a year.

During this whole period infant mortality was one of Quebec's most serious problems, especially in the cities, where it was uniformly higher than in the country, although the gap narrowed in the late 1920s (see Table 6). A large proportion of infant deaths was attributable to gastro-intestinal diseases. According to the historian Terry Copp, between 1906 and 1915, forty-two per cent of all deaths of children up to age two in Montreal was due to what was called "infantile diarrhea"; in 1927 this disease was still responsible for thirty-three per cent of the deaths in that age group. These infections were in large part the result of the poor quality of the water and milk drunk in Montreal.

While the water problem was more or less solved in 1914 with the opening of a filtration plant, it was another ten years before pasteurization of milk became a general practice. The establishment just before the First World War of child care centres called Gouttes de lait ("Milk Drops"), where uncontaminated milk and medical care were given to children and counselling was provided to mothers, had remarkable beneficial effects. In 1914, calculations showed that the death rate for children registered in the Gouttes de lait was a quarter the rate for children not in the program. Doctors in the Provincial Board of Health and its municipal counterpart in Montreal were acutely aware of the seriousness of the infant mortality situation and suggested ways to avoid this terrible calamity. In 1914, for example,

TABLE 6

Infant Mortality Rate, Quebec as a Whole and Montreal, 1871-1929 (per 1,000 live births)

Period	*Quebec as a Whole*	*Montreal*
1871	150.0	294.0
1891	179.4	212.7
1900-4	143.0	274.9
1905-9[1]	152.5	268.6
1910-14	170.0	220.2
1915-19	147.0	183.0
1920-24	134.0	160.6
1925-29	126.2	126.9

[1] Statistics available only for 1906, 1908 and 1909.

Sources: Jean Hamelin and Yves Roby, *Histoire économique du Québec, 1851-1896,* p. 55; Georges Langlois, *Histoire de la population canadienne-française,* pp. 263-64; Adélard Groulx, "La mortalité maternelle et la mortalité infantile à Montréal," *Union médicale du Canada* (December 1943), p. 1415.

the Montreal Board of Health drew up a regulation making the pasteurization of milk compulsory. However, neglect on the part of the city's leaders prevented this regulation from being adopted until 1925.

In the late 1920s, at long last, the situation improved significantly, especially in Montreal. However, in 1929 Montreal was still spending only thirty-nine cents per capita for public health, half of what twelve other large North American cities were spending; Montreal was in the process of increasing its public health expenditures at the very end of the period, and the figure reached sixty-four cents per capita in 1931. Despite the deficiencies of public health measures, Montreal's infant mortality rate declined in the late 1920s, dropping from 160.6 per thousand in 1920-24 to 126.8 per thousand in 1925-29. This was an improvement, but Montreal was still behind other large cities. Nor could the problem be resolved through public health policy alone, as it was largely the result of socio-economic conditions: living and working conditions, low income and education, and so on. We will examine this link in more detail later.

After the turn of the century, epidemics, contagious diseases and tuberculosis all slowly declined as causes of death; infant mortality also decreased. Concurrently, the proportion of deaths due to degenerative diseases such as cancer (seven per cent of all deaths in 1931) and heart disease (10.1 per cent in 1931) rose steadily. These diseases became increasingly significant in later years.

The demographic transition

In all countries, industrialization and urbanization have led to a major shift in demographic behaviour. This change from the demography of the pre-industrial era to that of the industrial era has been called the demographic "revolution" or "transition."

According to Hubert Charbonneau, from its founding to 1875, Quebec experienced a period of demographic stability characterized by high birth, fertility and marriage rates, resulting in a doubling of the population every twenty-five years, although the death rate was also high (Figure 1). In 1875 a new phase began, marked by a decline in the birth and death rates. This demographic transition, which lasted to 1930 and beyond, had characteristics peculiar to Quebec. In the usual model of the demographic transition, it is the death rate that declines first, as epidemics become less common and sanitary conditions improve. This decline in the death rate is followed sooner or later by a decline in the birth rate, and the process ends with the birth and death rates at a much lower level than they were at the beginning.

In Quebec, by contrast, the birth and death rates declined almost simultaneously, and also more slowly than elsewhere.

The Roman Catholic church's teaching on birth control, the educational level of the population and nationalist propaganda encouraging the "revenge of the cradle" were among the factors that slowed the decline in the birth rate. The death

FIGURE 1
Quebec's Age Pyramid, 1871, 1901, 1931
(in % of total population)

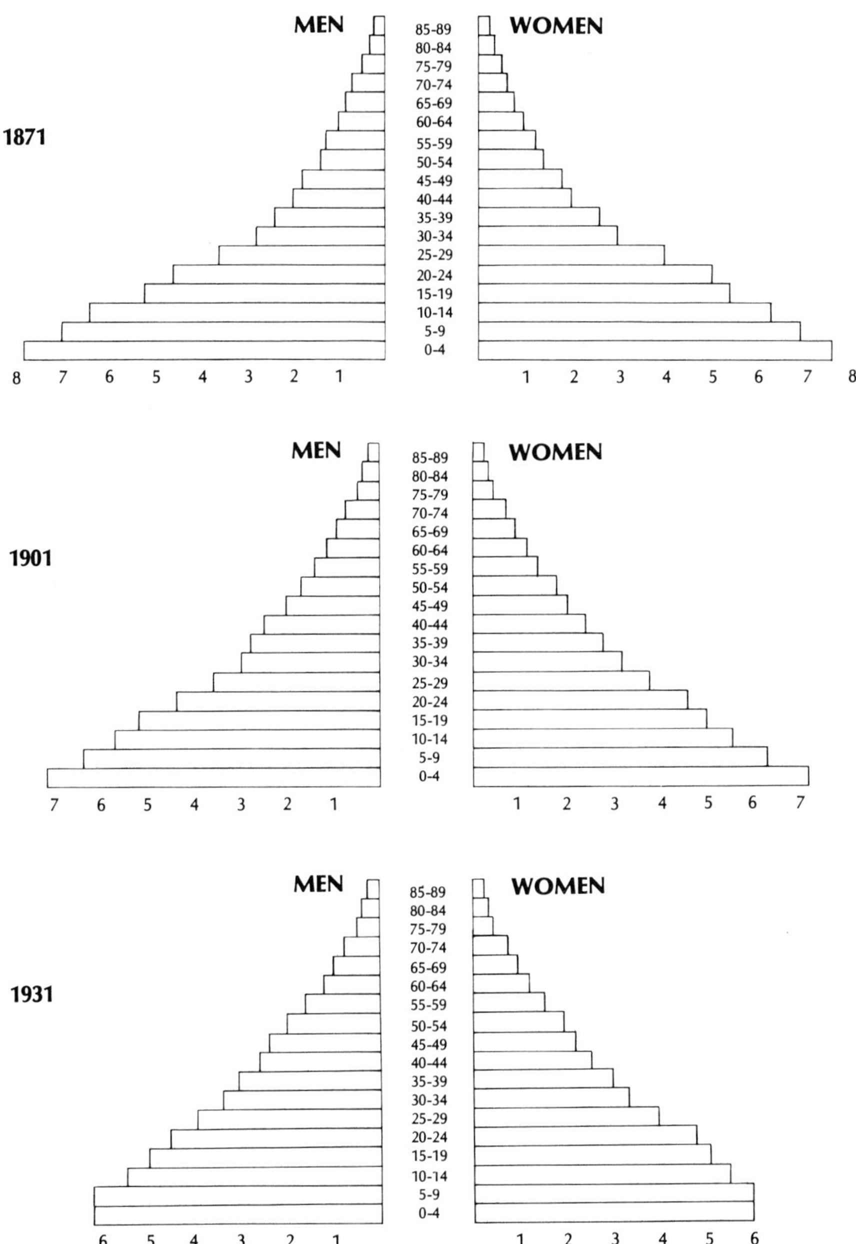

rate remained high because of the shortsightedness and negligence of Quebec's leaders, who were unable to take effective measures to reduce infant mortality and the ravages of tuberculosis. But these differences notwithstanding, the demographic transition did take place, and present-day Quebec is in a third phase, in which it fits the demographic pattern common to the industrialized western world.

Between 1871 and 1931, despite the demographic transition, Quebec maintained a high rate of natural increase. At the end of the nineteenth century, the birth rate was about thirty-nine per thousand and the death rate about twenty-two per thousand, while between 1900 and 1920 the rates were typically thirty-seven and eighteen, and between 1920 and 1930 they were thirty-three and thirteen. This is a substantial surplus of births over deaths for the whole period—seventeen to twenty per thousand. However, the total increase in Quebec's population (Table 1) doesn't correspond to this rate of natural increase, especially between 1871 and 1901. The reason for this difference is, of course, migration.

Migration

The "great haemorrhage"

For every decade between 1871 and 1931, Quebec's net migration was negative; more people left Quebec than entered it. Contemporaries were not only aware of this phenomenon but were taken aback by the scope of French-Canadian emigration to the United States. Antoine Labelle, curé of St-Jérôme and Quebec's "apostle of colonization," said that emigration would be "the graveyard of the race." When the geographer Raoul Blanchard, in the twentieth century, spoke of a haemorrhage and the squandering of Quebec's demographic surplus, he was far from the first to talk in such terms.

A look at the extent of French-Canadian emigration makes these cries of alarm from French Canada's élites understandable. Between 1840 and 1930 more than 900,000 Quebecers left their homeland (Table 7). The vast majority of these emigrants, ranging from two-thirds in some years to four-fifths in others, were French Canadians.

Starting in the 1830s, Quebecers crossed the American border to bale hay in Vermont or cut wood in Maine. This early emigration was seasonal or temporary, but the movement took on new dimensions after 1860 as a result of industrial development in the United States. A large number of people left Quebec for good, and whole families rather than individuals emigrated. We can see this trend by looking at the age and sex pyramids for 1871 and 1901, which do not show the irregularities that would be caused by a massive departure of young men. The reason for family emigration was that most emigrants found jobs in the textile mills of New England, which employed men, women and children.

TABLE 7
Estimated Net Emigration to the United States from Canada as a Whole and Quebec, 1840-1940

	Canada[1]		*Quebec*		
Period	*In 000's*	*% of Popu-lation*	*In 000's*	*% of Popu-lation*	*Quebec/ Canada (%)*
1840-50	75	4.3	35	5.4	47
1850-60	150	7.0	70	7.8	47
1860-70	300	10.7	100[2]	—	—
1870-80	375	11.0	120	10.1	32
1880-90	450	11.3	150	11.3	33
1890-1900	425	9.7	140	9.6	33
1900-10	325	6.4	100	6.0	31
1910-20	259	4.0	80	4.0	32
1920-30	450	6.0	130	5.6	29
1930-40	25	0.3	—	—	—
1840-1940	2,800	—	925	—	32

[1] For the pre-Confederation period, British North America; after 1867, present-day Canada minus Newfoundland.

[2] This figure is only a reasonable hypothesis; the author does not have data for this period.

Source: Yolande Lavoie, "Les mouvements migratoires des Canadiens entre leur pays et les Etats-Unis au XIXe et au XXe siècles," in Hubert Charbonneau, ed., *La population du Québec,* p. 78.

As Table 7 indicates, the critical period of emigration was the last three decades of the nineteenth century, during which Quebec lost ten per cent of its population. In the early twentieth century, the number of departures remained high, despite rapid economic growth in Quebec, but it represented a smaller percentage of the total population. The depression of the 1930s and the decision of the American government to place severe restrictions on immigration brought the migratory movement to an abrupt end.

Contemporaries tried to determine the reasons for this seemingly disastrous movement. Some saw the haemorrhage as being caused by the scarcity of land and the deficiencies of Quebec agriculture. The government was frequently blamed for inadequate roads and for its favouritism towards lumber merchants and speculators. The *habitant* was reproached for allowing himself to be seduced by the false attractions of the city and for succumbing to an unhealthy taste for luxury. In 1868 a committee of the Quebec legislative assembly expressed the opinion that the two main causes of the situation were the absence of industry and the low level of agricultural knowledge; these would be recurring themes in the decades that followed. Immediately after Confederation, while Quebec's political leaders tended to rely on private enterprise and the federal government to develop commerce and industry, they tried to modernize agriculture through a variety of measures. Later, the Quebec government, despite very limited means, undertook a daring railway policy, hoping that it would have the effect of checking emigration to the United States. These measures were highly inadequate, and in some cases it is even possible that they encouraged the exodus from the countryside. In their *Histoire économique du Québec*, Jean Hamelin and Yves Roby advance the hypothesis that the modernization of agriculture reduced the need for rural manpower, and that these surplus labourers' only option for survival was emigration.

In the early twentieth century, the Liberal governments of Premiers S.-N. Parent, Lomer Gouin and Alexandre Taschereau saw industrialization and the development of natural resources as the solution to the problem. Foreign investment was seen as a blessing — if capital was imported, Quebecers didn't have to be exported. The clergy, meanwhile, throughout the period persistently advocated the opening of new colonization regions to absorb the surplus population of older parts of Quebec.

Although Quebecers at the time were only imperfectly aware of it, emigration was not a movement limited to Quebec. Its effects on Canada as a whole were considerable (Table 7), and all the more disastrous in that the federal government's entire policy was geared towards settling the country. In addition, sixty million emigrants left Europe between 1846 and 1914; of these, sixty per cent went to the United States, eleven per cent to Brazil, and only 8.7 per cent to Canada.

According to Albert Faucher, the mechanization of agriculture and the development of new modes of transportation both had effects that encouraged massive population movements in this era. The largest number of emigrants were attracted to the United States, with its abundance of good land and its apparently unlimited economic potential. Emigrants generally leave their homelands for economic reasons, and Quebecers were no exception to this rule. If Quebec is looked at in its North American context, Faucher argues, then it can be seen to be a marginal region in an economic space containing different levels of development and unequal standards of living. While New Englanders went to the mid-west, Quebecers who were in economic difficulty or hoped to better themselves headed for New England, where they could find industrial jobs. These "Chinese of the East," as French Canadians were called in New England, were accustomed to a low standard of living and took the unskilled, low-wage jobs that were available in the textile mills and shoe factories.

Other factors also encouraged this southward emigration. The Canadian Shield inhibits expansion to the north and west, and directs the axis of migration along the St. Lawrence Valley in a southwesterly direction. The Canadian-American border presented few obstacles. And the orientation of a large part of the railway network made it easy for Quebecers to emigrate to neighbouring parts of the United States. Thus Faucher's continentalist approach stresses geo-economic factors and calls attention to regional disparities as the fundamental cause of this important episode in Quebec history.

Through this massive emigration, Quebec lost a significant portion of its population. By 1901 it could be said that there were almost as many French Canadians elsewhere in North America as there were in Quebec. No one doubted that the exodus was massive and an appropriate cause for concern. But in the context of the time, emigration was practically inevitable, and French Canadians were relatively fortunate in that they had an outlet close to their homeland, and soon became concentrated there in sufficient numbers to be able to ease the transition to the new society. They had their own parishes, schools and newspapers in a number of New England towns. But the Franco-Americans paid a price in terms of social mobility for their attachment to their French identity, as Léon Bouvier has shown in his comparative study of Irish, Polish, Italian and French-Canadian immigrants to the United States. Although no comparable study has been done of French Canadians who emigrated to other provinces of Canada during this period, it is not inconceivable that those who refused to become assimilated quickly into the dominant group suffered similar consequences.

Emigration helped relieve the population pressure that Quebec was experiencing. A high rate of natural increase, such as Quebec had in this period, involves substantial costs: housing, education, health, job creation. This necessitates an increase in capital formation equivalent to the rate of population growth. Without emigration, the standard of living in Quebec could well have been even lower and misery could have been more widespread.

Migration within Quebec

Not all Quebecers who uprooted themselves went to the United States; many of them moved to other parts of Canada or from one region to another within Quebec. At the beginning, attempts were made to discourage people from leaving Quebec; the clergy was especially active in this endeavour, but it gradually resigned itself to emigration and tried to direct the movement or at least provide a framework for it by sending priests to minister to the Franco-Americans. It tried to persuade those who had to leave Quebec to go to western Canada. This propaganda had little effect. Arthur Silver has tried to explain the unwillingness of French Canadians to exile themselves in the West by the conservatism and fear of adventure. But with Winnipeg at a distance of 3,200 kilometres from Montreal while the American border is only sixty kilometres away, it is hardly necessary to resort to psychological explanations of this sort. The geo-economic factors that Faucher invokes are considerably more convincing.

In any case, in 1901 there were only 84,465 Quebecers, French- and English-speaking, living in other provinces, according to Hamelin and Roby. Of these, 61,776 lived in Ontario, 17,315 in the West and 4,293 in New Brunswick. Most of the emigration to the rest of Canada was thus directed towards Ontario, and French-Canadian communities grew up in the southwestern part of the province and in eastern Ontario near the Quebec border. French-Canadian emigration to northern Ontario inspired that readily excitable visionary, Curé Labelle, and a few others to dream of a majority French-speaking Kingdom of the North stretching from northern Quebec to Winnipeg! Some French-Canadian élites, meanwhile, advocated colonization of new areas of Quebec, but the movement enjoyed only limited success, and according to Hamelin and Roby between 1851 and 1901 only some 50,000 Quebecers took this route.

Of those who did not emigrate to the United States, the vast majority of Quebecers who left their native farms and villages went to the cities of Quebec. We will save a detailed study of urbanization for chapter 7, but we will note here that while 22.8 per cent of Quebec's population was classified as urban in 1871, this proportion had risen to 63.1 per cent by 1931. Montreal Island absorbed the largest number of these migrants, and its population grew from 153,516 or 12.9 per cent of Quebec's population, in 1871 to 1,020,018—35.5 per cent of Quebec's population—in 1931. The population was highly mobile, and these migratory movements added up to a vast mixing of people that brought about major changes in the distribution of Quebecers over their territory (Table 8). Between 1871 and 1901, the population of the Saguenay-Lake St. John region increased by 61.1 per cent, that of the Eastern Townships by 49.8 per cent, that of Montreal Island by 141.7 per cent and that of the Outaouais by 65.3 per cent. Population increase in the Gaspé-Lower St. Lawrence and Trois-Rivières-St. Maurice Valley regions was a little over twenty-five per cent, or less than the average for Quebec as a whole.

Quebec City and its environs grew by only 13.5 per cent, while the environs of Montreal bore the brunt of the rural exodus, and experienced only an insignificant population growth of 1.8 per cent in this thirty-year period. Between 1901 and 1931 the Saguenay-Lake St. John region became industrialized and saw its population grow by 186.2 per cent, while Montreal Island's grew by 174.9 per cent, Abitibi-Temiscamingue's by 562.7 per cent, and the North Shore-New Quebec region's by 96.8 per cent. The population of the Gaspé-Lower St. Lawrence region increased by 56.4 per cent and that of the Trois-Rivières-St. Maurice Valley region by 55.3 per cent, while Quebec City and its environs did better than in the previous period and grew by 49.0 per cent. As the average increase for Quebec as a whole was 74.3 per cent, these three regions lagged behind and had slower than average growth. The Eastern Townships and the Outaouais, which had above-average growth in the previous period, were unable to maintain this pace and were now below average with 35.2 per cent and 27.0 per cent respectively. The environs of Montreal had an increase of 17.7 per cent, slightly better than in the last three decades of the nineteenth century.

TABLE 8

Population of Quebec by Regions, 1871, 1901 and 1931

Region	*1871*		*1901*		*1931*	
	Popu-lation	*% of Total*	*Popu-lation*	*% of Total*	*Popu-lation*	*% of Total*
Gaspé/Lower St. Lawrence	134,001	11.2	172,815	10.5	270,363	9.4
Saguenay/Lake St. John	22,980	1.9	37,028	2.3	105,977	3.7
Quebec City and environs	236,563	19.9	268,595	16.3	400,256	13.9
Trois-Rivières/St. Maurice Valley	98,294	8.3	124,328	7.5	193,173	6.7
Eastern Townships	138,960	11.7	208,164	12.6	281,494	9.8
Montreal environs	352,673	29.6	358,936	21.8	422,560	14.7
Montreal Island	153,516	12.9	371,086	22.5	1,020,018	35.5
Outaouais	54,439	4.6	89,998	5.5	114,357	4.0
Abitibi-Temiscamingue	—	—	6,685	0.4	44,301	1.5
North Shore/New Quebec	—	—	11,263	0.7	22,161	0.8

Sources: *Census of Canada,* 1901, I, 4 and 5: *Quebec Yearbook,* 1955, pp. 46-47.

Immigration

According to official statistics, some 1,550,154 immigrants entered Canada between 1871 and 1901. However, hundreds of thousands of them did not settle permanently, but either returned to their countries of origin or used Canada as a stepping-stone to the United States.

There is no data for Quebec in this period, but no doubt it received its share of these thousands of immigrants. Most of those who came to Quebec were from the British Isles or the United States; very few came from other countries, and only between 1.6 and 2.2 per cent of the population was of other than French or British ethnic origin. This percentage gives only a very rough indication of immigration to Quebec in this period, as people of "other" ethnic origin could have arrived in Quebec before 1871. In addition, in 1851, 10.4 per cent of Quebec's population was foreign-born, while in 1901 the foreign-born represented only 5.5 per cent of the population. It would appear from these figures that Quebec attracted few immigrants in the last three decades of the nineteenth century.

After the return of economic prosperity, Canada began to attract large numbers of immigrants. Between 1901 and 1931, 684,582 foreigners entered Quebec, 292,296 of them in the years 1910-15 alone. Nevertheless, Quebec's net migration was negative between 1901 and 1931. According to Nathan Keyfitz, there were 822,582 emigrants from Quebec during the period, counting only people over the age of ten. In other words, thousands of immigrants who came to Quebec were transients. However, some did settle in Quebec, as the foreign-born population, which represented 5.5 per cent of the total population in 1901, grew to 8.7

per cent of the total (250,095 people) in 1931. Figures for the ethnic composition of Quebec's population lead to the same conclusion: the proportion of the population that was of neither French nor British origin grew from 2.2 per cent in 1901 to 6.0 per cent in 1931. Thus, not only did Quebec benefit from immigration during this period, but its population became more varied. We will examine this in more detail later.

According to the British North America Act of 1867, responsibility for immigration was to be shared between the federal and provincial governments, but the constitution also stipulated that in case of conflict between the two levels of government the federal government was to prevail.

Immediately after Confederation, Quebec endeavoured to exercise its responsibility in this area by engaging a number of agents in foreign countries and by publishing pamphlets for prospective immigrants. In 1875, because of the economic situation and financial constraints, it effectively withdrew from direct participation in immigration. After that, its efforts were limited to maintaining a sub-agent in the federal immigration office in England until 1883, and to the odd sporadic measure.

The Canadian government, by contrast, considered immigration a priority and was very active in promoting it. Between 1871 and 1901 it succeeded in attracting almost one and a half million immigrants, but as about two million people left Canada during the same period, its policy could hardly be called a shining success, at least not until after the turn of the century, when circumstances improved. With the help of railway and steamship companies, for which immigration meant profits, the federal government attracted hundreds of thousands of immigrants each year. Immigrants were recruited not only in the United Kingdom, but also in all parts of central and eastern Europe and in the United States.

With more than 400,000 immigrants arriving in 1913 alone, Canadian trade unions criticized the level immigration had reached. Workers feared that this massive influx of manpower would have a negative influence on wages. Others feared the difficulties of integrating the newcomers into Canadian life. There was considerable hostility towards Asian and black immigrants, and the government took steps to restrict their numbers severely. There were even signs in some shop windows in western Canada reading "No English need apply." They were addressed to the indigent Britons who had been driven out of England by the economic difficulties of 1907-8.

In a similar vein, French-Canadian nationalists such as Henri Bourassa and Armand Lavergne attacked the poor selection of immigrants and criticized the almost total absence of immigrants from Belgium and France. They saw this policy as a threat to the English-French ethnic balance of the country. In this context, it is not surprising that evidence of racism and xenophobia could be found among French as well as English Canadians.

Quebec was favourable, however, to the federal government's efforts to repatriate Canadians who had gone to the United States. While the results of these

Immigrants in Quebec City, 1911.

efforts were not encouraging in the nineteenth century, the situation improved in the twentieth and especially in the 1920s. It is estimated that the Canadian government succeeded in repatriating more than 400,000 Canadians between 1900 and 1940, and that along with them came tens of thousands of Americans born of Canadian parents. While it is not known how many of these were French Canadians, we do know that 55,000 of the American immigrants to Canada counted in the 1931 census were of French ethnic origin.

The Quebec government also had a repatriation policy and undertook efforts in this direction at various times. In 1871 it appointed a priest as its repatriation agent in Massachusetts and between 1875 and 1879 it spent a little over $100,000 on repatriation, but the results were disappointing. For a decade, especially during the administration of Premier Honoré Mercier (1887-91) and his deputy minister of agriculture and colonization, Curé Labelle, new efforts were made to attract immigrants from France and Belgium to Quebec. But the few thousand who were recruited represented only an infinitesimal proportion of the immigrants who came to Canada. In 1928, the Quebec government again tried to repatriate Franco-Americans, but as in the past, hopes were disappointed; at the end of 1931, only 9,920 candidates for repatriation had been recruited, and the program had cost almost $400,000 in four years. On the whole, immigration policy did little to promote the interests of Quebec, and in any case Quebec was more concerned with keeping its population at home than with attracting newcomers.

Between 1871 and 1931, Quebec's high rate of natural increase compensated for its negative net migration. Unlike Ontario's growth, to which immigration made a significant contribution, Quebec's population growth was primarily the result of natural increase. Quebec's population aged somewhat, as can be seen by a comparison of the age pyramids for 1871 and 1931 (Figure 1), but it remained younger than Ontario's. This had important economic effects. Ontario's age structure was more favourable than Quebec's because its population was more heavily concentrated in the economically active age groups — from fifteen to sixty-four. In 1931, 392 of every thousand people in Ontario were economically active, while in Quebec the proportion was 357 per thousand. As Jacques Henripin has shown, this had the effect of lowering per capita income in Quebec in comparison with Ontario.

Between 1871 and 1931, Quebec's demographic behaviour tended towards conformity with the demographic behaviour of North America as a whole. But it was slow in reaching this point, and this delay was beneficial to French Canadians as an ethnic group, at least from a numerical standpoint. Whether it was also beneficial for the quality of life of Quebecers remains to be seen.

CHAPTER 3
ETHNIC AND LINGUISTIC GROUPS

Because relations between French Canadians and English Canadians in Quebec and in Canada as a whole have played such a large historical role, the ethnic composition of Quebec, the proportion of the population represented by different groups and the development of these groups over time are questions that merit our attention.

Ethnic Composition

In the debates leading up to Confederation, majority or minority status again became an important theme. The union of the two Canadas in 1840-41 had made French Canadians a minority, and this numerical weakness would become even more pronounced if all the British North American colonies were to unite. Some people feared that such a union would have undesirable political consequences for French Canada as a whole. On the other hand, the proposal's supporters maintained that since the new union would be a federal one it would give French Canadians more political power. They argued that the only alternative was annexation to the United States, where the French-speaking population would be completely engulfed.

Some spokesmen for the English minority in Lower Canada were also uneasy about the future, because under the new régime they would be dependent on the French-Canadian majority for at least some aspects of their community life. As we will see, they were provided with solid constitutional guarantees aimed at protecting them.

The 150,000 French Canadians outside Quebec were not so fortunate, and were made subject to the political whims of the English majorities in their respective provinces. The educational and linguistic rights of these French Canadians would be trampled on in New Brunswick, Manitoba, the Northwest Territories (when the provinces of Saskatchewan and Alberta were created) and in Ontario. Majority versus minority was an essential element of these ethnic disputes, although far from the only one.

In Manitoba, legislation promoting French-English equality was passed in 1870 when the two groups were roughly equal in number, whereas the rights of French-speaking Manitobans were abolished in the 1890s when they made up only about a seventh of the population. A similar pattern can be seen in Ontario, where relations between the two groups reached a crisis when the French-speaking population increased from five to eight per cent of the provincial total within a few decades (1881-1911).

The weight of numbers

Nevertheless, the French-Canadian minority continued to believe in the possibility of a Canada that would be both French and English. Overall population changes in Canada between 1871 and 1931 were reasonably reassuring, both in terms of the proportion of the Canadian population represented by the population of Quebec and in terms of the percentage of French Canadians in the population (Table 9).

The effects of French Canadians' extraordinary fertility balanced those of migration movements which were unfavourable to them. Up to 1901, their proportion in the population varied between twenty-nine and thirty-one per cent. The wave of immigration at the beginning of the century lowered that percentage by about two per cent. The population of Quebec followed the same pattern in

TABLE 9
Population of Canada, Population of Quebec and French-Canadian Population, 1871-1931

Year	Canada	Quebec	Quebec / Canada (%)	French Canadians	Fr. Can. / Canada (%)
1871	3,689,257	1,191,516	32.3	1,082,940	31.1
1881	4,324,810	1,359,029	31.4	1,298,929	30.0
1891	4,833,239	1,488,535	30.8	—	—
1901	5,371,315	1,648,898	30.7	1,649,371	30.7
1911	7,206,643	2,005,776	27.8	2,061,719	28.6
1921	8,787,949	2,360,510	26.9	2,452,743	27.9
1931	10,376,786	2,874,662	27.7	2,927,990	28.2

Source: Censuses of Canada.

relation to that of Canada as a whole, except that the decline in the proportion it represented was a little sharper. In all, despite Canada's territorial expansion and the influx of immigrants, both Quebec and French Canada almost succeeded in maintaining their relative numerical strength over the six-decade period.

The proportion of the French-Canadian population living outside Quebec increased steadily from 14.2 per cent in 1871 to a maximum of 22.9 per cent in 1921, and then began to decline. The notion of a Greater French Canada that formed part of nationalist ideology gained strength from the growth of the French-Canadian population outside Quebec.

In 1871, 85.8 per cent of all Canadians of French origin lived in Quebec, while in 1931 this proportion was only 77.5 per cent. Quebec remained the *foyer du Canada français*, but the 657,931 French Canadians outside Quebec could not be ignored. However, while in the nineteenth century Franco-Americans could also be considered part of French Canada, now there was no longer any basis for this belief. Nevertheless, the disputes between Irish Catholics and Franco-Americans in New England were followed with great interest in certain circles.

Ethnic origin — defined by the census as the nationality of the first male ancestor to arrive in America — is a fairly crude measure of a group's size. The criterion of mother tongue, which the census defines as the first language learned among those still spoken by an individual, gives a better reading. It is questionable whether people who no longer speak French should be considered part of the French population.

While there is a very high correlation between French ethnic origin and French mother tongue in Quebec, this is not as true for French Canadians outside Quebec. According to the 1931 census, 99,552 of the 657,931 Canadians of French origin outside Quebec no longer had French as their mother tongue. This indicates the extent to which French minorities became weakened and were assimilated in an English-speaking environment.

The ethnic composition of Quebec

The situation in Quebec appeared to be more favourable for French Canadians, and during the period we are studying their proportion of Quebec's population remained in the neighbourhood of eighty per cent (Table 10).

Data for 1851 and 1861 are included even though it is impossible to separate Quebecers of British origin from those of other origins for those years. During those decades, Quebec was only three-quarters French; starting from this minimum figure, French Canadians strengthened their hold on Quebec's territory. In half a century, their proportion increased from 75.2 per cent to 80.2 per cent of Quebec's population. During the next twenty years it remained stable despite heavy immigration and then declined to seventy-nine per cent.

TABLE 10
Distribution of Quebec's Population by Ethnic Origin, 1851-1931

	French		*British*		*Other*	
Year	*Number*	*%*	*Number*	*%*	*Number*	*%*
1851	669,528	75.2	—	—	—	—
1861	847,615	76.2	—	—	—	—
1871	929,817	78.0	243,041	20.4	18,658	1.6
1881	1,075,130	79.1	260,538	19.1	23,359	1.8
1901	1,322,115	80.2	290,169	17.6	36,614	2.2
1911	1,606,535	80.1	318,799	15.9	80,442	4.0
1921	1,889,269	80.0	356,943	15.1	114,453	4.9
1931	2,270,059	79.0	432,726	15.0	171,877	6.0

Source: *Quebec Yearbooks.*

Quebecers of British origin

The first settlers in some regions of Quebec were English-speaking; they came either directly from the United Kingdom or via the United States, as Loyalists or as farmers in search of good land. The first Quebecers of British origin settled in Quebec City and Montreal. With the coming of the Loyalists, and even more so with the large wave of immigration after 1815, major concentrations were established in the Eastern Townships, the Outaouais, the Gaspé and the plain south of Montreal.

Authorities in England channelled British immigration towards the Eastern Townships, so that in 1851, not surprisingly, sixty-six per cent of that region's population was of British origin. But from that time on an increasing number of French Canadians came into the Eastern Townships, and by 1871 they formed the majority there. In 1901, seventy-three per cent of the region's population was French Canadian, and only Brome, Missisquoi and Stanstead counties had British majorities. The British reacted by setting up colonization companies to attract their countrymen to the region, but these efforts met with little success. The industries that came to the urban areas of the Townships brought with them personnel of British origin and strengthened the British group in such towns as Granby, Waterloo and Magog. But the need for manpower also attracted French Canadians, who by 1931 made up eighty-four per cent of the population and were the majority everywhere except in Brome county. Of the 52,000 Quebecers of British origin in the region, 17,000 lived in urban areas; they were concentrated especially in Lennoxville, where they founded a university (Bishop's), in North Hatley, and near Lake Massawippi and Lake Memphremagog, where tourism allowed them to survive. The 35,000 rural residents of British origin in the

Townships were an aging population, as young people left the region. With no one to take their place, older people sold their lands to French Canadians and retired to the villages.

Some British Quebecers saw this dramatic population reversal as a conspiracy of the Roman Catholic church. In his book *The Tragedy of Quebec: The Expulsion of Its Protestant Farmers*, Robert Sellar virulently denounced this French-Canadian invasion. He was not the first. In 1876, the Montreal *Daily Witness* criticized the Quebec government for allotting $50,000 to a repatriation program for Franco-Americans. The *Witness* argued that the money would really be used to recruit French-Canadian settlers from traditionally French parts of Quebec to the Eastern Townships, and the author of the article added: "No English, Irish, Scotch or German need apply."

According to Raoul Blanchard, the Outaouais — the Quebec section of the Ottawa Valley — could be called a little Ireland in 1851 since nearly half its population was Irish; in addition, people of English, Scottish and Welsh origin made up more than twenty per cent of the population. But construction work attracted French Canadians, who formed a majority by 1881 and constituted seventy per cent of the population in 1931. Immigrants of British origin continued to settle in the Outaouais after they had stopped coming to the Eastern Townships, and as a result the British population was better able to resist the French-Canadian tide.

Beginning in the early nineteenth century, English-speaking settlers — Loyalists and immigrants from the United Kingdom — formed a majority in the Gaspé. The Gaspesian fishery was dominated by a few merchants from the Channel Islands, notably the Robin family. There were also some French Canadians and Acadians established there, and gradually more French Canadians from the Lower St. Lawrence joined them; by 1931 the population of the Gaspé was eighty per cent French.

There were 41,000 Quebecers of British origin in the plain south of Montreal in 1851; there were significant Scottish settlements in Huntingdon and Beauharnois counties. By 1931, all the counties in this area were dominated by French Canadians; their numbers had grown to 238,000, as compared with a British population of 22,000.

Montreal picked up the pieces of the English-speaking rural exodus. In 1871, 22.5 per cent of all Quebecers of British origin lived on Montreal Island; by 1901 this proportion had risen to 39.3 per cent and by 1931 it was 61.0 per cent. Outside Montreal Island there remained only 168,947 Quebecers of British origin, engulfed in a mass of 1,665,232 French Canadians. Only three counties — Pontiac in the Outaouais, Huntingdon southwest of Montreal and Brome in the Eastern Townships — still had British majorities.

This British group is not a homogeneous bloc. It has English, Scottish, Irish and Welsh components, along with natives of British possessions and Americans. (Census data do not identify Americans as a separate ethnic group since they are based on origin of the first male ancestor to arrive in America as the criterion of ethnicity.) The English, Scottish and Irish have been by far the largest of these groups, and each has grown and developed at its own pace (Table 11).

In 1871, more than half of Quebec's British population and 10.4 per cent of the population of Quebec as a whole was Irish; by 1931 only a quarter of the British group was Irish. A large number of Irish emigrated to Ontario and the United States.

Most of the Irish came in the first half of the nineteenth century, forced to leave their country by the desperate conditions that prevailed there, culminating in the Famine in the 1840s. They were very poor when they arrived in Quebec and, along with French Canadians, formed Quebec's first working class. Many of them built canals and railways and worked in the forest industry, on the docks in Quebec City and Montreal and around the Lachine Canal. For historical and religious reasons, relations between the Irish and other immigrants from the United Kingdom were not always cordial. On the other hand, while their Catholicism gave the Irish something in common with the French Canadians, language was a divisive factor, and the two groups tended to compete for the same jobs. Competition for labouring jobs between the Irish and French Canadians coming to the cities from rural Quebec degenerated into ethnic conflicts distinguished by fights on the docks and construction sites. The Catholic church made attempts to ease the tension between the two groups. The Montreal Irish had their own parish, St. Patrick's, where they were served by Irish priests, and from 1888 the Collège Sainte-Marie gave a full course in English to accommodate them. English-speaking Jesuits founded Loyola College in 1899.

While peaceful co-existence between Irish and French Canadians within the institutional framework of the Catholic church was established in Quebec, the same was not true in Ontario and New England, where there were intense struggles between the two groups for the control of churches and schools. On a personal level, marriage between Irish and French Canadians was facilitated by their common religion, and this led to assimilation that could work either way. Overall, Quebecers of Irish origin had succeeded in improving their lot by the early twentieth century.

TABLE 11

Quebecers of English, Scottish and Irish Origin, 1871, 1901 and 1931 (as % of total population)

Origin	*1871*	*1901*	*1931*
English	5.9	7.0	8.2
Scottish	4.2	3.6	3.0
Irish	10.4	7.0	3.8

Sources: H. Charbonneau and R. Maheu, *Les aspects démographiques de la question linguistique;* Censuses of Canada.

Scots began to settle in Quebec at the time of the conquest and quickly became dominant in the commercial sector. But not all Scots were fur-trading magnates like the McTavishes and McGillivrays. There were many Scottish farmers as well. Raoul Blanchard even reported that in Argenteuil county northwest of Montreal French Canadians took the best lands while Scottish farmers were forced to raise livestock in the uplands.

The Scottish population declined as a percentage of the total, while the proportion of English increased substantially; by the end of the period we are studying, more than half of all Quebecers of British origin were English. In absolute numbers, Quebec's population of English origin grew from 69,822 in 1871 to 234,739 in 1931. Not much is known about the history of this group in Quebec, but it should certainly not be assumed that all English Quebecers have been part of the bourgeoisie (capitalist class). While Quebec's bourgeoisie has indeed been dominated by an Anglo-Scottish bloc, English immigration to Quebec has included people of all classes: the urban poor and orphans sent to Canada by charitable societies to reduce the social burden in England; skilled workers in such fields as iron and steel and transportation equipment; and a substantial number of farmers.

Language and religion separated the English and Scottish group on the one hand from the French Canadians on the other, and each group set up its own institutional network as much as possible and kept its contacts with the other group at a minimum. In Quebec City, where ninety-two per cent of the population was French-speaking in 1931, the English-speaking group had its own newspaper, high school, and voluntary organizations and, as Blanchard noted, included a substantial number of people who didn't deign even to speak French. But the Anglo-Scottish group, unlike the Irish, were not in direct competition with the French Canadians. It seemed natural for the English-speaking minority to be dominant so long as it didn't interfere directly with the ways and customs of the majority, and this prevailing belief made it easier for the élites of the two groups to maintain harmony.

* * *

Ethnic groups of other than French and British origin were small in absolute numbers, growing from a total of 18,658 people in 1871 to 171,877 in 1931 (Table 12). But they constituted a true mosaic. In the first thirty years of the period this population barely doubled, while in the next thirty years, the years of the great wave of immigration of the early twentieth century, it nearly quintupled.

Ethnic diversification had hardly begun in 1871: native Indians and Germans accounted for eighty per cent of the population of other than French and British origin. By 1901 the Jewish and Italian groups had begun to grow, and these four major groups now made up seventy-five per cent of the "others." Thirty years later, while the native Indian and German groups had grown only slightly, there had been a considerable increase in the numbers of Jews and Italians. Quebec had

TABLE 12

Ethnic Groups of Other than French and British Origin in Quebec, 1871, 1901 and 1931

Group	*1871*	*1901*	*1931*
Native Indians	6,988	10,142	12,312
Inuit	—	—	1,159
Germans	7,963	6,923	10,616
Jews	74	7,607	60,087
Italians	539	2,805	24,845
Others	3,094	9,137	62,858
Total	18,658	36,614	171,877

Source: H. Charbonneau and R. Maheu, *Les aspects démographiques de la question linguistique*, pp. 309, 311 and 314.

also become more ethnically diverse, as only sixty-three per cent of the "others" were now constituted by these four groups. An additional eighteen ethnic groups with between 1,600 and 9,500 members in 1931 could be included to make the table more complete.

Native Indians and Inuit

As an aboriginal people, native Indians merit special attention, even though they made up only about 0.5 per cent of Quebec's population throughout the period we are studying. It is estimated that when the first whites came there were 220,000 native Indians in what is now Canada. As a result of the European arrival, their way of life sustained a shock of such magnitude that some people believed they would virtually disappear. The 1901 census counted only 93,460 Indians in Canada; this population decline is a good indication of the difficulties that the original inhabitants of the territory underwent.

The numbers of native Indians living in Quebec have been relatively small. In 1901, the 976 Métis and 9,166 Indians living there represented only 2.8 per cent and 9.8 per cent respectively of the Canadian total for these two groups, and in 1931 Quebec's 13,471 Indians and Inuit constituted 10.5 per cent of Canada's native population.

The vast majority of Quebec's Indians lived on reserves scattered throughout the province. The largest concentrations of Indians were in northern Quebec, where they lived by hunting, but there were also some near Quebec City and Montreal (Lorette, Caughnawaga and Oka).

The 1931 census counted 1,159 Inuit, all living in northern Quebec and making their living primarily from fishing. Both the nature of their habitat and their way of life made the Inuit a homogeneous group, and they had less contact

A group of Montagnais at Pointe-Bleue on Lake St. John, about 1890.

with whites than did the Indians. The 12,312 Indians consisted of two large families, Algonquins and Iroquois, subdivided in turn into a number of tribes: Naskapis, Crees, Montagnais, Micmacs, Hurons and others. Some tribes had quite different ways of life from others, which tended to isolate them from one another. On the one hand, the Crees and Montagnais of the North Shore preserved their ancestral way of life. They lived by hunting, with a hunting season lasting eight to ten months. When they left the reserve they took women and children with them, leaving only the old people behind. One result of this precarious mode of existence was a high rate of infant mortality. The Micmacs of Bonaventure county in the Gaspé, on the other hand, fished and farmed and lived much as did the neighbouring whites. The proximity of Caughnawaga to Montreal meant that its Iroquois population was heavily influenced by the city. Many of them worked in construction in Montreal, Ontario or the United States. There was little farming on the reserve and those who stayed there tried to make a living from tourism. In brief, the Indians were a heterogeneous group, and the slow growth of the Indian population is graphic evidence of their vulnerability and the misery in which they lived.

The native Indians had little contact with the Quebec government during the period we are studying. According to the constitution, they were a federal responsibility. For many years, the Indian Act of 1876 was the framework within which federal policy towards the Indians was carried out. This very paternalistic legislation was based on the proposition that it was necessary to protect the Indians from the whites by keeping them confined to reserves where attempts would be made gradually to "civilize" them. The reserve system was in effect before 1867, but it was greatly expanded when the federal government negotiated treaties with various Indian tribes in Ontario and the West between 1871 and 1923. In these treaties, the Indians relinquished vast expanses of land to the federal government in exchange for guaranteed rights on their reserves and some very meagre material advantages. Although there were a number of reserves in Quebec, some of them dating back to the French régime, no treaties had been negotiated with Quebec's native peoples. When Ungava (New Quebec) was added to Quebec in 1912, it was stipulated in the federal-provincial agreement that it would be the Quebec government's responsibility to negotiate with the Indians so as to extinguish their aboriginal rights over the territory. Through indifference or carelessness, the government of Premier Lomer Gouin, in office at the time, and its successors neglected to fulfil this responsibility. The question of Indian and Inuit rights became urgent when the James Bay project was undertaken in the 1970s.

The Germans

From the mid-eighteenth century to Confederation, many Germans came to Britain's North American colonies, so that in 1871 there were 202,991 Germans in Canada, 158,608 of them in Ontario and 31,942 in Nova Scotia. Although there were only 7,963 Germans in Quebec, they were the largest ethnic group after the French-Canadian and British groups.

The Germans settled in places where the British element predominated: there were 1,315 in Montreal, 3,023 in four counties in the Eastern Townships, 862 in western Quebec and 500 in three counties in the plain south of Montreal. Very few Germans came to Quebec in the sixty years following 1871, and in 1931 their numbers had risen to only 10,616.

The Jews

In 1871, only seventy-four Quebecers declared themselves to be of Jewish ethnic origin while 579 said they were of the Jewish religion, a fairly small number by either measure. The forbears of most of these Jews came from Britain or the United States; it was primarily a bourgeois population and a large number of its members were merchants.

The immigrants who started to come to Quebec towards the end of the century were very different. Large numbers of Jews emigrated to North America at this time to escape persecution in Russia and some of these came to Quebec. In 1900 it was estimated that there were 6,000 Russian Jews in Montreal, and in 1901 the Jewish population of Quebec was 7,607. During the next three decades, thousands of Jews left the Austro-Hungarian Empire and Poland, so that in 1931 there were 60,087 Quebecers of Jewish origin, four-fifths of them in Montreal. From the turn of the century on, they were the largest ethnic group in Quebec outside the French and British groups. Between 1911 and 1931 Jews constituted six to seven per cent of the population of Montreal; their concentration in certain neighbourhoods allowed them at a very early date to elect representatives of their community to the federal parliament, the Quebec legislature and city council.

The social characteristics of the late-nineteenth- and early-twentieth-century Jewish immigrants were different from those of the Jews who were previously established in Qubec. The new immigrants were poor; many of them worked in the clothing industry while some went into business as shopkeepers or pedlars. Unlike other immigrant groups, the Jews were supported by self-help institutions that Jews in Europe had set up as a result of centuries of persecution; institutions of this sort were established in Montreal. Jews made their mark in Quebec primarily in two areas: trade unionism on the one hand, and commerce and finance on the other.

The Italians

While the growth of the Italian community took place primarily in the early twentieth century, there were already some 1,400 Italians in Montreal in 1893. Canon Bruchési, who spoke Italian, succeeded in obtaining a "mission" for them; this became Mount Carmel parish in 1905. A second parish, served by Italian priests, was founded in 1911. As with the Irish, the Catholic church tried to respect the ethnic identity of its Italian parishioners. In general, relations between French and Italian Quebecers were good, as can be seen by the tendency of the Italians to choose French as their daily language and the large number of marriages between members of the two groups. A number of factors contributed towards bringing them together: Catholicism, Latin culture, a tendency to live in the same Montreal neighbourhoods and a similar socio-economic position.

The Italians who came early in the century worked mostly at labouring jobs. They were exploited ferociously not only by Canadian capitalists but also by some of their own countrymen. The most notable of these was one Cordasco, who played the role of middleman between the railway companies and the immigrants whom he brought over by the thousands, promising them jobs and extorting a substantial commission. When Mussolini, in power in Italy since 1922, decided to extend his influence to the Italian diaspora in the late 1920s, the result was a split in Montreal's Italian community. During the Second World War, the Canadian government made life very uncomfortable for some of those who had followed Il Duce and his fascist doctrine.

Montreal, a cosmopolitan city

A strong tendency to concentrate on Montreal Island was characteristic of all ethnic groups except the French Canadians and the native peoples (Table 13). The industrialization of Quebec along with the rural exodus brought French Canadians to the cities, where they became the majority. But in Montreal, the most important centre of economic activity, the proportion of French Canadians just barely stayed above sixty per cent, primarily because by far the heaviest concentrations of the British and other ethnic groups were to be found there (Tables 13 and 14).

In the mid-nineteenth century French Canadians were a minority in Montreal, and even in Quebec City they constituted only sixty per cent of the population. Quebecers of British origin who came to Montreal from the country and the "others" who concentrated there helped make Quebec's metropolis a highly

TABLE 13
Distribution of Ethnic Groups between Montreal Island and the Rest of Quebec, 1871, 1901 and 1931

	1871		*1901*		*1931*	
Origin	*Montreal Island*	*Rest of Quebec*	*Montreal Island*	*Rest of Quebec*	*Montreal Island*	*Rest of Quebec*
French	9.3	91.7	17.4	82.6	26.6	73.4
British	22.6	77.4	39.3	60.7	61.0	39.0
Other	12.7	87.3	44.3	55.7	78.7	21.3
Total pop.	12.0	88.0	21.9	78.1	35.9	64.1

Source: H. Charbonneau and R. Maheu, *Les aspects démographiques de la question linguistique.*

TABLE 14
Ethnic Composition of the Population of Montreal Island, 1871, 1901, 1931

	1871		*1901*		*1931*	
Origin	*Number*	*%*	*Number*	*%*	*Number*	*%*
French	86,846	60.3	230,217	63.9	604,827	60.2
British	54,824	38.1	113,897	31.6	263,779	26.3
Other	2,374	1.6	16,233	4.5	135,262	13.5
Total	144,044	100.0	360,347	100.0	1,003,868	100.0

Source: H. Charbonneau and R. Maheu, *Les aspects démographiques de la question linguistique,* p. 369.

colourful cosmopolitan city. The east end was overwhelmingly French, but other neighbourhoods had a Victorian appearance, and there were Jewish neighbourhoods, an Irish Griffintown, a Chinese section, and a black ghetto in the Saint-Antoine area, near Bonaventure Station, where a number of blacks were employed.

A French-Canadian Province

In the mid-nineteenth century French Canadians constituted three-quarters of the total population of Quebec and were concentrated in the St. Lawrence Valley, where the seigneurial system still prevailed. Raoul Blanchard described the situation around 1851 as follows:

> The French Canadians appeared to be hemmed in, surrounded by a British cordon. The position of the British was strengthened by their concentration in the Ottawa Valley, southwest of Montreal, and in the Eastern Townships; the British also penetrated the two cities, and thus struck deep into French territory. But the French Canadians were actively moving out from their base, and they would break down all the barriers, cover the whole province, and even spill across its borders.

By the 1840s and 1850s, the older areas of Quebec could no longer absorb the French-Canadian surplus population, and French Canadians began to infiltrate the areas held by the British groups. By 1901, the Eastern Townships had a French-Canadian majority; so did the Outaouais, which had been an English/Irish region since 1880. Meanwhile, French Canadians also settled in the new regions that were becoming open to colonization: Saguenay-Lake St. John, Temiscamingue and the area north of Montreal. In 1931, only three counties — Brome, Huntingdon and Pontiac — did not have French-Canadian majorities, and thirty-six of Quebec's seventy-four counties were more than ninety-five per cent French-Canadian. Overall, Quebec was Canada's most homogeneous province.

Linguistic Evolution

The Canadian census deals with language under two headings. Starting with the 1901 census, Canadians have been asked about their knowledge of the two official languages, English and French. Only people who say they can carry on a conversation in English and in French are considered bilingual for census purposes; a Canadian who speaks Italian and French is considered unilingual. The second heading is mother tongue, that is, the first language learned among those still spoken at the time of the census. This question first appeared in 1921, for people at least ten years old. In the 1931 census, measurement of mother tongue was extended to the whole population by making the assumption that the mother tongue of children under ten was the language spoken by their parents at home.

Interesting results can be obtained by correlating information about mother tongue with information about origin and languages spoken. In this fashion, a picture emerges of such phenomena as the assimilation of one group by another, language shifts within various ethnic groups and the relative force of attraction exerted by English and French.

According to the 1931 census, in every province except Quebec (which will be discussed below), there were fewer Canadians of French mother tongue than of French origin. This indicates that a number of Canadians of French origin no longer spoke French or else did not learn French as their first language. Taking the analysis somewhat further, 127,086 Canadians of French origin had English as their mother tongue and 5,210 listed a mother tongue other than French or English. In short, the French ethnic group outside Quebec effectively had lost twenty per cent of its numbers.

For Canadians of French origin in Quebec, the situation was different from what it was in the other provinces; there were more people of French mother tongue than of French origin. Conversely, there were fewer people of English and other mother tongue than of British and other ethnic origin (Table 15).

The existence of more people of French mother tongue than of French origin, as was the case in 1931 in Quebec, indicates that French Canadians remained faithful to their language and even succeeded in winning over some people of British or other ethnic origin. A very small proportion of the French-Canadian population of Quebec — 0.6 per cent — had a mother tongue other than French; 12,653 had English as their mother tongue and 665 listed some other language. On the other hand, 24,465 people of British origin and 10,987 from other ethnic groups had French as their mother tongue. The French language thus came out ahead: 35,452 gains as opposed to 13,318 losses.

The English language had a small negative balance (3,113). It is startling to realize that twice as many people of British origin were assimilated into the French-Canadian group than vice-versa — 24,465 as opposed to 12,653. This can

TABLE 15

Mother Tongue of Quebec's Population by Ethnic Group, 1931

Ethnic Origin	*English Mother Tongue*	*French Mother Tongue*	*Other Mother Tongue*	*Total*
British	406,883	24,465	1,428	432,726
French	12,653	2,256,741	665	2,270,059
Other	10,127	10,987	150,356	171,470
Total	429,613	2,292,193	152,449	2,874,255

Source: H. Charbonneau and R. Maheu, *Les aspects démographiques de la question linguistique*, p. 258.

be explained by the isolation of the people of British origin who remained in rural Quebec and probably also by marriages between French and Irish Catholics, which resulted in O'Neils, Johnsons and Ryans becoming Quebecers of French mother tongue although for census purposes they were still of British ethnic origin. However, the British group could hardly be described as weak, and its strength can be seen in its capacity to absorb members of the other groups. Of the 21,114 members of other groups who had one of the two official languages as their mother tongue, 10,127 had chosen English and 10,987 had chosen French. The French Canadians, who made up seventy-nine per cent of Quebec's population, attracted fifty-two per cent of the new Quebecers, while the British group, only fifteen per cent of the population, attracted forty-eight per cent, an indication of how strong the attraction of English was.

The other groups were losers in these language shifts, with a negative balance of 19,021. Because immigration was heavy in the first three decades of the century, the number of people listing a mother tongue other than French or English remained fairly high. Their children or grandchildren, however, would list French or English as their mother tongue. The tendency to choose French differed from group to group. In 1931, seventy-seven per cent of the Italians and 41.8 per cent of the Germans had chosen French, as compared with only 7.5 per cent of the Dutch and 18.2 per cent of the Jews.

The force of attraction exerted by English also shows up in an analysis of the data relating to the official languages. The author of the introduction to the 1901 census was in no doubt about this force of attraction: "And as English is now in a very large degree the language of commerce throughout the world, it is also desirable to ascertain to what extent citizens of French origin are able to speak it in addition to their own."

A number of constants relating to bilingualism in Canada showed up in the four censuses between 1901 and 1931. First of all, the rate of bilingualism — the proportion of the population able to speak both French and English — was not very high: 13.9 per cent in 1901, 7.4 per cent in 1911, 16.7 per cent in 1921 and 15.1 per cent in 1931. The large influx of people speaking other languages led to the drop in the rate between 1901 and 1911, while in the next ten years it more than doubled, probably as a result of the First World War; in 1931, it had returned to a level not much different from what it was at the beginning of the century. For each census in which it is possible to calculate the rate of bilingualism separately for Canadians of French origin and Canadians of British origin, the rate for French Canadians was almost ten times as high. Quebec was by far the most bilingual province in the country, with a rate of 29.3 per cent in 1931 (Table 16).

Charbonneau and Maheu standardized the percentages to make those of different censuses comparable with one another, and according to their calculations, 23.3 per cent of Quebecers of British origin and 30.6 of those of French origin were bilingual in 1931. In all the other provinces, the minority, understandably enough, had a much higher rate of bilingualism than the majority. Even if

TABLE 16
Distribution of Quebec's Population by Official Languages Spoken, 1931

Languages Spoken	*Number*	*%*
Only English	395,995	13.8
Only French	1,615,155	56.2
English and French	842,369	29.3
Neither English nor French	20,736	0.7

Source: H. Charbonneau and R. Maheu, *Les aspects démographiques de la question linguistique*, p. 24.

Quebecers of British origin were more bilingual than their fellows in the other provinces, the fact remains that they were not as bilingual as Quebec's French majority. The reason why French-speaking Quebecers agreed or were forced to speak English in such large numbers can be seen in the very close relationship between bilingualism and economic life in Quebec. Charbonneau and Maheu have shown that men are more bilingual than women in Quebec simply because they are more likely to be in the labour market. The rate of bilingualism varies significantly according to sex and age group. Thus, in 1931, boys and girls up to fourteen years of age had roughly the same rate of bilingualism — twenty-one per cent for boys and 20.5 per cent for girls; for the fifteen to nineteen age group, the age at which people entered the labour market, the rate rose to thirty-six per cent for boys and thirty-three per cent for girls; for the twenty to thirty-four group the rate was fifty per cent for men and thirty-six per cent for women; after the age of thirty-five the rate gradually declined, but it remained substantially higher for men, who were more likely to be in the labour market and needed English for promotions, than for women. As a result, even though there were only 432,726 Quebecers of British origin, 1,238,364 Quebecers spoke English.

Eloquent as they are, statistics don't tell the whole story. As is well known, the English language enjoyed enormous prestige during the period we are studying. The French-Canadian élite preached the need to learn English and prided itself on its bilingualism. A foreign observer, André Siegfried, was shocked by the English appearance of Quebec City and Montreal early in the century. He remarked that in Quebec City "English [is] the speech of the managers and French of the menials." In Montreal, he wrote, "visitors may pass whole weeks there, frequenting hotels, banks, shops, railway stations without ever imagining for a moment that the town is French by a great majority of its inhabitants. English society affects unconsciousness of this fact, and bears itself exactly as though it had no French neighbours. They seem to regard Montreal as their property." How could this phenomenon be explained? "Think of the Indian civil service, and you will understand better the rulers of Canada," Siegfried concluded. The situation in Quebec's smaller cities doesn't seem to have been much better. In Sherbrooke in 1912, although the vast majority of the population was French-speaking, not only

The English character of Montreal was clearly reflected in its signs.

did the city council conduct its meetings in English but the city employees were also all English-speaking and spoke only their own language. The most important part of the course at the technical school in Shawinigan consisted of learning English, since this was the only way a French-Canadian worker could obtain a promotion in the town's large factories. Michel Brunet reminds us that until 1925 cheques issued by the provincial government were in English only.

In the nineteenth century, some outspoken individuals — Arthur Buies, Jules-Paul Tardivel and Edmond de Nevers, to name only a few — criticized the lowly position of French as best they could, but with little effect. The struggle to protect the French language became much wider in the early twentieth century, and had the support of such movements as the Société du Bon Parler Français, the Ligue Nationaliste Canadienne, the Association Catholique de la Jeunesse Canadienne-Française, the Ligue des Droits du Français and the Action Française. These are generally termed nationalist organizations, and their major demands fell into three categories: respect for the language rights of French-speaking minorities, implementation of bilingualism at the federal level and a fair representation of French Canadians in the federal civil service, and making Quebec French again.

In the first area, they saw one province after another — Saskatchewan, Alberta, Ontario, Manitoba — bring in legislation that seriously interfered with the rights of French minorities. However, in 1927, after fifteen years of bitter struggle, they had the satisfaction of seeing Ontario repeal its famous Regulation 17.

In the area of federal bilingualism, the only result of their efforts consisted of two small victories: excise stamps became bilingual in 1923, as did postage stamps in 1927.

Their efforts to make Quebec French again in terms of both spoken language and appearance also met with little success, and their struggle never seemed to get beyond the starting point. Their only significant victory — and it was a modest one — was the passage in 1910 of what was called "la loi Lavergne."

Armand Lavergne was a young follower of nationalist leader Henri Bourassa, elected in 1904 to the federal House of Commons, where he twice introduced a bill making it compulsory for utilities to offer services in French. Although his bill was supported by a petition signed by 433,845 people, it was not accepted by the House. He took up the cause again in 1909 after being elected to the Quebec legislature. It was only on his second try, the next year, that the bill was accepted. With public opinion behind him, he succeeded in overcoming the reservations of the Liberals, who were afraid of upsetting English-speaking business circles. The act stipulated that railway, steamship, telephone, telegraph and electric companies would have to use both French and English in communicating with the public in Quebec.

If these modest victories are testimony to the zeal of the champions of the French language, they also indicate the inferior status and low prestige of the language of the majority of Quebecers.

PART II
1867-1896

THE ECONOMY

In the first thirty years after Confederation, Quebec's economy underwent profound changes. The choice of 1867 as a starting point for these changes is somewhat arbitrary because some of them, notably industrialization, were under way as early as the 1850s, while others such as the growth of dairy production did not appear before the 1870s and 1880s. Nevertheless, 1867 represents a significant turning point, since Confederation established a wider domestic market and a new economic entity, and this had a decisive effect on Quebec's subsequent development.

We will concentrate on two sectors of Quebec's economy — agriculture and industry. Some aspects of the wider economic context are necessary background to a discussion of these sectors, and they will be examined in the first chapter of this section. This chapter will look at the economic effects of Quebec's membership in the British Empire and Canadian Confederation, and at two major historiographic interpretations that endeavour to explain Canada's economic development and the changing external influences affecting Quebec. In the second chapter, the effects of internal factors will be examined — the domestic market, the communications network (especially railways), commercial and financial institutions, and the economic policies pursued by the Quebec government and the province's municipalities.

The third chapter is devoted to agriculture and the forest industry. During the period under consideration, these two sectors still dominated Quebec's economy, and most of the work force was employed in them. Quebec agriculture, after undergoing a serious crisis in the mid-nineteenth century, had embarked on a new course marked by specialization and technical modernization. The forest provided Quebec's main export commodity and was the basis for the development of peripheral areas. In these "colonization regions," agriculture and forestry were mutually dependent with the framework of the agro-forest system.

Industry is discussed in the fourth chapter. There were radical transformations in this sector and the face of Quebec was visibly changed as a result. Industrialization began in Montreal and from there its effects gradually spread throughout Quebec, so that by the end of the century large-scale industry was solidly established. Among the consequences of industrialization were increasingly rapid urbanization and growth in the importance of the Montreal region in Quebec's economy.

CHAPTER 4
THE WIDER CONTEXT

The Empire and Canada

While the development of Quebec's economy between 1867 and 1896 can be partly explained by factors specific to Quebec society, Quebec was also subject to wider economic currents operating on a world scale. The most important of these developments in the late nineteenth century were the rise of a handful of imperialist powers and the domination by these powers of economic blocs to which all parts of the planet were linked. The foremost of the imperialist powers was Britain.

Between London and New York

In the mid-nineteenth century, Britain reached a position of dominance, even hegemony, in the world economy. It became a great industrial nation, exporting its manufactured goods to all parts of the world. It was ahead of other countries technologically and its fleet allowed it to dominate international trade.

While Britain exported the products of its factories, it had to import raw materials in large quantities, being poor in natural resources except for iron and coal. Britain found it increasingly difficult to feed its population, and had to import foodstuffs from foreign sources. It also had to import other raw materials such as timber and cotton; the latter was particularly important since textiles were the leading British industrial product. In this way, Britain bought raw materials and sold manufactured goods in return, and nowhere was this system of exchange more highly developed than within the Empire.

The British Empire had developed gradually during the previous century. The colonies that constituted it were of two kinds. One group comprised the "white colonies" or colonies of settlement, the most significant of which were in North America, Australasia and southern Africa. The other consisted of colonies with previously established native populations of considerable size; these colonies, of which India was typical, were of interest principally as markets for British industry. The first group of colonies was expensive to administer, and starting in the mid-nineteenth century London made its political relationship with them more flexible by allowing the colonials to exercise a degree of autonomy. Colonies in the second group were kept under much more direct metropolitan control.

In addition to this formal empire there was another, more informal one — to use Eric Hobsbawm's phrase — which Britain dominated economically without administering directly. Most of the components of this empire were in South America and Asia, which were brought into the British orbit in the nineteenth century.

After 1873, Britain's position on the international chessboard changed. As other great industrial powers, especially France, Germany and the United States, developed to the point where they were serious competitors, British hegemony was eroded. The growth in Britain's export of manufactured goods slowed down, and since its imports remained high, it had to export capital and services (such as transportation and finance,) to avoid an unfavourable balance of payments. In this way, capital exports became an essential instrument of British imperialism in the late nineteenth century. A growing proportion of this capital was directed towards the white colonies — by now dominions — and Latin America.

British hegemony was called into question in another way as well. The other industrialized countries also wanted to build colonial empires to assure themselves of supplies of raw materials and create export markets. This was the era of the "race for colonies," which led to the partition of Africa and Asia. The situation forced Britain to tighten its hold on its own empire and to bring under direct political control some countries that until then had been part of its informal empire. Colonies thus became an important element in the struggles among the large capitalist powers.

Of these emerging empires, it was that of the United States that most directly affected Canada in general and Quebec in particular. Until the end of the century, American imperialism took the form of territorial expansion, primarily at the expense of Mexico but also, in the case of the Oregon Territory, at the expense of Britain. In 1898, however, the United States gained its first colonies by taking over the remnants of the Spanish empire in America (notably Cuba) and the Pacific (the Philippines). The Americans were latecomers in the race for colonies and their formal empire remained relatively small, but by the turn of the century they had an extensive informal empire. The heart of this empire was Latin America, where American interests dominated the economies of several countries and régimes friendly to the United States were installed.

Canada had the same function as other colonies within the British Empire — to provide the metropolis with raw materials and serve as a market for its manufactured goods. This had been its role since the French régime. Fish, furs, timber and wheat were Canada's major export commodities, and one or more of these staples was the linchpin of its economy at any given time.

At the time of Confederation, the situation was changing. The population of the country was growing and the economy was becoming more diversified. The loosening of political and economic restraints within the British Empire allowed for a certain amount of indigenous development. Economic links with the United States took on increasing importance relative to those with Britain. These changes were slow, and Canada's economy remained colonial in many respects. Statistics for external economic relations were compiled only for Canada as a whole so that separate data for Quebec do not exist, but it is clear that Quebec shared in the general tendencies.

During the period under consideration, Canada's trade balance was usually negative — that is, the value of its imports was greater than that of its exports. Canada continued to be an exporter of raw materials, with animal and agricultural products and timber representing more than three-quarters of its exports. Some of these commodities, such as sawn lumber or dairy products, underwent a certain amount of processing in Canada, but it did not go beyond the primary stage. The United Kingdom was Canada's major customer, accounting for fifty-seven per cent of its exports in 1896, followed by the United States with thirty-four per cent. There was thus little diversification of markets.

However, Britain was losing ground as a supplier to the Canadian market, and its share of Canadian imports in 1896 (thirty-one per cent) was smaller than that of the United States (fifty-one per cent). Canada's imports during the period consisted primarily of textiles and textile fibres, agricultural products and iron products.

If Britain was losing its dominance of merchandise exports and imports, the same was not true of the flow of capital. Between 1867 and 1900, foreign investment in Canada grew from $200 million to $1.305 billion. Britain continued to have by far the largest share, although this share declined from ninety-two to eighty-two per cent. Most British investment in Canada was portfolio investment, and it took the form primarily of purchases of railway and government bonds. American investment, small in 1867 ($15 million), reached $205 million, or sixteen per cent of the total, in 1900. Most of this was direct investment in companies, and for American capital, it was only the beginning. After 1900, the imperialism of both these great powers, as manifested in their capital exports, became much more conspicuous in Canada.

The Canadian bourgeoisie's strategy

In the mid-nineteenth century, the expanding Canadian bourgeoisie began to assert itself. It was limited in its claims to autonomy by its historic position as a creature of the British bourgeoisie and its growing dependence in the second half of the century on its American rival. Still, it tried to consolidate its economic power and to extend it beyond the borders of central Canada.

There were three avenues that the Canadian bourgeoisie could explore. It could aim to penetrate the sizeable British market, but there it came up against competition from a number of other countries. To reduce this competition, the Canadian bourgeoisie needed a British tariff wall aimed at protecting colonial products. But this was precisely the policy that London had rejected in gradually establishing free trade in the 1840s, and subsequent Canadian attempts to obtain an Empire tariff preference failed. Another possible direction for the Canadian bourgeoisie was to set its sights on the rapidly expanding North American market. For this to work, Canada and the United States had to grant each other reciprocal tariff concessions. This was accomplished with the Reciprocity Treaty of 1854, which eliminated customs duties between the two countries on raw materials and agricultural products. Over the next decade, the volume of trade between the two countries grew, but protectionism was a growing force in American manufacturing circles; under pressure from these interests, the United States government announced in 1865 that it did not intend to renew the treaty, and it was allowed to expire in 1866. In subsequent years, the Canadian government tried to revive the reciprocity treaty, but without success.

The Canadian bourgeoisie was thus forced to consider a third solution — to imitate the United States by building a large domestic market protected from foreign competition. During the second half of the nineteenth century, it put into effect a strategy for realization of this economic goal. The strategy involved participation by the government, which the Canadian bourgeoisie controlled, and had three main elements: the domestic market was to be expanded, an infrastructure was to be established to make communication easier and industrialization was to be encouraged through tariff policy.

To ensure a minimum level of development, it was important to increase the number of consumers and producers through territorial expansion and population growth. The geographic extension of the market occurred in five stages. The first was the unification of Upper and Lower Canada (Ontario and Quebec) in 1840, creating the united Province of Canada that became the base onto which additional territories were grafted. The first additions were in the east, where Confederation added two Atlantic provinces and a few hundred thousand consumers to the province of Canada in 1867. The next expansion was to the north and west, with the transfer of the Hudson's Bay Company's lands to the government of Canada in 1869. This immense tract of land, which became the Northwest Territories, was inhabited by native Indians, Métis and Inuit. It was hoped that the experience of the United States, where the settlement of the western plains was a significant source of development, would be repeated in Canada. To complete this westward expansion, access to the Pacific had to be obtained, and negotiations were undertaken leading to the entry of British Columbia into Confederation in 1871. The last stage of Canada's territorial expansion occurred in 1873, when

Prince Edward Island joined Confederation. In less than a decade, all the British North American territories except for Newfoundland had been united into a single economic and political structure.

Just as important as geographical extension was expanding the Canadian market in terms of population. Once again, the United States was used as a model. Attempts were made to encourage immigration from Europe by distributing promotional material and giving subsidies to companies that brought immigrants over; free homesteads were granted to settlers who went west. However, these policies were slow in being implemented and had little effect before the end of the century.

A transportation infrastructure — rivers and railways — was necessary to unify this geographically scattered market and attract new settlers to thinly populated regions. The St. Lawrence-Great Lakes axis had long been the main avenue of communication. But it is an avenue strewn with obstacles to navigation, and in the first half of the nineteenth century the Montreal bourgeoisie used all the means at its disposal to improve it with canals and thus make Montreal the principal transshipment depot between the North American interior and the ports of Europe. Standardization and organization of the canal network became possible with the Union of 1840 and was completed in 1848. Later in the nineteenth century, individual canals were widened but the structure of the network was not changed.

After 1850, the railway became the main instrument for unifying the British North American territories. Canada built three major railway networks in thirty years, aside from the many secondary and local lines. The first was the Grand Trunk, aimed at strengthening the union of Upper and Lower Canada; completed in 1854, it ran from Sarnia, Ontario, to Rivière-du-Loup, Quebec. The second, the Intercolonial, was built to support Canada's eastward expansion at the time of Confederation; it was constructed between 1867 and 1872 and linked Quebec, New Brunswick and Nova Scotia. The third, the Canadian Pacific, was tied to westward expansion; completed in 1885, it linked the central Canadian provinces with the Pacific Ocean.

Let us note in passing that the Canadian government played an important role in financing these large projects; it took responsibility for building the canals and the Intercolonial and gave generous subsidies to the private companies that owned the other two railways.

The Americans' refusal to give Canada free access to their market led the Canadian government to impose higher customs duties on foreign manufactured products. For the government, such tariffs had a twofold purpose: to obtain revenue and to protect Canadian industries from competition. The first tariff was put into effect under the Union régime, in 1857. It was not very protectionist and was aimed primarily at increasing government revenues. The depression of 1873-78 led the federal government to impose a protectionist tariff in 1879 under which most imported manufactured products came in at a duty of twenty-five to

The entrance to the Lachine Canal in Montreal.

thirty per cent. This high tariff was in effect for the rest of the period under consideration.

The three elements that formed the so-called "national policy" were now in place. In theory, the effect of these measures operating in concert should have been a substantial degree of economic development. Industry was protected by the tariff, which also brought increased revenues to the federal government and allowed it to subsidize railway construction. The railway facilitated the development of new territories and allowed western products to be brought to ports from which they could be taken via the river system to export markets. The opening up of new territories, especially in the West, created a market for industry, ensured the profitability of the railway and, in general, stimulated the growth of the Canadian economy.

This policy should have increased the autonomy of the Canadian bourgeoisie. It should not be forgotten, however, that it also met the needs of the metropolitan bourgeoisie, which was seeking to increase its profits by exporting capital.

The "national policy" of economic development was gradually implemented in the early years of Confederation and even before. What were its effects? Major Canadian historiographic debates revolve around this question.

Historians quickly recognized that the policy had little success between 1873 and 1896. The historical studies conducted by the Rowell-Sirois Commission in the 1930s concluded that the National Policy was a relative failure in this period. It was established that the settlement of the West, a fundamental part of the strategy, occurred very slowly, reducing the utilization and profitability of the railways and limiting the growth of industrial production. This interpretation was challenged during the 1960s, leading to a debate on the level of Canada's economic development and the scope of what has been called the Great Depression of 1873-96 which will be discussed later.

The historians who first questioned the effects of the development policy did not challenge the policy itself but simply conceded that unfavourable economic conditions made it impossible for it to produce the expected results before 1896. However, in the last few years, other historians have raised the problem of the nature of the policy, and questioned whether the inherent effect of its implementation would necessarily be the realization of its objectives.

Prominent among these critics have been John H. Dales and Alfred Dubuc who, during the 1960s, expressed a number of reservations about the National Policy. First of all, they questioned the harmonious relationship that was supposed to exist among its different elements. For example, channelling savings into massive railway investments may have restricted rather than stimulated the growth of the manufacturing sector. They also criticized the policy effect on regional development, and maintained that it did not encourage the different parts of Canada to function harmoniously; in promoting regional specialization, it accentuated the disparities among regions and the concentration of economic power in the hands of large central Canadian institutions.

The tariff policy has been a particular target of criticism. The ambiguity of a tariff that was supposed both to bring in government revenues and to protect domestic industry has been pointed out. Also, by supporting uncompetitive industries, the policy sacrificed quality to quantity; if it succeeded in raising overall national income, it was at the price of a drop in the standard of living, which paradoxically encouraged emigration to the United States. The resulting demand for labour could have led to an increase in wages and thus in the standard of living; instead, government policy favoured massive immigration, which put downward pressure on wages. In addition, the tariff allowed increased penetration of Canada by American capital. Unable to dispose of their United States-made products on the Canadian market, American entrepreneurs opted to establish subsidiaries in Canada.

From these and other questionable elements in the National Policy, a number

Donald Smith drives the last spike on the Canadian Pacific Railway, 1885.

of authors have concluded that the policy did not reach its objectives and led to anarchic rather than harmonious development in Canada.

The National Policy's impact on Quebec was considerable. Quebec is strategically situated within Canada, especially with respect to the transportation network; along with Ontario, it represents one of the largest population aggregations in the domestic market and one of the two areas of industrial concentration. In addition, during the period under consideration, Montreal was still the economic centre of Canada. The capitalist class was firmly established in Montreal, and it became the headquarters for the large institutions that backed the National Policy, notably the Bank of Montreal and Canadian Pacific. But Canadian development policies had specific effects on Quebec, and these must be considered separately. Here again, historical opinion is divided.

In his master's thesis, "La politique nationale et le développement industriel du Québec, 1870-1910," Jean-Yves Rivard concentrates on the effects of the tariff, which in his estimation were highly beneficial. He concludes that "in the long run, the tariff policy allowed a number of Quebec's important industries to develop, or at least to survive." He finds that the policy allowed large-scale enterprises to emerge where before there had been only small local establishments. Similarly, in their *Histoire économique du Québec*, Jean Hamelin and Yves Roby see the tariff of 1879 as a significant factor in the industrialization of Quebec.

While the policy may have led to overall industrial growth in Quebec, the growth it promoted may have been regionally imbalanced or uncontrolled. The other elements of the National Policy, railway construction and western settlement, also have to be taken into account. In his article "L'évolution économique du Canada et du Québec depuis la Confédération," François-Albert Angers examines the National Policy from another angle — that of investment policy. He maintains that the emphasis placed on the West slowed down Quebec's economic development, and that the diversion of investment to the West occurred at a cost to Quebec. In addition, except for Montreal, Quebec benefited much less than Ontario from railway investment. The historian Gaétan Gervais calculated that only 13.8 per cent of all federal railway subsidies between 1867 and 1896 went to Quebec while twenty-eight per cent went to Ontario. The National Policy seems to have widened the gap between Montreal and the rest of Quebec, leading to substantial inequalities in development. Ronald Rudin has shown that the large Montreal banks were not interested in the development of Quebec and preferred to invest in Ontario and the West. In intensifying corporate concentration, the National Policy may in the long run have helped make the French-Canadian bourgeoisie a marginal class.

In general, the criticisms expressed by John H. Dales and Alfred Dubuc for Canada as a whole are applicable to Quebec. It is worth considering the National Policy's effect on emigration, a movement that involved ten per cent of Quebec's population between 1870 and 1900. The policy encouraged development of a sort in Quebec, but it was not a very harmonious form of development and the marginal status of some of Quebec's regions was maintained or even accentuated.

Two Interpretations of Canada's Development

While there is disagreement among historians about the National Policy, there is also a wider debate about how the entire history of Canada's, and therefore Quebec's, economic development should be explained. The two theses around which this debate revolves were mentioned in chapter 1. The Laurentian thesis and the Faucher thesis will now be examined more closely.

The Laurentian thesis

The Laurentian thesis is the most important of all the theories of Canada's development. For a long time, it held unrivalled sway as an interpretation of Canada's economic and social history. Like all historiographic theses, it is closely tied to the society that inspired it and cannot be understood without taking into account the socio-political problems Canada was undergoing at the time it was conceived. It has its antecedents in the years following the execution of Louis Riel in 1885, years when Canada went through the first great crisis in its history. In this period the new Dominion was in the grip of a deep malaise, both economic and political in nature.

It was in this atmosphere that Goldwin Smith's essay *Canada and the Canadian Question*, with its theme of Canada's fragility, appeared in Toronto in 1891. The thesis of the essay was that since Canada's existence was based on an attempt to replace the dominant north-south lines of force with a single line oriented east-west, the country was an artificial creation. Smith saw Canada as a geographical absurdity, destined sooner or later to disappear and become part of the United States. A few years later, in 1906, the French political scientist André Siegfried restated part of Smith's argument.

In reaction to this thesis, other interpreters of Canadian history argued that Canada, far from being a geographical aberration, exists as a country precisely because of its geography. According to the Laurentian thesis, the St. Lawrence Valley, through the system of development it implies, is the foundation for Canada's existence as an economy and finally as a country. This thesis was formulated for the first time in the works of Harold A. Innis and W.A. Mackintosh in the 1920s; Donald G. Creighton is probably the best-known Canadian economic historian to have used it, and the appearance of his authoritative 1937 study, *The Commercial Empire of the St. Lawrence, 1760-1850* (later reissued as *The Empire of the St. Lawrence*), consecrated the Laurentian thesis as a fundamental element in the explanation of Canada's past.

All economic historians have made use of the Laurentian thesis to some degree; a notable example among recent Quebec historians is Fernand Ouellet, whose *Histoire économique et sociale du Québec 1760-1850* is inspired by this thesis. In the last few years, however, it has not been as much of a common denominator among historians as it once was, and has come under increasing criticism for being teleological — that is, for intentionally creating a history in which everything is determined by final causes, the seeds of which exist from the beginning. Looked at from the point of view of the Laurentian thesis, the history of Canada is a neat continuity, beginning with the fur trade in Champlain's time and culminating in the Dominion of Canada, which was badly in need of theories that could help strengthen its unity during the Second World War.

The main propositions that constitute the thesis can be summarized as follows. The St. Lawrence Valley constituted a system built around a staple, or easily exploitable natural resource that could find a buyer on the world market — hence the importance of the transportation network. Exploitation of the staple created capital which was invested in the system and fuelled economic growth. A few resources — fish, furs, timber and wheat — exploited in succession thus provided the foundation on which Canada's economic growth was based.

The St. Lawrence system was supported by the commercial activities of the Canadian bourgeoisie (in practice, essentially the Montreal and Toronto bourgeoisie). When the fur trade disappeared as a dominant activity, these merchants turned to exporting timber and wheat. At the same time, they looked beyond these two commodities, and early in the nineteenth century sought to control a much wider array of foreign trade. With the growth of the American mid-west and the resulting increase in import-export activities, they initially promoted canal-building to improve the navigability of the St. Lawrence and later backed railway construction. However, the bourgeoisie's schemes turned out to be somewhat less successful than had been hoped. Its next strategy was Confederation, through which it aimed to create a domestic market that would assure it of a solid economic base.

Remarkably, the St. Lawrence Valley, from the Atlantic to the Great Lakes, has been the territorial base for all these successive projects. Even western expansion was undertaken with a view towards linking the new territories to the main axis, notably through the railway. Indeed, the centres from which the economy has been run have always been located at strategic points in the St. Lawrence Valley: Quebec City until the nineteenth century, then Montreal, and finally Toronto, which established its dominance in the mid-twentieth century.

These are the major elements of the Laurentian interpretation. Examining it from the point of view of the history of Quebec, it is necessary to express a number of reservations about its validity. First, the primary aim of the thesis is to explain Canada's internal development, especially the relationships among its different regions. Thus, in its vision of the development of the Canadian economy, the thesis considers only phenomena in which these relationships are involved. But these are far from being the only processes in Canadian history, and there is another whole succession of phenomena in which regions are related to one another only peripherally, if at all — for example, what Fernand Ouellet refers to as the "disengagement" (*décrochage*) of pre-1850 Lower-Canadian agriculture. The inability of the Laurentian thesis to explain these phenomena is one of its weaknesses. In addition, since Quebec is of interest only as an element in a wider system, to look at Quebec from the vantage point of the thesis is to run the risk of paying attention only to Montreal and Quebec City.

Quebec's internal development eludes the Laurentian thesis. It has no explanation for the growth of Quebec's economy or society — or, for that matter, for the internal development of any other region of Canada, since it is really interested only in relationships among the regions. A final weakness of the thesis arises out of its emphasis on the role of a single generative commodity. If the source of this commodity changes, or if there is a shift to a new commodity produced in a different region, then the thesis shifts its attention to the new producing region and there is a corresponding tendency to underestimate the economic importance of other regions.

The thesis does give a clear picture of what the Canadian bourgeoisie intended to do, what it achieved and especially how it accomplished its ends. It also provides a justification for the bourgeoisie's economic design in the name of the higher interests of Canadian nationalism. The thesis implicitly regards the Canadian bourgeoisie as a group of dynamic entrepreneurs, on the model of the class that played such a large role in the development of the British economy. Some historians, however, challenge this interpretation.

In addition, while economic space is an interesting idea, the geographic dimension of economic space is not the only one. It is important not to lose sight of other significant variables, such as the nature of the dominant activity and modes of transportation. In this light, any changes in the economy or in transportation necessarily imply a redefinition of economic space.

Finally, if the staple theory is analysed as a theory of economic development, it becomes clear that it cannot really explain development, but at most describes it and highlights a historical phenomenon, the successive exploitation of a series of major commodities. This is necessarily so because of the extremely dependent nature of the Canadian economy at the time of the fur and timber trades. The real factors of economic development must be sought elsewhere, and were external to the Canadian economy. The wave of immigration between 1815 and 1860, for example, was more the result of economic difficulties in Ireland and England than of the internal dynamism of the Canadian economy.

The thesis has other limitations: it does not take economic diversification into account, and it appears to become increasingly difficult to apply after 1850. What it really constitutes is a description of Canada's pre-1850 economic base. The Canadian economy was an "economy of gathering," in which natural resources were exploited in the simplest possible way. This description applies not only to furs and timber but also to wheat, for the techniques used in early wheat farming were so rudimentary that it was not far removed from simple gathering.

In conclusion, the Laurentian thesis is interesting in that it highlights the role of the bourgeoisie of Montreal and Toronto in the creation and development of the Canadian economy. It cannot, however, pretend to explain everything, and especially not the development of a complex economy.

The Faucher thesis

This thesis was outlined for the first time in 1952 in an article by Albert Faucher, an economic historian at Laval Univesity, and Maurice Lamontagne, also of Laval. In subsequent works, Faucher developed some of the elements of the thesis on his own.

A former student of Harold Innis's at the University of Toronto, Faucher counters the Laurentian thesis with a continental vision in which technology is presented as a determining factor in economic development. In his view, the growth or stagnation of a given economic space depends in the final analysis on the combined state of its technology and natural resources. The borders of economic spaces do not necessarily coincide with those of political entities. Faucher identifies four major economic spaces in North America: Quebec and the Maritimes,

New England and the mid-Atlantic states, Ontario and the American mid-west, and the Canadian and American west and northwest. The inequality of these spaces in terms of natural resources and the general development of technology explain their different rates of growth.

Thus, according to Faucher, the economic history of North America is marked by the displacement of the centre of gravity from the seaports to the interior. The prosperity of the port cities of the east was based on an economy in which trade was the dominant activity and sea transport played a fundamental role. With industrialization, iron and coal became the key elements of economic growth, so that the poles of development moved to the interior regions that were rich in these resources. In the twentieth century, iron and coal have been partly replaced by electricity and new alloys, and regions that are better equipped to meet these new conditions have prospered as a result.

In these circumstances, Quebec went through a commercial era characterized by the predominance of trade and a technology based on wind and water; this era lasted until 1866. In the next period, lasting from 1866 to 1911, Quebec's growth slowed down; this was the period in which iron and the steam engine were dominant, as a result of which Quebec, poor in iron and coal, was left behind. In 1911, a new era begins in which Quebec was able to develop more quickly since it had one of the elements of the new resources-technology combination — hydroelectricity. Emphasizing that Quebec did not respond any differently from the other regions in the same economic space, Faucher concludes that its industrialization was only a local, regional manifestation of long-term economic development on a North America-wide scale.

This thesis has played a very important role in Quebec historiography. Faucher goes beyond the traditional explanation of French-Canadian economic inferiority, which emphasized cultural factors, and puts Quebec back into its North American continental context.

However, the thesis can be criticized for a number of deficiencies. Its analysis of factors of production tends to overestimate the importance of natural resources and technology and underestimates other, equally important factors such as labour and capital. The cultural factor is eliminated a little too quickly, for economic growth is inseparable from the elements of the society in which it occurs. Faucher underestimates the scope and effect of industrialization in Quebec in the second half of the nineteenth century, and his periodization has been challenged by recent research. In addition, he exaggerates the importance of iron smelting in industrialization, while at the same time ignoring the iron and steel industry that was established in Montreal.

Difficult Economic Circumstances

The emphasis in this book is on structural changes in Quebec's economy, such as industrialization or specialization in agriculture. Major changes of this nature do not happen all at once but are stretched out over a long period and occur in stages. They are affected by cyclical movements in the economy, which can slow down or accelerate the pace of change.

There are various kinds of economic cycles, but historians have been interested primarily in two of them, long-term and short-term cycles. In the history of capitalist countries, long-term cycles lasting about half a century have been identified. The relevant long-term cycle for the period being examined here lasted from 1850 to 1896. It can be divided into two phases — a phase of rising prices from 1850 to 1873 and one of falling prices from 1873 to 1896. An examination of the 1867-96 period is thus almost exclusively a look at Quebec during the second phase.

Long-term cycles are periodically disturbed by short-term cycles, each with its own phases of rising and falling prices. In their *Histoire économique du Québec*, Hamelin and Roby identified five such cycles for the period 1867-96 (Table 17).

These cycles will not all be examined in detail, but it will be valuable to look first at the period's most serious economic crisis, the depression of 1873-79. This was a depression of international dimensions, touched off by bank failures in Austria and the United States, whose repercussions began to be felt in Quebec in 1874. The Canadian banking system was seriously disrupted, and most Canadian banks went through a very difficult period. The Mechanics, the Stadacona and the Consolidated were among those that failed, while others had to suspend payments for a time; for some of these latter banks, notably the Banque Jacques-Cartier, this was the first step towards financial reorganization. Many companies went bankrupt. Industrialists had to reduce or even suspend production for a time. Unemployment was high and employers cut wages; when this was done in Quebec City in 1878, it provoked a construction workers' strike that escalated into a riot. The depression led employers and workers to demand a tariff policy that would protect Canadian industry. As Hamelin and Roby point out, "the depression of 1873-1879 had a profound effect on Quebec society.... It brought about new orientations. The closing of foreign markets and dumping gave rise to a determined protectionist movement; the relatively stable demand for butter and cheese on the English market oriented Quebec agriculture towards the dairy industry." These tendencies will be examined later on.

TABLE 17
Economic Cycles in Quebec, 1862-96

Cycle	*Expansion*	*Contraction*
1862-69	1862-67	1867-69
1870-79	1870-73	1873-79
1880-85	1880-82	1882-85
1886-91	1886-88	1888-91
1891-96	1891-94	1894-96

Source: Jean Hamelin and Yves Roby, *Histoire économique du Québec*, pp. 84-97.

The recovery phase that followed this long depression should also be noted. Although brief (1880-82), this phase brought about a wave of industrialization in Quebec. Adoption of a new customs policy by the Macdonald government in 1879 stimulated establishment of new industries, especially in the textile sector. The resumption of construction work on the Canadian Pacific Railway and new enthusiasm for settlement in Manitoba had positive effects on demand.

These periods of depression and prosperity all occurred within the context of the long-term trend towards falling prices that prevailed between 1873 and 1896. This period has proved a difficult one for historians to interpret, and two opposing interpretations have been advanced. Some historians refer to the whole period as a "great depression"; others, by contrast, see it as a period in which the establishment of an industrial economy led to significant progress. This is one of the great debates in Canadian historiography and we will try to give a brief outline of both sides.

For many Canadian historians, the 1873-96 period was one in which the hopes that had been held out for Canada were disappointed. It seemed that the economic goals of Confederation were not being achieved. The population grew slowly; worse yet, more than a million Canadians emigrated to the United States. Settlement of the West, which was supposed to strengthen east-west economic links and stimulate production in central Canada, was delayed. Industrialization turned out to be a slow process. Historians contrast the slow pace of Canadian economic growth with the dynamism of the United States in the same period; in the United States, westward expansion occurred at a hectic pace, industrialization was rapid and millions of immigrants swelled the population. Comparisons are also made between this period and its successor. Between 1896 and 1914, Canada had a high rate of growth and it finally seemed that the goals of Confederation were being achieved; the brilliance of the later period makes the earlier one appear all the more sombre. This interpretation of the "great depression" was dominant in Canadian historiography until the 1960s.

The first to challenge it was the economist Gordon Bertram. Bertram's interest was in industrial production, and he established that industrial growth between 1870 and 1890 in Canada was substantial, although not as rapid as in the first decade of the twentieth century. According to Bertram, there was no sudden discontinuity in 1896. Recent historical studies tend to confirm his hypothesis. For Quebec, while not directly taking a position on the interpretation of the "great depression," Hamelin and Roby have nevertheless presented an array of facts that demonstrate the scope of industrialization in the 1880s.

It is now recognized that the last three decades of the nineteenth century were not as black as originally had been believed. There was a significant degree of industrialization in Quebec in that period, while agriculture underwent profound changes. Still, economic growth was slower than in the United States in the same period or in Quebec between 1896 and 1914; it was also, in terms of job creation, not enough to retain Quebec's surplus population.

CHAPTER 5
INTERNAL FACTORS

The agricultural and industrial sectors dominated Quebec's economic life between 1867 and 1896. A number of contextual elements specific to Quebec — the home market, the transportation network, commercial and financial institutions and economic policies — are important to an understanding of their development.

An Expanding Market

In the last third of the nineteenth century, the growth of agricultural and industrial production in Quebec was based on an expansion of the home market. In principle, Quebec benefited from access to the extended Canadian market that Confederation provided. Quebec farmers and manufacturers could sell their products in the Maritimes, Ontario and the West. In return, products from the other regions of Canada had access to Quebec. Because of the emphasis historians have placed on the development of the West, the importance of the Quebec market has sometimes been forgotten. But as Hamelin and Roby have shown, changes in the home market played a determining role in the industrialization of Quebec. It should be remembered that between 1867 and the end of the century, more than thirty per cent of Canadian consumers lived in Quebec. In addition, the Quebec market was rapidly expanding both geographically and demographically and undergoing qualitative change.

Geographically, the Quebec market was growing in all directions. Colonization and the forest industries led to the opening up of new regions. Previously uninhabited areas of the St. Lawrence Lowlands, notably the Bois-Francs, became populated. Regions such as Temiscamingue, Saguenay-Lake St. John and Temiscouata were opened to permanent settlement. The market was also growing demographically: despite the large number of emigrants to the United States, Quebec's population increased by 38.3 per cent between 1871 and 1901, not a spectacular increase but not negligible either.

Even more important were the qualitative changes in the market. Through specialization, Quebecers were increasingly integrated into the market economy; from small independent producers hoping to attain a degree of self-sufficiency, they were transformed both into specialized producers and into consumers. Urbanization (Quebec's urban population increased by 140.6 per cent between 1871 and 1901) not only increased the number of consumers of manufactured goods; it also created an outlet for agricultural products, leading the farmer to improve the organization of his production. In rural Quebec, Hamelin and Roby have shown that agricultural specialization brought farm families increased income, allowing them to buy certain articles instead of making them.

These were slow, gradual changes, and their pace varied from region to region. It was a very different process from the rapid growth experienced by some American states in the same era. Nevertheless, the market did expand, providing the basis for increased production and industrial diversification.

But an effective means of reaching the consumer was also needed. In the last decades of the nineteenth century, an improved communications network, new methods of distribution and new merchandising techniques allowed the products of mechanized industry to be marketed on a larger scale. These changes will be examined more closely.

The Transportation Network

In a territory as large as Quebec, improvements in communication were a necessary foundation for the growth of commerce. While roads and rivers played a role in this process, in the second half of the nineteenth century it was the railway that caught the public fancy. It became not only the principal means of transportation, but also a sector in which investment was concentrated.

The railway mania

The introduction of this new mode of transportation represented a major technological breakthrough. For the first time in history, man had found a way of travelling quickly over land. The drastic reduction in the time it took to move people and goods was a highly significant change. In addition, since the train was much less dependent on good weather than competing modes, it became possible to deliver supplies with considerably greater regularity than ever before. The railway corporation was a large-scale enterprise, organized as a joint stock company, with a network of stations and facilities and numerous employees. The emergence of such an enterprise marked the beginning of the era of big business.

Quebec was a railway pioneer — the first train service in the British North American colonies, inaugurated in 1836, linked Laprairie, south of Montreal, with Saint-Jean on the Richelieu River. Its lead did not last long, however, and the railway fever of the late 1840s and early 1850s affected Ontario much more than it did Quebec.

In 1867, Quebec still did not have a highly developed railway network, with only 925 kilometres of track, while Ontario already had more than double that (2,241 km). The Quebec network consisted of one major road, the Grand Trunk, and a few small lines south and southeast of Montreal.

The Grand Trunk clearly dominated the railway scene. The company was formed in 1853, and by acquiring some existing lines and building new sections, it put together a main line from Sarnia, Ontario, to Rivière-du-Loup, Quebec, by 1860 (see Map 6, which shows the entire network at the end of the century). In Quebec, the Grand Trunk followed the north bank of the St. Lawrence from the Ontario border to Montreal, where it crossed the river on the Victoria Bridge (opened in 1859). Then it strayed from the south bank of the river, passing through Saint-Hyacinthe and Richmond; from Richmond, a major branch line linked the main line with Portland, Maine — which thus became Montreal's winter port — via Sherbrooke. The main line reached the river again at Lévis and then followed it to Rivière-du-Loup. Another branch line linked Victoriaville in the Bois-Francs region with the south bank of the river opposite Trois-Rivières.

A number of small lines ran south and southeast from Montreal to the United States border, where they linked up with American lines heading for New York and Boston. These lines formed a network centred on an axis consisting of the Richelieu River and Lake Champlain; this was the only region of Quebec in which there was a significant concentration of railways — even if its network didn't include the St. Lawrence and Industry Railway, which ran nineteen kilometres between the village of Industry (Joliette) and Lanoraie on the St. Lawrence, functioned only in the summer, and served mostly to transport wood.

Quebec's railway network was by no means satisfactory. The only part of Quebec that was favoured by the system was Montreal, strategically located on the main line of the Grand Trunk. This position allowed it to strengthen its ascendancy over central Canada, and it was also closely linked to cities on the east coast of the United States through international lines which became the royal roads for French Canadians emigrating to New England. All the Montreal-centred lines were intended primarily to carry interprovincial and international traffic and their owners had little interest in local or regional development. Some benefits accrued to centres along the railway such as Saint-Hyacinthe and Lévis, but the effects of

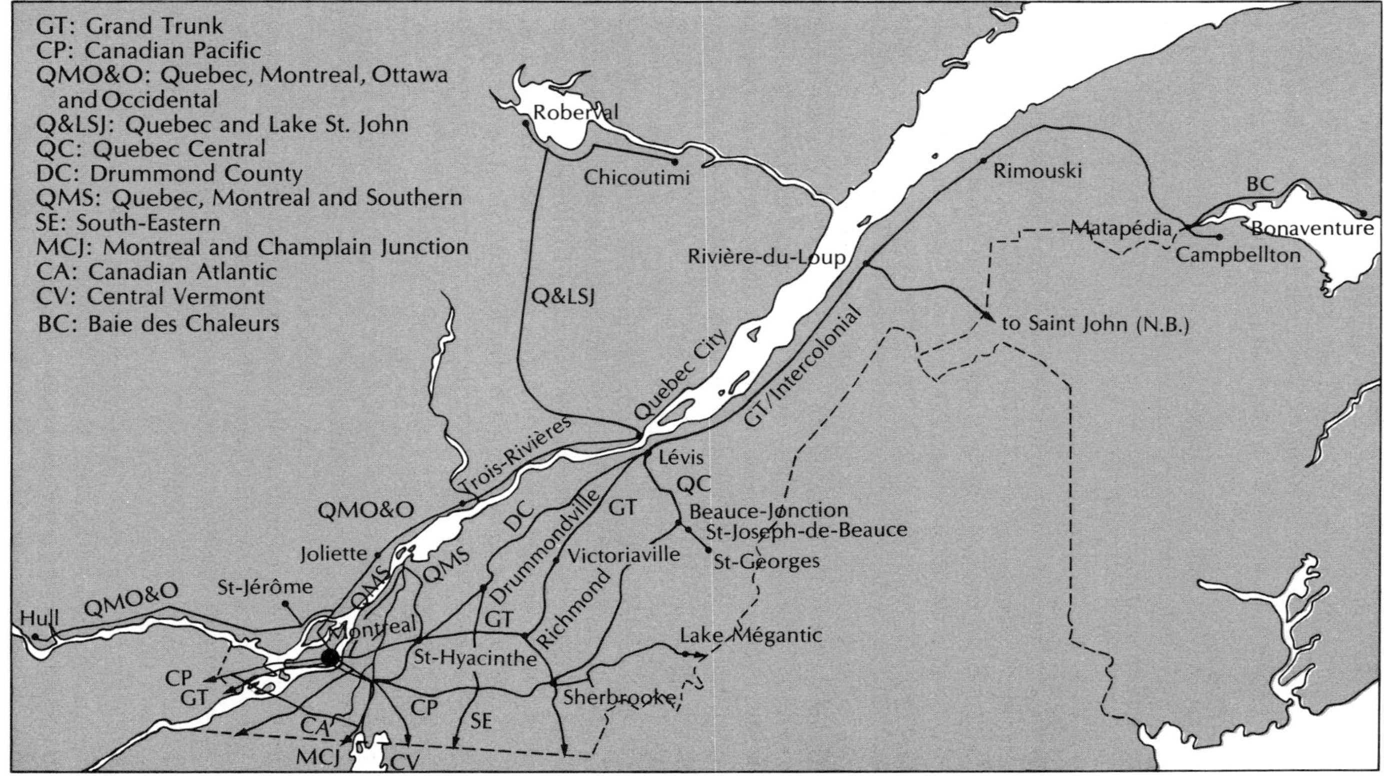

MAP 6: Major Railways in Late-Nineteenth-Century Quebec

this growth were limited. Important cities such as Quebec City and Trois-Rivières were left outside the system, and vast regions — the north bank of the St. Lawrence, the Outaouais, the Beauce — were entirely without railways. There were few branch lines, and the only real railway network was in the Richelieu Valley.

Immediately after Confederation, Quebec's political leaders and businessmen reacted to the railway infrastructure's inadequacy. In the late 1860s new railway projects were initiated and old ones that had lain dormant were taken off the shelf. The Quebec government opted to participate in financing these enterprises, and slowly developed a policy of aiding railways. The close ties between politicians and railway entrepreneurs made things easier. A number of these projects were hampered by the depression of 1873-79, but with the recovery of 1880 and increased efforts by the government, it was possible to complete most of them.

These projects were of two kinds. First there were the regional railways, called "colonization railways" as they were directed towards new regions and designed to serve the needs of the timber trade and colonization. There was considerable enthusiasm for these railways as a means of development in some peripheral regions, and they were built with substantial help from the Quebec government. There were also three new main lines. While two of these, the Intercolonial and the Canadian Pacific, were the result of federal initiatives, there was also one built by the Quebec government and directed more specifically towards Quebec goals — the Quebec, Montreal, Ottawa and Occidental (QMO&O).

Of these main lines, the Intercolonial was the first on which construction was begun. The idea of linking Quebec with the Maritimes by rail had been discussed for several years, and the representatives of New Brunswick and Nova Scotia had made it a condition of their entry into Confederation. The British North America Act obligated the federal government to build the railway; it began construction in 1868, and operated the railway after it was completed in 1876. The Intercolonial linked Rivière-du-Loup, the terminus of the Grand Trunk, with Halifax, Nova Scotia. In Quebec, it followed the St. Lawrence past Rimouski and then cut across the Matapedia Valley. In 1879 the Intercolonial acquired a western extension by buying the Lévis–Rivière-du-Loup line from the Grand Trunk. Thus, by the end of the 1870s, all railway transportation in eastern Quebec was under the control of an enterprise whose main purpose was to provide a direct link between Montreal and Halifax; the Intercolonial contributed only in a limited way to regional development in eastern Quebec. The Intercolonial was also subject to competition from the coasting trade, which was very important in the Lower St. Lawrence. The most direct positive effects of the line were felt in Rivière-du-Loup, eastern Quebec's only significant railway centre. The Intercolonial did, however, help end the historic isolation of the Lower St. Lawrence and the Gaspé.

More significant was the Quebec, Montreal, Ottawa and Occidental venture. Two distinct projects were at the origin of the QMO&O — the Montreal Colonization Railway and the Quebec North Shore Railway. The Montreal Colonization

Railway was initiated by Curé Labelle in 1869. The goals of Labelle and his supporters in building a railway between Montreal and Saint-Jérôme were to promote colonization and, even more important, to facilitate the delivery of firewood to Montreal. Labelle's promotion of the railway was sometimes spectacular. In January 1872 he descended on Montreal at the head of a caravan of twenty-four sleighs loaded with firewood, which he distributed to the poor; he took advantage of the opportunity to ask for a million-dollar grant for his railway from the city of Montreal. But colourful as such events were, the actions of financiers played a more determining role. A group of businessmen headed by the immensely rich shipping magnate Hugh Allan got involved in the project. In their hands it became a plan to build a line that would run along the north shore of the Ottawa River between Montreal and Ottawa, where it would link up with the proposed Pacific Railway; a branch line would run to Saint-Jérôme. The Montreal Colonization Railway Company became the rallying point for Montreal interests opposed to the Grand Trunk, and in 1872 the city of Montreal promised it a grant. But the Pacific Scandal, in which Allan was implicated, and the depression that set in after 1873 made it impossible for the enterprise to raise the capital it needed in England and it remained at a standstill.

The second railway, the Quebec North Shore, was a project of the Quebec City bourgeoisie and was designed to link the capital with Montreal by a north shore route. The railway was first proposed in the early 1850s but remained on the shelf for about twenty years. Reactivated around 1870, the company was promised a million-dollar municipal subsidy by Quebec City and could count on public lands that had been granted it by the government of the province of Canada. However, the North Shore Railway threatened to create serious competition for the Grand Trunk, which carried on a secret campaign against it in the City of London. As it happened, the North Shore Railway was unable to get the capital it needed in England, and its meagre financial resources did not allow construction to proceed very far.

In 1874, the Quebec government made completion of the two projects a priority, and faced with the repeated failure of their promoters to obtain financing in London, it decided to take the matter in hand. The two projects were joined together as the Quebec, Montreal, Ottawa and Occidental and construction became the responsibility of a government commission. The government assumed the costs of construction except for a total of $2.5 million promised by various municipalities including Quebec City and Montreal. This was a bold decision by a government faced with a depression and declining revenues, and it shows how high a priority the cabinet attached to the project. Construction proceeded smoothly; the Montreal-Hull link was completed in 1877 and the Montreal-Quebec City section in 1879. The choice of route in the Montreal area was highly controversial. Should the eastern and western sections link up at Montreal itself or at Sainte-Thérèse? If Sainte-Thérèse were chosen, there would be only a branch line to Montreal and some western traffic would be directed via the main line to Quebec City; if Montreal were chosen, Quebec City would get only local traffic and Montreal would benefit. The government chose the route that favoured Quebec City and there were angry protests in Montreal.

In any case, the railway was completed in 1879. Its construction had cost about $14 million. Soon after its completion the government announced its intention of selling it to private enterprise. In 1880, Premier Joseph-Adolphe Chapleau appointed his friend Louis-Adélard Sénécal general manager of the QMO&O. A well-to-do businessman, Sénécal was to play an important role in the deals that followed. Chapleau and Sénécal tried to sell the railway to the newly formed Canadian Pacific, but it was interested only in the Ottawa-Montreal section. In March 1882 a deal was concluded: Canadian Pacific bought the Ottawa-Montreal section for $4 million and a group of businessmen led by Sénécal bought the Montreal-Quebec City section, also for $4 million. There was an angry reaction; Chapleau's opponents accused him of favouritism towards his friend Sénécal, and the premier's supporters were branded as *sénécaleux*. Meanwhile, Sénécal did not lose any time, and after a few months sold most of his stock in the railway to the Grand Trunk at a substantial profit. Now the Quebec City bourgeoisie protested vigorously; the sale gave the Grand Trunk a monopoly of transportation between Montreal and Quebec City, with lines on both the north and south banks, and the Quebec capital would have no direct link with the new transcontinental. Representatives of the Quebec City region put pressure on the Macdonald government in Ottawa, demanding the transfer of the north shore railway to the Canadian Pacific. In 1885 the federal government required the Grand Trunk to sell it the Montreal-Quebec City section, which it then resold to the Canadian Pacific.

For the Quebec government, involvement in the QMO&O had resulted in the sale of the two sections in 1882 for $6 million less than the cost of construction. Nor had it received any federal subsidies, as had the builders of other railway projects of similar scope. Quebec MPs lobbied in Ottawa for a subsidy and in 1884, five years after work on the railway was completed, they obtained a commitment of $2.4 million, reducing the size of Quebec's gift to the Canadian Pacific to a little more than $3 million.

With the acquisition of the QMO&O, the Canadian Pacific Railway — third and last of the major systems — made its entry into Quebec; this Quebec section was a link in a vast network that, by 1885, connected Montreal with Vancouver. The plan to build a transcontinental railway was conceived in the wake of British Columbia's entry into Confederation in 1871, and the contract was awarded to a group headed by Hugh Allan in 1873. But there were improprieties involved in the deal, and their revelation brought on the "Pacific Scandal" and the fall of the Conservative government. The Liberals, in office during the 1873-78 depression, decided to build some sections of the transcontinental as a government project. The Conservatives returned to power just as the economic situation improved, and entrusted the railway to private enterprise. Thus in 1880 a group of Montreal businessmen, closely linked to the Bank of Montreal, formed a company to build and run the transcontinental.

Louis-Adélard Sénécal (1829-87), businessman and railway promoter.

They obtained a sumptuous contract in which they were granted $25 million in cash, 25 million acres of land, tax exemptions in perpetuity, a twenty-year monopoly in the West, and other advantages. Strengthened by this government support, the new company completed construction of the railway and then ran it at a profit. The CPR established its terminus at Montreal, undermining the Quebec City bourgeoisie's aspirations to reroute some western traffic to its advantage. The Montreal-Quebec City section became a line with primarily regional functions, helping to strengthen the economic links between Quebec City and Montreal. The CPR did have designs on an outlet to the Atlantic, but its plans did not include Quebec City. It chose instead the most direct route, which went from Montreal through the Eastern Townships, crossed the American border into northern Maine, and crossed back again into New Brunswick, where it reached Saint John. This line was opened in 1890.

The principal effect of the main lines was to strengthen Montreal's position as a metropolis whose influence spread over a vast hinterland, much of it located outside Quebec. However, other railway companies were established whose purpose was regional development; these were the "colonization roads." Despite promises of government subsidies, all these projects ran into serious financial difficulties, and it took a number of years to complete them. Promoters of colonization roads were on the look-out for ways to reduce costs, and when an American entrepreneur suggested in 1868 that wooden rails could be used, the idea met with an enthusiastic response. Within a few months there was a proliferation of wooden-rail projects, but enthusiasm began to wane as a result of the first actual experiment with their use, near Quebec City. After a year of operation, it was realized that the rails did not stand up well to the rigours of the climate and quickly became unusable. Railway promoters went back to conventional techniques.

The best-known colonization railway was the Quebec and Lake St. John Railway. It began with a 40-kilometre-long wooden railway between Quebec City and Gosford; this road was opened in 1870 and helped supply the capital with wood for heating and construction. When the wooden rails proved to be a failure, the enterprise went bankrupt. It was reorganized in 1880, this time as a proposed railway linking Quebec City with Lake St. John. After numerous financial difficulties, the main line reached Roberval in 1888, and a branch line to Chicoutimi was completed in 1892. Construction of the railway cost about $8.7 million, forty-five per cent of which was supplied by provincial, federal and municipal subsidies. While the railway facilitated communication between the Saguenay-Lake St. John region and the outside world, it was also an instrument through which the Quebec City bourgeoisie made the region part of its hinterland and imposed its economic dominance on the local bourgeoisie.

The other significant railway was the Quebec Central, which ran from Lévis through the Beauce to Sherbrooke. This enterprise had its origin in two distinct projects — the Lévis and Kennebec, which completed a line from Lévis to Saint-Joseph de Beauce in 1876, and the Quebec Central, between Sherbrooke and Beauce-Jonction, construction of which began in 1870 and was completed in 1880. The Lévis and Kennebec was acquired by the Quebec Central in 1881, and the expanded Quebec Central opened a branch line to Lac Mégantic in 1895. The railway thus established a presence in the northern Beauce and the eastern part of the Eastern Townships.

Other railway companies built lines in various parts of Quebec. There was the Baie des Chaleurs Railway, which ran along the bay from Matapedia, where it linked up with the Intercolonial, to Gaspé. Construction of this line began in 1882 and lasted a number of years; the project was accompanied by shady transactions that led to the "Baie des Chaleurs scandal" and brought about the fall of the government of Premier Honoré Mercier. A number of small companies, started by different promoters, built railways in the Laurentian region, between Hawkesbury and Quebec City. There was the Lower Laurentian Railway, the Great Northern of Canada and the Chateauguay and Northern; after the turn of the century, these lines became part of the Canadian Northern system. On the south shore of the St. Lawrence there were a number of small lines, mostly in the Richelieu Valley and the Eastern Townships; some of these enterprises were supported by American railway companies seeking access to the Quebec market. The Vermont Central, the Montreal, Portland and Boston, the Quebec, Montreal and Southern, the South-Eastern and the Lake Champlain and St. Lawrence Junction, among others, were all developed in this way; all these regional railways eventually became part of the major systems.

Quebec's efforts in the railway field were fruitful, and in 1901 the province had 5,600 km of track. Hamelin and Roby estimate the total cost of railway construction at $104,430,000, of which about sixty per cent was paid by various levels of government.

An inadequate road system

In the second half of the nineteenth century, the railway became the means of communication favoured by government and business, and the road system was something of a poor relation. With large sums of money being invested in railways, only a limited amount was left for roads.

The problem was one of both quantity and quality. An extensive network of small roads was needed to expand Quebec's inhabited territory and integrate new regions into the market. But the government's energies were devoted to railways and it didn't invest the amounts needed in roads, so that a number of regions and sub-regions remained isolated, wtihout adequate links to the province as a whole. Laying out a road was not enough; it also had to be passable. Nineteenth-century Quebec roads were in a pitiful state; they were badly maintained, and turned into mud-holes as soon as it rained. Many roads could be used effectively only in the wintertime, when the cold and the snow smoothed things out.

Conditions varied depending on the kind of road. Provincial roads linking major cities and towns or running between regions were sometimes better built. But since on these major routes the choice of rail transportation also often existed, there was little incentive to improve the roads and the amount of money set aside for this purpose after 1867 was clearly inadequate.

Rural transportation was in a worse state because there was no alternative to the roads. The Quebec railway network was made up primarily of main lines; there was a dearth of local lines. With the commercialization of agriculture, the construction and maintenance of good rural roads became necessary, and the need for colonization roads also became urgent in the last decades of the nineteenth

Running the Toll Gate, by Cornelius Krieghoff.

century. But here too financial resources were insufficient and badly distributed. Demands from agronomists and settlers that the situation be improved were without effect.

The cities and surrounding areas were better provided with roads. In cities such as Montreal and Quebec City, with their high concentration of population and trade and financially better endowed municipal governments, the main arteries were macadamized under municipal auspices. However, things were far from perfect, and muddy roads were still common in many urban neighbourhoods in the late nineteenth century. The outskirts of large cities were served by toll roads run by independent companies. These roads provided access to urban centres, and the importance of this function combined with the toll revenues led to their being generally better maintained than roads of other kinds.

Overall, Quebec's road system was the poor relation of its transportation infrastructure. Its deficiencies had both qualitative and quantitative effects on commerce and held back the development of rural regions.

The river system

Throughout the nineteenth century water transport played a very important role in Quebec's economic life. This is hardly surprising since one of the world's great rivers, the St. Lawrence, runs through Quebec, and the province is also dotted with other navigable rivers and lakes.

From the time of New France, Quebec's colonial situation and close links with the metropolitan centres of Europe made it dependent on maritime transport. As a departure point for goods exported to Europe, Quebec was tied into large-scale international trade, and from the early nineteenth century on, the Montreal bourgeoisie wanted to make Montreal the pivot of trade between Europe and North America. While it was only partially successful in realizing its ambitions, Montreal did become the most important port in Canada and one of the major ones on the continent.

A number of obstacles had to be overcome to reach that position. While the St. Lawrence is a magnificent access route, its navigation presented many dangers. Downstream from Montreal, there are scattered reefs and shoals, which were the cause of numerous shipwrecks and prevented most ocean-going ships from venturing beyond Quebec City. To reduce the number of accidents and attract ships to Montreal, it was necessary to dig a ship channel. The Montreal bourgeoisie took this project in hand and dug the first ship channel between Montreal and Quebec City, with a depth of 3.8 metres and a width of 22.8 metres, in 1850-51. After that it was repeatedly enlarged, and by the end of the century its dimensions were 8.4 metres by 137 metres.

There were obstacles of a different sort between Montreal and the Great Lakes, where numerous rapids made it necessary to build canals. The St. Lawrence canal system was completed in the mid-nineteenth century, but with the growth of traffic it had to be improved at the end of the century. Thus the Soulanges Canal replaced the Beauharnois Canal in 1899, and the Lachine Canal was enlarged.

Montreal was always a transshipment point in this system. Ocean-going ships of deep draught could not go farther than Montreal, and merchandise destined for Ontario and the West had to be unloaded there and loaded onto ships built especially for canal navigation. Montreal's port thus played an important role, and its Harbour Commission made sure it was adequately equipped. Extensive improvements to the harbour were carried out beginning in 1877.

In addition to the main St. Lawrence axis, oriented towards Europe and the Atlantic provinces in one direction and towards southern Ontario and the American mid-west in the other, there are two supplementary axes, both augmented by canals during the nineteenth century. First, there was the Ottawa, which served northeasten Ontario and western Quebec and was a transportation route for wood and agricultural products. There was also the Richelieu, which led to New York via Lake Champlain and the Hudson. For a long time, this was the main avenue of communication with the United States, and the town of Saint-Jean was the pivot of Montreal-New York trade. However, water transport along

Montreal harbour in 1875.

this route was in decline in the last quarter of the nineteenth century, probably because of the limited dimensions of the canals and railway competition.

Water transportation was not used only for interprovincial or international trade. There was also substantial local traffic in the form of the coasting trade. Little is known about it, but the many docks built here and there by the federal government are evidence that it once flourished. In some isolated regions, served poorly if at all by the railways, water was the principal mode of transportation.

* * *

Between 1867 and 1876, Quebec's transportation infrastructure was extended but balanced growth eluded it. At the end of the century, Quebec was endowed with excellent facilities for communicating with the outside world, but internal communications were badly underdeveloped. There was an imbalance among the different modes of transportation, with rail being favoured at the expense of road transport. In all cases, emphasis was placed on main arteries and local routes were neglected. There was also a regional imbalance; Montreal came off fairly well while peripheral regions were underequipped.

By the mid-nineteenth century, Montreal had become Canada's main nexus of communication. Its initial advantage resulting from its strategic position on the St. Lawrence was augmented by canals and harbour development. Railways heading east, south and west converged at Montreal, and Canada's two major railways, the Grand Trunk and the Canadian Pacific, established their administrative offices and maintenance workshops there. Through its control of communications, Montreal strengthened its ascendancy. As a result, the imbalance between it and its historic rival, Quebec City, grew; the other cities and towns of Quebec were left even further behind, and many became satellites of the metropolis.

The Commercial and Financial Sectors

The growth of transportation systems is related to the development of trade networks, another area in which Quebec underwent significant changes during the period being studied. Trade with the outside was gradually redirected from Britain, which clearly dominated Quebec's trade until the middle of the century, to the United States. Hamelin and Roby report that Britain's share of Quebec's imports in 1871 was sixty-five per cent while the United States accounted for twenty per cent; in 1901, the proportions were thirty-two per cent for Britain and forty-five per cent for the United States. Quebec's trade also became slightly more diversified geographically; in particular, trade with Germany, France and the Caribbean became significant. A portion of the timber trade with England passed through Quebec City, but with that one exception Montreal was the centre of most of Quebec's international trade. The increasing importance of relations with the United States and the movement of goods by rail accentuated Montreal's dominant position.

The penetration of the railway into Quebec's various regions also transformed the province's internal trade. The railway made possible a year-round regularity of supply that had been unknown until then. A sales instrument that made its appearance in the 1870s and 1880s, the catalogue, allowed big-city merchants to sell directly to consumers in rural areas, using the railway and the postal service for delivery.

Nevertheless, in the villages the most important retailer was still the local merchant. Relations between these merchants and their suppliers changed in the course of the period. Hamelin and Roby stress the importance of the travelling salesman, who "made his appearance in Quebec in the 1850s." He brought the merchant samples of the latest products and took orders. In the cities another new phenomenon, the department store, appeared, and new sales techniques were used. In Montreal, Henry Morgan brought retail trade to Sainte-Catherine Street in the 1890s; he was soon imitated by other larger merchants. Thus, towards the end of the century, new distribution and marketing techniques, many of them of American origin, were introduced into Quebec. Commercial methods were gradually but profoundly changed as a result.

The financial sector was dominated by the banks. The Canadian banking system was established slowly over the course of the nineteenth century, and was characterized by a fairly limited number of banks, governed by the Bank Act and

A page from the 1901-2 Eaton's catalogue.

established by acts of the federal parliament — hence the name "chartered bank." The operation of such a bank extended beyond its home base through the branch system.

The banking system, in turn, was dominated by a single large institution, the Bank of Montreal. It was the oldest bank in Canada, having been founded in 1817, and its stockholders and directors included the most eminent members of the Canadian bourgeoisie. In 1867, it had 15.7 per cent of the capital and 25.8 per cent of the assets of all Canadian chartered banks. However, it was faced with increasing competition, especially from Ontario banks, so that in 1896, while its share of the capital of Canadian banks had grown to 16.3 per cent, its share of total assets had delined to 18.6 per cent. Considering only banks having their head office in Quebec, the Bank of Montreal's share was 32.5 per cent of the capital and 37.4 per cent of the assets. The Bank of Montreal was the principal lender to the

The interior of Savage & Lyman's department store in 1876.

Quebec government, and it had a say in choosing the minister who occupied the post of provincial treasurer.

At the beginning of the period being examined, a number of new banks were founded in Quebec (Table 18). The depression of 1873-78 put an end to the establishment of new banks and placed some existing ones in a precarious financial position. The Canadian banking system's reputation for stability has been challenged by the economist Tom Naylor, who in his *History of Canadian Business* has shed light on the large number of bank failures and the improprieties that accompanied them.

Aside from the large institutions such as the Bank of Montreal, there were also a number of middle-sized banks in Quebec, carrying on activities primarily on a regional scale. The French-Canadian banks were in this category. The oldest was the Banque du Peuple, founded in 1835 by businessmen close to the Parti Patriote; weak management led to its closing in 1895. The Banque Jacques-Cartier was founded in 1861. Its president for a number of years was Jean-Louis Beaudry, who was also mayor of Montreal; he was followed by Senator Alphonse Desjardins, the major stockholder in the bank in the 1880s and 1890s. A run on the bank led it to suspend its activities in 1899; it was reogranized the next year as the Provincial Bank. The Banque d'Hochelaga, founded in 1874, was more successful

TABLE 18

Chartered Banks Headquartered in Quebec, 1867-1896

Bank	*City*	*Year Founded*	*Assets in 1896 ($ 000's)*
Bank of Montreal	Montreal	1817	59,289
Bank of British North America	Montreal	1836	12,687
Banque du Peuple	Montreal	1835	4,852
Banque Jacques-Cartier	Montreal	1861	3,040
Banque Ville-Marie	Montreal	1872	1,745
Banque d'Hochelaga	Montreal	1874	5,642
Molson's Bank	Montreal	1853	14,990
Merchants' Bank of Canada	Montreal	1861	23,895
Banque Nationale	Quebec City	1859	4,975
Quebec Bank	Quebec City	1818	11,205
Union Bank of Canada	Quebec City	1865	7,531
Banque de St-Jean	St-Jean	1873	528
Banque de St-Hyacinthe	St-Hyacinthe	1873	1,597
Eastern Townships Bank	Sherbrooke	1859	6,705
Mechanics' Bank[1]	Montreal	1865	—
Metropolitan Bank[1]	Montreal	1871	—
Exchange Bank of Canada[1]	Montreal	1872	—
Stadacona Bank[1]	Quebec City	1873	—

[1] Had gone out of business by 1896.

Sources: *Canada Year Books; Sessional Papers; Canada Gazette.*

than its rivals in overcoming the various crises and merged with the Banque Nationale (founded in 1859 in Quebec City) in 1923 to form the Banque Canadienne Nationale.

In the insurance field, only fire and life insurance developed to any extent in the nineteenth century. Most insurance companies in Quebec were subsidiaries of British companies, but a significant exception was Sun Life, which was founded in 1865 by representatives of the Montreal capitalist class and quickly rose to a leading position in the industry. There were also the mutual benefit societies, which will be dealt with in connection with charitable organizations.

Finally, the founding of the Crédit Foncier Franco-Canadien in 1881 deserves mention. The Crédit Foncier was established under the guidance of Premier Chapleau and was a joint enterprise of businessmen in Quebec and France. While the company's directors were Quebecers, most of the money came from France (notably from the Banque de Paris et des Pays-Bas). It specialized in mortgage loans and its impact was felt in rural areas. In his study of Hébertville in the Lake

St. James Street in Montreal, 1891. The building with columns in the centre is the head office of the Bank of Montreal.

St. John region, Normand Séguin has established that the Crédit Foncier replaced local merchants as the major lender.

Economic Policy

To complete this look at the context of Quebec's development, it is necessary to examine the role of the state. Was there such a thing as Quebec government economic policy in the late nineteenth century? While the government did not do any real economic planning, a political will was expressed in its actions and specific tendencies can be detected in its interventions in the economy. It is in this sense that one can speak — with caution — of a rudimentary form of economic policy. The dominant framework for this policy was economic liberalism. This meant that the government conceded the upper hand to private capital, which made the major decisions. Private capital guided and, in its own way, planned the economy.

The head office of the Banque Jacques-Cartier, 1873.

It expected the government to complement these activities by establishing a political and legal framework in which business could be carried on without too many constraints and by bearing the cost of certain infrastructure projects, either by taking charge of them itself or by subsidizing the private companies entrusted with them.

The Quebec government's room for manoeuvre, already narrow, was further limited by two institutional constraints. The first was the division of responsibilities within the Canadian federation. The major economic powers — money and banking, trade, customs duties — were given to the federal government. The provincial government's power to intervene was limited to works of a local nature. A further constraint on the Quebec government's power to intervene was its chronic financial weakness in the thirty years immediately following Confederation.

But despite these constraints, the Quebec government did intervene in the economy. It was not entirely without means at its disposal. It had the capacity to borrow, which it used to finance large public works. Another asset was the ownership of natural resources — crown lands and the forests that covered them, waterfalls, mineral rights. Through legislation, the government could also regulate activities with economic implications, without itself spending large amounts of money.

In *Les premières années du parlementarisme québécois*, the historian Marcel Hamelin has amply shown that Quebec's economic development was one of the major preoccupations of the politicians of the era. Their primary means of achieving development was railway construction, which they believed would stimulate trade, industry, forestry, agriculture and colonization. A number of ministers and members of the legislature were also directors or stockholders of railway companies, so that they were in the fortunate position of distributing government favours and benefiting from them at the same time.

Government subsidies took the form either of money or of grants of crown lands; the policy was subject to the availability of funds and the government borrowed money to finance it. Quebec government assistance to railways between 1867 and 1875 did not exceed $200,000, but by 1896 the cumulative total had reached $14.5 million, a little more than double the amount invested by the government of Ontario in the same period. This was a considerable financial effort that drained the government's resources and limited its ability to intervene in other sectors.

However, the government's ownership of crown lands allowed it to have some influence on the development of the agricultural and forest sectors. It favoured the growth of forest industries, which provided it with a significant source of revenue. As will be seen later, the government was satisfied with establishing an institutional framework while allowing entrepreneurs to develop Quebec's forests as they liked.

In the agricultural sector, government policy aimed at modernization and the

This 1875 cartoon shows Premier de Boucherville standing on a Quebec, Montreal, Ottawa and Occidental Railway engine and waving the flag of progress and prosperity. Railways were seen as the principal vehicle of economic development in the late nineteenth century.

propagation of new techniques. Here too, it only provided support for initiatives taken by others, in this case, agronomists and agricultural and colonization societies. It subsidized these societies and contributed to the construction of rural roads. But the government invested only limited resources in agriculture throughout the period, a policy that probably had the effect of slowing down change in this sector.

Quebec government policies were complemented by the actions of municipal authorities. Under the Union régime, the Canadian government had allowed municipalities to invest in railways crossing their territory. The provincial government continued this policy after 1867. Thus the city of Montreal granted a $1 million subsidy to the Montreal Colonization Railway and Quebec City offered the same amount to the North Shore Railway. In all, municipal subsidies to railways in Quebec totalled $4.3 million in 1896; the figure in this case is substantially less than the $11.3 million granted by Ontario municipalities.

From the 1880s on, municipalities increasingly tried to encourage another kind of investment — industry. In the eyes of local promoters and politicians, the establishment of an industry seemed the best way of boosting the growth of a town or village, attracting new people to it and providing its large property owners with quick profits.

Municipal assistance to private enterprise took two main forms: grants of money and exemptions from municipal taxes for periods of up to twenty years. This assistance became the subject of competitive bidding, as town governments tried to attract a company by offering better terms than their rivals. Entrepreneurs were well aware of this situation and did not hesitate to take advantage of it to reap the maximum possible benefit. In most cases, municipal assistance was an outright gift to a company that would have established in Quebec in any event. The taxpayers — tenants and small property owners — paid the costs. At the present stage of research, it is impossible to measure the size of municipal investment in industry. However, isolated surveys indicate that the system operated on a large scale.

Thus, both provincial and municipal economic policies were oriented towards encouraging modernization and development in Quebec. But the idea behind them was to provide private initiative with a framework and support, rather than direction.

CHAPTER 6

THE AGRICULTURAL AND FOREST SECTORS

In the nineteenth century, agriculture was the economic sector in which the largest number of Quebecers were employed, although other sectors were gradually gaining on it. It was an area in which significant changes were taking place, especially on the social and ideological levels. We will first examine agriculture proper, and then look at two activities that have historically been linked to it in Quebec: colonization and forestry.

The importance of agriculture in Quebec history is well known. However, its position as the employer of the majority of Quebec's economically active population accounts for only part of its status. In defiance of climatic and topographical reality, it inspired a belief that Quebec was fundamentally agricultural in character. This belief was held by significant elements in Quebec society and took on messianic overtones. Thus in 1895, Benjamin-Antoine-Testard de Montigny wrote proudly and confidently:

> Yes, agriculture is the calling of this people, that has so mysteriously established itself on our few acres of snow.... We have sometimes asked ourselves whether our country is an agricultural country and whether agriculture offers as many advantages here as commerce or manufacturing. It must be stated as an unchallengeable principle that Quebec soil is prodigiously fertile, and while in Europe it takes months and seasons for grains to ripen and they must be sown in the autumn, sowing is done here in April, May or even June, and all is ripe and harvested in August and September.

Attitudes of this sort were widespread among Quebec's élite, with the result that in some circles people seemed ready to farm almost any land that seemed arable, without any thought being given to what kind of agriculture was desirable or even feasible there. It has been noted, for instance, that because of climatic constraints, the growing season outside the St. Lawrence Lowlands is shorter than the minimum required. Nor was much thought given to the question of markets, so that efforts were concentrated on a single type of agriculture in places where attempts should have been made to adapt to other forms. In the pages that follow, the reality of agriculture in Quebec will be examined more closely.

Agriculture

At the time of Confederation, Quebec's population was overwhelmingly rural — 77.2 per cent in 1871. More than 900,000 Quebecers lived elsewhere than in incorporated entities with populations over 1,000. Twenty years later, the rural sector of the population was still preponderant, forming 66.4 per cent of the total. Census data do not distinguish between people who lived on farms and those who lived in villages, but it can be stated that the majority of the rural population lived on the 118,086 farms reported in the 1871 census. While the proportion of the population classified as rural declined slightly between 1871 and 1891, the purely argicultural sector appears to have grown steadily; the rural population increased by only 7.5 per cent between those two dates while the number of farms grew by 48.2 per cent. The total area of Quebec's farms grew by the same percentage, so that the increase can be attributed to a geographical extension of agriculture in Quebec. Towards the end of the century, probably a majority of Quebec's population lived on farms, and eighty-eight per cent of the farmers owned the land they worked.

If there is an activity where the weight of tradition is heavy, it is surely agriculture. It is a sector in which habits, once acquired, endure for a long time, making it important to look at agriculture in a historical perspective.

The agriculture practised in Quebec in the second half of the eighteenth century was very traditional. It was not integrated into a market economy; in other words, it was subsistence farming, based primarily on the needs of the local unit of consumption, the family. In this kind of agriculture, only surpluses, if there are any, are sold. The status of wheat cultivation and the archaic methods of preparing the land for crops are evidence of the traditional character of agricultural practices. European peasantries had given wheat cultivation pride of place from time immemorial. Other grains that can be made into bread, such as rye and buckwheat, followed in descending order of preference. The first farmers in New France brought this tradition with them; it took a number of years of crop failures before people realized that agriculture based on these crops was not necessarily profitable. Preparation of the land for crops was rudimentary; work done on the land was poor both in quantity and quality. Well into the nineteenth century Quebec farmers were still letting land lie fallow in the old way. A two-year rotation was used, and the part left fallow was completely unattended instead of being sown with clover or herbage. Finally, the practice of spreading fields with manure was not universal.

In the late eighteenth and early nineteenth centuries, Lower Canadian agriculture was similar to the extensive form of agriculture practised elsewhere in North America. The reason is very simple: because land was so plentiful, the easiest way to increase production was simply to increase the area under cultivation. However, the changes that began to occur in North American agriculture as a whole bypassed Lower Canada, and in the first half of the nineteenth century the Quebec farmer appeared to be clinging to old practices.

The factors that brought Quebec agriculture to a state of crisis are beginning to be fairly well known. At the end of the eighteenth century, the Quebec farmer faced the new prospect of selling his surplus wheat on the British market. Increased production initially met the demand, but it reached a plateau very quickly in the early nineteenth century, while the price of Canadian wheat continued to rise. A combination of factors seems to have been at the root of these problems. Increased production combined with rudimentary maintenance led to rapid deterioration of the soil. The supply of unused land suitable for wheat cultivation was soon exhausted. And there is a third factor that was long ignored: increasing consumption was an inevitable result of the continuing growth of the population. Thus, in the early nineteenth century, Quebec agriculture was faced with a serious problem; it could not increase production to meet external and internal demand. The situation rapidly worsened as a result of the relative overpopulation of the seigneuries and was further aggravated by the natural disasters that struck in the 1830s — the wheat midge and wheat rust, which attacked the already weakened crops.

Around 1850, these problems were far from being resolved but progress was being made in two important areas. First, the question of land — an increasing number of Quebec farmers, previously unwilling to leave the seigneurial zone, were settling in the Eastern Townships, and emigration to the United States was also helping to ease population pressure. Second, the question of crops — more and more land was being switched from wheat to peas and potatoes. However, this diversification of production had the unfortunate effect of completely disconnecting Quebec agriculture from the market; the Lower Canadian farmer had gone back to subsistence agriculture. Improvements to be sought in agriculture were identified at this time, and an 1850 report by Joseph-Charles Taché gave an accurate picture of the situation:

> Your Committee thus recapitulate: — the soil and climate of Lower Canada are favourable to agriculture — the people are laborious and intelligent; but they do not, however, derive from the soil more than one-fourth of what it can produce: the cause of this is, that the system of cultivation is bad. The principal defects of this system are: — first, the want of an appropriate rotation of crops; secondly, the want or bad application of manures; thirdly, the little care bestowed upon the breeding and keeping of cattle; fourthly, the want of

The harvest at Saint-Prime, near Lake St. John.

draining in certain places; fifthly, the want of attention given to the meadows, and the production of vegetables for feeding cattle; sixthly, the scarcity of improved agricultural implements.

After the middle of the century, specialization and technical improvement gradually transformed Quebec agriculture. Markets provided the initial impetus for these changes. Foreign markets expanded considerably, with the American market leading the way and Britain following. Initially, there had been no market for the replacement crops introduced to mitigate the effects of the collapse of the wheat crop in Quebec, but by about 1850 urbanization in the United States had created a strong demand for these crops. The Quebec horse, an especially hardy breed, also aroused great interest in the United States, and the great demand for horses led to real fears that the breed would become exhausted. While American and British needs were variable, Quebec became a supplier of oats and dairy products to these markets. Also significant was the market created by urbanization in Quebec, and Quebec agricultural products became more competitive in the domestic market as a result of the improvement of the communications network.

From 1850 on, however, American demand was the primary stimulus to changes in agriculture. The Reciprocity Treaty of 1854 was followed by unprecedented expansion, especially during the Civil War (1861-65). The depression that began in 1873 accelerated the move towards more suitable crops and improvements in technique, as in many cases diversification of production to

The Montreal Agricultural Fair, 1870.

meet a specific need was the farmer's only alternative to abandoning his farm.

It was at this time that Quebec farmers began to specialize in dairy production. In the Eastern Townships, the move towards specialization in the production of butter, primarily for sale on the New England market, had already begun by about 1850. Quebec's first cheese factory, opened in 1865, was in the Eastern Townships, as was its first butter factory, opened in 1869. According to Hamelin and Roby, it was about 1875 that Quebec agronomists and politicians chose to direct Quebec agriculture towards the dairy industry. In his annual report for that year, the minister of agriculture wrote: "The importance of developing this industry, which should become a national one, cannot be overemphasized."

In twenty years, specialization in dairy production changed the course of Quebec agriculture. Farmers turned first to cheese production and then, after 1880, to the production of butter. In the last decade of the century there was a rapid increase in the number of factories: from 162 butter and cheese factories in 1886, the number more than quadrupled to 728 about 1890, and then reached 1,992 ten years later. Spectacular as this increase was, there were problems associated with it. The quality of the finished products apparently suffered as a result of deficiencies in production, and wholesalers regarded Quebec butter as being too soft and oily, with a tendency to become rancid quickly.

Most of the problems occurred at the processing stage. Domestic production had begun to decline early on and had gradually disappeared as a result of the increasing number of factories. In Quebec, with its poor rural roads, small rural factories were built so that they would be easy for farmers to reach. This was not the situation in Ontario, where larger factories were built. The small factory faced a twofold problem: it often didn't have enough money to be able to afford a competent person to operate the factory, and its production was not year-round, since many farmers stopped making deliveries in November when their reserves of green fodder ran out. The drop in the prices of dairy products in 1895 and 1896 made people more aware of the deficiencies in production; many small factories closed and the Société d'Industrie Laitière, founded in 1882, asked the government to improve the roads. However, despite its difficulties, the dairy industry made lasting progress. It represented Quebec agriculture's first significant move towards specialization, and for a while it was able to meet British demand.

While Quebec as a whole specialized in the dairy industry, other forms of agriculture were important at a regional level. The Eastern Townships concentrated on livestock-raising and gardening in addition to dairy production; Chambly county, east of Montreal, raised horses for the American market; the Beauce, the Quebec City region, the St. Maurice Valley and Pontiac county grew hay both to feed horses in Quebec lumber camps and for the New England market. Bellechasse and Montmagny on the South Shore of the St. Lawrence below Quebec City concentrated on livestock-raising; the rural areas around Montreal and Quebec City specialized in market-gardening; and in the Joliette region tobacco-growing was taking hold. Wheat and peas, once Quebec's leading crops, declined to the point where they represented only an insignificant portion of agricultural production; in their place, oats and especially hay were grown. These two crops found a ready market in the lumber camps, in Montreal and in the United States. Quebec agriculture was thus multifaceted, and cannot be described as monoculture, but rather as mixed farming in which dairy production was dominant.

The overall result of these various changes was that the situation of the Quebec farmer was much better at the end of the period under consideration than at the time of Confederation. However, nowhere in Quebec was there a single commodity that provided the farmer with a substantial majority of his income, so that he had to earn his income from a variety of sources. What he could make from dairy production had to be supplemented by income from his livestock, his garden and the wooded portions of his farm, which in the aggregate represented a significant element in Quebec's supply of wood. Finally, what the farmer produced for his own consumption should not be underestimated. Self-sufficiency was still a fundamental objective.

These changes in agricultural production and the improvements in technique that allowed them to happen did not occur uniformly across Quebec. The regions most closely linked to the markets made the most progress. Thus, the move towards dairy production occurred in areas where agriculture was market-oriented, while in colonization regions agriculture was practised traditionally and grain production retained its importance. Hamelin and Roby note that wheat growing was still a significant activity in 1871 in the Chicoutimi, Rimouski and Charlevoix regions.

The government's efforts at guidance also contributed to the progress of agriculture in Quebec. Agricultural societies, which had languished in the first half of the century, grew both in size and number after 1850. After 1862, agricultural circles were also formed; while the societies were county-wide organizations, the circles worked at the parish level and were more effective as a result. The provincial Department of Agriculture provided speakers to the agricultural circles, which organized meetings in each parish. Towards the end of the century, the Catholic church appointed colonizing missionaries to help in these efforts at agricultural education. Other measures taken were the founding of newspapers directed at farmers and the opening of agricultural schools. But while newspapers proliferated, the high incidence of illiteracy among farmers limited their potential readership. The agricultural schools — the major ones were at Oka, Saint-Hyacinthe and La Pocatière — were organized somewhat haphazardly; the government respected the acquired rights of the schools' founders and refused to take steps to rationalize their activities, with the result that the schools suffered from a chronic shortage of students. Finally, the government also engaged a number of agricultural promoters, who were, in their own way, Quebec's first agronomists.

While these efforts were limited, their role in agricultural progress should not be underestimated. Quantity alone is not an adequate measure of the dissemination of information, and the actions of a few can help change a small society. Farm equipment was another area in which there were changes. In the second half of the nineteenth century, a variety of agricultural implements was invented and developed; a glance at the newspapers of the era gives an idea of the range of machinery offered. Mechanization, like the improvement of techniques, was related to the degree to which a region was linked to the market. The more prosperous older areas were in a better position than newer ones.

Despite these structural changes, there were also characteristics of Quebec agriculture that remained stable. These fall into three categories: the structure of the rural landscape, the structure of agrarian society, and the kind of agriculture practised. The rural landscape was dominated by the range system (see chapter 1) and the typical form of rural habitat that developed from it. Even today, a traveller in the Quebec countryside can see this characteristic of the landscape. Two elements in the structure of agrarian society, the parish and the family, were of supreme importance in Quebec. The parish was not only an institution of religious organization; it quickly became the basic institution in all of rural society and indeed of Quebec society as a whole. It grouped a number of ranges and became a basis for social and spatial identification; a person was spoken of as being from such and such a parish. The government quickly recognized this reality, and

Agricultural machinery manufactured by Matthew Moody at Terrebonne, north of Montreal.

when the first municipal code was drawn up, it used the parish as a base for rural municipalities, local institutions whose officials were elected and were responsible for governing the territory of the parish. The family played a fundamental role in rural Quebec, especially in areas where subsistence farming was practised. In these areas, the family was the basic unit of production and consumption, and determined the volume of agricultural production. Throughout the period, the rural family unit was characterized by its large size.

The third element of stability was the continuing presence of subsistence farming. Subsistence farmers are nearly self-sufficient and try to produce on the farm as many as possible of the goods consumed by its inhabitants. Agricultural specialization in Quebec during the period being studied led to a decline of subsistence farming; it slowly disappeared from areas that were close to cities or where specialization was most advanced. However, pockets of resistance where subsistence farming lingered could be found even in the most prosperous regions. Meanwhile, in the colonization regions, this kind of agriculture developed, and with the help of the growing forest industry, even managed to take root. Isolation from any form of market and the presence of a supplementary activity such as work in the forests — in other regions it was the mines or the fisheries — were the two conditions for the development of subsistence farming.

Colonization

The word "colonization" has a variety of meanings, but in the context of nineteenth-century Quebec it is used in a precise sense, which is captured by Esdras Minville's definition: "To colonize means to devote to agriculture a parcel of land that has previously been unoccupied, uncultivated and, in most cases, wooded.... Colonization is thus essentially the beginning of agriculture, and it is conceived, organized, and treated as such. The colonist is a potential farmer." A number of characteristic Quebec expressions were associated with colonization in this sense: *défrichement* (clearing), *terres neuves* (new lands), *faire de la terre* (to make land cultivable).

The dream of extending agriculture

Agricultural colonization is a very old phenomenon in Quebec, dating back to the earliest permanent white settlement. In the century following the conquest in 1760, the occupation of new lands intensified. This movement occurred naturally, as the surplus population of older parishes spilled over into areas that were still uninhabited.

Around the middle of the nineteenth century, there was a break in this gradual process. The St. Lawrence Lowlands, in which the best land in Quebec is located, were almost completely occupied, except for a few areas in the interior. Farmers' sons looking for land had to turn to peripheral areas, in the Laurentian and Appalachian foothills. In this way, regions such as the area north of Montreal, the St. Maurice Valley, the Saguenay-Lake St. John region, the back country south of the St. Lawrence and later Temiscamingue were opened to colonization. These regions were fairly isolated and often ill suited to agriculture. These new conditions discouraged many potential colonists.

Around the same time, another outlet for surplus rural population opened up — factory work in the cities and towns of Quebec and New England. From a strictly economic point of view, rural Quebecers were faced with the choice of remaining in agriculture by becoming colonists or leaving agriculture by becoming proletarians. Most of them chose the second solution.

The leading members of French-Canadian society were concerned about this new situation, and especially about emigration to the United States. The Quebec clergy reacted quickly and tried to take charge of the colonization movement so as to give it new impetus and organize it. The clergy had a number of motivations for this involvement, related to its overall goal of maintaining in Quebec a rural and traditional society in which the church would be assured of a large role. In the context of this goal it was important to stem the tide of emigration to the United States, which seemed to present a long-term threat to the very survival of the French-Canadian people. In addition, the roots of clerical power were more firmly embedded in rural Quebec and the exodus to the cities threatened the ideological and political ascendancy of the clergy. There were also financial considerations on which little research has yet been done; dioceses, seminaries and religious communities had invested heavily in rural Quebec and the development of colonization regions made these investments more profitable.

The clergy's strategy was two-pronged. The first prong was institutional, as parish priests and bishops took the initiative in founding colonization societies, with the aim of making it easier for colonists to settle in new regions. In addition, some priests got involved more directly, and personally founded new parishes in the colonization regions. These colonizing missionaries took on the role of defenders of and spokesmen for the colonists. Thus Curé Hébert of Kamouraska county spurred colonization in the Hébertville plain in the Lake St. John region, and Curé Brassard instigated development of the region north of Joliette. Most famous was Curé Labelle of Saint-Jérôme, who brought many colonists to the Laurentians north of Montreal; when Premier Honoré Mercier replaced the Department of Agriculture and Public Works with a Department of Agriculture and Colonization in 1888, he entrusted Curé Labelle with the position of deputy minister.

The second prong was ideological, and the clergy joined with some laymen in formulating a virtual ideology of colonization, a facet of what has been called the ideology of conservation (see chapter 16). According to this ideology, colonization fulfilled a national duty by strengthening the French presence in Quebec and in Canada, and also a Roman Catholic duty by helping to ensure the maintenance of moral values and ancestral virtues.

Antoine Labelle (1834-91), *curé* of Saint-Jérôme from 1868 to 1891 and deputy minister of agriculture and colonization from 1888 to 1891.

The colonization movement in Quebec thus went through a significant change after the middle of the century. Clerical involvement was only one aspect of this new situation, which was primarily a function of economic changes resulting from the increasing isolation of colonization zones and the appearance of a new outlet for rural manpower. There was also another change that affected the very nature of colonization. As it proceeded farther and farther into peripheral areas, colonization was no longer purely an extension of agriculture and became increasingly dependent on the forest.

The reality of an agro-forest economy

Ideally, colonization was supposed to be a stage in the development of agriculture. The colonist was supposed to settle in the forest, cut down the trees and, with a few years of hard work, transform his land into a farm. However, in the new colonization regions this ideal model became harder and harder to live up to. The main obstacle was that two economic interests were trying to co-exist in a single geographic space. The interest of one group was in timber, which it wanted to sell, and the interest of the other was in the land, which it wanted to exploit through agriculture.

The forest entrepreneurs usually came first to these regions, before the arrival of the first colonists. They wanted to keep the timber for themselves and were not interested in the extension of agriculture. They also needed plentiful, hardy and cheap labour for their lumber camps, and since these workers were only needed for part of the year, in winter, they would have to have other means of support. Where could such a worker be found if not on a farm?

Meanwhile, the colonist had to clear his land, and that took time. During that time he needed a supplementary income, and he found it in the forest industry. His path to becoming a real farmer was not smooth. The land in the new colonization regions was generally fairly poor and the climate was not very favourable, so that little more than subsistence farming was possible. Even in regions where the land and climate were better, distance from markets and poor communications delayed the start of specialized commercial agriculture. The colonist produced essentially to feed himself, and if he had a surplus his only outlet for it was the lumber camps.

Thus, the forest entrepreneur needed the colonist, who provided him with cheap labour and food for his camps. The colonist, in turn, needed the forest entrepreneur, who provided him with a necessary supplementary income and a market for his agricultural products. This situation was the basis of the agro-forest economy, which the historian Normand Séguin has defined as follows: "The agro-forest economy is defined by agricultural and forest activities co-existing in the same space and linked together in a complementary relationship. There are two conditions for its existence: (1) agriculture must have at most very weak links with commercial networks, and (2) agriculture must be clearly subordinate to the forest industry."

Beaudet Settlement in the Lake St. John region, late nineteenth century.

In such a system, the capitalist sector — the forest industry, in this case — is dominant and determines the pace of development. When the forest entrepreneurs have cut down all the trees in an area, they move elsewhere and the colonists follow them. New parishes are opened up while the older ones stagnate. As Séguin showed, the process can be seen clearly in the Saguenay-Lake St. John region. Settlement moved gradually from Chicoutimi, on the upper Saguenay, towards the western shore of Lake St. John.

Another characteristic of the system is that it is in the interest of the forest sector to hold back the development of agriculture and keep it at a subsistence level. The colonists are then forced to go to work in the forest to survive and since they are accustomed to a low standard of living, they are willing to work for low wages. This explains why the lumber merchants put pressure on the government to make it illegal for colonists — unlike other farmers — to sell wood cut on their own land; such sales would have made it possible for the colonist to free himself from the tutelage of the forest entrepreneur.

Only by breaking its ties with the forest industry could agriculture develop. The condition for that to happen was a market for agricultural products, and no such outlet developed until the peripheral areas of Quebec became urbanized in the twentieth century. Even then, only the areas with the best lands benefited. A significant portion of Quebec's colonization lands remained within the orbit of the agro-forest system until the middle of the twentieth century.

The Quebec government played an important role in the agro-forest system. In all the new colonization regions, the government was the initial owner of both the land and the forest. It possessed huge tracts of land called "crown lands," and its income from these lands was one of the major sources of government revenue.

Government policy was based on the development of crown lands both to bring in income and to encourage economic growth. The government brought in legislation and implemented policies to guide this development. Thus, woodcutting was carried out under a concession system; the government remained the nominal owner of the land but conceded the exclusive right to cut wood on it to forest entrepreneurs, who had to pay stumpage dues in return.

The system for conceding colonization lands was different, as the concession ultimately involved the definitive sale of the land. A colonist could obtain a 100-acre lot at a price that varied both with time and with the region where the lot was located, within a range of twenty to eighty cents an acre. He received a certificate and had to fulfil certain requirements, such as building a house, living in it and clearing part of his land, within a fixed period. When these conditions were met and the purchase price paid, the colonist received title to his land.

Government railway policy was also oriented towards the development of colonization regions. The Quebec government subsidized regional railways such as the Quebec and Lake St. John and the Baie des Chaleurs, and even the North Shore Railway was undertaken partly to facilitate the development of colonization regions. Roads were another area of government activity, and subsidies were given for colonization roads. The amounts set aside for this purpose were always inadequate and the roads that were built only partially met the needs of the colonists.

The overall effect of these various government policies was to establish the legal and administrative framework for development but not to stimulate it directly; the initiative was left to private capital, and the state had only a supporting role. Did these government policies favour the forest entrepreneur at the expense of the colonist? It should be no surprise that the answer is clearly yes. Many politicians were themselves linked to lumber or railway companies. The government was dominated by the bourgeoisie and served its interests first.

Thus, fairly precise limits were imposed on the colonist. Advocates of colonization criticized these measures, which they regarded as impediments to settlement. The policy of selling lots was unfavourably compared with the free-homestead system that prevailed in the United States. The government replied that by selling land it was keeping away land monopolizers and colonists who were not acting in good faith; besides, income from land sales was an essential part of the government's budget. The conditions imposed on the colonist in the first years after his entry were attacked as being too heavy; the regulation under which the colonist could not sell wood cut on his own land came in for special criticism for depriving him of an income that could have helped finance his attempt at settlement. Under pressure from the forest entrepreneurs, the government closed the best timber-

Squatters in the Lake St. John region.

lands to colonization. In addition, the government never acted on behalf of the "squatters" who settled illegally on crown lands.

In response to these criticisms, the government moved to take some measures to protect the colonist. The most significant was the Homestead Act (1868), which made it illegal to seize a colonist's land, equipment, animals or personal property. While this was an important step on the part of the government, it was not enough. The causes of the Quebec's government's failure to do more can be found in its financial weakness in the nineteenth century and its excessive dependence on revenue from crown lands. Another determining factor was pressure from the forest entrepreneurs who, overall, were clearly favoured by the government at the expense of the colonists.

A qualified success

The clergy's objective was to stop the rural exodus and emigration to the United States. It failed to achieve these goals. Hamelin and Roby have estimated that an average of 1,000 new settlers a year took up colonization lands during the period being studied, while ten times as many Quebecers left their homeland for the United States and another large contingent settled in Quebec cities.

Colonization did have the effect of extending considerably the portion of

Quebec's territory under cultivation. The colonists were true pioneers, and opened new regions to settlement. At the end of the century, Quebec was no longer confined to the St. Lawrence Lowlands. But this territorial expansion was accomplished by extending subsistence farming to peripheral regions, and the movement never really succeeded in transforming the colonist into a farmer who could make a living from what he produced on his land.

It must be acknowledged that it was unrealistic to try to develop some regions of Quebec through agriculture. Soil quality, relief and climate made most of the colonization regions less suitable for agriculture than the St. Lawrence Lowlands and made it impossible for the farmer to obtain a sufficient yield. The agro-forest system also had a limiting effect. The Quebec government tried only to provide a framework in which the dominant forces could act. The failure of agricultural colonization was the result of a number of factors, and the government was only partly to blame.

For it was not colonization but industrialization that would have made it possible to absorb the surplus population of rural Quebec. Quebec's failure to become sufficiently industrialized and urbanized meant that many of the people who left the countryside headed for the United States and also prevented Quebec agriculture from becoming more prosperous.

The Forest Industry

Throughout the nineteenth century, wood was Quebec's main export commodity and a major element in its economy. Wood is a material that can be used in a variety of ways, and different uses defined three stages in the development of Quebec's forest industry: squared timber, sawn lumber and pulpwood. Along with each of these uses came a characteristic set of conditions of exploitation and ramifications for the economy.

The major stages

Although the potential of the Quebec forest was recognized from the time of the French régime, it was not until the early nineteenth century that systematic development began. With Europe at war, England was forced to turn to its North American colonies for supplies of the wood it needed for naval construction. England granted a tariff preference to Canadian timber to encourage its development. Starting in the 1840s, this preference was gradually eliminated, forcing Canadian producers to compete with their Scandinavian rivals. England was still buying Quebec timber at the time of Confederation, but it was a declining market.

The largest part of this trade was in squared timber, mostly pine, of which the principal stands were found in the Outaouais region. Squared timber consisted of pieces of wood shaped roughly with an axe at the site where the wood was cut. These pieces were assembled into rafts, which were floated down tributaries of the

Loading squared timber at Quebec City, 1891.

St. Lawrence and then the St. Lawrence itself as far as Sillery, on the outskirts of Quebec City. There the rafts were taken apart; the timber was loaded onto ships — many of them built in Quebec City — and carried to England. Squared timber production presented some special problems. Only very tall, very straight trees were used, and it became necessary to travel farther and farther to find them. A substantial part of each tree cut down was wasted in the process of squaring. These difficulties, along with high costs and changes in markets, led to a decline in the production and use of squared timber starting in the 1860s and its complete disappearance in the early twentieth century.

The sawn lumber industry took up the slack. This change began to occur in the middle of the nineteenth century and was primarily related to American demand. Construction related to growing urbanization in the United States created a strong demand for lumber, which American forests could not fully satisfy. Canada quickly became the major supplier to the American market. This new market was not for squared timber, but for sawn lumber — boards and planks — and led to a very different kind of development. The lumber merchants were now able to use smaller trees and cut species that hitherto had been neglected. Logs were still floated, but over shorter distances. The wood was processed in sawmills which were established at the mouths of the major rivers in the lumber-producing regions. From the sawmills, it was carried to markets by boat or train. The expansion of the railway network in the second half of the nineteenth century facilitated the transportation of lumber to all parts of North America. Wood production for export in Quebec between 1867 and 1896 was dominated by the sawn lumber trade, which had replaced the trade in squared timber (Table 19). By the end of the century, however, it was a sector that appeared to have reached its peak. Lumber faced competition from other construction materials, such as iron, steel and bricks. However, once again a new use for wood came along to give the forest industry a new impetus.

Towards the end of the nineteenth century, a new commodity from Quebec's forests was in demand — pulpwood for use in the manufacture of paper. This industry had modest beginnings, and it was not until the early twentieth century that it really began to grow. This stage differed from the preceding ones in that the forest could be cut more systematically; small conifers, previously neglected, could be used. It also led to the establishment of processing plants (pulp mills and later paper mills) in the producing regions. But this happened slowly, and in the early days pulpwood was often exported to the United States without undergoing any processing.

Along with these three uses, the forest also supplied other commodities, mostly to the domestic market. The most important of these was firewood, at the time still the main fuel used for home heating. Some colonization regions specialized in supplying firewood to the cities. Thus the main function of the Quebec and Gosford Railway, opened in 1870, was to provide the capital with firewood, and fuel supply was an argument used by Curé Labelle in gaining support in Montreal for his proposed railway to the Laurentians. The forest also supplied wood in smaller quantities for laths, shingles, railway ties and stakes (Table 19).

TABLE 19
Principal Wood Products, Quebec, 1870-1900
(millions of cubic feet)

Product	*1870*	*1880*	*1890*	*1900*
Squared timber	24.3	25.7	17.3	5.5
Sawn lumber	173.0	205.0	266.0	258.0
Pulpwood	—	—	11.1	44.8
Firewood	280.9	327.5	304.2	276.3
Laths	0.6	2.9	15.5	—
Shingles	—	—	15.8	—
Staves	0.1	0.2	—	—
Ties	—	—	14.4	16.2
Posts	1.1	1.5	1.8	1.1
Stakes	—	—	19.3	15.6

Source: Esdras Minville, ed., *La Forêt*, p. 354.

The Eddy sawmill in Hull, 1874.

A key sector

Canadian statistics show that each year during the period under consideration wood and paper products made up between a fifth and a third of the value of Canadian exports. Statistics for Quebec are not available but forest products no doubt were Quebec's leading exports. Looking only at processing, it is clear that the sawmills constituted one of the most important industries in Quebec. William Ryan has calculated that the wood products group (not including paper) was in third place among Quebec manufacturing industries between 1870 and 1900, behind food and beverages and leather products. Wood products represented 17.1 per cent of the value of manufacturing production in 1870, and 11.1 per cent in 1900. In those same two years, paper products contributed 1.3 and 3.8 per cent respectively of manufacturing production. The forest and its derivatives were a key sector of Quebec's economy.

Lumberjacks' quarters in a lumber camp, about 1870.

Foreign demand played a determining role in development of the Quebec forest industry. A significant portion of Quebec's forest output was exported to Britain and the United States, which had many consequences. Quebec was not master of its own development, which was determined to an extent by decisions made elsewhere. Production in Quebec was subject to the hazards and price fluctuations of international trade. Because of the nature of foreign markets, the highest quality trees were systematically cut down, and the parts of the tree least in demand were wasted; the forest was pillaged, and reforestation was neglected. Foreign purchasers were interested only in the raw material; the processing done in Quebec—squaring or sawing—was primary processing, the only exception perhaps being naval construction in Quebec City. In this context, Quebec did not benefit fully from the spin-off effects that forest production might have had. Foreign demand also brought with it entrepreneurs of foreign origin, such as the Price family in the Saguenay and the Gilmours in the Outaouais, who carved out virtual forest empires in the peripheral regions of Quebec.

Quebec's forest production was not entirely externally oriented. Firewood, shingles, staves, stakes and ties were produced primarily for the domestic market, as was some of the sawn lumber. However, little is known about this relationship between the forest and the domestic market.

The forest industry in Quebec was also distinguished by the extent of the human resources devoted to it. Censuses of the time counted only between 3,000 and 5,000 lumberjacks, but this figure is far from being a true one, because most people who worked in the forest also had another occupation. These included all the farmers who maintained part of their land *en bois debout* (wooded). The surpluses they sold gave them a supplementary income without interfering with their primary activity, agriculture. As late as 1921, wood figured in the output of three-quarters of Quebec's farms. A more significant phenomenon was the lumber camp, found primarily in peripheral regions, where powerful entrepreneurs, or lumber barons as they were called, obtained huge concessions and hired crews of lumberjacks. These were mostly colonists from the surrounding areas who had become part of the agro-forest system; there were also day labourers and farmers' sons from older parts of Quebec whose presence on the farms was less important in the winter. The lumberjacks came to the camps in the fall and the cutting season lasted all winter. In the spring, some lumberjacks became drivers and took charge of floating the logs down the rivers to the sawmills at their mouths. These operations involved the participation of tens of thousands of men. Hamelin and Roby estimate that 20,000 men were employed in the forest industry during the 1880s in the Outaouais alone. There were, in addition, 12,000 to 14,000 men employed in sawmills in Quebec as a whole between 1870 and 1900, according to census data.

CHAPTER 7
INDUSTRY AND THE CITY

The radical change in the conditions of production occurring in England in the late eighteenth and early nineteenth centuries was labelled "the industrial revolution." It was in the second half of the nineteenth century that this process occurred in Quebec. Its effects were not felt in the economic sphere alone. Industrialization changed the social structure, modified the spatial distribution of the population by intensifying the process of urbanization, and profoundly affected the way people thought.

Industrialization

The pattern that industrialization has typically followed will be outlined briefly. In the transition from the pre-industrial to the industrial era, three stages are generally recognized: craft production, small-scale manufacturing, and mechanized industry.

In the pre-industrial era, the production of goods is fragmented, being carried out by a large number of small independent producers, or craftsmen. The craft system has three characteristic elements: the producer owns the means of production himself; the same person generally carries out the different stages in the production of a commodity; and the craftsman works independently and has at most a few employees, typically apprentices.

The second stage is reached when a capitalist has a number of craftsmen working under his command in a large workshop. In this system, a crucial distinction is introduced — ownership of the means of production is no longer in the hands of the workers, and is gradually transferred to the capitalist. In small-scale manufacturing, a functional division of labour is also established. Brought

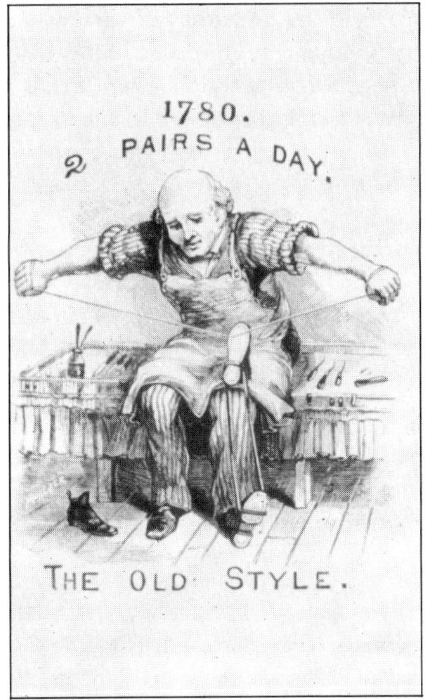

From craft to mechanized production.

together, the craftsmen no longer carry out all the stages in the production of a commodity, but instead each one performs a different operation, and efficiency is improved as a result. Some tasks become substantially simpler through this process and therefore can be carried out by unskilled workers, at lower cost to the employer. Thus, with small-scale manufacturing, production becomes better organized and productivity is improved; it is a transitional stage between craft production and mechanized industry.

The industrial revolution proper occurs with the advent of mechanized industry. The technological basis of the revolution is the machine; with the introduction of the machine, productivity is substantially increased and craft production gives way to mass production, with a significant reduction in cost. Because production now requires capital on a larger scale, the entrepreneur's hold on the means of production is strengthened and the producers take on more of the characteristics of proletarians. The machine allows the division of labour to be carried further and makes it more advantageous to employ unskilled labour. Not all the profits from increased productivity are distributed to the workers; some are retained by the owners of the means of production, who thus accumulate more capital. Finally, bringing together workers in a specific place speeds up the concentration of population in cities.

The process as a whole often extends over many decades, and for a while independent craftsmen can co-exist with large companies. The pace of industrialization also varies from sector to sector and from region to region. There is thus a transition period during which the economy of a country, viewed as a whole, is undergoing profound changes that presage the industrial era, while at the same time showing significant evidence of the continued presence of pre-industrial society.

For Quebec, this transition period was the second half of the nineteenth century. However, whether the general pattern of industrialization fits the Quebec case exactly is an open question, which at the present stage of research cannot be answered definitively. While the three major stages appeared in succession in some sectors, such as the shoe industry, in others they did not. Two ways in which Quebec's situation was a peculiar one should be pointed out. Since Quebec was a colony, and recently settled, in some cases the initial stage of craft production never developed. Some commodities, such as textiles, had traditionally been imported, and when domestic production in these sectors began it was possible to enter the industrial stage immediately. In addition, England and the United States became industrialized earlier than Quebec, so that Quebec benefited directly from experience acquired elsewhere; technological innovations that developed in other countries as the result of a long maturing process were imported into Quebec and introduced abruptly. In many cases, British or American entrepreneurs established factories in Quebec, bringing these innovations with them. In this context, it is conceivable that the intermediate stage of small-scale manufacturing was quite brief in Quebec, and in some cases avoided entirely.

From workshop to factory

The industrialization of Quebec in the second half of the nineteenth century occurred in two distinct stages. Although a few manufactories and mills were established as early as the 1820s or 1830s, the real beginnings of industrialization date to about 1850. The Union political régime facilitated the integration of Quebec and Ontario into a Canadian economic unit.

The completion of the canal system in 1848 and the subsequent building of the Grand Trunk improved the quality and speed of communications and thus contributed to unification of the domestic market. The large wave of immigration between 1840 and 1857 substantially increased the number of consumers and provided embryonic industries with cheap and abundant labour. These changes in the market and the labour pool were determining factors that made possible the establishment of mass production in Quebec. During this period, industry became concentrated in Montreal, which is at the hub of the Canadian market and enjoys significant location advantages. The redevelopment of the Lachine Canal, completed in 1848, made available large quantities of hydraulic energy to operate

Industry and workers' housing concentrated along the banks of the Lachine Canal in Montreal, late nineteenth century.

the machines in the factories. Within a few years, the southwest corner of Montreal had become Quebec's industrial centre. Four major sectors were developed in this period: milling, iron and iron products, wood and wood products, and shoes. The dominant sector was the shoe industry, in which the largest factories employed several hundred workers. Outside Montreal, the wood and wood products sector was probably the only one that became industrialized.

The process slowed down during the depression of 1873-78, but in the 1880s Quebec experienced a second period of industrialization. A number of factors contributed to this development, most notably the tariff of 1879, which sheltered industries from foreign competition and allowed them to grow. The effects of the growth of the Canadian market in the preceding years and the building of new railways were also felt. In general, industrialists profited from increased integration of the Canadian market and improved merchandising methods; Hamelin and Roby have also pointed out the significance of agricultural specialization in opening up rural markets to industry.

Whereas during the first period of industrialization labour was mostly of foreign origin, this time it was primarily indigenous. With reduced immigration and a large surplus population in the countryside, French Canadians became the new proletarians of Quebec industry. They were accustomed to a low standard of living on the land and too numerous for the available jobs. As a result they had to be satisfied with low wages; this situation attracted industries that needed large quantities of unskilled labour. Industrialization in this period was not limited to Montreal, although about fifty per cent of Quebec's production was concentrated there. Industry spread to the suburbs of Montreal — Hochelaga, Saint-Gabriel, Sainte-Cunégonde, Saint-Henri — to other towns in the Montreal region, such as Valleyfield, Saint-Hyacinthe, Saint-Jean and Sorel; and still farther afield to the Eastern Townships, concentrating in Sherbrooke, Magog, Coaticook and neighbouring communities. Outside Montreal and its satellite regions, the Quebec City-Lévis region also became industrialized; Trois-Rivières, however, attracted little industry.

In this period, industry also became diversified. The textile industry, protected by the tariff, became solidly established in Quebec. Industries such as railway equipment manufacturing, sugar refining, meat curing, clothing and tobacco products grew rapidly as well. Table 20 provides a rough picture of Quebec's industrial structure at the end of the period. First, there was a significant group of light manufacturing industries, based on the requirements of dress: textiles,

TABLE 20

Value of Manufacturing Production in Dollars, Quebec, 1861-1901

Group	*1861*	*1871*	*1881*	*1891*	*1901*
Food and beverages	3,830,307	18,650,000	22,440,000	34,700,000	33,099,000
Tobacco	262,050	1,430,000	1,750,000	3,600,000	8,231,000
Rubber	—	—	—	—	39,000
Leather	1,206,527	14,330,000	21,680,000	18,900,000	20,325,000
Textiles	788,316	1,340,000	2,400,000	4,300,000	12,352,000
Clothing	28,000	5,850,000	10,040,000	13,600,000	16,542,000
Wood	4,155,693	11,690,000	12,790,000	18,500,000	16,340,000
Pulp and paper	268,200	540,000	1,342,000	2,300,000	6,461,000
Iron and steel	1,472,680	3,130,000	4,220,000	7,600,000	12,842,000
Printing and publishing	—	1,250,000	1,830,000	2,300,000	3,510,000
Transportation equipment	648,041	2,910,000	3,600,000	9,900,000	8,058,000
Non-ferrous metals	—	—	—	—	1,497,000
Electrical appliances	47,300	—	—	400,000	1,815,000
Non-metallic mineral products	321,390	—	—	—	1,630,000
Oil and coal	—	—	—	—	245,000
Chemicals	130,600	—	—	—	4,138,000
Other	35,750	1,510,000	2,490,000	4,270,000	1,342,000
Census total	15,000,000	77,200,000	104,660,000	153,300,000	153,574,000
Total classified	13,194,854	62,630,000	84,582,000	120,370,000	148,467,000
Sample	87.9%	81.1%	80.8%	78.5%	96%

Source: Jean Hamelin and Yves Roby, *Histoire économique du Québec, 1851-1896,* p. 267.

clothing and shoes. This group accounted for about a third of Quebec's manufacturing production and employed cheap, plentiful labour. Industries in this group were established not only in the large cities but also in smaller centres in the Montreal region and the Eastern Townships. A second group consisted of technologically advanced industries, notably the manufacture of iron and steel products and railway rolling stock. These industries were concentrated primarily in the Montreal area and their work force, most of which was of British origin, was considerably more skilled than that of the first group. Other significant sectors were the food and beverages group, highly diverse and divided among a large number of enterprises, and the wood and wood products group; both of these depended on cheap labour. Each of the sectors that made up the industrial structure will be examined below in more detail.

The major sectors

Hamelin and Roby have compiled a table showing the major industrial sectors in Quebec during the period 1850-96 (Table 20). Some of the more significant features of the table will be pointed out here.

The food and beverages group is the largest in terms of value of production. However, food and beverages is a composite sector that lumps together a wide variety of industries. In most of these industries, production was carried out in small-scale factories scattered throughout Quebec. Three industries in succession dominated the sector: first, flour milling, until about 1880, when the major firms migrated to Manitoba as the West began to develop; then sugar refining, where two companies (Redpath and the St. Lawrence Sugar Refining Company) monopolized production; finally, in the 1890s, the dairy processing industry came to the fore as butter and cheese factories sprang up. This sector also included other significant industries: brewing, in which there were some long-established enterprises, such as the Molson family firm; biscuitmaking, from which the Viau family made its fortune; distilling; baking; and meat curing, which developed rapidly after 1880.

The wood products industry was a key one in Quebec throughout the nineteenth century. In the middle of the century significant changes took place in this industry; these were described in the section on the forest and wood-processing industries in chapter 6. With the transition from squared timber to sawn lumber, a wood-processing industry emerged, whereas exploitation of Quebec's timber resources had previously involved little more than gathering for export. The large sawmills that were established on the tributaries of the St. Lawrence after 1850 employed many workers. Their location near sources of timber helped decentralize Quebec's industry and its urban network. Small towns and villages, such as Hull in the Outaouais, Les Piles in the St. Maurice Valley, Chicoutimi in the Saguenay or Rivière-du-Loup in the Lower St. Lawrence owed their existence in part to the *moulin* (mill), which often was the source of livelihood for the majority of the population. A secondary wood products industry, in which lumber from the sawmills was further processed in response to industrial and construction needs, also developed. These door and sash, box, or cask factories were concentrated in the large cities. The pulp and paper industry, meanwhile, was still in its infancy, although mills began to spring up in the last two decades of the century. These were small-scale enterprises, however, and did not succeed in competing effectively with American producers. The meteoric rise of the paper industry had to wait for the twentieth century.

Among consumer industries, the three sectors based on the requirements of dress made significant progress; leather, textiles and clothing. An important shared characteristic of the three industries was their use of underpaid female labour.

The leather sector occupied second place in terms of the value of manufacturing production in Quebec, after food and beverages. The shoe industry clearly dominated this sector. It was concentrated in the two large cities, especially in Montreal, which alone produced between sixty and seventy-five per cent of all shoes sold in Canada towards the end of the century. Montreal's primacy in this industry went back a long way, and in the pre-industrial era a large number of shoemaker craftsmen had established themselves there. As a result, the transition from craft production to small-scale manufacturing to mechanized industry is unusually clear in this case (Table 21). The transition began in the 1850s, and less than twenty years later Montreal had a number of shoe-manufacturing enterprises employing between 200 and 500 workers each. During the first wave of industrialization in Quebec, the shoe industry was probably the one that grew most rapidly, but between 1880 and 1900 it tended to stabilize while other sectors took up the slack. The tanning industry, closely linked to shoe manufacturing, also made rapid progress, but according to Hamelin and Roby it declined in the face of American competition after 1880.

TABLE 21
Four Montreal Shoe-Manufacturing Enterprises, 1871

Characteristic	*J.-S. Courval*	*J.-D. Pelletier*	*E.-H. Thurston*	*Ames Millard*
Fixed capital ($)	264	10,000	30,000	200,000
Circulating capital ($)	500	30,000	30,000	380,000
Number of workers	3	25	73	341
Yearly wages paid ($)	312	10,000	15,600	84,000
Use of steam	no	no	yes	yes
Value of raw materials ($)	382	14,630	8,500	225,000
Number of pairs produced	520	18,176	27,000	316,000
Value of production ($)	2,080	36,000	45,000	470,000

Source: Census of Canada manuscript, 1871, Table 6, industrial census, Public Archives of Canada.

A shoe factory in 1875.

More than the shoe industry, the textile industry has become the symbol of Quebec's industrial structure in the historical literature. Its geographical concentration, the size of its mills, the composition of its work force and its financial structure make the textile industry perhaps the most striking illustration of large-scale capitalist production. It should be noted at the outset that only the cotton industry made significant inroads in Quebec; the woollen and silken industries attained only a marginal position, and Canadian production in these two areas became concentrated in Ontario. After a few more or less successful experiments, the Quebec cotton industry really got off the ground in 1873-74, with the establishment of the Victor Hudon mill in Hochelaga and the Montreal Cotton Company mill (set up by a group of Montreal businessmen, led by A.F. Gault) in Valleyfield. Given new impetus by the protective tarriff of 1879, the industry was able to win part of the Canadian market from English and American imports. The value of production grew steadily, and five new firms were established in Quebec between 1879 and 1884, leading to a crisis of overproduction. The manufacturers dealt with this crisis initially by agreeing to increase specialization of their mills and establish a price cartel; later, between 1889 and 1892, they established two trusts, the Dominion Cotton Mills Company and Canadian Coloured Cottons, which brought together firms in four provinces and represented seventy per cent of the mechanized mills in Canada. In 1905 Dominion Cotton merged with three other companies to form Dominion Textiles; the new trust was controlled by Montreal businessmen.

Thus, the textile industry represents one of the first examples in Quebec of the process of corporate concentration and monopolization. Cotton mills tended to locate not in Montreal proper but in the suburbs (Hochelaga and Saint-Henri) and in small towns outside the metropolitan area (Valleyfield, Chambly, Coaticook, Magog, Montmorency). Proximity to an abundant rural population available for low-paid work (Quebec mills recruited mostly women workers in the nineteenth century and also used child labour extensively) was one reason for this choice, but not the only one. According to Jacques Rouillard in *Les travailleurs du coton*, the availability of large quantities of hydraulic, and later hydroelectric, energy was a determining factor. At the end of the century, textiles had become an important industry in Quebec, and ranked in sixth place in terms of value of manufacturing production.

The clothing industry operated in a very different manner. It developed in Quebec during the 1860s, probably as a result of the Civil War in the United States, as Hamelin and Roby suggest, and had a significantly higher value of production than the textile industry. Clothing manufacture had not yet become concentrated; establishments were numerous and competition was intense. There were few large factories, as the ready-made clothing industry was based on its own particular form of employment, the "sweating system." Under this system, garments were sewn at home by women paid at extremely low rates on a piecework basis; the manufacturer did only the cutting in his establishment. Rural women often became caught up in this exploitative system, and through it were indirectly integrated into the urban labour market. At the turn of the century, the exploitation of poor immigrants of Jewish origin became characteristic of the clothing industry.

Heavy industry in Quebec was represented by the iron and steel sector and the manufacture of railway rolling stock. In the years after Confederation, the primary iron and steel industry was in the process of disappearing. The famous St. Maurice Forges, which had existed since the French régime, were closed in 1883, and other enterprises suffered a similar fate. In *Québec en Amérique au XIXe siècle*, Albert Faucher explains this decline by the technological development of the iron industry. Quebec's iron establishments used charcoal to transform bog ores into iron for casting into stoves and machinery, a technology that was becoming increasingly obsolete as the industrial era progressed. Because Quebec lacks mineral coal and its reserves of iron ore suitable to modern processes are not easily accessible and exploitable, the transition to the new iron technology did not take place. However, secondary processing of imported primary iron and steel did develop in Quebec. Rolling mills and factories producing such articles as nails, tools, boilers were established primarily in Montreal. The largest enterprise was the Montreal Rolling Mills Company, founded in 1869 by Morland and Watson, hardware wholesalers who were having difficulty obtaining supplies. Its rolling mills were modern installations with steam-driven machinery and employed 400 workers. Using pig iron imported from England, the company turned out a

The Victor Hudon textile mill in the Montreal suburb of Hochelaga, 1874.

variety of products; by 1881 it had become the largest Canadian producer of iron pipes.

The railway rolling stock industry, linked to iron and steel processing, became solidly established in Montreal and grew rapidly during the 1880s. Montreal became a centre for this industry because of its place in the communications network and its status as the administrative headquarters of the two large railway companies, the Grand Trunk and the Canadian Pacific, both of which also set up their shops in the city. At the Grand Trunk shops, in Point St. Charles in the southwestern part of the city, railway cars used by the company were built and all of its rolling stock was repaired and maintained; about 2,000 workers were employed in the 1880s. Canadian Pacific established its Angus Shops in the east end of the city.

The railway equipment industry is part of the transportation equipment sector; the other significant industry in the sector, shipbuilding, was clearly in decline after 1867. Primarily concentrated in Quebec City, it had reached its peak in the middle of the century. The growing demand for iron- or steel-hulled ships sounded the death-knell for the wooden sailing vessels built in the Quebec City shipyards.

In this sketch of late-nineteenth-century Quebec industry, a few other industries are worth mentioning — tobacco, in which Montreal dominated Canadian production; printing and publishing; cabinetmaking; and brickmaking, which grew as a result of the increasing use of bricks in construction. There were other industries as well, but their share of total manufacturing production was fairly small.

By the end of the nineteenth century, the industrialization of Quebec was well under way. Its main areas of concentration were food and beverages, wood, wearing apparel, and iron and steel, but it was becoming more diversified as the market grew. While industrialization had not proceeded far enough to employ all the available manpower and check emigration, it had begun to bring about profound changes in social relations and living conditions.

Urbanization

Because industrialization brings workers together in factories, the growth of cities and changes in the living conditions of urban populations are among its effects. In examining these effects, however, urbanization and industrialization should not be confused. Urbanization refers to a social process in which people are grouped together in cities; in that sense it is a very old phenomenon, but one whose characteristics change over time and vary from one economic system to another. Industrialization does not create urbanization, but rather speeds up its pace and changes some of its characteristics.

General characteristics

To describe and explain the growth of cities, geographers have developed the concept of urban function. An urban function is an economic activity that distinguishes a city, employs a significant portion of its population, and has a product that is intended for use outside the city. Until the middle of the nineteenth century, the function of Quebec's cities was essentially commercial. They were trading posts with a double role, covering both international trade, as the major staples — furs, lumber and wheat — were brought there to be shipped out, and internal distribution, as they provided goods and services to a growing rural hinterland.

Quebec's dominant urban centres, Montreal and Quebec City, are also among its oldest. The importance of these two cities, their control of economic activity and political power, and their attraction for a significant part of the population have been evident from the seventeenth century to the present day. As the area of Quebec under cultivation expanded in the late eighteenth and early nineteenth centuries, a network of villages — points of communication between city and country — appeared, forming the skeleton of Quebec's future urban network. The dominant position of Montreal and Quebec City was not the only characteristic of the urban network that was already apparent in the commercial era; the geographer Louis Trotier has pointed out others as well. Urban centres grew up primarily along the banks of the St. Lawrence and its tributaries, and were most densely concentrated and most clearly organized into a hierarchy in the Montreal plain (Map 7).

The 1850s and 1860s were a transition period in several respects. In those decades, the first effects of industrialization began to be felt, especially in Mont-

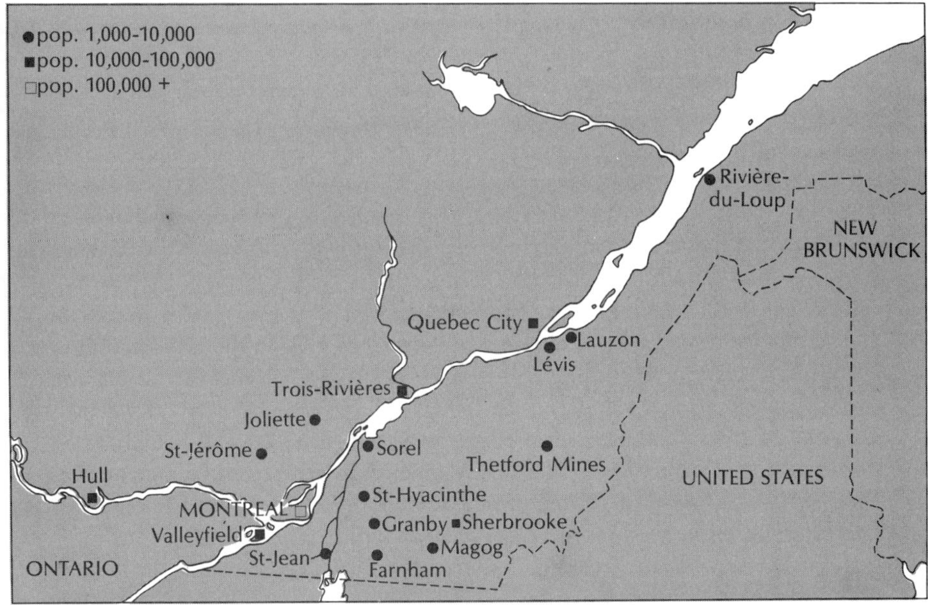

MAP 7: Quebec's Urban Network, 1901

real. Montreal's growth took off, and it definitively replaced Quebec City as the nerve centre of Quebec's economic life. The population gap between the two cities widened steadily from then on. In Quebec as a whole, the organization of the urban network was changed radically by the coming of the railway. The Grand Trunk main line became a second spinal column (after the St. Lawrence) through which part of Quebec's urban system was linked together. Thanks to the railway, some villages — Saint-Hyacinthe, Sherbrooke, Lévis, Rivière-du-Loup — became intermediate centres of regional significance and experienced a period of rapid growth. As urban areas grew, it became necessary to establish political structures on the local level. Between 1840 and 1870, a series of acts set up the municipal government system as it exists today.

After 1870, the industrial function clearly became the driving force behind urban growth in Quebec. Factories began to dot Quebec's territory, draining a portion of the surplus rural population towards the cities. The commercial function did not disappear, but rather remained a significant economic base for most of Quebec's urban centres. Its effects, however, were overshadowed by those of the new industrial establishments, which were generally built in already existing towns and villages, giving them a new impetus. Very few new towns were established in this period as a direct result of industry, and there was no radical change in the existing urban network. Rather, industrial centres were superimposed on commercial ones, and urban development became even more concentrated in the Montreal plain and its neighbouring region, the Eastern Townships.

The urban population

As a result of industrialization, the concentration of Quebec's population in cities increased, as can be seen by looking at the percentage of the population living in urban areas in a succession of census years (Table 22). The census definition of an urban area is an incorporated municipality with a population of 1,000 or more; in 1851, a little under fifteen per cent of Quebecers lived in urban areas, while fifty years later the figure was more than a third. The growth of the urban population began to accelerate in the decade 1871-81.

The degree of urbanization in Quebec followed a similar pattern to that of Canada as a whole. Table 22 shows no evidence of a lag in the urbanization of Quebec in relation to that of Canada, and the percentage of Quebec's population living in urban areas was higher than the Canadian percentage for every census year except 1891. There is a clearer gap between Quebec and its neighbouring province, Ontario. In the middle of the nineteenth century the two provinces showed a similar level of urbanization, but after 1871 Ontario clearly outpaced Quebec as a result of its more favourable economic circumstances.

Table 22 shows that Quebec underwent a significant change in the second half of the nineteenth century. But in giving us snapshots at a succession of fixed points in time, these figures can be misleading and do not always do justice to the complexity of the real world. It could be argued, for instance, that Quebec's population also underwent another process of urbanization. Throughout this period, the surplus population of the countryside flowed to the cities. Some of those who left rural Quebec remained in agriculture, in the American mid-west or western Canada, but cities were the destination for the largest part of Quebec's rural exodus. The weakness of Quebec's industrial structure relative to that of the United States made it impossible for Quebec cities to absorb all the surplus population. Those who were not absorbed within Quebec experienced urbanization outside Quebec, in the industrial towns of New England.

TABLE 22
Percentage of the Population Living in Urban Areas, Quebec, Ontario and Canada, 1851-1901

Year	*Quebec*	*Ontario*	*Canada*
1851	14.9	14.0	13.1
1861	16.6	18.5	15.8
1871	19.9	20.6	18.3
1881	23.8	27.1	23.3
1891	28.6	35.0	29.8
1901	36.1	40.3	34.9

Source: L.O. Stone, *Urban Development in Canada*, p. 29.

As was pointed out in chapter 2, migration was characteristic of North America as a whole in the second half of the nineteenth century, and it led to another phenomenon of continental significance. Much of the urban population of the time consisted of transients, either from overseas or from the rural hinterland, for whom the city was only a temporary place of residence. In a context of great geographical mobility, as people left, new arrivals came to take their place, so that the total number of people who lived in a city in a ten-year period was much larger than the population figure that showed up in a census. As major relay points in the continental communications network, Quebec City and Montreal saw part of their population periodically replaced in this way. The scope of the phenomenon has not been measured, but the geographer Raoul Blanchard examined the case of the Irish of Quebec City. For a few decades in the middle of the nineteenth century, they represented a significant proportion of the population of the city. Around 1871, with Quebec City in a period of economic stagnation, they left en masse, some for Montreal, some for other parts of North America.

Urbanization was brought about by these population movements as well as by industrialization. In the last few decades of the nineteenth century, the process was clearly under way in Quebec and could not be reversed. All regions of the province were affected by it, but its pace and scope differed from one region to another.

The major cities

Montreal: At the time of Confederation, Montreal was unquestionably the metropolis not only of Quebec but of Canada as a whole, and it maintained its dominant position throughout succeeding decades. During the period, it registered a consistently high rate of population increase, with the most rapid growth occurring between 1881 and 1891 (Table 23). In 1861, Montreal was a city of 90,000 people; adding the population of its still semi-rural suburbs gives a figure of almost exactly 100,000. At the end of the century Montreal proper, which now covered an expanded area, had a population of more than a quarter of a million, and adding the suburban municipalities brought the total to about 325,000, or half the urban population of Quebec.

As Raoul Blanchard pointed out, Montreal's rise was due to industry. A first period of industrial growth had occurred in the 1850s and 1860s, and was concentrated in the southwestern part of the city, especially along the Lachine Canal. Around 1867, Montreal's industrial structure was characterized by the presence of five major industries: sugar refining, flour milling, ironmaking, wood processing and shoemaking. In the 1880s, a second wave of manufacturing investment rounded out this early structure. Additional enterprises were founded in the existing sectors, while new ones such as meat curing, textiles, clothing, railway rolling stock and tobacco emerged. By the end of the nineteenth century Montreal had become an important industrial centre and accounted for half the

TABLE 23

Population of Major Urban Centres in Quebec, 1861-1901

Municipality	*1861*	*1871*	*1881*	*1891*	*1901*
Montreal Region					
City of Montreal	90,323	107,225	140,247	216,650	267,730
Montreal and suburbs[1]	100,723	126,314	170,745	250,165	324,880
Saint-Jérôme	—	1,159	2,032	2,868	3,619
Joliette	—	3,047	3,268	3,347	4,220
Sorel	4,778	5,636	5,791	6,669	7,057
Saint-Hyacinthe	3,695	3,746	5,321	7,016	9,210
Saint-Jean	3,317	3,022	4,314	4,722	4,030
Valleyfield	—	1,800	3,906	5,551	11,055
Quebec City Region					
City of Quebec	42,052	59,699	62,446	63,090	68,840
Lévis	—	6,691	5,597	7,301	7,783
Lauzon	—	—	3,556	3,551	3,416
Eastern Townships					
Sherbrooke	5,899	4,432	7,227	10,110	11,765
Magog	—	—	—	2,100	3,516
Granby	—	876	1,040	1,710	3,773
Thetford Mines	—	—	—	—	3,256
Coaticook	—	1,160	2,682	3,086	2,880
Farnham	—	1,317	1,880	2,822	3,114
Others					
Hull	—	3,800	6,890	11,264	13,993
Trois-Rivières	6,058	7,570	8,670	8,334	9,981
Chicoutimi	—	1,393	1,935	2,277	3,826
Rivière-du-Loup	—	1,541	2,291	4,175	4,569

[1] A suburb is defined here as a town or village on Montreal Island bordering Montreal.

Source: Censuses of Canada.

value of Quebec's manufacturing production. Illustrations from the era show a landscape dominated by factory smoke in the southwestern and eastern parts of the city.

The advantages accruing to Montreal from its position at the centre of the transportation system were another factor in its growth. It benefited from the substantial investments in infrastructure made in the nineteenth century (see chapter 5). The St. Lawrence River canals, the ship channel and the city's new

Saint-Urbain Street in Montreal, 1882. (Notre Dame church is in the background.)

harbour facilities made Montreal the focal point of water transportation. It was also the base of operations for the two major railway systems, the Grand Trunk and the Canadian Pacific, which established their administrative offices and maintenance shops there, and the centre of a web of railway lines extending in many directions. Transportation was an essential factor in the marketing and distribution of the goods that were manufactured in the city. Because Montreal was so well endowed with means of transportation, the concentration of industry in the city increased and its status as a metropolis for all of Canada was enhanced.

Towards the end of the nineteenth century, Montreal's capitalist class clearly dominated the economic activity of Canada as a whole. The most visible symbol of this domination was the ascendant Bank of Montreal-Canadian Pacific tandem. These two companies seemed to be almost ubiquitous in Canada. They were controlled by a close-knit group consisting of Donald Smith, George Stephen, R.B. Angus, William C. Van Horne and others, whose interests extended to a large number of companies in the financial, commercial, industrial and transportation sectors.

Spatial extension was another aspect of Montreal's growth, as the area within the city limits was systematically occupied and the city began to overflow into the suburbs. Montreal's city limits had been officially designated in the late eighteenth century; within them were large areas that were not yet urbanized. These areas gradually became inhabited as the nineteenth century progressed; at the time of Confederation this progress was not yet completed. Three wards near the city limits grew substantially in the decades after Confederation — Saint-Antoine in the west end and Saint-Jacques and Sainte-Marie in the east (Map 8). By the late nineteenth century, occupation of the city's original territory was almost complete, and the overflow of population into the new suburban municipalities that had been established from the late 1860s on had begun. The most important of these new suburbs were the industrial towns of Saint-Gabriel, Sainte-Cunégonde and Saint-Henri on the banks of the Lachine Canal to the west; Saint-Jean-Baptiste and Saint-Louis to the north; and Hochelaga and Maisonneuve to the east. Between 1871 and 1901, the population of these newly urbanized areas on Montreal Island grew from 11,000 to 130,000, or from four per cent to twenty per cent of the urban population of Quebec. At the end of the century, the largest part of the population increase in the metropolitan region was occurring in these new areas.

Montreal's municipal authorities wanted to adjust the region's political structures to these new demographic and economic realities, and tried to extend the city's territory by annexing suburban towns. The process began in 1883 with the annexation of Hochelaga; in the subsequent years, three more municipalities met the same fate. The phenomenon took on new dimensions in the early twentieth century, when the annexation of nineteen suburban municipalities in twelve years brought about a spectacular increase in Montreal's territorial size.

These small municipalities were typically the creation of a handful of real estate

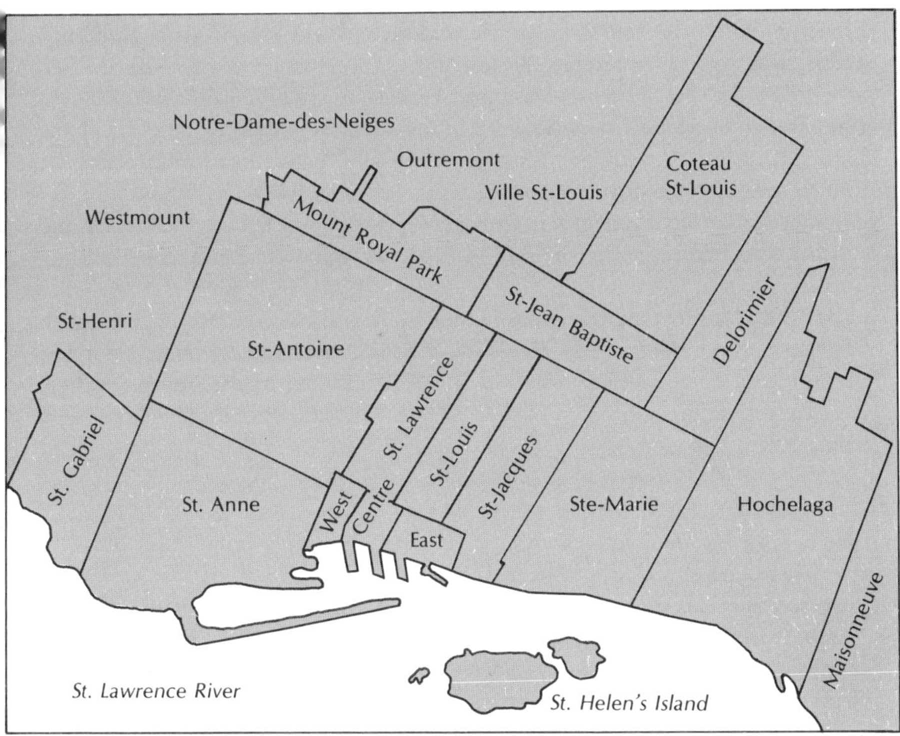

MAP 8: Montreal Wards in the Late Nineteenth Century

promoters, who wanted to develop land that they owned. Towards this end, they would incorporate a small town, in which they would then control the town council. Through tax exemptions or cash subsidies, they attracted companies whose employees became residents of the new town. The promoters themselves also used tax exemptions to start development projects, which the municipality financed through borrowing, the burden of which was ultimately borne by small property owners and tenants. A few years or decades later, the municipality was heavily in debt, and annexation to Montreal seemed appealing as a solution to its financial problems.

The period was thus one of rapid growth and change for Montreal. One of the most significant changes was in the city's ethnic composition. Mid-nineteenth-century Montreal was culturally and politically a British city, with an English-speaking majority between 1831 and 1865; the English-speaking proportion of the population reached a peak of fifty-seven per cent in 1844. This British preponderance was reflected in the city council, where decisions were made in the interests of the English-speaking majority. The appearance of the city also changed, and in the 1840s British-style architecture started to replace the old

French architecture that had characterized the city until then, although French architecture was never completely eliminated. The situation began to be reversed around 1865, when a French-speaking majority was re-established in the city as rural French Canadians came to work in the factories and immigration from the United Kingdom slowed down. Annexation of suburban municipalities with large French-speaking majorities intensified the processs. However, it was almost twenty years before the change in ethnic composition was felt on city council, and much longer before it was reflected in the city's appearance and major cultural institutions.

By 1896, Montreal had become not only a financial and commercial metropolis but also a great industrial city. However, as a result of its rapid growth, a number of problems of adjustment affected living conditions in the city: crowding, deficient sanitary conditions, a high death rate. These questions will be dealt with later.

Quebec City: The evolution of Quebec City during this period was very different from that of Montreal. Founded in 1608, Quebec City was the oldest city in the province, and had been the principal centre of New France and later of British North America. However, it had gradually lost its political pre-eminence to Ottawa, and at the time of Confederation it was entering a period of relative stagnation that lasted until the end of the century.

Quebec City's population grew by forty-two per cent between 1861 and 1871 (Table 22), but its growth in the three succeeding decades was very slow. A comparison between Quebec City and Montreal brings this slowdown into sharp focus. Throughout the first half of the nineteenth century, the population of the two cities was roughly the same. A clear gap began to appear in 1851, and by 1901, the Montreal urban area had a population five times as large as the Quebec City urban area. While twenty-two per cent of Quebec's urban population lived in the Quebec City area in 1871, that figure had fallen to 10.5 per cent in 1901.

The transition from the commercial era to the industrial era was difficult for Quebec City. The difficulties the city experienced in the late 1860s were identified by Raoul Blanchard. Most significant was the decline of the timber trade. From the early nineteenth century, Quebec City was the port from which the largest part of Canadian lumber exports to England were shipped. But the replacement of squared timber by sawn lumber and the redirection of trade from Britain to the United States changed the lines of communication, so that Quebec City was no longer the pivot of wood exports. Ships built in Quebec City had carried Canadian timber to England, where the ships were resold; the slowdown in timber shipments thus adversely affected the city's shipbuilding industry. This industry was also hurt by changes in maritime technology, as the wooden vessel was replaced by the iron- or steel-hulled ship. From the 1870s on, Quebec City's shipyards declined rapidly. The port of Quebec City also experienced difficulties

Little Champlain Street in Lower Town, Quebec City, about 1890.

as a result of competition from Montreal. The dredging of the ship channel made it possible for ocean-going vessels to sail upriver as far as Montreal, and Quebec City gradually lost its importance as a terminus for transatlantic lines. Thus, as Blanchard pointed out, all of Quebec City's maritime activity was in decline, with thousands of workers losing their jobs and having to seek employment elsewhere.

Quebec City was also not well integrated into the railway system. With the Grand Trunk running along the south shore, it was the Lévis area rather than Quebec City that developed; it was not until the early twentieth century that the two banks of the river were linked by a bridge. It was only in 1879 that the North Shore Railway, connecting Quebec City with Montreal, was opened to traffic, and this long wait for railway service did not help the city get out of its slump. When the capital of Canada was established at Ottawa in 1867 there was an exodus of civil servants, which was followed by the departure of the British garrison in 1871.

While there were many unfavourable elements in Quebec City's situation, they were partly counterbalanced by the development of some compensating factors. Having lost its pre-eminence on a Canada-wide scale, Quebec City increasingly became a regional metropolis for eastern and central Quebec. Quebec City's immediate hinterland is fairly limited, so that new regions had to be brought under its influence and dominated, a task which occupied the Quebec City bourgeoisie during the last three decades of the century. Its main instrument was the railway. Thus, the Quebec and Lake St. John Railway allowed it to dominate the Saguenay region, the Lévis and Kennebec brought the Beauce within its orbit, and the North Shore Railway strengthened its links with the region to the west of the city. Also during this period, Quebec City attracted some industrial establishments, especially shoe factories. Some of the jobs lost through the decline of maritime activities were made up for by this industrial growth, but not enough to retain all the city's surplus population. An attempt was also made to breathe new life into the maritime sector by significantly enlarging the city's harbour facilities; this project was completed in 1890.

Thus, Quebec City's stagnation in the late nineteenth century was due to the decline of its traditional economic activities; their replacement by new activities did not occur quickly enough to stabilize its population.

This situation also had significant effects on the city's ethnic composition. In 1861, about forty per cent of its population was of British origin: by 1901 this figure had declined to fifteen per cent. The decline was just as dramatic in absolute numbers — from 23,000 to 10,000 in the same period. This population was mostly Irish and consisted primarily of labourers in the harbour or the shipyards; they were the first to feel the effects of the slowdown in economic activity and had no choice but to leave the city. Thus, Quebec City became increasingly French in the late nineteenth century. As Blanchard noted, this change affected the bourgeoisie as well, and there were a growing number of French Canadians among the owners of the major enterprises.

The growth of the population, limited as it was, nevertheless brought about an expansion of the city's inhabited area. This occurred in the eastern part of the city, the population of which doubled between 1861 and 1901, especially in the neighbourhoods of Saint-Roch, Saint-Sauveur and Saint-Vallier, where new industries were established.

Other cities and towns: At the time of Confederation, Trois-Rivières was still the third largest city in Quebec, far behind Montreal and Quebec City; in the next three decades it was passed by Hull, Sherbrooke and Valleyfield in succession. Like Quebec City, Trois-Rivières was in a period of stagnation, and its population grew only from 6,098 to 9,981 in forty years; between 1881 and 1891, it even declined slightly. The reason for this situation was the decline of the timber trade in the last quarter of the century. The economy of Trois-Rivières' hinterland was essentially agricultural or agro-forest. It was not until the early twentieth century that hydroelectricity and the pulp and paper industry gave new impetus to the region's economy and brought about the development of an urban network

A bird's-eye view of Trois-Rivières, 1881.

(Cap-de-la-Madeleine, Shawinigan, Grand-Mère, La Tuque) for which Trois-Rivières was the bridgehead.

The situation was different in the Eastern Townships, where a relatively prosperous agricultural economy led to the growth of a network of villages. In the last quarter of the nineteenth century, factories were established in a number of these centres to make use of rural manpower, turning them into small towns, each with a population of barely 3,000 in 1901 — Magog, Granby, Coaticook, Farnham, Richmond, Windsor. Thetford Mines, whose growth was based on the asbestos-mining industry, was a special case. This little urban network was capped by a regional metropolis, Sherbrooke, which played a dominant role in the Eastern Townships during the period. Sherbrooke's location on the St. Francis River at its confluence with the Magog was advantageous, and it benefited further from being on the Grand Trunk Railway. It was both an industrial town and a service centre for the Eastern Townships as a whole.

There was also another regional network in Quebec, consisting of six satellite towns forming a ring around Montreal at a radius of about sixty kilometres — Saint-Jérôme, Joliette, Sorel, Saint-Hyacinthe, Saint-Jean and Valleyfield. Their combined population was more than 18,000 by 1871, and it was 40,000 in 1901. Industrial and commercial functions and a role as service centres all contributed to their growth. The town of Joliette is a representative case. Founded in 1824, it developed slowly until the middle of the century. It was the site of a large sawmill, and the forest industry was its main economic base. When neighbouring townships were opened to settlement, it quickly became a regional service centre, a development which brought new kinds of establishments to the town and introduced a form of economic activity that was both commercial and industrial. Typical of this process was the gradual evolution of a small ironworks into a plant where farm machinery was manufactured; another ironworks offered its customers a wide variety of iron goods, from machine parts to saucepans by way of *ferrures de moulin à laver* (iron parts for wood-frame washing machines). The population of Joliette at the turn of the century was 6,000; creation of a diocese of Joliette in 1904 was testimony to its importance.

At the end of the period, the process of urbanization in Quebec was well under way. Montreal's ascendancy had grown, while a network of small towns had developed primarily in the Montreal plain and the Eastern Townships.

SOCIETY

Along with the economic change that Quebec experienced in the second half of the nineteenth century came a challenge to its existing social organization. New social relationships were established, and groups organized themselves to defend their interests more effectively. Not all these developments occurred smoothly; old structures endured and change was sometimes slow. In the late nineteenth century, the slow pace of some changes could not escape attention.

Among the many aspects of Quebec's social history, a few are especially significant in the context of a synthesis such as this one. It is important at the outset to establish just what Quebec's social structure was in the late nineteenth century; thus, the first chapter of this section is devoted to a study of the main social classes. Next, the focus is on working and living conditions, both in the city and in the country. While the weight of tradition was still heavy in rural areas, it was less so in places where the effects of industrialization and urbanization were strongly felt, upsetting daily life and accentuating social problems. Attempts were made to deal with these problems through charity, but such attempts did not get at the root of the difficulties and their effectiveness was consequently limited.

The rise of Quebec's labour movement occurred between 1867 and 1896. First the different stages of unionization will be identified, and then workers' goals and governments' response to their demands will be examined. While conditions were difficult for workers, they were no less hard for women, who were considered second-class citizens; movements to change their status did not appear until the very end of the period. In the last chapter of this section, the development of two institutions that play an especially important role in social organization — the church and the school — will be examined.

CHAPTER 8
SOCIAL STRUCTURE

Quebec's economic structure, as described in the last section, had profound ramifications for its entire social structure. With the establishment of industrial capitalism, new relationships developed within society and new social classes emerged. Historians and sociologists, however, have taken a long time to acknowledge this fact, and have generally regarded French Canadians as a fairly homogeneous bloc, standing opposite an English-Canadian bloc.

For a long time, historians and sociologists described French-speaking Quebec as an essentially rural society, relatively egalitarian, with a social structure based on the family. This society was united by a common culture and religious values, and produced religious and political leaders who had their roots in the people and reflected their concerns. This thesis was expressed in its fullest form in the analyses carried out during the 1930s by the American sociologists Robert Redfield, Horace Miner and Everett Hughes, who saw French-speaking Quebec as a model case of a folk society. In their view, the main characteristics of such a society were that the family played a large role and was the basis of the social structure; the lives of individuals were governed by a coherent system of precepts and values; daily life was viewed in a religious context; oral tradition was accorded a prominent place; members of society were united through a cohesive network of relationships and society was somewhat isolated from the external world. Rural Quebec was seen by these sociologists as having many of these defining traits, and the disappearance of its folk society was regarded as having been brought about by twentieth-century urbanization.

This interpretation, originating in the United States, was very popular among Quebec sociologists in the 1940s and 1950s, but it was later abandoned. It was a far from adequate account of Quebec's social structure. The emphasis it placed on the family and kinship obscured social relationships of other kinds, such as relations of economic dependence and class relationships. In emphasizing rural Quebec's isolation, it underestimated the flow of ideas and people and the extent of relations with the urban world. In describing the society as essentially rural, it overlooked the massive exodus to the United States and the cities that had begun in the mid-nineteenth century and the industrialization and urbanization that Quebec had experienced well before the 1920s.

The concept of a social structure unique to Quebec emerged in the postwar era. Historians and sociologists after the Second World War saw late-nineteenth-century French-Canadian society as having been made up of two groups — the mass of the population, consisting of *habitants* confined to agriculture, and the élite, made up essentially of the clergy and members of the liberal professions. The élite tightly controlled Quebec's political, social and religious institutions and succeeded in guiding and directing the mass of the population. This interpretation put special emphasis on the leading role of the clergy within the élite. The theme of clerical control, already present in English-Canadian historical literature (in which Quebec was presented as a "priest-ridden society"), also found its way into French-Canadian historiography. Quebec intellectuals of the 1950s, struggling against the conservatism of the régime of Premier Maurice Duplessis, exaggerated the historical significance of clerical control.

During the 1960s, a new conception of Quebec society in the second half of the nineteenth century arose. This time, French Canadians were not the only group considered and the concept of class was introduced. Quebec society was divided in three: a bourgeoisie of British origin, which controlled the economy; a French-Canadian petty bourgeoisie, made up of members of the liberal professions, small businessmen and the clergy, which exercised institutional and ideological control; and the mass of rural French Canadians. This classification leaves a number of questions unanswered. Can the bourgeoisie be so closely identified with the English-speaking group? Were French Canadians totally absent from the bourgeoisie? How should farmers of British descent, still numerous in Quebec at the time, be classified? What about the thousands of unskilled workers who came from Ireland and England as well as the Quebec countryside? Could the ideological control of the petty bourgeoisie have been totally devoid of a material base? Were rural French Canadians really a homogeneous group? It was realized that one problem with these interpretations was the low level of historical knowledge about nineteenth-century Quebec.

Since the mid-1960s, research has progressed, making possible a more accurate view of Quebec's social structure in the past. Recent work that has been done in economic history has cast new light on the role and composition of the bourgeoisie, and research on the working class has allowed it to take its proper place on the historical stage. In addition, issues that have been raised with regard to Quebec's present-day social structure have inspired historians and sociologists to ask new questions about the past and define their concepts more sharply.

Quebec society in the second half of the nineteenth century now appears to have been much more complex than was allowed for in the monolithic view of it that prevailed for so long. There were a number of classes, and strata or segments within them. In addition, the social structure was changing, and there were groups that are difficult to classify. It is too early to develop a new overall interpretation. Using the latest knowledge, however, it is possible to get a sense of the situation, and describe the basic elements of Quebec's social structure at the time of industrialization.

The Bourgeoisie

At the top of Quebec society was the dominant class, the bourgeoisie, which controlled the major political and economic decisionmaking powers. Formation of the bourgeoisie was based on the accumulation of capital, which, in the case of the Quebec bourgeoisie (or, if you will, the Quebec section of the Canadian bourgeoisie), had six major sources: import-export trade, commercial credit, real estate speculation, water and railway transportation, large public works (railways, canals, aqueduct systems), and industrial production. The bourgeoisie is defined as the group that owns capital, and not only owns it, but also puts it to work through the employment of wage labour. In this way, the bourgeoisie is in a position to control the major economic institutions of the country and to have a determining effect on its political choices.

Historically, the origins of the Quebec bourgeoisie can be traced to the late eighteenth and early nineteenth centuries, to the agents or partners sent out by English and Scottish merchants or engaged by them from among the locals to represent their interests in the colony. Some of these representatives were quickly able to accumulate capital on their own account and reinvest it profitably in the colony; the case of Joseph Masson, who began as a clerk for a Scottish merchant, became a partner, and built a considerable fortune through his business acumen, is well known. The first source of capital accumulation was furs, which gave rise to the beaver aristocracy of McGills, McTavishes and McGillivrays. While the fur trade faded from the Quebec scene around 1821, the population growth and economic development of the British North American colonies opened up a variety of new paths to wealth.

Throughout the nineteenth century, the Quebec bourgeoisie maintained close relations with its parent class, the British bourgeoisie, from which it continued to draw capital and recruit new members. The nature of these relations changed over time, as what had been a formal relationship between a metropolis and its colony gave way to a more flexible association in which the colonials could advance their own interests and exercise a degree of autonomy. Banks and other institutions set up by the Quebec bourgeoisie were a concrete expression of the existence of these distinct interests. The Quebec bourgeoisie was solidly established by the time of Confederation, and continued to strengthen its position in succeeding decades.

With the growth of industrial capitalism, the bourgeoisie — like the proletariat — was a rising class. Its numbers were increasing rapidly, and it still contained a substantial number of "self-made men." Cases of poor but enterprising Scottish immigrants or destitute but daring French-Canadian farmers' sons who rose to its ranks were not legion, but they were not rare either. New societies tend to be mobile ones, and it is a characteristic of rising classes to recruit new blood. The historian T.W. Acheson has calculated that as late as 1885, about a third of the members of the Canadian industrial élite were the sons of farmers or craftsmen. But these cases became increasingly hard to find as time went on; as the twentieth century approached, the avenues for social mobility became narrower and the bourgeoisie tended more and more to recruit its new members from families within its own ranks.

The career of Jean-Baptiste Rolland (like that of Donald Smith, which will be examined later) illustrates how this process of mobility worked. Rolland was a farmer's son, born in Verchères in 1815, who arrived penniless in Montreal in 1832. He was hired as an apprentice typesetter and became a typesetter, then a printer. In 1842, he founded the bookselling business that was to become the basis of his fortune. He started by peddling books and paper in the countryside, then widened his activities to include publishing and bookbinding. Within a few years, the Rolland firm became one of the largest booksellers in Montreal and its owner had expanded into real estate promotion and residential construction. In 1881, in order to secure a better supply of paper for the firm, Rolland decided to manufacture it himself; the Rolland Paper Company established its mill in Saint-

Jean-Baptiste Rolland (1816-88), Montreal printer and bookseller who established a paper mill in Saint-Jérôme in 1882.

Jérôme and began production in 1882. When he died in 1888, Jean-Baptiste Rolland left an appreciable fortune and a substantial commercial and industrial enterprise to his four sons.

While there were a few success stories, there were also many failures. Competitive capitalism often allows those who make it to do so only by wiping out others. In the second half of the nineteenth century, there was a rapid turnover in the membership of the bourgeoisie, and bankruptcies were numerous. Nevertheless, the general growth of the economy swelled the ranks of the bourgeoisie.

That class dominated society, and had clear control of political institutions. Cabinets, parliaments and city councils included many businessmen, and their presence ensured that governments' economic objectives meshed smoothly with their own. They found outlets for this philanthropy by heading a variety of cultural and charitable institutions, and showed off their wealth in many ways, most typically by building luxurious residences.

A characteristic of the careers of many representatives of the Quebec bourgeoisie was the diversity of their interests. Their economic interests covered several sectors simultaneously — commerce, railways, manufacturing, banking, real estate. Some of them also pursued political careers while continuing to run their companies.

Historians have taken the sectors in which the Canadian bourgeoisie was involved as a basis for speculation about the nature of the bourgeoisie itself. Some historians, notably R.T. Naylor, have argued that the industrial sector was dominated by a commercial and financial bourgeoisie that was interested in making profits through financing and exchange rather than by developing production.

Essentially a conservative group, the commercial bourgeoisie blocked the emergence of an indigenous Canadian industrial bourgeoisie, and thus encouraged the industrialization of Canada by American subsidiaries. While this is a tempting interpretation, it is not based on much hard evidence. It has been forcefully challenged by the historian L.R. Macdonald, who questions the rigid distinction between industrial capital and commercial capital and the classification of railways as part of commercial capital; he argues that on the basis of the scale of their investments, railways have much more in common with industrial than with commercial capital. He also challenges the statement that the commercial bourgeoisie was essentially conservative, as opposed to a dynamic and innovative industrial bourgeoisie. At the present stage of research, the evidence seems to favour Macdonald's interpretation; rather than a black-and-white distinction between commercial and industrial sectors, the picture of the Canadian (and Quebec) bourgeoisie that emerges appears to consist of different shades of grey. While it is true that a number of industrial enterprises were set up or taken over by merchants, it is far from clear that their development was held back as a result. More commonly, the transfer of capital from the commercial to the industrial sector was an essential factor in the rise of industry. Far from being a conservative influence, the participation of commercial capital in industrial enterprises often brought about a better integration of production and distribution. Because his supplies of paper were irregular, Rolland, bookseller and merchant, established a paper mill. Similarly, it was to secure regular supplies that the Montreal textile merchants invested heavily upstream in the manufacture of cotton yarn during the 1870s and 1880s. These are only two examples. A study of late-nineteenth-century businessmen shows that they invested in several sectors simultaneously, and it is often difficult to categorize them exclusively as members of the commercial bourgeoisie or the industrial bourgeoisie.

However, it is possible to distinguish two levels or strata within the bourgeoisie. First, there is the big bourgeoisie, which possesses capital in large quantities and controls the leading economic institutions, such as the Bank of Montreal and Canadian Pacific. Its power in society is substantial and highly concentrated. Within a competitive system, it is powerful enough to impose its own solutions and it is the only group in a position to undertake the process of monopolization. The scope of Quebec's big bourgeoisie exceeded the boundaries of the province, and it operated in a Canadian and imperial context. It had few members, and they were concentrated in Montreal, Canada's most important financial centre. Most of them were English or Scottish, although some businessmen of other origins, including a few French Canadians, succeeded in gaining entry to the group. Donald Smith, Hugh Allan, George Stephen, William Macdonald and Louis-Joseph Forget were prominent members of this group.

The second stratum, the middle bougeoisie, had a much larger membership. With smaller amounts of capital at its disposal, it exercised control at an intermediate level, in middle-sized institutions that, while substantial enough, were far behind the Bank of Montreal in scale and influence. The line separating the two groups is not always easy to discern, and the purpose of this discussion is to look at an overall phenomenon rather then to classify individuals. Because its means were more limited, the field of operations of the middle bourgeoisie was generally regional.

The difference between the two strata can be seen more clearly by comparing two late-nineteenth-century bank presidents — Donald Smith (later Lord Strathcona) of the Bank of Montreal and Alphonse Desjardins (not to be confused with his namesake, the founder of the caisse populaire movement) of the Banque Jacques-Cartier. Born in Scotland in 1820, Smith arrived in Quebec in 1838, and began his career as a Hudson's Bay Company factor. Rising through the ranks, he became the company's chief commissioner for Canada in 1870, and later a director and governor. He was also one of the founders of the Canadian Pacific Railway in 1880, and held a succession of high offices in the Bank of Montreal — vice-president (1882-87), president (1887-1905) and honorary president (1905-14). Smith was thus simultaneously a major stockholder and key director of three companies that played a determining role in the economic history of Canada. He also participated in many other industrial, commercial and financial enterprises. He amassed an immense fortune during his career, and by the end of

Alphonse Desjardins (1841-1912), president of the Banque Jacques-Cartier, 1880-99. Not to be confused with his namesake, the founder of the caisse populaire movement.

Donald Smith (1820-1914), created Baron Strathcona and Mount Royal in 1897, was a key director of the Hudson's Bay Company, the CPR and the Bank of Montreal.

the century had become the richest member of the Montreal bourgeoisie. Meanwhile, Smith also carried on a successful political career; he was a member of the Canadian parliament for twenty years, and in 1897 was named to the British House of Lords. From 1896 until his death in 1914, he was Canadian High Commissioner in London.

Alphonse Desjardins was born in 1841 and died in 1912. His particular field of activity was the financial sector. He was president of the Banque Jacques-Cartier from 1880 until it closed in 1899, as well as the bank's principal stockholder for a number of years. He also sat on the boards of mortgage loan and insurance companies, and had interests outside the financial sector, as the founder of a company that manufactured bricks and as a promoter of urban real estate in Maisonneuve. A lawyer by training, he was politically active as well; he was one of the leaders of the ultramontane group in Montreal, and for a time was publisher of its newspaper, *Le Nouveau Monde*. From 1878 to 1892 he was a Conservative member of the federal House of Commons; appointed to the Senate in 1892, he served as a cabinet minister under prime ministers Mackenzie Bowell and Charles Tupper in 1896. In 1893-94, he was also mayor of Montreal. The defeat of the federal Conservative party in 1896 put an end to his political career. In 1899, Desjardins was elected president of the Chambre de Commerce du District de Montréal, testimony to the esteem in which he was held in French-speaking business circles.

Both Smith and Desjardins had interests in the banking, financial, industrial and real estate sectors and carried on active political careers at the federal level. But the bank over which Smith presided operated all over Canada and was the financial agent of governments, while the Banque Jacques-Cartier, with one-twentieth the assets of the Bank of Montreal, operated primarily in the Montreal region. Smith's real estate interests were on a large scale, involving a huge region, the Canadian West, while Desjardins' activities as a developer were confined to a small suburban town. Smith and Desjardins were both members of the bourgeoisie, but the degrees of control they held over the Quebec — and Canadian — economy were very different.

The presence of Quebec's middle bourgeoisie was felt through the province's network of regional banks — the Banque Nationale (Quebec City), the Eastern Townships Bank (Sherbrooke), the Banque de Saint-Hyacinthe, and the Banque de Saint-Jean. However, it was felt even more strongly in Montreal. Here too, financial institutions, notably the Banque d'Hochelaga and the Banque Jacques-Cartier, were among its manifestations. Some of the Montreal middle bourgeoisie's members, such as Rodier, Rolland, Beaubien, Beaudry, Rivard, Desjardins, Préfontaine, Viau, Cherrier, Barsalou and Delisle, are familiar figures, but there were many others and it would be valuable to know more about them.

The ethnic composition of the middle bourgeoisie appears to have been more varied than that of the upper bourgeoisie. Many of its members, of course, were English and Scottish, and there were some Irish as well. But the middle bourgeoisie was also marked by the presence of a significant number of French-Canadian businessmen, who were involved in all sectors of economic activity. Many of them represented that typically North American phenomenon, the lawyer-businessman with his finger in a number of pies. There can be no doubt that the presence of French Canadians in the bourgeoisie, while disproportionately small in relation to the percentage of the population as a whole that was French-speaking, was nevertheless substantial.

French-Canadian businessmen in the industrial sector had to overcome a serious handicap. Industrial technology in this period was almost always imported, either from Britain or from the United States. An American or British immigrant who built a factory in Quebec came with the necessary technological knowledge; he also retained contact with his country of origin so that he was part of an information network through which he could keep up with the latest technological advances. It was clearly much more difficult for a French-Canadian businessman to be part of an information network of this sort; some managed to do it, but it appears that most of them turned away from the industrial sector and concentrated instead on commercial and real estate activities. The real estate sector, neglected by historians, was very important in this context. The information network on which it depended was, to a much greater extent, internal to Quebec society. To make a good profit in land, it was necessary to know local conditions and to be able to control or influence city or town councils. This may be why so many French-Canadian businessmen were active as real estate speculators and promoters.

The Petty Bourgeoisie

Between the bourgeoisie on the one hand and the mass of farmers and workers on the other, there is an intermediate class that has played a major role in the history of Quebec. It consists in part of small entrepreneurs, retail merchants and other similar intermediaries who participate in the ownership and accumulation of capital, although in a peripheral way, and who employ at most a few wage labourers. Another important part of this class consists of members of the liberal professions.

In comparison with the operations of the bourgeoisie, capital accumulation by this class is on a very modest scale. While some of its members, such as the craftsman/small entrepreneur, accumulate capital through production, it is more common for capital to be accumulated through commercial credit and real estate operations, almost always carried on at the local level.

This class, the petty bourgeoisie, has been of interest to historians primarily because of its overwhelming presence in the institutional framework of Quebec society — parliaments, city and town councils, school boards, *fabriques* (boards of lay trustees responsible for parish financial affairs), charitable societies and other voluntary organizations. Elective positions in these institutions were easily monopolized by the petty bourgeoisie, which thus acquired a key organizational role in both urban and rural areas.

In a society that was still predominatly rural, the most characteristic manifestation of the petty bourgeoisie occurred at the village level. The village petty bourgeoisie was generally made up of the *curé*, the notary, the doctor and the principal merchants. Its domination showed up in several ways, most notably in the monopoly it held of elected administrative positions in various parish-level institutions; the same people were often churchwardens, school commissioners and town councillors. Power of this sort rested on economic foundations. The first to tap rural incomes was the *curé*, whose livelihood came from a portion of each farmer's harvest; the amount collected often went beyond the basic needs of the parish. In addition, the merchants and members of the liberal professions were generally owed money by the farmers, and a list of their debtors often constituted a virtual directory of the parish or at least a substantial part of it. If mortgage loans are examined, again the same people turn out to be involved. Thus, relations of dependency were established between the local *notables* and the mass of farmers, relations which were reflected in all aspects of rural life.

The petty bourgeoisie played a similar role in urban areas. In large cities, it operated primarily at the parish or neighbourhood level. Its economic and political power was comparable to that of the village petty bourgeoisie, although there were some differences, such as the greater prominence of the landlord-tenant relationship in an urban context.

Historians have so far paid little attention to relations between the petty bourgeoisie and the bourgeoisie, although there were clear dependency links between the two. Local merchants were closely tied to large-scale merchants who provided them with goods and, even more important, credit. Notaries and lawyers often served as representatives for large investors or loan companies such as the Crédit Foncier Franco-Canadien. Through its control of local institutions and its role in orienting the population ideologically, the petty bourgeoisie had an important function in maintaining social peace and institutional stability.

The role of the clergy in this area was especially significant, and it was willing to use its influence to help large investors. Within the clergy, there were hierarchies that must be kept in mind. While the influence of the parish priest was considerable, it was hardly felt beyond the local level. On the other hand, dioceses and major religious orders, the leaders of which often came from the bourgeoisie, had at their disposal substantial financial resources, accumulated over decades and usually free of taxation. They made investments, provided credit and financing, even acted like banks in regions where the banking system was still rudimentary. The interests of religious institutions at this level were quite close to those of the bourgeoisie. However, not much is known about this economic dimension of clerical power. In the army of male and female members of religious orders recruited primarily from the large families of rural Quebec, the clergy also had access to a source of cheap and abundant labour. The role of the Roman Catholic church in Quebec society will be discussed further in chapter 12.

Also associated with the petty bourgeoisie are the intellectuals — journalists, writers, teachers, artists. There were not many of them in Quebec in the period under study; journalists, heavily involved in the political and ideological debates of the time, were the most significant group. Not much research has yet been done on the living and working conditions of intellectuals; only a few well-known figures, such as Arthur Buies, journalist and later secretary to Curé Labelle, and William Dawson, principal of McGill University, have been studied.

The Working Class

There is no doubt that one of the most significant changes in the social structure during the period being studied was the emergence of the working class. The formation of this new class was a very conspicuous consequence of the rise of industrial capitalism; it began well before 1867, but took on new proportions in the last three decades of the nineteenth century. At the heart of this process was dismemberment of the craft system and its replacement by the capitalist form of production. The craftsman, a small independent producer, gradually lost control of the means of production and became a wage labourer working for an entrepreneur. Examples of this well-known process of proletarianization of the craftsman can be found in the report of the Labour Commission, which conducted an inquiry in 1887-88. A number of witnesses had begun their careers as craftsmen and had experienced a gradual deterioration of their working conditions; with mechanization and the fragmentation of tasks, their work became devalued.

But craftsmen were not the only source of recruitment for the new working class, and indeed often represented only a small part of the labour force in a factory. The entrepreneur had access to three other labour pools as well. The first was the large reservoir of unskilled labour in pre-industrial cities – forty per cent of the population of Montreal in 1825 consisted of labourers, journeymen and domestics. When women began to work in factories, the proportion of domestics dropped radically. In the early stages of industrialization, this urban pre-proletariat was one of the major sources of recruitment for the new working class. Another source was immigration. Poor immigrants from Ireland, Britain and, at the end of the century, eastern Europe, arrived regularly in Quebec City and Montreal. However, the number of such immigrants who arrived between 1867 and 1896 was very small, in comparison with earlier (1815-55) or later (1896-1914) periods. Therefore, the main source from which the working class was constituted was a third one — surplus labour from the Quebec countryside. Accustomed to a low standard of living and too numerous to be able to ask for very much, rural Quebecers took the new low-paying jobs offered by industry, which had the advantage of not requiring any special skill.

Capitalist methods of organizing work affected not only the industrial working class but people who worked in other sectors as well. Big business became a force in the commercial, transportation and service sectors, bringing with it hierarchical work relationships and, in many cases, difficult working conditions.

The conditions under which people worked varied widely. Proletarianization did not occur at the same rate in all places or in all sectors. Craftsmen were better able to resist the process and protect their working conditions in some sectors than in others, and a clear hierarchy developed within the industrial working class and among working people in general.

At the top of this hierarchy was what became known as the aristocracy of labour — skilled workers, with a trade that required training, such as typesetting, certain categories of ironwork, and some of the construction trades. The wages of these workers were well above the average. They were the most loyal and best organized members of the labour movement, and union leaders were recruited from their ranks. Office workers in the public and private sectors, who enjoyed a high status, were also part of this group. But with the growth of bureaucracies, hierarchies developed and working conditions changed in this area as well; one manifestation of this process was the more frequent employment of women in offices, at lower pay.

Workers in the Clendenning foundry in Montreal, 1872.

The largest group of workers was made up of those who were specialized but not highly trained, and performed a precise task in the production process. This was the group of low-paid industrial workers; women workers were concentrated in this category. It was a highly mobile population and efforts to organize it did not proceed very far in the nineteenth century.

Finally, there were workers who were neither skilled nor specialized. These were mostly day-labourers, who worked on the docks, in construction or in transportation. They too were poorly paid and not highly organized. Like domestics, they represented a diminishing proportion of the working population.

There has been no systematic study of the ethnic composition of the working class, but it would be wrong to assume that French Canadians were its only significant component. They were, no doubt, a majority of the working class after 1867. But there were also substantial numbers of workers of British origin — English, Irish and Scottish — who during the period tended to become concentrated in Montreal. At the very end of the century, the first contingents of eastern European Jews arrived; large numbers of them would be employed in the clothing industry. At the end of the nineteenth century, Quebec workers formed a class with significant elements of diversity, but with the common experience of highly difficult living and working conditions.

Office work in 1874: the head office of the Royal Canadian Insurance Company on St. James Street in Montreal.

Rural Quebecers

Between 1867 and 1897, a majority of Quebecers lived in the country. At the time, the word "class" was often used to categorize people according to the place where they lived and worked, so that the "agricultural class" was one of four classes into which the Canadian census of 1871 divided the working population. However, in the sense in which the word is used in this book, it would not be accurate to speak of an "agricultural class" or "rural class." For agricultural society was not homogeneous. First, it was divided between those who owned a piece of land and those who didn't — there were many day-labourers whose only means of livelihood was to go from farm to farm trying to sell their labour. Nor was mere ownership of his farm enough to place a farmer in the same class as a large landowner. The size of landholdings varied widely; in addition, many farmers were so heavily in debt that they owned their land only in a nominal sense. "Small independent producers" is another term that has been used as a catch-all for rural Quebecers, but it is subject to the same criticism; it too has the effect of obscuring fundamental distinctions within the rural population.

An attempt will be made to look at the divisions within rural Quebec, identify the major groups, and sketch the role they played. However, it should be noted at the outset that because rural history is a very weak aspect of Quebec — and Canadian — historiography, it will not be possible to cast light on all the interesting questions. At most, problems can be defined and working hypotheses developed.

Territorial units in the countryside were of two distinct kinds. The village was characterized by a grouping of houses, and was the place where religious and professional services and commercial activities were concentrated. The parish or township municipality was made up of the rural zone that surrounded the village. Some services were decentralized. Schools, for instance, were located not only in the village but in the ranges as well. The same was true for some manufacturing activities; butter and cheesemaking were carried out in small units in the ranges.

The importance of the family and the parish as units in rural Quebec has already been noted. There was also a very significant intermediate unit between them, the range. Socially, it was at the range level that the good neighbourliness and mutual assistance that characterized rural life took place. The range was one feature that identified the Quebec rural landscape; it survived the seigneurial system and even extended its domain with the expansion of settlement throughout the nineteenth century.

There were four distinct groups of people in the village. First there were the *notables* — notary, doctor, *curé* and local merchants. The *notables* were members of the petty bourgeoisie and constituted the dominant group in village society. They were also its link with the urban bourgeoisie; the merchants, for example, had customers and suppliers in the city as well as among the farmers. For the farmers, the merchants were also often substantial creditors. Then there was a small group of craftsmen, who made the few articles that the farmer could not or would not make for himself. The third group was hidden, consisting of people with small private incomes: farmers who had retired to the village, former craftsmen, former day-labourers. The day-labourers, who will be examined later, constituted the last group. The village was the social centre of rural life. It contained the parish church, and most of those who wielded a significant degree of power within rural society lived there. But the power of the village was not total, and there were *gros cultivateurs* (substantial farmers) in the parish who exercised considerable influence and had to be reckoned with by the village petty bourgeoisie.

Outside the village, there were three major groups in rural society: farmers, day-labourers and colonists in the new "colonization" areas. The farmers were not a homogeneous group. There is a classic distinction between the more prosperous farmers, who were constantly increasing the extent of their lands, and the rest. But this was not the only cleavage — proximity to an urban market, means of transportation to the market, and agricultural specialization were three other factors of differentiation. Quebec agriculture did not follow a single model, uniformly distributed over the territory; in addition to the factors already mentioned there were regional differences and climatic and geographical constraints. In the Montreal plain haying is done in late June, while in the Lower St. Lawrence region it is done in late July; this difference in itself has a significant effect on the orientation of agriculture.

The day-labourers were also a varied group. In the lowland parishes, the typical day-labourer was a genuine agricultural worker, who did farm work and, in the time-honoured expression, was paid *à gages* by the farmer; in other words, he was a "hired hand" who received wages for his work. In other areas, however, especially in the highlands, many day-labourers were in fact lumberjacks, whose livelihood came from the forest industry and who did little if any agricultural work as such. Some day-labourers were highly mobile, even unstable — bachelors who were not tied to any particular place and went from range to range and parish to parish looking for work. In other cases, the day-labourer lived in a village where he had a house and garden.

In the first half of the nineteenth century, with Lower Canada in the grip of an agricultural crisis and the population expanding rapidly, there was a substantial increase in the number of day-labourers. After 1850, as the crisis eased and large numbers of people left for the United States, the size of the group shrank. Towards the end of the century a form of sharecropping developed, especially on the fringes of urban areas; an agricultural day-labourer would farm a piece of land, and half the harvest would go to the owner of the land as rent.

At first glance, the colonists appear to have been a more homogeneous group that the other two. Since deprivation was common to all, there was not the same imbalance in living conditions and social distinctions were blurred. At least in their first years in a new region, colonists bore a greater resemblance to agricultural day-labourers than to the more prosperous farmers. Like a day-labourer, the colonist could often make a living only by doing some other work in addition to his farm labour, and unlike a well-off farmer, he practised a form of agriculture that did not generate a surplus. The absence of markets also made it impossible to stimulate agricultural production. The colonist was put in a situation of dependency; the combination of problems he faced was examined in chapter 6 under the heading of the agro-forest economy.

The same kind of dependency existed in the fishing villages of the North Shore, the Gaspé and the Magdalen Islands. In the nineteenth century, these areas were isolated from the rest of Quebec and were accessible only by boat. The inhabitants lived through fishing and subsistence agriculture. They were under the tutelage of merchants and trading companies, which exercised effective monopoly power as the only buyers of what they produced and the only sellers of commodities brought in from the outside.

But despite the significant social distinctions and forms of domination that existed in the countryside, social cleavages were tempered by an egalitarian tradition that dated back to the time when the first ranges were cleared. This was due in part to the way land was occupied in Quebec. Settlement filled one range and then spilled over into the next, until eventually a new parish had to be formed. Sometimes parents would establish their son on a farm, although there was no universally accepted pattern. There is no evidence that young people were the only ones who went to new ranges. The French social observer Charles-Henri-Philippe Gauldrée-Boileau studied a family in Saint-Irénée parish northeast of Quebec City in 1861 and 1862; when Léon Gérin, in one of his classic studies, took another look at the same family sixty years later, he found that it had moved to a distant region. Gérard Bouchard's recent research on the Saguenay region also shows the great geographical mobility of the population. After 1850 there was a new pattern. Young people would work for a few years in the mills of New England or in the Great Lakes region and come back to Quebec to buy a piece of land with their savings. This was a widespread phenomenon; it has been said that every parish in Quebec had members who had lived in the United States.

Thus, there were different groups in rural Quebec, in a hierarchical relationship to one another, and while traditions of egalitarianism and mutual assistance were mitigating factors, there were still perceptible social differences. It is also important to take into account regional diversity, which led to different kinds of agriculture and varying social conditions. For this era at least, it doesn't seeem accurate to speak of a homogeneous agricultural class.

It is not the purpose of this sketch of the social structure to examine all its aspects. Not only is each class complex, but there were also groups that don't fit comfortably into any of the classes just outlined. There were, for example, nomadic hunters and fishermen, most of them native Indians, who had their own social structure based on the tribe but were linked to the rest of Quebec society by dependency relationships established by the fur-trading companies. While class constitutes a fundamental cleavage within society, there are other cleavages as well — ethnicity, religion, regional identification, sex, age. Sometimes these reinforce the class structure; at other times, however, they are in conflict with it.

CHAPTER 9
LIVING CONDITIONS

The social inequalities outlined in chapter 8 influenced the conditions under which individuals lived. The class to which a person belonged affected the way he ate, the way he was housed, the way he died. The changes that Quebec was undergoing in the late nineteenth century were another significant influence on living conditions, and resulted in serious problems of adjustment. A reconstruction of all the facets of daily life in Quebec will not be attempted here, but some of these problems will be examined. Urban life (including the problems that arose out of factory work) and rural life will be discussed in turn, and then the role of private charity will be highlighted.

Urban Life

With industrialization and urbanization, large numbers of people were squeezed into a limited space. The newcomers were crowded into hastily built dwellings. With greater population density came changes in the quality of urban life, including increased risk of fire and deteriorating sanitary conditions. The demand for services grew, and it became necessary to build aqueducts and sewers, organize transportation facilities and regulate various aspects of city life.

Urban growth was sometimes rapid, and everywhere the organization of the old pre-industrial city cracked under its weight. New solutions had to be found, but the transition period was difficult. Institutions and leaders were ill prepared to deal with the new situation. Some problems were solved quickly, but more often it took several decades of tension and adjustment before a new equilibrium was reached. And the benefits of these changes were very unequally distributed.

Housing was an area where changes were especially conspicuous. In the com-

Donald Smith's house on Dorchester Street in Montreal.

mercial city, merchants and workers alike tended to live close to their work; they were massed together near the harbours of Quebec City and Montreal. With the growth of areas outside the old urban centres, a degree of geographical specialization appeared in the city, but neighbourhoods retained a socially heterogeneous character. Industrialization changed this pattern, and brought about a much clearer separation of residential areas.

Upper-class neighbourhoods were now clearly distinguishable from working-class neighbourhoods, and each had its characteristic environment. Generally located on high ground, upper-class neighbourhoods were airy, consisted of stone houses and green spaces, and were well provided with public services. These generous endowments were in marked contrast to those of the working-class neighbourhoods that grew up around the factories, where overcrowding and unhealthy conditions were the general rule and green spaces were nonexistent. Thus, the richer members of the bourgeoisie began to leave the old city of Montreal in the 1860s and settled on the slopes of Mount Royal, where they built luxurious residences that looked like small castles. Working-class neighbourhoods spread out under a pall of factory smoke along the St. Lawrence River and the Lachine Canal. A similar situation developed in Quebec City, where the bourgeoisie settled comfortably in Upper Town while the workers were crowded along the river banks, in the working-class neighbourhoods of Champlain on the St. Lawrence and Saint-Roch and Saint-Sauveur on the St. Charles. Even in smaller municipalities, a similar form of segregation existed, and the local *notables* all lived on one street.

Urban growth made it necessary to introduce new building techniques. Quick construction of a large number of houses was impossible with the old methods, in which heavy wooden planks were used, and the technology had to be adapted to the urban explosion. Innovations developed in the United States soon became widespread in Quebec. The new technique of building skeletons from simpler frames made out of two-by-fours made rapid standardized construction possible. Bricks were increasingly used for outside walls. As a result of new developments in iron and steel technology, metal skeletons could be built for large buildings; this made taller buildings feasible. There were changes in what cities looked like — in Old Montreal, for example, houses dating to the French régime gave way to multistorey commercial buildings. There was no order to the way these changes took place, and no planning was done by municipal authorities. Private capital was responsible for how land was disposed of, and the owners of a lot decided how it should be used. Regulations relating to construction were neither particularly restrictive nor widely respected.

The increase in population density was greatest in working-class neighbourhoods, where row housing was built and duplexes and triplexes increasingly replaced the old one-storey house. No systematic analysis of this process has been done for nineteenth-century Quebec. There were gross errors in the calculations done for Montreal by the city's health department. However, all indications are that overcrowding in Montreal was far from being as serious a problem as it was in large American cities such as New York and Chicago. In his study of a Montreal working-class neighbourhood in 1897, the reformer H.B. Ames found that the average density was fifty-five people per acre, or ninety-four people per acre if streets, parks, canals, docks and the like are taken out of the calculation. However, in Griffintown, a poor neighbourhood, the average density was 173 people per acre and in one especially densely populated block the figure reached 300. Figures on numbers of people per house showed similar disparities.

The increased population density and overcrowding brought about intensified public health problems. Pre-industrial cities were totally lacking in sanitary measures, but with their small populations, the damage caused by this deficiency was kept within bounds. The situation was different, however, now that hundreds of thousands of people were living in the same place, and a practice such as throwing garbage in the street or piling it up in the courtyard now became dangerous.

The first task of the municipal health services set up in the 1870s was to collect

Commercial buildings of this kind were an innovation in the second half of the nineteenth century.

A rear tenement typical of a working-class Montreal neighbourhood.

the animal carcasses and other waste that posed a hazard to citizens' health. Distribution of water by door-to-door salesmen could not satisfy the needs of a growing population for very long and construction of a piped water supply system became a priority. In Montreal, a modern water distribution system was put into service in the 1850s, but the water was not filtered and caused periodic typhoid epidemics. Few streets were paved; most of them were dirt roads, dusty in fine weather and muddy in the rain. Ames launched a crusade against privy pits, which still served 5,800 Montreal dwellings in 1896. Rear tenements, where the only windows looked out onto a courtyard and where living conditions were deplorable, were another target of his attacks. Many hastily built new dwellings were badly lit and badly ventilated.

Upper-class neighbourhoods escaped some of these problems, but the mass of the urban population was subject to diseases caused by seriously deficient sanitary conditions. Social inequality was clearly reflected in illness and death during the period. The French-speaking working-class Montreal ward of Sainte-Marie had an average death rate of 36.7 per thousand between 1877 and 1896, while in Saint-Antoine, an English-speaking, upper-class ward of the same city, the average rate was 18.7 per thousand. Montreal's high rate of infant mortality was also felt

Interior of a working-class dwelling visited by illness, 1873.

primarily in the working-class neighbourhoods of the east end. Although the low educational level of French-Canadian workers and their ignorance of elementary rules of hygiene have often been invoked to explain this situation, the real causes were socio-economic. Both on the job and at home, workers had to live in an environment that was dangerous to their health. Their education was deficient because they had to enter the labour market at an early age. Because of their inadequate income, they could have neither a high-quality dwelling nor a healthful, balanced diet. Access to health services was difficult because they couldn't afford them. The problem was not primarily cultural, but was rather the result of an economic system based on exploitation and inequality.

Living conditions in the cities improved very slowly. Such measures as were taken by public authorities were timid and never got to the root of the problems. In 1886, the Quebec legislature set up a provincial Hygiene Council and required municipalities to establish local health departments. These agencies had little power and had effects only over the long term.

City councils were concerned primarily with establishing basic services: aqueducts, sewers, gas (and electricity towards the end of the century), public transpor-

A typical house in a working-class neighbourhood (*faubourg Québec*) in east-central Montreal.

tation, police and fire protection. The growth of the urban population made fire protection a priority. Fire had been one of the scourges of the pre-industrial city. In Quebec City in 1845, two fires in succession destroyed all of one neighbourhood, Saint-Roch, and part of another, Saint-Jean. In Montreal, fire destroyed 1,200 buildings in 1852, leaving 9,000 people — a sixth of the city's population — homeless. With the establishment of a permanent fire department, fires of this sort were avoided, and after the 1860s there were no more disasters on the same scale.

Poor sanitary conditions in the industrial areas of Montreal resulted in frequent epidemics. A *Canadian Ilustrated News* illustration from 1875.

In most cases, municipal authorities preferred to entrust the running of public utilities to private enterprise, as was the practice in all large North American cities. The city council granted a company a franchise to operate a particular utility; most often, the franchise was exclusive, giving the company a monopoly in a particular field. In return, the company agreed to provide a specified quality and regularity of service at a given price. The agreement was usually formalized in a twenty-year contract.

Not all Quebec cities and towns had a full range of services; only the largest cities were well provided in this regard. In most cases, private enterprise distributed water, gas and electricity and operated public transportation. There were a

Saint-Roch neighbourhood in Quebec City after a fire in 1866.

few cases of municipal ownership — such as water distribution in the city of Montreal and electricity in Westmount — but these were exceptions. Municipal leaders typically justified private ownership on grounds of efficiency, but its main result was that the overriding objective of the franchise-holder was not to provide the public with the best possible service but rather to make the highest possible profit. The franchise-holder was able to take advantage of its monopoly position, and it was in its interest to keep rates high while cutting corners on quality and regularity of service. The profits made by the tramway, gas and electricity companies in Montreal in this way were nothing short of spectacular. In addition, the franchise system was a major source of political corruption. A company seeking a franchise or aiming to improve the terms of its contract needed the backing of a certain number of city councillors, and campaign contributions were a common means of ensuring this support.

All these utilities were essential means of progress in a large city, as can be seen by looking at public transportation. In the pre-industrial city, covering a small area, walking was the principal means of getting from one place to another. With industrialization and the growth of the city, thousands of workers had to be transported every day over increasing distances from their homes to their jobs, so that it became necessary to establish a public transportation service. The first streetcars made their appearance in North American cities in the middle of the

A flood in Montreal, a recurring problem in working-class wards.

nineteenth centry, and privately owned tramway services were established in Montreal and Quebec City in 1861. These early streetcars were horse-drawn vehicles moving on rails — in the winter they were equipped with runners. In the 1890s (1892 in Montreal), electric streetcars were introduced, providing faster and more reliable service. The electric streetcar itself acted as a stimulus to urban growth by promoting expansion into the suburbs and making possible the establishment of residential neighbourhoods at considerable distances from where people worked.

Thus, industrialization changed the face of the city. The rise of industrial capitalism encouraged technological progress — new construction methods and materials, the use of gas and electricity, the development of public transportation, and the like. But the benefits of urban growth were distributed in a highly unequal fashion. Class divisions were reflected in space, environment, architecture and other aspects of the conditions in which people lived. The quality of life — and even death — was not the same for everyone.

Working Conditions

The transition from craft to factory production, the stages of which were described in chapter 7, brought about radical changes in working conditions. In the interests of reducing production costs and increasing their profits, capitalists resorted to child labour, the employment of underpaid women workers, long working hours, and the contracting-out or "sweating system." Labour leaders and journalists drew the attention of governments and the public to the numerous abuses, and the reports of government inspectors and the information collected by the Royal Commission on the Relations of Labour and Capital (1886-89) presented a less than shining picture of working conditions in the factory.

The late-nineteenth-century Quebec worker generally had to work very long hours to earn his meagre wage. In the 1880s, the usual work week for factory workers was sixty hours, divided into six ten-hour days. However, employees were often called upon to work longer than that, and overtime was paid only at the regular rate. In the service and other sectors of the economy, the work week was often seventy-two hours — twelve hours a day. An extreme case was that of domestics, who worked from early in the morning until late at night and had only half a day off per week. Wages varied considerably from one trade to another. Skilled workers such as typesetters and workers in the building trades commanded higher than average wages. On the other hand, workers in the shoe, textile, clothing and tobacco industries and day-labourers were paid very low wages, substantially lower than the minimum needed to support a family. There was also the problem of irregular employment. Unemployment was often seasonal; water transportation and construction sectors practically came to a halt in the winter. Large factories laid off employees whenever there was a slowdown in orders, sometimes even shutting down temporarily. Unemployment was especially high in the winter and during depressions, and there was no insurance of any kind against these situations. Governments took no action, leaving the field to private charity. The unemployed could only survive by turning to agencies such as the St. Vincent de Paul Society.

Because of the low wages in many sectors and the irregularity of employment, a worker's income was generally inadequate. In most cases, the wages of the head of the household were not enough to support a family, and a family needed more than one income to make ends meet. Employers did not hesitate to take advantage of this situation.

Children were put on the labour market at a very early age by their parents, and employers were only too glad to hire them. The use of child labour was characteristic of the early stages of industrialization in most countries, and Quebec was no exception. The division of labour simplified tasks and so made possible the employment of children. It was not uncommon to see nine- or ten-year-old boys and girls in textile, shoe and cigar factories. Employers invented an artificial apprenticeship period for their young employees, lasting several months and

Inside a typical factory in the late nineteenth century.

sometimes even years. Paid only a small fraction of an adult worker's wage, these "apprentices" took home barely $1.50 a week. They were very badly treated by foremen and bosses. A number of witnesses before the 1886-89 royal commission testified about children who were beaten, punished or fined. Reformers were very concerned about this situation and demanded that the government outlaw child labour. However, because the system was in the interests of many powerful people, it did not disappear quickly, and it was only after several decades of effort by reformers and legislative measures that it was finally eliminated.

Women workers were another group exploited above and beyond the norm. The employment of women in light industry became widespread towards the end of the nineteenth century. They were an underpaid group; not only were women hired in low-paid sectors, but they were also paid systematically less than men for the same work, often only half as much as male workers. The sweating system, which was very common in the clothing industry, exploited women even further. The factory owner did only the cutting in his establishment; garments were sewn by women working for contractors at home or in small shops. These women were paid at ridiculously low rates on a piecework basis. With the growth of the

A work accident on a construction site, 1870.

clothing industry, the sweating system expanded into the country, ensnaring thousands of rural women in this web of exploitation. Sexist attitudes helped perpetuate the deplorable conditions under which women worked. The ideology of the woman as housewife and mother provided an easy justification for her working at home under the sweating system, while the idea that what the head of household brought home was a family's main income and what the woman earned was supplementary justified paying women lower wages than men. There was no effective challenge to this inequality between the sexes, although the Knights of Labor (see chapter 10) demanded that the principle of "equal work for equal pay" be applied.

Factory work was carried out under fairly primitive health and safety conditions. Observers criticized the overcrowding, the bad ventilation, the inadequate sanitary equipment. Machinery was not designed with the safety of workers in mind and accidents were common. The injured worker was not entitled to any statutory compensation and had to rely on benevolent or charitable organizations.

Workers were subject to the arbitrary rule of the boss and his foremen, since there was no job security and the employer could use any one of a number of pretexts to fire whomever he wanted to get rid of. Some bosses resorted to physical violence, penalties or fines when an employee made a mistake or was not sufficiently docile.

The most flagrant abuses were not necessarily committed by all bosses. On the whole, however, the working conditions that prevailed during the early stages of industrialization were deplorable and workers were exploited in many ways; only with a strong trade union organization could workers have fought these conditions effectively. Nor was exploitation limited to the factory; in general, the workers who were crowded into the cities lived under deplorable conditions.

Rural Life

In the last third of the nineteenth century, living and working conditions did not change as rapidly in the country as in the city. Of course, rural life was changing, but at a much slower pace, and in most cases, living and working conditions were still governed by tradition. This prevalence of traditional practices was one major characteristic of rural life; another was the lack of separation for most rural Quebecers — day-labourers were an exception — between place of residence and place of work. The farm was a unit of both production and consumption. While these two characteristics were general, there were also regional shadings; a farmer lived and worked under much more arduous conditions in colonization regions than in the older regions of Quebec.

The quality of housing was generally higher in the country than in the city, primarily because there was more space. The rural house was usually large enough to accommodate a family, although not every family member had his own room. The room that got the most use was the kitchen, which was the focal point of family life. It was here that the family had its meals and spent its evenings, which were devoted to a variety of maintenance and home manufacturing tasks.

As there have been few studies of rural housing, it is difficult to know how comfortable it was. Furniture seems often to have been purely functional and somewhat rough and ready, but heating the house in the winter did not pose the same problems as in the city, where the fuel supply was not always assured.

A dominant aspect of rural living conditions was home manufacture of most objects used in the household. Towards the end of the century, however, with the development of railway transportation and the introduction of catalogue sales, some of these home manufactures tended to disappear. In his classic study of Saint-Justin, Léon Gérin noted the change in the way the *habitant* was clothed;

Notre-Dame de Batiscan, east of Trois-Rivières, 1890.

linens and other homespun materials were replaced by commercially sold fabrics, especially cottons. Farm machinery soon underwent a similar development, and even the village blacksmith was left with only maintenance work as the farm became mechanized.

Food was available in sufficient quantities in rural Quebec, although there was little variety. Starches dominated the rural diet — potatoes were on the table at every meal, peas and bread at many of them. Meat, except for fat bacon, was a less common food. In the summer, this dietary base was supplemented with wild fruit and the harvest from the household garden. In the nineteenth century, game was plentiful in rural Quebec, especially in colonization regions, and constituted a welcome addition to the rural diet.

Although the country was free of the overcrowding that had so many deadly consequences in the city, health conditions were nevertheless far from ideal, and showed little improvement as time went on. There may have been a somewhat greater acceptance of doctors, but the *rammancheux* and *rebouteux* (bone setters) remained in business, and remedies were still prescribed by "empirics" with a "gift" for healing horses or cows. Infant mortality remained at a fairly high level.

Life in the country was lived according to the season. Spring was for sowing, summer for reaping, and fall for ploughing, while winter was a slack time. Farming activites were reduced to a minimum in the winter, and the farmer, after taking care of his animals, generally used the time to do maintenance and repair work or improve his house and equipment. Winter was also the season for visiting neighbours and relatives.

Maple Syrup Making, by Cornelius Krieghoff.

While working conditions in the country were different from those in the city, they were still hardly idyllic. The whole family had to participate in production on the farm. Children began to work and bear their share of the farm's responsibilities at a very early age, and old people were likewise expected to do farm work. The farmer woke up with the first glimmer of daylight, and when heavy work was in progress his day ended late. There were many technological innovations in agriculture in the last half of the nineteenth century, but even if some mechanization was very hesitantly introduced on Quebec farms, much of the work was still done in the traditional way. There were also some changes in working conditions as a result of agricultural specialization, which became widespread during the period.

Rural Quebecers who were not farmers lived and worked under very different conditions from those just described. This was especially true in the case of the day-labourers. The farmer's land provided him with a degree of comfort; the day-labourer, who had to survive on his wage alone, lived much more precariously. In the colonization regions, conditions were different again. The colonist might work in the forest during the winter, so that there was no slack season, and if the land was still being cleared the family was not able to live at all comfortably. In the first few years, the colonist's life was fairly rough. He started with a wooded lot; first he had to cut down trees and burn the wood. Then the ashes had to be sold and, more important, the stumps that remained had to be removed. Gradually, the area that could be farmed grew, and within a few years the farm became more or less viable: now the colonist could think about replacing his crude lodging with a real house. If he worked in the lumber camps, the farm and family life were adversely affected. And in addition to all these difficulties, the colonist lived in an area where not all basic services were provided.

It is important to recognize, in concluding this brief look at rural life, that not much is really known about living and working conditions. In the abundant literature devoted to Quebec rural life, its charms are highly exaggerated. The bards of ruralism present exceptional moments of rural life as typical and embellish a reality they find much too prosaic. It must be remembered that the presentation of rural life as healthy and natural was in reaction to another way of life that was regarded as much less so.

Charity

People's ideas about poverty and how to combat it vary from era to era. In the nineteenth century, these ideas were influenced by capitalism and its accompanying ideology, liberalism, so that poverty was viewed as an individual phenomenon, a person's failure to adapt to the economic and social system. Therefore, aid to the poor had to be directed towards helping them adapt, and people who showed promise of being able to change were the ones who deserved to be helped — this was the source of the distinction often encountered in nineteenth-century writing between the "deserving" poor and the rest. This general concept of poverty explains why public authorities had no interest in any form of organized assistance. During the period being studied here, the idea that the government was responsible for social security did not exist at either the federal or the provincial level. Except during an epidemic, when everyone's health was threatened, governments did not intervene directly, but only supported private initiatives with small grants. Instead of an integrated system, there was a collection of agencies with a variety of objectives trying in an uncoordinated fashion to alleviate the burden of the poor.

The churches played a fundamental role in the development of this collection of private agencies. According to Christian tradition, as interpreted by both Catholics and Protestants, charity was a person's duty. In the nineteenth century, most charitable activities, with the exception of the work of mutual benefit societies, were carried out under church auspices. The Catholic church did not limit itself to inspiring charitable works, but exercised a degree of control over how they were carried out. An interesting example is the case of the St. Vincent de Paul societies. Founded in France in 1837, these societies were introduced in Quebec before Confederation by Dr. Joseph Painchaud. The local priest was involved in the running of each society, ensuring direct church influence; in addition, the bishop

A nun serving soup to old people, about 1870.

could intervene at any time in matters of overall policy for the whole diocese. Thus, the church was involved in founding this agency and continued to play an important role in running it once it was set up.

The origins of private charity will not be examined here, except to say that solidarity among human beings has existed from time immemorial, especially in rural areas. However, this original form of spontaneous charity was clearly no longer enough when the population grew or when the number of people in need increased for reasons of economic structure or circumstance. Benevolent societies provided a channel for spontaneous charity and later developed it into a system. This happened with the traditional *guignolée*, originally a collection taken periodically by the whole parish, with the proceeds distributed to the poor. However, the St. Vincent de Paul societies, soon after they were organized, began to use the *guignolée* as a means of collecting contributions.

Generally established by members of the bourgeoisie for the express purpose of alleviating poverty in a city or town, the benevolent society was the prototype of organized private charity. Benevolent societies chose "their" beneficiaries, and supported themselves through the gifts of members, public campaigns, and benefit concerts and similar activities. Some were organized on the initiative of an individual, others at the suggestion of a church. In 1815, bourgeois women in Montreal founded the Female Benevolent Society of Montreal with the aim of helping the poor; in 1827, some women belonging to the *première société de Montréal* (Montreal high society) decided at a meeting attended by a priest to form the Association des Dames de Charité. These societies were very common in Quebec; every religious denomination had its own, and some were established on a purely ethnic basis.

Some charitable work was done by the Catholic clergy and religious communities. In many parishes, the *curé* or his *vicaire* attended to the poor on their regular visits to their parishioners; in the parish of Montreal, the poor were the concern of special priestly visitors. Some religious communities also dispensed charity directly. Often, the role of the clergy or the religious community was to channel contributions made by others.

The establishment of hospitals and hospices was a very old tradition among both Protestants and Catholics. In the period being studied, patients who could afford it were taken care of at home as much as possible. Only those who could not pay the cost of their treatment or whom the doctor could not cure at home went to the hospital. Towards the end of the century, however, the hospital increasingly became a place where all patients were cared for, and not only the poor.

Entrusting hospitals to religious communities was an old Catholic practice, and in the early days of New France hospital communities were established in the colony and took charge of running its hospitals. These institutions were financed in a variety of ways. Some communities were granted seigneuries or fiefs, the revenues from which were to be devoted to charitable works. In the nineteenth century some hospitals received government subsidies, although these did not

Hôtel-Dieu Hospital, Montreal's oldest and largest, in 1875.

make up the main part of their income. Protestant hospitals were organized somewhat differently, as there were no Protestant religious communities. The Montreal General Hospital, for example, was resolutely Protestant, but it was required to observe a degree of religious tolerance because different denominations co-existed in Montreal and because its personnel was non-religious. It was run by a board of directors and financed through donations, government subsidies and subscription campaigns. Some hospitals received large donations from local businessmen. Construction of the Royal Victoria Hospital in Montreal, which opened its doors in early 1894, was financed by a joint donation of a million dollars from Lord Strathcona and Lord Mount Stephen.

Hospices and refuges met a variety of needs. Hospices were institutions for the old and the chronically ill, while refuges provided shelter for people on the fringes of society — adolescent mothers, children who were more or less abandoned, juvenile delinquents, and the like. Institutions for the insane also fell into this category. This was one kind of patient whose care was subsidized by the government, although in very niggardly fashion. Much of what we said about hospitals is also applicable to insane asylums. Conditions in these institutions left something to be desired. Their meagre financial resources were partly responsible for this, but in addition, the methods used in treating the various categories of patients were somewhat behind the times. It was only after a famous British alienist visited Quebec around 1885 that centuries-old practices such as keeping the patients chained at all times were finally stopped.

The largest number and widest variety of charitable institutions were found in the city. In the countryside, with its religious homogeneity, services were organized more simply, with the parish and diocese as focal points. Each parish took care of its poor, while at the diocesan level there was typically a hospital run by a religious community in the cathedral town.

All these organizations were, in the final analysis, dependent on public donations. In addition to the duty of giving charity imposed by Christian morality, there was also an idea current among members of the nineteenth-century bourgeoisie that wealth entailed responsibility. According to this notion, once an individual had made his fortune, it was incumbent on him to attach his name to some great work, which he would subsidize with some degree of generosity. This idea of charity was divorced from the same person's other activities — the philanthropy of great industrialists didn't extend to paying higher wages to their employees. However, philanthropy of this sort was very common in bourgeois circles.

A few remarks should be made about the organization of charity as it has been described. The first is that charity was never regarded as a right, but rather as something that had to be earned. While assistance was provided to the needy who had no "shameful habits" — in other words, who did not drink to excess — the undeserving poor were refused help. The bourgeoisie saw alcoholism as the principal cause of poverty.

Second, the absence of social security gave rise to a multitude of mutual benefit societies; typically, an institution of this sort was part mutual aid association, part co-operative, and part health insurance agency. Life insurance was in its very early stages in this era, and only the wealthy could afford the premiums. The transition from craft production to wage labour created insecurity for the working class, and sickness and death were particular sources of anxiety. Therefore, with industrialization and urbanization, groups of workers organized themselves into mutual benefit societies to combat poverty, and an early function of these societies was to provide insurance against misfortune. Typical of these organizations was the Union Saint-Joseph, a working-class society founded in Montreal in the middle of the nineteenth century. Each member paid a subscription; from the proceeds, members were paid a small pension if they were sick and their widows received an indemnity when they died.

Finally, while philanthropy did bring a degree of distribution of wealth, as we saw earlier, in Quebec the contribution of philanthropists tended to be weighted towards the institutions that were closest to them culturally. Because of the ethnic distribution of the capitalist class, Anglo-Protestant charitable organizations quickly became the best endowed of Quebec's institutions. Ethnic and religious distinctions also had the effect of further compartmentalizing an already fragmented system of private charity. More or less impregnable ethnic and religious barriers were the rule. There were some exceptions, notably in the area of hospital services, but for the rest, it was to each group its own poor.

Aside from this network of agencies, the nucleus of a public system existed. In the British tradition, health conditions and the poor were the responsibility of parishes and municipalities, so that large cities in Quebec established health

A poor family's rigorous winter, 1872.

services fairly early on. While these were far from adequate, they did play a role in the gradual realization that social problems were a collective responsibility. Except in the case of the insane, the contribution of higher levels of government was limited to sporadic subsidies that bore a greater resemblance to large donations than to an assumption of collective responsibility.

The solutions offered by private charity were in no sense a match for the problems posed by inequalities in living conditions. Symptoms rather than causes were treated, and not even all the symptoms were adequately dealt with. The individualistic ideology of liberalism and Roman Catholic traditions were behind both this attitude and the low level of government intervention.

CHAPTER 10
THE LABOUR MOVEMENT

Ultimately, improvements in living and working conditions would be much less a consequence of the philanthropy of the rich than the result of organization of the working class. Workers responded to the concentration of capital by getting together and organizing themselves. They created their own institutions, and by the end of the nineteenth century these were a force to be reckoned with in Quebec.

The Rise of the Trade Union Movement

The first appearances of the trade union movement in Quebec were unassuming. Before the 1860s and 1870s, a few scattered unions were established, but nothing that could be called an organized labour movement. The first union was founded by the printers in Quebec City in 1827, and during the next four decades their example was followed by other workers. In most cases, these early unions were organized by skilled workers — typesetters, shoemakers, cigarmakers, moulders — who were well established before industrialization and saw the rise of the capitalist form of productive organization as a threat to their working conditions. Unions were also organized by construction workers, such as carpenters and joiners, and by transportation workers, such as stevedores and locomotive engineers. In addition, there were spontaneous movements by workers with no union organization, such as the strike of labourers working on the Lachine Canal in 1877.

Little is known about these organizations. For many of them, newspaper reports of a strike are the only evidence available. It is known, however, that unions were in a precarious position; they were not legally recognized, and could

The strike by unorganized labourers at Montreal harbour, 1877.

even be accused of being illegal. They had to face ferocious opposition from employers, who in most cases refused to recognize them as bargaining agents, and also had to overcome divisions among workers themselves. Highly skilled workers established the most successful unions, as employers could not easily replace them with strikebreakers if there was a conflict. Some early unions acted as benevolent societies, providing a small income to members in case of accident or illness; these unions generally had a more stable membership. Through the successes and failures of the early unions, a tradition of trade unionism was established on which the labour movement could build.

The weakness of the trade union movement before the 1870s is not surprising, as industrialization was still in its infancy. In other countries where industrialization took place earlier, the labour movement was also more advanced, and Quebec felt the impact of these developments. British and American immigrants, with trade union experience in their native countries, played a role in establishing and developing the Quebec labour movement. More significant was the entry into Quebec of foreign, especially American, labour organizations. A British organization, the Amalgamated Society of Engineers, had affiliated unions in Quebec and

Ontario by the mid-nineteenth century. Around 1867, the Knights of St. Crispin (named after the patron saint of shoemakers) extended their influence into Canada. But the two organizations that had the strongest influence on the Quebec labour movement during the period being examined were the Knights of Labor and the international craft unions affiliated with the American Federation of Labor.

Because of the prohibitions under which they were forced to function, some unions established themselves as secret societies, with initiation rites and secret proceedings. One legal obstacle was removed in 1872. There was a typesetters' strike in Toronto that year and its leaders were convicted of conspiracy in the courts. Prime Minister Sir John A. Macdonald saw that the embryonic labour movement represented a significant political interest; taking his cue from a British law passed the previous year, he brought in legislation declaring that the formation of a trade union did not constitute an act of conspiracy. However, this initial victory did not resolve all the legal problems, and it took another twenty years before the courts unequivocally recognized the legality of trade unions.

After 1867, the rise of the labour movement was accomplished in bursts of rapid growth which alternated with periods when growth was slower or gains were consolidated. The depression of the 1870s clearly had an inhibiting effect, while the 1880s were a highly fruitful period marked by the rapid growth of the Knights of Labor.

The Noble Order of the Knights of Labor was founded in the United States in 1869. It operated initially as a secret society, but dropped this policy in 1881. The Knights of Labor got off to a slow start but grew spectacularly during the 1880s, reaching a peak in 1886, and became the most important American labour organization.

The Knights expanded into Canada in 1881, and the first Quebec local assembly was founded in Montreal the next year. This resulted in the first conflict between the Roman Catholic clergy and the labour movement. Archbishop Taschereau of Quebec came out against the Knights of Labor and succeeded in having them condemned by the pope in 1884. Tensions within the church arose over this action. Bishop Fabre of Montreal, whose diocese included the majority of the Quebec membership of the Knights of Labor, did not share Taschereau's anti-union views. Neither did some American bishops, as many Irish-American Catholics belonged to the Knights. In 1887 the papal ban was lifted at the urging of Cardinal Gibbons, archbishop of Baltimore; after that, the Knights entered an initial phase of expansion in Quebec which saw twenty-four assemblies established by 1889. This was followed by a second period of growth in 1893-94 in which fifteen more assemblies were established.

The Knights favoured the organization of workers in local assemblies irrespective of their trade; they also accepted craft organizations in their ranks, however, so that two different kind of assemblies functioned side by side, and often in opposition to each other. A district assembly brought together a group of local assemblies; the Montreal district assembly was founded in 1885. Four years later, on the initiative of its French-Canadian members, it was divided in two, so that there was both a French-speaking and an English-speaking district assembly. A district assembly for the Quebec City region was established the same year, but the Montreal region, where sixty-four local assemblies were founded between 1882 and 1902, always had the largest membership. There were a few assemblies in Quebec City, and scattered ones in other towns.

In the United States, the Knights went into decline after 1886. That same year, a rival organization, the American Federation of Labor, which admitted only craft unions as affiliates, was founded. There was an intense battle between the two organizations over the next few years, but by the mid-1890s the AF of L had won a clear victory. The effects of these developments were felt, after a time lag, in Quebec.

Initially, the AF of L did not create a new kind of union; rather, it brought together existing organizations, some of them a number of years old. American craft unions had begun to establish locals in Quebec in the 1860s. These American unions began to call themselves "international" as soon as some Canadian locals became affiliated with them. Some of these unions or their members also belonged to the Knights of Labor, but gradually withdrew from the Knights after the founding of the AF of L.

The Knights of Labor in Quebec were more persistent than their American counterparts and remained a significant force until the turn of the century. The Canadian Knights even went so far as to break relations with the American organization in 1896. But in Canada, as in the United States, unions affiliated to the AF of L gained strength and, in the end, virtually monopolized the labour field.

The rivalry between the Knights of Labor and the international craft unions — at first latent, and then open — was rooted in significant ideological differences, which will be dealt with in chapter 16. It should be noted, however, that the tensions between the two rivals came into the open more slowly in Canada than in the United States, and they co-operated within umbrella organizations on both a local and a Canada-wide level.

The first attempt in Quebec to bring together various unions in one organization was launched in 1867, when a reform-minded lawyer, Médéric Lanctôt, founded the Grande Association, in which twenty-six Montreal craft groups were included. Lanctôt advocated the establishment of stores selling merchandise at cost price and supported workers in a number of strikes, but he was never able to reach his goal of bridging the gap between capital and labour. His Grande Association was short-lived; it was disbanded the same year it was founded, when Lanctôt went into politics.

More significant was the founding, initially in 1883 and then permanently in 1886, of the Canadian Trades and Labour Congress (after 1892, the Trades and Labour Congress of Canada), the first Canadian central labour body. The TLC included both Knights of Labor assemblies and AF of L unions, and was dominated by the Knights of Labor until the turn of the century. The local counterparts of the TLC were the labour councils; the Montreal Trades and Labour Council was founded in 1886, while the Quebec City council was established in 1890. The Congress did not provide for the establishment of comparable organizations on the provincial level, although it did set up provincial legislative committees; Quebec's was founded in 1891. The TLC, its committee and its labour councils brought workers' demands before the various levels of government.

The Goals of the Labour Movement

Thus, the period between 1867 and 1896 was a time of considerable growth and development for the Quebec labour movement. At the time of Confederation it was still a marginal phenomenon, while thirty years later it had emerged as a significant force in society. The goals the movement was seeking and the changes it succeeded in bringing about will now be examined.

The earliest labour grievances took the form of protests by craftsmen against changes introduced by capitalists in the organization of production, around the mid-nineteenth century. Thus, in 1849, Montreal's craft shoemakers waged a campaign against the Brown & Child Company, which was introducing machinery in its plant and employing unskilled labour. They were struggling for the survival of their jobs and the traditional pattern of their work, in a typical conflict between the craft system and capitalist organization of production. These attempts to hold back the coming of the capitalist system were doomed to failure, and between 1867 and 1896 they gradually died out; instead, workers' demands increasingly revolved around working conditions within the new system.

The main area of grievance in labour conflicts was clearly the wage level. Not only did workers want to be better paid, but they also had to fight attempts by their employers to cut wages during times of economic slowdown. In addition, Quebec workers joined in the continent-wide campaign to reduce the working day to nine and later to eight hours. In some conflicts, workers also demanded that the boss recognize the union as a bargaining agent and employ only union labour.

In addition to these specific demands that were the subject of labour conflicts, central labour bodies and local labour councils also put forward more general proposals that they sought to realize in the legislative arena. Protection against work accidents was their most important goal. The historian Fernand Harvey has summarized the proposals of the Knights of Labor as follows:

> health and safety measures in the factory, reduction of the work day to eight hours, legislation against the employment of children under fifteen years old, payment of wages on a weekly basis, equal pay for men and women, abolition of the fixed-wage contract, and the establishment of a bureau of labour statistics. In the area of working conditions, the program demanded that all labour unions be recognized on an equal basis, a system of binding arbitration be set up, contract labour for immigrants be abolished, and the use by some capitalists of convict labour be outlawed.

Jules Helbronner (1844-1921).

Other demands dealt more generally with the organization of the economy and society: support for co-operatives, nationalization of some companies, and the like. These demands will be discussed further in chapter 16.

Labour conflicts were, however, the most common occasion for the expression of workers' demands. The historians Jean Hamelin, Paul Larocque and Jacques Rouillard, authors of the *Répertoire des grèves dans la province de Québec au XIXe siècle*, unearthed 167 strikes occurring between 1850 and 1896, and suggest that the true figure is probably higher. In many of these, the workers were not organized in a union, and their strike was a spontaneous act of protest, often over a single demand, most commonly a raise in pay. Strikes waged by unions were better organized and had a greater chance of success.

There were a number of other ways of articulating demands. Meetings of the TLC and the labour councils were one, public demonstrations such as the march by the Grande Association in 1867 were another. There were the beginnings of a labour press, which voiced workers' demands and published information about the labour movement in other countries. A commercial newspaper with a large working-class readership, such as *La Presse* in Montreal, might also take pro-labour positions; the journalist Jules Helbronner wrote a labour column in *La Presse* under the pseudonym Jean-Baptiste Gagnepetit in which he exposed the deplorable working conditions in the factories. Many labour leaders of the era also saw politics as an important channel for their demands; this form of action will be discussed further in chapter 14.

Labour Legislation

The new working conditions introduced under the capitalist system led to many abuses. Labour leaders who sought to change the situation quickly realized that it was not enough to take action to improve conditions within one company. The government had to step in and impose minimum conditions on all companies.

Union demands for the adoption of pro-labour legislation were a never-ending refrain during the period. Unions sought the regulation of child labour, reduction in working hours, better health protection for workers, recognition of their political rights, and other similar measures. But the liberal philosphy of government that prevailed in this era left little room for intervention in this area. Many public officials at the time were businessmen, who regarded changes of this sort as burdens on themselves and thus had little enthusiasm for them. They were interested in labour issues only to the extent that they saw in them the possibility of immediate electoral advantage.

As already noted, the federal government took action in 1872 to remove some legal obstacles to the existence of trade unions. This, however, was the end of its legislative activity, and it abandoned the field to the provinces, which according to the constitution bore the primary responsibility for working conditions. The federal government's only other significant action was the establishment of the Royal Commission on the Relations of Labour and Capital in 1886. The commission included a number of labour members, and it carried out an in-depth study of working conditions and employer-employee relations. The considerable body of evidence it collected presented a stark picture of the situation of factory workers. Its work resulted in the issuing of two reports in 1889.

The inspiration for the majority report, which was labelled pro-union, was the program of the Knights of Labor. The minority on the commission, labelled pro-company, was made up of employers and journalists and produced a report that Fernand Harvey has termed "philanthropic." Even though the two groups based their reports on different conceptions, they ended up making fairly similar recommendations. However, according to Harvey, "those who hoped for an overview of the labour problem from the two reports were soon disappointed. The two groups of commissioners produced only a more or less orderly series of findings and recommendations dealing with various problems that had come up in the course of the inquiry."

Both groups of commissioners recommended that the work day be reduced to nine hours, that the work week for women and children be limited to fifty-four hours, and that the minimum working age for both girls and boys be established at fourteen years. In the area of workmen's compensation, the majority recommended that the indemnity to be paid be fixed by law; on this question, the minority went further, acknowledging that work accidents were a company responsibility and suggesting that compensation be handled through a universal insurance plan. The reports diverged somewhat more sharply in the area of labour relations. The pro-union report favoured the introduction of arbitration that would be binding on both parties and cover all points in dispute, while the minority suggested that arbitration boards be established whose recommendations would not be binding and would cover most of the points at issue but not wages. In addition to these major questions, the commissioners made many other recommendations aimed at improving the lot of the worker. But the two reports remained a dead letter. Part of the reason why was that some subjects they dealt with were outside the responsibility of the federal government; more significant, however, was the fact that the ruling classes were deeply conservative on social issues and disinclined to change the status quo.

The most significant Quebec legislation was the Factories Act, passed in 1885 and modeled after an Ontario act of 1883. The act set a ceiling on working hours, but it was high — sixty hours a week for women and children and seventy-two and a half hours for men — and some loopholes in the law made it easy for employers to exceed even this limit. The act made it illegal to employ a boy under twelve or a girl under fourteen without a certificate from the child's parents authorizing him or her to work. Other clauses dealt with job security and cleanliness in the workplace. In all, it was a very lenient act, and difficult to apply. It was three years before the government appointed the first inspectors responsible for making sure the legislation was honoured. Although only three inspectors were named for all of Quebec, they played an important role in increasing public awareness of labour matters. Examples of the exploitation of workers were criticized, sometimes vigorously, in their annual reports. In the course of time, they succeeded in getting the act amended to make it tougher and widen its area of application.

Until the end of the century, however, the Quebec government acted only very timidly on labour issues. Discouraged at the slow pace of government intervention, some labour leaders sought a solution in direct political action.

CHAPTER 11
THE STATUS OF WOMEN

For a long time, women were virtually absent from written history, although they constituted half the population or even more. Like workers, women gradually grew aware of their situation in society and endeavoured to organize to protect their rights. This was not to be a simple process, however, and women would have a long road to travel before they could overcome the structural inequality of which they were victims.

In the second half of the nineteenth century, in Quebec as in all western societies, a woman was in essence regarded as weak to the point of being inferior. She was defined by her role as wife and mother, at the service of her husband and children. It was universally agreed that her most important function was procreation. In this area, the Quebec woman's unstinting commitment to her duty, often at the risk of her life, leaves no room for doubt and is confirmed by the high birth rate statistics of the era. An unmarried woman was considered an incomplete woman who had not succeeded in realizing herself fully. A woman who entered a religious order, however, was an exception to this rule, for even though she remained a virgin she became married to Christ and often played a mother's role in caring for children and the sick. Inside or outside the church, women were always under the domination of men — the priest, the father, the husband and, in a deeper sense, the legislator who defined the legal and political rights of various members of society.

Women's Inferior Status

An examination of the Quebec Civil Code in effect after 1866 (Table 24) and the political rights accorded to women indicates that legal and political institutions enshrined and perpetuated women's inferior status. In essence, the Civil Code mandated the twofold principle of the authority of the husband and father within

TABLE 24

Legal Status of Married Women as Defined in the Quebec Civil Code, 1866-1915

(numbers in parentheses indicate relevant Civil Code articles)

A. *As a Person*
- (1) General incapacity (akin to minors and interdicted persons). She has, however, the right to make a will (184).
  - (a) Legally incapable of contracting (986).
  - (b) Legally incapable of offering a defence or suing before the courts (986).
- (2) Denied right to tutorship (282).
- (3) Denied right to be appointed curator (337a).

B. *Personal Relationship with Husband*
- (1) Submission to the husband. In return, the husband owes protection (174).
- (2) Nationality determined by the husband's (23).
- (3) Choice of domicile rests with the husband (83).
- (4) Choice of places of residence rests with the husband (175).
- (5) Exercise of civil rights in husband's name (customary law).
- (6) Double Standard principle: the husband is free to seek a separation on grounds of adultery; the wife can do so only if the husband keeps his concubine in the common household (187, 188).

C. *Financial Relationship with Husband*
- (1) Wife may not engage in a calling distinct from that of her husband (181).
- (2) Wife may not engage in commerce without her husband's consent (179).
- (3) In cases of legal community or property:
  - (a) The husband alone administers the property of the community (1292).
  - (b) The wife is responsible for her husband's debts. The contrary is not the case (1294).
- (4) In cases of separation of property:
  - (a) The wife cannot dispose of her property. She can, however, administer her property with the authorization of her husband or, failing the latter, that of a judge (1422).
  - (b) The husband cannot grant general authority to his wife: a special authorization is required for each act (1424).
  - (c) The wife cannot dispose of her professional earnings (1425).
- (5) Cannot accept a succession alone (643).

Table 24 (continued)

(6) Cannot make or accept a gift *inter vivos* (763). The husband can, however, make his wife the beneficiary of insurance on his life (1265).
(7) Cannot alone accept testamentary executorship (906).
(8) Cannot inherit from her intestate husband until after the twelve successoral degrees (637).

D. Family Status

(1) Cannot alone consent to marriage of a minor child (119).
(2) Cannot allow an unemancipated minor to leave the house (244).
(3) Does not have the right of correction of children (245). The wife has, however, the right of supervision over the children (customary law).
(4) Cannot exercise alone the right to tutorship of her minor children (282).

Source: Micheline Dumont Johnson, "History of the Status of Women in the Province of Quebec," p. 45.

the family. This principle implied the legal incapacity of the married woman; in other words, married women had the same legal status as minors and people deprived of their civil rights on grounds of mental disability. In this context, the married woman lost her autonomy and was subject to the authority of her husband, who was legally entitled to make all decisions concerning her civil rights and her children. The extent of this legal incapacity, which remained virtually unchanged until 1931, is clear from Table 24, the original idea for which came from Marie Gérin-Lajoie and which we have borrowed from Micheline Johnson.

Legal inferiority was compounded by very strict limitations on women's political rights. In this area, the situation of women actually deteriorated during the nineteenth century. At the beginning of the century, women had to fulfil the same conditions as men to be eligible to vote. As the Constitutional Act of 1791 did not specify that only men had the right to vote, no objection could be raised to women's voting. In 1849, however, the parliament of the Province of Canada formally abolished women's right to vote. It was not restored until 1918 at the federal level and 1940 at the provincial level.

The law was more flexible with regard to municipal and school board elections. Any property owner could vote or run for school board positions. But when a representative of a group of Montreal feminists ran for a position on the Protestant school board in 1899, male legislators quickly changed the law to make women ineligible for candidacy. On the municipal level, widows and adult unmarried women who owned property had the right to vote. However, the right to vote of a married women who owned property was exercised by her husband!

This patriarchal conception and the regression that occurred at the school board and provincial levels were expressions of the degraded political status of women in the late nineteenth century.

A Doubly Exploited Labour Force

While legal and political inequality was common to all women, their living conditions varied according to where they lived and what class and ethnic group they belonged to.

In rural areas, there was a division of labour based on sex, but since the family was the unit of production the subordinate position of women was not as pronounced as it was in urban areas. In the city, a woman's living conditions depended primarily on the social status of her husband or her father. A woman whose husband was upper class could afford the luxury of a maid and devote part of her time to social and cultural activities. The wife of a worker, on the other hand, shared her husband's hard life. If she stayed at home, she was completely dependent on her husband and received no direct compensation for her "invisible" work in the house.

With industrialization, however, a large number of girls and married women had the opportunity to work outside the home or to leave the country for the city. In the second half of the nineteenth century, there were more opportunities in the city for young women than for young men. This was reflected in population statistics — Susan Cross has compiled figures which show that while the two sexes were relatively equal in number both in the whole population of Quebec and in the group under sixteen years of age, there were many more young women than young men in Montreal and Quebec City.

Most girls between fifteen and twenty years old who went to the city in search of work found jobs as domestics or manual workers. The majority of the workers in industries such as textiles, clothing and rubber goods were women, while in the tobacco and shoe industries women constituted about forty per cent of the work force. These industries required large numbers of unskilled workers. Hiring women was all the more attractive to employers in that their wages were only half those of men. Exploitation was even more extreme in the clothing industry, where pieces cut out in the manufacturer's establishment were very often sewn by women at home or in small rural workshops. The income these workers were able to earn on a piecework basis under the sweating system was scandalously low.

Women's place in the industrial labour force was significant. In Montreal and its suburb of Hochelaga, thirty-three per cent of industrial workers in 1871 were women, while in 1891 the figure was twenty-eight per cent. While most female workers were girls, there were also undoubtedly some married women among them. There is clear evidence of this in the opening by the Grey Nuns of a number of free day-care centres called *salles d'asile* (shelter rooms). Between 1893 and 1897, some 9,000 children between two and seven years old were accommodated in these centres. At least at this time, the clergy apparently did not express any

Women working in a copper mine in Bolton, 1867.

reservations about married women working, no doubt because wages were so low and unemployment so common that women absolutely had to work. English-speaking women made some attempts during the 1890s to establish day-care centres, but none were successful.

Domestic work was another important source of employment. In Montreal, 3,657 women, or 6.4 per cent of the female population of the city, worked as domestics in 1871. Ten years later, the figure had grown to about 6,000, or 7.9 per cent of the female population. Working conditions in domestic service were

Domestic work was a major source of employment for women.

so exacting that girls preferred factory work, and there was frequent talk of a "crisis of domestic work." Upper-class women established agencies to recruit servants in the United Kingdom. There were even attempts to train girls between eight and twelve years old as domestics. Towards the end of the century, it was observed that French Canadians had replaced Irishwomen in this underpaid sector.

Women also worked in small businesses, stores and offices, but jobs in these sectors were sufficiently highly regarded that most were held by men. The telephone and the typewriter appeared towards the end of the century, but it was only later that these machines provided women with a significant source of employment.

One career possibility for women in the second half of the nineteenth century was teaching. Indeed, as the nineteenth century advanced, teaching increasingly became a woman's profession. The percentage of teaching positions in Roman Catholic public schools occupied by women climbed from 63.5 per cent in 1854 to 81.3 per cent in 1874, and it remained above eighty per cent for the rest of the century. It was in the interests of school commissioners to hire women teachers, since they were generally paid a third to half the salaries of male teachers. In addition, they did not have access to the same training as men. At the Laval Normal School in Quebec City, women were a small minority, and they were not admitted to the Jacques-Cartier Normal School in Montreal until 1899. The only options for women were to study in private schools run by religious communities or — more commonly for lay women — to receive no special training before becoming teachers.

The lay Catholic woman teacher in Quebec, disadvantaged by her lack of access to specialized training, faced a further obstacle in competition from nuns, who constituted more than thirty-five per cent of primary school teachers in the late nineteenth century. While lay women teachers had to appear before a board of examiners, nuns were exempt from this requirement.

The teaching profession was considerably more accessible to Protestant girls. The McGill Normal School accepted candidates of both sexes starting in 1857, and girls always formed a substantial majority. Protestant women teachers were paid significantly less than their male colleagues for doing the same work.

Another career possibility for women opened up in the hospital sector, where nursing was developing into a profession. It took a number of years and much effort to change things before nurses finally came to be treated as professionals rather than as servants. It was only in 1890 that the Montreal General Hospital offered a systematically organized professional course. In French-language hospitals, the nursing profession was monopolized by nuns, and it was not until 1897 that the first lay women were admitted as students at Notre-Dame Hospital.

Some upper-class women, especially in the English-speaking community, found an outlet for their talents in the various charitable organizations, although they were often assisted by a board of directors consisting of their husbands or other representatives of the bourgeoisie. It was harder for French-speaking women to penetrate this sector, since a near-monopoly of charitable work was held by nuns. There are many examples of charitable endeavours that were

A group of nuns, about 1870.

founded and administered by lay women but in the end taken over by nuns. This tendency was explicitly encouraged by the Catholic hierarchy, for which the social services were a power base, and acquiesced in by the government through its refusal to provide adequate financial support for such services.

Thus, entry into a religious community offered Catholic women in Quebec a splendid opportunity to exercise their talents, and this was undoubtedly one of the reasons why Quebec had such a large number of nuns. At the beginning of the twentieth century about 10,000 Quebec women, or roughly one per cent of the total female population of the province (as the historian Micheline Johnson has noted), were nuns. They were divided into thirty-seven communities and administered about 500 establishments. Their activities included education, care of the sick, missionary service, domestic work for the clergy, contemplation, and charitable works such as hospices, day-care centres and orphanages. Although they were under the tutelage of the hierarchy and the chaplain, these women could become administrators of very large institutions, be in charge of dozens or even hundreds of people and handle substantial sums of money.

The First Stages of Organization

Slowly, challenges developed to the pervasive discrimination to which women were subject. Until 1884, only male normal school graduates were eligible to go on to McGill College, but in that year McGill finally agreed to accept female candidates as well, although law and medicine were still closed to them. In 1890, Bishop's College in Montreal began to accept women into medicine, and by 1905 ten women had completed their medical studies. The opening up of university education was a springboard for women, and a number of university-educated women subsequently became active feminists. French-language universities remained closed to women throughout the nineteenth century, and the struggle to open them was not engaged in until later.

It was only towards the end of the century that women began to organize to demand their rights. The first major national women's association was the National Council of Women, founded in 1893 and presided over by Lady Aberdeen, wife of the governor general. This was an English-speaking movement, but its Montreal section, the Montreal Local Council of Women, was particularly dynamic and succeeded in recruiting some French-speaking women, who became the first generation of feminists in their community.

CHAPTER 12
TWO KEY INSTITUTIONS

A profile of Quebec society would not be complete without an examination of the two key institutions that were its organizational base. For both Protestants and Catholics, religion was very important in the nineteenth century, and churches' activities extended to many fields. Religion was also one of the basic elements of Quebec's dual school system. Contrary to what happened in other countries, where governments sought control of the school system, in Quebec the government was content not even to play an advisory role.

The Churches

The 1871 census reported that no fewer than forty different religions were practised in Quebec. Despite this characteristically North American religious diversity, one religion, Roman Catholicism, was overwhelmingly predominant, while Protestantism maintained a significant minority presence.

Catholicism was the religion of more than eighty-five per cent of Quebecers, while a little over fourteen per cent belonged to the various Protestant denominations. Adherents of other religions, along with people whose religion was not reported, constituted only 0.2 per cent of the population. It was the Protestant minority, divided into thirty-four separate denominations, that was responsible for the large degree of religious diversity. In broad outline, this situation prevailed until the end of the century.

The Protestant churches

Because of their minority situation, Protestant churches in Quebec maintained close links with allied institutions in the other provinces of Canada, the United

St. George's Church (Protestant), Montreal, in 1871.

States and Britain, so that Quebec Protestantism must be seen primarily as part of a larger movement. However, the strength of the Protestant minority in the Montreal region gave the Quebec metropolis a certain historic importance in the development of Canadian Protestantism. Montreal was something of a microcosm where all the major denominations were practised. On the other hand, the decline in Quebec's rural English-speaking population had adverse effects on the dynamism of Protestant communities outside Montreal.

One characteristic of Protestant churches was their tendency towards division. Briefly, the roots of this tendency in Canada go back to the period immediately after the American Revolution. The American experience led Britain to fear religious diversity, as the various sects seemed to it to be so many hotbeds of republicanism. Therefore, Britain tried to implement the principle of an established church in its remaining colonies and supported the Anglican denomination. However, this policy failed in Quebec because of the presence of the Catholic church, to which London was forced to grant de facto recognition. As a result, other Protestant denominations, especially in Ontario, demanded that the privileges accorded to the Anglican church be abolished, which was done in the middle of the nineteenth century. At the same time, a profusion of sects were introduced into Canada by immigrants and American preachers. For example, the

Presbyterians, one of the three large Protestant denominations in Quebec, were divided into six subgroups in 1871. Doctrinal questions were at the origin of many of these divisions. Thus, about 1860, there was a new split in the Presbyterian church as a result of the influence of twelve diehards, among them the Montreal industrialist John Redpath. A new church was opened, followed in 1864 by a new Presbyterian college.

Around the same time, however, a movement towards church unity began, and national and provincial synods were called in an effort to establish a common body of doctrine. The Presbyterians were the first to undertake the process of reunification, followed by the Methodists around 1874. The period after Confederation was thus marked by a lessening of rivalry among denominations and sects.

Quebec Protestantism was dominated by three denominations, which comprised more than eighty-four per cent of the total Protestant population in 1871; in order of size, these were the Anglicans, the Presbyterians and the Methodists. However, with the profusion of subgroups, only the Anglican church was a unified entity with a solid bloc of adherents. Twenty years later, the unity movement had had perceptible effects, and the Presbyterian and Methodist churches were no longer divided into a multiplicity of sects. In all, the figure of thirty-four distinct denominations or sects that had shown up in the 1871 census had been reduced to thirteen by 1891. The same three denominations still dominated Protestantism in Quebec, and now accounted for eighty-eight per cent of all Protestants.

Despite their divisions, the various denominations shared the great traditions of Protestantism — individual piety, considerable emphasis on the Bible, and a form of church organization in which a great deal of initiative was left to the laity. One notable distinction between these denominations and the Catholic church was the early appearance of secularization in Protestant charitable and educational institutions. Because of the profusion of sects, Quebec Protestants established common institutions that were recognized as Protestant but not linked to a particular denomination. The best example of this process was in the area of education, where a unified Protestant school system operated alongside the Catholic system. In general, Protestant institutions, whether schools, hospitals or charitable societies, were organically linked to a religion to a much lesser degree than their Catholic counterparts. This did not prevent the better organized Protestant churches from establishing institutions of their own, notably theological colleges.

While Protestant-Catholic relations had once been quite strained, Protestants slowly resigned themselves to accepting the Catholics' existence. Nevertheless, there were still incidents, such as the outbreaks of violence between Irish Catholics and Orangemen in the streets of Montreal in the 1870s. There was also the spectacular conversion to Protestantism in the late 1850s of Quebec's apostle of temperance, Abbé Chiniquy, who tried without much success to convert French Canadians. Gradually, however, Protestant missionary work among French Canadians, which had never been very effective, was abandoned. Religiously, Protestants and Catholics constituted two separate worlds, all but impermeable to each other.

The Catholic church triumphant

Throughout the nineteenth century, the Catholic church was preoccupied with the impact of the French Revolution and sought to combat the gradual penetration of liberal ideas. The revolutions of 1848, and especially the experience of Pope Pius IX, who had to flee from Rome, made the church's resistance all the more determined and strengthened its resolution to carry on the fight. In 1864, a document central to an understanding of the development of the church appeared. This was the *Syllabus of Errors*, which took the form of a catalogue of eighty propositions deemed unacceptable by the church; its list of condemned ideas ranged from rationalism to liberalism to socialism. The church vehemently attacked anything that it suspected of liberalism for most of the remainder of the century, until Pope Leo XIII reconciled the Vatican to modern ideas in his encyclical *Rerum Novarum* in 1891. Papal authority within the church was strengthened and ultramontanism encouraged by the Vatican Council, which resulted in the proclamation of papal infallibility in 1870.

At the time of Confederation, the Catholic church was enjoying a resurgence in Quebec. Between 1800 and 1837, the church had been in a position of weakness. The absence of full legal recognition meant that its material base was not secure; it was on the defensive against the rise of liberal ideas; and finally, it had insufficient personnel to give the population adequate guidance. Starting in the 1840s, however, two of these obstacles were removed. The church obtained full legal recognition, and the anticlericalism of some French-Canadian leaders was a casualty of the failure of the 1837-38 rebellion. This was the beginning of what has been called the Catholic reaction, during which a growing clergy organized the faithful and took them in hand. Supporting elements in this process were the founding of numerous organizations, the arrival of religious communities, improvements in religious practices and the increasing popularity of devotions. This period was also marked by a revival of clerical prestige and power within society.

In sum, the Catholic church appeared to be a very dynamic element in Quebec society at the time of Confederation, and it is thus not surprising that the clergy was increasing numerically. In addition, the political structure established in 1867 was favourable to church influence. The areas placed under provincial jurisdiction were to a large extent those in which the church was interested: education, public health, property and civil rights — in short, the areas that most immediately affected people's daily lives.

Thus, under the new constitution, for matters under provincial jurisdiction the church had to deal only with an assembly elected by a population that was more than eighty-five per cent Catholic. This new homogeneity meant increased power for the church. It still had to take politicians into account, but it could influence them through the very base of their power, their constituencies, and in any case most politicians were themselves Catholics or at least had to profess Catholicism publicly.

Montreal Cathedral, which Bishop Bourget modelled after St. Peter's in Rome.

Very quickly, the church came to occupy a privileged position. A material expression of its privilege was the tax-exempt status granted by the government to church property — this particular advantage also applied to Protestant churches. Another aspect of the church's privilege was the manner in which its influence extended to spheres that were not strictly religious. It was in charge of compiling and keeping records of births, marriages and deaths. The best example of this process, however, was education, where in the course of a few decades the church brought in religious teachers to replace lay ones and thus completely reorganized Quebec's teaching staffs. It went so far beyond the bounds of the religious domain that in the late nineteenth century it soon became a completely indispensable element in Quebec society.

The extent of the church's involvement in Quebec society could be seen when a region newly opened to colonization was being organized. Parishes had to be founded; schools had to be provided along with religious communities to run them; a diocese, colleges, hospitals and the like had to be established. It should also be noted that the network of parishes, and of dioceses at a higher level, formed a powerful means of communication, which the church could use in either direction — to collect information or to disseminate it, as it wished. This network was an important instrument of church power.

Some clergymen wanted to make extensive use of the church's strength to intervene in electoral politics, and their desire took concrete shape in the Catholic Program of 1871. Politicians, however, were overwhelmingly opposed to this tendency, and they forced the political activitists in the church into a steady retreat. The annulment by the courts in 1876 of election results in two constituencies on the grounds of undue influence exercised by *curés* during the campaign was an indication to the clergy of the bounds beyond which it could not go. At bottom, the church had much to lose in a direct confrontation with the state, which could retaliate by taking away the basis of its powers. An understanding was soon arrived at and limits to the clergy's political pretensions were established.

The quarter century preceding Confederation was a period of reorganization for the Catholic church; while this process involved some changes in worship and discipline, its main focus was strengthening the clergy. A number of religious orders were founded or came to Quebec during this period. Bishop Bourget of Montreal was a zealous recruiter; without going into details about his activities, it can be said that the clergy's capacity for exercising social control over the population of Quebec was improved. The available statistics are not extensive, but they give some indication of the changes that occurred. Thus the geographer Louis-Edmond Hamelin, in his study of the numerical evolution of the Quebec clergy, showed that the ratio of priests to practising Catholics increased considerably between 1850 and 1890 — from one priest for every 1,080 Catholics to one priest for every 510. In other words, the number of priests was growing; it more than doubled between 1860 and 1890. Religious communities, both of men and of women, were also growing. The sociologist Bernard Denault has shown that the total membership in religious communities of men increased from 243 in 1850 to 1,984 in 1901, while communities of women grew even more spectacularly, their membership jumping from 650 to 6,628. There were an additional 407 men and 2,973 women affiliated with Quebec communities but working outside the province in 1901.

While the communities of men were mostly branches of orders initially founded in Europe, the same was not true for the communities of women, most of which were founded in Quebec. Even when communities were initially founded by foreigners, they soon succeeded in recruiting most of their membership in Quebec.

Along with the numerical growth of the clergy and communities went an improvement in the quality of training. Seminaries and classical colleges were established all over Quebec; these schools provided preliminary training and channelled promising candidates towards diocesan institutions called *grands séminaires*. Here the future priest's education was completed — he studied theology and, in general, prepared to carry out his ministry.

The church had immense power and many people working for it, but it was not

Novice Grey Nuns, 1894. At the turn of the century 9,600 women were affiliated with Quebec religious communities.

monolithic. In the organization of the Catholic church, the bishop of a diocese plays a fundamental role in defining and directing church policy. With the increase in the number of dioceses in the second half of the nineteenth century, a degree of collegiality in church leadership developed. The dioceses of Trois-Rivières and Saint-Hyacinthe were established in 1852, Rimouski in 1867, Sherbrooke in 1874, Chicoutimi in 1878, Nicolet in 1885 and Valleyfield in 1892. In the latter part of the century, the assembly of Quebec bishops was a larger and more varied group than it had been previously, and differences of opinion developed on a number of points. The most celebrated issues were ultramontanism, on which the bishops were clearly divided into two camps; the Knights of Labor, on which the bishop of Montreal, more in touch with labour problems, did not show the same zeal as the archbishop of Quebec; and the university question, which pitted supporters of a Catholic university in Montreal against opponents of such an institution. Some debates could not be settled without the intervention of Rome, and apostolic delegates were sent to Quebec three times in the late nineteenth century — Mgr Conroy in 1877, Dom Henri Smeulders in 1883, and Mgr Merry del Val in 1897.

Another division of religious authority occurs in the relationship between bishops and religious communities. Although the primacy of the bishop in matters of church discipline is recognized by everyone, communities also have to endeavour to fulfil the goals assigned to them by their founders. A situation can easily arise in which these goals are not wholly compatible with the particular policy of a bishop. In addition, some communities have considerable political influence within the church, and a bishop has to be exceptionally cautious if he follows a course that goes against the wishes of one of the more powerful communities.

By far the most interesting conflict of this type was the quarrel between the Sulpicians and Bishop Bourget of Montreal over the division of Notre-Dame de Montréal parish. The quarrel ended with a victory for Bourget in 1875 after years of more or less open struggle. Its arcane details will not be described here, but in brief, the bishop wanted to divide the huge parish so that the Catholic population would be better served, while the Sulpicians, buttressed by their long-standing privileges, challenged the bishop's interference. Politicians became involved in the quarrel — including George-Étienne Cartier, who supported the Sulpician position — and the disagreement was taken to Rome, which finally recognized the bishop's authority. The Sulpicians, however, did not give up until the very end.

The power of the bishop was thus not unlimited, and there was a measure of internal discussion of church policy. An institution in which a broad consensus prevailed, as was undoubtedly the case in the Quebec church, should not be confused with a monolith.

Finally, in the area of church discipline and the determination of religious questions, the authority of the bishop was preponderant in his own diocese, but in this area as well the institution of provincial councils made possible discussion and confrontation of various episcopal points of view.

The Catholic church in Quebec was very close to the faithful. Two areas of church activity — the recruitment of secular clergy and acts of worship — demonstrated this characteristic. In the country, where the majority of Quebec Catholics lived, farmers' sons were recruited into the priesthood; such a pastor was a product of the same society as his flock, and knew the problems and particularities of their way of life from experience. There was no significant social distinction between higher clergy and lower clergy in the Quebec church; the hierarchy was fairly open and specific social groups do not seem to have monopolized any offices. The situation was different in the religious communities, where there was a clear division between fathers and brothers; from current research, no conclusions can be drawn about social origin as a factor in access to leadership positions.

Another manifestation of the clergy's closeness to the faithful was its encouragement of demonstrations of popular piety — parish or diocesan retreats or celebrations such as rogations and pilgrimages. These events were conducted with as much pomp as possible with the aim of attracting a large crowd. The clergy also watched the celebration of religious holidays closely, and reacted quickly to any feeling of dissatisfaction.

The church used other tools of organization as well — a variety of societies and associations, and Catholic newspapers. During the second half of the nineteenth century there was a proliferation of Catholic mutual benefit, charitable and

Ignace Bourget (1799-1885), bishop of Montreal from 1840 to 1876.

cultural societies. The church took a very active part in this network, through which it increased its capacity for social control. It also began to use newspapers to make known the Catholic position on particular problems.

The church's struggle against liberal ideas continued during the period of its resurgence. The circumstances of the pontificate of Pius IX (1846-78) encouraged this tendency. Pius was not hostile to liberal ideas at the beginning of his reign, but he was influenced by the revolutions of 1848 and never forgot that he was forced to flee from his states. His growing opposition to modern ideas culminated in his condemnation of them in the famous *Syllabus of Errors* in 1864. The perfervid enemies of liberalism in Quebec, led by Ignace Bourget, bishop of Montreal from 1840 to 1876, needed no further encouragement. The struggle against liberal ideas grew more and more intense until the bishop of Montreal finally triumphed over the Institut Canadien, which had come to symbolize everything hateful and harmful in liberalism from the Catholic point of view.

The Institut had been founded during the 1840s as a cultural organization that maintained a library and held lectures. Staunch republicans who advocated the separation of church and state, the young liberals of the Institut aroused the ire of the bishop, who used all the means at his disposal in an effort to destroy them. First, he founded a rival institute, then he imposed the penalty of interdict on the Institut Canadien's library, and finally, provoked by the Institut, denied the sacraments to members who refused to resign. The most famous episode in the struggle, the Guibord affair, began in 1869. Joseph Guibord, a printer and member of the Institut, died and Bourget refused to allow him to be buried in a Catholic cemetery. His decision was appealed, and in 1874 a court order finally

Joseph Guibord is buried under army protection, 1875.

forced the bishop to yield. However, he surrendered as gracelessly as he could, going so far as to deconsecrate the plot in the Catholic cemetery on Mount Royal where Guibord was finally laid to rest under army protection.

At about the same time, some 135 young Quebecers were sent to Italy to serve in the regiments of Zouaves that were defending the Papal States against attack by Garibaldi's troops (1868-70). Recruiting was carried out all over the province and several hundred Quebecers volunteered. This event was another indication of the lengths to which the church's struggle against liberal ideas and their consequences had gone. Tensions eased after the Institut Canadien effectively ceased to exist and Bourget resigned in 1876, but a distrust of liberalism, and of modern ideas generally, persisted in some clerical circles for a long time afterwards. Under Pius IX's successor, Leo XIII, who was much less hostile to some aspects of liberalism, Rome pursued a more conciliatory path, and in general the Quebec church followed its lead.

It is clear that some Catholics, both clerical and lay, dreamed of establishing a near-theocracy in Quebec. But although the church enjoyed immense power and had an influence on all aspects of the lives of Catholic Quebecers, their dreams were never realized. This was so first because state recognition was an essential element in the material basis of church power, and second because of the way the economy and population of Quebec developed. The church was able to organize its faithful, but its force of persuasion was not enough to stop the social and ideological changes that came with the development of capitalism. The influence of the Catholic church was significant in some areas, but it had little power over economic life and could not pretend to control government decisions. There, ultimately, lay the limits of its power.

The Educational System

Immediately after the Act of Union, the educational situation in Lower Canada was catastrophic. The superintendent of public instruction, Dr. J.-B. Meilleur, noted in his 1842 report that there were 804 primary schools operating in Lower Canada and that they served 4,935 pupils. Those figures were very small for a total population of about 700,000 including 111,244 children between the ages of five and fourteen.

Fortunately, the situation improved considerably in subsequent years, and by 1866 there were 3,589 primary schools in Lower Canada, with a total of 178,961 pupils. In addition, there were 237 other educational establishments, including some fifteen classical colleges, approximately the same number of industrial and commercial colleges, some academies and special schools, three normal schools and three universities. In all, 27,859 students were enrolled in these secondary and post-secondary institutions.

A school law passed in 1841 and another and more significant one passed in 1845-46 made this progress possible. The most notable virtue of this legislation was that it recognized the importance of the school commissions and the Catholic clergy while providing for co-ordination of the system by a superintendent. At about the same time, disaffection with education, resulting in part from a lack of information, manifested itself in a refusal to pay school taxes and led to what was known as the *la guerre des éteignoirs* (the war of the killjoys). These protests were calmed through co-operation between the superintendent and the clergy, and in their aftermath Dr. Meilleur obtained sufficient funds to support a staff of some twenty inspectors.

Dr. Meilleur was succeeded as superintendent in 1855 by P.-J.-O. Chauveau, who had been a minister in the Conservative government of the Province of Canada. Chauveau succeeded in giving a new impetus to the cause of education. He was convinced that educational progress depended on improving the quality of teachers, and his efforts were directed chiefly towards that goal. He succeeded in founding three large normal schools in 1857 and in establishing a pension fund for teachers, and was constantly demanding higher salaries for teachers so that the profession would attract — and keep — good candidates. He also founded the *Journal de l'Instruction publique* and the *Journal of Education*, which he tried to make into instruments of teacher training and professional information for teachers. Thus, the foundations of the Quebec school system were laid under the Union régime, but although the progress that was made was impressive there were still deficiencies to make up and shortcomings to correct.

In principle, the new federal constitution, under which education was an exclusive responsibility of the provinces, should have infused the Quebec school system with new vigour, but unfortunately the encouraging start that was made immediately after Confederation was followed by a long period of stagnation. Two issues — the educational rights of the Protestant minority and the role of the Catholic clergy — were exacerbated by Confederation, and the two groups involved got together to emasculate the government in the field of public instruction. Faced with this coalition, Quebec governments themselves helped build an administrative and financial structure that not only limited their own role in education but also contributed to fragmentation of the school system and ensured that the Protestants would enjoy special privileges in the area of school financing.

The Protestant minority

Under Confederation, the educational powers of the majority in each province were widened, and religious minorities were placed in the position of having to fight for their autonomy in this field.

During the last session of the parliament of the Province of Canada in 1866, the Confederation project almost came apart completely over this question. Through their spokesman in the cabinet, A.T. Galt, Quebec Protestants had the French-Canadian legislator Hector Langevin introduce a bill that would guarantee the autonomy of their school system. As the Catholics of Upper Canada had ventured to ask for a similar guarantee and had been stymied by the opposition of the Upper Canadian representatives in parliament, the representatives of Lower Canada were very reluctant to vote for the Langevin bill. The situation became bitter, the bill was withdrawn, and Galt resigned to save his honour. He had, however, been invited to the London Conference and his proposal was included in Article 93 of the British North America Act, which satisfied his coreligionists. This, however, was only a first step.

The next occurred in 1867, when the lieutenant governor of Quebec asked Joseph Cauchon to form the first government of the province. Representatives of the Protestant minority, angry with Cauchon because of his public opposition to the Langevin bill the previous year, refused to enter any ministry he headed, and Cauchon was unable to form a government. The minority had in effect vetoed the appointment of Cauchon, and the lieutenant governor called on P.-J.-O. Chauveau, who had been superintendent of public instruction for twelve years and had always maintained good relations with the Protestants. A few months after he assumed the premiership, Chauveau proposed major changes in the administrative and financial organization of the educational system. This reorganization, which would be completed by a later premier, Charles de Boucherville, fully satisfied the Protestant minority, which enjoyed a large degree of autonomy in the organization and control of its schools.

Structure and financing

Chauveau, who had been identified with the cause of education since 1855 and had just returned from a long period of study in Europe undertaken in his capacity as superintendent of public instruction, accepted the premiership in 1867 on the condition that he be allowed to continue his activities in the educational field. Thus in 1868 he established a Department of Public Instruction, headed initially by himself as minister. Quebec was the only province endowed with such a department. That a government not otherwise notable for its audacity should undertake such an innovation was rather surprising, and can be attributed to Chauveau's determination and experience. This measure could have signified a deep and lasting commitment to education on the government's part, but instead it was gradually emptied of its content.

In 1869, Chauveau introduced a bill to change the composition of the Council of Public Instruction, an advisory body that had existed since 1859 and was composed of ten Catholics — most of them laymen — and four Protestants. Under the change effected by Chauveau, the Council was divided into two denominational committees, a Catholic committee with five clerical and nine lay members and a Protestant committee comprising three clerics and four laymen. This division had been demanded by the Protestants over a period of years, and was aimed at giving them greater autonomy.

The process was carried considerably further in 1875 by another Conservative premier, de Boucherville, who after consulting Quebec's bishops decided to abolish the Department of Public Instruction. De Boucherville was of the opinion that a politician generally had neither the time nor the competence to take charge of education, and that this noble cause had to be kept away from politics. Under the proposed reform, the minister of public instruction would be replaced by a superintendent appointed for a long term. In general, the bishops were satisfied with this decision, although some wanted to go even further and give the clergy exclusive control over the education of Catholics.

The division of the Council of Public Instruction into two denominational committees was maintained. The Catholic committee would now be composed of all Catholic bishops whose dioceses were located wholly or partly in Quebec, along with an equal number of laymen appointed by the government. However, only the bishops could be represented by a substitute in case of absence, and thus were assured of a majority on the committee for all practical purposes. The Protestant committee was composed of as many members as there were laymen on the Catholic committee. The superintendent had to implement the policies formulated by the committees and was at their service. The full Council was to meet infrequently, and the two committees were to function separately. Protestants supported the measure, which gave them greater autonomy. Thus, in 1875-76, the Quebec government abdicated its responsibilities in favour of the Catholic church and the Protestant minority.

Between 1876 and 1896, even though the preponderance of the Catholic church in education was beyond challenge, some clerics were suspicious of any government intervention. Thus Gédéon Ouimet, as superintendent of schools, started a controversy by trying to establish a government "book deposit" to sell books and educational materials at cost price to school commissions that

Belmont School in Montreal, built in 1876.

requested them. Bookstores and some clerics got together to attack this instance of government interference. The superintendent and the government that supported him were forced to retreat on this question as they also were when they tried to standardize the choice of books used in the schools. Limited as they were, these two government initiatives nevertheless created tensions with the bishops. When Joseph-Alfred Mousseau became premier in 1882, he publicly and officially declared that he would not take any initiative without consulting and obtaining the assent of the two committees.

This promise was not binding on his successors, one of whom, Honoré Mercier, had long been interested in education. On a number of occasions, Mercier had come out in favour of compulsory education for children. But when he became premier with ultramontane support, he no longer dared to take up this cause, although he did hope to create a climate conducive to change. He asked five Conservative lay members of the Catholic committee to submit their resignations.

They refused vociferously. He had his government appoint him a member of the Catholic committee at the earliest opportunity. But because of the government's abdication of its power, Mercier could act only indirectly and in marginal areas.

The debates about the structure of the educational system were paralleled by controversies over school financing. The legislation of 1869 included some highly important financial clauses. It stipulated that school taxes paid by Protestants would go to Protestant school commissions while those paid by Catholics would go to Catholic school commissions. Since Protestants owned much more real estate than Catholics, this meant that Protestant schools received much more than they would have if all tax revenues were divided in proportion to population. J.-Adolphe Chapleau, a young member of the legislative assembly (and future premier), could not help pointing out that this criterion was unjust because "in the end, it is the tenant who pays the tax, and not only will he pay it, but in many cases the money will go to support schools that are not of the majority and not of his faith." The newspaper *Le Pays* estimated that Protestant schools would receive about $1.80 per child as compared to eighty-four cents for each Catholic child. This was part of a barrage of heavy criticism of the measure in the press, in which even Conservative newspapers joined. It was called a retrograde principle and referred to ironically as a compromise in which the majority showed an extraordinary spirit of sacrifice. Nevertheless, the law was passed unanimously. The Catholic clergy and Protestant spokesmen were as one in their wholehearted approval of the bill.

A different method of division was applied in the case of property belonging to companies, which were considered religiously "neutral." These "neutral" tax revenues were divided between Catholics and Protestants in proportion to their percentage of the population at the time of the last census. The same principle was applied to public funds directed to higher education. This did not come close to compensating for the inequality created by the division of school taxes according to the religion of the property owner.

At the end of the century, a delicate issue, the "Jewish school problem," divided Catholics and Protestants. The Protestants demanded that all non-Catholics be considered Protestants for school tax purposes, and also that the stockholders of companies be identified according to their religion. In taking this position, however, they were going too far. Even the most conciliatory bishops came out vigorously against their demand, which if implemented would have deprived Catholics of part of their revenue, and Cardinal Taschereau countered by saying that if the Protestants insisted on it, he would use his influence to try to have school funds distributed in proportion to population. The cardinal noted that "the existing division gives the Protestants a third of the funds available, while distribution according to population would reduce this figure to one-seventh."

Although property taxes were a very important element in school financing, the burden was borne first and foremost by parents, as education was not free in the nineteenth century. In 1874, about a million and a half dollars was spent for education in Quebec; this figure was equivalent to about three-quarters of the total provincial budget. However, about fifty per cent of the amount spent for education came from parents and more that thirty per cent came from property taxes. The rest consisted of subsidies paid by the Quebec government to school commissions and money allocated by the government for special schools, higher education, the teachers' savings plan and poor municipalities.

In the first thirty years after Confederation, the government abdicated its responsibilities in favour of the Catholic Church and the Protestant minority. The Protestants enjoyed not only a large degree of autonomy but an advantageous financial situation as well.

Educational institutions

Despite everything, the number of educational establishments increased during the period and the system developed bit by bit. The number of schools increased from 4,063 in 1870-71 to 5,863 in 1897-98, the number of pupils grew from 223,014 to 314,727, and the number of teachers increased by almost 100 per cent, from 5,424 to 10,493. To complete the elementary program required four or five years of study, divided into a primary course and a model course. Youths left school when they were ten or eleven years old, after their first communion. Inspectors were constantly deploring students' lack of diligence. Secondary institutions included academies, industrial colleges and classical colleges. Some people, including Chauveau himself, objected to the excessively large number of classical colleges, which trained lawyers and doctors for whom there was no future. Arthur Buies said ironically that the members of these two professions were highly useful — one group ruined you and the other killed you. Liberals advocated a more practical course of study with more science, mathematics and English instead of Greek and Latin. Some people criticized the distorted way in which catechism and religious history were taught in the schools. In addition to the encouragement given to the creation of industrial colleges and commercial academies, provision was also made for the establishment of special schools — art and trade schools, evening schools, schools for deaf mutes and the blind.

One of Premier Chauveau's goals that remained unfulfilled was the creation of model farms attached to the normal schools to promote the development of agriculture. Along with his sucessor Gédéon Ouimet, however, he did succeed in bringing about the establishment of a polytechnical school. The original initiative in this area was taken by McGill University, which asked for a subsidy from the government. Chauveau was very conscious of the need to train engineers and wanted to see French-speaking Quebecers represented in this area, so he offered a subsidy to Laval University for the creation of a similar school. After difficult negotiations, Laval refused the government's assistance, on the grounds both that the amount offered was not enough and that it feared government interference. Fortunately, the Montreal Catholic School Commission was less timid and agreed in 1873 to found the school, which remained under its jurisdiction until 1888.

The Plateau Commercial Academy in Montreal, built in 1876.

Not only did Laval University refuse to establish the polytechnical school, but it also energetically opposed the creation of a French-language university in Montreal, a proposal which had the enthusiastic support of Bishop Bourget, the Jesuits, and the doctors of the Victoria Medical School. The conflict went to Rome, which decided in favour of the creation of a Montreal branch of Laval in 1876. Meanwhile, the Protestants had a much more unified system, consisting of primary schools, high schools and two universities, Bishop's and McGill, which served the Protestant population adequately.

The teachers

Clearly one of the major problems during the period was the pitiful situation of lay teachers. Every year, the superintendent reminded the population that providing for the presence of competent teachers was the most urgent reform required and that accomplishing it meant paying teachers decently.

Students at the Jacques-Cartier Normal School in Montreal learning the rudiments of farming, 1896.

With the many reforms put into effect by Chauveau — normal schools, pedagogical journals, boards of examiners, pension fund — it was thought that the crucial problem of teacher training had been solved. But while these excellent reforms and initiatives contributed towards improving the quality of teachers, they had little effect on improving their wages and working conditions. Too often, school commissioners regarded teachers as labour to be hired at cheap rates, and showed little concern for competence and experience.

Normal school graduates were supposed to be the main source of the teacher supply, but after 1867 the number of normal school students no longer increased. A large number of graduates left teaching for other careers after fulfilling their obligation to teach for three years. In these conditions, teaching became more and more a woman's profession (Table 25).

Girls had limited access to advanced academic training, were hired at a very young age and were paid absurdly low salaries. Teaching was often viewed as a temporary occupation to be pursued while waiting to find a husband. The resurgence of male teachers at the end of the century was due to the massive entry

TABLE 25
Representation of Each Sex in the Teaching Profession, 1854-1898

Year	*Men (%)*	*Women (%)*
1854	36.5	63.5
1874	18.7	81.3
1887-88	16.5	83.5
1897-98	20.6	79.4

Source: André Labarrère-Paulé, *Les instituteurs laïques au Canada français 1836-1900*, pp. 300, 356, 439.

of the clergy into the teaching sector. Clericalization was another notable feature of the teaching profession in the second half of the nineteenth century (Table 26).

After 1837, a large number of religious communities came into existence in Quebec, some of them founded locally and others established as branches of communities based elsewhere. Members of these communities — Christian Brothers, Brothers of the Holy Cross, Brothers of the Sacred Heart, Clerics of St. Viator — taught in the primary and secondary schools, as did members of the secular clergy. Among male primary teachers, the proportion of clerics increased from 48.5 per cent in 1876-77 to 68.3 per cent in 1887-88. Considering only the Catholic sector, the proportion of clerics was 75.5 per cent in 1887-88 and reached 82.8 per cent in 1896-97.

Clericalization was less pronounced among women teachers despite the presence of a number of communities such as the Congregation de Notre Dame and the Sisters of the Holy Names of Jesus and Mary. In 1876-77, lay women constituted 79.1 per cent of women teachers; this figure was 73.3 per cent in 1887-88 and 64.5 per cent in 1896-97.

Clericalization of the teaching profession increased the Catholic church's influence over the population. It also allowed school commissioners to save money, since religious who lived communally and had no family obligations could be

TABLE 26
Clericalization of Catholic Teaching, 1853-1897

Year	*Lay (%)*	*Clerical (%)*
1853	89.5	10.5
1874	78.0	22.0
1876-77	65.3	34.7
1887-88	52.5	47.5
1896-97	55.7	44.3

Source: André Labarrère-Paulé, *Les instituteurs laïques au Canada français, 1836-1900*, pp. 300, 356, 439.

content with lower salaries. This phenomenon, however, made life impossible for lay teachers. A lay person who ended up in the profession despite all the obstacles had to act as the humble servant of the priest. Some people saw clericalization of the teaching profession as a danger to Quebec society, which was ill prepared to face the hard realities of secular life as a result.

The increasing role of women and the clergy in the teaching profession had the effect of keeping salaries low (Table 27). Catholics were paid only half as much as Protestants, while within each denomination women were paid much less than men.

In 1894, teachers asked to be paid monthly instead of every six months, so that they would not have to borrow — often at high interest rates — to survive, and the Council of Public Instruction granted their request. However, their meagre salaries were not raised, and the government did not agree to provide funds to augment the salaries of deserving teachers or to establish a minimum wage.

In 1896, the twenty-four boards of examiners which handed out diplomas for the asking were abolished and replaced by a more demanding central board. Only the central body and the normal schools were authorized to grant diplomas to lay teachers, while clerical teachers were still exempt from certification. The inspectors replaced their first visits with pedagogical conferences. In addition, it was determined in 1895 that a review of school legislation would be conducted, as the way the system was functioning was coming under increasing criticism.

A flutter was caused when the 1891 census showed that Quebec had the highest percentage of illiterates over twenty years of age. Some groups endeavoured to show that Quebec had reduced the percentage by 6.29 per cent between 1871 and 1891 and thus made more progress than the other provinces, or to attribute the situation to the Conquest, but their arguments fell on deaf ears. Somewhat unconvincing at best, these arguments were wholly unsatisfying to reform-minded people, prominent among whom were the Liberals, who came to power under Premier Félix-Gabriel Marchand in 1897.

TABLE 27
Average Annual Salaries of Quebec Teachers, 1894-1895
($)

	Primary Schools		*Model Schools and Academies*	
Teachers	*Men*	*Women*	*Men*	*Women*
Catholics without certificates	180	77	246	77
Catholics with certificates	233	103	442	133
Protestants	516	177	805	304

Source: André Labarrère-Paulé, *Les instituteurs laïques au Canada français, 1836-1900,* p. 451.

POLITICS

The full significance of political history becomes clear only when it is placed in its social and economic context. Political decisions cannot be wholly understood without taking into account the play of economic forces and relationships among social groups and classes. Conversely, as noted in the preceding pages, government intervention is an important factor in the evolution of social and economic structures.

The word "politics," of course, conjures up elections, parties and governments. But politics also means the state and all its organs through which the different aspects of power are expressed. The type of state that Quebec had in the second half of the nineteenth century is generally referred to as liberal, and a brief definition of the exact nature of this type of state will be given. Since state power is exercised at different levels of government, the distribution of powers among these different levels — municipal, provincial, federal, and for the era being studied, imperial — must also be analysed. In this context, the specific role and scope of activity of the Quebec state, a state with its own particular characteristics, institutions and personnel, can be better appreciated.

Quebec politics was dominated by the competition for power between the Conservative and Liberal parties. Before looking at the various governments that administered Quebec between 1867 and 1896, it is necessary to examine the organization of these parties and other aspects of the electoral process. While in preceding chapters the primary emphasis has been on structural phenomena, here the focus will shift to the role played by politicians, especially by premiers of Quebec. Finally, in the last chapter, the evolution of federal-provincial relations will be studied. Federalism can take on a variety of forms depending on the forces acting at any given time, and since Quebec has only a provincial state these different forms of federalism must be analysed.

CHAPTER 13
A LIBERAL STATE

In a liberal society, the state is supposed to be the expression of the citizenry as a whole and the objectives it pursues are supposed to serve the common good. In theory, this is achieved through a system of parliamentary democracy, in which those who are entrusted with management of the state are elected by the people. However, this theoretical vision does not correspond to reality, and in concrete terms state power is dominated by groups or classes with particular interests to protect.

This was especially true in Canada in general and Quebec in particular in the late nineteenth century. All women and a significant number of men were excluded from political representation. Powerful groups, formed into parties in which popular participation was almost nonexistent, struggled for political office. At this time, the state was clearly dominated by one social class, the bourgeoisie, and government policies advanced the interests of that class. The personnel of government either came from the bourgeoisie or was closely identified with it.

This domination, however, should not be seen mechanistically. Within the bouregoisie there are often tensions, conflicts betwen interest groups, and widely varying social ideas. In addition, in a liberal state, the power of the bourgeoisie is tempered by a number of factors. The first of these is the democratic system itself, however imperfect it may be. Because they must face the electorate periodically, the rulers in a democratic system have to explain their positions to the voters and cannot make autocratic decisions with impunity. The claims of groups with different interests are another mitigating factor. Thus the trade union movement, starting in the 1880s, could demand and obtain from the ruling bourgeoisie concessions that improved the lot of workers, while the clergy was sufficiently well organized to be able to impose its views in the field of education. Recognition of freedom of speech and freedom of the press can encourage the expression of opposition to the powers that be. Finally, the federal system, by dividing the exercise of state power between two levels of government, places limits on the actions that either can take.

Within this general framework, how state power and the control of the bourgeoisie were exercised in Quebec society in the late nineteenth century and how other groups expressed their resistance to this control will now be examined.

The Distribution of Powers

After 1867, the exercise of state power in Quebec was distributed among four levels of government — imperial, federal, provincial and municipal. Canada in 1867 was a colony of Great Britain and the British parliament in London exercised sovereignty over the country, as it did over the whole British Empire. However, the North American colonies had gradually acquired a large degree of autonomy, and in 1867 the imperial government maintained direct control only over external affairs. Canada did not have the right to sign treaties or to have embassies in foreign countries, and it was bound by treaties negotiated by Britain in the name of the Empire.

The constitution of 1867 assigned the major elements of state power to the federal and provincial governments. This constitution was an act of the British parliament known as the British North America (BNA) Act.

The 1867 constitution was federal, but it was based on a highly centralized form of federalism. In 146 articles, it outlined the main institutions of the country and endeavoured to define the responsibilities of the various governments with which it endowed the federation. It dealt with the distribution of powers, crucial in any federal constitution, primarily in Articles 91 and 92.

The provinces were given exclusive powers relating mostly to the social organization and cultural life of Canada's various communities — property and civil rights, health and social security, public lands, municipal institutions and works of a local nature, the administration of justice, and education. At a time when governments intervened little in these sectors, the powers accorded by Article 92 were considered essentially secondary.

The powers attributed to the central government by Article 91 were predominantly economic and military in nature. In particular, the central government was given the exclusive power to legislate in matters relating to trade and commerce, currency and coinage, banks, the postal service, defence, criminal law and Indians.

These powers were already significant at the time, and in themselves gave considerable importance to the federal government. But the centralist character of the union of 1867 becomes even clearer if other provisions scattered throughout the BNA Act are taken into account. Thus, the preamble to Article 91 assigned to the federal government what are called residual powers, or powers not specifically attributed to either level of government. The federal government was given the power to legislate "for the Peace, Order and good Government of Canada, in relation to all Matters not coming within the Classes of Subjects by this Act assigned exclusively to the Legislatures of the Provinces." By virtue of this preamble, the central government could, in case of emergency, legislate in any domain.

The unchallengeable predominance of the federal government was manifested in other ways as well. Agriculture and immigration were recognized as shared responsibilities, but in case of conflict between the federal government and the provinces the federal position was to prevail automatically. The federal government was given the right to disallow any provincial legislation, and in 1867 this right was not subject to any limitations. Provincial laws were to require the approval of the lieutenant governor, an official appointed by Ottawa, to become operative. In what is known as the declaratory power, the federal government could exercise its authority over "such Works as, although wholly situate within the Province, are before or after their execution declared by the Parliament of Canada to be for the general Advantage of Canada or for the Advantage of Two or more of the Provinces." Senators, who in a federal system should at least in principle be defenders of provincial interests, were to be appointed by the federal government, as were judges of the Supreme Court which Ottawa instituted in 1875.

The federal government was also made predominant in the financial sphere. While the provinces were given circumscribed powers and the right only to "Direct Taxation within the Province in order to the raising of revenue for Provincial Purposes," the federal government's powers were to extend to "the raising of Money by any Mode or System of Taxation." Not only was the federal government allowed to raise money through indirect taxes — the largest source of revenue in the nineteenth century — as well as direct ones, but it was also given the power to spend money for any purpose which it considered relevant, regardless of whether that purpose fell within its own jurisdiction or the provinces'. On the other hand, the provinces were given the right to borrow money on their own credit, and this power has been widely used. By going to the money markets, the provinces acquired some room to manoeuvre, and the heavy dependence on Ottawa that characterized the provinces' financial and political affairs in the nineteenth century was reduced.

The political system put into operation in 1867 was thus in no sense a confederation — that is, an association of sovereign states for limited ends — but rather a federation. Prime Minister Sir John A. Macdonald himself said that the system had all the advantages of a legislative union. This judgment was later confirmed by the jurist K.C. Wheare in his classic study of federalism, in which he categorized the Canadian case — in 1867 at least — as a case of "quasi-federalism."

In a federation comprising a number of ethnic groups, minorities try to have guarantees of their rights written into the constitution. In 1867, there were two groups trying to protect themselves — French Canadians and the Protestant minority in Quebec. Two articles in the BNA Act are significant in this regard. Article 93 allowed the federal government to intervene to protect the educational rights of minorities, even though education was under the exclusive jurisdiction of the provinces. For a number of reasons, this article turned out to be completely ineffective as a protective measure. First, minorities were defined only in religious terms. Second, only rights existing by law at the time of the union were protected. Finally, since intervention by the federal government was not made obligatory, legal and political constraints have in practice prevented Ottawa from imposing coercive measures on provinces that mistreat their minorities.

The other article of the BNA Act of special interest to minorities was Article 133, which stipulated that debates in the federal parliament and the Quebec legislature could be in French or English. The records and journals of these bodies had to be kept in both languages, and the laws that they passed had to be published in both French and English versions. Finally, either language could be used in pleading before the courts of Canada or Quebec. Despite these provisions, the bilingualism of the federal government was defined so restrictively that it was impossible to apply it in concrete terms; among the provinces, only Quebec became truly bilingual.

The problem of minority rights is linked with the question of the general meaning of the constitution, especially with regard to relations between the provinces and the federal government and between the English-speaking majority and the French-speaking minority.

For a long time, French-Canadian spokesmen attached great importance to the first paragraph of the BNA Act: "Whereas the Provinces of Canada, Nova Scotia, and New Brunswick have expressed their Desire to be federally united into One Dominion under the Crown of the United Kingdom of Great Britain and Ireland, with a Constitution similar in principle to that of the United Kingdom." The statement that it was the provinces which "expressed their Desire to be federally united" was supported by certain speeches of the Fathers of Confederation, and it led some people to interpret the BNA Act as a "compact," a "treaty," or an "agreement" among the provinces. A corollary of this intepretation was the idea that the constitution could be changed only with the unanimous agreement of the provinces, and that since the provinces gave up only some of their powers to the central government they retained their sovereignty over everything else. There have been many challenges to this theory, and nowadays, it is generally accepted that the BNA Act was a simple act of the British parliament and in no sense a treaty.

In addition to the theory of a pact among the provinces, another theory has taken root according to which Confederation was a compact between the two large "races" or nationalities of the era. This theory starts from the premise that the representatives of French Canada agreed to the union on two conditions: that it be federal, and that it guarantee French Canadians enough autonomy to protect their national character and special institutions, of which the most important at the time were French law, the Catholic religion and Quebec's distinctive educational system. From this, it was a short step to the conclusion that equality of the two "races" was confirmed by the pact of 1867. This theory does not stand up to the facts any better than the first one; the majority and the minority have been in conflict too often to talk about a compact guaranteeing their equality.

Apart from these great debates, applying the constitution raised many concrete problems which were resolved either by the play of political forces or by judicial interpretation. During the period being examined, the respective powers of the federal and provincial levels of government became more clearly defined through these processes.

The municipal level of government, the fourth and final level operating during the period, had no independent constitutional existence. Municipalities were the creatures of the provincial governments which defined their powers and reserved the right to limit or extend them at will. In Quebec, the municipal system had developed gradually under the old Union régime and was completed by the Municipal Code of 1870 and the Cities and Towns Act of 1876. The basic function of the municipalities was to provide public services of a local nature — roads, aqueducts, sewers, police, fire protection, public health. The scope of a municipality's functions and powers depended on whether it was a parish municipality, a village, a town or a city. In each county, the rural municipalities (villages and parishes) were grouped in a county council that administered territory not organized into municipalities and dealt with questions involving more than one municipality, such as a bridge joining two villages. Large cities such as Montreal or Quebec City had more extended powers, granted to them by virtue of special acts. Municipalities financed their activities through the property tax and other local taxes; in their borrowing activities they were subject to the control of the Quebec government.

The Role of the State

The role traditionally assigned to the state under the tenets of economic liberalism was much more modest than the role it has assumed today. Primacy was given to private enterprise, and the state was expected to play only an auxiliary role. The most important functions entrusted to it were ensuring respect for private property — notably by administering the judicial system — and financing infrastructure projects. This system was beginning to come under vigorous attack in the second half of the nineteenth century in countries that were either already industrialized or in the process of becoming so. A number of developments — population growth, urbanization, industrialization, the increasing complexity of the economy and the proliferation of economic actors — all helped create a need for intervention by a new kind of power. This new power had to stand above individual interests, be able to impose rules for the functioning of the system and have the capacity to provide or finance a wider variety of services than had been required in the past. The increased role of the state also provided entrepreneurs close to the centres of power with an opportunity to gain access to public resources for their own enrichment. Governments found themselves in a position where they had to intervene more and more, but private initiative still had the upper hand. Governments were more active, but their role was still auxiliary.

In Canada, the constitution gave the federal government both the largest share of the power to intervene in the economic sphere and the most substantial sources of revenue. In the first decades after Confederation, the Quebec government was in a situation of weakness that limited its capacity to act.

The weakness of the Quebec government

The period from 1867 to 1897 was characterized by the financial weakness of the Quebec government. The division of powers made in 1867 gave the provinces three main sources of revenue: a subsidy from the federal government, proceeds from the sale and exploitation of crown lands, and licences and other miscellaneous taxes. The constitution also allowed the provinces to impose direct taxes of all kinds, but since these were very unpopular, governments hesitated to resort to them, and for a long time the only direct tax of any importance was the property tax which municipalities were authorized to levy.

The agreement of 1867 anticipated that the federal government — which controlled the most significant source of revenue, customs duties — would contribute towards the financing of the provincial governments. The federal subsidy consisted of a fixed amount of $70,000 plus eighty cents for each inhabitant of Quebec enumerated in the 1861 census. No provision was made for readjustment of this amount to take account of population increase, so that the federal subsidy remained the same throughout the period. In 1869, the subsidy represented sixty per cent of Quebec's revenues, but this proportion decreased steadily; it was less than half of Quebec's revenues in 1874 and in 1896 only a quarter. In the 1880s, the Quebec government tried in vain to have the subsidy adjusted in line with the province's increased population.

The second source of revenue was exploitation of natural resources, especially public lands and forests. According to the historian Marcel Hamelin, the sale of lands, the concession of "timber berths" and the various taxes arising from the forest industries represented between twenty-five and thirty per cent of the province's revenues in the years immediately following Confederation; in 1896 they were still a quarter of the total. The government thus had an interest in stimulating the forest industry since its revenues would thereby be increased. However, this created a situation of dependency that made it difficult for the government to balance its budget when there was a drop in forest production, as happened during the depression of 1874-79 when revenues from the forests fell drastically.

The government also could count on revenue from miscellaneous taxes and

The old parliament building in Quebec City, destroyed by fire in 1883.

licences, especially liquor licences. Revenues were nevertheless insufficient to meet expenditures, and starting in the 1880s the government had to resort to direct taxes. Despite opposition from business circles, it chose to impose taxes whose greatest effect was on people with high incomes — corporation taxes, taxes on property transfers and succession duties.

Between 1869 and 1896, the revenues of the Quebec government increased from $1,651,321 to $4,327,910 while its current expenditures increased from $1,321,933 to $4,099,777. At the end of the period, governments still suffered serious financial difficulties, mostly as a result of heavy borrowing for railway construction.

In 1867, the Quebec government inherited part of the debt that had accumulated before Confederation. It was agreed that the federal government would assume a significant part of the founding provinces' debts, but in the case of the old Province of Canada there remained roughly $10.5 million that had to be shared between Quebec and Ontario. An arbitration commission was set up to decide the amount that should be attributed to each province, consisting of one representative from Quebec, one from Ontario and one from the federal government. Quebec and Ontario couldn't agree on the criteria by which the division should be made, and the discussions were dragged out until the federal representative decided to support Ontario's position. The Quebec arbitrator then withdrew from the discussions; the two others submitted their decision in 1870, and the portion of the debt that Quebec was required to assume was fixed at about $5 million. There was a general outcry in Quebec, and to resolve the question

Quebec put pressure on Ottawa to assume the entire pre-1867 debt. The pressure was kept up, and in 1873 the federal government accepted this solution and offered the other provinces proportional compensation. This agreement put Quebec in a position to borrow money to finance railway construction.

The central position of railways in Quebec's economic policy was indicated in chapter 5. Between 1874 and 1900, Quebec governments gave out $26,177,000 in subsidies for railway construction. Of this amount, Quebec got back $10.4 million through sale of the Quebec, Montreal, Ottawa and Occidental (QMO&O) and through a subsidy paid by the federal government for this same railway. These subsidies were paid to assist long-term borrowing, a method of financing that was also used for some public works. At the end of the century, Quebec's debt had reached $35 million. Interest payments weighed heavily on the annual budget; in 1896, debt servicing represented 36.5 per cent of current expenditures.

In that same year, the government's other significant areas of expenditure were the administration of justice (13.6 per cent), education (9 per cent), charitable institutions (8 per cent), agriculture and colonization (6.9 per cent) and public works (3.8 per cent). General expenses for legislation and civil administration represented eleven per cent of the total. The extent of the government's indebtedness thus seriously limited its capacity to intervene in sectors such as education and agriculture where the need for its presence was evident.

Nor was the weakness of the state purely financial. The inadequacies of the civil service, which was beset with problems of both quantity and quality, were another contributing factor. At the end of the century, the permanent staff of a department consisted on the average of about twenty people. Little is known about what the qualifications of these people were or what they did. There were some devoted but relatively obscure senior civil servants who provided the government apparatus with a degree of stability; in this category was Siméon Le Sage, a deputy minister for forty-two years. The celebrated Curé Labelle, deputy minister of agriculture and colonization under Premier Honoré Mercier, was more of a special case.

All observers agreed that the main problem with the government was patronage, which affected all aspects of its administrative activity. Patronage came into play most significantly in the area of hiring, since government jobs were reserved to friends of the ruling party. It also came into play in the division and distribution of public funds and in the implementation of government policy. This situation often led to a proliferation of isolated, badly co-ordinated actions and subsidies, with no logic except for their effect on the next election.

Municipal governments also played a significant role. Current revenues of the city of Montreal alone were equal to half those of the province of Quebec in 1869 and two-thirds of those of the province in 1896. At the end of the century, Montreal's debt was equal to three-quarters of the provincial debt. In financial terms, the economic activities of all the municipalities together outweighed those

The new Quebec parliament building, built between 1877 and 1885.

of the province. Although their spending was purely local in nature, it could sometimes have more than a local effect, as in the case of municipal railway subsidies. The fragmentation of decisionmaking units could give rise to waste and overbidding; thus municipalities tried to outbid one another in offering tax exemptions and subsidies to companies. At the municipal level, as at the provincial, corruption and patronage were widespread.

The sectors of activity

In the absence of in-depth historical studies of Quebec's legislation and public administration in this period, no more than a sketchy outline of their general orientation can be drawn. Certain kinds of activity require public spending. Some of these activities take the form of a public service provided by the state itself; in these cases, the state generally intends to recover part of the cost from the users of the service. The best example of this is the judicial system: the state builds, maintains and runs courthouses and prisons; it pays guards and other staff; it then recovers some of these expenses from the users of the system through court fees, fines, and the like. There are a large number of other cases where public spending is in the form of government subsidies to groups or companies — railway corporations, colonization companies, charitable institutions. All these actions requiring public expenditures were clearly limited by the weakness of the government's financial position.

But there are also many sectors of activity that require little or no government spending. These are situations where the state legislates to require groups or citizens to respect certain norms or meet certain objectives. There are many examples of this kind of government intervention; two will be examined here. In order to deal with the ever-present problem of public health, the Quebec legislature in 1886 authorized municipalities to take steps to promote public hygiene and forced them to set up health departments. At the same time, the legislature adopted a Factories Act establishing standards for working conditions in factories. Neither of these actions required much government spending, but both had the potential to affect society in a significant way.

These legislative measures, however, raise the question of the gap between law and reality. It isn't enough to pass a law; a government has to ensure its acceptance and, most important of all, see to its application. In this respect, government activity in the late nineteenth century seems to have been largely ineffective. To implement the Factories Act, the government appointed only three inspectors, who had to cover all of Quebec and visit hundreds of factories. Their effectiveness was clearly limited. The municipalities had to set up health departments, but nothing forced them to adopt public hygiene measures, so that there could be great disparities between one place and another. Those who broke the laws were generally able to escape prosecution fairly easily and when fines were imposed they were often ridiculously low. These difficulties can be traced to the inadequate staffing of the civil service, administrative inefficiency and patronage.

Taken as a whole, government intervention did not extend beyond a few sectors. The most important of these were ones that related to economic policy. The government's emphasis on railway construction, which drained a large part of its resources, has already been noted. The development of agriculture and colonization also had a significant place, but the resources allocated to these two sectors were insufficient. Another object of the government's attention was the public domain (lands, forests, mines), which was important both for the Quebec economy and for government revenues.

Social policy, by contrast, was almost nonexistent. Even taking into account the promotion of public health and legislation concerning factory work, which were exceptions to the general lack of activity in this field, the government's overall performance in the social sphere was far from daring. Aside from these two measures, the government left the initiative to private charities, contenting itself with giving out subsidies here and there. Only the maintenance of the mentally ill in asylums was fully covered by the state. In the field of education, the government withdrew from playing a direct role in 1875. As pointed out in chapter 12, it was left to an autonomous organ, the Council of Public Instruction, to oversee development of this sector. In the cultural sector, there was no policy; government activity was limited to acting as patron to a few artists and giving out the occasional subsidy.

One area where the presence of the state was most visible was the administration of justice which, during the nineteenth century, underwent a process of decentralization.

The municipalities devoted the bulk of their activities and expenditures to building a local infrastructure (aqueducts, sewers, roads) and protecting property (police and fire departments). It was noted in chapter 9 that some municipalities turned the management of certain public services over to private enterprise; this was often the case of water, gas, electricity, telephone and public transit systems. A portion of municipal revenues was set aside for education and turned over to the school commissions, which were responsible for the construction, maintenance and staffing of schools.

Institutions

The institutions — parliament and government — that provided the framework for the exercise of political power will be briefly described. The 1867 constitution gave Quebec a British-style parliamentary system with a bicameral legislature, made up of the Legislative Assembly and the Legislative Council. This was not new; Quebec had lived under similar institutions since 1791.

The Legislative Assembly was clearly the most important body. It was made up of sixty-five members, each representing an electoral constituency; this number was increased to seventy-three in 1890 and to seventy-four in 1897. The Assembly had two main responsibilities: to vote on legislation and to decide the fate of governments, which had to obtain the support of a majority of members. The representation of the population in the Assembly was distorted in several ways. With the growing urbanization of Quebec, rural areas became overrepresented in relation to urban areas. In addition, the areas where the English-speaking rural population was concentrated in 1867 were overrepresented through a special provision written into the constitution as a concession to the English minority. These areas, in the Eastern Townships and the Outaouais, were organized into twelve constituencies whose boundaries could not be changed without the agreement of a majority of the members from those constituencies; this provision was maintained even though, in the course of the period, some of the constituencies acquired French-speaking majorities.

Unlike Ontario, Quebec was given an upper house, the Legislative Council. This body was created to satisfy the desire of the French-Canadian political élite to give more prestige to the Quebec parliament and the wish to give another guarantee to the minority. During the last years of the Union régime, the Legislative Council of the Province of Canada was elective, but this system was not maintained for Quebec in 1867; instead, the twenty-four legislative councillors were appointed for life by the government. Laws passed by the Assembly had to be submitted to the Council, which could accept them, change them or even reject them (which it did several times during the nineteenth century). Bills, except for money bills, could also be introduced in the Council and passed by it before going to the Assembly, but this practice was rare. The Council represented a brake on the democratic system and was a factor leading to social conservatism.

The government is embodied in the Executive Council, more commonly known as the cabinet. In constitutional theory, the cabinet is headed by the lieutenant governor, but in practice the premier is the chief officer of the government. The lieutenant govenor is Quebec's chief of state. He represents the British sovereign, who is also the sovereign of Canada; he chooses the premier; and he must approve all laws before they can become operative. Since he is appointed by the federal government, he is in effect a federal representative, and he can refuse to sign a Quebec law or reserve it for the signification of the pleasure of the governor general of Canada. In the latter case, the law would not take effect unless explicitly assented to by the federal government. The constitutional evolution of the office of the lieutenant governor has been similar to that of the British monarchy, and the lieutenant governor has increasingly become a symbolic figure who leaves the actual task of governing to the cabinet. Between 1867 and 1896, lieutenant governors did intervene directly in the political process on several occasions, the most celebrated being two cases in which the lieutenant governor dismissed the government — Premier Charles de Boucherville was fired by Luc Letellier de Saint-Just in 1878, while Auguste-Réal Angers got rid of the Mercier government in 1891. But these were exceptional incidents and didn't prevent the gradual eclipse of the lieutenant governor.

Executive power is exercised by the cabinet, whose members are normally members of the Quebec parliament — in the period being studied either MLAs or legislative councillors. Under the rules of ministerial responsibility, the cabinet had to have the support of a majority in the Legislative Assembly in order to govern. The premier was generally an MLA, but between 1867 and 1897 there were two premiers who were legislative councillors, Charles-Boucher de Boucherville and John Jones Ross. During this period, the cabinet usually had six or seven members, chosen according to a variety of criteria — personal competence, party experience, ethnic and regional representation. The English-speaking minority was represented by three members in the cabinets of the period, usually two Protestants and one Irish Catholic. The speaker of the Legislative Council was in the cabinet, almost on an *ex officio* basis. The premier also tried to balance the representation of the Montreal and Quebec City regions. The cabinet was a small circle in which decisionmaking power was concentrated and on which pressure was exerted by the most influential groups in society.

There were few government departments. At first, in 1867, there were six — the departments of the Provincial Treasurer, the Attorney General, the Secretary and Registrar, Agriculture and Public Works, Crown Lands, and the Solicitor General. The Department of Public Instruction was added in 1868, and then abolished in 1875. The Department of Agriculture and Public Works was divided in 1888 into a Department of Agriculture and Colonization and a Department of Public Works. Between 1880 and 1888 there was also a Department of Railways.

Politicians

In countries that are governed according to parliamentary democracy, politicians generally come from an élite whose level of education and wealth is considerably higher than that of the population as a whole. Quebec is no exception to this rule, as the political scientist Robert Boily and the historian Marcel Hamelin have amply shown. In the period being examined, politicians were recruited primarily from the ranks of the bourgeoisie and the petty bourgeoisie. The working class was almost totally absent from parliament, while farmers, who made up the majority of the population, contributed only fifteen per cent of the MLAs during the period, many of these being wealthy farmers who were landed capitalists rather than small peasant producers.

The Legislative Assembly was dominated by professionals and businessmen, who made up almost ninety per cent of its membership. About two-thirds of the seats were occupied by lawyers (the largest single group), doctors and notaries who, as a result of their training and their place in society, were in a position to command the support of the electorate. However, their membership in the liberal professions was only the visible surface of a more complex situation, since many of these MLAs were also closely involved in business. Among the actual businessmen, a few — such as William Price and Louis-Adélard Sénécal — were heads of large companies. As sessions of the Assembly lasted only two or three months, they were able to participate in politics while continuing to run their corporations. Some businessmen, especially those involved in railway enterprises, saw their presence in Quebec City as a way of promoting their interests and obtaining government subsidies.

Cabinet ministers came from an even more restricted group than other legislators. Recruitment was much more strictly limited to the ranks of the bourgeoisie, and most ministers came from leading families, which were often represented simultaneously in politics, business, the judiciary and the clergy. Members of the liberal professions, and especially lawyers, clearly dominated the cabinet. All the premiers of the period were lawyers, except de Boucherville, who was a doctor. Another noteworthy aspect of cabinet composition at the time was the overrepresentation of English-speaking Quebecers, who usually occupied forty to fifty per cent of the cabinet posts.

The class background of politicians, and especially of cabinet ministers, indicates the direct control that the dominant class, the bourgeoisie, exercised over the state and its political institutions.

At the municipal level, a similar control by élites existed, but the élites were of a different order. In the villages and parishes, the local petty bourgeoisie — generally made up of lawyers, notaries and merchants — controlled the important posts, especially the positions of mayor and secretary-treasurer. In the towns and cities, land developers were an additional important group and used their presence on city council to influence urban development in a direction favourable to their interests.

Montreal city council in the early 1870s.

Municipal government in Montreal, which has been studied by the political scientist Guy Bourassa, was something of a special case. In an early period, from 1840 to 1873, Montreal city council resembled a private club of the capitalist class. The overwhelming majority of mayors and city councillors came from big business; members of the liberal professions were clearly in the minority. City council in this period was also dominated by English Montrealers. The situation began to change after 1873. There were still leaders of big business on city council, but there was also a growing number of representatives of the liberal professions and middle management; most of these, however, were still closely tied to the bourgeoisie. From 1887 on, French-speaking Montrealers were a majority on city council. Thus one social class, the bourgeoisie, dominated Montreal city government throughout the nineteenth century, just as it dominated the Quebec provincial government, even if the way in which its power was exercised differed somewhat from one level to the other.

CHAPTER 14
POLITICAL DEVELOPMENTS

Competition for political power takes place within the framework of a party system, and between 1867 and 1896 there were two large parties competing for the prize, the Conservatives and the Liberals. Both had been founded during the Union régime (1841-67) and were coalitions of a number of factions. There was no real third party in the post-1867 period. There was some political activity on the part of labour, but it was in its early stages and the few individuals elected through it quickly joined one or the other of the existing parties.

The Parties

Political parties were not yet highly structured, and in this situation it was possible for a certain number of independent MLAs to be elected. The Liberal and Conservative parties operated at both the federal and the provincial level; no clear distinction was made between the two.

Each party consisted of two ideologically distinct wings. The Liberal party had a radical left wing, heir to the tradition of the Rouges, and a centrist, moderate group. The Conservative party also had a centrist group, as well as an ultramontane right wing. There were forces bringing moderate Liberals and Conservatives together while the left and right wings tended to keep the two parties apart. Between 1867 and 1896, both parties moved gradually towards the right. In the Liberal party, the radicals became more and more a marginal group as the centrists tightened their hold, while the ultramontane wing increased its influence within the Conservative party.

The dominance of the Conservative party

Between 1867 and 1896, the Conservative party clearly dominated the political scene both in Canada as a whole and in Quebec. It was in power in Ottawa for twenty-four of these twenty-nine years, while in Quebec City it formed the government for all but about six years (see Table 28).

The Conservative party was older than Confederation. Its origins dated back to 1854, when a number of factions in Canada East (Quebec) and Canada West (Ontario) formed a coalition called the Liberal-Conservative party. There were two major groups in the Quebec wing of this coalition. The largest bloc was the group of French-Canadian reformers organized by Louis-Hippolyte LaFontaine after the Union of 1840. This group fought to obtain responsible government and other political reforms. In the 1850s, it identified itself more and more with the interests of Montreal big business while advocating the maintenance of French-Canadian cultural traditions. The other group was the Tories, English-speaking conservatives in Canada East who agreed to be discreet about their plans for assimilating the French Canadians in return for French-Canadian support of their economic policies.

The Conservative party's domination of the Quebec political scene began in this era, during which it succeeded, with the support of the clergy, in containing the rise of the Rouges. In the years before 1867, the Quebec wing of the Conservative party was dominated by George-Étienne Cartier. A former Patriote leader, Cartier became lawyer for the Grand Trunk Railway and the Sulpicians during the 1850s. His career followed a pattern common to a number of leading French-Canadian politicians of the time, and is evidence of the rise of French

TABLE 28
Quebec General Elections, 1867-1897

Year	Registered Voters	Valid Ballots	Seats	Liberals Elected	Conser-vatives Elected	Others Elected	Percentage of Popular Vote Lib.	Percentage of Popular Vote Cons.
1867	161,800	75,385	65	14	50	1	45	55
1871	172,369	60,395	65	20	45	—	35	65
1875	185,783	86,939	65	19	43	3	44	56
1878	217,825	134,475	65	30	33	2	49	51
1881	223,215	97,590	65	15	49	1	42	56
1886	234,844	146,850	65	31	28	6	51	49
1890	276,641	158,932	73	42	24	7	53	47
1892	290,335	174,725	73	21	51	1	45	55
1897	338,800	225,179	74	51	23	—	54	46

Source: *Quebec Yearbook*, 1966-67.

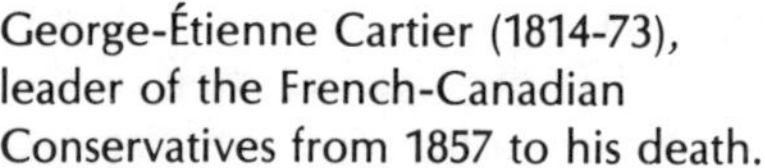

George-Étienne Cartier (1814-73), leader of the French-Canadian Conservatives from 1857 to his death.

Sir John A. Macdonald (1815-91), Conservative prime minister of Canada, 1867-73 and 1878-91.

Canadians within the bourgeoisie and the many ties of common interest that bound these French Canadians to English-speaking capitalists.

English- and French-speaking Conservatives alike upheld the principles of economic liberalism. They advocated policies directed towards encouraging infrastructure development, with the aim of promoting integration of the Canadian market and the growth of private enterprise. In doing this, they were effective representatives of the Montreal bourgeoisie, which hoped to control the development of Canada.

In addition to this consensus on economic policy, there was an agreement of sorts in the cultural sphere based on mutual respect between English- and French-speaking Conservatives. The English-speaking Conservatives, led by A.T. Galt, strongly defended the English minority's religious and educational rights and the existence of its own network of institutions. French-speaking Conservatives protected French-Canadian institutions in the religious, educational and legal sectors. At the time of Confederation, the two groups had reached a nonaggression pact that was no less effective for being unspoken.

The Conservative party was nevertheless a fragile configuration, with both ideological and regional differences contributing to its tensions and contradictions. Sir John A. Macdonald was the federal leader of the party from 1867 until his death in 1891, and was able to provide continuity and a degree of unity. But he was at odds with two reactionary wings that were on the rise within the party — the Orangemen in Ontario and the West and the ultramontanes in Quebec.

In Quebec, the rise of the ultramontanes was gradual. Around 1867, Cartier's leadership of the Quebec Conservatives was almost unchallenged. While a minister in the federal cabinet, he essentially ran the Quebec government by proxy and put his own stamp on the party in the form of an orientation known as the "Cartier school." Moderate for its time, the Cartier school emphasized economic development and religious toleration. Politically, it tried to follow a middle way between the radicalism of the Rouges and the extreme conservatism of the ultramontanes. This was an orientation that satisfied the ultramontanes less and less as time went on.

The ultramontane group was formed in the 1850s and 1860s to combat the liberalism of the Rouges; its primary field of activity was thus ideological struggle. In their effort to resist the rise of the Rouges, the ultramontanes supported the Conservative party, but after 1867 they went further and tried to make it their instrument.

While the differences between the ultramontanes and the Liberals were clear, it is not so easy to distinguish the ultramontanes from the Cartier school. Recent research on the subject tends to show that both wings of the Conservative party recruited their leaders from the bourgeoisie. Like the moderates, the leaders of the ultramontane wing were heavily involved in business and their conception of progress attracted them to economic liberalism. Quebec historiography has often given the impression that they were men of principle, upright and incorruptible. A closer examination reveals that they too had their manipulators skilled in placing public resources at the service of their personal interests. They were different from the moderates primarily in their conception of the social order. The ultramontanes wanted to organize society according to Catholic principles and give control of its main institutions to the church.

The ultramontane wing of the Conservative party first surfaced publicly during the 1871 Quebec election campaign, when it launched the Catholic Program, an attempt to create a Catholic political force in Quebec. According to the Program, voters were supposed to insist that candidates promise to make Catholic doctrine the basis of their political action; if the bishops requested changes in legislation, legislators loyal to the Program were expected to comply. The aim of the Catholic Program was thus a virtual subordination of the state to the church. Most candidates, Conservatives as well as Liberals, refused to accept the Program and only one *programmiste* was elected in 1871. It was a setback for the ultramontanes, but the episode had given them a chance to get organized.

After Cartier's death in 1873, the rivalry between the two wings of the party became more animated. It reached its climax between 1879 and 1883, when Adolphe Chapleau was the dominant figure in the party in Quebec. Chapleau adopted a policy of confrontation with the ultramontanes and tried to shut them out of power; he went so far as to try to come to an agreement with the moderate wing of the Liberal party in the hope of establishing a grand coalition of the centre. His association with the enterprising businessman Louis-Adélard Sénécal aroused suspicion and led to the epithet of *sénécalistes* which the ultramontanes — who themselves were know as *castors* (beavers) — attached to Chapleau and his supporters. The battle between the two wings of the party, carried on through pamphlets and editorials, threatened to result in an irreparable split, but a compromise was reached in early 1884. From that time on, the Cartier school shared power with the ultramontanes and the Quebec cabinet included representatives of both tendencies. This *modus vivendi* strengthened the position of the ultramontanes and emphasized their ascendancy in the party, with the result that some moderate Conservatives were tempted to switch to the Liberals.

This drift to the right was not the only cause of disunity within the Conservative party. There were also personality conflicts and regional tensions, one manifestation of which was the silent battle between Hector Langevin, a representative of the Quebec City region who succeeded Cartier as leader of the Quebec wing of federal party, and Chapleau, who represented the Montreal region and challenged Langevin's leadership.

Meanwhile, the Liberal party carried out a reorganization in Quebec under the leadership of Honoré Mercier and Wilfrid Laurier, and succeeded in attracting part of the Conservatives' constituency. It was helped in doing so by the national question, which reappeared during the Riel controversy in 1885. The hanging of Louis Riel allowed the Liberals to discredit French-Canadian Conservative ministers, and the Conservatives became, in the eyes of a section of the electorate, a party of Orangemen and *pendards* (hangers). The result of all these developments was that the voters became increasingly disenchanted with the Conservatives from the mid-1880s on.

The rise of the Liberal party

In the thirty years following Confederation, the Liberal party spent most of its time in opposition. It was difficult for them to make a dent in the domination of the Conservatives, although they succeeded in gradually widening their base of support.

In order to understand the difficulties the Liberal party underwent in the early years of Confederation, it is necessary to look at its predecessors during the Union period, especially the Rouges. In the late 1840s, young intellectuals grouped around the newspaper *L'Avenir* (the future) gradually broke with Louis-Hippolyte LaFontaine's reform party, which they criticized for being too conservative. Among these intellectuals were Jean-Baptiste-Eric Dorion, Joseph Papin, Joseph Doutre, Louis Labrèche-Viger, Charles Daoust and Charles Laberge. This was the first split in the French-Canadian bloc. The *L'Avenir* group, in the minority, developed a radical ideology, expressed admiration for European liberals and American-style democracy and were called Rouges (Reds) by their opponents. The Rouges wanted democratization of Quebec's institutions, serious reforms in the educational system, and a clear separation of church and state that would limit the church to the religious sector. The Rouges reached their apogee in the mid-1850s when they achieved an electoral breakthrough in the greater Montreal region.

They became the nucleus for a Liberal party made up of a variety of elements. Among these elements was the small group of Lower Canadian English-speaking Liberals, notably including Luther Holton and John Young, who cast their lot with their French-speaking colleagues. But the most important group was a growing number of French-Canadian politicians who, while maintaining democratic ideals, adopted a moderate attitude and tried to avoid conflicts with the church. Antoine-Aimé Dorion was the most prominent of these moderates.

The Quebec clergy considered the Rouges a serious threat. In Europe, liberals were forcefully attacking the privileges of the Catholic Church, including the temporal power of the papacy. Fearing repetition of this situation in Quebec, the clergy became more and more direct in its opposition to the Rouges, and its tactics included condemnations from the pulpit during election campaigns.

This situation forced the Rouges into retreat in the 1860s and reduced them to marginal status both within their party and in the electorate. In his study of the Rouges, Jean-Paul Bernard has shown that the 1867 election marked the end of Rougism. Liberals elected after that date were very different from the radicals of the 1850s. The radicals continued to work within the Liberal party, but only as a minority, and while certain reforms, especially in the educational field, were still advocated by some Liberals, they were substantially watered down.

Thus, the post-1867 Liberal party was no longer radical. It presented a moderate program similar to that of the Cartier school in the Conservative party. However, the more conservative faction in the clergy took several decades to recognize this new reality and continued to attack the Liberals. A number of Conservative party spokesmen covered the same ground and associated the Liberals with radicalism and anticlericalism.

Liberal party strategists tried to get out of this trap by taking a series of initiatives to dissociate the party publicly from Rougism and present a moderate image to the electorate. Thus at the time of the 1872 election, a group of young Liberals including Louis-Amable Jetté and Honoré Mercier founded the Parti National, which existed only for the one election and helped elect some Liberals.

The next year, the Pacific scandal brought the federal Liberal party to power in Ottawa. This was the opportunity for the Liberals to show their moderation. However, the party suffered from internal difficulties that manifested themselves in frequent changes of French-Canadian ministers. It was at this time that Wilfrid Laurier entered the cabinet and began his rise in the party. In Quebec, Henri-Gustave Joly had been Liberal leader since 1867; he was premier for a few months as a result of Lieutenant Governor Letellier de Saint-Just's dismissal of the de Boucherville cabinet, but the Liberals' electoral base was still not solid enough to give them a clear majority.

In the battle between the Liberals and the clergy, the most spectacular event was probably the disputed election in two constituencies in 1876. In Charlevoix and Bonaventure, the defeated Liberal candidates demanded that the election results be thrown out because of the undue influence exercised by the *curés* on behalf of the Conservatives. The final decisions of the courts (one case went all the way to the Supreme Court) were favourable to the Liberals.

The clergy's opposition to the Liberals was not unanimous. The archbishop of Quebec, Mgr Taschereau, a member of a leading Liberal family, did not approve of the ultramontanes' intransigence. The battles within the clergy were spirited and left the Catholic hierarchy in a state of agitation; to re-establish peace, Rome sent a special investigator, Mgr Conroy, in 1877. Wilfrid Laurier took advantage of the occasion to delivery a major speech on British-style "political liberalism," which was also practised in Canada and which he distinguished from the Catholic liberalism rejected by the church. Mgr Conroy accepted this argument and persuaded the bishops to forbid *curés* to take a position against a party or a candidate. This was a victory for the Liberals and put them in a better position relative to the church, although it did not eliminate the opposition of the ultramontane clergy.

The Liberal party's turn to the right became even more pronounced in the 1880s with the advent of new leaders. Wilfrid Laurier became the principal French-Canadian lieutenant in the federal Liberal party, and in 1887 he succeeded Edward Blake as party leader. In Quebec, Honoré Mercier became Liberal leader in 1883.

In 1885, their cause was aided by a spectacular event, the hanging of Louis Riel. The Indians and Métis of western Canada, led by Riel, rebelled against the federal government. This was the culmination of a conflict between two civilizations — on one side, the nomadic or semi-nomadic Indians and Métis had an economy based on hunting and considered the western plains their territory, while on the other, the much more technologically advanced whites wanted to develop the West through agricultural settlement. The whites robbed the original occupants of their lands, undermined their economy, and confined them to reserves or pushed them farther and farther north.

But in Quebec, as in Ontario, political and religious leaders twisted the meaning of this conflict. Because the Métis rebels were mostly French-speaking and Catholic, their struggle was presented as a step in the continuing battle between English and French Canadians. The 1885 uprising was put down by federal troops and Louis Riel was brought to justice in Regina and condemned to death for treason. French-Canadian public opinion demanded that the federal cabinet commute the sentence. English-Canadian public opinion, especially in Ontario and the West, demanded with equal force that Riel be hanged. Forced to choose between these two contradictory positions, the Macdonald government decided in favour of the majority: Riel would be hanged.

There was a heated public reaction in Quebec. The Conservative party became the "party of *pendards*." A stigma was attached to the three French-Canadian ministers in Ottawa who remained in their jobs. Some Conservatives, especially

Louis Riel (1844-85), leader of the Métis during the 1869-70 and 1884-85 rebellions, seen in the dock at his trial in Regina, where he was found guilty of treason and condemned to death.

from the ultramontane wing, broke with their party. Honoré Mercier assumed leadership of the dissatisfied French Canadians. He spoke at a famous rally in which 50,000 people gathered on the Champ-de-Mars in Montreal, and began his speech with the words: "Riel, our brother, is dead."

Mercier proposed a union of all French Canadians and towards that end established a new political organization; like the organization of 1872, it was called the Parti National. The new party was an alliance of the Liberal party and dissident Conservatives, and such radicalism as had been able to survive in the Liberal party was allowed to wither away. At the head of the Parti National, Mercier kept the popular reaction to the hanging of Riel alive, conducting a series of public meetings over the next year through which he perpetuated the discontent. This campaign lasted until the next election, held in the fall of 1886 and won by Mercier.

With Mercier's accession to power, the Liberals again demonstrated how far they had come from the radicalism of their predecessors, the Rouges. Through the combined efforts of the Mercier government and the federal leader, Wilfrid Laurier, the Liberal party sank deeper roots in Quebec soil. This process was temporarily slowed down in 1891 by the fall of Mercier as a result of the Baie des

Chaleurs railway scandal, but by the end of the century the Liberals were solidly installed in power at both levels of government and dominated the Quebec political scene.

Labour political action

The working class sought its own political goals through the two-party system, but its role was marginal. Labour political action arose as a result of the progress of the trade union movement. Very early on, union leaders realized that they would have to take action at the political level to obtain the reforms they were demanding. This action took the form of workers running as candidates in federal and provincial elections.

With the exception of Médéric Lanctôt's unsuccessful attempt to get elected in Montreal East in 1867, the earliest labour political activity took place in the 1880s. The main protagonists were the Knights of Labor, who advocated political action and presented candidates in working-class Montreal neighbourhoods in 1883, 1886 and 1887. They had their first success in 1888 in a federal byelection, when Alphonse Télésphore Lépine, a member of the Knights and secretary of the Montreal Trades and Labour Council, was elected member of parliament for Montreal East with the tacit support of the Conservative party. Two years later a workers' candidate, Joseph Béland, was elected to the Quebec Legislative Assembly, this time with the support of the Liberals. These were the only two elections in which the Knights of Labor were successful.

Alphonse Télésphore Lépine (1855-1943), labour member of parliament.

This labour political action was limited in nature. It was purely electoral and concentrated in a small number of ridings. It was not supported by an independent political organization, and labour MPs and MLAs had to work within one or the other of the big parties. They were in a position to attract attention to workers' problems through their intervention, but their political influence remained marginal.

Party organization and elections

In the nineteenth century, political parties did not yet take the form of membership organizations, and their structures were not well defined. In reality, a political party was the property of the MPs and MLAs and their organizers. There was an organizer for each district — Montreal, Trois-Rivières and Quebec City. He controlled the election fund and was responsible for the ridings in his district. At the local level, each riding and each parish also had its organizer. In the cities, parties also made use of another form of organization, the political club, which provided an opportunity for party chieftains and their leading supporters to get together.

However, the most visible element of a political organization was the party press. The newspapers of the time were, with a few exceptions, party organs. Each party — and even each faction within a party — aimed to have newspapers in Quebec City, Trois-Rivières, Montreal, Saint-Hyacinthe and other parts of Quebec. There was thus a proliferation of newspapers, many of which were ephemeral. Each of these papers developed and vigorously defended the positions of its party or faction.

Party organizations came into their own at election time. In many ridings, the quality of a party's organization could make the difference between victory and defeat. Elections were also marked by corruption, which had been institutionalized since the middle of the century and mostly took the form of patronage. An election victory was an opportunity for a party to distribute, directly from public funds, jobs and contracts to supporters who had contributed time or money to its success.

Abuses of power and violence were encouraged by the election laws in force at the time of Confederation. First of all, elections were not held on the same day in all ridings. The nomination of candidates in meetings was another practice open to abuse. A new election law in 1875 brought in a number of reforms, the most fundamental being the secret ballot. Among other changes were the replacement of nomination meetings by nomination forms that had to be signed by a certain number of voters, and the introduction of more severe measures — including cancellation of elections — to fight fraud, vote-buying and undue pressure on voters. The reform also provided for some control of election expenses; this was abandoned in 1892, but reintroduced in 1895.

The new rules established by the 1875 reform were the basis of the electoral system for a century. This law, which suppressed the most flagrant abuses, still did not completely eliminate fraudulent practices. Parties continued to buy votes and put pressure on voters, although somewhat more subtly. Substitution of voters, "telegraphing" (an elaborate vote-buying system) and the use of violence remained part of Quebec's electoral practices. In this context, success often depended on the power of a party's organization — its ability to have representatives at polling stations and provide services to voters. The historian Marcel Caya attributes some of the Liberal party's difficulties before 1886 to the weakness of its organization.

Another question that can be asked is who the voters were. Suffrage in Quebec was far from universal during the period. The political scientist André Bernard has calculated that the number of voters registered in 1871 represented only 14.8 per cent of the population. The right to vote depended on a property qualification — a voter had to own real estate of a certain minimum value fixed by law or, if a tenant, have an equivalent amount of income. Only males at least twenty-one years old and meeting these criteria were allowed to vote; women with sufficient property or income had not had the right to vote since 1849. In the course of the period, new laws increased the size of the electorate by granting the vote to additional categories of citizens, so that by the end of the century the electorate represented twenty per cent of the population. There was thus some progress, but property or income remained the basis of the system and women continued to be excluded.

The Succession of Governments

Between 1867 and 1897, there were ten premiers of Quebec, and they headed a total of twelve governments. That means that most premiers stayed in office a mere three or four years, and a few — Gédéon Ouimet, Henri-Gustave Joly, J.-Alfred Mousseau and Edmund James Flynn — held the position only a little more than a year. Three — Pierre-Joseph-Olivier Chauveau, J.-Adolphe Chapleau and Louis-Olivier Taillon — left the premiership to enter federal politics. This rapid succession of governments can be broken down into four distinct periods (see Table 29).

The Cartier school (1867-78)

The essential tasks of the governments that held office between 1867 and 1878 were establishing the institutions of the new state on a firm basis, developing the main elements of policy and creating instruments and economic development. Their activity was limited by the state's financial weakness, which was aggravated, from 1874 on, by the depression that struck the industrialized countries.

In 1867 Joseph Cauchon, a Quebec City politician, barely missed becoming the first premier of Quebec (see chapter 12). The lieutenant governor called on him to form a cabinet, but representatives of the English-speaking minority were categor-

TABLE 29
Premiers of Quebec, 1867-1897

Name	*Party*	*Date of Accession*
Chauveau, Pierre-J.-O.	Cons.	July 15, 1867
Ouimet, Gédéon	Cons.	February 27, 1873
Boucherville, Charles-B. de	Cons.	September 22, 1874
Joly, Henri-G.	Lib.	March 8, 1878
Chapleau, J.-Adolphe	Cons.	October 31, 1879
Mousseau, J.-Alfred	Cons.	July 31, 1882
Ross, John Jones	Cons.	January 23, 1884
Taillon, L.-Olivier	Cons.	January 25, 1887
Mercier, Honoré	Lib.	January 29, 1887
Boucherville, Charles-B. de	Cons.	December 21, 1891
Taillon, L.-Olivier	Cons.	December 16, 1892
Flynn, Edmund J.	Cons.	May 11, 1896
Marchand, F.-Gabriel	Lib.	May 24, 1897

Source: *Quebec Yearbook,* 1966-67.

ically opposed to him. They objected to his failure to commit himself to giving Protestants complete autonomy in the field of education. Cauchon thus did not become premier and Pierre-J.-O. Chauveau was appointed to the position instead.

Chauveau was a political associate of George-Étienne Cartier, and so with his accession it was the "Cartier school" that took power. He easily won the 1867 election, in which the Conservatives took fifty of the sixty-five seats. Until his entry into the cabinet, the new premier had been involved in education, and he had held the position of superintendent of public instruction. Wishing to continue his activities in this field, he established a Department of Public Instruction and headed it himself. His first task was to organize government institutions. He inherited some structures that had been created under the Union, such as the administration of justice (courts, prisons, and so on), but there was much work to be done in co-ordinating administrative machinery, organizing government departments and establishing a budget.

The government also had to define its role in the new federal system and identify the fields of activity on which it wanted to concentrate. Concern with Quebec's economic development dominated parliamentary debates. MLAs were haunted by the scope of emigration to the United States and wanted to stem this movement. Their solutions were economic: opening up new regions for colonization, encouraging modernization of agriculture, stimulating forest industries and accelerating industrialization. In Quebec as elsewhere, building railways appeared to be the magic solution; it would stimulate trade and industry and allow farmers and lumbermen to market their products. In 1869, the Chauveau administration

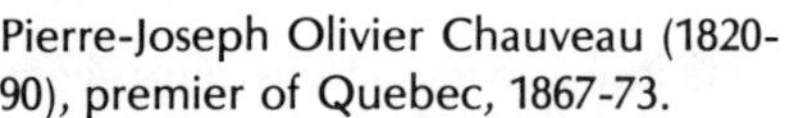

Pierre-Joseph Olivier Chauveau (1820-90), premier of Quebec, 1867-73.

Gédéon Ouimet (1823-1905), premier of Quebec, 1873-74.

adopted a policy of financial assistance to railways which led the Quebec government to commit large sums to the support of private railway companies.

The other plank in the Chauveau government's economic policy dealt with agriculture and colonization. The government reorganized the Department of Agriculture, encouraged establishment of colonization companies, exempted new colonists' goods from seizure, and subsidized the building of colonization roads.

However, the government's capacity to act was limited by its financial weakness. The first difficulty the Chauveau government had to face was the excess debt that had accumulated before 1867. Until that question was resolved, the government could not float large-scale loans. In addition, it had to work with limited current revenues; not even the steady increase in revenues from the forest sector during the favourable economic circumstances prevailing between 1867 and 1874 did much to improve the situation.

In the 1871 election, Chauveau was again victorious; he could now count on the support of about forty-five MLAs. The launching of the Catholic Program did not unduly disturb the course of events since only one *programmiste* was elected. It did, however, lead to the strengthening within the Conservative party of the ultramontane wing which opposed Chauveau and the Cartier school. Other problems — regional tensions and personality conflicts — led to wrangling within the party and brought about Chauveau's departure in 1873. One of his ministers, Gédéon Ouimet, succeeded him as premier. Ouimet also identified with the Cartier school and kept the ultramontanes out of power.

The Ouimet government continued the policies of the previous administration, but with the question of the debt resolved it was able to broaden the economic role of the state. It negotiated the first large Quebec loan, a $4-million issue in England. Most important, in 1874 it adopted a policy of subsidizing railways, and in particular of trying to speed up completion of two railway projects on the north shore of the St. Lawrence.

The Ouimet government had hardly any time to put its policies into practice before the Tanneries scandal erupted in 1874. A group of sharp land speculators succeeded in persuading the cabinet to exchange a parcel of land in the Montreal suburb of Saint-Henri des Tanneries, which the government owned and planned to use as the site of a hospital, for another piece of land which they claimed was of equal value but in reality was worth only a tenth as much. The affair mushroomed into a scandal and forced the Ouimet government to resign. According to the historian Marcel Hamelin, a scandal of this sort illustrates the carelessness that characterized public administration in Quebec and the corruption that reigned at the time.

The Conservatives' hold on power did not end with the fall of Ouimet. Charles-Eugène Boucher de Boucherville, a legislative councillor, stepped into the vacant premiership and formed a new cabinet with men who had not been involved in the scandal. The new premier introduced a major electoral reform that included, among other changes, the secret ballot, the use of nomination papers and the holding of elections on the same day in all ridings.

The 1875 election was held under the new electoral law. The Conservatives, having put the lid on their internal squabbles, retained power with little difficulty. In 1875, Premier de Boucherville reformed the educational system, after long

Charles Boucher de Boucherville (1822-1915), premier of Quebec, 1874-78 and 1891-92.

consultation with the bishops. The most important element of this reform was abolition of the Department of Public Instruction. Quebec's educational system would henceforth be administered by a senior civil servant, who was not accountable to the Legislative Assembly; his work would be under the control of the Council of Public Instruction and its Catholic and Protestant committees. In passing this law, the Legislative Assembly was for all practical purposes getting out of the field of education. The state ceded its prerogatives to the bishops and the Protestant leaders. It was a decision with serious consequences for the future of Quebec.

In another area, the de Boucherville government struggled with the severe depression that hit Quebec after 1874. One of Quebec's most important economic activities, the forest industry, was seriously affected, and the revenues that the government drew from it fell precipitously in 1874-75. Revenues from the sale of crown lands suffered the same fate.

But politicians devoted most of their attention to the railway question. In 1875, the government decided to take over the construction of the Quebec, Montreal, Ottawa and Occidental, on the north shore of the St. Lawrence and Ottawa rivers. The context in which this nationalization took place and the importance of this railway for Quebec's economic development were discussed in chapter 5. MLAs from the south shore demanded more assistance for their own railways, which were also in difficulty, and won their point in 1876. This policy forced the Quebec government to borrow substantial sums of money at a time when its ordinary revenues were undergoing a serious decline. The government had to impose new taxes; it was also counting on subsidies that a number of municipalities, among them Montreal and Quebec City, had promised for the north shore railway. In 1877, a misunderstanding occurred between the government and the municipalities over the route of the railway in the Montreal area. Invoking reasons of economy and efficiency, the government changed the route, deviating from the original plan. Most municipalities were dissatisfied with this change and refused to pay their share of the subsidy; the government introduced a bill to force them to pay. Protest meetings were held in Montreal, Quebec City and other municipalities. The Liberal party took up the affair and attacked the government unsparingly.

It was at this point that Lieutenant Governor Luc Letellier de Saint-Just entered the scene. Letellier was a Liberal who had been appointed to his position by the Liberal federal government of the time, and he wanted to put a Liberal government in power in Quebec. Using the municipalities bill and the premier's failure to consult him as a pretext, he dismissed the de Boucherville cabinet in March 1878 and called on the leader of the Liberal opposition, Henri-Gustave Joly, to replace him. His action was constitutionally dubious, and it became known as the "coup d'état of Letellier de Saint-Just."

Joly thus became the fourth premier of Quebec. With only a minority in the Legislative Assembly, he was unable to govern, and called an election in the hope of obtaining a majority.

Henri Gustave Joly (1829-1908), premier of Quebec, 1878-79, seen presenting a document to Lieutenant Governor Luc Letellier de Saint-Just.

Chapleau and the castors (1879-85)

Joly was in a position to take advantage of the discontent aroused by the policies of the de Boucherville government and improve the Liberals' standing in the 1878 election. He won about thirty seats, but it was not enough to assure him of a majority. A few independent Conservatives agreed to support him, allowing him to continue to govern, but his position was still precarious, and in the 1878 session, government bills were passed with a majority of only one vote. Byelections held in 1879 allowed Joly to increase this majority to four.

The Joly government also had to struggle with the effects of the depression. It cut government spending by eliminating some public positions and abolishing the provincial police. In June 1878, it had to face labour troubles as well. The contractors in charge of building the houses of parliament in Quebec City wanted to reduce wages from sixty to fifty cents a day. The workers protested by walking out and won the other construction workers of the city to their side. There were several demonstrations in the streets of Quebec City, and when some strikers looted a store the army was called out. The confrontation between strikers and soldiers ended with one dead and ten wounded.

Joly succeeded in completing the construction of the Quebec, Montreal, Ottawa and Occidental and calmed the tensions that had developed over the choice of the route. But he had to face strong opposition in the Legislative Assembly, led by Joseph-Adolphe Chapleau.

The Conservative party regained power in Ottawa in the fall of 1878 and a few months later decided to dismiss Luc Letellier de Saint-Just as lieutenant governor and replace him with a Conservative, Théodore Robitaille. Meanwhile, the Quebec Legislative Council, which had a Conservative majority, obstructed the Joly government by refusing to vote supply and thus leaving it without funds. Chapleau succeeded in persuading five government MLAs to change sides, and in the fall of 1879 the Joly government was defeated in the house and had to give way to a Conservative government headed by Chapleau.

The fifth premier of Quebec governed in favourable circumstances. The depression vanished, and the early 1880s witnessed an economic recovery stimulated by railway investments tied to the building of the Canadian Pacific and by the industrialization that followed adoption of the protective tariff of 1879.

The financial activity of the government was highlighted by its entry into the French market. Quebec floated its first loan in France in 1881, a $4-million issue handled principally by the Banque de Paris et des Pays Bas. This bank decided to invest further in Quebec by establishing a company, the Crédit Foncier Franco-Canadien, with the aim of lending to farmers, municipalities and parishes. Chapleau himself was involved in the creation of the Crédit Foncier.

Clearly the main question preoccupying the Chapleau administration, however, was the government railway. Chapleau appointed the businessman Louis-Adélard Sénécal manager of the enterprise. His chief priority was to sell the railway, which was costing the government a lot a money and forcing it to borrow heavily. The government wanted the QMO&O to become the Quebec link in the Canadian Pacific network, but the Canadian Pacific was interested at first only in the western portion between Ottawa and Montreal, which it bought in 1882; the eastern portion was sold to a financial syndicate led by Sénécal.

The ties betweeen Chapleau and Sénécal aroused opposition from some Con-

This cartoon shows Premier Chapleau trying to sell the Quebec, Montreal, Ottawa and Occidental Railway to the federal government.

servatives, notably the ultramontanes. The Conservative party had managed to re-establish its unity after the coup d'état in 1878 in order to mount an effective opposition to the Joly government, but Chapleau's accession to power reawakened hostilities. The tension between the two wings reached a peak. Chapleau systematically kept the ultramontanes out of power, while the ultramontanes in turn virulently attacked the premier's running of the province. To solve the problem, Chapleau hoped to establish a coalition of Liberal and Conservative "moderates," and even began negotiations with Honoré Mercier on this subject, but they came to naught.

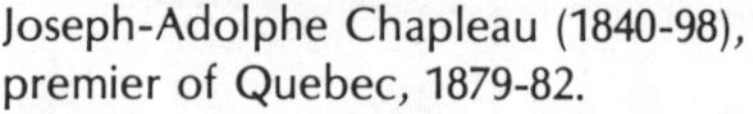

Joseph-Adolphe Chapleau (1840-98), premier of Quebec, 1879-82.

Joseph-Alfred Mousseau (1838-86), premier of Quebec, 1882-84.

The 1881 election, in which some fifty Conservative MLAs were elected, strengthened Chapleau's position in the party and in the Assembly. After the sale of the railway in 1882, he decided to switch to the federal scene where he hoped to become Macdonald's Quebec lieutenant. He quickly became a minister in Macdonald's cabinet, while another federal minister, Joseph-Alfred Mousseau, made the reverse switch and became premier of Quebec.

Under Chapleau's domination and lacking his stature, Mousseau was quickly placed in an uncomfortable position. The ultramontanes girded up for battle and intensified their attacks against the ruling group. Apart from the premier, their main target was the Chapleau-Sénécal tandem. Mousseau tried in vain to come to an agreement with the ultramontanes, and resigned for the sake of peace early in 1884.

He was replaced by John Jones Ross, who was fairly close to the ultramontanes. The fall of Mousseau marked the establishment of a new set of power relationships within the Conservative party and from this point on the ultramontanes had their place in the cabinet. On the Liberal side, Honoré Mercier succeeded Joly as party leader in 1883.

Mercier: The Quebec state asserts itself (1886-91)

Ross's accession to power ushered in a period of calm. The government seemed in no hurry to proceed with large projects. With their newly re-established unity and a large majority in the Assembly, the Conservatives did not feel seriously threatened by the Liberals. But in 1885, the quiet in Quebec City was disturbed by Riel's hanging. The effects of this event on party alignments have already been mentioned. The Quebec Conservative party felt the repercussions of the federal government's refusal to commute Riel's death sentence. Honoré Mercier founded the Parti National, made up mostly of Liberals but including some Conservatives, who became known as National Conservatives.

In the 1886 election, Mercier took full advantage of the Riel affair and the Parti National won a majority. The Conservatives tried to stay in power by wooing the National Conservatives away from Mercier, but without success. In a final manoeuvre, Ross resigned in favour of the ultramontane Louis-Olivier Taillon, but Taillon was premier only four days. When the session opened in January 1887, he was defeated in the house and had to resign. Honoré Mercier became premier of Quebec.

The Mercier government was characterized by its French-Canadian national-

John Jones Ross (1833-1901), premier of Quebec, 1884-87, began a period of ultramontane influence.

Louis-Olivier Taillon (1840-1923), premier of Quebec for a few days in 1887 and from 1892 to 1896.

ism. This theme was the integrating element that made possible the alliance between the Liberals and the National Conservatives. It was the central theme of the 1886 election and it strongly coloured Mercier's actions as premier.

The corollary of Mercier's exaltation of nationalism was a degree of social and political conservatism. To be sure of the support of the National Conservatives, the Liberals had to de-emphasize some of the more radical aspects of their program, notably educational reforms and measures that could be seen to increase government intervention or challenge traditional institutions.

Quebec nationalism can be expressed through demands that Ottawa respect provincial autonomy. Mercier's forceful assertion of these demands was an innovation in Quebec political life. He convoked the first interprovincial conference since Confederation, at Quebec City in 1887; five provincial premiers participated.

The advocacy of French-Canadian Catholic nationalism by a Quebec premier provoked negative reactions from English Protestants both in Quebec and in the other provinces of Canada. These reactions manifested themselves in the agitation that followed resolution of the Jesuit Estates question in 1888. This was unfinished business left over from the British Conquest. The British crown had seized the estates belonging to the Jesuits and appropriated for educational purposes the revenues that came from these estates. The return of the Jesuits to Quebec in the mid-nineteenth century raised the question of the retrocession of the estates or equivalent compensation to the Jesuit order.

Honoré Mercier (1840-94), premier of Quebec, 1887-91.

However, there was disagreement within the clergy on this point. The bishops reasoned that the estates should not go to the Jesuits alone but to the Catholic church in Quebec as a whole, for educational purposes. Because of this disagreement, successive premiers of Quebec failed to resolve the question. Mercier decided to negotiate directly with Rome. He offered the Catholic Church in Quebec compensation totalling $400,000, with the pope deciding how it should be divided between the Jesuits and other religious institutions. To make this decision acceptable to the minority, he offered $60,000 for English Protestant universities and colleges. There was great commotion among the Orangemen of Ontario, who took offence at the pope's intervening in a British country and argued that the minority had been unjustly treated. To fight Mercier's action, they founded the Equal Rights Association, which advocated English unilingualism in Canada and launched an anti-French-Canadian campaign in Ontario and Manitoba.

In the economic sphere, the Mercier government embarked on a major program of public expenditures — road building and paving and construction of iron bridges and railways. One result of its program was a substantial increase in borrowing. Particular emphasis was placed on the need to complete railways in remote parts of the province and colonization regions. Clearly the most important of these was the Quebec and Lake St. John Railway, which was inaugurated as far as Roberval in 1887 and reached Chicoutimi in 1893.

By bringing railways to these regions, the government had a larger objective in mind — it hoped to improve the lot of the regions' inhabitants, increase the profitability of their agriculture and make it easier for farmers in the regions to market their products. This was also the aim of the new Forest Act adopted in 1888, which was directed towards making a clearer separation between colonization regions and timber lands. But Mercier's most spectacular move in this area was to elevate colonization to the rank of a department with the creation of a Department of Agriculture and Colonization. What is more, he brought in Curé Labelle as deputy minister.

Taken together, Mercier's actions can be seen as a *politique de grandeur*, accompanied by pomp and showy gestures and aimed, like all *politiques de grandeur*, at outside recognition. During five years in power, Mercier went to France and Rome twice and participated in a major Catholic congress in Baltimore. He was received everywhere with full honours. France, Belgium and the Vatican conferred decorations on him.

Mercier's prestige and popularity grew, and in the 1890 election the Liberals obtained a clear majority of seats. But within a few months everything was thrown into uncertainty again. Corruption had taken root in the premier's entourage, and in 1891 the Baie des Chaleurs scandal broke out. The contractor in charge of building the Baie des Chaleurs railway had obtained from the government a subsidy of $175,000 to which he was not entitled. He had got it through the agency of Ernest Pacaud, the Liberal party treasurer, whom he had paid $100,000, making in possible for Pacaud to pay the debts of certain ministers. Even though a commission was unable to establish that Mercier knew of this transaction, Lieutenant Governor Auguste-Réal Angers fired the premier and called on de Boucherville to succeed him.

The end of a régime (1891-97)

De Boucherville was now premier for the second time. Since the 1890 election had given a large majority to the Liberals, he was faced with an Assembly that was hostile to him, and so called an election for early 1892. The Conservatives used the Baie des Chaleurs scandal and other cases of corruption against Mercier, and most of the National Conservatives separated from Mercier and returned to the Conservative fold. It was the end of the Parti National as Mercier had conceived it. The exploitation of the scandals led to a complete reversal of the results of the 1890 election. The Conservatives swept Quebec and found themselves back in power opposite a decimated Liberal party.

This massive return of Quebecers to the Conservatives was more an accident that a realignment of forces. The Conservative party was in decline. The old quarrels between ultramontanes and moderates started again. At the same time Wilfrid Laurier, the federal Liberal leader, solidly entrenched his party in Quebec and laid the groundwork for the fall of the Conservatives at both levels of government.

In Quebec, de Boucherville, who sat not in the Assembly but in the Legislative Council, remained at the head of the government for only a year, and in 1892 gave way to Louis-Olivier Taillon. Coming on the heels of Mercier and his *politique de grandeur*, the de Boucherville and Taillon administrations seemed fairly dull. It was a time for the government to lower its sights.

The two premiers operated under circumstances not particularly favourable to them. The first half of the 1890s was a period of slow economic growth, and Mercier's heavy spending had seriously burdened government finances. The Conservatives had to practise a policy of economy, abolishing some positions and postponing public works. They also had to impose new taxes that turned out to be highly unpopular.

Like others before it, the Taillon government turned to France for loans. In 1893, it negotiated a two-year renewal of a short-term loan that Mercier had floated in 1891, but it wanted to replace this loan with a long-term issue and opened negotiations on this question in 1894. The provincial treasurer, J.S. Hall, was against this projected French loan. Hall represented the large Montreal financial institutions in the cabinet and was closely linked to the Bank of Montreal group. He wanted to borrow on the English market instead and, faced with the opposition of the premier, resigned from the cabinet. The English-language press carried on a campaign against Taillon and the conflict over the financial question quickly acquired an ethnic flavour. There was a risk that the English-speaking MLAs would go over in a group to the opposition, but the government managed to fend off this threat.

Edmund James Flynn (1847-1927), premier of Quebec, 1896-97.

In the economic field, the de Boucherville and Taillon governments were characterized, according to the historian Robert Rumilly, by an emphasis on agricultural development, carried out not through spectacular moves but rather through a number of measures aimed at supporting the activities of regional groups and improving the quality of agricultural products. The conversion of Quebec agriculture to dairy production increased in scale in the 1890s. The government subsidized the establishment of a school for the dairy industry in Saint-Hyacinthe and encouraged the formation of agricultural circles and co-operatives.

The Quebec Conservatives were affected by the difficulties that the party was experiencing on the federal level. In Ottawa, the death of Sir John A. Macdonald, internal rivalries, the rapid succession of prime ministers (five in five years) and especially the debate surrounding the Manitoba Schools question weakened the party. During the 1896 election, Taillon agreed to resign as premier of Quebec to enter the federal struggle. It was a futile gesture as Wilfrid Laurier, as head of the Liberal party, won the election and became the first prime minister of French-Canadian origin since Confederation. In Quebec, Edmund James Flynn succeeded Taillon as the head of the government. But Laurier's victory and his increasing hold over Quebec made it clear that the end of the provincial Conservative régime, a régime that had dominated the Quebec political scene for thirty years, was not far off. With an election expected in 1897, Flynn tried to improve the image of his government, but he was unable to hold back the wave of popularity enjoyed by Laurier and the Liberals. The Liberals took two-thirds of the seats in the 1897 election and Félix-Gabriel Marchand became premier; this was the beginning of the Liberal reign that would last without interruption until 1936.

CHAPTER 15
THE FEDERAL GOVERNMENT AND QUEBEC

The new constitution that went into effect on July 1, 1867 instituted a system of government that had both a federal and a provincial level. What would be the attitude of Quebecers in general and their representatives in particular towards this new system? What share of the power in the new institutions and in the political decisionmaking process would be accorded to Quebec, and to French Canadians?

Quebecers and Federal Institutions

The régime was conceived by politicians meeting behind closed doors, and it is not surprising that it was greeted with little enthusiasm by French-speaking Quebecers. With the voters apparently more interested in discussing local problems than constitutional questions, the first federal election was in no sense a referendum on Confederation. The Rouges, led by Antoine-Aimé Dorion and supported by young nationalists grouped around the newspaper *L'Union Nationale* and the Club Saint-Jean-Baptiste, had been trying unsuccessfully since 1864 to rouse the people against the proposed federation. The Conservatives, led by George-Étienne Cartier and supported by powerful Montreal financial interests, London, and the clergy, maintained their hold on Quebec and succeeded in winning forty-five of its sixty-five seats. In the provincial election that was held at the same time (this didn't add to the clarity of the debate) the Conservatives did even better, electing fifty members in the sixty-five-seat house. The opposition, defeated, quickly resigned itself to Confederation as a *fait accompli*. For many years to come, the legitimacy of the new system would be challenged only by a few individuals on the margins of political life. Quebec, or at least its political élite, even appeared to regard the federal government as the more significant of the two. The domination of the Chauveau government by Cartier and Langevin in the era of the double mandate and the resignation of a premier of Quebec such as Chapleau to become an ordinary minister in Ottawa are indications of this attitude.

It was partly due to the considerable powers and financial resources at Ottawa's disposal. In addition, Ottawa appeared to be the only government in a position to protect French and Catholic minorities outside Quebec, and this too influenced French-speaking Quebecers. Meanwhile, English Quebecers also regarded Ottawa as the more significant political stage, although they did not neglect Quebec politics and were vigilant in defending their educational rights and the financial interests of business. The hierarchy of governments was also reflected in the political vocabulary that came into use. The head of the federal government bore the title of prime minister, while Quebec's leader was a premier; the lower house in Ottawa was called the House of Commons, just as in London, while the provincial lower houses were called legislative assemblies; the crown's representative in Ottawa was a governor general while its representative in Quebec City was a lieutenant governor; Ottawa had a parliament and Quebec City had a legislature.

French-speaking Quebecers did not show dissatisfaction towards the new régime even though it involved reduction in their influence in Ottawa. Under the Union régime, Upper and Lower Canada had equal representation in both houses of the legislature. Confederation decreased Quebec's relative strength. In the House of Commons, provinces were represented strictly in proportion to their population. Thus, Ontario had eighty-two seats to Quebec's sixty-five in 1867, and ninety-two to Quebec's sixty-five in 1896. Quebec's position became steadily worse as new provinces entered the federation; in 1867, Quebec had sixty-five seats in a 181-seat House, while in 1896 Quebec's representation had remained at sixty-five but the total number of members had increased to 213. Representation to the Senate was on a regional basis, and Quebec and Ontario each had twenty-four seats. But the total number of senators was seventy-two in 1867, while in 1896 it was eighty-one.

It should be noted, however, that French Canadians were a minority even under the Union régime. There were always some English-speaking members from Lower Canada elected to both houses of parliament. Immediately after Confederation, some fifteen of Quebec's representatives in the House of Commons, as well as a number of senators, were English-speaking. On the other hand, the French Canadians of Quebec had majority control of a provincial government under the new régime.

In the parliamentary system, the cabinet and especially the first minister enjoy considerable power. Confederation brought about significant changes in this area. Under the Union régime, the cabinet had been led jointly by an English Canadian and a French Canadian, and governments were identified by the names of both leaders: Baldwin-LaFontaine, Brown-Sicotte, Macdonald-Cartier and the like. Immediately after Confederation, Governor General Lord Monck called on Sir

John A. Macdonald alone to form a government, and thus made a clean break with this important tradition. In addition, Quebec had the right to only four cabinet posts, one of which was reserved for an English Quebecer. French Canadians outside Quebec were not represented, and instead of at least four French-Canadian ministers from Quebec as there had been in cabinets under the Union régime, there were now only three out of thirteen or fourteen. Thus, between 1867 and 1896, French-speaking Quebecers held from twenty-one to twenty-five per cent of the cabinet posts. The positions they did hold were generally secondary, such as secretary of state or revenue, or portfolios where patronage was important, such as public works, the post office or agriculture.

The Political Ascendancy of Ottawa

The instruments of the federal government's power over Quebec were not only constitutional and financial but political as well. The operation of the two-party system was very effective from this point of view. The Liberal and Conservative parties were both federal and provincial organizations, and federal politicians had close ties with their provincial counterparts. Under the Union régime, especially during the 1840s, French Canadians formed a sufficiently large and homogeneous group that they had the effective capacity to block the operation of parliamentary institutions. Lord Elgin, governor in the late 1840s, was very conscious of this phenomenon and explained to London that the institutions would function smoothly when the French Canadians were divided between the two major parties, Tory and Reform. In the 1850s and 1860s, even though French Canadians were active in both parties, the French-Canadian Conservatives were still a large enough group that their influence on the operation of the government was substantial. After Confederation, there was still a bloc of thirty-five or forty MPs that could threaten the government with defeat, but this threat was not as powerful as it had been before. Occasions arose when the French-speaking Quebec MPs exercised pressure to obtain a decision in their interest, such as the dismissal of Lieutenant Governor Letellier after his "coup d'état" or a grant of a few million dollars to the QMO&O Railway. But in general, French-speaking MPs were divided first by party, second by region, and finally by interests and personalities. Most of the time, the government could impose party discipline on them, as their re-election depended on it. The same party system operated at the provincial level, and provincial MLAs avoided criticizing their federal counterparts for fear of causing harm to their own party. With the Conservatives almost perpetually in power in both Ottawa and Quebec City, the party system was extremely effective in maintaining peace between the federal and Quebec governments; in this respect Quebec differed from the other provinces.

The double mandate, which allowed a member to have a seat in both Ottawa and Quebec City at the same time, was in effect between 1867 and 1873 and played a direct role in maintaining federal domination. The first Chauveau government in particular was accused of being under the sway of the federal government through Cartier and Langevin, who were ordinary MLAs in Quebec City but influential ministers in Ottawa. Abolition of the double mandate made federal dominance less visible, but parties still had the same workers and organizations at the two levels.

Relations between Governments

Macdonald and the other Fathers of Confederation hoped that Canada would become an increasingly centralized state, but events between 1867 and 1896 were not favourable to their aspirations. During these first thirty years, the provinces succeeded in establishing their identity while the federal government was deterred from pursuing its ambitions of centralizing the country.

The general framework

With the large size and diversity of the new Dominion of Canada, a less centralized form of federalism was a necessity. This tendency was further encouraged by the staunch traditions of autonomy in the former colonies which, though brought together by Confederation, did not acknowledge any great loyalty towards the new political entity it had created. The ethnic and religious tensions that tend to tear the country apart make its unification even more difficult. And the dissatisfaction of the provinces at the meagre resources accorded to them by the agreement reached in 1867 was exacerbated by the unfavourable economic situation that prevailed between 1873 and 1896.

The evolution towards a more decentralized federalism was endorsed and encouraged by the Privy Council in London, which served as the court of last resort in constitutional matters. Through its decisions, the Privy Council supported the autonomist views of the provincial leaders — and, no doubt, of the people who elected them, whose natural identification was more likely to be with the province than with the central government.

Starting with the federal election of 1867, Nova Scotia vigorously expressed its opposition to the new régime, under which it lost the autonomy it had previously enjoyed; of the eighteen MPs it sent to Ottawa in 1867, seventeen were opposed to Confederation. A veto from London and increased subsidies were needed before its desire to secede was quieted. Even then, in 1886 the government of Premier W.S. Fielding again threatened to take Nova Scotia out of Canada, which Fielding blamed for his province's economic difficulties.

Ottawa did not find much more cause for satisfaction in the West, where Manitoba and British Columbia were unhappy with the stagnation from which they suffered and the federal railway policy that held back their development. On top of the West's economic difficulties, there was also the problem of the Métis and Indians, many of whom followed Louis Riel in twice taking up arms against

Ottawa. These two rebellions had ramifications for relations between French and English Canadians and placed the federal government in a difficult situation. The schools questions in New Brunswick and later in Manitoba were additional burdens on the federal government; the two provinces appeared to be in competition to see which one could provide a clearer demonstration that federalism was not a miraculous solution to ethnic tensions. The inability of the federal government to intervene effectively in these conflicts as a result of pressure from the majority indirectly favoured provincial autonomy. The prestige of the federal government was weakened, at least in the eyes of French Canadians in Quebec and the other provinces.

As a crowning touch, even the richest and most influential province in the country was vigorously opposed to Ottawa's centralist views. Between 1867 and 1896, the fight for provincial autonomy was led by Ontario. The Ontario Liberal party, which formed the provincial opposition in the years following 1868, attacked the centralizing manoeuvres of the federal Conservatives. The Liberals were in favour of Confederation, but they emphatically reminded Ottawa that federalism meant union and separation at the same time. One basic reason for Ontario's support of Confederation was its wish to control its own local affairs and avoid what was referred to as "French domination." In addition, as the richest province, Ontario was relatively independent of Ottawa, even during hard times. People in Ontario were aware that as federal power and expenditures increased, so would the extent to which they would have to subsidize the less fortunate provinces. With the Liberals in power under Oliver Mowat, premier from 1872 to 1896, the Ontario government repeatedly and successfully challenged federal decisions, both before its consistently faithful electorate and before the highest court in the Empire, the British Privy Council.

Because the drafting of the BNA Act was uncommonly obscure, the courts were called upon to play an important role in interpreting it. In a series of decisions, notably between 1883 and 1896, the Privy Council interpreted the constitution in a way that was highly favourable to advocates of provincial autonomy. It came out against the idea that the provinces were subordinate to the federal government in the areas attributed to them by the constitution. The judges wrote in 1883: "Within these limits [Article 92] of subjects and areas the local legislature is supreme and has the same authority as the Imperial Parliament, or the Parliament of the Dominion, would have had under like circumstances."

By force of circumstance, this theory of the sovereignty of the provinces within their sphere of jurisdiction led to limitations on the federal right of disallowance and even on the general character of the preamble to Article 91, which authorizes the federal government "to make Laws for the Peace, Order and Good Government of Canada." The Privy Council regarded it as necessary to impose rigorous restrictions on the powers of the federal government, especially its residual powers and its "declaratory" power to invoke the national dimension of local problems. Failure to do this, the Council argued, "would practically destroy the

Cartoon commenting on centralization in the Macdonald era.

autonomy of the provinces." Similar reasoning led the Council to recognize the lieutenant governors as direct representatives of the crown in the provinces rather than ordinary civil servants — in other words, the provincial parliaments were not just local councils.

The struggle for provincial autonomy had a partisan aspect, in that Liberal premiers were able to combine business with pleasure in fighting the Macdonald Conservatives. It also had a patronage aspect that was very important at election time. But beyond these elements, it was a movement that corresponded to the pronounced individuality of the different regions of Canada, which helped tilt the new country towards decentralization.

The same constitution was in effect in 1896 as in 1867, but the interpretation that had been given to it had substantially changed the balance between the federal government and the provinces. The provincial governments had the support of their electorates in their struggle for autonomy. Carrying on the struggle individually or acting as a group, as at the time of the first interprovincial conference in 1887, they succeeded in gaining a degree of autonomy that was inherent in the logic of the federal system.

The case of Quebec

Between 1867 and 1896, all French-speaking politicians in Quebec were in favour of provincial autonomy in principle, but with the exception of Honoré Mercier, they did little in practice to advance the cause. The determining factor in federal-provincial relations was the partisan spirit that prevailed among both Conservatives and Liberals. The Conservatives held power in both Ottawa and Quebec City throughout the thirty-year period except for the years 1873-79 and 1887-91. The Quebec Conservatives were dominated by their federal colleagues, and didn't dare do anything that might hurt the federal wing of their party. The Liberals also acted from partisanship and took up the cause of autonomy when it coincided with their narrow political interest.

Unlike Ontario, Quebec was in a precarious financial situation, and as a result was more dependent on Ottawa and less sensitive to the question of provincial rights than Ontario was. Thus, soon after Confederation, Quebec abdicated its role in immigration policy, leaving Ottawa a clear field. By making minimal financial concessions (resolution of the Quebec-Ontario debt, subsidies for the QMO&O), Prime Minister Macdonald prevented autonomy from becoming a major issue in Quebec. The provincial Conservatives took the position that by obtaining more money for Quebec from Ottawa, they were making it possible to avoid imposing direct taxes and thus effectively defending provincial autonomy. Even George-Étienne Cartier shared this view. Cartier realized that the change from the unitary institutions of the Union régime to a provincial government that could be dominated by French-speaking Quebecers constituted political progress for the francophone population of Quebec. But he still argued that one advantage to the provincial government would be that this arrangement would not cost very much and would not have to resort to direct taxes because of the large subsidies it would receive from Ottawa. It was fifteen years before another point of view, that of Honoré Mercier, was heard. Going against the commonly held position, Mercier contended that "the day when we have to count, unavoidably and without any other recourse, on the government in Ottawa as our only instrument for extricating ourselves from the financial embarrassments we fall into — that will be the day of our national disgrace."

French-speaking Quebecers not only regarded Ottawa as the "big" government, but also counted on it to protect the religious and educational rights of French-Canadian minorities outside Quebec. Many English-speaking Canadians, meanwhile, opposed federal intervention in the name of provincial autonomy. As a result of the ethnic quarrels that arose and Ottawa's powerlessness to resolve them, French-speaking Quebecers gradually turned more towards the government of Quebec. With Honoré Mercier, premier from 1887 to 1891, provincial autonomy became the political expression of Quebec nationalism.

This new attitude had been gestating for a number of years, and the Liberals, almost perpetually in opposition, turned it to their political advantage by attacking the government for being under the sway of the federal Conservatives. They vigorously criticized the double mandate. Wilfrid Laurier said on this issue: "With the single mandate, Quebec is Quebec; with the double mandate, it only becomes an appendix to Ottawa." In this case, as in the affair of Letellier de Saint-Just's "coup d'état," the Liberals came to the defence of provincial autonomy. It should be noted, however, that this coincided with their partisan interest, and they were less favourable to autonomy in other circumstances, especially when they were in power in Ottawa.

Honoré Mercier's advocacy of autonomy, while not entirely free of partisanship, was unique in that it appeared to constitute a coherent line of thought. Mercier's thinking was influenced by that of Judge T.-J.-J. Loranger, who in turn borrowed ideas current in Ontario. In his *Lettres sur l'interprétation de la Constitution*, Judge Loranger argued that the provinces were not subordinate to the federal government; rather, each level of government was sovereign in its own area of jurisdiction. In addition, he maintained that the federal government was created by the provinces, and endowed by them only with certain powers to pursue goals that transcended provincial boundaries. Mercier used these ideas to support his campaign for provincial autonomy.

Along with these legal arguments, Mercier also put the case for autonomy on more nationalistic grounds. The Riel affair provided him with an opportunity to emphasize this dimension. In particular, he argued that in order to defend their rights French Canadians had to unite across party lines, even to the extent of forming a national party. On a deeper level, he concluded that French Canadians could be assured of their rights only in Quebec. As premier, he endeavoured to stimulate French-Canadian pride and emphasized the French and Catholic character of Quebec in his speeches.

However, neither Mercier nor any other premier of Quebec during the period questioned federalism as such. Thus Mercier, along with Premier Mowat of Ontario, convoked the first interprovincial conference in Quebec City in 1887; the federal government refused to participate. The two main demands of the

The first interprovincial conference, held in Quebec City in 1887, put Ottawa on guard against the possibility of a provincial common front. Seated from left to right are premiers A.G. Blair (New Brunswick), Honoré Mercier (Quebec), Sir Oliver Mowat (Ontario), W.S. Fielding (Nova Scotia) and John Norquay (Manitoba).

provinces were readjustment of the subsidies paid to the provinces and limitation of the central government's right of disallowance. Although the conference's impact on the federal government does not appear to have been great, Ottawa did have to note the possibility of a provincial common front against its policies.

Between 1867 and 1896, Quebec followed Ontario's lead in the struggle for provincial autonomy. However, the ethnic and religious conflicts that characterized the period had the effect of exacerbating French-Canadian nationalism. As a result, French-speaking Quebecers began to have a sense of the importance of their provincial government.

CULTURE AND IDEOLOGY

Apart from the material features of the economy and society, there are other realities of human life, located more at the level of artistic productions and of ideas. This is the area of discourse, writing, painting — in short, the area where language, in whatever form in takes, is used to render an account of reality and of its transformation.

It is there that a given society derives its vision of the past and its schemes for the future; it is also there that a society reveals its deepest values. We have chosen to deal with two of the principal manifestations of this society — ideologies and culture.

CHAPTER 16
NEW THEMES

In a society such as Quebec where a variety of groups co-exist — different social classes, different ethnic groups, special groups such as the clergy — a variety of ideologies may grow up; sometimes these ideologies will be compatible, while other times they will be opposed. Some ideologies are more rigorously developed or more widely diffused than others, and there is a strong temptation for the historian to pay attention only to those that are most articulately expressed. This has been the case in Quebec, where historians have emphasized the opposition between the most radical liberals and the most reactionary ultramontanes. For a long time, they pictured the last decades of the nineteenth century as being dominated by what is called the ideology of conservation or clerical-nationalist ideology, which was developed by the clergy and ruling élites and emphasized the Catholic, French, rural and conservative character of French-Canadian society. With recent research, a serious challenge to this view has begun, and it has been realized that the ideological landscape did not have the unclouded simplicity that had been attributed to it.

To get a clearer view of the situation, a number of themes will be examined and the positions of different groups on each of these questions will be compared. Three major components of the ideologies being examined will be looked at in turn — their views of socio-economic structures, their conceptions of the social and political order, and their definitions of the nation and nationalism. An attempt will then be made to see how these elements came together within the different ideological currents.

Ideologies and Socio-Economic Structures

To understand the first component of late-nineteenth-century Quebec ideologies, it is necessary to recall some elements of the economic context of the time. A large majority of the population of Quebec was rural and agricultural, but many of these people were trying to improve their lot by moving to the city or out of Quebec. The capitalist system was also developing in Quebec in the natural resources and industrial sectors.

The basic picture: economic liberalism

In Quebec, as elsewhere, in the second half of the nineteenth century, economic liberalism was clearly the ideology on the rise. It emphasized the individual more than the collectivity and regarded the progress of society as being composed of a sum of individual successes. An especially high value was attached to private ownership and enterprise. Liberalism was opposed to anything that might seem to have a socialist orientation and especially to trade unionism and collective action by the working class. It also emphasized the idea of progress, which was regarded as both necessary and beneficial. Economic development was seen as synonymous with progress. Statements of the need to encourage new investments, stimulate production and exchange, and develop agriculture, industry and commerce were common in this era. Liberal ideology valued individual effort, work and education; it maintained that success and wealth were accessible to everyone who worked hard and didn't give up. There was a place in the sun for everyone, and all the individual had to do was take it. Testimony to the validity of this principle was provided by the many "success stories" — biographies of poor immigrants and farmers' sons whose energy and talent led them to become powerful, rich and respected businessmen.

Economic liberalism was the ideology of the bourgeoisie. Its most forceful exponent was the economically dominant English-speaking bourgeoisie, and its most important vehicle was the English Montreal press. Other transmitters of the ideology were reports of the Board of Trade and the many publications appearing throughout the period that trumpeted the glory of economic development and material progress.

The French-speaking bourgeoisie, not to be outdone, came increasingly to share the ideology of economic liberalism, to which it added the idea of *rattrapage*, or catching up. French-Canadian businessmen had to have their place in the sun, their slice of the pie. They regarded it as self-evident that *rattrapage* would be achieved not through government intervention of any sort but through work and individual effort, although this belief did not prevent them from demanding their share of the generous support that the three levels of government gave to private enterprise. Marcel Hamelin has amply shown how Quebec politicians, between 1867 and 1896, forcefully expressed the ideology of economic liberalism. The same ideas were presented in the French-language business press, which grew up towards the end of the century and has been studied by the historian Yves Saint-Germain. The biographies of businessmen and studies of companies that appeared in newspapers and specialized publications were opportunities to emphasize the importance of personal effort and perseverance, rewarded by success and wealth. The French-speaking bourgeoisie, along with its political spokesmen, wanted full economic development for Quebec and supported improvements in agriculture.

Agriculturalism: the physiocratic reaction

Some elements within Quebec's ruling groups did not share the economic liberals' optimistic vision of the future or their goal of material progress. When they looked at Quebec society, they saw old socio-economic structures crumbling, the pre-eminence of rural life being challenged and thousands of farmers abandoning the land to settle in the cities of Quebec and the United States. The ideology they adopted in reaction to this was physiocratic, and is generally called agriculturalism; their advocacy of it was sometimes vociferous.

In the late nineteenth century, agriculture was still the occupation of a majority of Quebecers, and it was accorded a prominent place in social programs. But while businessmen discussed agriculture in terms of improved production, specialization and access to markets, agriculturalists spoke of traditions, moral values and ways of life and expressed themselves in theological terms. According to the historian Michel Brunet, "agriculturalism was above all a general way of thinking, a philosophy of life that idealized the past, condemned the present and was suspicious of the modern social order. It was a rejection of the contemporary industrial age based on a static conception of society." Agriculturalist thinkers saw agriculture as an ideal way of life in which the human being blossoms in communion with God and nature. In the city, by contrast, he was condemned to perdition; when the farmer came to the city, he lost his economic independence and the simple life gave way to a taste for luxury. The agriculturalists wanted to slow down the process of industrialization and stem the rural exodus through agricultural colonization.

The most prominent group espousing agriculturalism was the Roman Catholic clergy. Its resistance to change was a product of the profound conservatism that characterized the Catholic church as a whole in the nineteenth century. Rural society corresponded to the Catholic ideal, and it was in the countryside that the clergy could best exercise its spiritual and moral control. The country *curé* led his flock, sharing power only with a few *notables*, while in the city it was not easy for a priest to exercise the same degree of influence. Thus, a question of power was involved, and it is possible that the material base of this power entered into the church's thinking as well. The church had large investments in the countryside, and it might have seen the rural exodus as a threat to these investments. This is, however, only a hypothesis, as there has been little study by historians of the economic activities of the church and the clergy. It should also be noted that the agriculturalist clergy saw the rural character of the French-Canadian nation as one of its essential qualities, along with its Catholicism and its Frenchness.

Agriculturalists came from outside the clergy as well — lay intellectuals, farmers, and representatives of the petty and middle bourgeoisie adhered to the ideology. But it is clear that the Quebec bourgeoisie as a whole did not accept the tenets of agriculturalism, which constituted a negation of economic liberalism. It did not agree to put the brake on industrialization, curb the development of capitalism or slow down material progress. Marcel Hamelin has shown that members of the Quebec legislature just after Confederation spoke of agriculture in economic terms and that their speeches were not at all agriculturalist. The subsidies they gave to agriculture and colonization were responses to economic imperatives — as well as electoral considerations, since rural Quebecers constituted a majority of the electorate. To argue that the ruling classes in Quebec unanimously and unreservedly adhered to agriculturalism does not appear to correspond to the historical evidence. The clergy clearly represented a force and the ruling bourgeoisie had to reckon with it, but not at the price of a dilution of economic liberalism. Instead, it made concessions to the clergy in the area of social control.

Egalitarian resistance: the ideology of labour

In the late nineteenth century another ideology grew up, distinct from economic liberalism and agriculturalism. It came out of the labour movement and was egalitarian in nature. Developed primarily by the Knights of Labor in the 1880s and 1890s, this ideology challenged some postulates of economic liberalism. The Knights of Labor were not opposed to industrialization and technical progress, but they recognized that contrary to what the exponents of liberalism maintained, opportunity is not equal for everyone and diligent work is not generally rewarded with success and wealth. In their view, the capitalist system led mainly to the exploitation of labour by capital. The Knights advocated the redistribution of wealth, carried out by the workers on a basis of fairness, and proposed replacing wage labour with a co-operative system.

The Knights' best-known spokesman was Alphonse Télésphore Lépine, elected to the federal House of Commons by a working-class Montreal constituency in 1888. The egalitarian ideology, however, remained marginal in Quebec; the Knights of Labor were concentrated in Montreal and did not have newspapers at their disposal to propagate their ideas outside trade union circles.

A watered-down variant of egalitarian ideology began to be developed by the unions of the American Federation of Labor in the 1890s. The AF of L did not challenge capitalism and economic liberalism, but only sought to ensure workers a larger share of its rewards. It acknowledged that the system led to the concentration of capital, and maintained that to deal with it workers also had to become concentrated and bargain collectively instead of acting individually. The more radical versions of egalitarian ideology, socialism and communism, had no effective presence in Quebec, at least not in the form of organized groups.

Ideologies and Socio-Political Organization

Ideological divisions take on a somewhat different appearance when they are looked at from the point of view of socio-political organization. Late-nineteenth-century Quebec society was characterized by a widespread conservatism. Some people wanted to intensify this conservatism still further; the position of radicalism, on the other hand, was very much marginal.

A *widespread conservatism*

Historians have little difficulty agreeing that the late-nineteenth-century Canadian bourgeoisie was deeply conservative. This characteristic was especially clear in the attitude of businessmen and politicians towards the social problems created by industrialization. There was no perceptible willingness on their part to change the situation and come to terms with new social realities. Canada was always behind the United States and England in these areas and the fate to which the recommendations of the Royal Commission on the Relations of Labour and Capital were consigned accurately reflected the state of mind of Canada's ruling groups. Another manifestation of the prevailing conservatism was the continuing force of religious and family traditions. Religious divisions that had begun to crumble elsewhere remained intact in Canadian society in the late nineteenth century.

In Quebec, conservatism was accentuated by the presence of a powerful and well-organized Catholic clergy. The clergy was regarded as a stabilizing factor that could ensure the maintenance of the social order. It is not surprising that an alliance was formed between the bourgeoisie, both French- and English-speaking, and the clergy. Businessmen cultivated relations with *curés*, and the press and religious authorities got together to condemn the first attempts at unionization without a dissenting note. When a few priests, such as Father Honorat in the Saguenay region and Father Paradis in Temiscamingue, ventured to fight the exploitation that victimized their parishioners, they were quickly called to order or sent elsewhere.

While in most countries the power of the clergy declined relative to that of the state in the second half of the nineteenth century, in Quebec the reverse process appeared to be occurring. Not only the legal position but also the material base of the church was strengthened; its property was not taxable and it had the power to tax the Catholic population to pay the cost of its places of worship. Priests acted as representatives of the government in registering births, marriages and deaths. Most important, the proportion of the educational system controlled by the clergy was growing at all levels. Thus, the church was in a position to impose its moral and social ideas on Quebecers — respect for authority, obedience to episcopal commands, pre-eminence of the family, moral improvement, and formal condemnation of deviant phenomena.

The whole life of a Catholic Quebecer, from birth to death, was guided by the

The beginning of classes at the Quebec City Seminary. Values of obedience and respect for authority were inculcated by the clergy.

clergy. Voluntary associations were organized at the parish level, so that the parish served as an institutional as well as a religious framework. The school system, hospitals and social assistance agencies were all dominated or controlled by the church. Not many people escaped from the social model it advocated.

English Protestants were not subject to the social control of the Catholic clergy, by virtue of a tacit nonaggression pact in which each religious group agreed to respect the other's institutions. The position of the Protestant clergy within each denomination was not as important as that of the Catholic clergy within its religious group. Ideological cohesion, however, was maintained just as effectively in the Protestant community. Its protectors in this case were the most powerful members of the bourgeoisie, who through their philanthropic activities had tight control of the Protestant education, health and charitable systems.

The conservatism of the bourgeoisie and the clergy was expressed in many ways. One of its manifestations was attachment to tradition, which showed up especially clearly in the form of nationalism. French Canadians were rivalled in this area by English-Canadian leaders, who praised imperial traditions and emphasized the pioneer virtues of work and frugality. Glorification of work and effort was at the centre of all social conceptions. The inequalities existing in society were considered natural and willed by God. The human being would be rewarded for his deeds only in the hereafter; on earth, he had to accept deprivation and misfortune — also willed by God — without protest. Any challenge to the existing social order was thus to be condemned.

The family was the basic social unit, and was responsible for the individual, in charge of his education and his protection. Any attempt by the government to take the place of the family was viewed as an attack on the social order. When problems arose, private charity was to make up for the family's inadequacies. The need for philanthropy was an integral part of bourgeois ideology in the late nineteenth century. The whole field of social assistance thus remained a private domain; if the government provided subsidies, it was to do so without trying to influence the nature of social assistance.

Another manifestation of conservatism was respect for political institutions. Constitutional monarchy and British-style parliamentary government were almost never challenged. The political arena, however, was the subject of a debate. Should clerical control extend to political power and to directing people's thinking? This question was at the centre of a struggle between two minority groups within Quebec's élites, ultramontanes and radicals.

Ultraconservatism

Quebec's ultramontanes, both clerical and lay, represented the right wing of the Catholic church. In the name of maintaining the integrity of Catholic doctrine, they resisted the changes characteristic of the modern era. Their organized presence in Quebec dates from the mid-nineteenth century and can be attributed to three major factors. First, the success of the Catholic reaction of the 1840s gave rise to an atmosphere of religious enthusiasm in which the church looked for new fields of activity and increasingly sought to impose the views of the clergy on the population. Second, the ultramontanes felt the need to become better organized to resist the rise of the Rouges, who advocated radical ideas, notably secularization of the state, and achieved some political success. Finally, there was the influence of the European situation; in several countries, the church had had to give up some of its powers to the state, and in Italy, the papacy lost political control — what was called the temporal power of the pope — over its own territory, the Papal States. Fear of seeing the European experience repeated in Quebec stoked the fires of ultramontane zeal. These fires were fuelled still further by the many French priests and religious invited to Quebec by the bishop of Montreal, Mgr Bourget.

The basic principle of ultramontane thought was that divine right takes precedence over natural right. Since the church represents the power of God and the state the power of men, it follows that the church takes precedence over the state. According to the ultramontanes, the activities of politicians should be subject to episcopal commands and the laws they pass should be in conformity with the teachings of the church. In this context, it was a matter of course that *curés* and bishops should take positions on all political questions and indicate to Catholic voters which parties and candidates they should vote for. The presentation of a Catholic Program at the time of the 1871 election was an attempt by the ultramontanes to have these principles adopted by the population of Quebec.

Outside the realm of relations between church and state, the ultramontanes took generally ultraconservative positions on all social questions. They were intolerant — often virulently so — of anyone who did not share their views and took an especially hard line towards any idea that might bear any resemblance to what they called liberalism. Writing in the *Courrier du Canada* in 1884, the journalist Thomas Chapais professed his conservative faith in the following terms: "Our ideas, our tendencies, our aspirations are conservative. It is enough to say that the most conservative principles are our principles, the most conservative measures are our measures, the most conservative men are our men."

Not all clergymen agreed with ultramontane ideas. The hard core of the movement was in the dioceses of Montreal and Trois-Rivières, and its leaders were Mgr Bourget, bishop of Montreal until 1876, and Mgr Laflèche, bishop of

Louis-François Laflèche (1818-98), bishop of Trois-Rivières, 1870-98.

Trois-Rivières. The movement was weakened in the Montreal region by Bourget's resignation in 1876 and his replacement by a moderate, Mgr Fabre. These bishops were supported by hard-line laymen such as Senator François-Xavier Trudel, who published the newspaper *L'Étendard*, and Jules-Paul Tardivel, publisher of *La Vérité*. In trying to impose their views, the ultramontanes often clashed openly with more moderate elements within the church. They tried to obtain the support of the pope, but without success, especially during the reign of Leo XIII. By the end of the century, they were an increasingly marginal group within the clergy and society as a whole, engaged in a rearguard action, even though they had succeeded in gaining a position of influence in the Conservative party.

Ultramontane ideas were also strongly resisted by most politicians, who were not enthusiastic about the idea of being subject to the authority of the bishops, although they had no objection to using clerical influence when they needed it. English Protestant politicians were especially averse to clerical control, and their resistance gave strength to French-Canadian political leaders in their own struggle against church domination. However, by keeping up constant pressure, the ultramontanes undoubtedly helped accentuate the social conservatism of Quebec's ruling groups.

There were also English-Canadian ultraconservative groups — the Orangemen, the Equal Rights Association, the Protestant Protective Association and the like — and they were every bit as hard-line as the ultramontanes. These groups were racist and fiercely opposed to the Catholic church, and wanted to establish white Anglo-Saxon Protestant power. The two major non-WASP ethnic groups — the French Canadians and the Irish Catholics — became the Orangemen's main targets. The Protestant extremist organizations met with some success in Ontario and the West, but little is known about the degree to which they became established in Quebec. It appears that they were concentrated in the English-speaking rural regions of the province.

There were also some forms of puritanism that could be placed under the heading of extreme social conservatism and religious intransigence. Protestant groups tried to impose their moral conceptions on society as a whole. In particular, they demanded government action to enforce Sunday observance and prohibit the sale and consumption of alcoholic beverages. As a minority in Quebec, these puritanical Protestants could not hope to have the same success in imposing their views as in Ontario. They did have a degree of freedom to carry out their program, however, in municipalities where they formed the majority.

Reform: a marginal movement

Diametrically opposed to these tendencies was Quebec's tradition of political radicalism. This movement had reached a peak with the Patriotes in the 1830s and again with the Rouges in the 1850s; after 1867, the tradition was continued by a minority in the Liberal party. The radicals emphasized freedom of thought and freedom of the press, and this made them opponents of the clergy, which believed it had the responsibility to tell Catholics what they had the right to think.

Their main aim was to restrict the clergy to strictly religious questions, and they also demanded a clear separation between church and state. The radicals saw the school system as a symbol of clerical domination and concentrated their attacks in that area. They argued that the Quebec school system suffered from many weaknesses and that the clergy kept the people in ignorance. In consequence, they demanded the declericalization of the teaching profession, programs of study better adapted to the modern world, and wider access to education through such measures as free tuition and textbooks and compulsory schooling. They also attacked the privileges of the clergy — the tax exemptions and the special status accorded to clerical teachers, who did not have to undergo the competency tests required of their lay colleagues. Clerical pretensions to have the power to forbid particular newspapers and books and influence the way people voted were additional targets of the radicals.

The radicals advocated a more democratic society, but their ideas did not go much further than electoral democracy. While they demanded abolition of the Legislative Council and some of them favoured a republican form of government, they stopped short of advocating an egalitarian ideology. Their demands were essentially the product of a power struggle within the bourgeoisie; they were in no sense socialists and did not aim to establish a new set of power relationships that would benefit the peasants or the workers. The radicals were reformers who wanted to change some aspects of the social order but did not challenge society's socio-economic foundations.

Most newspapers that expressed radical ideas existed for only a short time. However, *La Patrie* of Montreal, by far the most significant of the radical newspapers, succeeded in staying alive by tempering its radicalism slightly. Old Rouges and young Liberals in the Montreal region provided most of the recruits to radical ranks. But the Liberal party and its leaders were determined to present a moderate image to the electorate, and their strategy had the effect of consigning the radicals to the margins.

Another minority tendency, the ideology of urban reform, began to grow up within the bourgeoisie in the 1880s. This new tendency was part of the larger North American progressive movement, but in Quebec it remained confined to a few elements within the Montreal bourgeoisie. Its most significant manifestation was the struggle against municipal corruption in Montreal. At the very end of the century, this ideology became somewhat more firmly established, and its adherents proposed a wide variety of social and political reforms.

Egalitarians: an isolated group

The most forceful and coherent exponents of the socio-political program of egalitarianism were the Knights of Labor. The Knights placed more emphasis on the advancement of the working class than on class struggle. Their labour relations strategy was not one of conflict, and they had, in principle, no particular attachment to the strike weapon, favouring compulsory arbitration instead. Their preferred instrument for improving the lot of the working class was education, especially adult education — evening courses, technical schools, public libraries and the like. They also demanded that the government adopt legislation with the aim of improving working conditions and placing workers on an equal footing with the representatives of capital. To obtain legislation favourable to the workers, they undertook direct political action and supported labour candidates in some elections.

The Knights of Labor developed an ideology that aimed to benefit the working class as a whole. This constituted a clear difference between the Knights and the American Federation of Labor, which expressed narrower conceptions and was interested essentially in unionized craft workers and their immediate working conditions. The basic activity of AF of L unions was negotiation of collective agreements. There were few references in its ideology to the general problems of the working class or to educational questions. Despite their minority position, the adherents of the egalitarian ideology of the labour unions succeeded in gaining a hearing; several members of the Royal Commission on the Relations of Labour and Capital came from the Knights of Labor, and Alphonse Télésphore Lépine expressed the views of the Knights in the Canadian parliament. However, their political influence was not strong enough to win easy acceptance for the reforms they proposed.

Forms of Nationalism

In general, one key concept in a nationalist ideology is that the nation is the basic unit in relation to which social ideas are defined. Such ideologies have occupied an important place in Quebec and Canadian history, because many leaders of opinion have tried to rally the population around this concept. In essence, nationalism is an instrument for unifying a people and cementing over the class distinctions that divide it. However, classes try to use nationalism to defend their own interests and privileges, and in the end, the relations existing among different classes determine the real content of nationalism.

It follows that very different meanings can be attached to the idea of the nation depending on who defines it and in what context and circumstances the definition is worked out. The presence of one or more of the following factors is invoked as evidence that a group constitutes a nation: a common history, an identity that distinguishes the group from its neighbours, concentration in a particular territory, a common language, a common religion, and common traditions.

However, a society does not have to have all these characteristics in order to be designated a nation. Every nation is a special case. Some sociologists go so far as to maintain that the only determining criterion is subjective. In other words, if the members of a society are convinced that they all belong to the same nation, then a nation exists. The nation should not be confused with the state; they are two distinct realities, one a sociological and the other a political entity. In some circumstances, a group finds it to its advantage to link the two terms, either to dominate a weaker group or to give more prestige to the state. The nation is a reality, but nationalism is an ideology, which is to say that it is a doctrine formulated by individuals and groups. Therefore, there is not one nationalism, but different forms of nationalism that change with time.

French-Canadian nationalism

No matter how the word nation is defined, there is no doubt that French Canadians in the nineteenth century perceived themselves and were perceived by others as a nation. At first, this nation was known as *la nation canadienne*; later, after the Act of Union, the term *la nation canadienne-française* gradually became more common.

When the next round of constitutional change was under discussion, the nation was one of the concepts that participants in the Confederation debates were called upon to define. While their conceptions were expressed in imprecise language, the same idea of the nation was shared by all — politicians, bishops and journalists, supporters and opponents of Confederation. In their view, it was a group's distinctive characteristics that made it a nation. In the case of the French Canadians, four such characteristics — language, laws, institutions and religion — stood out, and were rooted in something still more basic, a common history. It was regarded as imperative that these characteristics be preserved. In this ideology, French Canadians did not have a well-defined territorial base. Meanwhile, because of the way problems were dealt with in the federal framework, politicians treated French Canadians as if they existed only in Quebec, so that little attention was paid to the approximately 150,000 Canadians of French origin who lived in other provinces, except indirectly in the context of the religious question, as an overwhelming majority of them were Catholics.

The problem of the nation's territorial base was related to another problem, that of its governmental framework. From its beginnings, the French-Canadian nation had never been in control of a state structure. It had been ruled by metropolitan governments — France initially, and then England after the Conquest. However, with the introduction of parliamentary institutions under English rule in 1791, French-Canadian politicians came to demand self-government, at least in internal affairs. London refused and rebellion ensued. After the Act of Union, with French Canadians in a minority position and London wanting to get rid of the burden of its colonies, responsible government was granted to the province of Canada.

In granting the French Canadians of Quebec a state in which they would be a majority, Confederation marked a step forward. The new state, however, was only a provincial one, under the tutelage of federal and imperial levels of government. In the view of some French-Canadian leaders, this provincial state was enough to ensure that the institutions particular to their nation would be protected. Others disagreed, believing that the constitution gave too much power to the central government, where English Canadians would have majority control. The position that the French-Canadian nation would be able to flourish within the Canadian nation, under the protection of the crown and within the framework of the Empire, prevailed. The opponents of this position eventually came to accept the idea that the French-Canadian nation was defined by its cultural components, while the new Canadian nationality was only a political structure. French-Canadian representatives might have ideological differences on other matters, and might be divided between adherents and opponents of economic liberalism, social conservatism or radicalism. But whether they came from the capitalist class or the petty bourgeoisie, they all shared the same form of nationalism, essentially cultural in content.

In the last third of the nineteenth century, however, the idea of the nation entertained by the various individuals and groups whose view of the situation carried some weight became clearer, and their proposals for action became more specific. The nationalist ideology that developed took the political dimension into account to a somewhat greater extent.

Moderate politicians and intellectuals, whether Conservative or Liberal (there was a gradual reconciliation between moderates in the two parties as the period progressed), agreed on the essentials, even if partisan political considerations led them to advocate different ways of reaching their goals. Slowly, it was realized that French Canada was not limited to Quebec. French Canadians in Quebec discovered the Acadians and Franco-Manitobans, as well as the Franco-Americans, whom they tried to repatriate and invited to their great national celebrations. They dreamed of a "Greater French Canada," but they also recognized Quebec as the *foyer* (home) of this French Canada. The periodic school and language controversies made politicians aware — although in a confused fashion — of the need to promote the autonomy of Quebec. With Mercier, provincial autonomy became the political expression of French-Canadian nationalism. As Liberal leader, Mercier did not hesitate to form an alliance with the National Conservatives during the Riel affair. However, he was faithful to the ideas of his time in consistently defining the French-Canadian nation as essentially Catholic and French. He maintained that the French Canadians of Quebec had to unite across party lines and he criticized politics for its role in dividing and weakening the nation.

The ultramontanes emphasized the primarily religious character of the nation. As Mgr Laflèche said, "Faith is the most powerful support of nations." One corollary of this ultramontane conception was that each people had received a mission from Providence. The history of the French-Canadian people demonstrated that its mission was to spread Catholicism in America.

The ultramontanes, who were also very conservative, taught that authority came from God; as a result, established institutions — including the Empire and Confederation — were to be obeyed. However, when these authorities attacked the Catholic religion, the ultramontanes had to fight them. Thus, they took nationalist positions when Catholics in New Brunswick were denied some of their educational rights and when the Manitoba Schools question and the Riel affair arose. One ultramontane thinker, Jules-Paul Tardivel, went so far as to become an advocate of French-Canadian independence, on the grounds that French Canada's interests were travestied within the federal system. Tardivel was far from a revolutionary, and his suggestion was not that people should work actively for independence but rather that they should await the hour chosen by Providence, which decides the destiny of nations. It should be noted that Tardivel had few disciples, although his religious zeal was admired and his newspaper (*La Vérité*) read within a limited circle.

In the first thirty years after Confederation, greater precision was attached to the conceptions that made up the French-Canadian nationalist ideology. The ideology and its variants were widely shared among the French-speaking ruling classes, and spread by politicians, members of the clergy and journalists. At particular moments, notably at the time of the Riel affair, the élites were able to mobilize the masses by appealing to their nationalist feelings. On the other hand, the ideological arguments of the ruling classes inviting French Canadians to remain in Quebec and colonize new regions of the province were not enough to prevent hundreds of thousands of them from emigrating to the United States. In the cities, some trade union organizations tried to make workers aware of their own specific interests, which were very much neglected in the clerical-conservative arguments. The Knights of Labor established French-speaking assemblies and were, on the whole, more sensitive to the cultural particularity of their members than were the international unions affiliated with the American Federation of Labor. This was one reason the Knights were popular among French-Canadian workers.

English-Canadian nationalism and imperialism

Meanwhile, British North Americans were taking on the identity of Canadians, a process that was encouraged by both the Act of Union and Confederation. This movement was slow outside central Canada, and English Canadians had their differences. But they were brought together by their common membership in the British Empire; some also emphasized their refusal to be Americans, even though they shared the English language, Protestantism as the majority religion, and — sometimes — antipapism with their southern neighbours. Canadian nationalism held little attraction for French Canadians and Irish Catholics, and language and religion were deeply divisive factors within the new dominion. The conflict between French-Canadian and English-Canadian nationalism after 1867 occurred not so much within Quebec as between Quebec and Ontario, and later between Quebec and English Canada as a whole.

While most English Canadians accepted or at least resigned themselves to the existence of a majority French and Catholic province in 1867, they had no intention of making Canada a bilingual and bicultural country. The creation of the province of Manitoba and the first and second Riel rebellions sparked conflicts between Quebec and Ontario. With forty-five per cent of the total population of the new dominion, Ontario was the foundation-stone of Canada. In the second half of the nineteenth century it was "expansionist and aggressive," as the historian P.B. Waite has pointed out, and it wanted to make the West a replica of its own British and Anglo-Protestant society. While about eighty-five per cent of Quebec's population was Catholic, about eighty-three per cent of Ontario's was Protestant, and Ontario was more heavily English-speaking than Quebec was French-speaking.

Like its French-Canadian counterpart, English-Canadian nationalism in the nineteenth century was based primarily on ethnic origin, language and religion. The reactions of English Canada to ethnic conflicts and the ideology of its various political and religious movements — the Canada First Movement, the imperialist movement, the Orange Order, the Protestant Protective Association — provide striking indications of this. As far as English Canadians were concerned, the whole of British North America was their country. Within this entity, the existence of a bilingual and mostly Catholic Quebec was tolerated, but apart from that, the country was to be British. D'Alton McCarthy and the Equal Rights Association launched a campaign in which the issue was raised in brutal terms; this campaign led to the *de facto* abolition of Catholic and French schools in Manitoba.

While belonging to the Empire, Canada enjoyed a large degree of autonomy in internal affairs. In the 1880s and 1890s, however, renewed emphasis was placed on the imperial connection with the growth of the imperialist movement. The imperialists were not impressed with Goldwin Smith's argument that because of geography Canada was destined to be annexed to the United States. On the contrary, the imperialists replied, history is stronger than geography; Canada had been born out of a rejection of the American Revolution and would survive if it cast its lot with the Empire. Thus, an élite in English Canada expressed its Canadian nationalism through imperialism. By instituting a protectionist tariff policy, the Canadian bourgeoisie was trying to build economic barriers against American penetration; these barriers were fragile, and it was very much in the bourgeoisie's interest to strengthen them by building ideological barriers as well.

Their vision of Canada, however, left little room for French Canadians. The historian Carl Berger has provided an apt summary of their attitude: "All imperialists were either unwilling or unable to recognize the French Canadians as anything more than a picturesque, unprogressive and potentially troublesome minority group with certain privileges guaranteed by imperial legislation."

For Canadian nationalists, the important tasks of the first thirty years after

Confederation were unifying British North America from the Atlantic to the Pacific, building a market that could resist American annexation, and settling this immense territory by drawing from the population of the British Isles and the United States. Canadians in general, however, went where their economic interests led them, moving to the United States with barely a second thought and often coming back to Canada later just as easily. In the same way, workers joined international craft unions or the Knights of Labor and were not much interested in nationalism, although their spokesmen did take positions on the protectionist tariff measures that were cleverly labelled the "national policy."

The economy, society and nation are three major themes on which ideologies focus. While there was hardly a profusion of ideological currents in the late nineteenth century, there were enough of them so that it would be a mistake to talk of unanimity. In essence, these ideologies were developed and debated (when there was debate) within the ruling classes, the bourgeoisie and petty bourgeoisie. However, the correspondence between class and ideology was not one-to-one. Thus, within the bourgeoisie, the French-speaking group shared the economic liberalism and social conservatism of the English-speaking group, but its nationalism was a distinguishing element. The French-speaking bourgeoisie's views on the nation and social organization were the same as those of the clergy, but it took a very different position from the clergy on economic development and political control.

In the last decades of the nineteenth century, three major ideological currents, each with a number of variants, gradually emerged. The *liberal* ideology was that of the bourgeoisie, both English- and French-speaking, and part of the petty bourgeoisie. It was characterized by adherence to the principles of economic liberalism and conservatism on socio-political questions. Political radicalism, in which secularization of the state was a key demand, constituted a minority current within this ideology. Nationalism was an important element in the ideology, but its content was different for different groups. French-speaking nationalists tried to encourage the development of French-Canadian culture within the Canadian political entity, while English-Canadian nationalism took the form of British patriotism in the context of the Empire, linked to a respect for French-Canadian traditions.

The *ideology of conservation* was espoused by the clergy and part of the petty bourgeoisie. It was centred on French-Canadian nationalism, of which the main components were the French language, French customs, the Roman Catholic religion and the rural way of life. It advocated a Catholic social order, with the church in a position of leadership and control. The ultramontane minority within this current even wanted to extend this control to political activities.

The *egalitarian* ideology, advocated principally by the Knights of Labor, had a more limited impact. Its goals were an improved position for the working class and a reduction in social inequality. The American Federation of Labor concentrated more on strictly trade union activities.

In addition to the content of these different ideologies, there is also the question of their dissemination. A variety of means were used towards this end; political speeches, patriotic speeches, education and political clubs were among the oral outlets, while the printed media included newspapers (in which editorials, news articles, features, pictures and advertisements all had a role), pamphlets, books and posters. The clergy was in an advantageous position in the Catholic community in this respect, and used its control of the religious apparatus, its power in the school system, and its printed materials to disseminate its message with considerable impact. Economic liberalism, the ideology of the bourgeoisie, was disseminated through the mass-circulation press that began to develop in the 1880s. Radicals and trade unionists had less powerful means at their disposal, and the circulation of their press was limited. It is very hard to evaluate the degree of influence these different media had. A church sermon, a sensational article, a Saint-Jean-Baptiste Day parade — which is the most effective means of gaining the adherence of the population to an ideological position?

Finally, it is impossible to study ideologies in Quebec without bringing up the question of their relationship to similar currents elsewhere in the world. Borders are not effective barriers to the circulation of ideas and people, and can be surmounted in various ways. Late-nineteenth-century Quebec businessmen and political and religious leaders travelled, primarily to the United States, England, France and Rome. Foreign publications were read in Quebec. Quebec radicals took their inspiration from European liberals. The ultramontanes drew from French ultraconservative ideas. The Vatican defined the official thinking of the Roman Catholic church. The idea of progress and the myth of individual success were shared by businessmen on both sides of the Atlantic. The program of the trade unions was partly American in origin. In this context, were Quebec's ideological currents autonomous, were they parallel to currents in other countries or was the relationship one of colonialism? What was the role of foreign influences? At present it is virtually impossible to answer these questions.

CHAPTER 17
CULTURE

The traditional view of the production of culture has stressed its artistic aspects, and the concepts and standards according to which it has been analysed have been esthetic in nature. Thus there are great works, produced at different times, and these can be explained only through a notion of immutable and transcendental beauty. This conception has long been challenged in the area of literary criticism, but opposition to it in the area of art criticism is more recent.

In reality the production of culture, like all human production, can only be understood if the conditions under which works are produced are taken into account. As the sociologist Pierre Francastel has written, "a work of art . . . is a meeting-place of minds. It is a signal, a relay-station, in the same manner as any other language. It is just as absurd to think that buildings or paintings could have an independent existence outside the twofold effort of the artist and the viewer, as it is to believe in the existence of words that, in combination, constitute languages independently of usage." It is in this spirit that the discussion of cultural output in this book is undertaken. Cultural products are intelligible signals that bear witness to the social reality that produced them.

Perhaps even more than in other fields, the deficiencies of the historical literature must be mentioned. Because the study of cultural production is still fragmented and compartmentalized into disciplines, it is very difficult to trace the relationships between social developments in literature, music or architecture.

The culture of a society is multidimensional, and in this discussion only a few dimensions of Quebec culture could be given the attention they deserve. First, it was decided to concentrate on two sectors, literature and painting, with a few glances at sculpture. These sectors will serve as illustrations and help cast light on the relationships between culture and society. This decision meant, however, that music, architecture, the performing arts and other sectors would be passed by. Second, in addition to the production aspect of culture discussed here, there are questions relating to its dissemination and consumption that are not treated. Finally, no attempt is made to deal with popular culture, despite its clear importance for the history of Quebec. Not much is known about this form of culture, but discoveries are beginning to be made as the work of anthropologists, enthnographers and folklorists progresses.

Literature*

In the last third of the nineteenth century, a gap had opened up between the official rhetoric of clerical-nationalist ideology and the reality of Quebec culture. The literary sector provides a good illustration of that gap. While literary ideologues and critics imposed on writers the often fruitless course of defending national, religious and conservative values, the daily diet of the reading public was a foreign literature that presented a very different vision of the world.

French influence

Despite what has long been written and said, the ties between France and its former colony, especially in the area of intellectual influence, remained very close throughout the nineteenth century. With improvements in printing, French books enjoyed increased circulation (as did newspapers), and they came regularly and in considerable numbers to the banks of the St. Lawrence. The advertising done by bookstores and salesmen whenever a ship came in from an English port is a good indication of the public's continuing interest in French literature. People were interested in political, scientific, philosophical and religious works, but also in poetry and especially in novels, starting with the rise of romanticism in the 1830s and 1840s.

There was some appreciation of the officially honoured titles of the great writers of the time — Balzac, Stendhal, Chateaubriand — but the most sought-after books, starting in the 1830s, were historical novels, fantasies and, later, the various twists and turns of Eugène Sue's serial *Les Mystères de Paris*, as well as popular melodrama in its innumerable variations. The public was so partial to this kind of literature that Henri-Émile Chevalier, a French writer newly landed in Montreal, hastened to write *Les Mystères de Montréal* and a dozen more novels that combined all the elements of contemporary popular French, American and English novels on an exotic Canadian canvas.

The main novelistic devices of this genre were intrigues with complicated ramifications, miraculous discoveries, mysterious crimes and passions run wild, and its stock characters were the virtuous orphan girl, the reformed prostitute and

---

*This section was written by Sylvain Simard.

the socialist aristocrat. It is difficult to evaluate its impact or the extent of its distribution, for these books were not only sold in bookstores in Montreal, Trois-Rivières and Quebec City but were also undoubtedly a common item in the suitcases of travelling salesmen. In addition, they reached the public through serialization in the newspapers. It was clearly a limited public, as there were still a large number of illiterates in 1867, but the circulation of books and newspapers increased steadily during the period.

In the 1880s, there were the beginnings of a popular press in *La Patrie* and *La Presse*, daily newspapers that followed European and American models and were among the chief disseminators of liberal ideology. Some of the success of this new style of newspaper was due to its alluring front page, almost all of which was devoted to serialized novels. The daily formula of *La Minerve, L'Évènement, Le Journal de Québec, Le National* and *Le Pays* also unfailingly included the works of Georges Ohnet, Alexandre Dumas, Eugène Sue and the many other popular writers who fed the public's insatiable hunger for such novels. The absence of any copyright convention governing this source of material made it free and unlimited and hence all the more attractive. Although carefully censored, these novels still transmitted some of the values characteristic of their societies and countries of origin, values opposed to the prevailing religious conservatism of Quebec.

The moralist reaction

In reaction to the foreign, "modern" ideas filtering into Quebec, some French-Canadian writers wanted to direct its emerging indigenous literature towards a different end. According to these writers, the French-Canadian people lived a peaceful, calm life; therefore, it would be useless to look for the spiciness of imported books (passions, crimes, suicides) in the new works Quebec would produce. Abbé Henri-Raymond Casgrain, whose vision deeply influenced Quebec prose and poetry, argued that Canadian literature had to be "essentially believing and religious." It had to "encourage sound doctrines," "promote love of the good, admiration for the beautiful and knowledge of the true" and above all "make the people moral" by opening their hearts to all these noble sentiments. In this spirit, he urged writers to show the holiness of agriculture in their works, draw their subjects from the great deeds of their heroic ancestors under the French régime, and revive the beautiful legends of yesteryear.

This nationalist imperative was echoed a few years later by Hector Fabre, a highly cultured man widely known as a Francophile, who warned the Canadian literary community against trying to transpose realities and sensibilities typical of France to the banks of the St. Lawrence. Such a transposition was improper, he maintained, and the French imports would be unable to survive the journey. French-Canadian literature was thus assigned an active role in the struggle to maintain French-Canadian cultural and ideological specificity. This struggle was a holy war, and woe be to those few writers who would try, even for a moment, to desert their positions at the front.

A hundred writers

Who were the writers of the last third of the nineteenth century? There were not very many of them — about a hundred — and none was able to earn his living through his literary activity. Thus, they were to be found on the editorial staffs of newspapers and in the translation departments, clerks' offices, libraries and archives of the federal and provincial parliaments. These were the only jobs that allowed them at least the minimum amount of time needed for creative work. Their social origins have not been studied with any precision, but it can be concluded that most of them came from the countryside; only in the last years of the century did writers of urban origin begin to appear. A typical writer would have gone to a classical college and then tried his hand at law; relatively poor and without professional or technical qualifications, he needed the friendship of politicians to be assured of a well-paying job.

Vulnerable and dependent as they were, it is not surprising that with the exception of a few radicals — the pamphleteer Arthur Buies, the poet Louis-Honoré Fréchette, the novelist Honoré Beaugrand — they were the servile singers of clerical-conservative esthetic and ideology. Even Buies and Fréchette, despite their visceral anticlericalism, extolled the agricultural mystique and colonization as the sacred mission of the French race in America; their vision of the world was not much different from that of traditionalists such as Octave Crémazie or Basile Routhier.

Honoré Beaugrand, however, struck out on a new course by openly and deliberately writing of American-style capitalism in glowing terms. His novel *Jeanne la Fileuse* (Jeanne the spinner) first appeared in serial form in the *République* of Fall River, Massachusetts, in 1875, and then again in *La Patrie*, Beaugrand's own newspaper, five years later; it was published in book form in 1888. This dependence on serial publication was typical for the French-Canadian literature of the era. While most of his contemporaries stuck to the stereotypes of conservatism and inward-looking nationalism, Beaugrand decided to write a vigorous defence of the Franco-Americans, whom he saw as being unjustly criticized in Quebec. The picture he paints of working conditions in the New England textile mills is favourable.

A gulf was being created between two kinds of culture. On the one hand, the mass-circulation press presented its daily dose of the "exotic" esthetic of French novels and American success stories to a growing public; on the other, the national writers reached only a very small audience with their stilted genres (epic poems, pastoral novels) and worn-out subjects (historical novels and essays on the conquest of the land or the glory of the papal zouaves). On one side, the official culture, the rhetoric of the élites endlessly proclaiming the superiority of the ancestral way of life through whole literary forms marshalled to do battle for the prevailing conformism and mediocrity. Opposed to it, a more "popular" literature, a culture comprising both reality and lived experience on the one hand and escapism on the other. No serious study of this unofficial literature has ever been done. Much could be learned from such a study about the links between popular culture and a society under the spell of industrial development.

It should be emphasized that the nineteenth century was, above all, the century of the novel. The church was aware of this, and after first condemning the novel as an inherently dangerous form, soon decided "to fight the enemy with its own weapons," as Jules-Paul Tardivel put it. In this spirit, 175,000 copies of Quebec works in a collection edited by Abbé Casgrain and subsidized by the Quebec government were distributed to students.

In the prevailing climate, there was no indigenous theatre. There were, however, numerous appearances by touring companies from France and the United States, and audiences for theatre were not lacking, if the triumphal reception given Sarah Bernhardt when she came to Montreal in 1880 is any indication. Her performances played to packed houses although they were explicitly condemned by Bishop Fabre.

Poetry reached only a limited public, but it was not without significance. Poets were fairly numerous, and about eighty collections of poetry were published between 1867 and 1896 as opposed to some thirty novels. And yet paradoxically, these poets did not — except for Fréchette and to a lesser extent William Chapman — occupy a very high position in a society where literary audiences were so small.

Poetry

Professor David Hayne has identified three phases in French-Canadian romantic poetry between 1860 and 1890. From 1859 to 1866, while the Canadian government was based in Quebec City, two reviews, *Les Soirées Canadiennes* and *Le Foyer Canadien*, served as outlets for poetry. Between 1867 and 1875 poetry declined markedly, despite the publication of Fréchette's *La voix d'un exilé* and modest collections by Abbé Casgrain and Benjamin Sulte. After 1875, poets born around 1850 took up the slack. The poetry of this last period was strongly influenced by the French romantic esthetic of the years 1820-50, and with the exception of part of Fréchette's work and some poems by Pamphile Le May, Alfred Garneau and William Chapman, is astoundingly poor. The French model served as a yoke that prevented not only any originality of form but also any interest in the revitalization that the realist and Parnassian movements represented. This vague collective romanticism is a clear reflection of the limited cultural choices imposed on Quebec writers by morality, religion and ideology, which not only kept them away from the esthetic revolutions of the second half of the century, but also prevented them from achieving poetic individuality, and therefore authenticity.

The work of Louis-Honoré Fréchette is an exception, however. Fréchette was constantly in the public eye for forty years, and after Crémazie went into exile he represented French-Canadian poetry almost single-handedly. Recognized at a very early age as an imaginative and talented poet, he was awarded the Prix Monthyon by the Académie Française in 1880. He was consecrated as the *barde national*, the official poet, called upon to celebrate an inauguration or a festival with a work written for the occasion, and crowds lionized him. Despite all this, it was not forgotten that Fréchette was actively anticlerical and strongly liberal, and lauded the French republic in a society that had little sympathy for this destructive and regicidal *mauvaise France*. He was an admirer of Lamartine, Chateaubriand and above all Victor Hugo, whose work he tried to duplicate in a Quebec context. His imitations of Lamartine and especially Hugo were not without sensitivity, and his poetry, based on these models, is endowed with verbal invention, evocative images, and a life and strength that make the reader forget its weaknesses. The following verses, taken from his *Légende d'un peuple* — a Canadian version of Hugo's *Légende des siècles* — exhibit these qualities:

Amérique! — salut à toi, beau sol natal!*
Toi, la reine et l'orgueil du monde occidental!
Toi qui, comme Vénus, montes du sein de l'onde,
Et du poids de ta conque équilibres le monde!

Quand, le front couronné de tes arbres géants,
Vierge, tu secouais au bord des océans,
Ton voile aux plis baignés de lueurs éclatantes;
Quand drapés dans leurs flots de lianes flottantes,
Tes grands bois ténébreux, tout pleins d'oiseaux chanteurs
Imprégnèrent les verts de leurs âcres senteurs;
Quand ton mouvant réseau d'aurores boréales
Révéla les splendeurs de tes nuits idéales;
Quand tes fleurs sans fin, quand tes sommets neigeux,
Tes tropiques brûlants, tes pôles orageux,
Eurent montré de loin leurs grandeurs infinies,
Niagaras grondants, blondes Californies!
Amérique, au contact de ta jeune beauté,
On sentit reverdir la veille humanité!

**America! — hail to you, fair native soil!*
To you, queen and pride of the western world!
To you who, like Venus, rise from the deep,
And with the strength of your trumpet keep the world in balance!

When, your brow crowned with giant trees,
Virgin, on the banks of the ocean, you cast off
Your veil of folds bathed in flashes of light;
When, draped in billows of waving woody vines,
Your great shadowy forests, filled with singing birds,
Impregnated the greens with their pungent smells;
When your shifting web of northern lights
Revealed the splendours of your ideal nights;
When your endless flowers, when your snowy peaks,
Your burning tropics, your stormy poles,

Louis Honoré Fréchette (1839-1908), *barde national* of Quebec.

Fréchette devoted thousands of verses to celebrating the epic of the Canadian people and the glory of its ancestors. Although he challenged the clerical-conservative ideology in his articles, essays and speeches, his poetry still took its inspiration from François-Xavier Garneau's history and Crémazie's patriotism. In Fréchette, the individual is still pushed into the background by the exigencies of the collective struggle for national and religious integrity. Nor would one look to Fréchette's work, any more than to the novels and pamphlets of the time, for a grasp of increasing urbanization and industrialization and the social change they indicated.

The novel

To a large degree, Quebec fiction was written in reaction to the so-called "light" literature of the time — French, English and American serials — and so was devoted to showing the honest and peaceful way of life of hard-working Canadian peasants. Patrice Lacombe's *La terre paternelle* (1844) and P.-J.-O. Chauveau's *Charles Guérin* (1853) were early evidence of this decision to let the "old countries" have a monopoly on "blood-stained novels" and inflamed passions.

Showed their infinite grandeur from afar,
Roaring Niagara, blond California!
America, in contact with your young beauty,
Old humanity seemed to bloom again!

Having chosen to write propaganda, Quebec novelists were constrained by their submission to ideological models and stereotypes. The most significant illustrations of this submission are two novels by Antoine Gérin-Lajoie, *Jean Rivard le défricheur* (Jean Rivard the settler) and *Jean Rivard, économiste*. Like other writers of the era, Gérin-Lajoie maintains that his intention is not to write a novel; rather, he is narrating the true adventures "of a young man without wealth, born in a humble situation, who succeeded in raising himself through his own merit to financial independence and his country's highest honour." When Gérin-Lajoie says he is not writing a novel, he means that his character is only an instrument and his story is an example. Its purpose is to convince his countrymen who read it of the pre-eminence of the country over the city and of colonizing new regions over any liberal profession — in other words, to persuade them that the dead end of education must be abandoned in favour of the fertile soil.

The protagonist, Jean Rivard, has just finished his course in rhetoric at the Nicolet seminary when his father dies. With only fifty louis as an inheritance, he has to give up his studies. Offered the choice between pursuing a career in law — the path for a young man who has no powerful friends and is destined for mediocrity — and settling on a small plot in an old overpopulated parish in the St. Lawrence Valley, he rejects both and decides to colonize a piece of land in Bristol township. Jean chooses a lot, buys it at a good price, and plunges into the forest, accompanied by his "hired man," Pierre Gagnon, his "man Friday" and comic foil. The land very quickly gives its first fruits, and the log cabin that shelters the unclouded marital bliss of Jean Rivard and Louise Routhier, the model wife and mother, soon gives way to a comfortable house. Small agricultural industries (potash and maple sugar) are started, a road linking Rivardville with civilization is opened, and with the help of these enterprises our hero is soon enjoying prosperity of a sort.

In the sequel, *Jean Rivard, économiste*, Gérin-Lajoie presents the social philosophy that he has drawn from Frédéric Le Play and his disciples. With the influx of new settlers, the pioneer colony has to organize itself into a social structure — that is, found a parish and establish regulatory bodies for education, commerce and industry. The guiding spirit of this enterprise is, of course, Jean Rivard. When he attains "his country's highest honour" by becoming mayor and then a member of parliament, Rivard remains faithful to the bucolic imagery of the story and comes back to cultivate his fields.

Make no mistake about it, the story seems like a fable not because it has been caricatured in this brief summary but because the novel itself, despite its author's disclaimer, is based on the techniques of fable-writing. Gérin-Lajoie's intention may have been to write a realistic work, but in his narrative he engages deliberately in the fantastic and the epic. The harvests and levels of production are miraculous, credits and commercial opportunities arise providentially, nature is totally subject to the hero, *deus ex machina* intervenes. Everything, including total freedom from the rules of verisimilitude, is at Jean Rivard's disposal to make him living proof of the soundness of his creator's social theories. Thus, the reader can only smile at the naïve contrast that Gérin-Lajoie sets up between the city and the country through Rivard's correspondence with Gustave Charmesnil, his schoolmate who made the wrong choice. A prisoner of the city, the slave of a liberal profession, poor Gustave is portrayed as a victim whose only wish is to escape to the quiet of the country.

The real impact of a book of this sort is hard to measure. Could it inspire others to become pioneers, other Rivards-in-paradise? It is doubtful. The book was reissued seven times during the nineteenth century, but the important factors in its success were probably persuasion by the conservative élites and the story's charm — despite the author's intention — as a novel. The Manichaean dichotomy between city and country appears again in other nineteenth-century novels of rural life, in which agriculture is dealt with as an idyllic escape rather than a subject for description. Even later, in the novels of the *terroir* school, the treatment of agriculture would continue to reflect their authors' rejection of a day-to-day reality that was difficult and not very glorious.

Similarly, it is Roger Le Moine's thesis that many writers, profoundly influenced by the failure of the 1837 rebellion, took refuge in the historical novel as an escape from material poverty and political impotence. In taking their inspiration from the studies of Garneau and Abbé Ferland and the many monographs on the heroes of New France, the historical novelists were trying to demonstrate the relativity of historical fortunes and to use the glory of a mythical past to lend prestige to a conquered people. At the same time, they were making use of a genre that had proved its worth in England and France with the works of Scott, Balzac, Dumas and others.

The past as it was evoked in the historical novel, subject as it was to the ideological parameters of the nineteenth century, had little in common with the actual history of the French régime. The heroes and heroines of these novels are caricatures — darkly handsome Canadiens, noble in both the literal and the figurative sense of the word, and brown-haired orphan girls with alabaster skin and wasp waists. The heroines swoon romantically whenever the opportunity presents itself, while remaining heroic and pure. The heroine of Joseph Marmette's *Chevalier de Mornac* is captured by Mains Sanglantes (Bloody Hands), an Indian chief who is as lecherous as he is cruel and is capable of making martyrs of twenty victims in a single day. But a contemptuous stare from the heroine stops him in his tracks, and he lays down his arms before this veritable Joan of Arc, subdued by the noble look of this model of virginal love who wants to keep her purity intact for her fiancé.

In the same realistic vein, it should be noted that the villains are never Canadiens but rather "others — Englishmen, Iroquois, "bad" Frenchmen whose ugliness betrays the blackness of their souls. The plots of these novels contain few surprises: the virtuous young man wants to marry the young orphan girl; she is abducted; guided only by his better nature, he manages, despite a series of pitfalls — is it necessary to go on? The structure of the novel is reinforced with a profusion of historical details tacked on during lulls in the plot. However, with the exception of the novels of Laure Conan and Napoléon Bourassa's *Jacques et Marie*, none of these works made intelligent use of the documentation with which they were fleshed out. Also missing is the art of characterization that marks the works of, say, James Fenimore Cooper. Noteworthy in this regard is the treatment of the *coureur de bois*, an authentic figure on whom an original literary type could have been based. Scorned when he is not simply ignored, the roving frontiersman of New France appears only to be condemned in the name of a moral standard of stability and the sedentary life; a person who escapes from the laws of the group cannot be a hero.

A special place, however, should be reserved for Laure Conan's *Angéline de Montbrun* (1884), the only work of the genre that is of interest today for other than socio-historical reasons. Alternating the highly contrasted literary forms of the epistolary novel and the intimate journal, the author lays bare the complex soul of a person who rejects human happiness after the death of her father and takes refuge in spirituality. The modern reader, accustomed to Freudian analysis, may read between the lines and find a naïve recounting of an incestuous relationship, but the narrative owes nothing to the psychoanalytic clichés of today's confessions and achieves a deeply authentic resonance of suffering.

Laure Conan (1845-1924).

The essay

The literary essay in the strict sense of the term would have to be considered a minor genre in Quebec in the nineteenth century. For the literary élite, pumped full of religious transcendence in the classical colleges, engaging in the disquieting endeavour of introspective writing was not a high priority. Quebec essayists used their talents primarily to serve the cause of the clerical-nationalist ideology; more than the poets and novelists, they were both its foot-soldiers and its theoreticians. At a distance from concrete reality, caught up in conventional rhetoric, enclosed in the dogmatism of a narrow ideology, they provide evidence of a sort that cultural life in their time was expanding, but they also indicate its limitations.

However many speeches, articles, sermons and lectures were produced, these were for the most part the work of minority groups with no real influence on public opinion. Because there were two major tendencies — radical liberalism and ultramontanism — among the essayists of the time, many historians and sociologists have made the mistake of seeing the nineteenth century as being limited to the confrontation between these two tendencies. On one side, the anticlerical writers Arthur Buies, Joseph Doutre, Louis-Antoine Dessaulles; on the other ultrareactionaries such as Jules-Paul Tardivel, Louis-François Laflèche, Thomas Chapais and Adolphe Routhier. This Manichaean vision can be the basis for clear and convincing analyses, but it obscures a fundamental fact — the ideologies expressed and advocated by these writers were marginal.

Buies's pamphlets were brilliant descriptions of the effects of clericalism on Quebec's cultural development, but he was a freelance whose struggle was out of step with his times and doomed to failure. Jules-Paul Tardivel, who published an *intégriste** newspaper in the manner of Louis Veuillot in France, was condemned by the religious hierarchy a number of times. His ultramontanism, which some have tried to treat as emblematic of religious conservatism in Canada, was in fact representative only of himself and a few fanatics. The Roman Catholic church in Canada, which supported Cartier and Macdonald, could hardly be identified with the proposals of a Tardivel who attacked the railway as representing the leprosy of materialism in America!

A better way to come close to the realities of the era would be to read the serene and spiritual works of Hector Fabre. Fabre was a journalist, politician and diplomat whose positions are a mixture of conservatism and moderate liberalism and whose ambivalence is an accurate reflection of the attitude of Quebec intellectuals towards American technical progress and the seductive esthetic and philosophical controversies taking place in France. His ambiguities were more characteristic of French-Canadian thought than the dogmatic certainties that historians have portrayed as the cutting edge of larger movements.

**Intégrisme* is "the state of mind of certain Catholics who, wishing to maintain the integrity of the doctrine, are loath to adapt to the conditions of modern society" (Larousse).

Only high literature — that is, written literature — has been discussed here. A serious study of what is generally called "popular literature" that would provide a frame of reference for it has not yet been done. The influence of tales and legends on the novel allows us to catch a glimpse of the existence of a rich and complex oral culture that did not hesitate to break official taboos. Our discussion has also been limited to literature written in French. Montreal was Canada's financial centre and the seat of its most important university (McGill), but if existing studies are to be trusted — especially that of Carl F. Klinck — only a very limited English-language literature was produced in Quebec. Rosanna Eleanor Mullins (Mrs. J.-L. Leprohon, 1829-1879) and William Kirby (1817-1906), the author of *The Golden Dog*, were novelists who wrote entirely within the tradition of the French-language historical novel, while the bilingual work of the erudite James MacPherson LeMoine fit in well with the literary context of Quebec City. While original works were appearing in Halifax and Toronto, the literature of nineteenth-century English-speaking Montrealers ironically remained obedient to the currents of French culture.

Painting and Sculpture*

Works of art are a reflection of the society in which they are created. Today, this simple statement is sometimes challenged in the name of a new consciousness of the uniqueness of the plastic arts relative to all other forms of expression. According to this view, to reduce works of art to simple ideological products of society would be to ignore their specific character and confuse them with all other forms of ideological discourse. If painters and sculptors had wanted only to transmit ideas, they would not have created paintings or sculptures. They would have gone to a public place and made political or other speeches. But this is not what they did, and when they did engage in an endeavour of this sort it was often largely unrelated to their artistic activity. In ignoring this fact, the sociology of art misses its mark.

This position, generally termed *formalist* because it is more interested in the form of works than in their content, undoubtedly contains much truth. It is not the content of works in the plastic arts that gives them their specificity, for they share this content with verbal discourse. Their specific character comes from the form — nonverbal in one case, verbal in the other — in which this content is set.

It is nevertheless true that works of art would not exist but for a particular combination of circumstances under which they are created and disseminated. There are no works of art without artists and patrons, and there are no artists or patrons without an ideology. The conditions under which a work of art is produced deserve to be studied. This is the point of view that will be adopted here, in all due awareness of what it leaves out.

---

*This section was written by François-Marc Gagnon.

The golden dog, subject of William Kirby's famous novel.

A conservative tradition

Among the conditions under which works of art exist and are disseminated, the most important are those of an ideological nature. As has been noted, the ideological landscape of the period being studied was a varied one, even if it was dominated by conservatism. This observation is confirmed by the persistence of certain forms of expression in sculpture and painting. Thus, at the beginning of the period, Ferdinand Villeneuve (1831-1909) was still sculpting gilded wooden statuettes in the old style, such as the one he did for the church at Saint-Isidore-de-Dorchester in the Chaudière valley in about 1865. Henri Angers (1870-1963) perpetuated this style even further. As late as 1909, he executed four large wooden scupltures representing the four evangelists "in the spirit of the old sculptors of yesteryear" for Saint-Ambroise church in Loretteville near Quebec City. Painters showed the same tendency. The mid-nineteenth-century "greats" of Quebec painting were dying out at the beginning of the period, except for Antoine Plamondon, who did not die until 1895, fifteen years after he was named first vice-president of the Royal Canadian Academy. Théophile Hamel died in 1870, Cornelius Krieghoff two years later. But their style did not die out with them. Two disciples of Théophile Hamel, Ludger Ruelland (1827-96) and Joseph-Arthur-Eugène Hamel (1845-1932), the elder Hamel's nephew, kept their master's style alive until the end of the century, continuing to paint portraits in the face of competition from photography, which eventually defeated them on their own ground.

Napoléon Bourassa and his influence

These examples of *survivance* are indications of the conservatism of the period but not of any great creativity. Meanwhile, Napoléon Bourassa (1827-1916) tried to do something other than simply repeat the formulas of his predecessors. Not that Bourassa can be considered a revolutionary. He was an ardent nationalist who married the daughter of Louis-Joseph Papineau and was profoundly influenced by the ideology of the Nazarenes while in Rome and Florence during the 1850s. The Nazarenes were German painters whose goal was both to develop a new form of romanticism and to express their religious feelings openly in their paintings. Their indirect influence on religious sensibility in Quebec was great, as not only Bourassa but also Ozias Leduc, at the beginning of his career, came under their spell. The Nazarenes' interest in the Middle Ages made a particularly strong impression on Bourassa; like them, he wanted to return to the old forms of association, the guild and corporation, in which artists had been organized. Needless to say, these anachronistic endeavours were no more successful in Quebec than in Germany, but they did provide artists with some opportunities to collaborate on collective projects that were important in their time.

The one in which Bourassa was most interested was Notre-Dame-de-Lourdes chapel in Montreal, which he wanted to do as a collective work; like a medieval headmaster, he surrounded himself with apprentices to whom he hoped to transmit the secrets of his art. Bourassa was also interested in mural painting which, until his time, had been confined to religious subjects. He correctly perceived that Quebecers would be interested in murals on great historical subjects, and this genre developed considerably in Quebec thanks to him. His *Apotheosis of Christopher Columbus*, on which he worked for six years (1859-65), is evidence of his commitment to this form.

Napoléon Bourassa (1827-1916).

Bourassa was also convinced of the importance of developing art education in Quebec. His efforts in this area, first undertaken in 1877, were preceded by the initiative of Abbé Chabert, who six years earlier had begun giving classes in painting and sculpture in Montreal's Arts et Manufactures schools. The promise of these early efforts would be fulfilled only much later, with the establishment of the École des Beaux-Arts in Quebec City in 1921 and a similar school in Montreal the following year.

One student who worked under Bourassa on the Notre-Dame-de-Lourdes project was a young sculptor, Louis-Philippe Hébert (1850-1917), who later became famous. Born in Sainte-Sophie-d'Halifax in the Bois-Francs region, he went to Rome in 1869 on a foolish escapade in an attempt to defend the interests of the Vatican under Pope Pius IX. When he came back, he settled in Montreal, and joined Bourassa's group of apprentices at Notre-Dame-de-Lourdes in 1871. His was a precocious talent, and belongs to the period being studied since he produced his works before 1893. Like his master, he contributed towards extending the range of traditional sculpture in Quebec beyond religious statuary. He won fame primarily through his large historical monuments, executed in the academic style and very popular as a result. His monument to Jacques Cartier in Ottawa (1885) is well known, and his monument to Maisonneuve on Montreal's Place d'Armes (1893) is even more renowned. In the meantime, he was commissioned to do a series of historical sculptures for the façade of the new parliament building in Quebec City in 1887.

The rest of Hébert's career is of less interest here. Wishing to complete his training in Paris, he succeeded in having his work shown regularly in the salons of the very conservative Société des Artistes Français between 1893 and 1913. He died in Montreal in 1917.

Despite everything, the work of Hébert, like that of Bourassa, is evidence of the general conservatism of the period. While they were more innovative than the painters and sculptors who only repeated the formulas of the past, their development did not involve any real break in tradition.

If it can be stated that the artists discussed until now were in some sense linked to the clerical-nationalist ideological current, another group sprang up reflecting the rather vague form of liberalism that was gaining more and more ground towards the end of the century. This current developed outside the traditional channels through which the arts were disseminated, the church and the portrait-hungry bourgeoisie. Between 1867 and 1896, the first art institutions were established and private individuals began to acquire a taste for collecting art. It was in the new artistic circles created in this way that new tendencies and new styles developed.

An innovative current

The most significant of these institutions was without doubt the Art Association of Montreal, which became the Montreal Museum of Fine Arts in 1948. The Art

The gallery of the Art Association of Montreal, inaugurated in 1879.

Association was for a long time the only forum where artists could show their works publicly in Canada. Even after a number of Canadian art institutions were established — such as the Ontario Society of Artists in Toronto in 1872 and the Royal Canadian Academy of Arts and the National Gallery of Canada in 1880 — Montreal continued to be the artistic capital of the country. Thus, despite its avowed "national" pretensions, the Royal Canadian Academy of Arts, after presenting its first annual exhibition in Ottawa in March 1880, showed the works from the exhibition in Montreal. Montreal was the major market for art; after all, it was where the money was, and also the collectors.

The collections accumulated by the leading businessmen of the time were so opulent and ambitious as to beggar the imagination. Sir William Van Horne had eclectic tastes and collected both old masters such as El Greco, Constable, Rembrandt, Hals and Reynolds and "moderns" such as Théodore Rousseau, Renoir and Monet. James Ross had a Ruisdaël and a Rembrandt. R.B. Angus had a magnificent Constable and the Turner in Lord Strathcona's collection was no less extraordinary. These Montreal millionaires did not collect only foreign art; they were prepared to encourage Canadian painting to the extent that it corresponded to their taste and training. They contributed greatly towards making Montreal Canada's art capital of the era.

It is hardly surprising that their taste ran primarily to landscapes. The setting for their railways and other projects was an immense country, and they were not insensitive to its visual aspects. The painters of the period naturally shared their enthusiasm, and landscape painting was by far the most common genre. Painters ventured down the St. Lawrence as far as the Maritimes, north of Toronto and even past the Great Lakes to the West to bring back images of the country's vast scale and luminous sky. The first school of Canadian landscape painting dates from this era. Joseph Légaré preceded these painters in time, but he remained an isolated case, an exception that proves the rule.

Sunrise on the Saguenay (1880) by Lucius R. O'Brien (1832-91) is probably one of the key works of the period. The fearsome vertical walls of rock on the left fade into a luminous haze. Small sailboats at the foot of the cliff indicate the scale of the composition. Light pervades the entire right side of the painting and suggests limitless expansion in this direction. All these characteristics had been brought together ten years earlier in a painting by A. Allan Edson (1846-88), *Mount Orford and the Owl's Head from Lake Memphremagog*. There are no people in Edson's scene, but a boat in the foreground takes their place. The haze is another element in this grandiose composition that presages O'Brien.

In late 1885, the last spike was driven on the Canadian Pacific Railway, bringing such unity as can be given a country by a ribbon of iron. Artists were commissioned to celebrate the event, and the vogue for landscapes reached new heights. In the years following 1885, almost every Canadian landscape painter of any consequence travelled to western Canada to paint the Rocky Mountains as an invited guest of the CPR. These artists produced a considerable number of large canvases aiming to express the grandiose, even sublime character of that part of the country. Thus, in the painting *In the Rocky Mountains* (1886) by John Arthur Fraser (1838-98), not only are the mountains placed in the background, but small human figures and a canoe by a lake in the foreground appear to make the mountain all the more overwhelming. The placement of the subject (the mountain recedes towards the left) suggests a forceful lighted expansion beyond the canvas. This contributes to the impression of the sublime that this large composition (110.4 x 120.7 cm) evokes. The same observations could apply to the numerous views of British Columbia forests that dominated exhibitions in Montreal and Toronto towards the end of the nineteenth century, of which Lucius O'Brien's *A British Columbian Forest* is perhaps the best example.

Lucius R. O'Brien (1832-99), *Sunrise on the Saguenay*, 1880.

The Montreal collectors' passion for large and picturesque landscapes did not exclude other tastes. Following the lead of their American counterparts, they were also interested in French painting, especially in the painters of the Barbizon school. The school took its name from a small village near the forest of Fontainebleau where a number of painters, grouped around Jean-Baptiste Camille Corot (1796-1875), did their work; notable members of the group were Théodore Rousseau (1812-67) and Jean-François Millet (1814-75). These painters attached great importance to the expression of emotion and as a result studied nature in a more intimate and affectionate manner than previous artists. The great trees of the forest of Fontainebleau, especially oaks, became Théodore Rousseau's favourite subject. Millet's inspiration was more varied, and he introduced human figures in his landscapes. His *Sower*, shown at the Salon of 1850, and his *Angelus* are widely known. But Millet's subject is less the individual himself than the dignity of work. His goal is not so much to represent individuals, the members of a class in society, as to portray exemplary figures and actions. This observation is important in understanding the psychology of the businessmen who collected Millet and his Canadian imitators.

Allan A. Edson (1846-88), *Mount Orford Morning*, 1870, now titled *Mount Orford and the Owl's Head from Lake Memphremagog.*

With their taste for the French masters of the Barbizon school, the Montreal collectors also took an interest in painters who could be called the Canadian representatives of the same tendency. The following anecdote is an indication of the seriousness of their commitment to these painters. In 1882, Oscar Wilde made a stop in Toronto as part of his celebrated North American tour. He was given a warm welcome, and in return for this reception deigned to express an interest in local art. He soon became enamoured of the work of the Ontario painter Homer Watson (1855-1936), in whom he saw a "Canadian Constable." He even ordered a painting from the artist, which contributed to Watson's success when it was delivered in 1888. But in his enthusiasm, Wilde took the still more astonishing step of offering to guide Watson around English art circles if the painter agreed to leave his native village of Doon near Kitchener and come back with him to London.

It might be expected that Watson would jump at the opportunity, but he did nothing of the sort. He was at the time earning a modest living by selling his paintings and was not about to give up a bird in the hand for two in the bush. His main customers were the Montreal collectors; he had made his first significant sale to Alexander C. Hutchison, a Montreal architect, in 1877. It was not until five years after Wilde issued his invitation that Watson went to England, where his mission fulfilled its promise. Wilde brought him in contact with the painter James Whistler and introduced him at the Chelsea Club in London.

The trip to London was far from being harmful to Watson's career. But it was in

John Arthur Fraser (1838-98), *In the Rocky Mountains,* now entitled *Unidentified Landscape.*

Montreal, after Watson's return to Canada in 1891, that the full significance of his recognition by Wilde and art circles in England was perceived. His *Log-Cutting in the Woods* (1893) won first prize at the spring salon of the Art Association of Montreal and was soon acquired by Lord Strathcona. This success again attracted attention to him and gave his career in Montreal a new impetus. His most important patron was James Ross, who bought a number of paintings and invited Watson and his wife to accompany him on cruises to Nova Scotia. Ross also pulled strings to assure Watson of a major London exhibition at the prestigious Goupil Gallery.

The Montreal collectors' infatuation with Watson is traceable to their taste for the painters of the Barbizon school, and perhaps also to their interest in the French realist tendency, a reflection of which they professed to find in Watson's style. During his stay in Europe (1887-91), Watson spent a short time in Paris and came in contact with the works of Millet, Daubigny, Corot, Théodore Rousseau,

Mauve and others. There is no doubt that his painting was influenced by this contact. *Log-Cutting in the Woods*, which shows two lumberjacks in the foreground sawing a tree trunk placed on the ground, is completely in the spirit of Millet.

With only a derivative and belated awareness of the Barbizon school, Watson remained on the margins of the tendency it inspired. The major representative of the tendency in Quebec was Horatio Walker (1858-1938). The son of a forest entrepreneur, Walker worked for the firm of Notman-Fraser in Toronto and then settled in New York in 1878, returning occasionally to Canada. In 1881 he went to Europe, where he became aware of the importance of Millet's work. Back in New York in 1883, he acquired a summer house on the Île d'Orléans in Quebec, and thereafter lived alternately in the United States and Canada. Although he sold his paintings primarily in the United States, he was not ignored by the Montreal collectors; Charles Porteous, among others, gave him steady encouragement. Towards the end of his life he retired to the Île d'Orléans, where he was visited by Mgr Albert Tessier, who filmed the painter on his own turf. Horatio Walker can be linked unreservedly to the Barbizon school. Walker himself described what his work was about in the following passage quoted by J. Russell Harper:

> The pastoral life of the people of our countryside, the noble work of the habitant, the magnificent panoramas which surround him, the different aspects of our seasons, the calm of our mornings and the serenity of our evenings, the movement of ebb and flow of our tides which I have observed on the shores of my island which truly is the sacred temple of the muses and a gift of the gods to men: such are the preferred subjects of my paintings. I have passed the greatest part of my life in trying to paint the poetry, the easy joys, the hard daily work of rural life, the sylvan beauty in which is spent the peaceable life of the habitant, the gesture of the wood cutter and the ploughman, the bright colours of sunrise and sunset, the song of the clock, the daily tasks of the farmyard, all the activity which goes on from morning to evening, in the neighbourhood of the barn.

While it is easy to understand what motivated the Montreal collectors to buy large picturesque landscapes showing Canada as a vast country to be exploited and transformed, the origins of their attraction to the paintings of Watson and Walker, influenced by the Barbizon school, are more puzzling. What could these powerful Montreal businessmen have had in common with the world of workers in the forest or French-Canadian rustics on the Île d'Orléans? Were they motivated by the pleasure of hanging images of the proletariat and peasantry they exploited on the walls of their Montreal mansions? Or were they secret adherents of agriculturalism beneath the trappings of economic liberalism? These hypotheses only have to be formulated for their absurdity to be seen.

It is closer to the mark to note that the countryside and the world of workers in the forest presented in the paintings of Watson and Walker have been heavily interpreted. It is not peasants that are presented so much as traditional peasant

Homer Ransford Watson (1855-1936), *Log-Cutting in the Woods,* 1894.

virtues, which the quotation from Walker cited above identifies with perfect accuracy — hard work, a life governed by the rhythms of nature (daily and seasonal cycles), and "easy joys."

This idealized vision of peasant life bears little relationship to reality. In this vision, peasant life appears highly austere, even sullen. Surely the pious couple in Millet's *Angelus* got to celebrate Mardi Gras! It is not clear that this worthy ideal of virtue corresponded to actual peasant patterns of the time. After all, the Patriotes of 1837 had recruited from the ranks of the peasantry. In truth, the image of work, endurance and stability was much closer to the ideal that the class of capitalist entrepreneurs set out for itself. The popularity of these painters with Montreal's top businessmen does not confirm the significance of agriculturalist ideology; rather, it proves that painting peasants at work was not enough to make one an advocate of the *retour à la terre*. In other words, there is not necessarily a one-to-one relationship between the subject-matter of a painting and an ideology, since the painter is able to treat his themes symbolically. We believe that this is the case here, and that the peasants and workers in the paintings of Watson and Walker are really only symbols through which liberal ideology saw fit to express its own aspirations.

PART THREE
1896-1929

THE ECONOMY

Three major processes highlighted development of the Quebec economy between 1896 and 1929. The first was the impressive growth of new sectors based on the exploitation of natural resources, a phenomenon closely linked to the introduction of hydroelectricity on a massive scale. As a result of the second process, the trend towards monopoly, corporate financial structures were transformed and huge entities were established to produce and sell goods. The final process was urbanization, which meant not only the growth of existing urban agglomerations but also the establishment of new cities and towns and, conversely, a declining role for the countryside in all aspects of the economy.

The international economic climate that prevailed during this era played an integral part in these processes. The trend towards falling prices that had marked the previous period reversed itself in 1896, signalling the start of an unprecedented phase of prosperity in the industrialized countries. The cautious atmosphere of the preceding decades gave way to a widespread mood of euphoria; both prices and profits were on the rise and the period seemed to be something of a golden age of capitalism. Almost all countries have evocative phrases to describe these years — "la belle époque" in France, "Edwardian splendour" in Britain, the "Gilded Age" in the United States. The ruling classes looked towards the future with increasing optimism, and the great success stories of the bourgeoisie reached a peak in this era.

In the United States, Rockefeller, Carnegie and Morgan were at the height of their glory and spent their money with unparalleled extravagance; Vanderbilt had a virtual Renaissance palace built in North Carolina. The French chocolate magnate Menier bought Anticosti Island in Quebec to use as his own private hunting grounds and as a base for trying his hand at the forest industry. In Montreal, the luxurious mansions of the Sainte-Antoine district and Westmount were evidence of a new affluence. As an economic dependency of the United

States and Britain, Canada benefited from the new international climate. Wilfrid Laurier declared optimistically that the twentieth century belonged to Canada. It should be noted, however, that the period did not have the same significance for other classes in society. Workers were especially hard hit by the negative effects of inflation, and their living conditions did not improve at a pace with the growing enthusiasm and profits of the bourgeoisie.

All in all, then, the years between 1896 and 1929 were stamped with the seal of prosperity, and this was undoubtedly one reason why the Depression that began in 1929 had such an impact on the imagination. However, as in the years 1873-96, there was a succession of shorter cycles, each with phases of rising and falling prices. These cycles corresponded to short-term fluctuations; in reality, the period was marked by a long movement of rising prices lasting from 1896 to 1920, followed by a movement of falling prices.

Between 1896 and 1913, prosperity was based on three elements—development of the Canadian West, railway construction, and industrial growth in central Canada. In Canadian historical literature, this is the period of the "wheat boom." As wheat prices rose in foreign markets, production in the Canadian West grew rapidly, and wheat acreage was extended beyond what prudence should have dictated; to increase production, wheat was planted in areas where climatic conditions were unfavourable. This was also the era in which two new transcontinental railways were built. And finally, in Quebec and Ontario investment picked up again at the turn of the century and brought about significant industrial growth, to the extent that it has been maintained that the industrialization of Quebec dates from this time.

Along with these initiatives, there was also a substantial increase in foreign investment, mostly of British and American origin. This private investment had a clear spillover effect on public spending, as the different levels of government committed large sums for a variety of purposes; even municipal governments promised subsidies to companies that established themselves within their jurisdictions. Two small recessions, in 1904 and 1907, appeared to be nothing more than chance occurrences.

By 1912, inflation had become a serious problem in Canada, and the contraction of the imperial powers in the world touched off a recession in 1913. The impact of the new conditions was felt in a tightening capital market and in export markets for agricultural products. The recession was initially exacerbated by the First World War, which disturbed economic circuits and production and aggravated unemployment.

Slowly, however, the situation improved. As more men enlisted, the number of unemployed decreased, and the military needs of Canada and its allies stimulated both agricultural and industrial production. Like all foodstuffs, Canadian wheat became a strategic material for the allies. During these years, governments encouraged the growth of productivity in agriculture, bringing about overinvestment on the part of farmers. The war also had a stimulating effect on industry. Traditional sectors such as textiles and footwear had to meet military needs, while new ones, such as the armaments industry, were created. In the last years of the war, Canadian industry operated at full capacity.

The return of peace raised the question of the reconversion of the economy. The years 1920-22 were a period of recession; both agriculture and industry were affected and prices fell with brutal suddenness, making the recession's impact all the greater. Farmers, who had been led to increase their productive capacity, now found themselves burdened with surpluses and heavy debts. Even more serious, the return of peace was accompanied by the closing of European agricultural markets, as each country wanted to protect its own production. Industry underwent a similar crisis of overproduction and reconversion.

The economy began to recover in 1923-24, and starting in 1925 investment and production grew in unprecedented fashion, especially in the industrial sector. These were the "mad years," which came to an abrupt end one Thursday in October 1929. The Wall Street crash was not in itself the cause of the "great depression" that followed; rather, it was a symptom, and perhaps the detonator. The crash was primarily a crisis of confidence pertaining to the financial world and the stock exchange. The collapse of the market value of stocks did not in principle entail a collapse of the real value of corporate assets. In other words, if the shares of a company lost eighty per cent of their value on the market, this did not in any sense mean that the company's factories had lost eighty per cent of their real value. However, in a climate of overinvestment, it could mean that the company would be driven into bankruptcy because creditors would demand repayment and the company would no longer be able to obtain financing. Overinvestment means growth in productive capacity, but it also means a higher debt level and necessitates an increasingly active market to provide an outlet for production. Nothing of the sort happened, and a crisis became inevitable. The depression was all the more striking in contrast with the long period of prosperity that had begun in 1896. There had been recessions in that period, but never a panic such as this.

In analysing the period, the rise of new sectors based on natural resources and manufacturing production will be looked at first. Then, after an examination of changes in capitalism, the development of commerce and communications will be looked at, followed by urbanization and agricultural production. The section will end with a brief survey of economic policies.

CHAPTER 18

NATURAL RESOURCES AND INDUSTRIALIZATION

In the late nineteenth century, Quebec's industrial structure was characterized primarily by the presence of light manufacturing industries employing cheap and plentiful labour and secondarily by the existence of an equipment industry concentrated in Montreal. The products of these industries were intended essentially for the Canadian market. Only one important sector, the sawn lumber industry, was based on natural resources and directed towards an external market.

Starting at the very end of the century, however, the use of natural resources served as the basis for the development of a number of new sectors. Within a few years, these sectors — hydroelectricity, pulp and paper, aluminum smelting, chemicals and mining — profoundly changed Quebec's industrial structure.

A New Industrial Front

These new industries shared a number of characteristics that distinguished them from the industries of the preceding era. An initial area of difference was their location. Traditional industries, based on abundant labour, tended to establish themselves close to the largest pools of rural population. Because of the nature of their products — consumer goods and equipment intended for the Canadian market — locations near the major railways were also highly desirable. This explains the heavy concentration of industry in the St. Lawrence Valley, especially in the Montreal plain. The new industries had to respond to different imperatives. They established themselves either close to raw materials so as to reduce transportation costs, or else close to sources of electrical energy. A number of these new industries located outside the old industrial zone, on the periphery of Quebec's inhabited area, in the colonization regions or the towns that served as outlets for these regions.

Most of the new industries were based on late-nineteenth-century technological advances, and the complex and costly technology they required was imported from Europe or, more typically, the United States. Because of the nature of the production process and the equipment required, production units of considerable size generally had to be built. The investment required was also substantial, often of the order of several million dollars, and the small local industrialist was forced to give way to powerful corporations with solid financial support.

Quebec and even Canadian demand was not large enough to support development based on resource exploitation. Instead, this development was governed by foreign demand, partly British but mostly American. Unlike previous industries, the new sectors were largely export-oriented, and this raised the question of the extent to which the product would be processed in Quebec before being exported. In most cases, only primary processing would be done in Quebec, and finished products would be manufactured in the United States; Quebec would export wood pulp newsprint to serve the American publishing industry, and aluminum ingots to be manufactured into finished aluminum products south of the border.

Because of the size of the investment required, the determining role of American demand and the need to import technology, American capital was a leading factor in the development of resource-based industries. The economic historian Albert Faucher has written of the "continental character" of this phase of industrialization. But while American capital was the driving force, English-Canadian capitalists linked to the large Montreal banks also played a role in this development, especially in the paper and hydroelectric industries. The position of French-Canadian entrepreneurs, however, was marginal.

Because of their technological complexity, these new industries needed skilled engineers and technicians who commanded high salaries. Thus, a technical school was established in the St. Maurice Valley to meet the manpower needs of the paper mills. The demand for unskilled workers, however, also remained high. The growth of the paper industry, for instance, led to an increase in woodcutting operations, and this meant a greater demand for lumberjacks, most of whom were farmers or colonists. Overall, the new industries employed mostly male workers.

The Major Sectors

Hydroelectricity

At the heart of these changes was the emergence of Quebec as one of the world's major producers of hydroelectricity. Although the existence of electricity had been known for a long time, its large-scale production began only in the late nineteenth century. Electrical energy produced by a generator was used in the 1870s, but it was in 1882 that Thomas Edison inaugurated his first electric generating station in New York. In subsequent years, thanks to the work of Edison, George Westinghouse and other inventors, industrial production of electricity was begun and distribution problems were solved. The first generating stations, however, were small in scale and used thermal energy. The harnessing of the American Falls at Niagara, completed in 1895, inaugurated the era of electricity generated by water power.

The production of electricity from thermal sources in Quebec began in the 1880s, when several companies were established in Montreal; at the same time, small dams were built on a number of rivers. Construction of the first large dam, at Shawinigan, began in 1898, only three years after completion of the Niagara plant. Thus, Quebec entered the electric age at almost the same time as the United States. Quebec, especially its northern region, formed by the Canadian Shield, is rich both in terms of the number of rivers within its borders and in terms of the size of their flow and drop. This considerable energy potential was initially developed by American capital and technology. Hydroelectric production capacity grew rapidly during the first three decades of the twentieth century, from 83,000 kilowatts in 1900 to 2,322,000 kilowatts in 1930. The rate of growth was especially high in the period before the First World War, when the first large dams were built, and during the 1920s, when large-scale generating stations on the Saguenay, the Ottawa and the St. Lawrence were brought into production.

There was a rapid tendency towards monopoly in this sector, at least within each region, as it was not profitable to set up multiple distribution networks within the same territory. A few giants emerged during the period. The Shawinigan Water and Power Company was by far the largest producer. Organized for the purpose of building the Shawinigan dam, it became solidly established in the St. Maurice Valley and along part of the south bank of the St. Lawrence. It provided electricity to Montreal, and in 1923 it took control of the Quebec Power Company, which served the Quebec City market and its surrounding region. Shawinigan exercised leadership of a sort and was responsible for a number of technological innovations.

Montreal Light, Heat and Power was the product of a merger of several gas and electricity companies under the guidance of powerful Montreal financiers. It was essentially a distribution company that bought electricity produced by other enterprises, especially Shawinigan. It exploited — in every sense of the word — the rich Montreal market, where it made profits that the economist John H. Dales has described as "fabulous."

Three other large companies shared the Quebec market. The Southern Canada Power Company produced electricity in the Eastern Townships region. During the 1920s, two additional large companies were established — the Gatineau Power Company, which served the Outaouais and part of the Laurentian region and sold a significant portion of its output to Ontario, and the Duke-Price Power Company, which produced electricity in the Saguenay primarily to meet the needs of the Alcan aluminum smelter and the Price Paper Company. There were also many small local or municipal enterprises, with a negligible share of the market.

The abundance of electrical energy and its availability for sale to industrial

The Shawinigan dam in 1929.

entrepreneurs at a fairly low cost led to the establishment of industries that consumed large quantities of it — aluminum smelting and chemicals. Similarly, pulp and paper mills used surplus energy from the generating stations to meet their needs. According to Dales, Shawinigan, at least in its early days, played an active role in this area. Seeking a market for its product, it brought about the establishment of a number of industries in the St. Maurice Valley.

Pulp and paper

Clearly the most important of the new industries was pulp and paper. Small paper-manufacturing enterprises had been established in Quebec in the nineteenth century, but the industry did not develop beyond a very modest scale. In the first three decades of the twentieth century, by contrast, its growth was extremely rapid. How can this growth be explained?

The electric age: poles, wires and streetcars on St. James Street in Montreal, 1910.

A series of nineteenth-century technological innovations made it feasible to manufacture paper from wood pulp; especially important was the invention of the Fourdrinier paper machine, which made possible continuous production. Machines of this kind first appeared in Quebec during the 1880s. The resinous woods of which Quebec forests had substantial reserves were in great demand because of their particular suitability for newsprint manufacture. But innovations and resources were not enough. A market was also necessary, and a determining factor in the industry's development was American demand, which in the early twentieth century was increasing rapidly. There were two major reasons for this growth — the rise of the mass-circulation press and changes in advertising that resulted in substantially larger newspapers.

In meeting this burgeoning demand, American producers were at an increasing disadvantage relative to their Canadian rivals. First of all, American forest resources had been abused and had become largely depleted, and there were growing conservation movements that aimed to limit the use of what remained. In addition, the species of wood available in many regions of the United States were less suited to newsprint manufacture than the conifers of the Canadian forests. It became more and more difficult for Americans to produce newsprint as cheaply as it was being manufactured in Canada. During the period, a regional division of labour was realized in North America. American manufacturers began to specialize in products other than newsprint, notably fine papers, while Canada became the major newsprint producer, ultimately supplying about eighty per cent of the North American market. And within Canada, Quebec was the largest producing province.

The value of Quebec's pulp and paper output grew from $5 million in 1900 to $14 million in 1910; it had increased to $75 million by 1922 and reached a peak of $130 million in 1929. Overall, the paper products sector was in ninth place among Quebec's industrial products in both 1900 and 1910, with 3.8 and five per cent respectively of gross value of production. By 1922, it had climbed to second place, with about twelve per cent of the total.

The first modern enterprise established in Quebec in this sector was the Laurentide Company, founded at Grand-Mère in 1877 by John Forman, a Montrealer of Scottish origin who had gone into partnership with American industrialists already active in the paper industry. In 1896, the company was bought by an American investor and a group of Canadian financiers linked to the Bank of Montreal and Canadian Pacific. A pioneer in its field, Laurentide was solidly based, and according to the sociologist Jorge Niosi was the largest Canadian newsprint producer between 1898 and 1919. The reorganization of Laurentide coincided with the first wave of new pulp and paper enterprises in Quebec, which occurred at the turn of the century and was conspicuous primarily in two regions that had already established a reputation for forest production.

In the St. Maurice Valley, Laurentide at Grand-Mère was soon joined by other enterprises. The Brown Corporation, an American company, established a mill at

La Tuque in 1900, while the Belgo Canadian Pulp and Paper Company was founded at Shawinigan by Belgian interests the same year. In the Saguenay-Lake St. John region, the Compagnie de Pulpe de Chicoutimi, headed by J.-E.-A. Dubuc, was founded in 1898 and became a major producer within a few years. Other establishments, such as Damase Jalbert's mill at Val-Jalbert, also entered the field, as did the Price Company, already an important influence in the region as a result of its forest operations and sawmills. Mills were opened in other regions as well. This early period of the Quebec pulp and paper industry was characterized by small-scale enterprises, most of which initially produced only pulp and exported it to be processed into paper in the United States or England. Quickly, however, profitability considerations led Quebec producers to manufacture their own newsprint.

Another stage in the northward migration of the North American pulp and paper industry arose out of changes in government policies between 1900 and 1913. To encourage increased processing of wood within the province, the Quebec government banned the export of pulpwood cut on public land in 1910, following the example of Ontario, which had adopted a similar measure ten years earlier. The American government countered in 1911 by imposing a tariff on paper originating in regions where such an embargo existed. The main victims of this measure were American newsprint purchasers, who had to pay a higher price for their paper; they put pressure on Washington and achieved repeal of the tariff in 1913.

Very heavy investments were made in the pulp and paper industry in Quebec, especially between 1915 and 1925. Existing mills were enlarged and new enterprises were established as a result of the heavy demand for newsprint. This race to invest in the pulp and paper sector quickly had negative effects. Production capacity exceeded demand and competition between the companies resulted in a price war starting in 1925. Some paper companies were eliminated, including the Dubuc group of Chicoutimi. Mills were closed; when the Val-Jalbert mill shut down in 1927 the townspeople left, and a ghost town still stands in mute witness to the ferocity of the paper war.

Financiers tried to find a solution in concentration. The most significant movement in this direction in Quebec involved the group of companies linked to the Royal Bank and its president, Herbert Holt. Five large paper companies — St. Maurice Paper of Trois-Rivières, Wayagamack Pulp and Paper of Cap-de-la-Madeleine, Belgo Paper of Shawinigan, Laurentide of Grand-Mère, and Port Alfred Pulp and Paper — and their subsidiaries were merged into the Canada Power and Paper Company. This company, founded in 1928, became Consolidated Paper three years later. But the merger movement only carried the price war to another level. In the late 1920s, the sector was dominated by a few giants — International Paper, an American company with a subsidiary called Canadian International Paper (CIP) in Canada; Canada Power and Paper; Abitibi Power and Paper, which had a few mills in Quebec although it operated principally in

J.-E.-A. Dubuc's pulp mill at Chicoutimi, early twentieth century.

Ontario; and the Price Company, which had been present in Quebec for more than a century.

The major Canadian producers tried to resolve the crisis through agreements fixing a base price for newsprint that would allow all the companies to make a profit. These attempts failed, primarily because of the refusal of the powerful International Paper Company to participate. At this stage, the war pitted the Canadian paper companies grouped around the Royal Bank on one side against International Paper, linked to the Rockefeller group of banks, on the other; it ended in the late 1920s with a victory for the American group.

Aluminum smelting and chemicals

Aluminum and chemical products were two new industries established in Quebec between 1897 and 1929. In both these industries, the production process requires large quantities of electrical energy, so that they tend to locate where electricity is abundant and cheap. Proximity to an energy source is more important than proximity to raw materials in determining factory location, and this was especially true during the period under consideration, when huge quantities of energy could

A new town: Arvida and its aluminum smelter in 1928.

not be transported cheaply over long distances with the existing technology. Thus, in the case of aluminum the raw material, bauxite, was imported from British Guiana. Reduction was accomplished through electrolysis, a new process whose industrial application dated from the late 1880s. The construction of the Shawinigan dam led to the establishment in that town of an aluminum smelter, which came into service in 1901. Another step was taken around 1924 with the construction of a smelter at Arvida in the Saguenay region by the Aluminum Company of America (Alcoa); this project was linked to the harnessing of the Saguenay River at Île Maligne. Alcoa spawned the Aluminum Company of Canada (Alcan), which inherited the Arvida smelter.

In the chemical industry, an electrical process for manufacturing calcium carbide was discovered in the late nineteenth century. At the instigation of Shawinigan Water and Power, seeking outlets for its electricity, a company specializing in this product was established in 1901; the Canada Carbide Company became a subsidiary of Shawinigan Water and Power. Acetylene, acetic acid and a large number of chemical products used in industry are obtained from calcium carbide. With the need for war matériel between 1914 and 1918, demand

The Canadian Electro-Products factory at Shawinigan, 1918.

in this sector was strong, and a number of related enterprises centred around Canada Carbide were established as a result. Shawinigan became one of Canada's major chemical centres. The industry managed to overcome the postwar recession without too much difficulty and underwent renewed expansion in the 1920s. While the Quebec chemical industry was not limited to calcium carbide and its derivatives, it owed part of its growth to this product and the electricity with which it was manufactured.

Mining

Mining was a late development among the new resource-oriented sectors. The image of Quebec as an area rich in mineral resources is a twentieth-century phenomenon. Unlike the other sectors examined in this chapter, mining as it developed in Quebec was not primarily an industrial activity; rather, it consisted

An asbestos mine at Black Lake, 1888.

of the extraction of raw materials that were exported and processed elsewhere. Nevertheless, some producers considered it advantageous to do a certain amount of primary processing locally. They would build concentrators and sometimes a refinery to eliminate some of the waste material, so that a higher-grade ore would be obtained and transportation costs would be reduced. Industrialization linked to mining in Quebec rarely went beyond primary processing of this sort. Despite this limited impact, the mining sector still brought notable changes to the economies of particular regions, such as the Eastern Townships and especially the Abitibi region (mining development of the North Shore was a later development).

Immediately before the First World War, there was still very little mining in Quebec. Such activity as existed was dominated by products of two kinds. First, there were construction materials, primarily stone and sand, extracted in quarries scattered throughout the territory. Only on the outskirts of large cities was the size of these enterprises substantial. The other significant activity was asbestos mining,

The main street of Rouyn, which was to become a centre of mining activity in the Abitibi region, 1924.

which began to develop in the Eastern Townships in the 1880s and 1890s; Quebec quickly became the world's leading producer of this commodity. While output was rising in terms of volume in the early twentieth century, its value remained low because Quebec mines contained mostly short fibres, which sold at a substantially lower price than long fibres. Asbestos was extracted near five major mining centres: Asbestos, Coleraine, Black Lake, Thetford Mines and East Broughton. After being extracted, the ore was separated from the rock in which it was embedded, but no further processing was done in Quebec. Mechanization of the mills in which the separation was effected began in the period being studied. Further stages of processing were done in the purchasing countries, primarily the United States and European nations.

Asbestos production was still very unstable. There were a large number of mining companies, and competition among them was fierce. When demand or prices rose, new mines were put into production, only to be closed when there was a crisis. Some mines were operated directly by American purchasers, such as the Johns-Manville Corporation, which thus assured themselves of a steady supply of asbestos. The independent producers tried a number of times to organize to reduce competition and limit the disastrous effects of overproduction, but these efforts were repeatedly stymied by the entry of new competitors. Finally, in 1925, eleven companies were brought together in the Asbestos Corporation, which became the leading producer. This reorganization contributed to stabilization of the industry at the end of the period.

The Noranda Mines smelter at Rouyn, 1927.

At the time the Asbestos Corporation was founded, mining exploration was also under way at the other extremity of Quebec, in the Abitibi region. The zone lying roughly between Rouyn and Val d'Or contains significant reserves of metals, principally copper, gold, zinc and silver, found in proportions that vary from location to location; in the Val d'Or area, as the name indicates, gold is predominant, while the area around Rouyn is rich primarily in copper. This geological structure is an extension of a similar zone in northeastern Ontario that had already been opened to mining development. The Abitibi only became part of Quebec in 1898, and communication with the rest of Quebec was difficult until the National Transcontinental Railway was built just before the First World War. With the coming of the railway, agro-forest colonization was undertaken in the Abitibi, beginning about 1912.

Although were were earlier attempts, serious mineral exploration in the Abitibi began only around 1920, when prospectors, most of them from Ontario, began looking for gold mines. While gold was found, the major discovery of the period was the Horne mine in Rouyn township, which contained some gold but mostly copper. This mine was developed by Noranda Mines Limited, which began construction of its installations in 1926. The company built a smelter and a concentrator at Noranda, and production began in 1927. In 1929 a subsidiary of Noranda Mines, Canadian Copper Refiners, built a refinery in Montreal East to process the ore coming from Noranda. Other mineral discoveries were made in the 1920s and 1930s in the Rouyn, Malartic and Val d'Or-Bourlamaque areas, but in most cases production began only after 1930.

Thus, it was in the late 1920s that mining activities became an important part of the Quebec economy. Output continued to be dominated by construction materials, but the relative significance of these products was on the decline; they represented sixty per cent of the total value of production in 1910 and forty per cent in 1929. Next came industrial minerals, which represented about a third of total production in 1929; this group was dominated by asbestos, production of which grew fairly steadily, from 30,000 tons a year at the end of the nineteenth century to 300,000 tons in 1929. The most significant change occurred in the area of metal production; metals' share of the total value of mineral production grew from two per cent in 1910 to twenty-nine per cent in 1929. Metal production in 1929 was dominated by copper, with gold, zinc, silver and lead some distance behind.

The overall value of mineral production grew from $1.6 million in 1898 to $46.5 million in 1929. The sector continued to be characterized by very limited processing within Quebec, except in the case of copper and some construction materials.

CHAPTER 19
MANUFACTURING PRODUCTION

The new and sometimes spectacular installations of the resource-oriented industries and their entry into new regions made them an object of interest, even fascination, in their early days. Historians have also been affected by this infatuation, and some of them have tended to identify the industrialization of Quebec with these sectors and to have seen their establishment as the sign of Quebec's industrial takeoff. This is, at the very least, a truncated vision of Quebec's economic history.

As noted in chapter 7, during the second half of the nineteenth century Quebec became endowed with a manufacturing structure based primarily on light industry (shoes, textiles, clothing) and secondarily on heavy industry (iron and steel, transportation equipment). This existing structure did not disappear in the twentieth century. Rather, it was extensively reorganized, and it continued to dominate manufacturing production even if its proportion of the total decreased.

The Growth of the Traditional Sectors

The manufacturing structure was based on the Canadian domestic market, which was expanding rapidly in the early twentieth century. The decade preceding the First World War was the period of the largest wave of immigration in Canadian history, half of which was directed towards the industrial centres of the East while the other half provided agricultural settlers for the West. The arrival of these new consumers was an initial stimulus to production. Two other factors contributed to a growth in demand for manufactured products — the commercialization of agriculture, which integrated rural Quebecers into the consumption circuit, and urbanization.

Existing firms entered into a phase of considerable growth. Many expanded their plants; in some cases, this required a move to the suburbs, as the phenomenal

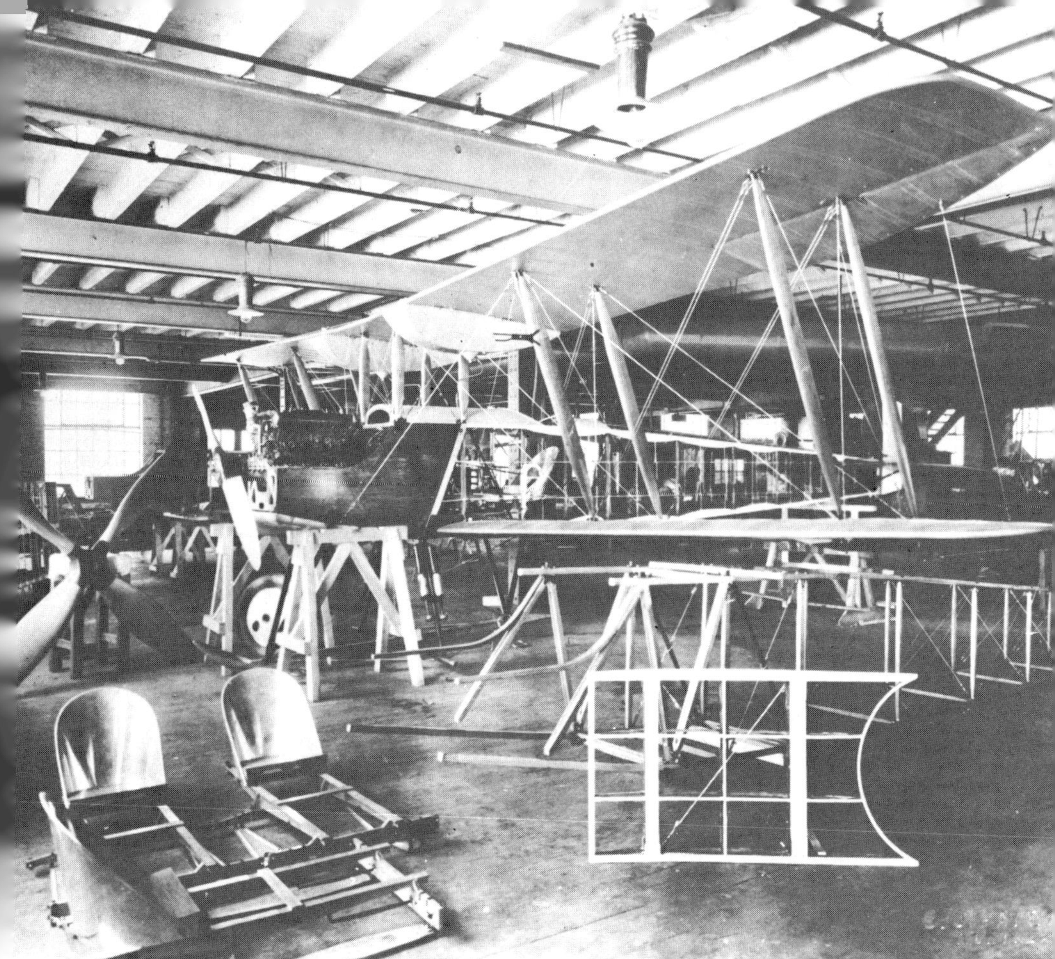

The Canadian Vickers aircraft plant in Montreal, 1920.

growth of the suburbs of Montreal in the early twentieth century attests. The suburban industrial town of Maisonneuve developed in this manner, attracting firms that had been established in Montreal for a number of years, or even several decades, and had to expand their plants. Moving made it possible for these firms to increase production to a new order of magnitude within a short time.

Little is known about another important factor — the rationalization of production through improved management techniques and the use of increasingly complex machines. The conditions of production in the factories were changed by the introduction of electricity. The steam engine was gradually replaced by the electric motor, which was much more efficient and self-contained. In large companies, personnel management methods replaced the paternalistic relations that had characterized the previous era.

Having increased their efficiency and productivity, and having in some cases been merged in the move towards corporate concentration, companies were in a position to extend the range of their products. Sometimes, diversification took the form of specialization of factories or workshops within a single company; in other cases, subsidiaries were established and given the responsibility of manufacturing particular products.

Industrial diversification took place not only within a given firm, but also in the manufacturing structure as a whole. Sectors based on new technology that had previously been at most marginally represented in Quebec developed during the era, the best examples being petroleum products and electrical appliances.

The gross value of manufacturing production in Quebec (Table 30) took a considerable leap during the period, from about $154 million in 1900 to $1.1 billion in 1929. Value added — the figure obtained by eliminating the cost of raw materials used in manufacturing a product from the calculation — grew in similar fashion; its rate of increase was even slightly higher than that of gross value. There were two sub-periods of especially rapid growth, 1900-10 and 1925-29. Data expressed in current dollars can be misleading, since Canada had a high rate of inflation in the second decade of the century, especially during the war. Through the use of data expressed in constant dollars, these figures can be deflated and a better idea of the real level of production can be obtained. The historian Marc Vallières has calculated the average annual rate of growth for each of the three decades under consideration using data expressed in constant dollars (Table 31). His figures clearly indicate the rapid growth during the first and third decades.

TABLE 30

Gross Value of Quebec Manufacturing Production and Value Added, 1900-1929 ($000's)

Year	*Gross Value, Current $*	*Value Added, Current $*	*Gross Value, Constant $*[1]	*Value Added, Constant $*[1]
1900	153,574	68,593	246,112	109,725
1910	340,117	159,111	433,270	202,689
1917	766,100	380,900	514,506	255,809
1918	857,800	403,700	516,747	243,193
1919	916,500	420,200	524,614	240,527
1920	1,053,000	499,600	518,209	245,866
1921	729,500	339,800	508,717	236,960
1922	679,300	346,000	535,726	272,871
1923	784,086	383,423	614,006	300,253
1924	746,859	361,603	576,720	279,230
1925	788,067	376,349	588,989	281,278
1926	867,620	426,435	665,863	327,272
1927	951,604	477,268	747,528	374,916
1928	1,023,269	520,600	814,705	414,491
1929	1,106,475	569,828	888,022	457,326

[1] 1935-39:100.

Source: Marc Vallières, *Les industries manufacturières du Québec 1900-1959*, pp. 132, 136, 145, 149.

Quebec's share of overall Canadian production, however, declined somewhat, especially during the first two decades. The gross value of Quebec's production represented 32.9 per cent of the Canadian total in 1900 but only 26.6 per cent of the total in 1918; after that, the percentage rose slightly, remaining between twenty-eight and twenty-nine per cent from 1919 to 1929. Ontario had much better success in maintaining its position, so that the gap between Quebec and Ontario widened a little, especially between 1900 and 1918 (Figure 2).

Table 31, which shows the distribution by sector of Quebec's industrial production for different years, gives an idea of the development of Quebec's industrial structure. This table shows elements of change, but also remarkable continuity. Leather goods (principally shoes), so important in the nineteenth century, underwent a spectacular decline, from second place with 13.7 per cent of the total value of production to tenth place with only 3.5 per cent of the total. Wood products were also on the decline, sliding from fourth to eighth place. Conversely, paper products rose rapidly, from ninth to second place.

FIGURE 2
Percentage of Gross Value of Canadian Manufacturing Production Accounted for by Quebec and Ontario, 1900-1930

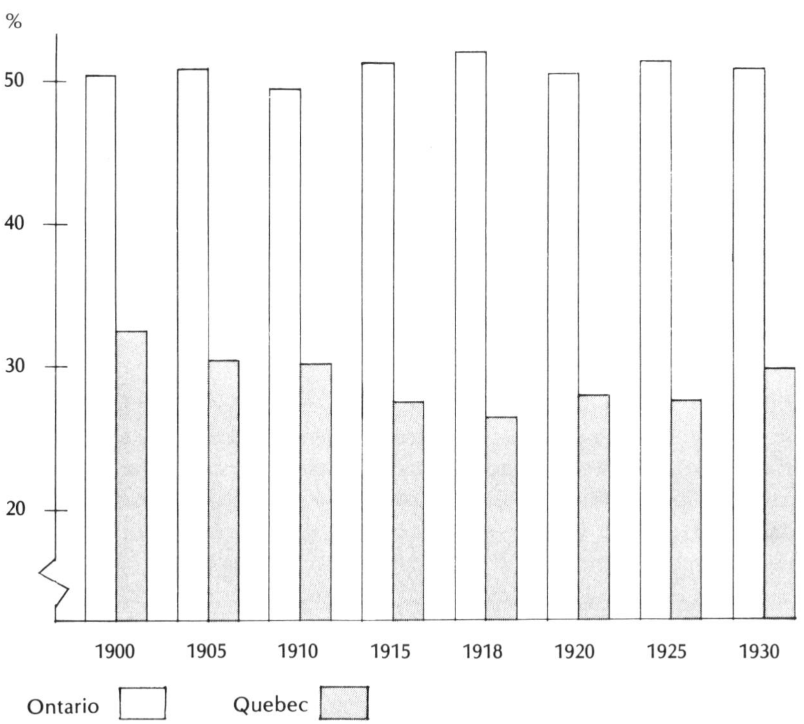

TABLE 31
Average Annual Rate of Growth of Quebec Manufacturing Production, 1900-1930 (in terms of gross value and value added, constant dollars, for each decade)

	Rate of Growth (%)	
Decade	*Gross Value, Constant $*	*Value Added, Constant $*
1900-10	5.51	5.94
1910-20	1.79	0.14
1920-30	5.07	6.08

Source: Marc Vaillières, *Les industries manufacturières du Québec 1900-1959*, p. 45.

The food and beverages sector remained the leader, with about one-fifth of the gross value of production. This was a very diversified sector. It included highly concentrated industries such as sugar refining, brewing and distilling, as well as industries in which competition continued to prevail, with many establishments scattered over the province — butter and cheese plants, bakeries, biscuit factories. This sector represented a much lower proportion of value added, since the cost of agricultural products was such a large component of the gross value of production.

Table 32 shows clearly the rise of the new resource-oriented sectors. Paper, non-ferrous metals, non-metallic minerals and chemical products represented only a little over nine per cent of Quebec manufacturing production in 1900; by 1929 their share had climbed to twenty-two per cent. Their proportion of value added was even greater (eleven per cent in 1900, twenty-six per cent in 1929); it should be noted, however, that until 1934 value-added statistics included fuel and electricity costs, and the industries in question used large quantities of these factors. Each sector increased its share of production during the period, but paper products was by far the largest of the four.

The overall picture of manufacturing production was changed significantly by the rise of these four sectors. But Quebec industry's dependence on sectors that produced consumer goods and used cheap labour was a major characteristic that did not disappear. While the shoe industry declined in relative terms, the clothing, textile and tobacco industries all maintained their positions. Even the shoe industry underwent a period of expansion in the early part of the century, although it did not grow as quickly as other sectors. In the 1920s, production reached a plateau and the industry was no longer a factor in Quebec's industrial growth. Clothing manufacture was in third place in both 1900 and 1930, although its share declined slightly; during the period, the sector represented

TABLE 32
Percentage of Total Gross Value of Quebec Manufacturing Production for Each Group of Industries, 1900-1929

Rank in 1900	*Rank in 1929*	*Group*	% *1900*	*1910*	*1922*	*1929*
1	1	Food and beverages	22.2	17.1	22.6	18.3
2	10	Leather products	13.7	9.1	5.3	3.5
3	3	Clothing	11.1	11.7	9.5	9.7
4	8	Wood products	11.0	13.1	6.3	5.4
5	6	Iron and steel products	8.6	8.7	5.3	7.1
6	4	Textile products	8.3	7.4	10.1	7.7
7	7	Tobacco and tobacco products	5.5	5.6	8.4	6.7
8	5	Transportation equipment	5.4	8.7	3.0	7.4
9	2	Paper products	4.3	5.0	11.8	12.5
10	9	Chemical products	2.8	2.7	5.3	4.1
11	12	Printing, publishing, etc.	2.4	1.8	3.1	2.9
12	14	Electrical appliances and equipment	1.2	2.4	1.5	2.5
13	15	Non-metallic mineral products	1.1	1.8	2.0	2.3
14	11	Non-ferrous metal products	1.0	3.3	1.2	3.3
15	13	Miscellaneous manufacturing	0.9	1.1	1.4	2.6
16	17	Rubber goods	0.3	0.3	1.5	1.8
17	16	Products of petroleum and coal	0.2	0.3	2.0	2.2

Source: Marc Vaillières, *Les industries manufacturières du Québec 1900-1959,* pp. 170, 172. The groups follow the classification system established by the Dominion Bureau of Statistics.

about ten or eleven per cent of Quebec manufacturing production. Textiles followed close behind and climbed from sixth to fourth place. Tobacco remained in seventh place and increased its share of the total; its growth was due to the spread of cigarette smoking. Overall, the share of these four sectors declined from thirty-eight to twenty-three per cent of total gross value of production. Nevertheless, they continued to be important elements in the manufacturing structure and employed substantial numbers of Quebecers.

Engines at the Canadian Pacific shops in Montreal, 1914-18.

The iron and steel products sector was closely associated with railway equipment in the nineteenth century. Together, these two sectors represented about fourteen per cent of production in both 1900 and 1929, although there was considerable variation in the course of the period. In the iron and steel sector, Quebec was increasingly outdistanced by Ontario. Quebec had no steel mill, and specialized in processing iron and steel that had been refined elsewhere into finished and semi-finished products. However, the sector's position in Quebec's manufacturing structure was not negligible — fifth place in 1900 and sixth place in 1929, as its share of the total declined slightly. The transportation equipment sector benefited from the presence in Montreal of the major railway workshops. While it climbed from eighth to fifth place, its share of production fluctuated considerably. A new component of this sector, the automobile industry, bypassed Quebec in favour of Ontario.

Finally, the progress of two relatively new sectors is worth noting — electrical appliances and products of petroleum and coal. Their place in the industrial structure, however, remained fairly small; in 1929 they represented only 2.5 and 2.2 per cent respectively of the value of production. Thus, Quebec industry retained its traditional sectors and a structure inherited from the nineteenth century. But it also underwent a phase of modernization and diversification between 1900 and 1929, and the relative positions of many sectors changed as a result.

A Lagging Economy?

What was the overall place of industry in the Quebec economy as a whole? All appearances indicated that its share of the total production of goods and services was growing, but it is not easy to measure this growth with precision. An initial way of trying to answer the question would be to compare industry with the other major sector of production, agriculture. To do this, it is necessary to call upon the estimates of the gross value of agricultural production established by the economist André Raynauld (see chapter 23). It can be seen that the gross value of manufacturing production was 3.3 times that of agriculture in 1900, and 6.7 times that of agriculture in 1929.

Figures published in the *Canada Year Book* dealing with the net value of production in Quebec indicate that between 1922 and 1929 agriculture's share fell from 29.3 per cent to 19.7 per cent, while the share represented by the manufacturing industry rose from 40.9 per cent to 47.3 per cent. Among the other sectors, the most significant were the forest industry and construction, each representing between ten and twelve per cent of the total. While these two sets of figures are far from perfect, they do indicate an order of magnitude. It is possible to conclude from them that industry was the most important sector of the economy throughout the period and that its share of production was growing.

Its impact on the labour market was also far from negligible. The manufacturing sector employed about a fifth of total manpower, although its share declined slightly, from 21.7 per cent in 1911 to 20.5 per cent in 1921 to 19.6 per cent in 1931. Quebec's percentage of manpower employed in industry in 1931 was higher than the Canadian average (sixteen per cent) but lower than the Ontario figure (twenty-two per cent). In absolute terms, manpower employed in industry

The Murphy sawmill at Rivière-à-Pierre, in Portneuf county west of Quebec City.

increased from 141,921 in 1911 to 201,273 in 1931. The decline in its share of the total was due to the rapid rise of the service sector.

The question of the scale of the industrialization of Quebec is related to the debate about Quebec's so-called economic lag, on which there is an abundant literature. According to a number of writers, Quebec's industrial takeoff occurred significantly later than that of other regions of Canada, especially Ontario. The well-known Faucher-Lamontagne thesis, discussed in chapter 4, is a notable expression of this interpretation. Faucher and Lamontagne argue that the years between 1866 and 1911 were a period of industrial lag for Quebec because of its lack of coal and iron, the two basic materials for an industrial economy. Quebec's real industrial takeoff, according to them, occurred after 1911, and was a result of the growth of the new resource-oriented sectors.

There has been much criticism of the thesis of Quebec's economic lag in the last two decades, notably by the economists John H. Dales and André Raynauld. The thesis was based on a knowledge of economic history that was still embryonic. As noted in chapter 7, more recent research has made it possible to demonstrate the importance of Quebec's initial, late-nineteenth-century industrial base, and the significance within that base of the iron and steel sector. On the basis of this research, the new resource-oriented sectors can also be seen in a more accurate perspective, as a powerful stimulus to — but still only a partial dimension of — the industrialization of Quebec.

To be sure, levels of production in Quebec and Ontario showed a gap in

Ontario's favour, but this should not lead to the conclusion that Quebec's development was slow or lagged behind. André Raynauld has shown that over the long term the rates of growth of Quebec and Ontario industries were entirely comparable. He concludes that between 1870 and 1957, "manufacturing production grew at an annual rate of 5.48 per cent in Ontario and 5.53 per cent in Quebec." While the gap might have widened during a short period — as in the decade 1910-20 — it narrowed again in later years. According to Raynauld, "the problem in Quebec is not one of lagging growth but rather of growth with structural and demographic characteristics different from those of some of the other provinces of the country." Specifically, Quebec's industrial structure included a higher ratio of light industry to heavy industry than Ontario's. In addition, Quebec's high birth rate meant that it had a younger population and thus a lower rate of participation in the labour force. The income obtained by people with jobs was therefore distributed among a larger number of people outside the labour market, so that per capita income was lower in Quebec than in Ontario.

This question of the so-called economic lag, implying a comparison between Quebec and Ontario, should not be confused with what has been called the economic inferiority of French Canadians within Quebec. In the historical literature, this latter problem refers to the minority position of French-Canadian entrepreneurs in the control of Quebec's economy; it will be discussed in chapter 25.

By whatever measure and whatever point of comparison, there is no doubt that in the first decades of the twentieth century Quebec had attained the status of an industrial society, in which the production of manufactured goods was the driving force of the economy.

CHAPTER 20
MONOPOLY CAPITALISM AND FOREIGN INVESTMENT

Competition and Concentration

In the late nineteenth and early twentieth centuries, capitalism underwent significant changes in industrialized countries. This was the era of the transformation from competitive to monopoly capitalism. At a time when most businesses were still modest in size, it was relatively easy for enterprising individuals to go into business, so that in the second half of the nineteenth century there was a proliferation of enterprises in competition with one another. But price wars soon became ruinous, and businessmen turned to monopolization as a check on competition. Their first recourse was the cartel, or agreement among companies to fix prices or divide up the market. There was a spate of such agreements towards the end of the nineteenth century, but they were difficult to maintain, since there was always a competitor that would break the agreement in an effort to increase its share of the market.

Businessmen then resorted to a more radical solution — corporate concentration through the formation of a trust. The more powerful company formed in this way was then able to eliminate recalcitrant competitors and dominate the market. In Canada, the concentration movement began in the 1880s, but did not build up significant momentum until the early twentieth century. Two main forms of concentration were current at the time. The best known and most spectacular was horizontal concentration, or mergers between companies operating in the same sector and manufacturing the same product. There was also vertical concentration, in which companies performing different stages in the production of a commodity were integrated.

The development of the joint stock company, which gradually replaced the traditional family enterprise, made concentration easier. A merger became a financial operation, as new shares were issued, the value of corporate assets was artificially inflated, and the promoters of the merger were in a position to make substantial profits through speculation.

Not much is known about the role of financial institutions in the concentration movement in Canada. In a number of European countries, the major banks gained control of industrial enterprises and initiated the concentration movement; the term finance capital — the result of a merger between banking capital and industrial capital under banker domination — refers to such cases. In Canada, financial networks centred on the major banks have been identified by the historian Gilles Piédalue. However, it cannot be concluded from the existence of these networks that the Canadian banks controlled industrial corporations. It appears rather that there were financial groups that sought control of banks, railways, and commercial, industrial or utility companies at the same time. It was these financial groups, headed by such men as Herbert Holt, Louis-Joseph Forget and Max Aitken, that brought about Canada's major corporate mergers.

The role of American companies in the process of monopolization in Canada must also be taken into account. When American parent corporations merged, Canadian subsidiaries did the same. Thus, the creation of a trust in the shoe-manufacturing machinery industry in the United States, the United Shoe Machinery Company, was closely followed by the establishment of a similar trust in Canada, the United Shoe Machinery Company of Canada. Sometimes, an entirely new Canadian subsidiary was created after establishment of the trust in the United States. Constitution of a Canadian subsidiary through purchase by the American trust of existing Canadian companies was another frequent occurrence. Monopolization, of course, was only one aspect of the penetration of foreign capital into Canada.

It is difficult to treat the Quebec case separately when dealing with the question of monopolies. The great monopolies established in the twentieth century were Canada-wide or at least Ontario-Quebec institutions. The problem therefore has to be dealt with in its wider context. During the period under consideration, the process of monopolization occurred in two distinct stages, the first in the years preceding the First World War and the second during the 1920s.

The early years of the twentieth century were characterized first of all by a significant concentration movement in the banking sector. The number of chartered banks in Canada fell from thirty-seven in 1896 to twenty-two in 1914. The Canadian banking system became considerably more centralized and a number of regional banks were absorbed by large Montreal and Toronto institutions. The field was dominated by three banks — the Bank of Montreal and the Royal Bank, with their head offices in Montreal, and the Toronto-based Canadian Bank of Commerce. Another manifestation of financial centralization was the proliferation of bank branches, the number of which grew from 533 in 1896 to to 3,049 in 1914. The concentration movement in other sectors was probably made easier by bank mergers.

Louis-Joseph Forget (1853-1911), Montreal financier.

Max Aitken (1879-1964), financier, created Lord Beaverbrook in 1917.

The most spectacular examples of concentration in the 1900-14 period occurred in the utility, textile, iron and steel, and cement sectors, and in some industries in the food and beverages sector. Montreal Light, Heat and Power is a good example of utility concentration. Formed in 1901 under the aegis of Louis-Joseph Forget and Herbert Holt, it brought together a gas company and three electric companies. Its purchase of its major competitor at a very high price in 1903 gave it a monopoly of gas and electricity distribution in Montreal. In this situation, it was able to charge Montreal consumers high rates and make considerable profits which were periodically camouflaged through financial reorganizations of the company.

In the textile sector, there was an initial wave of concentration in 1890-92, when Dominion Cotton Mills Limited and Canadian Coloured Cottons were formed, each of them bringing together seven mills. A new stage was initiated in 1904 with the creation of the Dominion Textile Company, which absorbed four companies — Dominion Cotton Mills Limited, the Merchants Cotton Company Limited, the Montmorency Cotton Mills Company Limited and the Colonial Bleaching and Printing Company Limited. The financial group that brought about this operation spent only $500,000 and obtained shares of Dominion Textile valued at $5 million in return, thereby receiving a gift of $4.5 million. As dividends were paid on this artificially inflated capital, the promoters enjoyed an average annual return of ninety-eight per cent on their real investment in subsequent decades. Such profits could be made only by charging the consumer high prices for textiles.

This example illustrates the extent to which corporate concentration could be profitable for its promoters. The second wave of concentrations peaked between 1909 and 1912, when fifty-eight mergers involving 247 companies were consummated. Especially noteworthy were the creation of Canada Cement in 1909 and the Steel Company of Canada (Stelco) in 1910. Formed under the aegis of the financier Max Aitken, Canada Cement brought together eleven cement companies. Among the various iron and steel enterprises in Quebec and Ontario that became part of Stelco was the largest Quebec producer, Montreal Rolling Mills; in this particular case, one result of the operation was a shift of the decisionmaking centre to Ontario.

Thus, just before the First World War, the process of concentration and monopolization had occurred in a number of industries. Other sectors, however, had escaped it. This latter category included both new sectors such as pulp and paper and mining and older industries where a large number of companies co-existed — notably shoes, clothing and most of the food and beverages sector.

The concentration movement resumed on an even larger scale during the 1920s. The bank merger movement was completed; of the nineteen chartered banks in operation at the end of the war, only eleven remained in 1929. Between 1923 and 1929, there were 228 mergers in Canada, involving the absorption of 644 companies. This movement touched a wide variety of sectors, and was especially pronounced in the food and beverages sector, where it affected the brewing, distilling, canning, dairy products and other industries, and in pulp and paper. The reorganization of the pulp and paper sector was particularly important for Quebec. Most of the existing paper companies were caught up in it, with the most spectacular merger undoubtedly being the creation of the Canada Power and Paper Company, discussed above (see chapter 18).

Foreign Investment

From the time of the initial establishment of New France, Quebec — and Canada — have always been heavily dependent on foreign investment for their development. With the flow of foreign capital, it has been possible to compensate for the shortage of domestic capital and build up the country more rapidly; on the other hand, foreign capital has also had significant negative consequences. After the initial investment is in place, its economic benefits are often felt in the investing country more than in Canada, since income is exported in a variety of forms — profits, interest, purchases of goods and services — and research and development are done outside Canada. More generally, because of the presence of foreign capital, important decisions concerning Canada's economic development are made in other countries, placing Canada in a state of dependence and giving it the characteristics of a satellite.

While this state of dependence has been a feature of all Canadian history, it took on a new dimension in the early decades of the twentieth century, when significant changes occurred in the nature and origin of foreign investment. Here again, the available data do not make it possible to treat the Quebec case separately and the question has to be dealt with for Canada as a whole.

The first change was the new scale of foreign investment, which increased from $1.2 billion in 1900 to $7.6 billion in 1930 (Table 33). There are two periods of especially rapid growth — 1905-14 and the 1920s.

Along with this substantial growth in the amount of money invested by foreigners, there was also a radical change in the origin of foreign capital in Canada (Table 34). In 1900, capital from the United Kingdom was overwhelmingly dominant — eighty-five per cent of the total. By 1930, American capital was in the majority (sixty-one per cent), while British investment represented only a little over a third of the total. This change became highly conspicuous during the First World War and the same trend continued through the 1920s. With a share ranging from one to five per cent, other countries were at no time a significant factor.

The shift from dependence on Britain to dependence on the United States also changed the nature of foreign capital in Canada. British investment was primarily portfolio investment — in other words, loans in the forms of bonds. In particular, major expenditures on infrastructure — railway building and public works of all

TABLE 33
Foreign Investment in Canada
1900-1930

Year	*Investment in Millions of $*
1900	1,232
1905	1,540
1910	2,529
1913	3,746
1914	3,837
1916	4,323
1918	4,526
1920	4,870
1922	5,207
1924	5,616
1926	6,003
1930	7,614

Source: M.C. Urquhart and K.A.H. Buckley, *Historical Statistics of Canada,* p. 169.

TABLE 34
Percentage Distribution of Foreign Investment in Canada by Country of Origin, 1900-1930

Year	*United Kingdom*	*United States*	*Other Countries*
1900	85	14	1
1905	79	19	2
1910	77	19	4
1913	75	21	5
1914	72	23	5
1916	66	30	4
1918	60	36	4
1920	53	44	3
1922	47	50	3
1924	42	55	3
1926	44	53	3
1930	36	61	3

Source: M.C. Urquhart and K.A.H. Buckley, *Historical Statistics of Canada,* p. 169.

kinds — were financed through such loans. American investment, on the other hand, was primarily direct investment, in the form of corporate stock. Americans were not satisfied with the role of lender, and instead directly owned the companies they invested in; they also made heavy investments in production. For Canada, the transition from British investment to American investment thus meant increased foreign control of its economy through direct ownership. The steps in this change will now be examined more closely.

Between 1896 and 1914, rapid economic growth, massive immigration and the settlement of the Canadian West created a need for heavy investment. One of the most important accomplishments of this period was construction of two new transcontinental railways, and it was in large part financed by British capital. The British invested about $2 billion in Canada during the period, primarily in the form of bonds. Britain was the most important financial power in the world, and it exported its capital to every continent.

The United States also became a supplier of capital during this period, but American investment was concentrated primarily in Latin America and the Caribbean. American investment in Canada grew substantially between 1900 and 1914, from $168 million to $881 million. Manufacturing and mineral exploration were the two sectors where American investment was heaviest, and the establishment of subsidiaries was the primary instrument of American penetration. American investment was directed towards two objectives — supplying American industry with raw materials (as in the mining and pulp and paper sectors) and penetrating a new market with products invented and developed in

Chiclets

REALLY DELIGHTFUL

The Dainty Mint Covered Candy Coated Chewing Gum

(Chiclets, l'excellente Gomme à Mâcher recouverte de sucre à la menthe poivrée véritablement délicieuse).

Chiclets pour la digestion — Les femmes au goût difficile se servent de Chiclets à leurs lunchs et à leurs thés — comme menthes d'après-diner — aux parties de bridge et à toutes les réunions sociales où s'impose le besoin d'un bonbon croutillant. Les Chiclets sont le raffinement de la gomme à mâcher pour les gens raffinés.

The Quebec market was penetrated by a wide range of American products.

the United States by manufacturing or assembling them in Canadian branch plants.

These trends were modified by the First World War. While savings were heavily encouraged and the Canadian government financed its war effort almost entirely through internal borrowing (amounting to about $2 billion), foreign investment between 1914 and 1918 nevertheless totalled $1 billion. The largest part of this sum came from the United States. Britain, which had to finance its own war effort, reduced its capital exports radically, to the point where there was British disinvestment in Canada starting in 1915. The United States, which entered the war only in 1917, did not have the same problem, and was in a position to replace Britain as the major supplier of capital.

The tendencies that had shown up during the war continued in the postwar years. Savings played a proportionally larger role in economic development than they had previously. As a result of the financing of the war effort, the importance of Canadians' savings was now recognized, and as a result of the progress made by financial institutions, it was now easier to collect them. The banks had an extensive network of branches, while financial institutions of other kinds, especially insurance companies, were also growing. The large brokerage firms such as Wood, Gundy and Company, Nesbitt, Thomson and Company and A.E. Ames and Company were instrumental in the area of corporate financing, as interest in the stock market grew spectacularly during the 1920s.

Foreign investment thus was relatively less important, but it became much more direct and visible during the 1920s. The relative position of the British, which had begun to decline during the war, continued its slide, although the total volume of British investment remained high — about $2.8 billion in 1930. American capital, meanwhile, made a substantial leap forward, from $1.6 billion in 1918 to $4.7 billion in 1930. The American presence was concentrated primarily in natural resource exploitation and industrial production. Canada thus increasingly became a branch plant of the United States; it supplied the U.S. with raw materials while Canadians bought products that were invented elsewhere and partially assembled in Canada with foreign technology and capital.

From Robin Hood flour to Kellogg cereals, from Westinghouse electrical appliances to Ford cars, Quebecers became more and more familiar with American products made in Canada. While they contributed to the profitability of American investment in industry, Quebecers benefited very little from it, since most plants were established in Ontario. In 1931, only sixteen per cent of all American factories in Canada were in Quebec.

At the end of the period, the Canadian bourgeoisie maintained its dominance of the old industrial sectors that had been developed in the nineteenth century — iron and steel, textiles, clothing, shoes, food and beverages — while Americans dominated the new industrial sectors. In 1932, Americans controlled eighty-two per cent of automobile production and sixty-eight per cent of electrical appliance production; they were solidly established in the petroleum industry, pharmaceuticals, rubber, machinery, and non-metallic minerals. In the pulp and paper industry, the scene of a lively struggle between the Canadian and American bourgeoisie in the late 1920s, Americans controlled about a third of production. In 1930, Canada was well on its way to becoming integrated into the American empire.

CHAPTER 21
COMMERCE AND COMMUNICATIONS

Transportation

In the area of transportation, this period represented a break with the past. Before the First World War, large amounts of money were invested in conventional modes — railways and navigation — but this situation was changed dramatically by the rise of the automobile, which gave new life to the road system. At the end of the period, commercial aviation added a new element of change to the transportation sector.

The last railway boom

The Quebec government no longer played an active role in railway construction after 1897, but the federal government took up the slack. With one transcontinental system, the Canadian Pacific, already in place, Ottawa encouraged the establishment of two new ones. The settlement of the prairies and the phenomenal increase in wheat production created imposing arguments in favour of improved transportation facilities for shipping grain east. Two groups succeeded in obtaining the support of the federal government — the Grand Trunk and the Canadian Northern.

The Grand Trunk proposed to the federal government that it extend its main line to the West. The existing line served the southern parts of Ontario and Quebec and had outlets to the sea at Montreal during the navigation season and Portland, Maine, when Montreal was blocked by ice. Prime Minister Laurier wanted a Canadian winter terminus in the Maritimes. He also wanted the new transcontinental to follow a route that would include Quebec City and encourage the opening up of new northern regions. This was a response to the wishes of businessmen in the Quebec City and Saguenay-Lake St. John regions who dreamed of a railway to James Bay that would make it possible to colonize the clayey lands of the Canadian Shield.

The Grand Trunk had little interest in this northward orientation, and its agreement with the federal government stipulated that a Grand Trunk subsidiary, the Grand Trunk Pacific, would build only the western portion of the new transcontinental, between Winnipeg and Prince Rupert. The eastern part, christened the National Transcontinental, would be the responsibility of the federal government itself. This railway would have its eastern terminus at Moncton, cross the St. Lawrence at Quebec City and the St. Maurice near La Tuque, and then head west through the Abitibi region and northern Ontario to Winnipeg (Map 9). According to the agreement, when construction was completed the National Transcontinental would be leased to the Grand Trunk. The new system was completed on the eve of the First World War, and made possible the opening of the Abitibi to colonization starting in 1912.

The third transcontinental system, the Canadian Northern, was built up gradually over a period of some twenty years. It was the work of two promoters, William Mackenzie and Donald Mann, who began in 1896 to buy small railway

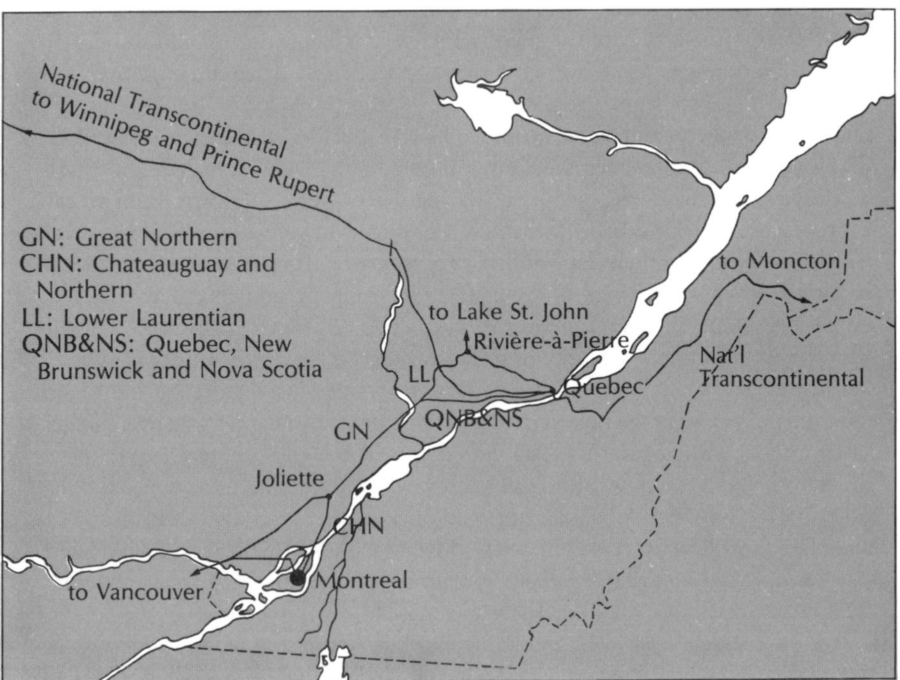

MAP 9: New Railway Lines Built in the Early Twentieth Century

Collapse of the central span of Quebec City's Quebec Bridge in 1916, the second such major accident that occurred during construction. In 1907, the superstructure had collapsed.

companies and build up a network of lines in Manitoba. By the turn of the century their operations stretched from Lake Superior to western Manitoba, and their main line was extended to Edmonton, Alberta, soon after. Mackenzie and Mann also began to acquire small railway companies in the East — in Ontario, Quebec and Nova Scotia — in the hope of some day integrating them into a transcontinental system.

In 1903, Mackenzie and Mann made their entry into Quebec by acquiring the Great Northern Railway of Canada, and through it a network of railways serving the colonization regions on the north shore of the St. Lawrence and Ottawa rivers. The main line ran from Proulx-Jonction, in the St. Maurice Valley, through Shawinigan, Joliette and Saint-Jérôme to Hawkesbury, on the Ontario side of the Ottawa, where it connected with other lines running west. The Great Northern had extended its line eastward by acquiring the Lower Laurentian Railway; the Lower Laurentian linked up with the Quebec and Lake St. John Railway, over which the Great Northern had running rights, giving it access to Quebec City. It had two other subsidiaries as well. The Chateauguay and Northern Railway established a link between Joliette and the east end of Montreal in 1903, and the Montfort and Gatineau Colonization Railway served the region north of Lachute.

This little network of railways ran at a deficit, but when Mackenzie and Mann took it over in 1903 they hoped to make it profitable by integrating it into a larger system. That same year they established a new subsidiary, the Quebec, New Brunswick and Nova Scotia Railway, with the objective of linking Quebec and the Maritimes. Construction was begun only on a line between the Great Northern main line and Quebec City. In 1906, Mackenzie and Mann reorganized their Quebec holdings into the Canadian Northern Quebec Railway, and they acquired the Quebec and Lake St. John Railway the next year.

It took another few years and some assistance from the federal government before the Canadian Northern's promoters linked up the various components of

The Canadian Northern Railway tunnel under Mount Royal in Montreal.

their Canadian network and created a new transcontinental. By 1915 the task was complete and Canadian Northern trains could run from Quebec City to Vancouver. The Quebec section was made up of previously acquired lines. However, the Canadian Northern still had to find a way of establishing a connection with downtown Montreal without making costly expropriations, and it adopted the bold solution of building a tunnel under Mount Royal through which its trains could reach the centre of the city.

Carried along by the general optimism that prevailed in the decade preceding the war, the federal government encouraged the creation of these two new transcontinentals, but they very quickly became a burden. There was not enough east-west traffic to make three large systems economic. Construction costs turned out to be much higher than had been foreseen, and the Grand Trunk refused to lease the National Transcontinental for this reason. These problems were aggravated by the war, which resulted in economic difficulties that had severe repercussions for the new railways. The federal government, having guaranteed the payment of interest on the railways' construction loans, was also affected. Unable to obtain further financing on the London market, the companies could no longer make these interest payments, and while the government provided them with temporary financial aid, it also had to find a permanent solution.

It decided to nationalize all the major systems except the Canadian Pacific and set up a government-owned corporation, Canadian National Railways, to administer them. Integration took place between 1920 and 1923 and brought five major components under Canadian National's control — the Grand Trunk, Intercolonial, National Transcontinental, Grand Trunk Pacific and Canadian Northern. The head office of the new company was established in Montreal, which was already the headquarters of Canadian Pacific and was thus confirmed in its role of railway transportation capital of Canada.

Harbours and navigation

During the period, substantial amounts of money were invested in the development of Canadian harbour facilities. The growth of wheat production on the prairies, which had provided the justification for the expansion of Canada's railway system, also made it necessary to build storage and loading facilities at ports that were terminal points for ocean-going ships. The general increase in the volume of imports and exports resulting from population growth was another justification for such projects.

Large redevelopment projects at the port of Montreal were successfully undertaken in the twenty years preceding the First World War. When these projects were completed, the face of the harbour was completely changed. The work was done by the Montreal Harbour Commission with the help of long-term loans from the federal government.

The first objective was to increase the docking area and to accommodate vessels of deeper draught. This required dredging the riverbed. Most of the old wharves were replaced with high-level quays, some of them in the form of jetties extending into the river. The available space was also increased by building new quays in the eastern part of the harbour, in the Hochelaga-Maisonneuve area. In 1914, the entire river bank from the mouth of the Lachine Canal to Maisonneuve was encased in concrete. Farther east, at Longue-Pointe and Montreal East, docks were built in some places to meet the needs of large companies, principally cement manufacturers and refineries.

The new, higher quays were safe from floods, and a wall was built to protect the lower parts of the city. Permanent facilities, safe from spring floods, could now be built in the harbour area — huge merchandise sheds, an integrated railway network and grain handling facilities (elevators and a system of conveyers to where the ships were anchored).

These changes made Montreal the major port for grain exports to Europe. After 1922 it had to meet competition from Vancouver, which began to export

Montreal harbour in 1928.

Canadian wheat through the Panama Canal. Other cities on the St. Lawrence wanted their share of the pie, and grain elevators were built at Quebec City and Sorel at the end of the period; Trois-Rivières didn't get a grain elevator until 1938.

In other aspects of water transportation, conditions also improved. With the exception of coasting schooners, sailing vessels disappeared. Faster ships made it possible to reduce the time required to cross the Atlantic. On the St. Lawrence, icebreakers were introduced in 1908, and the use of wireless telegraphy made it possible to be aware of ice conditions in the Gulf and thus reduced navigational risks.

The emergence of the automobile

In a period of less then twenty years, transportation priorities were turned upside down by the coming of the automobile. The first cars were objects of curiosity and seemed to be reserved for eccentric sportsmen. Once cars began to be mass-produced, however, their use spread quickly.

TABLE 35
Number of Motor Vehicles Registered in Quebec and Ontario, 1906-1930

Year	*Quebec*	*Ontario*
1906	167	1,176
1910	786	4,230
1915	10,112	46,520
1920	41,562	177,561
1925	97,418	342,174
1930	178,548	562,506

Source: M.C. Urquhart and K.A.H. Buckley, *Historical Statistics of Canada*, p. 550.

The growth in the number of vehicles in Quebec was very rapid, although Quebec remained far behind Ontario in the use of this new means of transportation (Table 35). Two aspects of the phenomenon will be examined here: the impact of specific kinds of vehicles on transportation systems and the effect of all motor vehicles on the road network.

The private car was not the only kind of vehicle to be introduced; use of the motor-taxi, bus and truck became widespread at the same time. The taxi and bus brought significant changes to passenger transportation, making urban transport faster and more flexible while the bus also increasingly replaced the train as a means of intercity travel. In addition, railways were now subject to competition from trucks for their freight business, but this development had only a limited impact before 1930. In the cities, the truck driver rapidly replaced the carter and the taxi driver replaced the coachman.

The motor vehicle also had a decisive effect on the quality of the road network. Most nineteenth-century roads were in very poor condition and were completely unsuited to the automobile. But road improvement was the responsibility of municipal governments, which were not interested in raising taxes to finance investment in roads. The idea of government subsidies to municipalities for road work had been accepted in principle in the nineteenth century, but the sum involved had remained small.

By the early twentieth century reform had become an urgent necessity. Automobile associations demanded change, and a pressure group, the Good Roads Association, lobbied the Quebec government. The government adopted a policy of improving rural roads in 1907, but it wasn't until the passage of the Good Roads Act in 1912 that the new era really began. The government placed a sum of $10 million at the disposal of the municipalities for the purpose of improving the road network. A roads section was established within the Department of Agriculture, and it became a separate department in 1914.

A particularly important consideration in improving the road network was

The presence of automobiles made it necessary to clear the streets of snow in the winter.

encouraging the growth of tourism. The first modern road in Quebec, built in 1912-13, linked Montreal with the American border. After the war, roads became one of the government's major priorities and occupied the largest share of the provincial budget.

Air transportation

The airplane was invented at the beginning of the century, but in its early days it was primarily a recreational mode of transportation. It was not until the 1920s that commercial use of the airplane really began. At the very end of the 1920s, civil aviation in Canada was growing rapidly, with substantial increases in the number of passengers and the volume of merchandise and mail transported. While the airplane was responsible for changes in communication with isolated

The Jacques Cartier Bridge under construction in Montreal, 1928.

regions and mining towns poorly served by conventional modes, it had only a very limited effect on Quebec's overall transportation picture during the period.

Communications

Apart from transportation, other means of communication also underwent change and played a new role in economic activity. In the late nineteenth century the oldest of the media, the newspaper, was radically overhauled. In this, Quebec followed the example of the United States. The nineteenth-century Quebec newspaper had been more a journal of opinion than a newspaper in the modern sense. It had a small circulation and was closely linked to a political group.

Starting in the 1880s and 1890s, this press gave way to the cheap large-circulation newspapers, directed not to a small group of cultivated readers but to the general public. The growing concentration of the population in cities and the much higher rate of literacy in Quebec created a market for this new kind of newspaper. It attracted readers by emphasizing immediacy, human interest and sensation, by using photography and illustration liberally, and by developing special sections that could interest different audiences. In Quebec, the Montreal *Daily Star* and *La Presse* were the pioneers of this kind of journalism and they were soon imitated by a number of other publications. In Montreal in the early twentieth century, *La Presse* and *La Patrie* tried to out-sensationalize each other in a bid for readers. *La Presse* was the largest daily in Canada in 1899 with a circulation of 63,000; just before the war, it had a circulation of 120,000.

Another noteworthy change in the newspaper was the increased amount of space devoted to advertising. Large newspapers introduced a classified advertising section, while commercial enterprises bought full-page advertisements to make their products known. Thus, marketing techniques were changed and advertising revenue represented an increased proportion of newspaper companies' income. Newspaper advertising was also widely used for war propaganda during the First World War.

While the electric telegraph had been used since the mid-nineteenth century, wireless telegraphy was not introduced until the early twentieth century. At the beginning, wireless was used primarily to transmit commercial information and as a navigation aid, but a few years later a way was found of using it to transmit the human voice, and the development of radio became possible.

In 1920, the Marconi Company began operating Canada's first radio station in Montreal. Two years later, the first French-language station, CKAC, was licensed. This new means of communication began to become very popular in the late 1920s. From the beginning, private radio stations broadcast considerable amounts of advertising.

Commerce and Credit

How goods and services are exchanged represents an important aspect of economic development. Unfortunately, historical studies are often deficient in this area and it is not possible to make more than a few general remarks.

International trade

It is very difficult to study Quebec's external trade separately for the period 1896-1929, as the available statistical data are for Canada as a whole and cannot always be allocated by province. It is known that Quebec played an important role in Canadian external trade, if only as an intermediary. A large share of the Canadian products exported to Europe — notably western grain — passed through the port of Montreal. Montreal also handled some western grain exported to the United States and American grain bound for Europe. However, Quebec's position as an intermediary was less important in Canada-United States trade, which could be carried on directly by railway or Great Lakes shipping.

But Quebec was not only a passageway; it also exported its own products, especially raw materials. In first place among these exports came forest products — wood pulp, newsprint, pulpwood and sawn lumber. The United States was the main customer for these products, although some of Quebec's pulp and paper output was shipped to England. Mineral products, notably asbestos and copper, were also sold on foreign markets.

Quebec was also an importer of raw materials — bauxite for its aluminum smelters, cotton for its textile mills, sugar for its refineries, coal to heat its houses and factories. In addition, it imported a large number of manufactured goods and foodstuffs.

The structures and institutions of external trade varied from commodity to commodity. The grain exporters were concentrated in Montreal, where they were organized in the Corn Exchange; they had close links with shipowners. In the case of newsprint, the paper companies themselves took charge of finding foreign customers and shipping their products, sometimes establishing sales companies for this purpose. Trade in sawn lumber was much more decentralized and fragmented, as forest entrepreneurs in the producing regions established links with American importers. It is thus difficult to draw a precise picture of institutions engaging in international trade for Quebec as a whole.

Internal commerce

Great variety and fragmentation were also characteristic of internal commerce. Using a study carried out by the economist François-Albert Angers for 1930, it is possible to describe the situation in this sector at the end of the period.

Two levels should be distinguished — wholesale and retail trade. In 1930, there were 2,932 wholesale establishments in Quebec, with net sales totalling $904,796,000. In addition to wholesale firms as such, wholesale trade included manufacturers' sales outlets, agents, brokers, chain stores' warehouses, and the like. Already, sales were heavily concentrated in the hands of very large enterprises. Only twelve per cent of the establishments had sales of more than $500,000, but they controlled seventy-one per cent of total sales. Wholesale trade was also geographically concentrated, with sixty-three per cent of all establishments, accounting for eighty-five per cent of total sales, located in Montreal.

Retail trade was more fragmented, with 34,286 establishments enumerated for 1930. About half of these sold food products — as in groceries, butcher shops, confectioners' shops. Retail trade was highly varied, and the census classified it into 123 separate categories. In many of these, small establishments were the general rule, but in some sectors concentration had begun with the coming of large stores or chains. According to Angers, in 1930, seven department stores representing only 0.02 per cent of the total number of establishments did eight per cent of all retail business. The 175 chain-store enterprises accounted for eighteen per cent of all retail sales. The geographical distribution of retail trade differed considerably from that of wholesale trade, as only thirty-seven per cent of retail establishments were in Montreal; these establishments, however, accounted for sixty per cent of total sales.

Morgan's department store in Montreal, 1930.

Financial sector

In the financial sector, chartered banks continued to be the most important institutions throughout the period. The banks underwent a significant reorganization, the most striking features of which were corporate concentration and the proliferation of branches.

In Quebec, the period was marked by the disappearance of a number of banks, especially banks headquartered outside Montreal. The Banque de Saint-Jean and the Banque de Saint-Hyacinthe both failed in 1908. The Union Bank of Canada moved its head office from Quebec City to Winnipeg in 1913, while the Sherbrooke-based Eastern Townships Bank was absorbed by the Canadian Bank of Commerce in 1912. The Banque de Québec fell under the control of the Royal Bank in 1917 and the Banque Nationale, with its head office in Quebec City, just managed to avoid failure by joining with the Banque d'Hochelaga to form the Banque Canadienne Nationale.

Even in Montreal a number of banks disappeared. The Banque Ville-Marie failed in 1899. The Banque Jacques-Cartier, in difficulty in 1899, was reorganized the following year under the name of the Provincial Bank of Canada. The Bank of Montreal absorbed a number of banks in succession — the Bank of British North

America (1918), the Merchants' Bank (1922) and Molson's Bank (1925), all with their head offices in Montreal.

At the end of the period, four banks had their head offices in Montreal: the two largest banks in Canada (the Bank of Montreal and the Royal Bank) and the two institutions controlled by French Canadians (the Banque Canadienne Nationale and the Provincial Bank). Barclay's Bank, a subsidiary of a British institution, established itself in Montreal in 1929 but did not amount to much. The other five Canadian banks had their head offices in Toronto. The assets of all Quebec-based banks grew considerably during the period, from $147,124,000 in 1896 to $2,066,927,000 in 1929.

This does not mean that the banks provided Quebec with good service. Quality of service apparently varied considerably from one part of Quebec to another, and Montreal was much better served than other centres. The historian Ronald Rudin has concluded that, at least before 1914, the large Montreal-based English-Canadian banks showed little interest in Quebec's internal development. They had very few branches in cities and towns outside Montreal and rarely issued loans to French-Canadian entrepreneurs, who turned to the French-Canadian banks in search of financing. These banks tried to meet their needs, but had limited capital resources.

Just before the First World War, banking services in Quebec were among the worst in Canada. In 1912, Quebec had only one bank branch for every 4,547 inhabitants, while the Canadian average was one for every 2,606. After the war, the branch network was extended considerably, and the French-Canadian banks were primarily responsible for this. In 1923, the French-Canadian banks had 319 branches, or more than half the total of 632 bank branches in Quebec. They also had several hundred sub-agencies, the primary purpose of which was to collect deposits. In 1929, the 1,169 branches and sub-agencies in Quebec were divided among the banks as follows: Banque Canadienne Nationale, 524; Provincial Bank of Canada, 281; Bank of Montreal, 130; Royal Bank, 89; others, 145. Clearly, not all these outlets were of equal importance, but their distribution is a good indication of the inequality of access to the large pools of capital represented by the major English-Canadian banks.

It was in response to the inadequacy of existing savings and credit institutions that the caisses populaires were founded. The initiative for the caisses came from Alphonse Desjardins, a former journalist who had become a stenographer in the House of Commons in Ottawa. His goal was to fight the scourge of usury, with its disastrous effects on workers and farmers, and although he studied the systems of people's banks in Germany and Italy and took his inspiration from them, his formula was original. He hoped to make the habit of saving money — at least on a modest scale — more widespread, and to give workers and rural Quebecers easier access to credit. In December 1900, he founded his first caisse populaire in Lévis; when it began operation the next month, its capital was only $26. An initial expansion beyond these extremely modest beginnings was made possible by the passage of the Quebec Cooperative Syndicates Act by the legislature in 1906. This

Canada's financial hub: St. James Street in Montreal.

legal recognition allowed Desjardins to found a large number of new caisses; in most cases, a parish served as the base for the new institution.

Desjardins was dependent on the active support of the Quebec clergy. In many parishes, the *curé* was the real organizer of the caisse populaire. The bishops, especially Mgr Bégin of the diocese of Quebec, supported Desjardins' movement, and some priests became propagandists for it, preparing pamphlets and making speeches. Clerical support was a determining factor in the early decades, for Desjardins faced strong opposition, especially from the Retail Merchants' Association and the Banque Nationale, which regarded the caisses populaires as competition. The growth of the movement did not stop with Desjardins' death in 1920. At the end of the period, there were 178 caisses in Quebec with 44,835 members and total assets of $11 million. This was still not much compared to the assets of the banks (Table 36), but in the light of the sectors of society in which the caisses were active their growth to this level represented an important step.

Alongside the chartered banks and the caisses populaires existed another set of institutions, like the caisses unique to Quebec. These were the two savings banks, the Montreal City and District Savings Bank and the Caisse d'Économie de Notre-Dame de Québec, both founded in the mid-nineteenth century. In 1929, they had total assets of $77.6 million.

The financial sector is not limited to banks and bank-like institutions, and during the period under consideration there was a proliferation of financial

TABLE 36
Assets of Banks Headquartered in Quebec, 1913-1929
($000's)

Bank	*1913*	*1923*	*1929*
Bank of Montreal	241,991	663,661	896,936
Bank of British North America	63,975	—	—
Merchants' Bank	83,217	—	—
Molson's Bank	50,302	73,261	—
Royal Bank of Canada	178,624	536,778	962,028
Quebec Bank	21,179	—	—
Banque Canadienne Nationale	—	—	154,539
Banque d'Hochelaga	32,530	71,593	—
Banque Nationale	24,213	52,864	—
Provincial Bank of Canada	13,077	36,939	53,424
Union Bank of Canada	79,567	—	—
Barclay's Bank	—	—	4,542
Total	788,675	1,435,096	2,071,469
Total assets of all Canadian banks	1,551,263	2,700,424	3,521,089

Source: *Canada Year Books.*

Alphonse Desjardins (1854-1920), founder of the caisses populaires.

intermediaries. Most important were the insurance companies, which were of three types — life, fire and general insurance. The life insurance companies, which had huge reservoirs of savings and represented a powerful economic lever, were of particular significance. Aside from the British and American companies operating in Canada, there were also a large number of Canadian life insurance companies. At the end of the period the sector was heavily dominated by a single company, Sun Life, the head office of which was in Montreal. The French-Canadian presence in the life insurance field was minimal. In the area of general insurance, the period was marked by the growth of new services such as automobile insurance and theft insurance.

Trust companies played an increasingly significant role as financial intermediaries. Acting as administrators of the assets of individuals or estates and as agents for corporations, they intervened in a number of sectors of the economy. Two Montreal companies, Royal Trust (linked to the Bank of Montreal group) and Montreal Trust (with ties to the Royal Bank), controlled more than sixty per cent of the assets of Canadian trust companies in 1926.

The development of joint stock companies and corporate mergers created conditions favourable to the growth of brokerage houses and investment firms. In the stock market speculation fever of the late 1920s, stockbrokers attained a new, if temporary, prominence. Other kinds of financial intermediaries, such as finance companies and small-loan companies, also made their appearance during the period. But the proliferation of institutions did not mean that economic power became dispersed. It continued to be concentrated in the hands of the directors of a few banks, life insurance companies and trust companies.

CHAPTER 22
QUEBEC: AN URBAN SOCIETY

In the early decades of the twentieth century, Quebec became more clearly an urban society. Most of its population lived in cities and towns, and urbanization extended, in varying degrees, to all parts of the province. In addition, there were changes in the layout of the urban network and the organization of cities and towns.

Widespread Urban Growth

At the turn of the century, a little over a third of Quebec's population lived in cities and towns (Table 37). Thirty years later, that figure had climbed to almost sixty per cent. The growth of the urban population was steady, and with each census the proportion of Quebec's population classified as urban increased about eight percentage points over the last one.

The proportion of Quebec's population classified as urban was consistently higher than the Canadian average, and the gap between the two was widening. Comparing Quebec with Ontario, the two provinces became urbanized at roughly

TABLE 37
Percentage of Population Living in Urban Areas, Quebec, Ontario and Canada, 1901-1931

Year	*Quebec*	*Ontario*	*Canada*
1901	36.1	40.3	34.9
1911	44.5	49.5	41.8
1921	51.8	58.8	47.4
1931	59.5	63.1	52.5

Source: L.O. Stone, *Urban Development in Canada*, p. 29.

the same rate. However, the lead that Ontario had established in the nineteenth century was maintained; it widened between 1911 and 1921 and then narrowed again during the 1920s, so that in 1931 it was less than four percentage points.

The 1921 census was the first to show that Quebec had become mainly an urban society. According to the historian William Ryan, the fifty per cent mark was passed about 1915. Some traditionalist intellectuals, editors of *Le Devoir* or *L'Action Française*, were alarmed by the evidence presented in the 1921 census and argued that urbanization should be slowed down, but their proposal met with little success.

As seen in chapter 3, some ethnic groups had a greater tendency to live in urban areas than others. The British group was increasingly concentrated in Montreal, although some rural counties still had substantial populations of British origin. The great majority of immigrants of other origins also settled in Montreal. A lower proportion of French Canadians lived in urban areas, but this proportion was rising rapidly during the period.

The overall proportion of the population classified as urban also obscures significant regional variations. The Montreal plain was much more heavily urban than the Gaspé, and the rate of urbanization was more rapid in some regions than in others. At the end of the nineteenth century, the main characteristics of the Quebec urban network were the importance of the two major poles, Montreal and Quebec City, and the existence of a series of small urban areas in the Montreal plain and the Eastern Townships (Map 1, page xx). Between 1897 and 1929, rapid urbanization occurred in regions on the periphery of this initial network — the St. Maurice Valley, the Saguenay-Lake St. John region and, at the end of the period, the Abitibi region.

Urbanization in these areas was closely related to natural resource development, as location factors for the new pulp and paper mills, chemical factories and aluminum smelters led to the creation of urban areas outside the existing network.

The St. Maurice Valley (Maskinongé, Saint-Maurice and Champlain counties) was still largely rural in 1901 and 1911, but urbanization took place very rapidly after that; in 1931, sixty per cent of the region's population was urban (Table 38). Only 2.6 per cent of Quebec's urban population lived in the St. Maurice Valley at the turn of the century, but thirty years later that figure had risen to 4.8 per cent.

Urbanization of the Saguenay-Lake St. John region (Chicoutimi and Lac Saint-Jean counties) followed a similar pattern. The pulp and paper and aluminum industries brought change to what had been a rural region based on an agro-forest economy. The region's urban population grew quickly and steadily during the thirty-year period, reaching 53.8 per cent of its total population in 1931. The region's share of Quebec's total urban population grew from 1.1 per cent to 3.1 per cent.

Thus in 1931, the St. Maurice Valley and Saguenay-Lake St. John regions accounted for nearly eight per cent of Quebec's urban population. This northward extension of Quebec's network of cities, however, was not enough to change the existing urban fabric significantly. Its most prominent characteristic, the dominance of Montreal, was not challenged. Montreal Island's share of the urban population of Quebec was 52.9 per cent in 1901. It increased to 56.2 per cent in 1911, fell back to 54.0 per cent in 1921 and was 54.7 per cent in 1931. However, the share of other components of the system tended to decrease during the thirty-year period. The proportion held by Quebec City and its suburbs fell from 10.5 per cent to 7.8 per cent; cities and towns in the Montreal plain, from 7.3 per cent to 4.9 per cent; the Eastern Townships and Bois-Francs, from 9.6 per cent to 7.9 per cent. Urban growth was thus a general phenomenon, but it was more rapid in Montreal and the new cities and towns of northern Quebec.

The increase in the number of urban municipalities was another sign of the growing urbanization of Quebec (Table 39). While some municipalities disappeared through mergers, others were incorporated elsewhere in the province. Some of these municipalities were suburbs of a large city; while legally distinct from the city, they formed part of what the census today recognizes as an urban complex. There were ten urban complexes with 5,000 inhabitants or more in 1901, thirteen such complexes in 1911, seventeen in 1921 and twenty in 1931. However, with the exception of Montreal and Quebec City, most of these complexes remained small in scale. Quebec really had no middle-sized cities. The only towns that could aspire to such a position were Sherbrooke, Hull and Trois-Rivières/Cap-de-la-Madeleine, and their populations were only between 29,000 and 43,000 in 1931.

Industry continued to rate high among urban functions and to be a significant generator of growth. Thus, for example, the rapid growth of Montreal and the proliferation of suburban municipalities in the years preceding the First World War can be explained by the expansion of manufacturing in those years. Resource-oriented industry was the key factor in the growth, sometimes even in the creation, of towns in the St. Maurice Valley and Saguenay-Lake St. John regions. However, heavy dependence on one or two industries could also lead to instability — when there was a slowdown in the dominant sectors, the entire economy of the town would be affected. During the period, a large number of

TABLE 38
Urban Population in the St. Maurice Valley and Saguenay/Lake St. John Regions, 1901-1931

	Percentage of Region's Population Classified as Urban		*Region's Urban Population as a Percentage of Quebec's Urban Population*	
Year	*St. Maurice Valley*	*Saguenay/ Lake St. John*	*St. Maurice Valley*	*Saguenay/ Lake St. John*
1901	22.2	19.3	2.6	1.1
1911	23.8	31.8	2.3	1.7
1921	52.9	44.0	4.8	2.4
1931	60.2	53.8	4.8	3.1

Source: Censuses of Canada.

towns had a limited industrial base, and because of the lack of diversification the fate of these towns was closely tied to the companies on which they were dependent.

In addition to the industrial function, the service sector also became a generator of urban growth. While 26.5 per cent of the jobs in Quebec were in this sector in 1901, that figure had grown to 40.4 per cent by 1931. Service activities—financial institutions, administrative services, hospitals, colleges and universities—became more heavily concentrated in the cities; this centralization was closely related to the concentration of population in the cities, which it both resulted from and helped accentuate. The specialized nature of some of these services was another limiting factor on the extent to which they could be dispersed throughout the province. The effect of the rise of the service sector was thus to encourage the growth and dominance of metropolitan centres.

The period under consideration was also marked by changes in the internal distribution of activities within Quebec's cities, especially in the Montreal region. With improvements in public transportation, wider areas became urbanized and suburban municipalities were established; some aspects of specialization within the urban space became more pronounced as a result. The scope of these transformations will become clearer as Quebec's major cities and towns are examined.

Metropolis and Capital

Changes in the population of Quebec's major cities and towns — those with more than 3,000 inhabitants — during the period are shown in Table 40. There were about forty such cities and towns, in addition to the Montreal and Quebec City metropolitan areas. An examination of each is beyond the scope of this book; in any case, it would be impossible given the embryonic state of research in urban history. In this section, the largest cities will be examined in detail and then an attempt will be made to put together a composite picture of the others, region by region.

TABLE 39

Number of Cities, Towns and Villages Incorporated in Quebec, 1901-1931

Year	*Cities*[1]	*Towns*	*Villages*
1901	11	40	138
1911	8	65	160
1921	21	86	251
1931	25	97	301

[1]A town with more than 6,000 inhabitants is eligible for the title of city; this title does not give it any additional powers.

Source: *Census of Canada*, 1951.

Montreal

By far the most notable characteristic of Quebec's urban landscape was the prominence of Montreal. The urban population of Montreal Island was over 345,000 in 1901, and just under a million in 1931. In other words, at the end of the period the island was home to about thirty per cent of Quebec's population, and more than half its urban population. Most of the island's residents lived in the city of Montreal, which grew from 267,730 inhabitants to 818,577.

This impressive growth was the result of a number of factors, related as much to the advantages accumulated by Montreal in the nineteenth century as to new circumstances appearing in the twentieth.

Montreal's economy continued to be based on industry. Value of production for Montreal and its suburbs increased from $87.4 million, representing fifty-five per cent of the Quebec total, in 1900 to $731.9 million, or sixty-three per cent of the Quebec total, in 1929. Montreal participated in the two major periods of industrial growth in Canada as a whole. The fifteen years preceding the First World War were a period of rapid expansion for Montreal industry, as the city took advantage of its well-established and diversified industrial structure. New demand stimulated existing enterprises to expand their establishments substantially; the shoe industry, for example, got its second wind during this period. Expansion of this nature meant that larger factories had to be built, and many of these new plants were established in suburban areas.

Industrial growth was slowed down by the war, but when it resumed in the 1920s Montreal was again fully represented. The shoe industry entered a period of stagnation, but Montreal's other traditional sectors — clothing, textiles, tobacco, iron and steel products — continued to grow. In addition, new sectors such as electrical appliances and petroleum developed. With the exception of the clothing industry, centred around St. Lawrence Boulevard and Bleury Street in downtown Montreal, industrial establishments were concentrated primarily along two major axes: the waterway — canal and river — between Lachine and Montreal East, and the railway running through the interior of the island between Outremont and Maisonneuve. Thus, conventional means of transportation continued to be determining location factors. Montreal retained its pre-eminence in the transportation field, and continued to be the headquarters for the major railway systems. After the Grand Trunk and Canadian Northern were nationalized, the administrative offices of the Canadian National Railways were set up in Montreal. The extensive improvements to Montreal harbour carried out early in the century confirmed the city in its role as Canada's leading port, and the growth of the Canadian West made it the pivot for wheat exports to Europe.

The war, however, marked an end to substantial investments in these classical means of transportation. With the rise of the car and the truck, it became necessary to improve the road system and build new bridges around the island. The most spectacular project in this area was the Harbour Bridge (later named the

Downtown Montreal, 1929.

Jacques Cartier Bridge), which was officially opened in 1930 and joined Montreal with Longueuil on the south shore of the St. Lawrence.

An increasingly significant factor in Montreal's economic growth was the rise of commercial, financial and service activities. Its position as one of Canada's two major financial centres, along with Toronto, was accentuated by concentration in the banking field. As noted in chapter 21, Montreal was the headquarters for the two most powerful banks in the country, the Bank of Montreal and the Royal Bank. The head offices of the two French-Canadian banks remaining after the merger of 1923 were also in Montreal. Apart from the banks there was an increasing number of insurance companies, brokerage houses and other financial institutions in the city. The new tall buildings that began to go up on St. James Street in the 1920s were testimony to the presence and importance of Montreal's financial corporations.

In addition to the financial sector, a large number of other specialized services such as universities, large hospitals and cultural services were concentrated in Montreal and strengthened its influence over neighbouring regions. But many other services, such as retail trade and personal services, were directed essentially to the local population. The rapidly increasing numbers of people employed in these sectors were evidence of the extent to which Montreal's growth was self-generating; the very size of the city's population created a demand for goods and services that became a factor of growth. Jobs as car dealers, garage mechanics, insurance agents, telephone operators or office clerks represented new possibilities both for long-established Montrealers and for new arrivals in the metropolis.

Montreal was like a magnet to rural Quebecers, who came there by the tens of thousands in the hope of improving their lot. While the rural exodus continued, the United States was on the decline as a destination and a substantial proportion of Quebecers who left the countryside now ended up in Montreal. Montreal's population was also augmented by heavy immigration from England and southern and eastern Europe. Few of these newcomers found the wealth and success promised by the promoters' handbills, and the vast majority of them lived and worked under difficult conditions.

Between 1901 and 1931, Montreal's population increased by more than 600,000. This growth brought significant changes to its urbanized space, extending the area it covered and accentuating the degree to which it was specialized. The city now stretched in all directions. An initial group of suburbs had grown up in a belt around Montreal proper towards the end of the nineteenth century, and in the early twentieth century the city was encircled by a second belt. This was the heyday of a number of small municipalities, the most substantial of which were Verdun, Ville-Émard and Westmount in the west, Outremont, Saint-Louis and DeLorimier in the north and Maisonneuve and Longue-Pointe in the east.

Typically, a municipality of this sort was dominated by a small group of real estate promoters and local entrepreneurs who hoped to make a quick profit by stimulating the "progress" of their town in a variety of ways, and it grew and developed in an unruly fashion as a result. Town councils often fought with one another to attract companies to their municipalities, and their divided state left them in a poor position to resist pressure from the large utility corporations. Montreal's political leaders wanted to eliminate competition among suburban muncipalities by integrating them. Once the large capital investments were in place, the promoters were only too happy to have the population of Montreal as a whole pay part of the bill. Thus, the annexation movement benefited a variety of interests, and it picked up speed in the early part of the century.

Montreal had hitherto annexed only four suburban municipalities, between 1883 and 1893. There was a pause of twelve years before annexation was resumed, but between 1905 and 1918 Montreal absorbed nineteen municipalities, eleven of them in 1910 alone (Map 10). Only the two bourgeois enclaves of Outremont and Westmount and a few towns such as Verdun and Lachine on the periphery of Montreal's urbanized space retained their separate identities. The territory that became part of the city of Montreal as a result of these annexations was far from being fully occupied, and it became populated gradually over the next forty years. Among the remaining independent municipalities, only Verdun and Outremont grew substantially during the 1920s.

Public transportation was an important factor in Montreal's territorial growth.

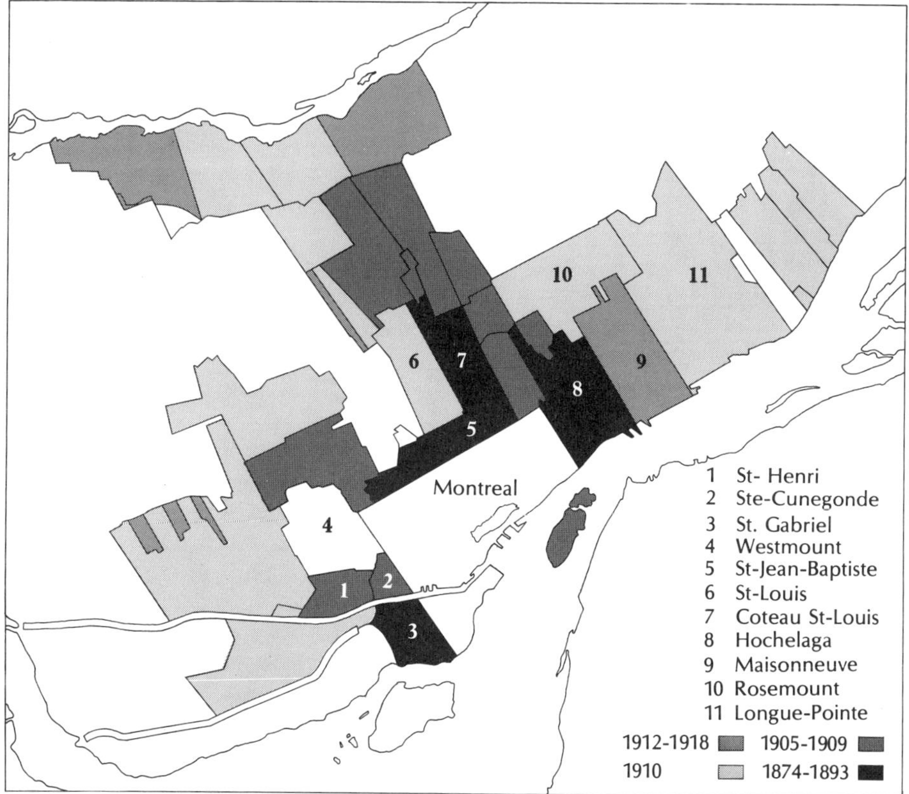

MAP 10: Annexation in Montreal, 1883-1918

Electric streetcars, first introduced in 1892, made it possible to transport thousands of workers quickly and reliably, so that it was no longer necessary to live close to one's workplace; specifically residential neighbourhoods and suburbs grew up as a result. Promoters played an important role in determining how urban space became specialized, especially in small suburban towns, where they exercised considerable influence over the town council. However, an interest in public planning also began to appear early in the century. The urban development ideas then in fashion emphasized great tree-lined boulevards, parks and majestic public buildings.

The most ambitious project in this area was undertaken by the town of Maisonneuve between 1910 and 1915. The group of businessmen that ran the town at the time launched a huge improvement project with the goal of making Maisonneuve the "garden of Montreal." Construction was begun on four major public buildings (city hall, market, public bath and fire station), some of them copied from American architectural models. Three great avenues were also part of

The streetcar encouraged urban expansion and growth of the suburbs.

the project — Pie IX Boulevard, running north-south from one end of the island to the other; Morgan Boulevard, site of two of the new public buildings; and Sherbrooke Street, at the top of the slope leading down to the harbour. It was intended to round out the project with a huge park, where cultural and sports facilities would be built. However, Maisonneuve Park could not be brought to fruition as scheduled because of the war, and was developed only gradually over subsequent decades.

Maisonneuve had few imitators. There were only limited efforts at planning on an island-wide scale, and a Metropolitan Parks Commission, established in 1912, remained inoperative for want of funds. Some towns adopted a zoning policy to achieve better separation of the residential function from commercial or industrial activities or to ensure greater homogeneity in wealthy residential neighbourhoods. There should be no illusions, however, about the public nature of these interventions. Promoters remained highly influential in town councils, and planning was often only the official seal of approval for private projects. Public investment, as in the case of Maisonneuve, was aimed at increasing the profitability of private projects.

DEMAIN, LA CITE DE MAISONNEUVE CELEBRERA

La JOURNEE de MAISONNEUVE

A une réunion récente du Conseil de Ville de Maisonneuve, grâce à l'initiative du leader, le conseil décidait de célébrer, dimanche le 27 mai, la "Journée de Maisonneuve".

Le but de cette fête est de faire connaître au public en général et aux manufacturiers en particulier les immenses ressources au point de vue industriel, commercial, aussi comme placement financier que possède cette ville progressive.

Toutes les dispositions nécessaires ont été prises pour faire de cette fête un événement qui fera époque dans l'histoire de la ville de Maisonneuve.

Maisonneuve's *politique de grandeur* and urban promotion campaign. The ad reads: "TOMORROW, THE CITY OF MAISONNEUVE WILL CELEBRATE MAISONNEUVE DAY. . . . The goal of this celebration is to make the public in general and manufacturers in particular aware of this progressive town's immense resources from the industrial and commercial point of view and as a financial investment. . . ." The public market, city hall, fountain and public bath are shown at the bottom.

A number of major utilities were still in the hands of private enterprise. In Montreal, water distribution had been taken over by the city in the mid-nineteenth century, but the private Montreal Water and Power Company distributed water in suburban municipalities and continued to do so even after they were annexed by Montreal. Gas and electricity distribution was controlled by the Montreal Light, Heat and Power Company, while public transportation was provided by the Montreal Street Railway Company, later the Montreal Tramways Company. These companies had an almost total monopoly and their exploitation of the Montreal market provided them with high profits. The utility trusts had numerous critics, and many businessmen advocated municipal ownership so that service would be provided cheaply. But their efforts had little success, for the utility companies assured themselves of powerful political support by contributing to election funds. The only municipal takeover was the purchase of the Montreal Water and Power Company system by the city of Montreal in 1927. The city paid $14 million for the system, a sum that represented a substantial gain for the financiers who owned it.

Jean Versailles was one of many promoters who launched urban development projects in the Montreal suburbs in the early twentieth century, promising quick profits to land buyers. One of his ads is shown above. It reads: "SPECULATORS! Take my Advice while there is still Time!!! I have at the Moment A NUMBER OF LOTS TO SELL on Terms that are Extremely Advantageous from both the Speculative and the Investment point of view."

With the growth of its population, the extension of its territory and the concentration of economic activities in its urban space, Montreal's metropolitan function and cosmopolitan character evolved. Until the end of the nineteenth century, Montreal's population had been essentially of French and British origin, but this situation changed in the first three decades of the twentieth century, as noted in chapter 3. The population of Montreal Island included 16,233 people of other origins, representing 4.5 per cent of the total, in 1901; this figure had grown to 135,262, or 13.5 per cent of the total, by 1931. Eastern European Jews made up about half of this group, with Italians a fairly distant second.

Montreal's cosmopolitan character was only one of the features that distinguished it from the other cities and towns of Quebec. Montreal had become a large North American city, with all the problems of scale that such a situation involved, but also with the advantages of dynamism, diversity and openness to the world that it allowed.

Quebec City

While Quebec City grew at a slower rate than its historic rival, its progress in this period nevertheless presents a marked contrast to the relative stagnation of the preceding one. In thirty years, its population grew from 68,840 to 130,594; the inclusion of its near suburbs adds about another 10,000 to that figure. Across the St. Lawrence on the south shore, Lévis and Lauzon had a combined population equal to about fifteen per cent of that of the capital.

Part of this growth was due to industry. The city's industrial structure was characterized by the use of cheap labour to produce consumer goods. Shoes were the leading industry, followed by corsets, tobacco and clothing.

Quebec City's position in the transportation network also improved. It was served by the two new transcontinental railways — the Canadian Northern had its eastern terminus at Quebec City and the National Transcontinental crossed the St. Lawrence there. The construction of the Quebec Bridge was both a significant and a spectacular event; it was punctuated by two major accidents, of which the collapse of the superstructure in 1907 was the more serious. Opened in 1917, the bridge made communication with the south shore easier and more reliable. The harbour continued to be a major element in Quebec City's economic activity, since large transatlantic vessels had to stop there, being unable to continue upriver to Montreal. Quebec City was thus the port of entry for most of the immigrants who came to Quebec during the period. Significant improvements to the harbour were carried out at the end of the nineteenth century.

Another part of Quebec City's growth was due to its role as capital of Quebec. While government activity was modest by present-day standards, it contributed to the employment of an increasing number of people.

The Canada-wide corporate concentration movement had the effect of relegating the Quebec City bourgeoisie to a relatively marginal position. In one manifestation of this process, local businessmen lost their leading position in regional railway companies, as the Quebec and Lake St. John railway was absorbed by the Canadian Northern and the Quebec Central was leased to the Canadian Pacific. The city's two banks — the Banque de Québec and the Banque Nationale — were also absorbed by larger institutions. The Quebec City bourgeoisie did not disappear, however, and continued to play a role on a regional level. Quebec City was the metropolis for all of eastern Quebec. Its businessmen supplied local merchants on both sides of the St. Lawrence downriver as far as the Gaspé and the north shore. For these areas, it was the big city where people made important purchases and obtained specialized services.

Extension of Quebec City's urbanized space and growth of its population proceeded towards the north and east, in the Saint-Roch, Saint-Sauveur, Saint Vallier and Limoilou areas (Map 11). The city's Upper Town continued to be occupied by major religious and governmental organizations and by the bourgeoisie. Expansion to the suburbs was highly limited and was concentrated in the

Quebec City in the early twentieth century.

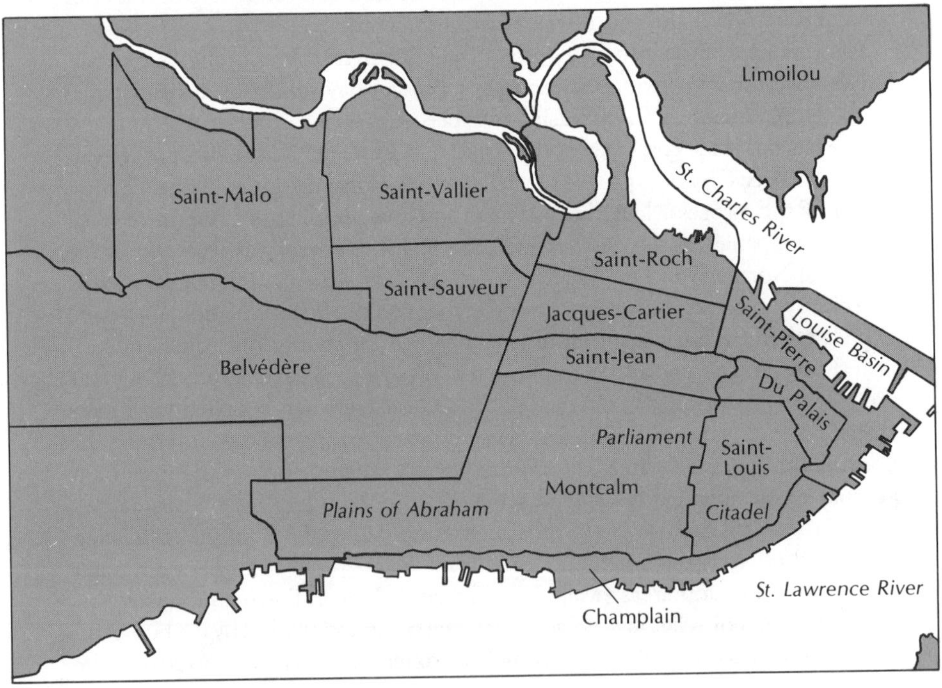

MAP 11: Quebec City Wards, about 1914

northeast, towards Giffard and Beauport. Farther east, the textile town of Montmorency had a population of 4,575 in 1931.

Other Cities and Towns

The importance of the six satellite towns forming a ring around Montreal diminished during the period. Saint-Jérôme, Joliette and Saint-Jean grew at a faster rate than Sorel and Saint-Hyacinthe, while Valleyfield, heavily dependent on the cotton industry, seemed to have reached a plateau; its population actually declined. With better and faster communication between Montreal and rural regions, these towns appear to have lost their former position as relay points.

In the Eastern Townships/Bois-Francs region, the old structure was maintained (Table 40). This structure was characterized by a network of small towns spread out over the region, most of them dependent on one or two large companies. Some of the older towns — Coaticook, Farnham, Magog — appeared to be running out of steam, while others grew very quickly; this latter group consisted of industrial towns such as Drummondville, Victoriaville and Granby and mining towns such as Thetford Mines and Asbestos.

Sherbrooke emerged more clearly as the regional metropolis and its population grew rapidly, accounting for an increasing proportion of the population of the region as a whole — 4.8 per cent in 1901 and 9.1 per cent in 1931. The cities and towns of the Eastern Townships thus appeared to be a balanced and structured subsystem of Quebec's urban network. The relative importance of this subsystem was declining, however, and none of these cities and towns was really able to act as a counterweight to the polarizing force of Montreal and Quebec City.

In the St. Maurice Valley, urbanization was a new phenomenon, as noted previously. There were three major urban poles in the region. The most important was Trois-Rivières, which accounted for thirteen per cent of the region's population in 1901; with the inclusion of the new town of Cap-de-la-Madeleine, this figure had risen to a little over thirty per cent by 1931. An old trading post founded by Laviolette in the seventeenth century, Trois-Rivières became one of the world capitals of the paper industry in the twentieth. It grew rapidly, especially between 1911 and 1931 (Table 40), and its role as regional metropolis was given new impetus by the general growth of the region. Grand-Mère and Shawinigan constituted a second urban pole, accounting for about fifteen per cent of the region's population in 1931. Shawinigan was a typical "company town." The municipality did not exist when the waterfall was sold in 1897. Creation of the town of Shawinigan Falls was the work of the Shawinigan Water and Power Company, which planned the town's layout and facilities itself. After a few years, population growth and economic diversification made it possible for the municipality to free itself from the company's tutelage. The St. Maurice Valley's third urban pole was much farther north; it consisted of the pulp and paper town of La Tuque and accounted for more than five per cent of the region's population in 1931.

TABLE 40
Population of Major Urban Centres in Quebec, 1901-1931

Municipality	*1901*	*1911*	*1921*	*1931*
Montreal Region				
City of Montreal	267,730	467,986	618,506	818,577
Montreal Island (urban population)	346,061	543,449	714,466	991,768
Saint-Jérôme	3,619	3,473	5,491	8,967
Joliette	4,220	6,346	9,116	10,765
Sorel	7,057	8,420	8,174	9,320
Saint-Hyacinthe	9,210	9,797	10,859	13,448
Saint-Jean	4,030	5,903	7,734	11,256
Valleyfield	11,055	9,449	9,215	11,411
Lachute	2,022	2,407	2,592	3,906
Sainte-Thérèse	—	—	—	3,292
Longueuil	2,835	3,972	4,682	5,407
Saint-Lambert	1,362	3,344	3,890	6,075
Beauharnois	1,976	2,015	2,540	3,729
Quebec City Region				
City of Quebec	68,840	78,710	95,193	130,594
Quebec City and suburbs	68,840	78,710	101,084	141,091
Lévis	7,783	7,452	10,470	11,724
Lauzon	3,416	3,978	4,966	7,084
Montmorency	—	1,717	1,904	4,575
Eastern Townships Region				
Sherbrooke	11,765	16,405	23,515	28,933
Magog	3,516	3,978	5,159	6,302
Coaticook	2,880	3,165	3,554	4,044
Farnham	3,114	3,560	3,343	4,205
Thetford Mines	3,256	7,261	7,886	10,701
Victoriaville	1,693	3,028	3,769	6,213
Drummondville	1,450	1,725	2,852	6,609
Asbestos	783	2,224	2,189	4,396
Granby	3,773	4,750	6,785	10,587
East Angus	—	—	3,802	3,566
Lac Mégantic	1,883	2,816	3,140	3,911

TABLE 40 (continued)

Municipality	*1901*	*1911*	*1921*	*1931*
St. Maurice Valley Region				
Trois-Rivières	9,981	13,691	22,267	35,450
Cap-de-la-Madeleine	—	—	6,738	8,748
Shawinigan	2,768	4,265	10,625	15,345
Grand-Mère	2,511	4,783	7,631	6,461
La Tuque	—	2,934	5,603	7,871
Saguenay/Lake St. John Region				
Chicoutimi	3,826	5,880	8,937	11,877
Jonquière	—	2,354	4,851	9,448
Kénogami	—	—	2,557	4,500
Alma	—	—	850	3,970
Eastern Quebec				
Montmagny	1,919	2,617	4,145	3,927
Rivière-du-Loup	4,569	6,774	7,703	8,499
Rimouski	1,804	3,097	3,612	5,589
Mont-Joli	822	2,141	2,799	3,143
Matane (St-Jérôme de)	1,176	2,056	3,050	4,757
Western Quebec				
Hull	13,993	18,222	24,117	29,433
Buckingham	2,936	3,854	3,835	4,638
Rouyn	—	—	—	3,225
Aylmer	2,291	3,109	2,970	2,835

Source: Censuses of Canada.

Like the St. Maurice Valley, the Saguenay-Lake St. John region had a regional metropolis that predated the resource-oriented industries but was given a new impetus with the arrival of these industries. Chicoutimi was the region's most important centre in 1901, accounting for ten per cent of its population; it was still pre-eminent in 1931, making up thirteen per cent of the region's population with the inclusion of two suburban municipalities. Other towns in the region were all very recently established, and their existence was closely linked to electricity, paper and aluminum production. The twin towns of Jonquière and Kénogami had a population comparable to that of the Chicoutimi agglomeration in 1931; Alma also grew rapidly during the 1920s. Another twin, Bagotville/Port-Alfred, had a combined population of about 5,000 in 1931.

A street in Sherbrooke, 1912.

There was no structure with a comparable level of development in eastern Quebec. The region's economy was based on agriculture, fishing and the forest industry, activities that do not lead to the creation of large urban areas. Instead, there were commercial and service centres in the region; in some of these, notably Rimouski, the religious function was significant.

Western Quebec had no urban network worthy of the name. Hull was the only important centre, with a population of almost 30,000 in 1931. Its economy was based on forest products and the Eddy paper mill; the proximity of the federal capital, Ottawa, was another factor influencing its growth.

From the turn of the century on, Quebec's urban character became increasingly pronounced. The city became the symbol of job creation and prosperity, draining a portion of the rural population and drawing the remainder ever more deeply into the consumption circuit it controlled.

CHAPTER 23
THE ECONOMY OF RURAL QUEBEC

The relative importance of the agricultural sector in the Quebec economy diminished during the first three decades of the twentieth century. There were also radical changes in the sector, which became increasingly apparent after the First World War. At the heart of these changes were the final decline of grain cultivation and the rise of dairy production.

The Producers

Population figures are one indication of agriculture's changing position in the Quebec economy as a whole. There are three yardsticks that can be looked at: rural population, agricultural population and agricultural manpower. Between 1891 and 1931, Quebec's population grew by 93.1 per cent, while the increase in the rural population was only 7.3 per cent. This gives an idea of the scope of internal migration within Quebec during those years. Clearly, the countryside was being abandoned in favour of the cities; the proportion of the population classified as rural fell from 66.4 per cent in 1891 to 36.9 per cent in 1931.

These figures are for the rural population as a whole and include people who lived in villages. The situation for the agricultural population proper, that is, people whose employment was directly linked to agriculture, was slightly different. According to G.V. Haythorne's estimates in *Land and Labour*, Quebec's agricultural population declined by about five per cent between 1891 and 1931. It decreased between 1891 and 1901, then increased slightly, reaching a peak in 1911; after that date the decline was steady.

A look at the change over time in the proportion of Quebec's total manpower accounted for by agricultural manpower reveals a similar trend. In 1891, more

A farm in the Joliette region, 1925.

than forty-five per cent of Quebec's manpower was classified as agricultural; by 1931, this proportion had fallen to thirty per cent.

There was a degree of stability in the composition of agricultural manpower during the forty-year period. Farmers consistently represented more than half of all agricultural manpower, while members of a farmer's family working on the farm constituted about forty per cent and hired labourers about a tenth. These figures indicate that the family was the main source of agricultural labour. By way of comparison, hired labourers on the average accounted for 15.3 per cent of agricultural manpower in Canada as a whole during the same period; the figure for Ontario was 17.1 per cent. This structure was changing slowly, however; while farmers were fifty-nine per cent of the agricultural labour force in 1891, they were only fifty per cent in 1931, and the proportion of wage labourers grew from 7.3 to 10.6 per cent.

These figures suggest that while the relative importance of agriculture in the economy was declining and people were leaving the countryside, agricultural employment was somewhat more stable. Agricultural manpower was not as heavily hit by the declining trend as other indicators, and this indicates that despite everything the sector did retain some vitality.

Using figures for the total number of farms, changes in the regional distribution of Quebec's agricultural population between 1891 and 1931 can be studied.

Quebec can be divided into three parts for this purpose. The area of the St. Lawrence Lowlands around Montreal underwent a relative decline, from thirty-two per cent of Quebec's farms in 1891 to 23.7 per cent in 1931. The second part, consisting of the eastern portion of the St. Lawrence Lowlands — from Sorel to the Quebec City area — and the Eastern Townships, was remarkably stable, with forty-five per cent of Quebec's farms. In the regions constituting the remaining part there were various tendencies — a decline in the Outaouais, increases in the Lower St. Lawrence, Gaspé, Lake St. John and Abitibi-Temiscamingue regions. The most dramatic increase was in Abitibi-Temiscamingue, which went from a negligible quantity in 1891 to about three per cent of Quebec's farms in 1931. An analysis of changes in the regional distribution of agricultural population confirms these tendencies. These changes were the product of two phenomena — the rural exodus, which had a steady effect on the Montreal plain, as Raoul Blanchard noted, and the colonization movement of the early part of the twentieth century. It should be pointed out that the number of farms must not be confused with their output or productivity.

A More Balanced Output

It is not easy to estimate the agricultural sector's share of Quebec's total output before the 1920s. Judging by tendencies apparent during the 1920s and by changes in the population, it is a reasonable hypothesis that its share was gradually declining. Changes occurring between 1922 and 1929 can be see in Table 41.

But while the relative importance of agricultural output was declining as a result of the rise of new sectors in the economy, the total value of agricultural output was

TABLE 41
Percentage Distribution by Sector of Net Production, 1922, 1926, 1929

Sector	*1922*	*1926*	*1929*
Agriculture	29.3	24.3	19.7
Forestry	12.7	11.6	10.1
Fisheries	0.3	0.4	0.3
Trapping	0.5	0.3	0.2
Mining	2.4	3.0	4.4
Electric power	3.0	3.0	3.9
Construction	9.4	12.0	12.3
Custom and repair	1.5	1.5	1.9
Manufactures	40.9	43.9	47.3

Source: *Canada Year Book*, 1932.

TABLE 42
Gross Value of Agricultural Production, 1890-1929
(in thousands of current dollars)

Year	Gross Value	Year	Gross Value
1890	42,105	1919	257,723
1900	46,188	1920	266,367
1910	69,570	1921	184,068
1911	91,883	1922	154,085
1912	65,040	1923	135,679
1913	79,363	1924	142,713
1914	87,720	1925	161,613
1915	92,090	1926	159,492
1916	93,988	1927	158,943
1917	135,392	1928	168,475
1918	231,056	1929	165,288

Source: André Raynauld, *Croissance et structure économiques*, p. 590.

nevertheless growing (Table 42). The fluctuations of the annual figures reflect both the vagaries of the economic cycle and major tendencies in the development of Quebec agriculture.

Table 42 clearly shows the growth in the gross value of agricultural production; the combined effects of overproduction during the war and inflation are conspicuous in the figures for 1917-20. Starting in 1921, agricultural prices fell sharply, returning approximately to prewar levels. The general recovery of 1924-25 and the rise in the value of production towards 1929 can be seen here as well.

More clearly than before, Quebec agriculture was mixed farming; the farmer's income came from field crops — hay, grains, potatoes and the like — on the one hand and dairy production on the other. Dairy products included butter and cheese as well as milk, and pork production was in a sense a complement to the dairy industry, as it allowed the farmer to put whey, a dairy by-product, to highly economic use.

According to calculations carried out by the economist André Raynauld, field crops constituted eighty per cent of Quebec's agricultural production in the 1900-10 period, while dairy products accounted for twenty per cent. These figures give only an order of magnitude, as there were other elements in gross agricultural output as well. Table 43 is more detailed, and shows the range of major sectors that made up agricultural income. The main elements, in descending order of importance, were field crops, dairy products, livestock, and poultry; this last was a recently developed sector. In 1929, these four sectors constituted ninety-four per cent of agricultural income. The table shows that the rise of the

TABLE 43
Percentage Distribution of Agricultural Income by Components, 1918-1929

Source of Income	1918	1920	1922	1923	1927	1929
Field crops	69.3	71.7	62.0	57.2	50.6	48.0
Farm animals	10.2	6.7	6.9	6.6	11.7	13.0
Wool	1.0	0.4	0.4	0.5	0.5	0.4
Dairy products	14.5	15.8	21.9	26.3	27.2	28.1
Fruits and vegetables	2.0	1.7	2.8	3.1	2.6	2.5
Poultry and eggs	1.3	1.2	3.5	3.8	5.2	5.0
Fur farming	-	—	—	—	0.3	0.9
Maple products	1.1	1.5	1.6	1.5	1.1	1.5
Tobacco	0.6	0.6	0.7	0.7	0.5	0.4
Clover and grass seed	—	0.2	0.1	0.2	0.1	—
Honey	—	—	—	—	0.2	0.2

Source: *Canada Year Books* and *Quebec Yearbooks*.

dairy industry compensated for the steady decline of field crops, which was interrupted in the pre-1929 era only by the period of overproduction due to the war.

The 1896-1929 period was also marked by the definitive replacement of wheat cultivation by other field crops, especially hay and oats and, to a lesser extent, barley and buckwheat. As a result of wartime provincial and federal government programs aimed at boosting agricultural production, wheat made a strong comeback, and the harvest increased from 932,000 bushels in 1911 to more than six million in 1918. But this was only a temporary phenomenon, and with the end of the war wheat resumed its decline.

Farmers were slow to give up hay cultivation, which had been very profitable towards the end of the nineteenth century. Quebec had a surplus of hay, as farmers produced more than was needed for their dairy herds. According to Raoul Blanchard, there was a substantial decline in the demand for hay following the rise of the automobile in the 1920s, but farmers were slow in adapting and hesitated to abandon a crop that didn't require too much work. The popularity of oats also seemed to be a function more of the ease with which they could be grown than of their value as fodder; highly nourishing for horses, oats are less valuable for other livestock. However, according to observers, they were not a very demanding crop; most important, they did not require high-quality soils, and this was why they found favour with farmers. A basic problem remained — the soil was exhausted and harvests reflected its exhaustion. It took time for the use of chemical fertilizers to become widespread, and in the meantime the livestock and

A farm at Cap-à-l'Aigle, on the north shore of the St. Lawrence east of Quebec City, 1910.

dairy industry suffered as a result of the insufficiency of certain elements in the animals' rations.

Dairy production grew steadily, and its share of agricultural income increased from 14.5 per cent in 1918 to 28.1 per cent in 1929. But despite this growth, the industry had some fairly serious problems. From the time New Zealand dairy products began to penetrate the British market in 1910, export markets for Canadian products tended to decline. Between 1901 and 1911, cheese output in Quebec also suffered from the province's tendency to specialize in butter production. According to Normand Perron, the Quebec industry was struggling with problems of quality that were recognized as early as 1896, and its products did not succeed in establishing themselves in foreign markets. In the early 1920s, a period of stagnation for the dairy industry began; cheese exports declined, despite a moderate increase in the number of cattle and the number of producers.

Conditions at the local level were responsible for this stagnation. Each parish held onto its own dairy processing establishment, so that production units were

Collecting milk, 1910.

small and costs were high. The lactation period lasted only from April-May to October-November, and dairy processing had to adapt to these constraints. However, with improvements in the animals' winter rations, these problems seemed to be on their way to being solved and it appeared possible to extend the lactation period. Raoul Blanchard noted that the practice of mixing the cows' feed with straw in the wintertime was slowly abandoned. Overall, dairy production made gradual progress between 1896 and 1929; towards the end of the period, however, the industry seemed to be incapable of diversifying beyond butter and cheese production, and the result was a degree of stagnation.

It is difficult to generalize about Quebec agriculture during the period. On the one hand, a portion of Quebec agriculture developed in close contact with specific urban markets and was constantly trying to adapt to these markets; on the other hand, subsistence agriculture, as defined in chapter 6 for the 1867-96 period, lingered. Subsistence agriculture was declining slowly, and the extent of this decline in a region was directly related to its proximity to an urban market. Both forms of agriculture were based on the family; few wage labourers were employed and the family was the basic unit of production and consumption.

In addition to these fundamental characteristics of Quebec agriculture as a whole, regional and local specialization merits a brief discussion. Throughout Quebec, regionally specific forms of agriculture were gradually emerging. The best known of these is market gardening near the large cities, especially Montreal. Pipe tobacco was a long-standing specialty of the Joliette region; this industry was about to be dramatically changed by the introduction of yellow cigarette tobacco, which occurred about 1935. Apples were grown around Montreal, notably in the municipalities of Saint-Hilaire, Rougemont, Saint-Bruno and Oka. According to Raoul Blanchard, apple trees were planted in these areas very early on, as far back as the French régime, although an additional contribution was made to the industry by Americans in the nineteenth century. It was not until the early twentieth century that an apple industry linked to urban markets really took hold. All these specialties were particular to a very small area — to the point where it is possible to speak of specialization on a parish level — and all were a function of the proximity of an urban market.

Expanding Markets

The traditional markets for Quebec agriculture were the cities and towns of Quebec and, for some products, the United States and England. As a city grew, it provided farmers in the immediate vicinity with an outlet for certain kinds of products — vegetables, dairy products, meat. Montreal polarized the agriculture of an entire region, but the same effect also existed elsewhere on a more modest scale. Raoul Blanchard mentions the case of Rivière Croche (now La Croche) in 1931, where thirty-five farm families lived exclusively by supplying La Tuque and the lumber camp at Haute Croche (area of the upper reach of Rivière Croche). Near every city or town, there was at least one parish where agriculture was oriented to urban needs.

It was primarily to satisfy American demand that Quebec agriculture had turned to hay production in the last quarter of the nineteenth century. Demand was stimulated by the war economy, and remained fairly strong through most of the 1920s. According to Blanchard, it was the farmers of the Montreal plain who put the most effort into specializing in hay production; he mentioned the case of one parish that shipped up to 500 carloads of hay a year. It is not surprising that hay alone accounted for half the total value of field crops for the years 1910, 1920 and 1930. It produced very satisfactory yields and found a buyer more easily than other crops.

Another product that found a significant American market was milk, sold to New York state. Production for this market was undertaken primarily by farmers in the Montreal region and the area near the Ontario border. Rapid shipment by rail was essential in this case, so that production became concentrated in a very specific area where railway service was good. Quebec exports to Britain consisted primarily of cheese and bacon. The British market had been supplied mostly by Ontario bacon, but Quebec began to penetrate it after the First World War.

A market on Montreal's Champ-de-Mars, about 1925.

The hay market in Montreal, 1917.

In addition to these traditional outlets, Quebec agriculture served new, more diversified markets between 1896 and 1929; some of these were ephemeral, others less so. There was an outlet for hay in western Canada as a result of the growing specialization of the prairies in wheat cultivation. This market lasted until horses were replaced by cars and tractors. Similarly, war markets absorbed Quebec's excessive output of grain, but as soon as the war ended farmers were faced with a surplus. The markets tied to urban consumption were the most lasting ones, and market gardening and poultry raising offered the best possibilities.

Farms and Farming Techniques

There was a drop in the number of farms in Quebec between 1891 and 1931, from 174,996 to 135,957; at the same time, there was a steady increase in the size of the average Quebec farm. These two developments indicate that small farms were gradually disappearing. In 1901, the average farm covered an area of 103 acres, of which fifty-three acres was cultivated; twenty years later, average farm size was 127 acres, of which sixty-six acres was cultivated.

The movement towards concentration was at its strongest between the 1911 and 1921 censuses, in other words at the time of the First World War. Before inquiring into the causes of the movement, let us look at how Quebec farms were distributed according to size.

Table 44 shows a clear decline in the number of small farms; while in 1901 almost a quarter of Quebec farms were under fifty acres in size, this proportion had declined to eighteen per cent by 1931. The largest increase was in the 101-200 acre category. The table also clearly shows the changes that took place during the decade encompassing the First World War.

This movement towards concentration did not affect all parts of Quebec uniformly. According to the agronomist René Monette, "large farms were in outlying regions, small ones were near major urban centres, and middle-sized ones

TABLE 44
Percentage Distribution of Farms by Size, 1901-1931

Farm Size	*1901*	*1911*	*1921*	*1931*
10 acres or less	9.7	10.7	5.1	5.2
11-50 acres	14.3	14.8	12.5	13.1
51-100 acres	32.7	32.8	33.4	33.8
101-200 acres	31.6	30.8	35.7	37.5
201 acres or more	11.7	10.9	13.3	10.4

Source: Esdras Minville, *L'agriculture*, p. 490.

Ploughing in the Baie Saint-Paul region, on the north shore of the St. Lawrence east of Quebec City, 1929.

were in the areas in between." In the peripheral areas, the size of the wooded—and thus still undeveloped—portions of farms explains their larger scale. As a result, an increase in average farm size in these regions does not necessarily indicate an increase in output or productivity. Farm size was a function of a number of variables, including the price of land and the proportion of the farm left *en bois debout* (wooded). According to Gérard Filion in the study *Notre milieu* (1942), the range of land values in Quebec was from $17,700 for a piece of land on Montreal Island or neighbouring Île Jésus to $2,700 for a piece of land of equal size in the Gaspé. A calculation of average price per acre shows a greater range, from $230 for gardening lands on Île Jésus and Île Bizard near Montreal to $25 in Labelle county, in the Laurentian mountains.

There were other factors bearing on the increase in average farm size. In Raoul Blanchard's view, farmers in the Montreal plain went into debt to buy more land and machinery so that they could grow hay. For Gérard Filion, three reasons account for the increase in average farm size—exhaustion of the soil, the use of machinery, and speculative agriculture near large urban centres. The historian

Pigs helping clear land in the Abitibi region, 1923.

Robert Migner has emphasized the importance of war markets in leading farmers to go into debt to increase their investment in both land and machinery.

Given the present state of knowledge about Quebec agriculture, it would be premature to outline the characteristics of an average Quebec farm. However, the following characteristics were reported in a study carried out in 1925 by the Union Catholique des Cultivateurs and cited by Robert Migner. The average farm had an area of 100 acres, of which fifty-six acres was cultivated. Its principal field crops were hay, grain and potatoes, and its other major products were milk, slaughter animals, eggs and wool.

Mechanization appears to have proceeded rapidly, especially if numbers of cars and trucks, and to a lesser extent tractors, are taken as an index. At the time of the 1921 census less than seven per cent of Quebec farms had vehicles — 9,549 cars or trucks for 137,619 farms. Tractors were even rarer, numbering only 944. Ten years later, there were 30,410 vehicles on 135,957 farms, for a proportion of twenty-two per cent. The number of tractors had grown to 2,281. The more rapid increase in the number of vehicles relative to the number of tractors indicates that the horse continued to be a very important source of energy in farm work, while the car and truck were replacing it as a means of transporting people and foodstuffs. However, this does not mean that there was no other power source on the Quebec farm, as stationary gasoline engines played a very important role. There were 27,113 of these engines in 1921, or about one for every five farms, and 34,033, or about one for every four farms, in 1931.

The mechanization of agriculture in Bolton, in the Eastern Townships, 1912.

Mechanization, however, cannot be reduced to these elements alone, and the amount of farm machinery as such had been growing steadily since the second half of the nineteenth century. However, statistical data are still too sketchy and, in particular, too discontinuous in time for any definitive conclusion to be drawn on this point. The fact remains that even if agriculture was less mechanized in Quebec than in Ontario or the West, the difference was only one of degree.

According to some observers, the problems of Quebec agriculture, generally speaking, were related less to mechanization than to the slow rate at which new techniques of preparing the soil were adopted and to the question of yields. Everyone agreed that the soil was exhausted because it was insufficiently fertilized, and this insufficiency was related in turn to the inadequacy of sources of credit. The question of agricultural credit had been a live issue in the countryside for a long time, but it was not until the 1920s that systematic demands were made, notably through the Union Catholique des Cultivateurs (UCC). At the end of the period, in 1928, the Quebec government decided to participate in the federal agicultural credit plan, and it was put into effect the following year.

The Quebec Department of Agriculture played a very important role with respect to agricultural institutions. Government activity in this area, which had initially been limited to giving out subsidies to agricultural societies, became more and more direct. In the dissemination of knowledge and techniques, the turning point was 1913, when the government hired its first agronomists. According to the sociologist Bruno Jean, this step was an indication of the government's

A subsistence farm in the Baie Saint-Paul region, on the north shore of the St. Lawrence east of Quebec City, 1929.

commitment to rationalizing and increasing agricultural production. The agronomists had a number of instruments at their disposal, notably experimental and model farms. The first experimental farms were set up by the federal government; six were established in Quebec between 1911 and 1928. The model farms belonged to farmers who contracted with the Department of Agriculture to use selected seeds and specific farming practices, and served as a means of popularizing these innovations in the various regions of Quebec.

Agricultural education made progress: in addition to the three institutions of higher education in agriculture — the school at Sainte-Anne-de-la-Pocatière (1858), the Oka Agricultural Institute (1893) and Macdonald College (1907) — agricultural middle schools began to be opened in 1926 with the intention of decentralizing secondary agricultural education. Finally, agricultural newspapers continued to serve as a means of popularizing knowledge.

Colonization and the Forest Industry

In chapter 6, the links between colonization as such and the forest industry were examined for the 1867-96 period; the complementary relationship between these

A lumber camp on Lac Vlimeux, late nineteenth century.

two activities was still the dominant feature of economic life in the colonization regions between 1896 and 1929.

The colonization movement continued to open up new areas of Quebec after 1896. The movement reached the Laurentian and Appalachian highlands before 1880, and colonists pushed ever further into the highlands in search of new lands. There was also a drive to the northwest, as settlement began on the Hudson Bay side of the Canadian Shield. With the war, the movement lost some of its vigour; ironically, it was at this very time (1914) that Louis Hémon put the spotlight on a family of *faiseurs de terres* and immortalized the Lake St. John region as the prototype of a colonization area with his famous novel *Maria Chapdelaine*.

At the beginning of the century, the Lake St. John, Outaouais, Temiscamingue, Lower St. Lawrence and Gaspé regions were being actively colonized. In the Lake St. John region, one of the oldest colonization areas, settlement was virtually complete by 1910. Colonization was proceeding in the vast area covered by the Outaouais and Temiscamingue regions, especially around Lake Temiscamingue and in the Rouge River valley, gateway to Labelle county in the Laurentians. A little farther east, the Matawin River Valley, in Berthier and Joliette counties, was also being colonized. In the lower St. Lawrence region, the back country and the Matapedia Valley were being settled at this time, while in the Gaspé, the Baie des Chaleurs coast was a particularly active area.

The last region of Quebec to be opened up to colonization of this kind was the Abitibi, which was almost inaccessible until the National Transcontinental was

A colonization road in the Abitibi region.

built in 1912. The region was first opened to agriculture around this time, but it was not until the 1930s that attempts were made to settle large numbers of colonists there.

The clergy continued to play a dominant role during this period; priests were the force behind the movement and the colonizing missionary was still an important figure. The government took charge of publicity, notably by publishing brochures and maps. But its most important contribution was the construction and maintenance of roads which, according to Esdras Minville, absorbed the largest part of the colonization budget. Before 1921, important items in the budget other than roads were grants to colonization societies and financial aid for immigration and publicity. In 1923, the government began to pay bonuses for land clearing.

Colonization was closely tied to the growth of the forest industry and agriculture in the colonization regions always had trouble progressing beyond the subsistence stage. Sometimes, especially in the Abitibi and the Gaspé, other industries such as mining and fishing replaced the forest industry as a complementary activity. In all cases, G.V. Haythorne's verdict was borne out — whenever agriculture is complementary to another economic activity, it is agriculture that

TABLE 45
Principal Wood Products, Quebec, 1900-1930
(in millions of cubic feet)

Product	*1900*	*1910*	*1920*	*1930*
Squared timber	5.5	0.2	—	—
Sawn lumber	258.0	158.0	183.0	137.0
Pulpwood	44.8	92.0	184.0	283.0
Firewood	276.3	258.8	303.0	286.8
Laths	—	4.8	5.8	4.5
Shingles	—	9.7	7.0	4.3
Ties	16.2	5.7	12.2	6.6
Posts	1.1	—	0.5	0.6
Stakes	15.6	—	0.1	0.2
Spools	—	—	13.3	0.6

Source: Esdras Minville, *La forêt*, p. 354

suffers. Population growth in the colonization zones was not negligible, but the surplus population of the countryside continued to be attracted in greater numbers to the United States and the rapidly growing cities of Quebec.

The Quebec forest industry's first period of expansion was related to squared timber, and the second to sawn lumber for construction. Towards the end of the nineteenth century, the industry was on its way to its third period of expansion, caused by the rise of the pulp and paper industry. A table of Quebec's major wood products (Table 45) clearly shows the rapid increase in pulpwood production between 1900 and 1930 — almost 600 per cent in these thirty years.

The persistence of two other important sectors deserves to be noted, however — firewood, which was produced for the Quebec market and was not replaced by other fuels until quite late, and sawn lumber, which declined substantially but nevertheless continued to represent a significant proportion of total production.

The forest remained a basic sector of the Quebec economy. Its importance may not show up in manpower statistics, since farmers who divided their time between farm and forest were counted as farmers; G.V. Haythorne estimated that seventy-five per cent of all forest workers came from the farms. But when the large share of Quebec manufacturing represented by forest products is recalled (see chapter 19), the pre-eminence of the forest industry becomes clear.

CHAPTER 24
ECONOMIC POLICIES

The economic changes whose main characteristics were outlined in the preceding chapters demanded a response from governments. One part of governmental adaptation to economic change was an institutional readjustment, which will be discussed in chapter 31. In addition, governments had a whole array of policies relating to economic development. The role of the Quebec government in this area grew and became more focused; it developed new strategies and its policies were widely debated in Quebec society. Federal policies, especially during the war, also had a significant impact on Quebec's development.

Quebec Government Policies

At the end of the nineteenth century, government action in the economic sphere underwent a major change of direction. Subsidies to railways and aid to colonization gave way to a policy of support for natural resource development and industrialization.

New orientations

There were two factors behind this change of course. Quebec's hydraulic resources, public lands and mineral wealth were owned by the government, so that when Canadian and foreign markets for these resources opened up it had to become involved. In addition, the Liberal governments that held power in Quebec City after 1897 were clearly interested in taking advantage of the new circumstances.

As a result, the Liberals put new economic policies into effect and held fast to them throughout the period. They had two objectives. One was to use natural resources to put government finances back into a sound position, Quebec having undergone a period of financial difficulty between 1892 and 1897. Income from public lands presented the largest source of government revenue at the time; it was thus in the government's interest to encourage demand for hydraulic and forest resources, and the increased revenue that resulted from this policy put Quebec's finances on a sound basis within a few years. The other objective was to stimulate economic development and create jobs, for in the Liberal way of thinking development was synonymous with progress. Convinced that industry and not colonization was the key to stemming the tide of emigration to the United States, the Liberals made the creation of industrial jobs a priority.

One striking characteristic of these new economic policies was the almost total abandonment of assistance to railways and colonization. As noted in chapter 5, the government had devoted a great deal of financial effort in preceding decades to providing Quebec with regional railways. This goal was largely reached by the end of the century, and government subsidies to railway companies came to an almost complete halt, although the federal government picked up the slack after a fashion, subsidizing two new transcontinental lines running though Quebec between 1903 and 1915. At the same time, colonization was no longer a major preoccupation. This became clear in 1901, when Premier Simon-Napoléon Parent abolished the Department of Colonization and turned its functions over to the Department of Public Works. This move aroused the opposition of the nationalist movement and sections of the clergy, and the Department of Colonization was revived in 1905, but subsequent efforts in this area were only concessions to politically vocal traditional elements, and did not involve a very strong commitment by the government.

Legislation and other measures taken by successive governments between 1897 and 1936 encouraged natural resource development by large companies, which were accorded numerous and extensive privileges and given huge tracts of land. Quebec's natural resources, especially its hydroelectric potential, were dangled before American investors in an effort to persuade them to establish factories in the province. This policy was particularly evident during the 1920s, when according to the historian Yves Roby, "the Liberals appeared to have mobilized for a vast industrial promotion campaign."

There were very close links between public officials and the directors of large companies. It was not unusual for cabinet ministers to act as solicitors for large companies or to sit on their boards of directors. These practices became common under the régime of Premier Louis-Alexandre Taschereau (1920-36).

The government's intervention on the question of the pulp and paper cartel is a good illustration of the form its activity took. With the co-operation of the premier of Ontario, Premier Taschereau tried to persuade a recalcitrant company, International Paper, to raise its prices and join the Newsprint Institute, which the other paper companies had set up in an effort to bring the industry out of its slump. However, his intervention failed to change the company's course.

Another goal of government policy was to provide Quebec with infrastructure. In abandoning its railway policy, the government was not getting out of the transportation sector; the long-neglected road network was the new focus of its attention. The rapid spread of the automobile made it necessary for the government to act forcefully in this area, and the adoption of the "good roads" policy in 1912 and the establishment of the Department of Roads in 1914 were evidence of the new direction it was taking. During the 1920s, roads were by far the largest item in the Quebec budget.

Nationalism and development

There were reactions to the rapid development of natural resources and the government's highly accommodating attitude towards American capital, especially from nationalist circles, grouped around Henri Bourassa before the war and Lionel Groulx and the journal *L'Action Française* during the 1920s. The nationalists put pressure on the Quebec government, arguing that natural resource development should benefit Quebecers first, and more specificially the French-Canadian bourgeoisie. They concentrated on three points: the ownership of resources, the participation of French-Canadian capital, and processing in Quebec.

The question of ownership came up initially in relation to waterfalls suitable for hydroelectric development. The government's policy was to sell these waterfalls to the highest bidder. The nationalists and their Conservative allies demanded that outright sale be replaced by a long-term lease (ninety-nine years), at the end of which the waterfall would revert to the government. The government acceded to this demand in 1907.

A more effective way of achieving public ownership would have been for the government to take charge of electricity production itself. This was the solution that Ontario adopted with the establishment of Ontario Hydro in 1906. But the Quebec government was not interested in public ownership of production and the nationalists did not press the issue. It was not until the 1930s that there was a large-scale public debate on the question of ownership of electricity by the Quebec government. Before 1930, more consideration was given to solutions on a local level, such as municipal ownership. Some municipalities, notably Sherbrooke and Westmount, owned their own electric utilities, but these were exceptions. In most cases, electrical energy was produced and distributed by private companies. Municipal ownership was an issue principally in Montreal, where the powerful Montreal Light, Heat and Power Company charged high rates and made fabulous profits. But any time the suggestion of municipal ownership came up it was successfully resisted by the company.

The question of ownership came up in a somewhat different way in relation to forests. In the mid-nineteenth century, the government of the province of Canada had put an end to the sale of forests located on crown lands; subsequently, forest entrepreneurs obtained renewable annual concessions for a fee. Nationalists criticized the scale of the concessions given out by the Liberal government, and proposed that only immediately exploitable energy and forest resources should be conceded, so that ownership of the rest would be retained for future generations. They did not succeed in winning their point on this question.

Another major subject of debate was the participation of French-Canadian capital in resource development. For the Liberals, it mattered little where the money came from — the highest bidder won. They wanted to industrialize Quebec and were convinced that it could not be done without American capital. The sale of the falls at Shawinigan is a good illustration of their attitude. After reaching an agreement with two local entrepreneurs, the previous Conservative government had put the falls up for auction at a bid price of $10,000. But before the auction could take place the Conservatives lost the 1897 election to the Liberals, and the new minister of lands and forests, S.-N. Parent, quickly modified the conditions of sale. Not only was the bid price raised to $50,000, but the eventual buyer would also have to spend $2 million in the eighteen months following the sale, pay out $200,000 a year in wages and agree to bring the station into operation within twenty months. The new conditions were well beyond the means of the two French-Canadian entrepreneurs, and the falls were bought by an American capitalist who raised most of the required capital in the United States.

While the nationalists were united on the goal of an improved position for French-Canadian capitalists in Quebec's economic development, they did not agree on the means. Most of them proposed voluntary solutions — getting businessmen together to pool their resources, a buy-Quebec policy, and the like. A minority, less wedded to tradition, wanted the government to intervene in favour of the French-Canadian bourgeoisie.

The Liberal party had little sympathy for this kind of intervention. While it was desirable, in the Liberal view, for French Canadians to increase their participation in economic development, they would have to do it within the framework of free enterprise, through their own individual efforts. At most, the government could encourage them in this direction by establishing specialized schools that would make it possible to train a larger number of French-Canadian businessmen and technicians. In a few cases, however, circumstances required the government to deviate from this rule. Thus, the Taschereau government intervened in 1923 to save one of the three French-Canadian banks, the Banque Nationale, from failure. The troubled institution, to which a large part of the Quebec City bourgeoisie was linked, was merged through government efforts with the Banque d'Hochelaga to form the Banque Canadienne Nationale. But this was an isolated action on the government's part, and it remained an exceptional case.

A third question on which economic policy debates focused was processing in Quebec. Natural resource development could have significant spinoff effects if raw materials were processed locally rather than exported in an unprocessed state.

Aiming to create jobs, Liberal governments hoped to persuade the companies that exploited Quebec's natural resources to process the raw materials within the province, but they were reluctant to resort to coercive measures to attain this goal. While the nationalist movement demanded policies with some firmness to them, the Liberals were afraid that investors would go elsewhere if Quebec insisted on too much.

Because of the strong American demand for newsprint, however, the government did have more room to manoeuvre in the pulp and paper sector. At the end of the nineteenth century, Quebec imposed a duty on exports of unprocessed pulpwood cut on public lands. The nationalist movement wanted more. It demanded that the government ban such exports outright, as Ontario did in 1900. This demand was echoed by Canadian producers. The government of Premier Lomer Gouin yielded to the pressure in 1910, proclaiming that henceforth all wood cut on public lands would have to be processed in Quebec. The measure did not apply to wood cut on privately-owned land, but along with a number of other factors it contributed towards accelerating the northward migration of the pulp and paper industry on a continental scale.

Electricity exports aroused similar concerns. In 1924, Premier Taschereau resisted a proposal by a group of capitalists to finance the construction of a dam at Carillon on the condition that most of the electricity produced would be exported to the United States. For the premier, to allow electricity exports would have been equivalent to abandoning his policy of using energy to attract companies and create jobs. In the mining sector, however, the government's policy consisted of *laissez-faire* in its purest form, and it did not intervene to encourage producers to process raw materials locally.

To implement nationalist policies would have meant looking to the longer term, but the government's concerns, on the whole, did not go beyond the short run. It aimed to industrialize at any cost and create jobs immediately, and as a result it favoured a policy of development by and for foreign interests.

The Impact of Federal Policies

The Quebec government's economic policies were focused on natural resources, over which it had jurisdiction. However, it was the federal government that had most of the power in economic matters, and the impact of its policies was felt in Quebec. Two areas will be examined here — the pursuit of the National Policy and the government's intervention in the economy during the war.

The National Policy

Between 1896 and 1929, the federal government continued to pursue the National Policy, which was based on three elements — tariff protection for Canadian industries, aid to railways, and encouragement to immigration and western development.

When the federal Liberals took power in 1896, they maintained the tariff policy of the previous Conservative government, although they modified it in some respects. The most significant of these modifications was the adoption of British preference, by virtue of which commodities imported from Britain were admitted at a lower rate. In 1910, however, the Liberal party changed its position as a result of pressure from western farmers. It negotiated a reciprocity agreement with the United States, under which customs duties on specified commodities would have been abolished or reduced. When the Laurier government was defeated in the 1911 election, this proposed agreement was abandoned, and the old tariff policy was maintained right up to the depression of the 1930s.

Sectors protected by the tariff accounted for a significant portion of Quebec industry. It was thus not surprising that industrialists and labour unions in Quebec were enthusiastic supporters of the "national" tariff policy. One of the effects of the policy, however, was to encourage American penetration, since the establishment of Canadian subsidiaries was a way of getting around the tariff wall and securing the entry of American products into Canada. In this way, the National Policy chiefly served to industrialize Ontario, where large numbers of subsidiaries of American corporations were established.

The second aspect of the National Policy was railway construction. Early in the century, huge sums of money were invested in construction of two new transcontinental lines. Industrial growth induced by railway development was limited to the Montreal area. For Quebec City, the transcontinentals meant a new role as a communications centre and an expanded sphere of influence. However, since the new lines, especially the National Transcontinental, ran through sparsely populated areas of Quebec, they had only a limited impact. The National Transcontinental did make it possible to open up the Abitibi region to colonization; later, it also facilitated the shipping of some of that region's mining output.

The third element of the National Policy, immigration, was focused on western settlement. The federal government was very active in this area, and immigrants arrived in large numbers in the years before the war and during the 1920s. Immigrants who went west represented a new consumer market for Quebec industry. In addition, half the newcomers settled in Quebec and Ontario. In Quebec, many of them went to the construction camps and new mining towns of the north, but most immigrants ended up in urban areas, especially Montreal. Jews from eastern Europe or Italians, they formed the new cheap labour pool for the manufacturing and construction industries.

The effects of the war

When war broke out in 1914, parts of the Canadian economy were seriously disturbed. With the approval of parliament, the federal government assumed extraordinary powers to control economic activity. Even though these new powers were not fully used, they brought about an unprecedented degree of

Women workers in a munitions factory in Verdun, an example of the federal government's economic mobilization for war production during the First World War.

government intervention. Inexperience prevented the government from carrying out the initiatives undertaken under these powers as effectively as it might have.

Its objective was to centralize production decisions so that the war effort could be maximized. Canada became one of the Allies' main suppliers. A series of agencies was established to control munitions, food and fuel supplies. Production in Canadian industry slowed at the beginning of the conflict, but it was redirected towards war production and operated at full capacity in 1918. Ontario industry benefited most, with Quebec second. The war also had a significant impact on Quebec agriculture, making it possible for farms to become better equipped and stimulating the production of foodstuffs.

The federal government tried to block loans floated by provincial governments on foreign financial markets, a move that would have extended its control over the provinces. Premier Gouin of Quebec protested vigorously, and Ottawa had to withdraw the measure.

To finance its war effort, the federal government had to resort to new financial instruments. First it increased customs duties; then it had to levy new taxes — a tax on corporate profits and, most notably, an income tax, which it imposed in 1917 and was supposed to abolish at the end of the war. But tapping savings in this way proved insufficient, and the government had to borrow heavily. It went first to New York, then turned to the domestic market for the first time, offering "Victory Bonds" to Canadians.

When the war ended, the federal government had to remain active in the economic sphere to facilitate the conversion to a peacetime economy. While it tried to get out as quickly as possible, in an effort to return to normal and leave the control of economic activity to private enterprise, it was clear that there were loose ends to be tied up. The heavy war debt combined with the indebtedness incurred as a result of railway construction forced the government to maintain the income tax, contrary to its initial intention. In the same way, it continued the shared-cost programs it had imposed on the provinces during the war.

SOCIETY

Socially, there was no break with the past in Quebec after 1900 as fundamental as the break that had occurred in the last decades of the previous century. The rise of an industrial bourgeoisie, the transformation of craftsmen into proletarians and the formation of a working class in the late nineteenth century were basic changes, while the period after 1900 was characterized more by the consolidation and expansion of this new social structure. Corporate concentration helped the bourgeoisie increase its power, and the working segments of society grew in size as large numbers of migrants from the countryside and from foreign lands became part of the proletariat. The bourgeoisie, proletariat and petty bourgeoisie all established organizations in an effort to strengthen their respective positions.

The coming of innovations such as electricity and the automobile and the increasingly urban character of Quebec might foster the illusion that there was a significant change in living conditions. But closer examination makes it clear that living conditions for the bulk of the population remained difficult and improvements occurred at a very slow pace. In matters such as housing conditions, the quality of the environment, women's rights and access to education, groups that sought reform were up against fierce resistance, and had to be satisfied with fragmentary and incomplete progress.

CHAPTER 25
BOURGEOISIE AND PETTY BOURGEOISIE

As the economic structure of Quebec, and of Canada more generally, evolved towards monopoly capitalism, a corresponding phenomenon occurred in the social sphere — the power of the capitalist class increased substantially.

The Capitalist Class and the Concentration of Power

The growth of the bourgeoisie's power was especially conspicuous in the financial sector. Three banks — the Bank of Montreal, the Royal Bank and the Canadian Bank of Commerce — together held a third of the assets of all banks in 1900. Thirty years later, their share of the total had increased to seventy-two per cent. Two trust companies, Royal Trust and Montreal Trust, held sixty-two per cent of the assets of all trust companies in 1926. The life insurance industry was more competitive, but it was still dominated by two large companies, Sun Life and Canada Life, in both 1900 and 1930. The result of this situation was that immense financial resources were placed in the hands of a small number of directors, who through their ability to accept or reject applications for loans and other forms of financing had the power of life or death over the vast majority of commercial and industrial corporations. Small and middle-sized companies were especially vulnerable in this regard, because only the soundest companies could finance enough of their operations internally to avoid recourse to the financial institutions.

In the industrial and commercial sectors, monopolization made it possible for corporations to control markets, fix prices, decide which products would or would not be made and impose these choices on consumers through heavy advertising.

But concentration of power went even further, for there were increasingly close

The St. James's Club in Montreal.

links among the leading figures in large financial, commercial and industrial corporations. In this way networks were established; in most cases such a network had a financial institution at its centre. By identifying interlocking directorships among different companies, the historian Gilles Piédalue was able to pinpoint these large networks for 1930. While the presence of directors sitting on the boards of two companies does not necessarily imply the control of one of these companies by the other (although this is often the case), it does demonstrate, at a minimum, that there are networks of information and co-operation.

Some capitalists sat on a great many boards of directors and had considerable influence; their opinions counted for much with businessmen and political leaders. In some cases they represented fortunes passed on from one generation to another. One such was Montagu Allan, the son of Hugh Allan, who had been one of the richest capitalists in Montreal at the time of Confederation. By 1912, Montagu Allan had collected twenty-four directorships, including six presidencies. Herbert S. Holt's fortune was more recently acquired. An immigrant of Irish Protestant origin and an engineer by training, he began his career as a contractor working on the construction of the Canadian Pacific Railway in the 1880s. He rose rapidly in Montreal in the succeeding decade and ended up as president of the Royal Bank (1908-34) and a director of many companies (Table 46).

TABLE 46
Directorships Held by Herbert S. Holt, 1912

President	Director
Montreal Light, Heat and Power Co.	Montreal Cotton Co.
Royal Bank of Canada	Shawinigan Water and Power Co.
Montreal Trust Co.	Canadian General Electric Co.
Colonial Bleaching and Printing Co.	Carlton Hotel Co.
Kaministiquia Power Co.	Canadian Pacific Railway Co.
Montreal Gas Co.	Ogilvie Flour Mills Co.
Calgary Power Co.	National Trust Co.
Imperial Writing Machine Co.	Canadian Car Co.
Vice-President	London Street Railway Co.
Steel Co. of Canada	Toledo Railways and Light Co.
American Bankers Association	Sun Life Assurance Co.
Permanent Insurance Agency	Imperial Life Assurance Co.
Dominion Textile Co.	Monterey Railway and Light Co.
Canada Paper Co.	

Source: H.J. Morgan, *The Canadian Men and Women of the Time*, p. 544.

Herbert Samuel Holt (1856-1941).

Louis-Joseph Forget represented another career profile — that of the securities broker who realized substantial financial gains and obtained blocks of shares in numerous companies through his participation in corporate reorganizations and mergers. Max Aitken and Arthur J. Nesbitt are other examples of this pattern. Forget's nephew and partner, Rodolphe Forget, was also a very active financier.

Finally, Lomer Gouin, premier of Quebec between 1905 and 1920, represented another kind of member of the capitalist class — that of the politician whose experience and influence can be very valuable. While he presided over the destiny of Quebec, he sat on a number of boards of directors; powerful businessmen had direct access to him and he took their wishes into account when he formulated his policies. When he retired from public life, positions on the boards of the mighty Bank of Montreal and other corporations opened up to him. He became something of a spokesman in political circles for the Bank of Montreal group.

This capitalist class operated on a Canada-wide and often on an international scale. Its activities went well beyond the boundaries of Quebec, even though almost half its members still had their base of operations in Quebec, primarily in Montreal. The work done by the historians Acheson and Piédalue on the characteristics of directors of the largest Canadian corporations established that forty-nine per cent of these directors lived in the "St. Lawrence region" (Quebec and eastern Ontario as far as Kingston) in 1910; twenty years later, forty-six per cent still lived in the same region. But the "peninsular Ontario" region, with Toronto at its centre, was gaining in importance, as the proportion of directors living in the region increased from twenty-seven to thirty-eight per cent over the same twenty-year period.

The capitalist class recruited its members from a more limited circle than it had in the nineteenth century. In 1885, the sons of farmers and craftsmen constituted thirty-two per cent of the directors of the largest Canadian corporations, but this figure had declined to sixteen per cent by 1910 and to zero by 1930. At the end of the period, all directors were the sons of members of the liberal professions, businessmen, manufacturers or managers. There were very few French Canadians in the group — 2.4 per cent in 1910 and 4.6 per cent in 1930, according to Piédalue.

Thus, Quebec society was clearly dominated between 1897 and 1930 by a capitalist class that had substantially increased its power and control over the economy while restricting its recruitment. It was overwhelmingly English-speaking and concentrated in Montreal. However, this capitalist class had to reckon with other groups in society, and among these groups was the largest part of the Quebec bourgeoisie.

The Decline of the Middle Bourgeoisie

The impact of concentration and monopolization was strongly felt by the middle bourgeoisie. This group lost a large number of its economic instruments, as many middle-sized companies were swallowed up in mergers and driven out of the market when they couldn't compete with the monopolies. The middle bourgeoisie was also forced to surrender a number of its vehicles of economic development. Regional railways were integrated into the large systems, while regionally-based banks disappeared, the only exceptions being two Montreal banks that were havens for French-Canadian capital. The result was a loss of economic autonomy and influence for this segment of the bourgeoisie. It did not disappear however, and it maintained an active presence in some fields.

Some sectors were less strongly affected by monopolization than others and remained strongly competitive. Shoes, clothing, sawn lumber, doors and sashes, printing and a number of other industries continued to be characterized by the presence of a large number of middle-sized enterprises. The same was true for a number of areas of wholesale trade, while the entire real estate sector was scarcely touched by monopolization. These fields were the major components of the middle bourgeoisie's economic base. Even in the monopoly sectors, an independent company with a regional base and a geographically concentrated market could sometimes survive and remain profitable, although such a company would represent only a small percentage of total production. In the early decades of the twentieth century, it was still possible to carve out a career or start a business in new fields or expanding sectors.

An important characteristic of the middle bourgeoisie was the regional scale of its economic base, although some entrepreneurs extended their operations over a larger area. Companies at this level often retained a family dimension, and there is little evidence of networks of companies like those of the big bourgeoisie.

The middle bourgeoisie appears to have been very active in politics — at the municipal level, in the provincial government and in political parties. Government contracts of all sorts contributed to the rise of many members of the group. While the big bourgeoisie was able to make sure that provincial and federal government policies served its interests, the middle bourgeoisie was highly skilled at influencing and using municipal government policies, as well as Quebec government policies in some cases. In the economy as a whole, the middle bourgeoisie was relegated to a secondary position. It became something of a marginal group in society, but it did not disappear.

The Position of French Canadians

As has been noted, French Canadians were a marginal group within the big bourgeoisie. Even in 1930, only 4.6 per cent of the directors of large Canadian corporations were French Canadians. The best-known figure of the era was Senator Louis-Joseph Forget, securities broker and director of numerous corporations, who died in 1910. Senator Frédéric-Liguori Béïque, classified as a "millionaire" by the *Montreal Star* in 1911, was a director of the Banque d'Hochelaga and later of the Banque Canadienne Nationale; he became president of the BCN in 1929. He also sat on the board of Canadian Pacific from 1917 on, and was named to the executive committee of that powerful company in 1929. His son-in-law,

Frédéric L. Béïque (1845-1933).

J.-E.-A. Dubuc (1871-1942).

Beaudry Leman, general manager of the Banque Canadienne Nationale, was also a director of Shawinigan Water and Power and other companies.

These men were exceptions, however. Almost all French-Canadian businessment operated at the level of the middle bourgeoisie, and were affected by the reduction of this group to a marginal position. In the move towards corporate concentration, institutions were established on a Canada-wide and sometimes a North-America-wide scale, and there were no French-Canadian monopolies. A number of businesses owned by French Canadians were integrated into larger entities, and French-Canadian entrepreneurs disappeared from the scene. But this dispossession should not be looked at in ethnic terms alone, as many other businessmen of a variety of origins were also relegated to a secondary position in the context of the transition to monopoly capitalism.

On the other hand, there were still fields open to the middle bourgeoisie and the period did see the rise of new French-Canadian entrepreneurs. J.-E.-A. Dubuc was one of these. Starting out as a bank branch manager, Dubuc became the leading figure in the Compagnie de Pulpe de Chicoutimi, and in this capacity he put up mills, built a harbour (Port-Alfred) and exported pulp to England. The company did not survive the paper war of the mid-1920s, but the Dubuc family continued to play a significant role in the economy and politics of the Saguenay region. In the Montreal area, Joseph Versailles, a securities broker, founded the municipality of Montreal East and established a cement business that endeavoured to compete with the cement trust. In Sorel, Joseph Simard, starting as a simple clerk, began to buy the enterprises that became the basis of his industrial empire. The Dufresne brothers (Oscar and Marius) of Maisonneuve were representative of the numerous French-Canadian entrepreneurs for whom real estate promotion and urban development constituted a significant sector of activity; while not exclusive of other interests, it contributed substantially to their enrichment.

The scale of these French-Canadian enterprises remained small in the Canadian context. The French-Canadian banks represented only six to seven per cent of the assets of all banks. In his 1936 work *Mesure de notre taille* (Measuring Our Size), Victor Barbeau tried to evaluate the position of French Canadians in the economy. In most sectors, he concluded that their position was "nonexistent," "microscopic" or "modest." Of some sixty sectors included in a table, about ten merited being classified as "good" or "satisfactory" and only three — agricultural products, leather and butter — as "excellent." Although the study was done a few years after the close of the period under consideration, it reflected a trend that was already evident at the time. The possibility that French Canadians maintained a minority interest in some corporations cannot be excluded, but this hypothesis would be difficult to test.

For French-Canadian businessmen, however, as for the middle bourgeoisie as a whole, reduction to a marginal position did not mean disappearance. The French-Canadian businessman still had a solid local or regional economic base. He used provincial and municipal patronage to his advantage, and his economic base allowed him to exercise a degree of power with local or regional dimensions in the economic, political and social spheres.

Bourgeois Institutions

The Quebec bourgeoisie had at its disposal institutions that acted as vehicles for its point of view and provided opportunities for discussion and co-ordination. Among these institutions were the economic interest groups, a category that included chambers of commerce but was clearly dominated in terms of importance and influence by the Montreal Board of Trade, the voice of Montreal's big and middle bourgeoisie. Although the most important French-Canadian businessmen belonged to the Board of Trade, it was an overwhelmingly English-speaking institution. It represented Montreal commercial interests first and foremost, and was especially active on all issues concerning the harbour. It also intervened in municipal politics, supporting administrative reform programs. Industrial capitalists, although members of the Board of Trade, considered themselves better represented by the Canadian Manufacturers Association, which had its head office in Toronto and local sections in Quebec.

The French-Canadian bourgeoisie, a small minority in both these institutions, had organizations of its own in the form of the chambers of commerce. The Montreal chamber was particularly active. It often conducted joint activities with the Board of Trade, an indication of class solidarity transcending ethnic divisions, but its interventions aimed at supporting French-Canadian economic interests represented a divergence from the Board. Contrary to the Board of Trade, which promoted Canada-wide development, the chamber was very interested in the development of Quebec. In 1902, the Montreal chamber launched a drive to organize chambers of commerce in other Quebec cities and towns. It also proposed that a federation of all Quebec chambers of commerce be established; this was accomplished in 1909. As the historian Ronald Rudin has noted, the Board of Trade openly refused to get involved with either of these endeavours, although it had previously supported similar efforts outside Quebec. The French-speaking chambers also differed significantly from the Board of Trade in recruiting part of their membership from outside the bourgeoisie, specifically from the petty bourgeoisie. The chambers thus did not have the same economic clout as the Board of Trade.

In addition to these well-organized institutions, there were many other interest groups, established to promote or defend a particular cause. Some were ephemeral, and were dissolved as soon as their goals were achieved. In 1918, for example, a group of holders of Maisonneuve municipal bonds was formed to make Premier Gouin aware of its members' fears about the financial situation of the municipality and hence about the security of their investments. This intervention appears to have been an important factor in the Gouin government's decision to force the annexation of Maisonneuve to Montreal.

The bourgeoisie also made use of the many institutions that provided opportunities for discussion and consultation: secret organizations such as the Freemasons or the Ordre de Jacques-Cartier; private clubs with very selective recruitment, such as the St. James's Club, the Mount Royal Club, the Garrison Club and the Club Saint-Denis; and philanthropic and cultural associations, in which representatives of the bourgeoisie often monopolized the leading positions.

The existence of the business press should also be noted. Major publications included the *Journal of Commerce*, the *Financial Times*, the *Moniteur du commerce* and the *Prix courant*, and there were also numerous specialized periodicals aimed at specific groups such as bankers, manufacturers and merchants. More significant was the bourgeoisie's ability to disseminate its ideas through the media, especially the large-circulation daily press.

The Petty Bourgeoisie

The petty bourgeoisie also felt the effects of concentration. The suppliers — wholesalers or manufacturers — with whom small entrepreneurs and merchants now had to deal were large companies that could fix credit terms. These small businessmen had to operate under precarious conditions and were clearly becoming marginal in the economy as a whole. Intense competition was another aspect of their situation, and the struggle for survival was constant.

Initially, urbanization encouraged the proliferation of small businesses. To have one's own business was synonymous with social advancement, and there were always new arrivals ready to start enterprises of their own. In particular, small business was a way for immigrants to climb the social ladder, so that competition often had cultural implications. Alongside small merchants of French-Canadian or British origin, there appeared Jewish, Syrian or other small merchants, and this ethnic diversification increased tensions. Meanwhile, as time went on urbanization also favoured the rise of chain or branch stores, and this represented a new setback for the small independent merchant. Viewed from the late 1920s, the petty bourgeoisie's traditional economic base appeared to be precarious.

However, expansion of the political, legal and cultural sectors provided new roles for a section of the petty bourgeoisie The bourgeoisie began to withdraw from the direct exercise of political power during the period, leaving it increasingly to professional politicians for whom it was a career of a sort. But the most significant development was the growth of the intermediate salaried strata of society that constitute what is known as the new petty bourgeoisie — managers, intellectuals, journalists, teachers. Thus, for example, university professors were more influential in the 1920s than they had ever been before. Men such as Abbé Lionel Groulx and Édouard Montpetit took part in public debates. In the health sector, doctors and other health professionals played an increasingly important role. This position of intermediary between the power structure and the population opened up new avenues for the petty bourgeoisie.

CHAPTER 26
THE WORKING CLASS AND THE LABOUR MOVEMENT

As noted earlier (see chapters 8 and 10), among the effects of industrialization in Quebec were the growth of a working class and the birth of a movement — the trade union movement — through which this class defended its interests. Between 1896 and 1929, these developments continued and even increased in scope. The period is best broken up into two stages, with the First World War as the dividing line.

Initially, at the turn of the century, the labour movement went through an era of significant growth. The period began with the final victory of the unions affiliated to the American Federation of Labor over the Knights of Labor and the national unions. For the next two decades, large international unions dominated the Quebec trade union movement. It was a period of expansion and militancy that even spilled over into political action, with the formation of the Parti Ouvrier. In 1921, fourteen per cent of the labour force was unionized.

The Catholic clergy had tried to resist this new force in the era of the Knights of Labor, but ultimately had been forced reluctantly to accept it. Then, as time went on, it increasingly regarded the growth of international unionism of American origin as a threat from both the religious and the national point of view. The growing resistance of the clergy, the ethnic tensions that emerged during the war and the fears aroused by the 1919 Winnipeg General Strike led to the emergence of a new force — the Catholic unions. The 1920s were marked by the existence of two competing forms of trade union organization. At the same time, expansion of the labour movement came to an end and its militancy ebbed.

Militancy and Expansion, 1896-1914

In 1896, the Trades and Labour Congress of Canada (TLC) included both the Canadian sections of the international unions affiliated to the AF of L and some Canadian national unions, most of them Knights of Labor assemblies that had broken with the American Knights. There was considerable tension between the two groups. In the years that followed, the international unions entered a phase of expansion and the number of locals affiliated with them increased significantly. Although the Knights of Labor played a very active role in the leadership of the TLC, they were reduced to a minority. The 1902 TLC convention in Berlin, Ontario (now Kitchener) decided to resolve the difficulty by expelling the Knights of Labor and all national unions operating in the same fields as existing international unions. The TLC was henceforth tightly bound to the AF of L and its president, Samuel Gompers.

The expelled unions, most of which were in Quebec, formed a new organization, the National Trades and Labor Congress of Canada (NTLC). These national unions were most active in the shoe, construction and textile industries; their stronghold was Quebec City, where they dominated the trade union movement. In a bid to increase its membership in English Canada, the NTLC became the Canadian Federation of Labour (CFL) in 1908. However, the new organization did not represent a significant force alongside the TLC. In Quebec, after an initial period of growth, its membership faded away in the years before the First World War. The expansionism of the international unions brought about the elimination of a number of national unions in Montreal, while in Quebec City internal dissension resulted in disaffection with the CFL and withdrawal of a number of unions from the Federation. These unions did not disappear, however, and some later became Catholic unions.

Thus, membership in an American international union became the rule in the Canadian trade union movement. In 1914, the number of unionized workers in Canada was estimated at about 166,000; of these, 134,348 were members of American international unions. They were not necessarily members of the TLC, which represented only 80,000 workers in 1914. Precise statistics for Quebec are difficult to obtain. There were 136 union locals in Quebec in 1901 and 329 in 1916, but the size of their membership is unknown. The statistics gathered by the historian Jacques Rouillard establish that the major gains during this period of expansion were made by the international unions. In 1901 the national unions, with sixty-two locals, were almost neck-and-neck with the internationals, which had seventy-four. In 1916, however, the internationals had 236 locals, as compared with seventy for the national and twenty-three for the Catholic unions. It should be noted that the number of locals is not an adequate measure of the relative strength of these organizations, since the size of their membership varied greatly.

Many unions were ephemeral. Employers succeeded in smashing some of them through a variety of tactics. It was common for employers to refuse to recognize the union as a bargaining agent; union leaders and workers who had signed up were fired; and employers supported the establishment of company unions to counter an organization they considered too militant. The workers themselves often wavered and did not give steady support; membership might rise dramatically after successful negotiations or a strike victory, but the loss of support that followed a strategic error or defeat in a conflict with the employer might be enough to kill the union. Inter-union rivalries, especially between national and international unions, also had negative effects.

But if trade unions came and went, trade unionism remained. Despite the difficulties and setbacks, the labour movement broadened its base and made appreciable progress in the early part of the century. This was a period of militancy, as shown both by labour's demands and by its political activity. There has been no systematic analysis of union demands and labour conflicts in this era. According to Terry Copp, the union movement's demands were concentrated on two major goals — wage increases (or wage maintenance in the face of threatened reductions) and job security. The period before the war was characterized by a large number of strikes.

The cotton mills, which were among the largest employers in Quebec, were the scene of many work stoppages; Jacques Rouillard has found evidence of thirty-six between 1900 and 1915. In 1908, textile strikes accounted for ninety per cent of all work days lost in the entire manufacturing sector. However, because textile workers were not highly skilled and were therefore easily replaceable, they had limited bargaining power and their demands were met in only twenty-two per cent of the cases. These strikes occurred at the major cotton mills in Montreal, Valleyfield, Magog and Montmorency.

The heavy concentration of workers in Montreal made Quebec's largest city its main trouble spot for labour conflicts. In addition to the textile workers, Montreal's tobacco and clothing workers frequently went on strike. Work stoppages were common in the construction sector as well, and there were major conflicts at the two large railway corporations, at the streetcar company and on the docks. In Quebec City, a strike in the shoe industry in 1901 had long-term repercussions because of the intervention of the clergy in the conflict. Another manifestation of trade union militancy was political action, notably the formation of the Parti Ouvrier and the election of Alphonse Verville as federal member of parliament for Maisonneuve in 1906. This dimension of labour activity will be discussed in chapter 32.

The labour ferment of the early twentieth century can be explained by a number of factors. The tradition of militancy associated with the Knights of Labor survived the demise of the organization. In addition, the conditions under which workers lived and worked, especially the inadequacy of their wages, resulted in waves of exasperation that showed up in the large number of strikes. Immigrant workers who came to Quebec in large numbers in the early years of the century

Workers building a railway bridge, 1898.

often brought experience of trade union militancy with them from their countries of origin; thus, English and eastern European Jewish workers played a significant role in the development of the Quebec trade union movement. The influence of the international unions was also important. The largest and best organized of the internationals were in a position to take charge of trade union activity and pay organizers to establish new locals. As they were interested only in craft unions, they brought together the most highly skilled workers, in other words the workers who were best able to obtain concessions from their employers.

While the American international unions were flourishing, Catholic unionism was getting its start, although on a very small scale. The open opposition of the archbishop of Quebec to trade unionism in the 1880s had given way by the early twentieth century to a desire to establish clerical control of unionized workers and their organizations. The first evidence of this new spirit appeared in 1901 in Quebec City, where a strike pitted workers in the shoe industry against their employers. To resolve the conflict, both sides agreed to accept the archbishop of

Quebec, Mgr Bégin, as an arbitrator. Mgr Bégin recognized the workers' right to organize, but suggested that they change the constitution of their union to bring it into greater conformity with the views of the church and accept the appointment of a chaplain.

Another step was taken in 1907, when Abbé Eugène Lapointe, a future bishop of Chicoutimi, established the Fédération Ouvrière de Chicoutimi to bring together the workers in the Dubuc pulp mills. This organization, which had many of the characteristics of a company union, was looked upon very favourably by the employers. It was avowedly Catholic and admitted only Catholic workers to membership. It got off to a slow start, but was reorganized in 1912 into the Fédération Ouvrière Mutuelle du Nord, with branches in the major cities and towns in the Saguenay region. Catholic unions were also established in Montreal and Trois-Rivières, but this remained a small-scale movement before 1914.

Competition and Weakness 1914-29

The rise of Catholic unionism was a postwar phenomenon, and the events of the 1914-19 period, especially the conscription crisis and the Winnipeg General Strike, contributed to it.

The outbreak of the First World War led to tensions within the Canadian labour movement. On the one hand, there was the anti-militarist tradition within trade unionism and the belief of some trade union leaders that this was an imperialist war, waged on the backs of the workers. On the other hand, there was a tendency to support the war effort, especially out of patriotism. Opposition between these two tendencies continued throughout the war. In Quebec, French Canadians' lack of enthusiasm for the war effort and their widespread rejection of compulsory military service constituted an additional factor. During the conscription crisis in 1917, a minority of delegates to the TLC convention wanted to resist conscription by declaring a general strike, but the majority decided not to challenge the government's measure openly. In tacitly supporting conscription in this way, the TLC was influenced by the policy of the AF of L, as Gompers wholeheartedly backed the American war effort. This policy of the American trade union leadership contributed to the isolation of Quebec and other Canadian trade unionists who wanted to resist conscription. In the view of many French-Canadian trade unionists, the Canadian central organization was taking a position that went against their interests.

They were not the only ones who were disappointed. Western Canadian trade union leaders, considerably more radical than their eastern counterparts, considered themselves constrained by the limits imposed on them by the AF of L and its Canadian branch. This situation led some of them to lay the foundation for a new labour organization. But the trade union movement in the West was important for Quebec chiefly because of another development, the Winnipeg General Strike. The general strike was declared in May 1919 by the Winnipeg Trades and Labour Council to support union demands, and it lasted a little over a month. The

Workers in a foundry during the First World War.

strike committee was master of the city and its actions were free from violence. Demonstrations in support of the strikers were held in major cities across Canada.

The bourgeoisie, in Winnipeg and in Canada as a whole, reacted very strongly to the strike. Political leaders labelled it a revolutionary situation inspired by Bolsheviks. Seeing that the strikers were succeeding, they decided to crush the movement by force and sent in the Royal North West Mounted Police. The RNWMP took the offensive and fired on a crowd of strikers. This had the desired effect and the established order regained control. In Quebec, the Winnipeg General Strike aroused fears among nationalist intellectuals and members of the clergy, who saw it as evidence of the growth of socialism and the dangers of international unionism. The Bolshevik Revolution of October 1917 in Russia also had a strong impact on them. Increasingly, they saw the establishment of Catholic unions as the solution.

The clergy and the nationalist intellectuals were opposed to the international unions for two main reasons. One was that these unions were religiously neutral and susceptible to a variety of tendencies that could go against the social doctrine preached by the church; in their view, this situation was an open invitation to socialism. Second, because of their international character, these unions were subject to directives from outside the country, and they regarded this as a threat to French-Canadian culture. The recent example of the war and the conscription crisis was there to remind them that orders from Washington could go against the national interests of French Canadians.

A group of priests and laymen began to organize a response to this threat in the form of a new kind of union, national in character, with its centre of decision remaining in Canada, and made up exclusively of Catholics, under the firm guidance of a chaplain. They gained the support of a number of French-Canadian trade unionists who had become disillusioned with the international unions as a result of recent events. The best known was Alfred Charpentier, a former member of the Bricklayers, Masons and Plasterers' International Union of America, who "converted" to Catholic unionism about 1917 and soon became one of the leaders of the movement.

From 1918 on, the movement grew in scope and new unions were founded at a faster pace. Catholic unionism was supported by a network of Catholic institutions, and its message was disseminated by its chaplains and brought to all the industrial centres of Quebec. It soon became necessary to organize these new unions into a federation. Delegates to a convention held in Hull in 1921 founded the Canadian and Catholic Confederation of Labour (CCCL).

Despite its name, the new federation recruited its members principally among French-speaking Quebecers. At the time of its founding it claimed to have 45,000 members, but this was clearly an exaggeration; according to Jacques Rouillard's estimates, it had 17,600 members in 120 locals in 1922. Thus, the CCCL represented about a quarter of all unionized workers in Quebec. This, however, was its best performance during the period, as after 1921 it went into a phase of stagnation and even relative decline. The Catholic unions were strongest in Quebec City and the smaller industrial centres; they were very much a minority in Montreal, where the international unions were dominant.

National unions that did not define themselves as Catholic and continued to be rejected by the TLC organized a new federation in 1927, the All-Canadian Congress of Labour (ACCL), with the Canadian Brotherhood of Railway Employees as its main component. However, the ACCL was not a very strong organization. During the 1920s, the number of national unions in Quebec varied between thirty and forty, but not all were affiliated with the ACCL. Catholic unions and national unions represented about a third of Quebec's unionized workers at the time.

The TLC, which defined itself as the federation of the Canadian branches of international unions, continued to dominate the trade union field. It was, however, in a phase of stagnation in the 1920s, and the number of Quebec locals affiliated with it actually fell from 334 in 1921 to 314 in 1926. Labour demands had been stimulated by the rapid postwar inflation of 1918 and 1919, but the economic slowdown and unemployment of the early 1920s led to a noticeable ebbing of militancy and a decline in membership, from which the trade union movement was slow in recovering. The international unions reduced their recruiting efforts, except possibly in the clothing industry.

The international unions' adherence to craft unionism prevented them from responding adequately to the needs of significant groups of workers — unskilled labour and employees of giant corporations where a number of crafts were represented. It would have been possible to adapt to this situation by establishing industrial unions grouping all the workers in an industry regardless of their craft or skills, but the international unions rejected this solution. Communist organizers appeared in some unions during the period, but they had only a limited role before 1930.

The 1920s thus were characterized by division within the labour movement and a marked slowdown in its organizational efforts. Militancy was in decline and labour political activity was reduced to almost nothing. These dismal years present a contrast to the dynamism of the trade union movement of the early years of the century.

Labour Legislation

Very slowly and after a delay of several years, the Quebec government began to implement some of the recommendations made in 1889 by the Royal Commission on the Relations of Labour and Capital and reiterated by the trade union movement. In the first three decades of the twentieth century, significant Quebec labour legislation dealt with accidents, placement services, women and children in the labour market, conciliation and arbitration, and legal recognition of unions. This was not much for a thirty-year period.

As the pace of industrialization speeded up, the problem of work accidents and their victims' loss of income and seniority became acute. Between 1890 and 1907, inspectors of industrial establishments enumerated 4,608 accidents, 263 of them fatal ones. As employers did not report all accidents, the number of victims was undoubtedly higher.

The worker who was the victim of an accident, or his family in case of a fatality, had to go to court in order to be compensated. The worker had to prove that the employer was responsible for the accident, and it was practically impossible for him to undertake costly legal proceedings. It was a long-standing demand of the unions that the government correct this situation, which was a source of misery for hundreds of working-class families.

The government conducted an inquiry and then, like other provincial governments, proposed legislation to remedy the situation. The Workmen's Compensation Act of 1909 enshrined the principle of "professional risk" — an employee

SEPT HOMMES SONT BROYES A MORT, HIER, A KENOGAMI

Un terrible accident est arrivé à la nouvelle pulperie que construit la Canadian Stewart Co., pour la compagnie Price.--Les victimes sont presque toutes des Canadiens-Français.

(Du correspondant de la PRESSE)

Jonquière, 2. — Un terribe accident, qui a causé la mort de 7 personnes, est arrivé, hier après-midi, vers quatre heures, à Kenogami. Les victimes, qui étaient à l'emploi de la Canadian Stewart Company, qui construit une pulperie pour la compagnie Price ,travaillaient sous un concasseur, lorsqu'une poutre surchargée céda. Les hommes furent broyés à mort. Six d'entre eux sont canadiens-français et le septième est anglais. Quelques-uns sont mariés et père de famille. Parmi les victimes on compte un de nos concitoyens, M. Girard. Ce dernier est marié mais n'a pas d'enfants.Les autres sont tous des étrangers et ne sont pas connus ici. Le coroner doit tenir une enquête.

LES VICTIMES

Québec, 2 — Une dépêche de Jonquières nous apprend que les victimes de l'accident de Kenogami sont les suivantes: Frank Aubut, Joseph et Edmond Plourde, de Saint-Godfroi de Bonaventure; Jean Huard, de Paspébiac, comté Bonaventure; Daniel Durcel, Baie Saint-Paul; David Girard, Jonquières, et J. Chardoux, Suisse.

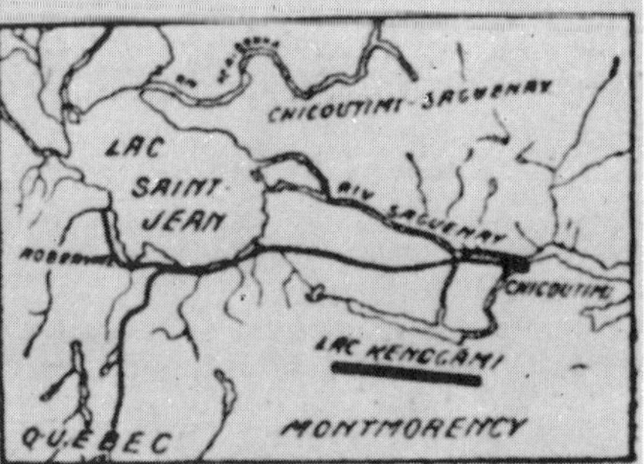

CARTE INDIQUANT où se trouve Kenogami, le théâtre d'un terrible accident qui a coûté la vie à sept ouvriers, dont six Canadiens-français.

Work accidents were one of the most important labour issues in the early twentieth century. This story from the July 2, 1912 *La Presse* is headlined: "SEVEN MEN CRUSHED TO DEATH, YESTERDAY, AT KENOGAMI. A terrible accident happened at the new pulp mill being built by Canadian Stewart Co. for the Price Company. The victims were almost all French Canadians."

would be compensated in case of an accident independently of whether he or his employer was at fault. The compensation to which the worker was entitled, however, was equal to only fifty per cent of his pay.

In 1926, the government amended the law under pressure from the unions. One amendment required employers to take out a policy with a recognized insurance company so that workers would be protected even if the employer went out of business. Another raised compensation to two-thirds of the worker's usual pay. The new act went into effect after two years of delaying tactics by the government. In the end, the government decided to establish a Workmen's Compensation Commission similar to the one in existence in Ontario; this new body would serve as a tribunal in work accident cases and determine the amount of compensation in each case. Workers could not appeal decisions of the Commission to the ordinary courts. While the new legislation did improve the treatment of accident victims, it had serious deficiencies, notably its silence on the question of industrial diseases. The problem to which it was addressed was unquestionably critical, as in 1929 alone 21,377 accidents were reported, of which 152 led to the death of the victim and 2,497 to a permanent disability.

Apart from accidents, unemployment continued to be one of the major problems faced by working people. There was no systematic protection against this scourge and there is much testimony to the misery suffered by families whose breadwinners were unemployed. There are no statistics that would make it possible to measure the scope of unemployment, but it is clear that it was a sizeable phenomenon. It took two forms, one tied to economic fluctuations and the other tied to seasonal slowdowns in some economic activities; dockworkers on the St. Lawrence and construction workers were unemployed every winter, whatever the state of the economy.

The only legislation during the period that was aimed at reducing unemployment had reference to the establishment of public placement offices to operate alongside private services. The public services offered their service free, while the government in 1914 limited the fee that a private service could charge to $3. In 1918, the federal government offered to pay part of the costs incurred by the provinces in providing this service if they would agree to co-ordinate their efforts. The goal of these offices, which represented only a very partial solution to the problem of unemployment, was to encourage a better matching of supply and demand on the labour market; in this capacity, they were well regarded by both employers and workers. Between 1911 and 1929, more than 240,000 workers got jobs through Quebec's five public placement offices. In 1929 alone, the offices succeeded in placing 27,330 of the 52,000 people who came to them looking for jobs. But they could do nothing for the other 25,000 people, surplus labourers who had to try to survive on public or private charity. This is an indication of just how limited the legislation was.

If governments did almost nothing for the unemployed, they were forced to make a few gestures towards the most vulnerable workers — women and children.

A private placement office, 1924.

The abuses to which these workers were subject, especially in relation to age of entry onto the labour market, hours of work, and wages, had long been under attack from a number of groups.

The best, if not the only, way to prevent exploitation of children on the labour market was to institute compulsory schooling, as demanded by some unions and liberals who were labelled as "radicals." The clergy was especially hostile to this solution. The government, which on the one hand did not want to do battle with the Roman Catholic church and on the other hand wanted to steal the thunder from the advocates of compulsory schooling, tried to correct the situation through a variety of legislative contortions.

Legislation adopted in 1907 made it compulsory for workers between the ages of twelve and sixteen who could not read or write fluently to take evening courses. This was a cruel measure, as the inspectors of industrial establishments pointed out; how could a youth who worked ten hours a day, six days a week, be required to take evening courses in addition? Thus, in 1910, the government imposed an outright ban on the employment of illiterates under sixteen years of age. Literate youths were covered by an 1885 law that established a minimum age of employment of twelve years for boys and fourteen years for girls. In 1910, the minimum age for working in an industrial establishment was set at fourteen years. Unfortunately, the legislation did not cover the thousands of children who worked elsewhere than in industrial establishments — grocery delivery boys, store clerks, stockboys, domestics. It also ignored those who were not directly on the labour market, such as girls who had to stay at home to raise their younger brothers and sisters.

Circumstances also required the government to limit working hours for women and children. Gradually, in some sectors, the work week was reduced from sixty to fifty-five hours, and in 1919, a Women's Minimum Wage Commission was given legislative authorization, although the commission was not really established until 1925, as will be seen later (see chapter 28). On the whole, this "protective" legislation was difficult to apply, and it was not overly disturbing to employers.

Another sector that attracted the attention of governments was labour relations. From the beginning of the century, attempts were made to reduce the number of conflicts. In 1900, the federal government began to offer conciliation and arbitration services to labour and management; it was imitated by the Quebec government in 1901. Recourse to these services was voluntary and they did not make binding decisions. Government intervention in this sector led to the establishment of specialized services that gradually became departments of labour, in both Ottawa and Quebec City.

In 1907, the federal government proposed to make conciliation compulsory in a number of sectors. In 1925, however, the British Privy Council ruled that it was exceeding its powers in intervening so broadly in a field that affected property and civil rights and was thus primarily a provincial responsibility. The Council did recognize, however, that Ottawa could intervene in specific sectors directly under its jurisdiction, such as railways. Provincial governments also attempted to establish a framework for labour relations and possibly reduce strikes in this way. Thus in 1921, after strikes by firemen and policemen in Montreal and other municipal workers in both Montreal and Quebec City, the Quebec government decided to make recourse to conciliation and arbitration compulsory for labour and management in these sectors before a strike or lockout could be called.

The government also tried to provide a better framework for the trade union movement with the Professional Syndicates Act of 1924, which made it possible for trade unions to gain full legal recognition. In principle, such legislation protected unionized workers, but it also contained restrictive clauses, such as the requirement that the officers and two-thirds of the members of a recognized union be British subjects. Under Quebec law, as under its federal counterpart, unions were not required to obtain legal recognition. The Catholic unions were pleased with the Quebec law, which they had been demanding for a number of years, while the international unions were more favourably disposed towards Ottawa's legislation.

In Quebec, labour relations were as far as possible considered individual relations, and thus a matter for the Civil Code. Employers benefited as a direct result of this individualistic view. Slowly, under pressure from workers, the government was required to intervene at least to limit the worst abuses, and in the end it admitted that labour issues had a collective character. There was also pressure in the opposite direction from employers to obtain more control over unions and to limit strikes. But overall, the government rarely took the initiative and was satisfied with minimal legislation during this period of heavy industrialization.

CHAPTER 27
RURAL QUEBECERS

In discussing rural Quebec, it is necessary to make the same distinctions as for the preceding period (see chapter 8); not everyone who is categorized as rural lived on a farm and there were social differences in the countryside as well. In 1931, Quebec had a rural population of 1,060,649, only seventy-three per cent of whom lived on farms. In other words, more than a quarter of the rural population lived in villages; this group included day-labourers, craftsmen, merchants, people with independent incomes, and members of the liberal professions. There were also 135,957 farms enumerated in 1931, with an average of 5.7 persons per farm and a large work force made up primarily of family members who worked without pay. Farmers were not a socially homogeneous group, and a 100-acre farm in a new colonization region had little in common with a farm of similar size on Île Jésus. There were all degrees of agriculture from commercial production, highly specialized or tied to urban markets to subsistence farming. In this period as in the preceding one, even if rural society may appear homogeneous at first glance, it contains many shadings on closer examination.

In the early 1920s, agriculture was severely affected by the recession; not only did prices collapse, as noted earlier (see chapter 23), but in the period of overproduction during the war, farmers had gone heavily into debt to buy land or machinery. In these circumstances, which were not limited to Quebec, farmers sought to strengthen their co-operative organizations and establish a trade association. There had been agricultural associations in the nineteenth century, but they had been either organized or controlled by the government or the clergy. The agricultural circles, which became widespread after 1876, were the best-known example. The government had quickly gained control of these organizations by manipulating grants, and had reduced their activities to sponsoring lectures and

A corn-husking party, a characteristic entertainment in rural Quebec. This engraving is by Edmond-Joseph Massicotte.

contests. In the end, the farmers had been left without organizations that were truly theirs. At the turn of the century, however, a new kind of organization began to appear.

Farmers' Co-operatives

In the United States, it was the Grange movement, founded in 1867, that played the role of pioneer in co-operation among farmers. It quickly spread to Canada and was especially strong in Ontario, where the Grangers succeeded in getting the provincial government to hold an inquiry into the state of agriculture in 1879. But this was not the only influence on the Canadian co-operative movement. The first consumers' co-operatives were established by workers of British origin and took much of their inspiration from the English model. In Quebec, there were other influences as well, from France and especially from Belgium; Abbé Allaire, who spearheaded the Quebec co-operative movement during the first two decades of the twentieth century, used as his model a Belgian Catholic farmers' co-operative.

The first co-operative institutions among farmers were fire insurance co-operatives and butter and cheese manufacturing enterprises, which began to be established in the mid-nineteenth century. About thirty fire insurance co-operatives were founded before 1900, the earliest dating from 1852. The two initial butter and cheese co-operatives were established at Baie-du-Febvre (now Baieville) near Nicolet and Rivière-Ouelle in the Lower St. Lawrence region; there were a number of such organizations after 1883, all focused primarily on production. In 1891, the Société d'Industrie Laitière de la Province de Québec, founded nine years earlier, began organizing a new kind of association in the butter and cheese industry. The chief purpose of the *syndicats* it promoted was to improve the quality of the industry's products, and towards this end the Société established an inspection service and arranged for the dissemination of new techniques by visiting teachers.

The agricultural co-operative movement really got off the ground in the early years of the twentieth century. In 1903, the first local agricultural co-operative was founded in Shefford county. The movement rapidly grew in scope, and was helped along by an act governing co-operatives passed in 1906. At the time of the First World War, there was a confederation of agricultural co-operatives with about a hundred member organizations; however, it disbanded in 1920.

Central co-operatives, organizing farmers on the basis of a product or a service, began to be founded a few years after the local co-operatives. In 1911, the Société Coopérative Agriçole des Fromagers de Québec (Quebec Cheese Co-operative) was founded in Montreal at the instigation of the Société d'Industrie Laitière; its activities rapidly expanded to include poultry products, honey and even livestock products, notably bacon. The next year, a purchasing pool, the Comptoir Coopératif de Montréal, was established, with agricultural circles, co-operatives and individuals as members. Finally, in 1914, the Société Coopérative des Producteurs de Grains de Semence de Québec (Quebec Seed Grain Producers' Co-operative Corporation) was founded, with the goal of providing farmers with better-quality seed.

In the early 1920s, the idea of merging these three co-operatives was in the air. However, as noted above, these were years of agricultural crisis, and this circumstance gave the merger movement an unexpected twist and changed its scope and complexion. Similarly, the critical state of agriculture gave a new direction to the initiative that eventually resulted in formation of the Union Catholique des Cultivateurs. In general, starting at the end of the war there was great ferment among Canadian farmers, and farmer militancy rose rapidly, making governments uneasy. A group that had originated in western Canada, the United Farmers, gradually established itself in western Quebec; in 1920, it came to an agreement with another farmers' organization, the Union des Cultivateurs (see below), to divide up counties between the two groups and pursue the common goal of forming an agrarian party. This was realized with the founding of the Farmer-Progressive Party of Quebec to contest the 1921 federal election; by this time the United Farmers were 5,000 strong. The new party ran candidates in twenty-one constituencies, and while it did not succeed in making a dent in the solid Liberal bloc, it did get eleven per cent of the vote. What was even more disturbing to the provincial government of Premier Taschereau was that influential members of farmers' organizations openly supported the new party. At the time, the United Farmers were in power in three provinces and played an important role in Ottawa.

According to Firmin Létourneau, it was the rise of the United Farmers that spurred the Quebec minister of agriculture, J.-E. Caron, to decide to merge the three co-operatives on his own initiative. This allowed him to get the jump on his adversary J.-Noé Ponton, editor of the influential *Bulletin des Agriculteurs* and one of the United Farmers' most enthusiastic propagandists. Recovering from the election defeat of the United Farmers, Ponton had revived the issue of association of the co-operatives in the *Bulletin* in 1922, and Caron had reason to fear that the United Farmers would be the beneficiaries of the merger.

J.-N. Ponton was one of the farmers' movement's more noteworthy figures. Born in 1886, he was a student at the Sherbrooke seminary before doing specialized studies at the agricultural college in Guelph, Ontario. It was said that he was the first French Canadian to complete advanced studies in agronomy. He was appointed professor of rural engineering at the Oka Agricultural Institute in 1916, but resigned after a few years to run a farm. He served briefly with the federal Department of Agriculture in 1919, and became the editor of the *Bulletin des Agriculteurs*, the organ of the Société Coopérative Agricole des Fromagers de Québec, the next year. In the pages of the *Bulletin*, he attacked the Quebec minister of agriculture; at the same time that he became actively involved in politics, he also bought the newspaper and made it an effective instrument of struggle and propaganda. Despite the open hostility of Agriculture Minister Caron, he succeeded in increasing its circulation from 5,000 in 1922 to 12,000 two years later. His death in 1929 ended a period of activity that had lasted only fifteen years, but in that short time his dynamism had contributed towards changing rural Quebec.

After the merger of 1922, the struggle was carried on within the new Coopérative Fédérée; "the annual meetings of the Coopérative Fédérée," Firmin Létourneau reports, "degenerated into meetings filled with conflict: Mr. Caron and his friends on one side, Ponton and his friends on the other." This little war did not end until 1929, when a new minister of agriculture established a committee of inquiry into the co-operative. The committee recommended that the organization be turned over to its members, and this was done in 1930. Thus, at the very end of the period, conditions were favourable to a new start for the co-operative movement; the efforts of the Union Catholique des Cultivateurs, which was increasingly establishing itself as the representative organization of Quebec farmers, constituted another important factor encouraging the movement's development.

Farmers' Organizations

Consciousness of their common problems and interests began to grow among Quebec farmers towards the end of the First World War. Until then, they had dutifully followed the advice of their political and religious leaders. There had been no opposition to the campaign to intensify production, as the prices paid for agricultural products acted as an incentive. Conscription of young farmers and farm boys between twenty and twenty-two years of age was an initial stimulus to collective awareness. In May 1918, the Comptoir Coopératif de Montréal decided to join the United Farmers of Ontario in demonstrating in Ottawa against the government's decision, and about 2,000 farmers answered the call.

The success of the demonstration encouraged farmers to form an association. The founding convention was held in August 1918 in Saint-Hyacinthe; the mayor of Saint-Hyacinthe, T.-D. Bouchard, considered a radical although he was also a Liberal MLA, managed to intrude into the debates and influence the direction of the Association. According to historian Robert Migner, his actions were undoubtedly based on an understanding with the minister of agriculture, who feared the possibility of an autonomous movement. At a subsequent meeting, Bouchard himself was chosen as the movement's organizer and his proposal to call the association the Union des Agriculteurs de la Province de Québec was adopted after he had succeeded in having six of his supporters elected as directors. In December 1918, however, farmer activists disappointed with the turn of events founded a rival organization, the Union des Cultivateurs de la Province de Québec, at a meeting in Saint-Jérôme. Contacts between the two organizations quickly proliferated, and despite the opposition of Agriculture Minister Caron, they merged in July 1919. The new Union des Cultivateurs had only 500 members in January 1920. Caron still entertained the hope of controlling the organization; as he said, "I am not afraid of seeing our farmers form associations, so long as these associations do not lead to class struggle."

After the Farmer-Progressive party episode, the idea of a farmers' organization made increasing headway. In October 1924, J.-N. Ponton and his supporters sponsored a convention in Quebec City to form a new organization. Only 600 farmers were expected, but 2,400 came. At this convention, the Union Catholique des Cultivateurs de la Province de Québec was founded; its initial leaders were two men who had been instrumental in forming the organization — Laurent Barré, a farmer, and Firmin Létourneau, an agronomist.

Credibility was the new organization's major problem. In an attempt to neutralize the influence of Agriculture Minister Caron, for whom every farmers' organization represented a potential political party, the UCC's leaders turned to the Catholic church. But there were conditions attached to support from the church, which would not accept an organization that was too politically involved or too radical. The tension between Ponton, whose *Bulletin des Agriculteurs* had become the UCC's semi-official organ, and Caron was one specific obstacle to church approval; UCC President Laurent Barré's militancy was another. At the 1926

Laurent Barré (1886-1964), first president of the Union Catholique des Cultivateurs.

convention, with the organization indisputably on the rise with a membership of 13,000, Barré and Ponton decided to give way and resigned to secure the support of Quebec's Catholic bishops. The UCC lost a dynamic president and a fighting newspaper, but finally, in 1928, the bishops endorsed the UCC, while insisting that it remain politically neutral.

The UCC was based on a two-tier structure — parish circles at the local level and a central office at the provincial level. Later, an intermediate level, the diocesan federation, was also established. By 1929, the UCC clearly had the upper hand over other farmers' organizations, as membership of the United Farmers had steadily declined. With the appointment of a new minister of agriculture in 1929, the UCC obtained official legal recognition under the Companies Act. However, representation from the Montreal region, which had been the scene of intense activity in the early days of farmer militancy, had declined considerably by this time. The early years of the UCC were taken up primarily with problems of internal organization; however, an examination of the resolutions at its annual conventions shows that the Union tried to deal with the major problems faced by farmers, especially long-term agricultural credit, colonization, and the financing of rural schools.

In the first thirty years of the century, rural Quebec did not submit passively to the changes it was undergoing. The rise of rural militancy that came out of the First World War was evidence of a real desire for a new order. There was no follow-up to the political experiment of the Farmer-Progressive party, but the co-operative movement and the Union Catholique des Cultivateurs resulted in more sustained initiatives, and both were to flourish after the close of the period being studied.

CHAPTER 28
LIVING CONDITIONS

Rural Life

In general, living conditions in rural Quebec were not radically different from what they had been in the preceding period. Gradually, however, some elements of change began to be noted, which were roundly criticized by advocates of a more traditional form of rural society. The following quotation from the introduction to *La campagne canadienne*, a novel by the Jesuit Adélard Dugré, is indicative of how these changes were perceived in 1925: "Even in the countryside, our old customs are no longer entirely safe. For a long time now, but especially since the invasion of our peaceful parishes by mass-circulation newspapers, cars and department-store catalogues, our good people glory in adopting American speech, styles and manners."

The innovations that would bring the deepest changes were still to come; it was only in succeeding decades that electricity and radio would become widespread. The impact of the automobile, however, had begun to be felt. If the railway had allowed the influence of the major urban centres to penetrate rural Quebec, the automobile brought about the rise of regional centres that could now benefit fully from their proximity to the countryside. While it had been easier to communicate with the major centres by rail than with regional centres by horse over poor roads, the coming of the automobile re-established the network of towns and villages as the base of the communications structure in rural Quebec. This change was not perceptible, however, until the end of the period.

Dependence on the cycles of plant growth and animal reproduction was a continuing characteristic of rural life. The expansion of the dairy industry, however, made farm work more constant; daily care of the herd left less slack time than the seasonal work involved in growing field crops. The distinctions between

Adults and children alike worked in the fields.

the different forms of agriculture in Quebec remained as sharp as in the previous period; living conditions were not the same in older areas as they were in the new colonization regions.

There was no sharp distinction between living conditions and working conditions in the countryside. One characteristic of the farmer's work life was that his income came from a number of sources. The cases of farmers who were also lumberjacks or fishermen are perhaps the best known, but all farmers were involved in other activities to some degree — selling firewood, making maple sugar, supplying road contractors with rock for crushing. Participation in road work proved to be a particularly significant source of income, and some farmers also took jobs either directly in road building or in transporting materials.

Health conditions in the countryside were slow to improve. Water quality remained a problem, and medical care was unequally distributed and relatively inaccessible. From 1915 on, Quebec's 1,158 municipalities were grouped into ten districts for purposes of sanitary inspection, and this centralization appears to

Hand-weaving in Saint-Bruno.

have contributed towards improving water quality and reducing infant mortality and death from tuberculosis. It was only in 1925, however, that the government, with the help of the Rockefeller Foundation, organized a system of county health units that turned out to be more effective in taking preventive measures.

Given the current state of knowledge of living conditions in rural Quebec, there is not much more that can be said. It is hardly necessary to add that the abundant literature glorifying the life of the farmer has been a long-standing hindrance to awareness of the reality of rural life.

A Culture of Poverty

With the rapid urban growth that took place early in the century, physical and social facilities in the cities soon proved inadequate in terms of both quality and quantity, and the quality of life was seriously compromised as a result. The effects of the cities' failure to adapt to new conditions were not distributed equally through the social structure, and were felt with particular intensity in working-class neighbourhoods. Three aspects of the urban infrastructure are important in this regard: housing and the urban environment; health and sanitation; and welfare and income security. Historical studies of living conditions in the cities are still few in number, and all concentrate on Montreal. It is true that the scope of urban problems was greatest there, but can conclusions based on the Montreal experience be applied to the other cities of Quebec? There are no studies that would make it possible to answer that question definitively.

The problems of overpopulation experienced by New York and Chicago were still unknown in late-nineteenth-century Montreal. As new residents arrived in the city in large numbers, however, available housing was no longer sufficient to meet the demand, and several families sometimes had to crowd into a single dwelling. With the migration of wealthier Montrealers to the suburbs, their former residences became available and were subdivided into several apartments, but this division often was poorly planned. Thus, Montreal's housing pool deteriorated and there was a proliferation of slums.

To meet the new demand, houses were built quickly, almost on an assembly-line basis. The characteristic Montreal house dates from this period, and has either two storeys with three dwellings or else three storeys with five dwellings. Adorned with Montreal's famous outside staircases, these houses are long and narrow, with an inside hall connecting the rooms in each dwelling. A number of contemporary observers pointed out the deficiencies of these badly lit and poorly ventilated houses. Landlords, however, had very wide latitude as the city had no building code; the only restrictions were a few sanitation regulations, and these were difficult to enforce.

Political leaders were much more concerned with respecting the rights of landlords and private enterprise than with defending the interests of tenants, although more than eighty per cent of Montreal dwellings were rented. Montreal was thus a city of tenants, and because of their low incomes very few of them could aspire to eventual home ownership.

In most neighbourhoods, it was not housing alone but rather the whole urban environment that was deficient — factories caused pollution, there were few trees or green spaces, and public facilities were inadequate. Reformers proposed that playgrounds or garden cities be built, but the ideas of the city's leaders in matters of urban environment ran more towards grandiose projects — majestic buildings facing onto great tree-lined boulevards, with a few large parks. There was little concern with what the environment was like off the boulevards, on the side streets where most Montrealers lived.

Montreal's housing and the urban environment were not conducive to good health and were a major cause of the city's poor health record. Montreal was distinguished by its extremely high death rate, higher than any other large western city. This situation, which had existed during the preceding period as well, persisted throughout the early decades of the twentieth century. It was not until after the First World War that the death rate declined significantly, but it still remained consistently higher than that of Toronto, for example (Figure 3).

The main component of Montreal's death rate was clearly infant mortality (Figure 4). Before the war, nearly one child in three died before reaching the age of a year. Sanitary measures adopted by the city government led to a rapid decline in the infant mortality rate after the war, but here too, the rate remained higher than Toronto's. The general decline was not equally distributed throughout the city,

FIGURE 3

General Mortality Rate, Montreal and Toronto, 1897-1931 (deaths per 1,000 population)

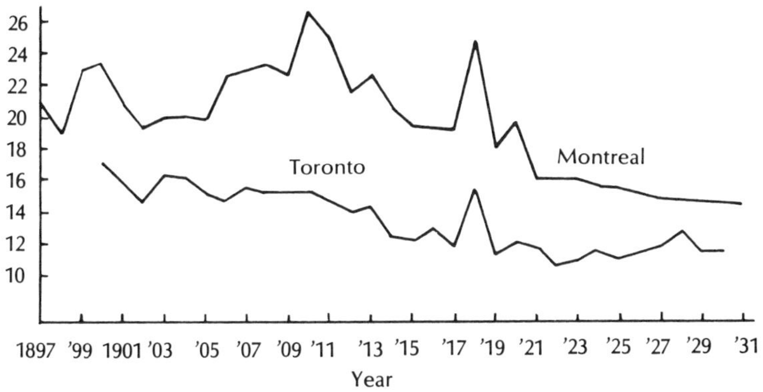

FIGURE 4

Infant Mortality Rate, Montreal and Toronto, 1897-1931 (deaths up to 1 year of age per 1,000 live births)

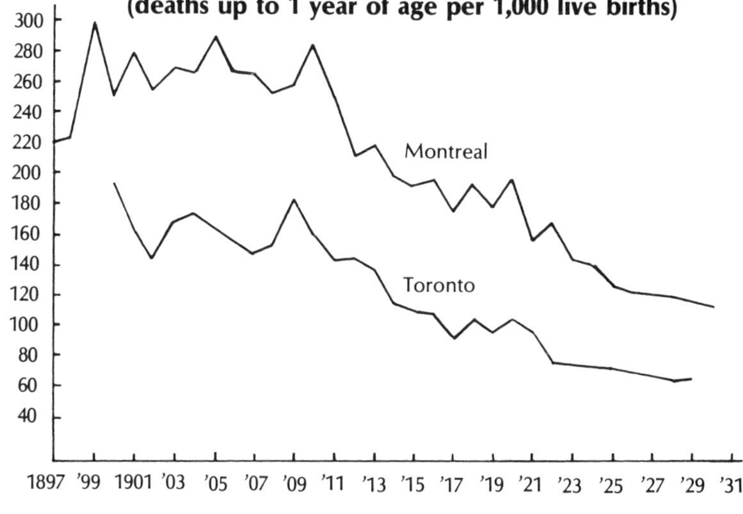

Source: Terry Copp, *The Anatomy of Poverty*, p. 167.

and there were significant differences from neighbourhood to neighbourhood. In 1922, working-class neighbourhoods in the east and southwest of the city still had very high infant mortality rates, while rates in the west end of the city were very low; the rate in Sainte-Marie or Saint-Henri was four times as high as it was in Westmount (Map 12).

The poor quality of the water and milk distributed in Montreal was a major cause of infant mortality. The situation improved when measures providing for filtration of water and pasteurization of milk were adopted, but the wide gap due to social inequality was not eliminated. It was because a large part of the Montreal working class lived in poverty that the quality of food and housing was so poor, with the clear negative effects that this had on health.

Nor was infant mortality the only problem. Montrealers, especially working-class Montrealers, were the victims of a variety of illnesses. Tuberculosis, for example, took a large number of lives in the early part of the century. Between 1900 and 1908, the mortality rate from tuberculosis was more than 200 deaths per 100,000 residents; according to the historian Terry Copp, this was the highest rate reported for any large North American city. While Montreal's rate declined after the war, it was still three times as high as Toronto's during the 1920s.

Nevertheless, there were significant changes in the area of public health during the period. The activities of Montreal's Board of Health, which in the 1880s had been limited to sanitary inspection (garbage removal, condemnation of unhealthful dwellings, collection of statistics on illnesses), took on increased scope around 1900. One factor in this change was a new willingness on the part of doctors, especially public health doctors, to take a stand in demanding a variety of measures relating to vaccination, nutrition and modernization of the city's network of public health institutions. Meanwhile, municipal and provincial authorities were reluctant to impose coercive measures or to devote significant amounts of money to public health. Improving the sanitary conditions in which people lived did not appear to be a priority for their political leaders.

Despite this resistance, public health doctors did obtain reforms that led to a slow decline in the death rate. They also had the support of private associations such as the Montreal Anti-Tuberculosis and General Health League. Made up mostly of businessmen, such associations were based on both the philanthropic tradition and their members' interest — which they fully understood — in having workers in better health.

The most significant reforms concerned water and milk supplies, reforms that affected the whole population. It was not until 1914 that Montrealers were provided with filtered water; the risk of a typhoid epidemic, especially in the summertime, was reduced as a result. In the suburbs, the private Montreal Water and Power Company initially resisted the idea of filtering its water, but finally agreed under pressure from the bourgeois municipality of Westmount, which succeeded where the working-class suburbs of Saint-Henri, Saint-Louis and Maisonneuve had failed.

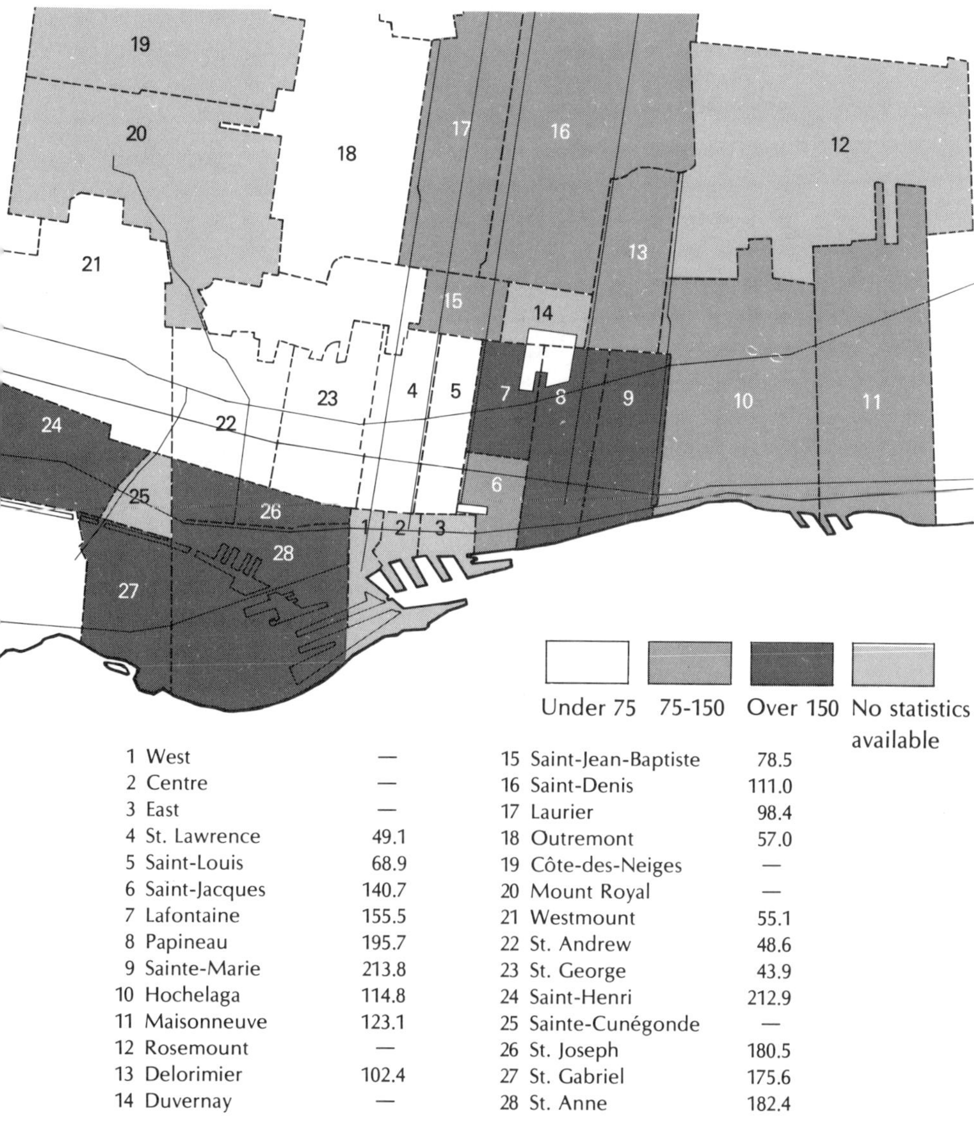

1	West	—	15	Saint-Jean-Baptiste	78.5
2	Centre	—	16	Saint-Denis	111.0
3	East	—	17	Laurier	98.4
4	St. Lawrence	49.1	18	Outremont	57.0
5	Saint-Louis	68.9	19	Côte-des-Neiges	—
6	Saint-Jacques	140.7	20	Mount Royal	—
7	Lafontaine	155.5	21	Westmount	55.1
8	Papineau	195.7	22	St. Andrew	48.6
9	Sainte-Marie	213.8	23	St. George	43.9
10	Hochelaga	114.8	24	Saint-Henri	212.9
11	Maisonneuve	123.1	25	Sainte-Cunégonde	—
12	Rosemount	—	26	St. Joseph	180.5
13	Delorimier	102.4	27	St. Gabriel	175.6
14	Duvernay	—	28	St. Anne	182.4

Adapted from: Canada, Department of the Interior, *Atlas of Canada 1915.*
Data from: Montreal Board of Health, *Annual Report,* 1922.
Source: Terry Copp, *The Anatomy of Poverty,* p. 98.

MAP 12: Infant Mortality Rate in the Various Wards of Montreal, 1922
(deaths up to 1 year of age per 1,000 live births)

The *Goutte de lait* in Ste-Justine Hospital, 1912.

The milk distributed in Montreal at the beginning of the century was of very poor quality, and some of it was unfit for consumption. The struggle for pasteurization lasted a number of years. In 1914, only a quarter of the milk consumed in Montreal was pasteurized, and the large dairies limited distribution of pasteurized milk to the wealthy neighbourhoods of the city's west end. Pasteurization of milk became widespread in the course of the next decade, but it was not required by law until 1926. To get around this problem in the years before the war, the city subsidized the Gouttes de lait (milk drops), depots set up in different neighbourhoods where good-quality milk was distributed free to children.

In the 1920s there was increased activity aimed at improving sanitation for children, as dispensaries operated by the municipal government proliferated in the city's neighbourhoods. In addition, a group of upper-class women led by Justine Lacoste-de-Gaspé-Beaubien established the Sainte-Justine hospital for children in 1907. The Royal Edward Institute and the Institut Bruchési were established to treat tuberculosis; the Hôpital du Sacré-Coeur, built in the 1920s, was also intended primarily for tubercular patients. Despite these advances, the network of health institutions remained insufficient to meet the needs of the

Charity in the English-speaking community: the Ladies Benevolent Institution.

population, especially that part of the population that was in no position to pay the cost of treatment.

Inadequate incomes were at the heart of Montreal's difficult living conditions. Terry Copp has estimated that between 1897 and 1929 the majority of the working class in Montreal lived below the poverty line. A family needed two incomes and reasonably steady work to make ends meet. In a number of sectors, such as construction or work related to the harbour, seasonal unemployment was heavy and workers went without income as a result.

Families hit by unemployment or illness still had to turn to private institutions. The government was involved in financing these organizations to a greater extent than before, but it did not try to influence their orientation. Copp summed up the spirit that underlay private charity at the time as follows:

> The poor posed a problem of some delicacy. A society conditioned to laissez-faire principles found pauperism an abhorrent idea; the concept of making one's way in the world was the very foundation stone of the social order. Yet, obstinately, the destitute insisted on being there. Fear of social disorder if the

> minimum needs of the poor were not met, as well as raw consciences, impelled the better classes to provide charity. But, in the laissez-faire context, it was necessarily stern charity, charity designed to be as uncomfortable and as demeaning as possible. Such a charitable system would meet the Christian duty of caring for real needs, while discouraging the vicious from seeking to make an easy life of pauperism.

There were attempts, especially in the English-speaking sector, to make charity more professional. The Charities Organization Society (1900) and the Montreal Council of Social Agencies (1919) were established with the aim of improving co-ordination of benevolent institutions' activities. But this modernization was in appearance only. The new organizations did not attack the roots of poverty, which they continued to regard as a curable individual problem rather than as a social phenomenon caused by unemployment, low wages or illness. As a result, they emphasized working with individuals likely to succeed in freeing themselves from the condition of poverty. While French-speaking Catholic institutions such as the St. Vincent de Paul societies made more of an effort to adapt to the needs of each client rather than adopting rigid norms, they still took an individual approach that could relieve misery but could not contribute towards a reduction of poverty.

A Hesitant Government

It was only with great trepidation that the Quebec government took action in the welfare and public health sectors before 1920; these sectors accounted for less than ten per cent of its expenditures, and what it did spend was devoted primarily to lunatic asylums. Other services were left to charitable institutions, and secondarily to the municipalities, which were authorized, but not obligated, by the 1871 Municipal Code to take care of their poor. In 1920, provincial and municipal contributions to hospitals, hospices, orphanages, day nurseries and other institutions amounted to only $372,677, or less than six per cent of these institutions' total expenses. By contrast, the Quebec government spent $974,483 to keep 5,491 lunatics in hospitals in the same year.

Private institutions, meanwhile, were overflowing. In 1901, there were only twenty-four hospitals and about seventy hospices and other benevolent institutions; an additional forty-two hospitals were opened between 1901 and 1929 and they tried to meet the enormous needs of the population as best they could. The 183 institutions in existence in 1920 cared for 20,915 people while struggling with very serious financial difficulties. The government had been required to intervene the year before to make good a deficit of a quarter of a million dollars, but it hadn't really solved the problem. It had avoided facing up to its responsibilities by legally authorizing institutions to refuse to hospitalize an indigent if the municipality in which he resided did not make a commitment to pay the costs incurred.

It was only in 1921 that the first major piece of legislation in the welfare field was adopted. The Taschereau government's Public Charities Act stipulated that

Nuns played an important role in benevolent institutions.

the costs of hospitalizing an indigent would be shared equally by the institution, the municipality and the province. These subsidies were available only for indigents, that is for people who could prove that neither they nor their relatives had the means of paying for the care they received. According to the beliefs held by legislators at the time, each individual or his family was responsible for the costs involved in illness or any other social problem.

Although it met an urgent need, the act aroused strong resistance in clerical and conservative circles. The influential publisher of *Le Devoir*, Henri Bourassa, attacked it in a series of editorials that was later published as a pamphlet. In his view, the act was the beginning of statism and laicization, and thus a "powerful threat to free charity"; it infringed the rights and responsibilities of individuals, families, religious communities and private institutions. Premier Taschereau was astonished at this attack and replied: "There is no question of government control over public assistance institutions. Charity does wonders that no government could accomplish, and all of its power to act should properly be left to it. We simply want to help our hospitals and all our charitable works as much as possible."

This statement was not enough to convince the act's opponents. In a confidential letter to the premier in 1922, the Catholic bishops demanded that the act be amended so that the government would not exercise any control over the funds paid out to the institutions. Taschereau's reply was highly pertinent; it was impossible for a responsible government to turn a million dollars over to a group of institutions without making sure that it could account for how the public funds it had allocated were used. Institutions slowly resigned themselves to the new order and registered with the government's plan, but some bishops continued to resist. There were discreet negotiations between the bishops and the government, which resulted in an amendment to the Public Charities Act in 1925. This amendment stated that nothing in the act or its regulations would infringe the rights of the bishops over religious communities or the moral, religious or disciplinary interests of the communities.

A struggle over principle of this sort between church and state gives the impression that each side was trying to protect its own power base rather than looking for solutions to real problems. Whatever the limitations of the act, the provincial and municipal governments were able to use the amusement tax, a meal tax and a portion of the revenue from liquor sales to pay out millions of dollars to charitable institutions. Only the poorest were helped, however, and even they were able to benefit only if they were hospitalized.

The government also had to take more active measures specifically related to health. Until the 1920s, it tried to shift the responsibility for this area to the municipalities and private institutions. A provincial agency, the Provincial Board of Health, had been in existence since 1886; it provided information and encouraged municipalities and the population to effect reforms. But the Board had few means at its disposal. The government did not want to get involved financially and was afraid to exercise its authority over the municipalities. In 1922, however, the government agreed to devote $500,000 to the establishment of anti-tuberculosis dispensaries and Gouttes de lait. Also significant was the establishment of health units in 1925; made up of doctors and nurses, their goal was education and prevention in rural Quebec. In 1929, four health units served some 151,300 people. These agencies were well regarded by rural Quebecers and proved to be suited to their needs, and by 1931 there were twenty-three units serving more than 800,000 people.

The federal government also began to be concerned with social legislation, and set up a Department of Health immediately after the war. One of the era's most significant pieces of social legislation came from Ottawa — the Old-Age Pensions Act of 1927. This measure, which had long been demanded by the trade union movement, was addressed only to people seventy years of age and older with incomes not greater than $365 a year, for whom it provided a government pension of up to $20 a month.

The act stipulated that costs would be shared equally between the provinces and Ottawa, so that its implementation in Quebec required the co-operation of the

The Meurling Refuge for the homeless in Montreal.

Quebec government. Premier Taschereau, however, refused consent, and did not relent until just before his resignation in 1936. He based his refusal on three arguments — first, that old-age pensions were a provincial responsibility and the federal government had no right to legislate in this area; second, that his government would have to raise taxes to provide its share; and finally, in the tradition of social conservatism, that such a measure undermined private charity and could encourage people to be irresponsible about providing for their future and about meeting their filial obligation to help their parents. Thus, for a number of years, Quebecers paid taxes to Ottawa that contributed towards old-age pensions distributed in the other provinces. The problem was made more acute by the depression of the 1930s, and Taschereau had to yield to pressure from public opinion at the very end of his premiership.

In the area of housing, however, the two levels of government co-operated without conflict, undoubtedly because rapid urbanization had created problems that were too pressing to be evaded. While about eighty per cent of rural families owned property, the corresponding figure for urban families was less than a third; in Montreal, it was only about twenty per cent.

Just before the First World War, the Quebec government adopted legislation to encourage construction of urban housing by authorizing municipalities to guarantee loans to certain real estate development companies. Limited and unprepossessing though it was, the act was never implemented because of the war; it was the federal government that took up the slack by putting $25 million in loans at the disposal of the provinces for housing construction in 1919. Quebec's share came to about $8.6 million, but it should be noted that this money was only lent to the municipalities, which had to pay back principal and interest. Between 1919 and 1924, twenty-eight municipalities borrowed more than $7 million to build some 2,100 dwellings, considerably fewer than what was needed.

Other problems also demanded the government's attention: the adoption of children, Sunday observance, children's attendance at movies, and prohibition. In these areas, the government had to take the views of the Catholic church into account, and church spokesmen frequently took it to task. Thus, its 1924 adoption legislation was criticized on the grounds that it did not specify that the foster parents had to be married and of the same religion as the child. The government changed the law as a result. Similarly, the government was accused of not being strict in implementing the law that required industries and businesses — with some exceptions — to close on Sundays. The government tried to avoid the issue because powerful economic interests, notably in the pulp and paper industry, were involved. It was also criticized for allowing what was called the "Jewish privilege" — the special authorization for Jews to work on Sunday. This criticism, with its antisemitic overtones, grew in intensity during the depression. Clerical pressure also forced the government to ban attendance at movies for children under sixteen. On the question of prohibition, however, the government was much bolder and refused to go along with the prohibition sentiment then current in North America. Instead, it established the Quebec Liquor Commission and gave it a monopoly of wine and hard liquor sales. The Commission made substantial profits and represented a source of wealth for the government. There is no doubt that patronage flourished within the Liquor Commission, but the bitter fruits of the prohibition crusade — dubious concoctions sold as liquor, and the likes of Al Capone — were avoided in Quebec.

The findings of the Quebec Social Insurance Commission, established in 1930, were testimony to the inadequacy of the modest advances made in the 1920s. The depression was still more dramatic evidence that these steps were nowhere near sufficient to deal with the problems of an industrialized country.

CHAPTER 29
WOMEN AND THE FEMINIST MOVEMENT

The feminist movement, in gestation in the late nineteenth century, became a force in the first three decades of the twentieth. As Quebec became more industrialized and more urbanized, some women became aware of the unjust situation imposed on them within society. The First World War accelerated this tendency, so that Idola Saint-Jean could write in 1929: "The last war — for which women were, thank God, in no way responsible — by leading man to the slaughter, forced woman to become a productive member of society. She fulfilled every kind of responsibility, did every sort of work. As a result, she became aware of her capacities, and having once put them at the service of humanity, she no longer wants to return to the incomplete life she lived before the war." In fact, however, only very limited progress had been made since the war, as the feminists' efforts came up against the conservatism of the existing élites. They had not worked in vain, however; they had learned how to organize, and women's role in Quebec's economic and social life was steadily growing.

In 1901, the 84,612 women with paying jobs represented 15.6 per cent of Quebec's total employed population, while in 1931 there were 202,000 women representing 19.7 per cent of the employed population. This percentage was slightly higher than Ontario's. A higher proportion of women was employed in the manufacturing and service sectors in Quebec than in Ontario, while the proportion of women in the commercial, financial and office work sectors was higher in Ontario. It is also noteworthy that the proportion of married women among Quebec's women workers was substantially lower than the Canadian average. In 1931, 6.9 per cent of Quebec's women workers were married, 7.4 per cent were widowed or divorced and 85.7 per cent were single. The presence of women in the labour market was especially significant in Montreal, where they

The number of women working in factories increased considerably during the First World War.

represented 25.4 per cent of the employed population in 1931. The vast majority of women at the time worked in manufacturing (23.4 per cent), personal services (29.3 per cent), office jobs (18.9 per cent) and professional services (11.6 per cent).

A striking characteristic of women's work was its concentration in the lowest-paid jobs. Thus, average pay for women was equal to about fifty-six per cent of the average pay for men in 1931. This wage discrimination made women prime candidates for work in industries requiring cheap labour, such as clothing, textiles, tobacco and shoes. A large proportion of women workers were employed in personal services — domestics, charwomen, hairdressers, waitresses. This sector was characterized by the absence of legal protection for women employed in it, high turnover and fluctuations related to turns in the economic cycle; the number of domestics declined during times of prosperity and increased during depressions. The historians Marie Lavigne and Jennifer Stoddart have pointed out that it "appeared to act as a labour reserve for the manufacturing sector." Domestics had to work long hours and be constantly available to serve their employers. It is hardly surprising that they preferred, when possible, to submit to the arduous routine of factory work, which at least left them some freedom after work hours.

In the early twentieth century, women began to be employed in office work, until then a male preserve. Many women found jobs in stores as full- or part-time saleswomen. These women worked long hours. Pressure was put on the government to make it obligatory for stores to allow saleswomen to sit down when there were no customers; such a *loi des sièges* ("seat law") was passed, but it was frequently ignored.

Women had little access to the liberal professions. It was not until 1930 that they were allowed to practise medicine and accounting, and they were still legally barred from becoming lawyers or notaries. Teaching and nursing were the only careers that were open to them. On the French-speaking side, both these professions were controlled by nuns, who represented stiff competition for lay women and kept salaries low. Religious communities, however, were increasingly unable to fulfil the requirements of Quebec hospitals. While fifty-seven per cent of nurses in 1923 were nuns, this proportion had fallen to forty per cent by 1928. In the teaching profession, the poor position of Catholic women teachers was especially conspicuous. Their average salary amounted to a meagre $387 a year, while for Protestant women teachers it was $1,068. In both communities, there was flagrant discrimination against women in comparison with men doing the same work. Average annual salaries for men teachers were $1,553 for Catholics and $2,351 for Protestants.

While women were singled out for particularly shameless exploitation on the labour market, governments, the clergy and even trade unions continued to believe that woman's place was in the home. If she was in the labour market, that was only a temporary situation prior to marriage. Governments took a few timid protective measures for humanitarian reasons, but these measures insulted women by lumping them with children in the category of minors, and were in any case almost completely ineffective.

Office work in 1924: an increasing number of women worked as secretaries and stenographers.

Thus, the work week for women was limited to a legal maximum that stood initially at sixty hours and was progressively reduced to fifty-five. The law, however, applied only to industrial establishments, and employers could obtain special exemptions from it. The government's Women's Minimum Wage Act, passed in 1919, provided for establishment of a commission composed of three people, one of whom could be a woman. However, the commission was not set up until 1925, all its members were male, and in practice, the effect of the law was extremely limited. The commissioners started from the principle that working women had no dependents, and they did not want to disturb the market; as a result, they established a very low minimum wage. The commission's regulations applied only to particular sectors, and not to the labour market as a whole. And employers found a way of partially getting around even the clearly inadequate minimum wages decreed by the commission from 1927 on. They were allowed to pay "apprentices" less than the minimum wage — and apprenticeship could last several years.

A nun managing the pharmacy in a hospital.

In addition to legislation concerning working hours and minimum wages, there was a ban on using women in certain hazardous jobs and a provision for female inspectors to visit industrial establishments. But these inspectors, like their male counterparts, had little power, and there were not enough of them to keep watch effectively. They did, however, make recommendations each year aimed at improving working conditions; the need to reduce promiscuity in factories by providing women with separate cafeterias and washrooms and the importance of improving hygienic conditions were repeated concerns.

If women could expect little help from governments, they could not count on much more from trade unions. In general, unions also operated on the assumption that woman's place was in the home. Equality between the sexes was not one of their priorities, although some did advocate equal work for equal pay or demand special protective measures for women and children.

In addition to the unions, there were associations for female store employees, industrial workers, Montreal Catholic teachers and *aides ménagères* (low-status maids) established by the Fédération Nationale Saint-Jean-Baptiste (FNSJB), a feminist organization discussed below. These were not unions but rather religiously oriented mutual help and educational organizations, in which upper-class women generally had considerable influence. The FNSJB campaigned for the *loi des sièges*, and tried to convince retailers to make voluntary reductions in their store hours. Its intervention was crucial in securing withdrawal of a bill that would have excluded women from positions as stenographers in Superior Court. Overall, however, the FNSJB associations were not very militant — understandably, since the president of the industrial workers' association was the wife of the industrialist J.-B. Rolland and the president of the store employees' association was the wife of the owner of a large Montreal department store, Dupuis et Frères. The associations achieved few results; it is hardly surprising, for instance, that domestics would not be very enthusiastic about the very bourgeois idea of having them take home economics courses in their limited leisure time.

Ladylike Feminism

In this context of discrimination and inequality, women began to pay increasing attention to the idea of organizing to demand their rights. The Montreal section of the National Council of Women of Canada, founded in 1893, managed to recruit some bourgeoise French-Canadian women — Marie Gérin-Lajoie, Josephine Dandurand, Caroline Béïque and others — who fought their first battles as part of this mainly English Protestant movement.

These women also worked after 1902 as patrons of the Saint-Jean-Baptiste Society, which was in financial difficulties after building the Monument National in Montreal and needed their help in raising funds. By now used to working together, they founded the first French-speaking feminist organization in 1907 — the Fédération Nationale Saint-Jean-Baptiste, aimed at bringing together all agencies that dealt with French-Canadian Catholic women. Caroline Béïque, the first president of the movement, took pains to make it clear that her brand of feminism was based on a Christian view of woman's role. The clergy, hesitant though it was about women's causes, could not object to this movement, and the guidelines for action for Christian feminists were established by the archbishop of Montreal himself, Mgr Bruchési: "Since the word *féminisme* has been introduced into our language, I accept it, but I claim a Christian meaning for it, and I ask permission to define it as follows: the zealous pursuit by woman of all the noble causes in the sphere that Providence has assigned to her." He enumerated some of the things that "good feminism" so defined should not include: "There will be no talk in your meetings of the emancipation of woman, of the neglect of her rights, of her having been relegated to the shadows, of the responsibilities, public offices and professions to which she should be admitted on an equal basis with man." It appears that the clergy had to make some concessions to the movement, but still hoped to be able to guide it if not to control it completely.

The FNSJB began with twenty-two affiliated associations that grouped several thousand members and were divided into three broad areas — charity, education, and working women. The federation held annual conventions, organized study weeks, and starting in 1913 published a monthly organ, *La Bonne Parole*, of which 2,000 copies were distributed. It worked intensely on a number of fronts. The efforts of its members led to the founding of the Sainte-Justine Hospital for children, which had a woman as its president. They worked zealously in support of the Gouttes de lait, which did so much to fight the scourge of infant mortality; organized lectures on hygiene; established a service to help mothers; demanded special courts for children; fought alcoholism and white slavery (forced prostitution); insisted on the presence of policewomen in police stations; and worked for causes such as the Red Cross and the Fonds Patriotique.

They fought for reforms, but their struggles were centred on home and family, which they regarded as woman's natural place; in short, their activities were compatible with clerical-nationalist ideology. Even Henri Bourassa, who has often been criticized as a male chauvinist, had to give them access to the columns of *Le Devoir*. When Christian feminists endeavoured to deal with such questions as the right to vote or education, they ran the risk of going outside what Mgr Bruchési called the sphere providence had assigned to them, and had to take multiple precautions. English-speaking feminists did not have the same fears, and were often the ones who took the initiative in struggles that challenged the legal and political system.

The Struggle for Equality and the Right to Vote

At the turn of the century, women had extremely limited political rights. In school commission elections, women had the right to vote and be candidates if they were property owners; in municipal elections, they could vote if they were widowed or single. In 1902, Montreal aldermen considered withdrawing the municipal franchise from women tenants; Marie Gérin-Lajoie, speaking for the Montreal section of the National Council of Women, successfully protested against this attempt. Women failed, however, in their effort to have the municipal franchise extended to married women in 1926.

No women had the right to vote at either the provincial or the federal level. With the rise of feminism and "suffragette" demonstrations, especially in Britain and the United States, Canadian feminists began to organize as well. They founded the Montreal Suffrage Association in 1913, but there was little French-Canadian participation in this movement. The federal government's extension of the right to vote in 1917 to women who were army employees or had close relatives in the army opened up a vigorous debate. What started out as a political manoeuvre to get more votes for conscription led the next year to legislation granting the right to vote in federal elections to all adult women.

A number of French-Canadian MPs, senators, journalists and clerics vainly resisted the measure, which in their view was a threat to the social order.

Marie Gérin-Lajoie (1867-1945).

According to Henri Bourassa, for example, "sexual differences imply differences in sexual function, and differences in sexual function create differences in social function. The alleged 'right' to vote is only an aspect of the *functions*, the social *responsibilities*, that devolve on man as a result perhaps of his physical or mental structure but primarily of his position and duties as head of the family." For these opponents of women's suffrage, woman's function was motherhood, her place was in the home, and political inequality was based on biology. A number of other arguments were used as well — woman would inevitably be sullied if she descended into the political arena, families would be divided, women did not have the abilities needed to participate in political life, and so on.

All Canadian women were able to exercise their right to vote in the 1921 federal election, and a year later women's suffrage was extended to the provincial level everywhere except in Quebec, which refused to yield. Marie Gérin-Lajoie undertook to convince some of Quebec's bishops that nothing in Catholic doctrine was violated by women voting. Along with an English-speaking colleague, she also worked actively in founding the Provincial Franchise Committee, which tried to mobilize women to put pressure on members of the legislature. At the same time a group of women, encouraged by the bishops and especially Mgr Eugène Roy of Quebec, got tens of thousands of signatures on a petition opposing women's suffrage. Gérin-Lajoie tried to get around this opposition by appealing to the Vatican. She went to Rome, where the World Union of Catholic Women's Organizations was holding its convention, in an effort to obtain the support of this influential organization. The convention came out in favour of women's suffrage, but at the last minute it added a proviso at the express request of the pope's representative, Cardinal Merry del Val, leaving it up to the bishops in each country to decide whether or not it was advisable to endorse this suggestion. As Luigi Trifiro has pointed out, it may not be a coincidence that Henri Bourassa, an influential figure in some church circles and a fierce opponent of women's suffrage, was in Rome at the time of the convention.

Marie Gérin-Lajoie's efforts failed on the political level as well. Before going to Rome, she was a member of a feminist delegation that met Premier Taschereau, who said flatly that not only was he opposed to their demand but their cause would never succeed as long as he was in power. As a result of these failures and pressure from the clergy, Gérin-Lajoie resigned from the Provincial Committee in 1922. It was not until 1927 that another French-Canadian feminist, Idola Saint-Jean, picked up the torch by founding the Alliance Canadienne pour le Vote des Femmes au Québec. She pressed for a debate on the question in the Legislative Assembly, and a bill to give women the right to vote was introduced by a sympathetic MLA, but it was defeated, as similar bills would be each year until 1940. In 1928, Thérèse Casgrain became president of the League for Women's Rights and participated in the annual "pilgrimage" to Quebec City. Once again, another group of women with episcopal support reacted against the feminists' initiatives and organized the Ligue Catholique Féminine. Within a few months, this organization succeeded in bringing 10,000 women into its ranks.

The only consolation in the political arena was a feminist victory in a long legal struggle to make it possible for women to be appointed to the Senate on an equal basis with men. In 1928, the Supreme Court of Canada ruled against them, but this judgment was overturned by the Judicial Committee of the Privy Council in London the next year. Unlike their Canadian colleagues, the learned British judges reasoned that when the word "person" was used in the Canadian constitution it applied to women as well as men.

Feminists also had to fight for access to higher education. In 1908, after lengthy negotiations, the bishops agreed to found a classical college for girls. The college was called the École d'Enseignement Supérieur pour Jeunes Filles and was run by the sisters of the Congrégation de Notre Dame, who later renamed it the Collège Marguerite-Bourgeoys. It was not until 1925 that a second classical college for girls, the Collège Sillery in Quebec City, was opened. The threatened establishment of a lay college persuaded the bishops to set up this institution. Most candidates for entry into these schools were nuns and girls from good families. Other girls were channelled into government-subsidized domestic science schools. In 1929, there were 119 such schools with 21,219 students.

Another arena of feminist struggle concerned women's legal rights. In 1929, a commission of women's civil rights was established, fulfilling a demand of the League for Women's Rights. The commission was chaired by Judge Dorion, and its mandate was to study the Civil Code in relation to marriage law; a demand by women to be represented on the commission was rejected. The commission submitted its report in 1930 and proposed a number of amendments, the most significant of which referred to the income received by married women. It recommended that a woman be allowed to dispose of the product of her own labour, without the authorization of her husband. However, it refused to suggest changes in the articles of the code dealing with adultery, which stipulated that "a husband may demand the separation on the ground of his wife's adultery. A wife may demand the separation on the ground of her husband's adultery, if he keeps his concubine in their common habitation." In justifying this fundamentally unjust law, the commissioners maintained that "despite what is said, it is well known that the heartache inflicted on a woman is not generally as intense as that suffered by a man who is deceived by his wife."

As can be seen, while women were able to attain some limited advances in the first three decades of the twentieth century, the road to true equality remained long and hard.

CHAPTER 30
RELIGION AND EDUCATION

Religious Institutions

The balance among the various religious denominations remained substantially the same as in the previous period; in both 1901 and 1931, Roman Catholics made up more than eighty-five per cent of the population and the Protestant denominations constituted a significant minority of between twelve and thirteen per cent. There were, however, three noteworthy changes: the proportion of Catholics declined by one per cent, the proportion of Protestants declined by a similar amount, and a rise in the percentage of Jews and Greek Orthodox made up the difference. In 1901, Jews represented only 0.4 per cent of the population, but their proportion rose to 2.1 per cent by 1931. There were no Greek Orthodox in 1901, while in 1931 they constituted 0.3 per cent of the population.

These changes corresponded to the population movements of the first third of the twentieth century; immigrants were now coming to Canada in general and Quebec in particular not only from the United Kingdom but also from central and eastern Europe. This new immigration had a greater impact than can be seen in the overall changes in percentage because the immigrants were overwhelmingly concentrated in Montreal.

Minority religions

This section will deal essentially with Protestantism and Judaism, as there were no other minority religions with substantial numbers of adherents in Quebec.

As Canada, especially western Canada, grew, there was a westward movement in the centre of gravity of Canadian Protestantism. As a result, even more than in the immediate post-Confederation period, Quebec Protestantism was tied to Canadian Protestantism as a whole and had few of the features of an autonomous entity. Three denominations comprised a majority of Quebec Protestants. In 1901, Anglicans, Methodists and Presbyterians constituted eighty-six per cent of Quebec Protestants, while in 1931, Anglicans, members of the United Church of Canada (which absorbed the Methodists in 1925) and Presbyterians accounted for 87.4 per cent. Thus, the same three groups remained dominant, as they had been since Confederation, while the other Protestant denominations divided up what was left. The Anglicans continued to be the single largest group, representing in the neighbourhood of forty per cent of the Protestant population in both 1901 and 1931. The Presbyterians held second place in 1901, but were dislodged from this position with the founding of the United Church. In 1931, the United Church represented about twenty-six per cent of Quebec Protestants, while only 17.5 per cent were Presbyterians.

The founding of the United Church was the most significant development in Canadian Protestantism during the period. It was the product of an ecumenical spirit that began by gaining ground within each church; then, at their general meeting in Winnipeg in 1902, the Presbyterians appealed to the other churches for unity. Presbyterians, Methodists and Congregationalists soon began discussions on matters of doctrine and church organization; not only did a common set of beliefs have to be worked out but the different clergies had to be integrated and the administrative structures made compatible as well. The Methodists and Congregationalists were ready to merge before the First World War, but the Presbyterians were unable to agree among themselves, and it was in a strained atmosphere that the United Church was finally founded in 1925. It brought together the Methodists, the Congregationalists and some Presbyterians; many other Presbyterians, however, chose to remain faithful to their old denomination.

Quebec Protestantism felt the repercussions of the formation of the new church. The figure of 59,000 continuing Presbyterians in 1931 is evidence that there was a strong group that refused to join the new denomination. It is impossible to tell to what extent the increase of five per cent in the proportion represented by the Anglican church can be explained by these difficulties, or whether in fact it was related at all. It is clear, however, that Protestantism developed in the same manner in Quebec as elsewhere in Canada, and the tide towards unity ebbed in the late 1920s as a large number of Presbyterians not only remained outside the new United Church but directed proselytizing efforts towards its members.

The late nineteenth century was marked by the appearance of a number of new Protestant sects which, unlike earlier sects, developed in urban areas. The best known was the Salvation Army, founded in 1883, which devoted itself to the care of the urban masses that had been more or less abandoned by the recognized churches. Despite their small numbers in Quebec — a few hundred in 1901 and a thousand in 1931 — members of the Salvation Army, with their open-air meetings, initially upset the established churches. According to the historian H.R. Walsh, the first reaction to the Salvation Army in Montreal and Quebec City was rather harsh and mass arrests took place, but the sect was gradually accepted, especially after the First World War. Its activities contributed towards making the more established churches aware that they tended to pay attention only to their own communities, dominated by representatives of the bourgeoisie, and thus neglected certain concerns and social groups. At the turn of the century another sect, the Jehovah's Witnesses, made its appearance in Quebec.

As in the preceding period, there continued to be widespread respect for the great traditions of Protestantism. In the first third of the twentieth century, however, there were major controversies over the Scriptures, with traditionalists on one side and new critics who based their arguments on new forms of analysis on the other. Interchurch relations continued to be marked by a division into spheres of influence; in particular, the Protestant denominations and the Catholic church directed only very discreet missionary efforts towards each other's members.

In the late nineteenth century, a movement called the Social Gospel began to develop within Protestantism. This movement was based on a growing awareness among Protestant ministers of the flagrant inequalities caused by the expansion of industrial capitalism, and was comparable to the developments that occurred in the Catholic church in the wake of the encyclical *Rerum Novarum*. In Canada, the Social Gospel movement played a role for several decades, but as a result of the polarization brought about by the Winnipeg General Strike, the ministers' sympathy for the working class waned.

The arrival of a large number of Jews at the turn of the century changed the religious make-up of Quebec. Jews had lived in Montreal for a long time, and the city's first synagogue had been founded in 1777, but their numbers had been small. Between 1901 and 1931, the proportion represented by the Jewish religion increased from less than one per cent to 2.1 per cent; there were as many Jews in Quebec in 1931 as there were Presbyterians — about 60,000, concentrated in Montreal.

How this new religious group should be integrated into Quebec society quickly became an issue, especially in relation to the school system, as public education was organized on a denominational basis. Would there be Jewish public schools or should Jewish pupils be integrated into the Catholic or Protestant system? This question will be dealt with later. In the area of charitable institutions, however, the Jews quite rapidly organized their own network.

While manifestations of overt hostility between Protestants and Catholics had died out, relations between Jews and Catholics were tense. The integration of such a large group of Jews gave rise to demonstrations of antisemitism; as the 1930s approached and antisemitism became widespread in the western world, it increased in Quebec as well. Similar attitudes characterized relations between Jews and Protestants, although they were expressed more discreetly.

The ubiquitous Catholic church

The Catholic church was the principal denomination with a share of the population that stayed consistently above eighty-five per cent and a steadily growing clergy, and its position remained very strong between 1896 and 1929. The geographer Louis-Edmond Hamelin has calculated both the variation in the numerical size of the Quebec clergy over time and — a more revealing statistic — the ratio of priests to church adherents. The changes in this ratio between 1901 and 1931 indicate that the church's presence was increasingly difficult to escape.

Even higher figures are obtained by adding members of religious communities to the secular clergy. The total number of religious of both sexes living in Quebec increased from 8,612 in 1901 to 25,332 in 1931; according to the sociologist Bernard Denault, this represented one religious for every 166 Catholics in 1901 and one for every 97 in 1931. This ratio is eloquent testimony to the tight rein under which the church kept Quebec Catholics. The parish was not the only field of activity for religious, and at most half of them did parish work; the rest worked as teachers or in hospitals and similar institutions. These were the three bases of the church's activity: the parish, the school, social assistance. New sees were established as they were needed — Joliette in 1904, Gaspé in 1922. In addition, the vicariate apostolic of the Gulf of St. Lawrence was established in 1905.

Growing urbanization was an obstacle to implementation of the church's strategy of social control. While in rural Quebec religious structures coincided perfectly with social and economic units, the same was not true in the city. Thus, in urban areas, the church's tactics were first to establish a large number of parishes so as to divide the territory as minutely as possible, and then to set up a panoply of organizations aimed at ensuring effective leadership of the population. The large number of clergy at its command made it possible for the church to keep all bases covered, co-ordinating the establishment of parishes and the founding of organizations of all kinds, some related to religious practice, others not. The church operated at three levels. The first was the parish level; here, church projects were local in nature and heavily influenced by the *curé*. The second was the institutional level; the services for which the church took responsibility — schools and hospitals — generally transcended parish boundaries. Finally, there was the diocesan level; agencies that operated at this level were outside the direct control of the *curés* and were linked more closely to the hierarchy of the diocese or to a religious community. At any one of these levels, the church's activities might be concerned with religion as such, charity or recreation, and its mode of operation depended on which was involved.

Some examples from Montreal will help clarify the kinds of activities the Catholic church conducted. In a parish chosen at random, Saint-Jean-Baptiste de Montréal, there were seven religious and charitable organizations that tried to bring Catholics together, taking into account who they were and what they wanted to do. Women had a choice between the Dames de la Charité and the Dames de

A country school in 1915.

Sainte-Anne, girls could belong to the Congrégation de la Sainte-Vierge, and for men there were the Ligue du Sacré-Coeur, the Garde d'Honneur, the Congrégation des Hommes and the Conférence Saint-Vincent-de-Paul. Curé L.-A. Dubuc also had other institutions at his disposal that helped him increase his control. Thus, starting in 1919, working mothers sent their children to a nursery school operated by nuns; Curé Dubuc also kept close watch over the mother's aid service and the Goutte de lait.

In the area of charity, in addition to the Conférence Saint-Vincent-de-Paul there was the Auclair Hospice, run by nuns who also visited the poor and sick in the parish. The church's presence was also strengthened by the religious communities that took charge of the parish's three academies. Raffles and pilgrimages were among the other activities organized by the *curé* to keep up the enthusiasm of his flock. Finally, there was a *bulletin paroissial*, containing a column written by one of the parish's vicars. While the exact composition of the institutional network varied from one parish to another, depending largely on finances, the basic pattern was common to all urban parishes.

The presence of religious communities in educational and health institutions was overwhelming, to the point where it could almost be called a monopoly. The most novel developments of the period occurred at the diocesan level.

In his 1891 encyclical *Rerum Novarum*, Pope Leo XIII argued "that some opportune remedy must be found quickly for the misery and wretchedness pressing so unjustly on the majority of the working class." Therefore, the pope proposed that the church organize a program of Catholic social action, taking into account the new conditions created by the industrial revolution. However, it was not until ten years later that the Quebec church got into step and developed what was called the "social doctrine" of the church. This doctrine had three major objectives. It was based on an acceptance by the church of the rights of workers to organize, but the church also wanted to guide them so as to steer them away from the dangers of religious neutrality and socialism. Rejecting class struggle, the church wanted to establish a wider solidarity, based on Christian charity and transcending narrow class interests. It hoped to achieve this goal by training an élite of Catholic activists that would work within a network of associations that it set about organizing. As a participant in the first *semaine sociale*, held in Montreal in 1920, wrote: "In first place, the church. Every social question is at bottom a moral question, and every moral question is a religious question."

Clearly one of the most important of the new organizations was the Montreal-based École Sociale Populaire (ESP), founded in 1911 and headed by the Jesuit Joseph-Papin Archambault. A similar organization, the Action Sociale, had already been started in Quebec City; publication of a daily newspaper quickly became the main focus of its activity. The ESP was given the responsibility of being a major instrument in developing the social doctrine of the church and applying it to the Quebec situation. It also became the main training centre for the new Catholic activists, whose task was to go back and work in their own peer groups. The school published pamphlets and organized closed retreats. As an extension of its teaching activity, it initiated the *semaines sociales du Canada* in 1920; for a week each year, several hundred people attended a series of colloquia on subjects related to the social doctrine of the church.

The church's organizational efforts also extended to specific social or occupational groups for which special associations were established, not necessarily linked to a parish. These organizations often imitated French or Belgian models. The best-known example is the Catholic trade union movement, discussed in chapter 26. From 1925 on, the Union Catholique des Cultivateurs extended this form of church activity into the countryside. The Association des Voyageurs de Commerce (Commercial Travellers' Association) tried to provide guidance to a group of working people whose wanderings made them especially vulnerable to temptation. But the greatest efforts were devoted to organizing youth. The Association Catholique de la Jeunesse Canadienne-française (ACJC — Catholic Association of French-Canadian Youth) was founded in 1903-4, again following a French model; it brought together students from different colleges. Later additions to Catholic youth activity were the Catholic scouts and, in the late 1920s, the Catholic action youth movements. In 1927, Abbé Aimé Boileau organized the first young workers' group in Saint-Édouard parish in Montreal; it was the beginning of a Catholic workers' youth movement, the Jeunesse Ouvrière Catholique, that grew rapidly.

The inspector and the *curé* visit the village school at Saint-Euphémie in Montmagny county, early in the century

All these new organizations were based on very clear social concerns. There was also an older group of Catholic associations, the mutual societies, which continued to play a significant role in the early twentieth century. Notable among these were the Alliance Nationale, with 2,292 members in 1900, and the Artisans Canadiens-Français, with 14,457 members. While the rise of insurance companies eventually led to the disappearance of these Catholic mutual societies, the kind of activity they represented was continued with the growth of the caisses populaires. These were not religious organizations as such, but they spread and sank roots with the help of the Catholic organizational structure. The church also used its influence in rural areas to promote the agricultural co-operatives founded by Abbé Allaire, following the Belgian Catholic model of the Boerenbond.

The growth of Catholic activism also brought about significant changes in Catholic journalism. Members of the clergy increasingly tried to lay the foundations for a Catholic press, and founded or bought newspapers in various parts of French Canada. *Le Droit* in Ottawa was founded by the Oblates, while *L'Action Catholique*, in Quebec City and *Le Bien Public* in Trois-Rivières were also clerical endeavours. In Joliette, the clergy bought *L'Action Populaire* in 1918 and a cleric was appointed to the editorship. Before 1896, Catholic journalism had been dominated by individuals, generally laymen, who published journals of opinion under religious and clerical influence. In the twentieth century, however, the emphasis switched to direct intervention by the clergy, which sought to have its own journalistic outlets so that it could disseminate its directives more widely and try to impose a Catholic view of the day's events. In Montreal, however, Henri Bourassa's *Le Devoir*, the last bastion of the independent Catholic press, appeared to be maintaining the older tradition of Catholic journalism; the clergy left the field to *Le Devoir* and never tried to found or buy a significant newspaper. The Catholic press as a whole had only limited success in the face of the rapid growth of mass-circulation newspapers in the major centres.

While the Quebec Catholic church continued to look to Rome for inspiration, it took time for the effects of some new Vatican policies to be felt in Quebec. *Rerum Novarum*, for example, was out for ten years before the Quebec church expressed its first reaction. The social doctrine of the church as it eventually developed was heavily influenced by clerical-nationalist ideology, and social problems were often treated in a nationalist spirit. In Quebec, the encyclical did not result in any truly deep thinking on the question of industrialization and especially on the making of the working class. As Jean Hamelin has pointed out, the encyclical "introduced a social dimension into the ideology that, while narrow, was at least wide enough to give workers a place in the proposed earthly city."

The separation of church and state in France in 1905 also had a definite if unexpected effect on the religious climate in Quebec. Many French religious came to Quebec in the wake of this development and their activities in Quebec were marked by a deep suspicion of the state.

Overall, the church sought to play a leading role in society. Its position and its institutions gave it the means not only to influence the ideological orientation of its followers but also to make its presence felt in a number of areas, notably in developing and disseminating nationalist thought. While the details of how nationalist thinking was worked out will be discussed in chapter 35, it is worth noting here that Catholic values and the definition of French-Canadian nationalism were jumbled together. The role of the ACJC in Quebec's educational institutions was significant in this regard. The church had the clear intention of defining nationalism itself and imposing its own values. Jean Hamelin has pointed out the problems that the power of the church created: "The central position it occupied in the power structure gave teeth to its moral authority and allowed it to limit its old enemy, the state, to secondary roles." The controversy over the Marchand government's proposed educational reform, discussed below, is a good illustration of its influence.

The church also tried to make its influence felt in all aspects of Quebec Catholics' cultural life. While it supported the Protestants of Quebec and Canada as a whole in their campaign for Sunday observance and their crusade against alcohol, it also had causes of its own — it attacked "animated photography" and popular newspapers, whose mass circulation was enough to make them a little too independent of clerical fulminations. For many years, Archbishop Bruchési of Montreal resisted the establishment of a public library in the city. There was a promise of a substantial grant from the Carnegie Foundation to buy books, but the church insisted on maintaining its control and would not accept a neutral, lay institution. The Sulpicians sought to fill the gap by establishing the Saint-Sulpice Library — later the Bibliothèque Nationale (national library) — on Saint-Denis Street in the east-central part of the city.

An examination of the actions of the Quebec Catholic church during these years leads to two conclusions. One is that it was a powerful church that gloried in its predominant position and did not hesitate to intervene wherever it saw a threat to the faith. Rome recognized it as a national church and the holding of a eucharistic congress in Montreal in 1910 was striking confirmation of its new maturity and renown. On the other hand, however, it was an anxious church, afraid of all the innovations of the twentieth century and constantly looking to the past to find the ideal society it was seeking.

Ubiquitous as it was, the church's power was not without limits. It was unable to penetrate the economic sphere in the city as it had in the country. A significant part of its social program consisted of bringing Catholic workers and employers together in a spirit of Christian charity, which proved impossible in the Quebec context. In addition, its very *raison d'être* as well as its programs and attitudes led the church to play an important role in the cultural sphere. This, however, was an area where it did not have a monopoly and had to reckon with innovations such as movies and radio; the influence of these new inventions was quickly felt and limited the power of the church.

These limits are clearly visible in two important cases. The very moderate success of the Catholic trade union movement shows that in the industrial sphere there were other forces besides the church; and in its battle against movies, the church had to lower its sights and be satisfied with a smaller degree of regulation than it had hoped for.

Despite these limits, however, the church was a formidable entity in Quebec,

Representatives of the Roman Catholic hierarchy and Prime Minister Laurier at the Eucharistic Congress in Montreal in 1910.

drawing its strength not only from religious belief but also in large part from the near-monopoly it held over a number of services that were indispensable to Quebec society, such as health, public charity and education. These services, along with its administrative role, gave the church the foundation for the power it exercised.

Education

Looking through the statistics published annually by the superintendent of public instruction or reading most of what was written about education at the time, one could get the impression that the educational system was not only healthy but also making rapid progress. Students, teachers and educational establishments were all becoming more numerous, and the sums devoted to education were increasing as well.

In fact, however, the Quebec educational system was fragmented and uncoordinated and contained flagrant inequalities. The establishment of a public system of professional and technical schools was an advance for government involvement in education, but in other areas progress was rather slow and defenders of the status quo generally had the upper hand over reformers, as an analysis of the major controversies of the period will make clear. A look at the jumble of educational structures and programs and an examination of the system's personnel and resources lead to the same conclusions.

The major controversies

The period was marked by three major controversies: the attempt to establish a Department of Public Instruction, the question of compulsory education and the problem of Jewish schools. In all three cases, the battle was won by defenders of the status quo.

In the 1897 election campaign, the Liberals promised changes in education, and once in power under Premier Félix-Gabriel Marchand, they acted promptly to fulfil this promise, introducing a bill containing substantial changes in the foundations of the educational system. A Department of Public Instruction was to be instituted and the quasi-judicial powers held by the superintendent of public instruction were to be turned over to the courts. The bill would have allowed the government to appoint two inspectors general on its own authority and the Protestant and Catholic committees to require all teachers, whether clerical or lay, to have a "certificate of competency." Finally, the books and instructional materials used in the schools were to be chosen by the minister of public instruction and approved by the committees.

The bill touched off a major conflict between the bishops and the government. It got a cool reception from the Catholic committee, which saw it as a serious encroachment on its power and influence. The superintendent of public instruction in office at the time wrote that "it was to all appearances political interference in the educational sphere with all that that entails, and a mortal blow to the act that had functioned harmoniously since 1875."

Soon after the bill was introduced, Archbishop Bruchési of Montreal went to Rome. Rightly fearing the pressure that the archbishop would put on the Vatican, Premier Marchand quickly wrote to Rome to express his point of view. A few days later, he received a telegram from Mgr Bruchési: "Pope asks you delay public instruction bill."

With the support of Lieutenant Governor J.-Adolphe Chapleau, the premier again wrote to Rome to explain the purpose of the proposed reform, which was essentially directed at giving back to the government the powers it needed to fulfil its responsibilities in the educational field. Mgr Bruchési wrote back to Quebec City saying that the pope himself did not want the government to proceed with the bill. Marchand wrote to Chapleau that he could not repudiate his commitment to reform the educational system; if he had to withdraw the bill, several ministers, himself included, would resign and there would be a great popular outcry. The lieutenant governor wrote to the Vatican secretary of state, Cardinal Rampolla, to

Paul Bruchési (1855-1939), archbishop of Montreal, 1897-1939.

inform Rome of Marchand's decision. The cardinal replied by telegram that the pope "did not intend to exercise pressure that could lead the minister to resign." Mgr Merry del Val, influential in the Vatican and in close touch with the situation in Quebec, wrote to Chapleau that Mgr Bruchési's "manner of interpreting the Holy Father's thinking seemed to me very strange."

With this double disavowal of Mgr Bruchési by Rome, the government had no reason to be unduly afraid of clerical opposition. The bill was introduced in the assembly and vigorously defended by Provincial Secretary Joseph-Éme Robidoux who, while offering the reassurance that "we will keep the crucifix on the walls of our schools," explained that with the creation of a department, the superintendent of public instruction, who had the powers of a minister but was not responsible to the legislature, would be replaced by a minister who would be truly responsible in accordance with the spirit of parliamentary institutions. He added, "It is the government's duty to create the future of a nation. . . . If the government is responsible for the end, it must have the means."

On his return to Quebec, Mgr Bruchési continued his fight against the bill with the support of other bishops, but the assembly passed it by a large majority. The bishops found allies, however, in the Legislative Council, which had a Conservative majority and rejected the bill by a vote of thirteen to nine. Mgr Bruchési quickly wrote to his friend Thomas Chapais, who had led the fight in the council: "You have killed the BILL. Now those ministers should understand what a mistake they made in not following my advice and not yielding to my request."

In January 1899, Marchand introduced a new bill, which amounted to an admission of surrender. There would be no Department of Public Instruction, and the basic structures of the system would remain intact. However, the government would be able to appoint and remove inspectors, and commissioners would have to standardize the books used in each municipality. There was also a provision for the government to buy the author's rights to a textbook and distribute it free to children. Despite Thomas Chapais' warning that this modest reform constituted "official communism and state socialism," the measure was accepted. But Quebec was not to have a Department of Education until 1964.

The Legislative Council acted as the instrument of powerful conservative forces in vetoing the reform of the educational system. But the government could have overcome this opposition by appointing a few legislative councillors at an appropriate time, or, even more effectively, by conducting a vigorous campaign to bring public opinion onto its side and thus put pressure on the Conservatives. It could also have neutralized the opposition of the bishops by using the documents it had received from the Vatican. What then was the reason for its surrender to clerical opposition? Its attitude can be explained by the pressure put on it by Prime Minister Laurier, who wanted to avoid conflict with the Catholic church and neutralize clerical opposition to his party. He also needed the bishops' acceptance of the compromise solution to the Manitoba Schools question that he had negotiated with the Greenway provincial government. Mgr Langevin of St. Boniface had criticized the agreement, and the federal Liberals were counting heavily on Mgr Bruchési to calm him. Even more important, they wanted the archbishop to influence the Vatican, which had to make a statement on the agreement, to view it favourably. In return, the prime minister used his influence to get Marchand not to interfere with the prerogatives of the Catholic church in Quebec.

A look at the dealings between the archbishop and the prime minister shows that relations between the two men were very close. Thus, during a meeting with Laurier, Mgr Bruchési expressed his concern about the financial situation of his diocese, especially the $200,000 debt incurred by the cathedral. On January 13, 1898, Laurier wrote to Mgr Bruchési that he would be able to help the archbishop as soon as the negotiations with Mgr Langevin in Manitoba were completed. Laurier said that Donald Smith (Lord Strathcona of Canadian Pacific and the Bank of Montreal) was very interested in the Manitoba Schools question and "when I can tell him that Mgr Langevin is satisfied and all the schools are under the authority of the law and Your Excellency gave me powerful help in obtaining this result, I will be surprised if he does not show his gratitude in a tangible manner." Mgr Bruchési, meanwhile, wrote to a correspondent that he was very happy that the Quebec government had given up on its educational reform and added: "You will guess what influence was exercised." We can guess without difficulty, especially since immediately before this remark he mentions that he had met with Laurier and discussed the Manitoba Schools question with him.

It is not surprising that on Marchand's death, Provincial Secretary Robidoux, who had not only been the vigorous advocate of a Department of Public Instruction but had persisted in his misguided ways by coming out in favour of free textbooks, was prevented from succeeding him as premier. Similarly, when Lomer Gouin became premier in 1905, he had to promise Mgr Bruchési and Laurier that he would not touch the foundations of the educational system, according to Robert Rumilly. Thus, despite his personal convictions, Gouin had to resist the "radicals" in his party who demanded compulsory education.

The question of compulsory schooling was another central theme of debates on education during the period. There were scattered discussions of the question from 1875 on, but it was in 1901 that it first reached the floor of the Legislative Assembly. An MLA named Boucher de Grosbois introduced a bill to require parents to send their children between the ages of eight and thirteen to school at least sixteen weeks each year; violators were to be fined. The bill was rejected by a vote of fifty-five to seven. The next year a citizens' group composed of politicians, journalists and teachers met in Montreal and founded the Ligue de l'Enseignement (Education League). The league stated that "public instruction is a government responsibility" on which the people's future depended, and demanded compulsory education. It was vigorously attacked as a Masonic organization that wanted to promote "schools that are lay, compulsory and free." As Rumilly has explained, Mgr Bruchési eventually succeeded in breaking up the league, which evoked the spectre of French radicals such as Jules Ferry and Léon Gambetta.

The problem surfaced again a decade later, when the Protestant committee itself asked for a compulsory education law for Protestants. The bill was discussed in the assembly, but it was rejected by a vote of sixty-two to six.

The Liberal MLA T.-D. Bouchard came out in favour of compulsory schooling in 1912 and delivered an impassioned plea for the idea in 1916. Meanwhile, another unsuccessful effort in favour of compulsory schooling had been undertaken by some English-speaking Quebecers. Battle was joined once again in 1918, when the Drummondville and Saint-Jérôme school commissions asked the government to authorize school commissions in cities and towns of more than 1,000 people to institute compulsory education for children between the ages of seven and fourteen. T.-D. Bouchard once again came out in favour of the idea, and campaigned for it in his newspaper, *Le Clairon* of Saint-Hyacinthe. The controversy took on considerable proportions, and the question was debated in speeches, articles, pamphlets and books. Senator Raoul Dandurand gathered signatures on a petition and presented it to Mgr Bruchési, demanding that he pass it on to the Council of Public Instruction. But despite a vigorous campaign, neither the CPI nor the government would budge, and the controversy lasted into the 1930s. It might be thought that adoption of the principle of compulsory education by the Vatican itself in 1931 would have been enough to persuade the Quebec bishops that compulsory schooling did not necessarily mean government control of education. Such a supposition would be wrong, however, and it was not until 1943 that the government instituted compulsory education for children under fourteen.

The third major controversy had to do with the Jewish minority, which grew very rapidly in the early decades of the twentieth century. While there had been only a few hundred Jewish schoolchildren in the nineteenth century, 12,000 of the 30,000 pupils in Montreal's Protestant schools in 1924 were of Jewish origin. Neither the Jews nor the Protestants were satisfied with their forced co-existence, and the government, in trying to resolve the problem equitably, managed to upset everybody, including the Catholics.

From 1894 on, Jews had attended Protestant schools and paid their taxes to the Protestant commission. This agreement was renewed in 1903, but it came under fire in the 1920s. The Protestants threatened not to renew the agreement on the grounds that the place of the Jewish minority in the Protestant school system had become disproportionate and the revenue brought in under the agreement concluded in 1903 was insufficient to cover the costs of teaching Jewish children. The Jews considered themselves unjustly treated because they were not represented on the school commission, let alone the Council of Public Instruction.

The threatened closure of the Protestant schools to Jewish children raised a number of questions. Since the BNA Act provided only for Catholic and Protestant schools, what would happen to the Jews if the two recognized groups refused to accept them? Could a Jew be a school commissioner? Could the government allow the Jews to have a separate school system? These questions were brought before the courts, and the legal entanglements lasted until 1928, when the Privy Council in London ruled that the provincial government could establish separate schools for the Jews.

The provincial secretary proposed that a Jewish Committee of Public Instruction be established to watch over the interests of Jewish children attending Protestant schools; the cost of their education would be met out of the taxes paid by Jews and part of the revenue collected from neutral taxpayers. In exchange, Jews would not be eligible to sit on the Protestant committee of the Council of Public Instruction. The government submitted this solution to authorized representatives of the Jewish community and the Protestant school system. At the same time, however, two Jewish MLAs came out in favour of a separate school system under the administrative and financial jurisdiction of the Jewish community.

The Catholic bishops, who had not been consulted, were uneasy about these proposals, and the archbishop of Quebec, Cardinal Rouleau, wrote to Premier Taschereau in 1930 to express his opposition to it. He asked whether a Jewish school system would not violate the constitution of the country, which provided only for Christian schools, and suggested that there was a danger of the Jewish committee's being free of the authority of the CPI. Finally, he said that with the establishment of a Jewish committee, there would be no guarantee "against the encroachments of Bolshevik propaganda, when even with the current provisions for supervision, it is said that there are Jewish — or Russian-Jewish — schools with Bolshevik tendencies in this very province."

Apart from the antisemitism, hidden or otherwise, that came out in this debate, what both the Protestants and the Catholics were worried about was the loss of their monopoly in the educational field. Their chief fear was that Jews would be admitted to the Council of Public Instruction; even a few Jewish seats on the Protestant committee or the school commissions constituted a prospect to be dreaded. Another cause for concern was that if they granted separate schools to the Jews they might subsequently have to do the same for other groups. As of 1930 it was reported that there were twenty-two groups demanding special classes. The Catholic bishops in particular were worried that this situation might entail a risk of government intervention and an end to denominational schools.

Nevertheless, the government legislated a Jewish school commission into existence in 1930, in the hope that an agreement would be reached between the Jews and the Protestants. Such an agreement was in fact concluded soon afterwards. It was to be in effect for fifteen years, and essentially brought matters back to the *status quo ante*, except for the presence of the Jewish school commission to supervise the agreement. The two Jewish MLAs, however, resisted the proposal and their opposition gave rise to a vigorous debate, as the Jewish community was itself deeply divided over the proper course to follow. This led to the resignation of the members of the Jewish school commission, and for all practical purposes, the previous situation was restored.

These three major controversies — Department of Public Instruction, compulsory education, and Jewish schools — are good illustrations of the obsession among Catholic and Protestant authorities with the possibility that their monopoly in the field of public education might be encroached upon by the government or by some other group. They vigorously defended the denominational status quo, which enshrined their power. While the Protestants were not unduly upset by the prospect of free textbooks, free tuition or even compulsory education, the Catholic bishops saw these proposals as veiled threats that would necessarily bring about government intervention and neutral schools.

A jumble of structures and programs

The educational system was composed of two autonomous subsystems, Protestant and Catholic, which were completely separate from each other. Each side had a private sector and a public sector, and each of these was made up of different levels, poorly defined and badly co-ordinated. There were a variety of authorities responsible for schools and programs, and this confused and fragmented structure was very difficult to reform.

The need to introduce changes in the public primary system was felt early in the century, but it took some twenty years before anything was actually done. The primary course was limited to four years, on paper at least, until 1923, when it was finally agreed that this was unrealistic and the decision was made to extend the course to six years and bring some order to the primary program. A happy result of this reform was that many pupils went to school for two extra years. It was also agreed that primary school proper would be capped with an additional two-year course, to be called the complementary primary course. In the seventh and eighth grades, a pupil had the choice of industrial, commercial, agricultural and domestic science options. This addition of two years also made it possible for some students to continue their education. But they were only a small minority — in Montreal in 1926, according to a commission of inquiry chaired by Lomer Gouin, ninety-four per cent of Catholic children left school after the sixth grade. In Montreal in particular, a ninth and a tenth grade were gradually added to the primary course, although there was no official program for these two years. It was not until 1929 that the establishment of a three-year superior primary course was agreed upon. However, there was no co-ordination between this embryonic superior primary course and institutions of higher education, which was a serious deficiency of the Catholic public system.

The Protestants, on the other hand, had a long-established and well-oiled system in which a student could go smoothly from primary school to high school and thence to university. The Protestant system was also structurally more unified and coherent. From 1925 on, all Protestant schools on Montreal Island were under the authority of a single school commission, which had distinct advantages in the areas of finances, administration and teaching. The Catholics of Montreal eventually imitated them, but imperfectly and only after two commissions of inquiry had cast light on all the weaknesses of the situation in the city, where authority over Catholic education was fragmented among some forty school commissions.

Secondary education was dominated by the high schools on the Protestant side and the classical colleges on the Catholic side. The classical colleges offered a post-primary course lasting eight years. There were some thirty-six such colleges in 1930, thirty-four for boys and two for girls. The colleges were private institutions which accepted boarding students and were run by members of the clergy. Most of them were seminaries, and their main function was to prepare youths for the priesthood and the traditional liberal professions, law and medicine. Education for scientific careers was shockingly neglected. With secondary education monopolized by the classical colleges, the system was clearly inadequate to meet the needs of an industrialized country that required skilled workers and specialists in science and management. It was because of these increasingly evident requirements that the government intervened directly in education.

In 1907, the Gouin government announced that two technical schools would be established, one in Montreal and the other in Quebec City, to "provide our manufacturers with educated producers, highly skilled overseers, experienced foremen and élite workers." Technical schools in Trois-Rivières and Hull were opened in the 1920s. There were also private but subsidized technical schools in Shawinigan, Sherbrooke and Lachine. In 1926, the government established the Corporation des Écoles Techniques, headed by Augustin Frigon, to co-ordinate development of the technical school system. The technical schools offered both trade courses, which a student could enter upon completion of the sixth grade, and technical courses, which required completion of the ninth grade. Given the deficiencies of the public system, however, not as many students were recruited as had been hoped.

In the nineteenth century, the government had put some effort into developing higher vocational education; it continued to work towards this goal by establishing a surveying school (1907) and a forestry school (1910), both connected with Laval University. Just as it had been behind the establishment of the École Polytechnique in Montreal in 1873, the government now brought about the creation of the École des Hautes Études Commerciales (HEC — school of higher commercial studies). Accusations were heard in some circles that the government was trying to interfere in the educational field, as all the technical schools and the HEC were responsible to the government and outside the authority of the Council of Public Instruction. The government was attacked for wasting public funds on the HEC, which was having trouble recruiting students and for which scholarships had to be given. Another cause for concern was that these schools were neutral, but Gouin cleverly answered this criticism by explaining that this was inevitable since otherwise it would be necessary to have twice the number of schools, which would be too expensive.

Two fine arts schools, one in Quebec City and the other in Montreal, were added to this network of major institutions in the 1920s. These Écoles de Beaux-Arts were objects of special attention from the government that had founded them, and received generous subsidies. The government also encouraged expansion of the normal school system, but these schools were under the jurisdiction of the Catholic committee.

Quebec had four universities, two French (Laval and its Montreal branch) and two English (McGill and Bishop's). The University of Montreal gained its independence from Laval in 1919-20. It launched a public campaign for funds and collected $4 million, $2 million from the public and $1 million each from the Sulpicians and the government. In addition to the traditional faculties, the new university had affiliated schools including the Polytechnique, the HEC after 1914, the Oka Agricultural Institute and a school of veterinary medicine, and added a science faculty and a social science school in 1920. In 1929, bursting with optimism, it decided to build a huge building on Mount Royal. The depression made this dream very difficult to realize and the building was not completed until 1942. The growth of the University of Montreal acted as a stimulus to Laval, which also established a chemistry school that became the nucleus of a science faculty in 1920.

On the English side, Bishop's University, a small college in Lennoxville, gave up its faculty of medicine to concentrate on arts, theology and teacher training. Meanwhile, the rise of McGill University continued. A gift of several million dollars from the industrialist Sir William Macdonald made it possible for McGill to establish its teacher training college and a large agricultural school in Sainte-Anne-de-Bellevue at the western end of Montreal Island. Macdonald's philan-

The Technical School in Quebec City.

thropy was also the foundation for three buildings on the downtown Montreal campus — physics, chemistry and engineering. McGill even had an affiliated college in British Columbia, which later became the University of British Columbia.

The unequal position of French-language and English-language universities shows up clearly in a comparison of their endowment funds, made up principally of gifts from rich individuals and corporations. While Laval and its Montreal branch had a total endowment of $15,000 in 1915, McGill's endowment was $6,720,896. This did not prevent the government from giving McGill proportionally as much money as the other universities. Thus, when it made donations of $1 million each to Laval and the University of Montreal in 1920, it quickly gave a similar amount to McGill.

Teachers and students

To round out the picture of the educational system sketched in the preceding pages, an attempt will be made to get an idea of how well it met the needs of the population by measuring the numbers of students and teachers in the system. Judging by a glance at Table 47, the first three decades of the twentieth century

TABLE 47
Students and Teachers in Quebec Schools, 1901, 1931

Characteristic	*1901*	*1931*
Schools	6,098	8,448
Teachers	11,511	25,793
Students registered	330,173	653,351
5-19-year-olds registered	57.8%	67.2%
5-24-year-olds registered	45.7%	53.4%

Source: Louis-Philippe Audet, *Histoire de l'enseignement au Québec*, vol. 2, p. 279.

appear to have been marked by fairly substantial growth. The table shows several positive developments — the number of teachers grew more rapidly than the number of students, and the number of students expressed as a percentage of the total population between five and nineteen or five and twenty-four years of age increased considerably.

It is difficult to analyse these data any further as the table is too general. It is certain, however, that if the major religious groups could be compared, Protestants would have the advantage over Catholics. In addition, it is practically impossible to measure actual school attendance, since it is well known that at the time there was a considerable difference between a registered pupil and a pupil actually in school. There is reason to believe that not only were statistics in this area not always properly collected, but there were also financial or ideological advantages to be gained in some cases by inflating them. Despite these deficiencies in the data, conclusions can nevertheless be drawn from the qualitative and quantitative information available that show that the progress made was highly relative.

At the primary level, there were complaints that the quality of the schools and the teaching was not high enough and that pupils were not diligent in attending classes. A one-room range school, built at a cost of $1,200, where pupils between the ages of six and fourteen were taught by a seventeen-year-old girl who was paid less than $200 a year, had its charm but also its limitations. This was, however, the most common kind of school in the 1,100 or so municipalities counted in the 1931 census. Nor was the situation any better on Montreal Island, where responsibility was divided among some forty school commissions before the First World War. The present state of knowledge does not make it possible to measure students' diligence in attending school, but there were reasons why some people demanded a compulsory school attendance law. Children left school at the age of ten or eleven, after their first communion, and few went beyond the sixth grade. The new program instituted in 1923, however, led to a significant improvement, and there were roughly 175,000 Catholic pupils in the seventh and eighth grades.

The Domestic Science School in Roberval, in the Lake St. John region, 1905.

Catholics who wanted to pursue their education could go to the technical and vocational schools, the normal schools, the domestic science schools or the classical colleges, while Protestants went to high school. There were some 4,000 students in the seven technical schools in operation in 1929, but this figure included evening students, who must have represented a fairly high proportion of the total as only seventy-six students received diplomas in that year. The twenty normal schools and the 119 domestic science schools were educational outlets reserved for girls. While 1,744 girls were being trained to become teachers (as compared with 177 boys), 21,219 others were being prepared for the "domestic life." Nuns and girls from upper-class families had access to the two women's classical colleges. Boys could enter a preparatory course in the vocational schools (HEC, Polytechnique, Écoles des Beaux-Arts, agricultural schools); these schools were part of the higher education system but were unable to recruit classical college graduates and had to be satisfied with less qualified entrants. There were perhaps between 1,000 and 2,000 students in regular attendance at these institutions. The thirty-four classical colleges accounted for most of the secondary level students; they had 1,072 teachers, of whom fewer than a hundred were lay, and 11,200 students.

While the significance of the 1923 reform shows up clearly in this statistical material, it is also clear that after the eighth grade there was a bottleneck that affected the other levels of education and was potentially very damaging to

French-speaking students. There were hardly any outlets for girls, for most of whom the only choices were to go to normal school or be sidetracked into a domestic school. For boys, there were the technical and vocational schools, but these accommodated only a tiny minority. The classical colleges were the dominant institutions at the secondary level and the gateways to the universities and other higher institutions; but the colleges were all private and few people had access to them.

The existence of the public, lay high school, which covered the ninth through eleventh grades and in which young people could complete their basic education and prepare for university, was a significant advantage of the Protestant system. In 1929, there were more than 18,000 students in Protestant high schools. On the Catholic side, it was only in 1929 that it was agreed to extend public education through the eleventh grade with the establishment of the superior primary schools, but even after these schools were developed, their graduates did not have full access to university, as did Protestant students who completed eleven years.

University education, the last link in the chain, was deeply affected by the rest of the system. Both French-speaking universities were under the tutelage of the Catholic church, while McGill was under the direction of businessmen.

In 1901, the situation of the French-language universities (Laval and its Montreal branch) was a near disaster — they had only 153 professors and 1,175 students, as compared with 254 professors and 1,208 students on the Protestant side. The two systems were not strictly comparable because of the differences between the high school and the classical college, but even if the comparison is limited to corresponding faculties — theology, law, medicine and applied science — the superiority of the Protestant system is clear. By 1929, a clear improvement was evident on the Catholic side, but there was still progress to be made (Table 48).

These data would have to be closely examined, as there are reasons for suspecting that the figure of 2,022 Catholic science students in 1929 is false. The French-language science faculties had been in existence less than ten years and were badly equipped; the few science professors at Laval and the University of Montreal were constantly deploring the limited means at their disposal and the

TABLE 48

Catholic and Protestant Students in Selected Faculties in Quebec Universities, 1901, 1929

	Theology		*Law*		*Medicine*		*Applied Science*	
Year	*C*	*P*	*C*	*P*	*C*	*P*	*C*	*P*
1901	406	7	198	47	344	493	39	340
1929	647	28	268	82	920	563	2,022	1,078

Source: *Quebec Yearbook*, 1930.

lack of scientific preparation in the classical colleges. The 2,000 students were clearly not all in full-time attendance, and the number of graduates was small. According to Raymond Duchesne, the École Polytechnique, for example, produced an average of only six or seven new engineers a year between 1877 and 1920. Even in 1929, there were only about twenty students in fifth year in the school. A similar situation prevailed at the HEC, where only seventeen regular students completed the course.

Teacher training continued to be one of the educational system's major problems. Most teachers were trained on the job, and their accreditation consisted of a diploma issued by the Central Board of Catholic Examiners. The élite of the teacher corps received a year of training in a normal school; the program was extended to two years in the 1920s. For male and female religious, no examination or diploma was required, and the habit was sufficient accreditation.

The establishment of the Central Board of Catholic Examiners in 1898 to replace the local boards that had existed until then was an attempt to improve the situation by imposing higher standards in the competency examinations. But it was not until 1939 that all teachers were required to hold a diploma from a normal school. The number of normal schools grew steadily in the early twentieth century, from the three that had been in operation since the system was founded in 1857 to twenty in 1929. In 1931, ten training colleges for religious were authorized to grant teachers' diplomas. Despite the progress that was made, most Catholic teachers in 1929 had diplomas only from the Board of Examiners. The situation was better on the Protestant side, as most teachers were normal school graduates. In addition, while the Protestant teacher training college was affiliated with McGill University, which required that entrants be high school graduates, a Catholic student could be admitted to one of the normal schools scattered throughout Quebec upon completion of the sixth grade.

Teaching remained essentially a woman's profession. More than eighty per cent of the teachers in Quebec's primary and high schools in 1928 were women. It was also a profession in which male and female Catholic religious were numerous. In the educational system as a whole, the Catholic church was represented by 1,272 priests, 2,577 brothers and 6,630 nuns. Clerics and religious constituted forty-three per cent of the total number of teachers at all levels. If just the Catholic side were considered, this percentage of clerical and religious teachers would be even higher, as very few Protestant clergymen were teachers. A third characteristic of the teaching profession was the low salary level and the payment of unequal salaries for the same work depending on a teacher's sex and ethnic group. Thus, in the Catholic school system in 1929, a male teacher was paid an average of $1,553 while a female teacher was paid $387; the Protestant schools paid men an average of $2,351 and women an average of $1,068.

Catholic teachers were answerable to the church for what they taught. Not only were many of the teachers themselves clerics or religious, but all teaching in the public primary system and the normal schools was controlled by the church through its predominant position on the Catholic committee. The church was also in full control of the classical colleges and the two French-language universities. The only sector in which its influence was not preponderant was technical and vocational education, where responsibility lay with the government and government-owned corporations. Some people wanted this sector too to be placed under the control of the Catholic committee, but the government resisted this demand.

While the church held a monopoly at the university level, it didn't have the competence to play a role in every faculty and had to give way to lay teachers in some areas. Thus, at the Polytechnique and the HEC and in the faculties of medicine, law and science, the professors were specialists and most were laymen, although there were exceptions, such as Abbé Alexandre Vachon, who was trained in science at the Massachusetts Institute of Technology, and Brother Marie-Victorin, a remarkable self-taught botanist. In addition, the church had to depend, at least to a certain extent, on subsidies from the government, which made a special effort to develop the institutions of higher learning that had been founded on its initiative and the science faculties. The life of a university professor at the time was far from luxurious; professors were paid miserable salaries and had to work outside the university to make ends meet.

Clearly one of the most noteworthy developments of the period was the growth of technical and vocational schools and the science faculties. French-speaking Quebec had few specialists in these areas, and the government recruited specialists in Europe, especially in France, Switzerland and Belgium. It also established a modest scholarship system to make it possible for Quebecers, such as the economist Édouard Montpetit, to study in Europe for a few years. In 1922, the government increased the number of scholarships it was authorized to grant professors to study in Europe from five to fifteen. The few local scientists also played a role in scientific training; many of these were medical doctors, and others were self-taught.

In 1923, the Association Canadienne-Française pour l'Avancement des Sciences (ACFAS) was established on the initiative of Brother Marie-Victorin, with the aim of bringing together the various scientific organizations that had grown up in the previous few years. The government and the University of Montreal founded the Institut Scientifique Franco-Canadien the next year to encourage scientific exchanges between France and Quebec. In 1927, the government gave a $100,000 grant to Dr. J.E. Gendreau to found the Institut de radium (Radium Institute). Marie-Victorin and Adrien Pouliot, a Laval University mathematician, started a controversy by demanding publicly that science play a larger role in secondary education. While the process that this small group of scientists set in motion would have results later on, the immediate fruits of their initiative were limited.

In all, the first three decades of the twentieth century were a period of modest progress in education. The near-monopoly of the Catholic church and the Protestant minority in the educational field and the marginal role of the government

Marie-Victorin (1885-1944), Christian Brother and botanist.

constituted one of the great weaknesses of the system. After the failure of Marchand's attempt to set up a Department of Public Instruction in 1897, a decade went by before the government took any further action in the area of education. The Gouin and Taschereau governments deserve credit for their efforts to develop technical and vocational education at the secondary and university levels. In other areas, however, the provincial government was consigned to an auxiliary role. The Catholic church and the Protestant minority took pains to prevent the government from expanding its role and make sure that their autonomy would be encroached upon as little as possible. Unlike the Catholics, the Protestants had the resources to make something of their autonomous position. Their development was not held back by the government's abdication; they were ahead of the Catholics from every point of view and the political status quo suited them perfectly.

In this context it is not surprising that, out of total expenditures calculated at a little over $32 million for education in 1929, the government spent only about $4 million. The rest was accounted for by local school taxes ($17.6 million), tuition fees ($600,000) and the share of independent institutions, estimated at about $10 million.

The Catholic public system was inadequate, teachers were poorly trained, and too many school commissions refused to pay teachers suitable salaries or provide proper facilities. Moreover, the modest gains that were made in the first three decades of the century were threatened by the depression that struck in 1929.

POLITICS

In the first third of the twentieth century, some of the characteristics the Quebec state exhibits today began to appear. Changes occurring in a number of areas of Quebec life had their effects on the role of the government and political parties. The government was not quite so passive as before and introduced a greater degree of regulation into Quebec's economic and social affairs. Similar changes occurred in the area of public administration, which gradually took shape and became more specialized and complex; this process could be seen, for example, in the large cities, where municipal governments made efforts to eliminate amateurism, ad hoc administration and corruption.

Increasingly, party leaders became the focal points of their respective organizations. As a result of the problems created by the electoral map and political corruption, Quebec's political life became noticeably less democratic in the course of the period. Third parties appeared, but with the possible exception of the nationalist movement they remained on the margins of Quebec politics. Clearly the most striking phenomenon of the period was the dominance of the Liberal party; which gave the province the first of the long "reigns" that have been a feature of twentieth-century Quebec; first elected in 1897, the Liberals were still in office in 1929. The period was also marked by a resurgence of provincial autonomy, which showed up in the fiscal and economic sectors as well as in the increased independence of provincial political party leaders from their federal counterparts.

The analysis of Quebec's political development in the following pages is divided into four parts. The state's new role in society will be looked at first, and then political parties, governments and federal-provincial relations will be examined in succession.

CHAPTER 31
NEW ROLES FOR THE STATE

In the early twentieth century, Quebec in a sense was still living in the golden age of liberalism. Political leaders gave priority to economic development and private enterprise, and saw the role of the government only as auxiliary. This view of things was to be brutually challenged by the depression of the 1930s. But even before that, between 1896 and 1929, there was a visible change in the nature of government intervention.

New Directions

As noted earlier, the main factor that caused government activity to take new directions was the scope of the social problems brought about by industrialization and urbanization. The extent of seasonal unemployment was an argument in favour of the establishment of employment services; the large number of work accidents made it necessary to institute some form of compensation; the evolution of labour relations towards collective bargaining and the conflicts between employers and workers that resulted from this development created the need for instruments of conciliation; the weakening of family structures that followed the rural exodus made the introduction of old-age pensions essential; with the increasing cost of poor relief, the government was required to contribute towards financing it; and the high death rate and poor sanitary conditions in the large cities brought about a greater degree of government intervention in the health field.

Another development leading to increased state intervention was the creation of monopolies, especially in the utility sector, where companies were the targets of opposition from citizens' groups complaining about excessively high rates, exorbitant profits and poor service. The government played the role of protector of the public against the powerful trusts a little more than it had before, although still very hesitantly in the pre-1930 period. Even with its more frequent interventions, the government's actions were no threat to private initiative; except in a few areas such as alcohol distribution, it did not go into business for itself. Its activity was more in the nature of support for private initiative, along with a degree of regulation.

The government's regulatory power was exercised primarily through a new group of institutions — government commissions and boards. These institutions also sometimes had a co-ordinating role, notably in the utility sector, where the government invested in infrastucture to the advantage of all companies in the field. These new government activities were financed in a manner analogous to insurance, involving the collection of money (as premiums or taxes) earmarked for specific purposes.

Under the Public Charities Act of 1921 (see chapter 28), the cost of maintaining indigents in private institutions was to be shared equally by the Quebec government, the municipality and the institution. The provincial and municipal share of this agreement was to be financed through a special amusement tax, half the proceeds of which were to go to the municipality that collected it and the other half to the province. The Public Charities Fund established in this way was administered by civil servants who were empowered to review the manner in which it was used by the institutions. While such a control measure seems routine today, at the time it aroused opposition on the grounds that it constituted government intervention in the internal affairs of religious communities. And, as noted earlier, in the end the Taschereau government amended the act to satisfy the bishops who were unhappy with it.

Some groups wanted the government's role to extend to protecting the moral standards of the population. The hope was entertained that alcohol would be banished from Quebec, or at least that its manufacture and sale would be heavily controlled. Sunday observance was also a controversial subject. Sunday work had become common in the large paper mills, and Quebec's bishops wanted the government to ban this practice. Groups with puritanical inclinations and mostly Protestant memberships went further and wanted various forms of recreation outlawed on Sunday. The Catholic clergy felt especially threatened by movies, whose contents it could not control, and there were demands that movies be closed to children and banned entirely on Sunday, the only day most workers had off.

Public Finances

The Quebec government had been financially strapped in the first thirty years after Confederation, but the situation changed radically after 1897. Natural resource development and new taxes led to a sizeable increase in government revenues, while the public spending policy of the successive Liberal governments was very conservative and cautious.

Government revenues increased tenfold in the first three decades of the twentieth century, from $4 million to $40 million (Table 49). Expenditures increased at roughly the same rate, but since the government regarded a surplus as a mark of sound administration it took care to make sure that expenditures were less than revenues.

TABLE 49
Current Revenues and Expenditures of the Quebec Government, 1897-1929 ($000's)

Fiscal Year	*Revenues*	*Expenditures*	*Surplus*
1897-98	4,178	4,365	-187
1902-3	4,700	4,596	104
1907-8	6,017	4,981	1,036
1912-13	8,383	7,954	429
1917-18	13,806	11,672	2,135
1922-23	21,635	20,190	1,444
1927-28	34,808	32,821	1,987
1928-29	39,976	35,964	4,012

Source: *Quebec Yearbook.*

Government revenues became considerably more diversified over the period; while the traditional sources of revenue were maintained, their relative importance declined (Table 50). The federal subsidy, adjusted again in 1907, still represented a quarter of the province's revenues just before the First World War, but as the subsidy remained nearly constant its share of the total diminished rapidly after that and was less than six per cent by the end of the period. Licence

TABLE 50
Percentage Distribution of Quebec Government Revenues, 1912, 1929

Source	*1912(%)*	*1929(%)*
Federal subsidies	25.4	5.8
Lands and forests	20.6	16.3
Duty on successions and stamps	15.2	10.5
Licences	17.6	8.0
Motor Vehicle Law	0.6	12.2
Taxes on commercial corporations	9.6	7.7
Miscellaneous	11.0	39.5

Source: *Quebec Yearbook*, 1929.

duties and revenues from the legal system represented only eight per cent of the total in 1929. Revenue from natural resource development (lands and forests) continued to represent a substantial element in public finances, although its share too was declining. There were also new sources of revenue that provided rapidly increasing amounts of money — taxes collected under the Motor Vehicle Law and income from the Quebec Liquor Commission, which was a major component of the "other" category and made a substantial contribution to government revenues.

On the expenditure side, the most spectacular change came in the area of roads (Table 51). This category does not include spending for road building, which was financed from borrowing; it represents only the cost of highway maintenance, which was assumed by the province under the Taschereau government to relieve some of the burden on the municipalities.

In addition to its current budget, the government administered an "extraordinary budget consisting of loans and certain funds in trust or deposit." Among the items financed out of this budget were expenditures for construction of public buildings, roads, bridges and dams, loans to municipalities for road building, the government's participation in public assistance, and the repayment of loans. The size of this budget varied considerably from one year to the next, depending on how much construction work was in progress and what loans fell due.

In 1897 Quebec's debt, incurred primarily to finance railway construction, amounted to $24 million. Once in power, the Liberals systematically avoided borrowing, and the debt varied between $24 and $25 million until the war. But additional borrowing was needed to finance the roads policy adopted in 1912, so that the consolidated debt had reached almost $57 million by the end of the period. Despite this increase, Quebec still had one of the lowest levels of per capita debt among the Canadian provinces.

TABLE 51
Percentage Distribution of Quebec Government Expenditures, 1912 and 1929

Expenditures	*1912(%)*	*1929(%)*
Debt servicing	15.3	12.1
Public instruction	15.9	10.0
Administration of justice	12.1	6.6
Public works and labour	8.0	6.1
Agriculture	12.0	5.8
Roads	—	21.0
Lands and forests	4.3	6.0
Colonization, mines and fisheries	4.3	6.2
Miscellaneous	28.1	26.2

Source: *Quebec Yearbook.*

Municipalities accounted for a substantial share of public spending in the province. The total current revenues of Quebec's municipalities continued to be significantly greater than those of the provincial government. Municipalities also resorted to borrowing on a large scale to finance the construction of sewers, streets, and the like. Total municipal debt was $182 million in 1915 and reached $301 million in 1927, with Montreal alone accounting for $164 million, or a little over half the total. School commissions, whose total current revenues grew from $11 million in 1918-19 to $21 million in 1927-28, were also borrowers on a considerable scale, with liabilities of $35 million in 1918-19 and $67 million in 1927-28.

The Bureaucracy

Another manifestation of the changing role of the state was the remodelling of its administrative structure with the establishment of new departments and agencies and the reorganization of older ones. Three new departments were created. With the greater frequency of government intervention in the labour field, a labour section was set up within the Department of Public Works in 1905; it eventually became a separate department, although not until 1931. The government's new road building policies entailed the organization of a Department of Roads in 1914. Finally, in 1918, the Department of Municipal Affairs was created to make it possible for the government to have more control over Quebec's municipalities and to co-ordinate their activities. In addition, a number of existing departments were reorganized, notably in the areas of lands and forests, fisheries, mines and colonization. In some cases, existing entities were given new functions; thus, the office of the provincial secretary acquired an expanded role in encouraging the arts and education at the initiative of Athanase David, provincial secretary under Taschereau. At the end of the period, Quebec had nine departments in addition to the premier's office. Specialized offices and services were established within these departments, and the provincial government became increasingly complex.

A new development was the establishment of semi-independent government boards and commissions. The Water-Course Commission, established in 1914, was responsible for supervising the use of the province's rivers and building dams to regulate their flow; these dams resulted in increased capacity for private electric power stations and the companies that benefited from them reimbursed the commission for their cost. The Quebec Liquor Commission (1921) had a monopoly of liquor sales and administered the issuance and supervision of liquor licences held by hotels and other outlets. The Women's Minimum Wage Commission was established on paper in 1919 but was not actually set up until 1925. The task of the Workmen's Compensation Commission, established in 1928, was to determine the amount of compensation to be paid to accident victims.

Another important development in the way state power was organized was the administrative reorganization of Quebec's large cities, especially Montreal. The city of Montreal had a mayor, but most of the power was in the hands of the city

The establishment of a Liquor Commission was one of the more controversial projects undertaken by Premier Taschereau.

councillors, elected on a ward basis. City council was divided up into badly co-ordinated committees, each controlling a sector of the city's administration. Businessmen complained about the inefficiency of this system and the corruption

Brochure de combat Rodrigue Langlois

Scandale

du parc de

MAISONNEUVE

Ils ont fait Maisonneuve,.............
Contribuables, faites Maison nette

The corruption that was an integral part of political life sometimes erupted into scandal. The "Maisonneuve Park scandal" had to do with a land expropriation in which middlemen made substantial profits by reselling the land several times. Playing on the word *Maisonneuve,* the pamphlet invites taxpayers to "clean house."

it led to; they wanted the city to be administered like a corporation and provide cheap, well-run services. Groups were organized to lobby for reform. They demanded that the municipal civil service be recruited on the basis of competence rather than patronage and that services be run by "experts." Their program also included reducing patronage and corruption by limiting the power of the city councillors and having them elected on a city-wide rather than a ward basis so that they would be under less pressure from the electorate.

The efforts of a "citizens' committee" set up by the Board of Trade and the Chamber of Commerce led to the appointment of a commission of inquiry by the provincial government in 1909. The commission laid bare the widespread corruption and patronage at city hall. The citizens' committee's proposals for administrative reform were then put to a referendum and, after being accepted, went into effect in 1910. Many functions of city council were transferred to a new four-member board of control, which was to be elected by the city as a whole and have the real power in the municipal administration. When this new structure did not produce the anticipated results, businessmen again put pressure on the provincial government, which replaced it with a still less democratic system in 1918. City council was cut in size and its powers were reduced even further; the city was run by a five-member administrative commission comprising three directors of municipal services and two members appointed by Quebec City. In 1921, however, Montreal's population, which wanted the city's autonomy restored, finally got the upper hand. It put an end to the attempt by the Montreal bourgeoisie and the Quebec government to put the city under their trusteeship and tilted the balance back towards democracy. Under the new system, members of city council were elected on a ward basis and chose an executive committee responsible for running the municipal administration from their own ranks.

Politicians

The changes that took place during the period were also reflected in the social origins of Quebec's politicians. Even though sessions of the legislature lasted only two or three months each year, a seat in the legislative assembly was an increasingly time-consuming position. With the strengthening of the party system, the MLA became more of an organization man; he was the link between the party and the voters and could do what had to be done to keep his constituency in his party's column. This new role created a need for professional politicians, who were recruited from the petty bourgeoisie rather than the bourgeoisie. Not many big businessmen were left in the assembly; their place was taken by small merchants and lawyers. English-speaking members were also less numerous than before.

The cabinet, however, continued to be recruited from an élite linked to the bourgeoisie. At this level, social origins and family ties were still important. It was the cabinet, assured of the loyalty of its troops in the assembly, that exercised real political power. Under the successive Liberal governments that held office between 1897 and 1929, the most influential ministers were very close to the bourgeoisie. They sat on the boards of directors of numerous corporations and paid close attention to businessmen's wishes. Businessmen could therefore withdraw from direct political action with equanimity. Their real power remained untouched by the change in the profile of Quebec's politicians.

CHAPTER 32
POLITICAL PARTIES AND MOVEMENTS

As noted earlier, the Quebec political scene between 1897 and 1929 was characterized by the unchallenged domination of the Liberal party. The Conservative party constituted the main opposition to the Liberals, but found it difficult to carve out a position for itself and did not offer a real alternative. There was a kind of ideological consensus, with the two parties presenting ideas that were not vastly different from each other. The task of offering a real alternative was left to third parties.

Party Structure

Both major parties had an élitist leadership, as did the nationalist movement. Party leaders, with the help of a handful of the more influential organizers and members of parliament, kept a firm hand on their organizations. Parties were not membership organizations, and had supporters instead of members.

Party loyalty was assured through the patronage system, especially in the case of the party in power — the Liberals in the period being studied. The growth of the government's financial resources and scope of activity allowed patronage to become more bountiful and reach a larger number of people. Roads, which became a major area of government intervention, are a good example of this process. Road building benefited the population by improving communication, and regions to be helped in this way could be chosen so as to favour voters faithful to the party in power. Roads could also have happy side-effects for voters who supported the government — construction or maintenance contracts and the opportunity for farmers to find part-time jobs or supply materials. The Conservatives accused the Liberals of using roads expenditures for patronage purposes. The existence of patronage is a well-known phenomenon, but there have been no systematic studies that would make it possible to get a true picture of its scope or describe all its characteristics.

The highly partisan press was another significant institution, and one that was changing as the mass-circulation press grew. The Liberals had two major daily newspapers — *Le Soleil* in Quebec City and *Le Canada* in Montreal. The Conservative party could rely on *L'Événement* and the *Quebec Chronicle* in Quebec City and the *Star* and *La Patrie* in Montreal; originally Liberal, *La Patrie* switched to the Conservatives around 1905. There were also regional newspapers that were politically aligned, as well as others that supported a particular party but were not partisan newspapers in the sense of having to take orders from political leaders. An example of the latter was *La Presse* in Montreal, which from 1904 on supported the Liberals but maintained an independent editorial policy.

Most of the time, a newspaper would support the same party at both levels of government. The large English-language newspapers, however, constituted an exception to this rule; Conservative at the federal level, they kept their distance from the provincial Conservatives, who were too close to the French-Canadian nationalist movement, and instead supported the Liberals, whose policies were viewed favourably in the business community.

There was no clear distinction between federal and provincial levels in terms of party organization. The parties did not have separate structures for the two levels and the same teams of organizers operated in both federal and provincial elections. Tasks were divided more on a regional basis than according to levels of government. Thus, Senator Raoul Dandurand, Liberal party organizer in the Montreal region, played a key role in both federal and provincial elections. At least in the case of the Liberal party, the federal leader was especially influential, and played a very direct role in choosing the provincial leader.

The Liberal Party: Stability and Continuity

During this period, the Liberal party enjoyed unusual stability. It remained in power nearly forty years (from 1897 to 1936) and two of its four leaders had fifteen-year terms of office. After the defeat of Honoré Mercier in 1892, Félix-Gabriel Marchand became party leader and leader of the opposition; his victory in the 1897 election gave him the premiership. Marchand died in 1900 and was succeeded by Simon-Napoléon Parent, whose autocratic methods provoked a revolt among his supporters that forced him to resign in 1905 (see chapter 33). Lomer Gouin replaced him and kept a firm hand on the leadership until his resignation in 1920. There was a smooth transition as his handpicked successor, Louis-Alexandre Taschereau, took over and remained party leader until 1936. Thus, from 1897 on, the party leader, chosen by the MLAs and organizers, automatically became premier, without having to have his appointment ratified by the voters. In addition, Parent, Gouin and Taschereau were all ministers in their predecessors' cabinets before succeeding to the premiership; this was another factor contributing to the large degree of continuity between one leader and the next.

During these four decades, the Liberals remained faithful to a single set of major political principles — economic growth through the development of natural resources and support for foreign capital; hesitant social policies; limited educational reforms aimed at more effectively gearing the system to the needs of the economy. In their essentials, these positions remained unchallenged throughout the period, although each leader put his stamp on the party by emphasizing one aspect or another of the program.

Underneath this stability, there were internal tensions within the Liberal party. The old radical tradition inherited from the Rouges was still represented within the party by a few MLAs and organizers and voiced by some newspapers. But the radical group did not count for much with the party leadership, which generally suppressed it or kept it in the background. The most vocal radicals were eliminated — Godfroy Langlois was sent off to be Quebec's representative in Brussels and T.-D. Bouchard was taught a lesson in moderation through an electoral defeat at the hands of an independent Liberal.

But intraparty rivalries were not only ideological in character; they also had to do with personalities and styles of operating. S.-N. Parent gradually lost the support of his legislative caucus as a result of his method of governing; Lomer Gouin became the leader of the malcontents and forced the premier's resignation. The Parent-Gouin rivalry also had a regional basis, and represented the old friction between Quebec City, Parent's bailiwick, and Gouin's stronghold of Montreal.

There were also tensions between federal MPs and provincial MLAs. The federal leader, Wilfrid Laurier, kept the party under virtual tutelage; in reaction to this control, Lomer Gouin established some distance between himself and Ottawa when he took over in Quebec City. At the constituency level, friction within the party was exacerbated by the weakness of the opposition. Liberal candidates were almost certain to be elected, and there were many Liberal supporters who hoped to become MLAs. It was tempting for those who were not chosen by the party leadership to run as independent Liberals.

All these tensions were not enough to cause the party to break up. The most serious threat to party unity occurred in 1905 with the caucus revolt against the party leader, but dissatisfaction was so widespread at the time that Parent had no choice but to resign. It was not until the 1930s, after the close of the period being examined here, that the tensions within the party exploded.

The Trials of the Conservative Party

The Conservatives had dominated the Quebec political scene throughout the second half of the nineteenth century, but the 1897 election marked the beginning of a prolonged stay in opposition. The Conservatives' difficulties were of three kinds. The first of these had to do with the electoral system. As a result of the "first-past-the-post" method of voting — with each constituency electing a single member by a simple plurality on one ballot — and the distorted electoral map, the number of seats held by the Conservatives was significantly lower than their real strength among the voters throughout the period; this phenomenon will be discussed later. A second difficulty arose out of the Liberal party's swing to the right and identification with big business, which made it hard for the Conservatives to establish a genuinely distinctive program; the Liberals kept the initiative in this area and the Conservatives were constantly struggling to catch up. They were sometimes able to deal with this problem by coming to an arrangement with the nationalist movement, but only at the cost of the not inconsiderable support they had within the English-speaking business community. The harmful side-effects of federal politics constituted a third difficulty for the Conservatives. The federal Conservative party did not have French-Canadian leaders with the prestige of Wilfrid Laurier or Ernest Lapointe, and its conscription policy during the war and pro-imperialist orientation had additional negative effects on its Quebec constituency.

There were five main stages in the development of the Quebec Conservative party between 1897 and 1929. The first was a period of disarray (1897-1908). The party reeled from its double defeat in the 1896 federal election and the 1897 provincial election, and former Premier Edmund James Flynn led his decimated forces as best he could. The brutal methods of Premier S.-N. Parent, who called snap elections in 1900 and 1904 and didn't give the Conservatives time to get organized, added to the confusion within the party. After his defeat in 1904 Flynn had to give up the party leadership to Évariste Leblanc. In 1908, the party began to gain strength again as a result of its electoral and parliamentary alliance with Henri Bourassa's nationalists. After Leblanc was defeated in the 1908 election, Mathias Tellier became leader of the opposition, and with the very active support of Bourassa, who won a provincial seat in the same election, was able to press the government hard in the Legislative Assembly.

After 1912, however, the party again went into a period of decline that lasted until 1920. The opposition was weakened by Bourassa's retirement from active politics, and the hopes stirred by the accession of the Conservative party to power in Ottawa with nationalist support in 1911 were quickly dashed. The Borden government's imperialist policies discredited the Quebec party. The conscription crisis of 1917 had even clearer effects. The federal Conservative party became the party of English Canada and French Canadians swung overwhelmingly into the Liberal column. Meanwhile, in Ontario, the Conservative provincial government adopted Regulation 17, which seriously limited the study of the French language in the bilingual schools, thus challenging the traditional rights of Franco-Ontarians. The Quebec Conservative party, led by Philémon Cousineau in 1915-16, felt the repercussions of these external events.

For Arthur Sauvé, the new leader of the opposition after the 1916 election, the

Arthur Sauvé (1874-1944), leader of the Conservative opposition in Quebec, 1916-29.

only solution was to establish a very clear demarcation between the provincial and federal wings of the party. His more nationalistic attitude incurred the displeasure of the party's English-speaking members, but the depression that struck Quebec in the early 1920s gave added weight to his criticism of the Liberal government. The party succeeded in gaining considerable support in the major urban centres, but it won only a relatively small number of seats as a result of the distortions of the electoral map. Thus, Sauvé's attempt at rebuilding the party during his tenure as leader (1916-29) was a failure in electoral terms. In 1929 the party entered a new phase, marked by a tendency towards populism, with the election to the party leadership of the mayor of Montreal, Camillien Houde.

The Nationalist Movement

A new political movement was born at the turn of the century as a reaction against the resurgence of English imperialism. Referred to as the nationalist movement, it was at first closely identified with an individual, Henri Bourassa, who put his stamp on it ideologically and, up to a point, prevented it from becoming a genuine political party. Imperialism became a hot issue in Canada in 1899 when Britain, drawn by gold in the Transvaal, went to war against the Boers in South Africa. The British colonial secretary, Joseph Chamberlain, along with some English Canadians, advocated a commitment by Canada on the side of the mother country. Prime Minister Laurier was very hesitant, but had to yield to English-Canadian pressure.

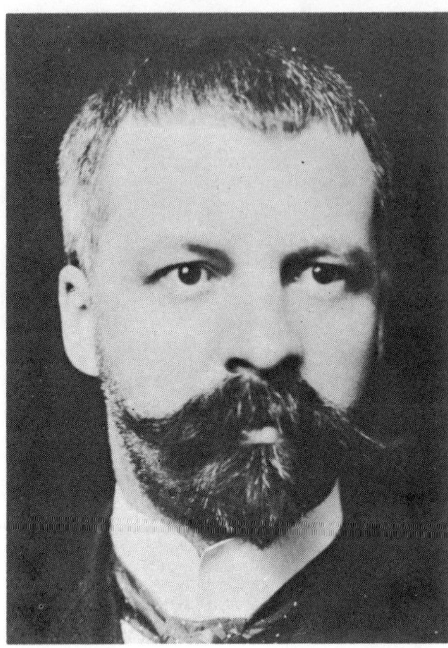

Henri Bourassa (1868-1952), nationalist leader and founder of *Le Devoir*.

Henri Bourassa, grandson of Louis-Joseph Papineau and a young Liberal MP, resigned his seat in the House of Commons in protest against the government's failure to consult parliament before making such a serious commitment. Bourassa was re-elected without opposition in his constituency of Labelle, and on his return to the Commons he tirelessly fought against imperialism and upheld the banner of Canadian nationalism. Bourassa used his numerous speeches in the House as an opportunity to elaborate further on what his nationalism meant. He argued that it was absolutely essential for Canada to assert and maintain its autonomy relative to the mother country if it didn't want to founder in colonial insignificance. But while resisting imperialism was, in Bourassa's view, crucial to the harmonious development of the country, it was not sufficient. Harmonious development was based on co-existence and co-operation between French and English Canadians, so that respect for cultural duality was also essential, especially in the area of language and religious rights. Furthermore, Canadians were heirs to an economic and intellectual birthright, and in developing it had to remain their own masters as much as possible.

The vigorous struggle that Bourassa waged, sometimes against his own party, won him the admiration of French Canada's youth. In 1903, a group of his disciples decided to establish a movement with the aim of disseminating the ideas he had put forward. The guiding spirits in this movement were young journalists — Olivar Asselin, Armand Lavergne, Omer Héroux and Jules Fournier — and it chose the name Ligue Nationaliste Canadienne (Canadian Nationalist League). It published a manifesto that had Bourassa's approval and took its inspiration from his writings and speeches. The 1903 manifesto became the league's political program, the content of which was subsequently developed and made more precise through Bourassa's public speeches and writings.

The program of the Ligue Nationaliste Canadienne had three major planks. The first dealt with the area of relations between Canada and England, where the league demanded "the widest possible political, commercial and military autonomy compatible with maintaining the colonial link." Specifically, the idea of participating in an imperial parliament should be rejected, Canada should have the right to be directly represented internationally and negotiate trade agreements, and finally, Canada should not participate in the wars of the British Empire and the militia command should be Canadianized.

The league's program was much less innovative in the area of federal-provincial relations. It demanded "the widest possible autonomy compatible with maintaining the federal link," placing renewed emphasis on the need to preserve the rights guaranteed to the provinces in 1867 and ensure that the right of minorities to separate schools was respected. It advocated increased federal subsidies to the provinces and a takeover of the administration of criminal justice by the federal government. It also demanded that civil court judges be appointed by the provinces.

Finally, the league proposed that Canada as a whole adopt "an exclusively Canadian policy of economic and intellectual development." This goal took concrete form in a number of proposals. Some of these were directed primarily to the federal government which, in the league's view, should make its customs policy conform more closely to Canadian interests, stop subsidizing private companies and keep tighter control over transportation rates and railway routes. The proposals directed to the provincial government were mostly in the area of resource management — colonization should be more actively supported, waterfalls should be leased rather than sold, and forest development policies should be changed in order to ensure conservation. This was the nucleus of the economic program of the nationalist movement. The movement also demanded development of patriotic education and support for literature and the arts, and advocated legislation guaranteeing job security and freedom of association.

To disseminate its program, the league organized public meetings and invited Henri Bourassa to speak. A more systematic organ of dissemination was established in 1904 in the form of a weekly newspaper, *Le Nationaliste*, founded with Bourassa's financial and editorial support. The paper provided an outlet for the league's young journalists and, most important, gave the movement a valuable tool for developing its ideas and making them known. *Le Nationaliste* quickly became a *journal de combat*, directly involved in the political arena. Ideas were developed through criticism of the policies of the parties in power in Ottawa and Quebec City, which aroused antagonism towards the editors in political circles. Thus the league, which at the beginning had defined itself as an educational movement distinct from the political parties, gradually intervened in the political process and was inexorably dragged onto the electoral stage.

After the Boer War, when Laurier's policy shifted towards Canadian autonomy within the Empire, Bourassa emphasized the other aspects of his program more strongly — minority education rights and the development of the Canadian economy by and for Canadians. As agriculture, colonization and natural resource development were provincial responsibilities, Bourassa and the young nationalists became more and more biting in their criticism of Quebec government policies. Thus, even though he was still a Liberal MP in Ottawa, Bourassa became a formidable opponent of the Quebec Liberals.

In 1907, this opposition changed into open hostility, especially on the questions of colonization policy, natural resource development and political corruption. A provincial cabinet minister, Adélard Turgeon, challenged Bourassa to resign his seat in the Commons and run against him in his constituency of Bellechasse. Bourassa somewhat rashly accepted the dare and was defeated. In the provincial general election of 1908, however, the nationalist movement plunged into the fray. Bourassa ran against Lomer Gouin in Saint-Jacques and his friend Armand Lavergne gave up his seat in Ottawa to run provincially. Bourassa was supported by the provincial Conservatives and contributed greatly to the Conservative resurgence. He even succeeded in defeating Premier Gouin in Saint-Jacques. The nationalists were not a serious threat to the Liberals in terms of the election outcome as they ran only two candidates, but the enthusiasm unleashed by Bourassa and Lavergne and their unspoken alliance with the Conservatives, who professed to accept the nationalists' ideas, were somewhat unnerving to the Liberals.

The 1908 election increased Conservative strength from five to thirteen MLAs, not counting the two nationalist candidates elected, and between 1908 and 1912 the Gouin government had to face a much more vigorous opposition than before. Moreover, starting in 1910 the nationalist movement had a daily newspaper, *Le Devoir*, founded and edited by Henri Bourassa. It was with some regret that Bourassa had taken part in the 1908 election, as he had long been convinced that the movement of which he was the leader should direct its efforts first and foremost towards the education of the voters, held captive by the partisan press. To ensure that his newspaper would remain independent of the old parties, Bourassa managed to persuade its financial backers to give him full authority over the paper as long as he remained its editor.

Bourassa and *Le Devoir* shifted some of their attention away from the provincial scene in 1911, as their main concern was the imperialist question, which was being discussed primarily in the federal parliament. The nationalists were increasingly disappointed with the positions taken by the Laurier government which, under pressure from Britain, proposed to establish a Canadian navy that would be placed at the service of the mother country in time of war. Outraged at Laurier's imperialism, they took an active part in the 1911 federal election on the side of the Conservatives, who were very hesitant about taking a clear position on the naval question. Nevertheless, with nationalist support the Conservatives won twenty-seven seats in Quebec, up from eleven. A number of these Conservatives elected in Quebec were actually disciples of Bourassa, who could have played a significant role in determining the direction taken by the federal Conservatives if he had agreed to become directly involved in federal politics.

As it was, however, the independent or nationalist Conservatives were left without leadership and as a result were absorbed by the Conservative party or reduced to a marginal role. The policies of the federal Conservatives turned out to be even more imperialist than Laurier's and not very favourable to the protection of minority rights. In the 1912 provincial election Bourassa, disappointed with politics, did not run as a candidate or take part in the campaign. However, the nationalists continued to support the Conservatives, who won fifteen seats and forty-five per cent of the popular vote. Armand Lavergne, the only nationalist elected, supported the opposition. After six years of direct involvement in political struggles, the nationalist movement's electoral activity as such came to an end with this campaign. There are two aspects of this activity that are worth discussing in more detail: the type of organization it involved and the kinds of support the movement gained.

One major difficulty from which the nationalist movement suffered was the weakness of its organization. This was the result of Henri Bourassa's refusal to found a genuine political party. Throughout his career, Bourassa was an opponent of *l'esprit de parti* — the group cohesion to which members of a party caucus in a parliamentary body had to submit. He sang the praises of the independent member of parliament, who voted according to his conscience instead of following party orders, an idea that went against the reality of how British-style parliamentary institutions function. Rather than turn his movement into a party, Bourassa gave it the task of encouraging the election of independents and members of the existing parties who were prepared to support its program.

Thus, the nationalist movement did not have a well-defined organization. Everything centred on Bourassa himself, and Bourassa began to see himself as the nation's guide. The movement's leadership was very élitist and carried the cult of personality further than the other parties. It was also dependent on the enthusiasm of Quebec's youth, for whom Bourassa was the new hero.

At the large meetings sponsored by the nationalists, Bourassa as main speaker gave long, articulate and well-documented speeches. During election campaigns these meetings took on a different character, attracting large numbers of supporters as well as people with nothing better to do for whom such meetings were a form of entertainment in the era before radio and television. The fiery manner of Bourassa and the young speakers who shared the platform with him contributed to the success of meetings of this sort. The movement's newspapers, *Le Nationaliste* and later *Le Devoir*, provided more scope for it to criticize the government and develop the different aspects of its program. They established a line of communication among the movement's supporters and gave them up-to-date information about the activities of the leader. They were not, however, mass-circulation newspapers. Their circulation was small and the public they reached was made up primarily of students, intellectuals, clergy and politicians.

Despite the weaknesses of its organization, the nationalist movement did gain support, although its strength is difficult to measure precisely. Its most conspicuous backers were students in the classical colleges, to whom Bourassa was an irresistibly attractive figure in the early part of the century. Some classical college students acquired nationalist beliefs at this time that were retained throughout their careers and were to find expression in the Action Libérale Nationale in the 1930s. A group of priests teaching in the classical colleges established the Association Catholique de la Jeunesse Canadienne-française (ACJC) in 1903. This organization emphasized both Catholicism and French-Canadian nationalism, and was fertile ground in which the ideas of the nationalist movement easily took root. These ideas were also warmly received by the clergy, intellectuals and many representatives of the liberal professions, who formed a substantial part of the leadership of *Le Devoir*.

The nationalist movement also received tactical support from the Conservative party, which benefited from the dissatisfaction with the Liberal government aroused by Bourassa's criticisms. As the nationalists themselves ran very few candidates, the electoral fruits of the movement's activities were reaped primarily by the Conservatives. This explains why the businessmen who agreed to finance *Le Devoir* were for the most part well-known Conservatives.

It is beyond question that Bourassa and his disciples helped enliven political discussion in Quebec in the early part of the century. They reinvigorated the moribund Conservative opposition and forced the Gouin government to manage natural resource development in a manner that was more logical and more beneficial to Quebec as a whole. In strictly electoral terms, the nationalists' influence was mostly indirect, since the movement did not give rise to a party. However, the nationalist movement did succeed in influencing the Liberal party at both the federal and the provincial level. To maintain their hold over Quebec, the Liberals had to appear to favour Canadian autonomy relative to Britain and provincial autonomy relative to the federal government. The Quebec Conservatives, meanwhile, tried to come to an agreement with the nationalists and take advantage of their influence. Towards this end, they dissociated themselves in the 1920s from the federal Conservatives, who were much more resistant to nationalist ideas.

But in the end, the nationalists proved unable to implement their political program of Canadian independence and equality between French and English Canadians. While their mistrust of British imperialism was soundly based, they could not understand that in English Canada imperialism was the political expression of English-Canadian nationalism. English Canadians were agreed or at least resigned to accepting some language and religious rights for French Canadians within Quebec, but not in the other provinces. In all, the nationalist movement had little success in convincing English-speaking Canadians either of the validity of its stand on the imperialist question or of the need to respect Canada's cultural duality.

The failure of the nationalists as a political movement brought about their departure from the electoral scene just before the war. This did not mean the disappearance of the nationalists but rather their redirection towards another form of activity. As a result of Regulation 17 in Ontario, ethnic tensions during the war, and the conscription crisis of 1917, Bourassa's disciples came to doubt that pan-Canadian nationalism in a bilingual and bicultural country was feasible. They turned increasingly towards a Quebec-centred French-Canadian nationalism and went so far as to flirt temporarily with the idea of Quebec independence.

During the 1920s, they completely abandoned electoral political activity and concentrated instead on intellectual activity through their publications, the education of students, and organization through such groups as the ACJC and the Action Française. The rise of a new nationalist leader, the priest and teacher Lionel Groulx, was an indication of this new direction. Bourassa, meanwhile, attacked the nationalism of his former disciples, now more French-Canadian than Canadian, and became increasingly estranged from them. He returned to the federal political scene, winning a seat in the 1925 election, but his political position now was strictly personal and he made no attempt to re-establish the movement he had headed before the war.

The Parti Ouvrier

For about ten years at the beginning of the century, the Parti Ouvrier (Labour party) played a very active role on the Montreal political stage, offering the population a labour alternative and winning some electoral victories. It reflected the dynamism and militancy that infused the Montreal labour movement at the time.

As noted in chapter 14, the labour movement had become politically active in the 1880s at the impetus of the Knights of Labor. However, its activity was sporadic and limited to election times. At the beginning of the twentieth century, the movement took a further step by establishing a permanent organization devoted to political action. The first attempt to establish a labour party occurred in Montreal in 1899. The party's crushing defeat in the election of 1900 led to its disappearance, but it rose out of its ashes after the 1904 provincial election, in which some labour candidates made a good showing although none was elected; this was enough to rekindle the fervour of the advocates of a permanent organization. The Montreal Trades and Labour Council took responsibility for establishing the Parti Ouvrier, and the party was formally founded in December 1904.

Its platform was aimed at protecting the interests of workers and included the nationalization of banks and utilities; free government-administered unemployment insurance, health insurance and old-age pensions; and free and compulsory education. Other parts of its platform were inspired by the North American populist movement — election of judges by the people, the referendum, and abolition of the Senate. There were also a number of policies dealing with working conditions — establishment of employers' responsibility for work accidents, the eight-hour work day, a ban on the employment of children under fourteen and convicts, and the like. Finally, there were policies aimed at making the electoral process more democratic — "one man, one vote," universal suffrage, abolition of the property qualification.

Three kinds of member organizations constituted the party and were represented in its structure: the Montreal Trades and Labour Council, trade unions and, most important, the labour clubs. These clubs were organized on the basis of regions corresponding to electoral constituencies, and brought together union and non-union workers from a variety of trades.

The Parti Ouvrier was essentially a Montreal institution, although it also ran candidates in Quebec City and some other cities and towns. It won its first electoral victory in 1906 in a federal byelection in the working-class Montreal constituency of Maisonneuve, where the party's candidate was Alphonse Verville, president of the Trades and Labour Congress of Canada. Verville's Liberal opponent was J.-O. Grothé, an industrialist who was reviled by working people because of his employment practices. The election of Verville was a victory for the labour movement, but it remained an isolated phenomenon. Although Verville was subsequently re-elected, the two major parties managed to stymie all other labour candidates by choosing candidates with populist appeal. In addition, Verville himself took a very moderate stance in the House of Commons, supporting the Liberals most of the time. He demanded reforms that would benefit working people in the spirit of his party's program, but as an isolated individual he was unable to bend the government from its course. At the provincial level, the Parti Ouvrier did not win any seats.

As a result of the difficulty of making a real breakthrough at the federal or provincial level, the Parti Ouvrier increasingly directed its activities towards the municipal political scene, where it believed it could have a more concrete effect on working-class living conditions. It won its greatest victory in 1910, when it elected a candidate, Joseph Ainey, to the city's four-member Board of Control, and a number of others to city council.

Starting in 1912, the party went into a phase of rapid decline. There was a split which led to the establishment of a rival organization, the Fédération des Clubs Municipaux (Federation of Municipal Clubs). Most of the unions that had been members of the party withdrew and the number of labour clubs declined. By the beginning of the war, the party was only a shadow of what it had been. Its weakness was undoubtedly related to the difficulties encountered by the trade union movement with the rise of unemployment just before the war.

The Reform Associations

Elements within the bourgeoisie also established new political organizations operating on the municipal scene. These were urban reform groups, which, as we have seen, aimed at cleaning up municipal politics and eliminating corruption. They first appeared in the late nineteenth century, recruiting their members from the Montreal bourgeoisie and especially from its English-speaking segment; they found it more difficult to attract French-Canadian businessmen to their ranks. Élitist and anti-democratic in character, these groups wanted the city to be run like a corporation. This meant that the power of locally-elected city councillors, too vulnerable to pressure from the electorate, would be reduced and a more technocratic form of administration would be established.

Grouped around H.B. Ames and Hormisdas Laporte, the reformers initially organized in the last years of the nineteenth century to fight the political machine that Raymond Préfontaine had built at city hall. They founded associations with various names that succeeded in electing a number of candidates. In 1900, the reform party managed to defeat the chiefs of the Préfontaine machine, and the reformers were now in a position to clean up municipal finances and improve sanitary conditions in the city. Their work was impeded, however, by the ethnic divisions and inter-neighbourhood rivalries that characterized city council, and corruption and patronage returned, stronger than ever, after 1902.

In 1908, the Board of Trade and the Chamber of Commerce got together to establish the Citizens' Committee, which later became the Citizens' Association. Through the efforts of this body, an inquiry was carried out and a new administrative system was adopted. Between 1910 and 1914 the reformers dominated the newly instituted Board of Control but they didn't eliminate corruption. With the victory of a group dominated by Médéric Martin in 1914, the reform experiment ended.

The reformers succeeded in making municipal administration a little more efficient despite the limitations of their activities. But as an élitist and bourgeois movement they were unable to obtain widespread popular support, except in 1910 when revelations of scandal created favourable circumstances for the adoption of their proposals for administrative reorganization. A man such as Médéric Martin, mayor after 1914, could brand them as well-heeled Anglophones protecting the interests of the city's west end and find a ready audience among the French-speaking and working-class population; using this formula, Martin won re-election a number of times.

Electoral Legislation and Practice

While electoral legislation was reformed significantly between 1867 and 1897, no comparable action was taken during the next period. The reforms of 1875 and 1895 improved the system in a number of ways: the secret ballot was introduced, electoral qualifications were reduced, election expenses were controlled. The general aims of the legislation were to clarify the rules of the game, extend the right to vote to a wider class of people, reduce fraud and curtail the physical violence and intimidation that compromised the voter's freedom. But with the Liberals winning uninterrupted victories after 1897, there was little incentive for them to change the system that served their interests so well. The only reform they carried out was an extension of the right to vote. Despite this measure, the electoral system became less democratic, as control over election expenses was ended and the electoral map became increasingly distorted.

This regression was especially evident in the area of the control of election expenses. In 1903, the Parent government removed the ceiling on election expenses stipulated by the 1895 legislation, and at the same time reduced the penalties for people convicted of electoral law violations. In 1926, the Liberals abolished the requirement that candidates make public their financial statements. The only remaining restriction was the provision that candidates' expenditures had to be carried out by a special agent, and this disappeared in 1932. Israël Tarte, Liberal organizer in the 1896 and 1897 elections, observed that elections are not won by prayers, and the Liberals were convinced of the truth of this maxim.

There was only one notable piece of progressive electoral legislation brought in by the Liberals. This measure, introduced by the Gouin government in 1912, contributed significantly to making the right to vote more democratic and allowed the Liberals to boast that they put the principle of "one man, one vote" into practice. They did this by abolishing the plural vote, which had made it possible for a citizen who owned property in a number of constituencies to vote in each of those constituencies. The 1912 legislation stipulated that a voter could cast his ballot only in the constituency where he was domiciled. There was no great debate over this measure, but it was a reform of some significance. In a number of constituencies in commercial areas, especially in Montreal, there was a significant reduction in the size of the voters' list, which gave more power to the real residents of the area. According to Jean Hamelin, in some cases the plural vote represented up to ten per cent of the voters' list.

The 1912 legislation also widened access to the ballot box by substantially lowering the income requirement, establishing it at an average of $10 per month. For all practical purposes, Quebec now had universal male suffrage. In 1915, however, Indians were carefully and specifically excluded with a stipulation that "Indians and individuals of Indian blood domiciled on land reserved for Indians" did not have the right to vote. Also, of course, the so-called universal suffrage of the time was only semi-universal, as it did not extend to women. As noted in chapter 29, it was only after many struggles that women obtained the right to vote — in 1918 in federal elections and in 1940 in Quebec.

With these important reservations, it remains true that the right to vote was widened considerably. In 1871, the electorate represented 14.8 per cent of the total population, while in 1912, after eliminating multiple listings due to the plural vote, the electorate represented 23.9 per cent of the population.

While implementation of "one man, one vote" corrected an inequity based on wealth, it did not mean that every voter had a vote that carried equal weight. This brings up the question of the electoral map or, more precisely, the substantial differences in population between one constituency and another. In 1927, for example, the fifteen constituencies in the Montreal region had an average population of 58,607, while in the four Quebec City constituencies the average was 28,225 and in the rest of the province it was only 23,420. That same year, the constituency of Montreal-Mercier alone had a population equal to that of the eight smallest constituencies in Quebec! Thus, as the political scientist Harold Angell has noted, the twenty-one smallest constituencies represented only 12.5 per cent of the population while the twenty-one largest ones represented forty-three per cent. As in general it was rural constituencies that were small and urban ones that were large, the rural population was overrepresented and the urban population underrepresented. Overall, as Angell has pointed out, only twenty-nine seats in the Legislative Assembly represented urban constituencies in 1926, as compared to fifty-six representing rural constituencies.

This distorted electoral map made rural voters extremely important and helped determine party strategy. To attract rural support, the Conservatives constantly attacked the government for not doing enough for farmers and colonists. The Liberals continued to push industrialization but argued that rural Quebecers benefited from the effects of this policy. A key element of their strategy consisted of stamping out any suggestion of political organization in rural Quebec, and they used patronage on a large scale and in a variety of forms to maintain their hold over this crucial power base. The dependence of rural society made it especially susceptible to patronage, and this situation, combined with the overrepresentation of rural Quebec, was highly beneficial to the party in power. The historian Richard Hofstadter observed this same situation in the United States, and noted that it got worse with increasing urbanization. As the rural population became smaller, it could be more easily controlled and "bought," while at the same time governments had ever greater financial resources as the number of urban taxpayers grew.

Politicians argued that in establishing the boundaries of a constituency, not only the number of voters but also such things as the geographical and historical characteristics of the area and means of communication had to be taken into account. Despite these arguments, the political system still had to maintain a certain balance among the different constituencies if it was to remain credible as a democratic process; increasingly as the period under study progressed, this balance was not maintained.

While the electoral map was periodically redrawn, this was done at the initiative of the ruling party rather than of an independent commission, and in general, with few exceptions, these changes always served the interests of the party in power. Through gerrymandering — manipulation of the electoral map for partisan purposes — new constituencies were established with boundaries that were favourable to the Liberals or made it possible to neutralize an opponent. A second effect of changes in the electoral map was to reduce the underrepresentation of some voters. Between 1897 and 1930, the number of seats in the Assembly was increased from seventy-four to ninety. Only seven of these sixteen new seats were urban ones, which was not nearly enough to close the huge gap between the size of rural and urban constituencies.

The electoral map combined with the first-past-the-post system had the effect of creating an imbalance between the proportion of the electorate voting for a party and the number of seats it obtained. Thus, the Liberals were systematically overrepresented and the Conservatives systematically underrepresented. In 1923, for example, the Conservatives obtained only 24.7 per cent of the seats in the Assembly with forty-four per cent of the popular vote, and in 1927, with thirty-seven per cent of the popular vote, they obtained only ten seats out of eighty-five, or 11.8 per cent. This massive distortion of election results clearly did not encourage voter participation or faith in the democratic system. The deficiencies of the system had the effect of demobilizing the opposition, as can be seen by the frequency of elections by acclamation. In 1904 and 1919, this situation reached the point where the number of Liberals elected by acclamation was large enough to ensure that the governing party would have an absolute majority of seats in the Assembly even before any ballots were cast.

The Liberals' record in the area of electoral legislation between 1897 and 1929 was hardly glorious. The system served them well and they had little reason to change it. The opposition criticized the government for being corrupt, but it was unable to defeat the Liberals and failed to tackle the crucial problem of the electoral map. The nationalists were disgusted with partisan politics and as they hoped that the rural population, "more wholesome" than people in the cities, would one day vote correctly, they too were held back from criticizing the massive disproportion between urban and rural constituencies. It took the excesses of the 1931 and 1935 elections to spark a brief round of indignation.

CHAPTER 33
THE REIGN OF THE LIBERALS

Premiers in Laurier's Shadow: Marchand and Parent

As we have seen, the years 1896-97 were an economic turning point. They also marked the beginning of a new political era with the accession of Wilfrid Laurier to the office of prime minister of Canada. It was the first time since Confederation that the federal government had been headed by a French Canadian, and this aroused high hopes among Quebecers.

Laurier's victory in the 1896 federal election was not won without a struggle. Almost all of Quebec's bishops supported the Conservatives, who had promised to bring in special legislation to re-establish the educational rights of Manitoba's French-Canadian minority. Laurier came out against such a measure, arguing that it would be impossible to implement and that the only way of solving the problem was to negotiate a compromise with the Manitoba government. He promised to negotiate a satisfactory agreement if he was elected and asked to voters to place their trust in him.

The bishops were not prepared to give him carte blanche in this way, but the Liberals nevertheless won a smashing victory in Quebec, taking forty-nine seats as compared with only sixteen for the Conservatives. Since this thirty-three seat margin in Quebec was about equal to Laurier's majority in the House of Commons, Quebec's role in the election was clearly decisive.

Laurier had engaged in battle with the bishops and won, but unlike some of his supporters, he did not want to get involved in a war between church and state. In an effort to restore calm in episcopal circles, he sent a delegation to Rome, which resulted in the appointment by the pope of Mgr Merry del Val to inquire into the situation. Laurier's dealings with the Vatican were not to be without consequence for the future of Quebec.

TABLE 52
Quebec Provincial General Elections, 1897-1931

Year	*Regis-tered Voters*	*Valid Ballots*	*Seats*	*Number Elected*			*Vote %*	
				Lib.	*Cons.*	*Others*	*Lib.*	*Cons.*
1897	338,800	225,179	74	51	23	—	54.3	45.7
1900	350,517	103,422	74	67	7	—	56.3	43.8
1904	381,933	113,453	74	68	6	—	67.7	25.4
1908	415,801	243,869	74	58	13	3	55.3	39.9
1912	479,521	291,148	81	64	15	2	54.3	45.1
1916	486,136	208,462	81	75	6	—	64.6	35.1
1919	480,120	129,636	81	74	5	2	70.0	23.7
1923	513,224	290,649	85	64	19	2	55.3	44.4
1927	567,907	318,012	85	75	9	1	62.7	36.6
1931	639,005	489,695	90	79	11	—	55.6	44.2

Source: *Quebec Yearbook, 1967-1968.*

The provincial Conservatives were still in power in Quebec City at the time of Laurier's victory, but they felt seriously threatened. Last elected in 1892, they waited until 1897 before facing the electorate again. The Quebec Liberals, under the leadership of F.-G. Marchand, received such massive support from their federal colleagues that it appeared that Quebecers were voting more for Laurier than for Marchand. The provincial leader's authority was not very great in Laurier's eyes. Consideration had been given in some Liberal circles to getting rid of him just before the election, but he had managed to navigate his way around the shoals; his position was strengthened by the results of the election, in which he won fifty-one of the seventy-four seats in the Legislative Assembly (see Table 52).

Marchand was, in fact, a very experienced politician. An MLA since 1867, he had been a minister in the Joly government and speaker of the Assembly under Mercier. He was a notary by profession but a writer and journalist by inclination. His newspaper, *Le Canada français*, had made him a figure of some note in his home town of Saint-Jean, where he was also a school commissioner. Putting together a cabinet proved to be difficult, as Marchand had to take into account the spoken and unspoken wishes of the federal Liberals, who had played a decisive role in the election. It seems that Laurier wanted Marchand's cabinet to be made up of moderates who would not arouse hostility from the clergy.

The Liberals had promised to clean up Quebec's financial situation, stimulate natural resource development and reform the educational system. As a result of budget cuts and improvement in the economic situation, the Marchand government was able to announce small surpluses in the second and third years of its

Wilfrid Laurier (1841-1919), prime minister of Canada, 1896-1911.

term. This achievement won the government considerable acclaim and was regarded as a sure sign of effective administration. The natural resource sector was entrusted to the minister of lands, S.-N. Parent. Under his guidance, both Quebec's economic activity and the public coffers grew as the government's income from forest and waterfall development increased considerably.

As soon as he came to power, Premier Marchand began drafting a major bill aimed at substantially reforming the educational system. As noted in chapter 30, however, his plan to replace the superintendent of public instruction with a minister was fiercely opposed by the bishops and led to a quarrel of major proportions between church and state. The conflict was not settled without the interference of the Vatican and the federal government in Quebec's affairs. This concluding battle between the Liberals and the bishops brought to an end the church-state quarrels that had characterized the party's relations with the Catholic hierarchy since the time of Papineau. There would be further skirmishes, and the clergy would vigilantly guard its privileges, but there would be no more conflicts on the same scale as before.

Marchand died after three years in office, his work uncompleted. His record was nevertheless adequate, at least in financial terms. The provincial secretary, Joseph-Emé Robidoux, who had eloquently defended the government's proposal to establish a Department of Public Instruction and supported free textbooks, hoped to succeed him, but he was considered too radical and was shunted aside. Simon-Napoléon Parent, a lawyer, mayor of Quebec City, president of the Quebec Bridge Company, director of *Le Soleil* and Quebec Light Heat and Power,

Félix-Gabriel Marchand (1832-1900), premier of Quebec, 1897-1900.

Simon-Napoléon Parent (1855-1920), premier of Quebec, 1900-5.

and minister of lands, forests and fisheries since 1897, was considered a better candidate. While Parent's reputation as an administrator and an important businessman stood in his favour, his unswerving loyalty to Laurier and his position as chief dispenser of patronage — municipal, provincial and federal — in the Quebec City area were undoubtedly his chief claims to the succession.

Almost immediately after he was sworn in as premier, Parent plunged into the federal election campaign of 1900. Despite the crisis touched off by Canadian participation in the Boer War, Laurier, whom French Canadians greatly admired, won easily. Soon after Laurier's victory, Premier Parent called a provincial election. His hasty action was not very democratic, but he wanted to take advantage of the Liberal wave that was sweeping Quebec in 1900.

The Conservatives, in a fairly demoralized state, accused Parent of being a paid agent of Laurier and endangering Quebec's autonomy. They also charged him with squandering the national birthright for the benefit of foreigners. These charges evidently made little impression with the voters, as thirty-five Liberals were elected by acclamation and thirty-two more won seats on election day, while the Conservative contingent in the Assembly was reduced to seven. In the constituencies where voting took place, the Liberals took 56.3 per cent of the popular vote, compared with 43.8 per cent for the Conservatives.

Parent was acutely aware that hydroelecricity and the growing importance of the Quebec forest to the North American economy were leading the province into a new economic era. Even after he became premier, he retained the lands, mines and fisheries portfolio and in 1904 he announced with great pleasure that his department had earned the treasury a record amount of $1.36 million. The burgeoning sales of waterfalls and forest rights made it possible for his government to announce a surplus each year.

While the government's economic policy appeared profitable in the short run, its opponents criticized the Liberals for giving Quebec's birthright away to foreigners. It didn't matter to Parent whether the capital was foreign or indigenous; he was interested only in natural resource development, economic growth and job creation. His policies were beneficial to capitalists, as shown by his action in lowering the export duty on pulpwood from $1.50 to $.65 a cord. He was afraid of appearing to demand too much of capitalists who "provide the population with work" — in some regions, the lumber camps were the main source of income for colonists and a significant supplementary source for farmers. The premier was so thoroughly convinced of the need to take the side of the forest entrepreneurs that he abolished the Department of Colonization outright. Through this measure, he made enemies among conservatives and nationalists for whom colonization was a very important activity. In addition, Parent was showered with accusations of poor administration of public lands and corruption in his capacity as minister of lands.

In short, under Parent Quebec had a "business government," as it was called by *La Presse*, which summed up the 1901 session of the Assembly as follows: "The session that has just been completed in Quebec City bears the stamp of a great practical spirit. The dream of those who have wanted to introduce business principles pure and simple into our provincial institutions has been realized." This was true for the entire span of the Parent administration, from 1900 to 1905. In 1904, Parent won another easy election victory by using the same tactic as in 1900, sneaking in on the coattails of Laurier, who had just been re-elected again in Ottawa. On November 4, just after Laurier's victory, Parent dissolved the Assembly and called an election for November 25, with nominations to close on November 18! The Conservatives, demoralized by the defeat of their party in the federal election, had to choose candidates in sixty-four constituencies in thirteen days. The Conservative leader, Edmund James Flynn, considered suggesting to his supporters that they boycott the election and not run any candidates to protest the antidemocratic attitude of the government. His suggestion was not followed, and the Liberals won sixty-eight seats, thirty-eight of them by acclamation, as opposed to six for the Conservatives, whose share of the popular vote fell to 25.4 per cent.

It was, however, a dubious victory for Parent. With no strong Conservative opposition on the electoral stage, a reaction against the premier's pro-business and autocratic methods grew up in his own party. He was publicly accused of corruption by some federal Liberals, including Henri Bourassa and, most notably, two senators, Joseph-Hormisdas Legris and Philippe-Auguste Choquette. In a number of constituencies, there was a battle between pro-Parent and anti-Parent Liberals. After the election, the party was divided and Parent's position was compromised to the extent that not even Laurier himself was able to prevent his fall. Some ministers quit the cabinet, obtained support from a majority of the Liberal caucus in the Assembly and forced the premier to resign.

Lomer Gouin

Lomer Gouin was a lawyer and son-in-law of former Premier Honoré Mercier, and was considered a radical because he supported educational reform. His political career began with a defeat at the federal level, but he succeeded in getting elected as a Montreal alderman and a provincial MLA in 1897 and became minister of colonization and public works in 1900. Three years later he showed that he was prepared to clash with Laurier himself, as he vigorously espoused a constitutional amendment that would raise the federal subsidy to the provinces. Gouin saw himself as following in Mercier's footsteps, and unlike Parent did not consider himself bound to the federal leader.

His standing as an important figure in the party was high enough that in 1905 he was able to take the leadership of the movement that overthrew Parent. Once he had achieved power, he remained there for fifteen years. This long reign represented a contrast to the premiers who had preceded Gouin, none of whom had remained in office for more than six years. Gouin's strength was consultation and

Lomer Gouin (1861-1929), premier of Quebec, 1905-20.

compromise rather than decisive action; he used these skills to impose his authority within the party and succeeded in making his administration very stable. Under his leadership, the government broadened its scope of activity and became more modern. Although its financial means were still limited and it continued to pay lip service to economic liberalism in its purest form, the government was increasingly involved in regulating the province's economic life — especially the natural resource sector — and was more active in infrastructure development, manpower training and modernizing the state apparatus.

Nevertheless, Gouin was a cautious administrator. He was proud of the budget surpluses he announced each year, and he endeavoured to reduce the provincial debt despite the government's ambitious roads program. His conservative fiscal management won him almost unanimous acclaim. The government was able both to obtain an increase in the federal subsidy and to draw substantial revenues from the public domain; most important, it made increasing use of its fiscal powers and levied a variety of taxes: corporate taxes, a tax on stock exchange transactions, a liquor tax, a tax on automobiles. Overall, however, Gouin's administration was, if not timid, at least very cautious in the financial sphere; it is not clear, for instance, that the government benefited as much as it could have from natural resource development.

Ontario brought the production and distribution of electricity under public ownership in 1906, but the Gouin government did not follow its lead; instead, under pressure from the nationalists, it brought in a series of measures to eliminate the worst abuses. Thus, it no longer sold hydraulic resources but leased them on a long-term basis; in some cases, it also tried to dampen speculation and encourage industrialization by requiring leaseholders to use their sites within a fairly short period time. With similar ends in mind, it established the Water-Course Commission in 1914.

In 1910, the government placed an embargo on the export of pulpwood cut on public lands; the wood now had to be processed into pulp or paper before being exported. There is no doubt that this measure stimulated the pulp and paper industry, the output of which rose from $7.4 million in 1905 to $64.5 million in 1919.

The government also devoted considerable effort to developing the road network, as roads were regarded as a key factor in economic growth. In the colonization regions, roads were necessary to put agriculture on a commercial basis and develop the forest industry; in the cities and towns, they were important not only for industry and commerce but also for personal travel by car, an increasingly popular activity in the 1910s and 1920s. The government tried, of course, to shift some of the financial burden of road building onto the municipalities. Increasingly, however, it was called upon to assume the greater share of road expenditures and take charge of planning and organizing development of the road system. This turned out to have highly beneficial consequences for the government at election time.

Education was another cause to which the Gouin government gave a new impetus. Gouin himself considered education the principal instrument of individual and collective advancement. He became a member of the Catholic committee of the Council of Public Instruction in 1898, and throughout his public career was actively concerned with education. In 1920, after his resignation as premier, he became president of the University of Montreal, and chaired two commissions of inquiry into the Montreal Catholic School Commission. There is no doubt that he was in favour of profound changes in the educational system, but he had to reckon with the clergy and he was forced to disavow — at least officially — his "radical" friends who advocated compulsory education. He also had to reckon with the municipalities, more concerned with keeping taxes as low as possible than with achieving progress in education. Thus, the reforms carried out by the Gouin government were limited ones. Teachers' salaries remained at a pathetic level, education was neither free nor compulsory, and the public education system suffered from many deficiencies. However, as noted in chapter 30, Gouin succeeded in establishing under government authority a system of vocational and technical education that developed alongside the general education system; this new system comprised the École des Hautes Études Commerciales, the technical schools, and other institutions.

While Gouin quickly imposed his authority as party leader and premier, he was vigorously challenged by the nationalists, who criticized him for tolerating corruption, turning Quebec's natural resources over to foreigners, and neglecting agriculture and colonization. The moribund Conservative opposition could only take heart in the virulent attacks that Henri Bourassa, Armand Lavergne and the newspaper *Le Nationaliste* unleashed against the government. As noted in chapter 32, Conservatives and nationalists pooled their efforts in 1908 to try to beat the Liberals; after a particularly lively campaign, they won a moral victory but only thirteen seats, with almost forty-five per cent of the popular vote. The Liberals still had a solid majority, but they had lost ten seats and about twelve per cent of the vote. In addition, Premier Gouin had suffered a humiliating defeat in the constituency of Saint-Jacques at the hands of Henri Bourassa, although he had taken the precaution of running in another constituency (Portneuf) at the same time, as the law permitted. The nationalist leader, elected in both Saint-Jacques and Saint-Hyacinthe, came out of the election with increased stature. Between 1908 and 1912, the government was pressed hard by the opposition and had to turn in a better legislative performance; these were undoubtedly the Gouin government's most productive years.

Despite Bourassa's retirement from the political scene, the nationalists continued to support the Conservatives. But the imperialism of the federal Conservatives, who came to power in Ottawa in 1911, the question of French schools in Ontario and wartime policies all helped turn the tide again towards the Liberals, who knew how to take full advantage of the situation. During the 1916 election campaign, Bourassa, although he had some reservations about the Gouin government, wrote a vitriolic editorial attacking the provincial Conservative leader. Meanwhile, Armand Lavergne decided not to run in his constituency. The Conservatives also had no program and had lost the initiative to the Liberals, who won easily, taking seventy-five seats — twenty-three by acclamation — as opposed to only six for the Conservatives, who nevertheless managed to retain thirty-five per cent of the popular vote. The conscription crisis of 1917 only made the Conservatives' situation worse. In the 1919 Quebec election, they won only five seats and 23.7 per cent of the popular vote, their lowest percentage since Confederation. The Liberals were victorious with seventy per cent of the vote and seventy-four seats, of which they won forty-three by acclamation.

The war not only allowed Gouin to defeat his opponents easily, but also provided an opportunity for him to win the respect of the nationalists. In a way, Gouin became the leading political spokesman of the French-Canadian people. He did, of course, participate actively in the Canadian war effort. The Quebec government sent gifts to England and Gouin endorsed charity campaigns, war bond sales and voluntary enlistment. But he vigorously opposed conscription and advised Laurier to do the same, whatever might happen; otherwise, Gouin warned, Quebec would fall to the nationalists. After conscription took effect Gouin allowed a member of his caucus, J.-N. Francoeur, to present a sensational motion: "This chamber is of the opinion that the province of Quebec would be inclined to accept the breaking of the 1867 confederation agreement if, in the other provinces, it was thought that the province of Quebec was an obstacle to the progress and development of Canada."

With a large number of reporters from both the French- and the English-language press in attendance, a series of MLAs took the floor to attack the slanders perpetrated against Quebec and the French-Canadian people and denounce the unjust fate reserved for French-speaking minorities, especially in Ontario. Gouin himself delivered a major speech that was eagerly anticipated. But despite all their criticisms, Gouin and the other speakers continued to profess their faith in federalism and their attachment to Canada. French Canadians were grateful to Gouin for having expressed their grievances while English Canadians were satisfied because Quebec was observing the law and not issuing a challenge to the federal system. Since the nationalists were also federalists, they could only support Gouin and wait for their chance to take revenge against the Conservatives. The Francoeur motion, which was only symbolic in any case, was withdrawn before a vote on it could be taken.

Canada was deeply divided by conscription, and the tension reached a breaking point in March and April 1918. A riot broke out in Quebec City and the federal government sent in the army; four civilians were killed and a number of others were injured. The image of the Conservative party, already damaged by Regulation 17, which limited teaching in French in Ontario schools, was further tarnished. The Gouin government had authorized Quebec's Catholic school commissions to provide financial aid to the French schools in Ontario that were

FETE DU JOUR: Saint Thomas

BEAU ET FROID

LA PRESSE

Le plus fort tirage des journaux du Canada tout entier, plus de 140,000 copies par jour

34me ANNEE—No 42 EDITION QUOTIDIENNE—MONTREAL VENDREDI 21 DECEMBRE 1917

POUR FAIRE SORTIR QUEBEC DE LA CONFEDERATION CANADIENNE

(Spécial à la "Presse")

Québec, 21.—A la séance d'aujourd'hui, à l'Assemblée Législative, M. J.-N. Francoeur, député libéral de Lotbinière, a donné avis qu'à la prochaine séance de l'assemblée législative, il proposera la motion suivante :

"Que cette Chambre est d'avis que la province de Québec serait disposée à accepter la rupture du pacte fédéral de 1867, si, dans l'opinion des autres provinces, la dite province est un obstacle à l'union, au progrès et au développement du Canada." M. Francoeur est le président du comité des bills privés.

LE REFERENDUM EN AUSTRALIE

LES ANTICONSCRIPTIONNISTES AUSTRALIENS ONT DEJA OBTENU UNE MAJORITE DE 150,000 VOIX

Jusqu'ici les dépêches indiquent que les citoyens du Commonwealth vont se prononcer contre la conscription, mais par une majorité beaucoup plus forte que l'an dernier.

REVIREMENT D'OPINION A VICTORIA

LES PREMIERS RAPPORTS

LE RAPPORT DE LA COMMISSION DES TRAMWAYS

ARRESTATION DE 150 AGITATEURS

LA RUSSIE ET LE JAPON UNIS CONTRE LA GRANDE-BRETAGNE

NOS DEPUTES EN VACANCES

LE DUC DE CONNAUGHT MALADE EN ANGLETERRE

UNE JOLIE FORTUNE

LA CRISE DU CHARBON

MESSAGE FRATERNEL

MOT D'ENCOURAGEMENT ET DE SYMPATHIE D'UN JOURNALISTE ONTARIEN

La province de Québec n'est pas isolée, ayant avec elle la grande majorité des provinces maritimes. —"Parler de châtier Québec est absurde".

"LA GUERRE METTRA FIN A LA GUERRE"

HERTLING A L'AUTORISATION DE CONCLURE LA PAIX

Le Kaiser donne à son chancelier le pouvoir de mettre fin à la guerre.—Qu'adviendra-t-il ? —Voyage significatif du secrétaire des affaires étrangères.

DES SCENES D'ENTHOUSIASME

VON HERTLING, chancelier impérial allemand

AIDE DE L'ARGENTINE

UNE GRANDE FOULE AU MARCHE DE NOEL

UN PAYS LOYAL

LA MAISON SWIFT GARDE SES SECRETS

PRECIEUSE CARGAISON

DE RUDES COMBATS AU FRONT FRANCAIS

UNE CATASTROPHE

UNE PERTE SENSIBLE

The Francoeur motion caused a sensation in the Quebec press. The headline in *La Presse* reads: "TO TAKE QUEBEC OUT OF THE CANADIAN CONFEDERATION."

resisting Regulation 17. The Quebec Conservative leader, Philémon Cousineau, had opposed the government's measure, and this gaffe gained him the hostility of the nationalists.

More generally, Gouin, like his father-in-law Honoré Mercier, staked out a position as a defender of provincial autonomy; while remaining an orthodox Liberal, he managed to keep his distance from Laurier. In 1920, Gouin resigned at the height of his reputation, leaving one of his ministers, Louis-Alexandre Taschereau, to succeed him. Gouin later returned to active politics at the federal level and became minister of justice.

Louis-Alexandre Taschereau

The new administration of Louis-Alexandre Taschereau remained in power until 1936. Taschereau had been in the Legislative Assembly since 1900 and in the cabinet since 1907, and came from a distinguished family that had produced lieutenant governors, a federal minister, a supreme court justice and a cardinal. The new premier himself was a lawyer and businessman who was thoroughly accustomed to political life and administration. Secure in his large majority in the Assembly, he brought in two major bills that aroused considerable public discussion: the Public Charities Act and the bill to establish the Liquor Commission. In other areas he followed in the footsteps of Lomer Gouin, especially in education and roads policy. The recession of 1921-22, however, forced the government to slow down its activities, as its policy was still to remain faithful to the sacred principle of the balanced budget.

As noted in chapter 27, postwar readjustment and the recession that followed made life extremely difficult for Quebec's farmers; there was an increase not only in emigration to the cities and the United States, but also in militancy and attempts at political action. The government, especially Agriculture Minister J.-E. Caron, took great pains to counter this embryonic agrarian protest, which threatened the Liberals' political base. The situation was not much brighter in the cities, especially in Montreal, where there were complaints about the rising cost of living and the control of the city by business and the provincial government. The clergy, the nationalists and the Conservatives were once again advocating the *retour à la terre* (the return to the land) as a cure for emigration. The Taschereau government believed that, on the contrary, the solution was industrialization, but it bowed to the pressure by bringing in modest increases in credit for agriculture and colonization.

It looked as if the 1923 election would be difficult for the government. The federal Liberals lent a helping hand to their provincial colleagues, while the provincial Conservatives, afraid of reviving the memory of conscription, waged their campaign on their own. The Conservatives attacked the government for its policy of excessive industrialization that benefited foreigners and accused it of neglecting agriculture and colonization, which they regarded as priorities. They

Louis-Alexandre Taschereau (1867-1952), premier of Quebec 1920-36.

attacked the government's tendency towards state control, as manifested in the Public Charities Act and the Liquor Commission, "which is poisoning our race." They promised to have more respect for municipal autonomy, especially with regard to Montreal, and denounced the tyranny and corruption of a Liberal government that had been in power too long.

Many of the Conservatives' accusations echoed the criticisms of nationalist and clerical spokesmen. *Le Devoir* and *L'Action Catholique* supported Conservative leader Arthur Sauvé; Henri Bourassa vigorously attacked the Liberal government in a series of editorials, while Armand Lavergne ran against Taschereau in the constituency of Montmorency. It looked like a return to 1908, when Bourassa, in tacit alliance with the Conservatives, ran against Gouin in Saint-Jacques. This support from the nationalists made Sauvé suspect in the eyes of the English-language press and the Conservatives' financial backers, while the Liberals eagerly recalled the nationalists' "treason" that led to the defeat of Laurier in 1911 and his replacement by the pro-conscription Conservatives.

But the war was over, Sauvé had dissociated himself from the federal Conservatives and his criticisms struck a responsive chord in the population. The Conservatives received 44.4 per cent of the popular vote, almost double their vote in 1919. They won an impressive victory on Montreal Island, taking thirteen of the fifteen seats, as well as two of the four Quebec City seats and the urban constituencies of Sherbrooke and Beauharnois. However, they were unable to make a dent in rural Quebec, which remained a Liberal stronghold, paradoxical as that may seem for a party whose policies were based on industrialization. In any case, the Conservatives now had nineteen seats in the Assembly instead of five, but the Liberals, with sixty-four seats, still had a solid majority.

The 1927 election was similar to that of 1923 in terms of issues and what was at stake, but circumstances were no longer the same. Economic conditions were much better, the policy of industrialization based on natural resource development appeared to be bearing fruit, and output was increasing in nearly all sectors of the economy.

The Taschereau government was not slow in claiming credit for this prosperity. In fact, the Liberals had been untiring in their efforts to attract foreign capital to Quebec, taking every opportunity to extol the province's abundant natural resources, its hydroelectric potential, its docile and hard-working labour force and its government sympathetic to private enterprise. Hoping to attract even more corporations and create more jobs to stem the flow of Quebecers to the south, the government opposed the idea of a St. Lawrence seaway and electricity exports to the United States. Taschereau never stopped reiterating that it was better to import foreign capital than to export Quebecers to the United States. The government strongly upheld its accomplishments — the Liquor Commission; the Workmen's Compensation Act, which it had undertaken to improve; the metropolitan commission, which aimed to achieve a better distribution of the fiscal burden of the municipalities.

The Conservatives, again under Sauvé's leadership, were divided and short of ideas and had limited means at their disposal. The Conservative English-language newspapers did not support them and the Montreal business community was hostile to them. Again, their only allies were the nationalists and the clerical press. The opposition attacked foreign control of the Quebec economy and intensive industrialization at the expense of farmers and colonists. There was an attempt to make a scandal out of what the Conservatives called "the Lake St. John tragedy," an operation in which the Duke-Price Company had purchased arable land and then flooded it to increase its potential electricity output.

Sauvé went down to his third consecutive defeat; discouraged, he submitted his resignation. He was succeeded by Camillien Houde, the mayor of Montreal and an MLA. The depression that began in 1929 and the results of the 1930 federal election, in which the Conservatives returned to power and made a breakthrough in Quebec, augured well for the new leader. But Houde ran into the same difficulties as his predecessor, and the long Liberal reign lasted yet another few years.

Thus, during the first three decades of the twentieth century, the political scene was dominated by the Liberals, who obtained between fifty-four and seventy per cent of the popular vote in the nine elections held between 1897 and 1927. There were even two occasions, in 1904 and 1919, when the Liberals won a majority of seats in the Assembly before election day as a result of the large number of candidates elected by acclamation. As noted in chapter 32, Liberal strength was amplified to an extraordinary degree by the voting system and the electoral map; they won more than ninety per cent of the seats on four occasions and never obtained less than sixty-nine per cent. This situation was beneficial to the party in power in terms of organization, financing and that great political gift, patronage.

It must be said that in terms of both political theory and action, the Liberals were more coherent and dynamic than the Conservatives, who never seemed to gain the initiative from their rivals on the ideological level. There is also reason to believe that the Liberals' industrialization policy was approved of not only by urban Quebecers, but also by the rural population, which benefited from its side-effects.

A final factor in the Liberals' favour was the support of their federal colleagues, who maintained their image as defenders of French-Canadian interests, while the provincial Conservatives were continually forced to dissociate themselves from the federal party and its anti-French image. These circumstances created the impression that the Liberals were invincible, and help explain why the nationalists became discouraged and despaired of political parties and the possibility of democratic change through the political system.

CHAPTER 34
FEDERAL-PROVINCIAL RELATIONS

In the 1867-96 period, the balance between the federal government and the provinces was modified substantially. The main feature of the balance that prevailed during the first three decades of the twentieth century was the sovereignty of the provinces in areas under their jurisdiction; for practical purposes, the powers of the federal government were limited to those listed in Article 91 of the BNA Act. This made for a form of federalism where, in theory, the two levels of government had equal status instead of one's being subordinate to the other; however, the theory did not apply during the war when, as a result of the emergency powers granted to it under the constitution, the federal government was dominant.

A New Balance

In 1896, a new set of circumstances favoured provincial autonomy. First, there was the coming to power in Ottawa of the Liberals who, while in opposition, had often advocated greater respect for provincial rights. In addition, the first Laurier government included no fewer than four former provincial premiers—Joly of Quebec, Blair of New Brunswick, Fielding of Nova Scotia and Mowat of Ontario; both Fielding and Mowat had been vigorous defenders of provincial autonomy. At the same time, Canada was entering an era of economic prosperity, largely based on the development of natural resources, a provincial responsibility. At the turn of the century, Quebec, Ontario and British Columbia were becoming involved in a new phase of industrialization, in which forests, hydraulic power and mines were increasingly important. It is significant that in this period governments preferred to resolve constitutional problems through federal-provincial or interprovincial conferences rather than by resorting to disallowance or Privy Council decisions. While between 1867 and 1896 there had been only one interprovincial conference, in which Ottawa had refused to participate, in the 1896-1930 period there were no fewer than seven formal meetings between the two levels of government.

Three stages in the development of federal-provincial relations can be identified: 1896-1914, the wartime period, and the 1920s. The first was marked by financial demands on the part of the provinces. As federal subsidies were fixed, they represented a steadily declining share of provincial revenues, while the needs of the provinces were increasing with rapid urbanization and population growth. In 1902, the provincial premiers joined forces to demand increased subsidies. On this occasion their demand was refused, but four years later Prime Minister Laurier called a federal-provincial conference, at the end of which he agreed to increase the subsidies by about a third and readjust them according to population at each census. The next conference, in 1910, did not discuss federal subsidies, but dealt only with the representation of the maritime provinces in the House of Commons. In 1913, however, the provinces took up the torch again and demanded that each year, in addition to the statutory subsidies, the federal government pay them ten per cent of its proceeds from excise taxes and customs duties.

Despite the increases provided for in 1907, federal subsidies represented only 28.6 per cent of provincial revenues by 1913, while proceeds from the public domain and the sale of permits and licences represented fifty per cent. To provide the remaining part of their revenues, the provinces had to resort increasingly to direct taxes (20.7 per cent). Just before the war, total provincial expenditures reached a level equivalent to half those of the federal government, a milestone that provides evidence of the increasing role played by the provincial governments in Canada's physical development and social organization.

The outbreak of war in 1914 put a stop to this trend and gave new impetus to federal centralization. Citing the emergency situation, the federal government had the War Measures Act passed, giving it wide powers to mobilize the population and the economy. The war effort made it necessary for the government to resort to borrowing and use its fiscal powers to the maximum. The government levied a tax on corporate profits for the first time in 1916 and the first personal income tax in 1917; it intended to withdraw from these tax fields, hitherto considered exclusively provincial, after the war. The government also considered placing controls on provincial borrowing but, faced with protests from Quebec and Ontario, never put this measure into effect.

As a result of the country's spectacular war effort, the productive capacity of the Canadian economy grew considerably and Canada established its presence on the international stage. On the debit side, however, the country was deeply divided ethnically, socially and regionally. The enormous needs the provinces had to fulfil made them all the more critical of the Conservative government. Ottawa refused to abandon the two major direct tax fields it had occupied during the war, offering instead to provide aid to the neediest provinces in the form of loans. In this way, it came to use a financial instrument that would play a very important role later on — conditional subsidies for specific programs. This method of financing had been used for the first time in 1912 for agricultural programs and had not aroused any opposition at the time; now, Ottawa used it for programs in the areas of health (venereal disease) and education (technical education).

But Ottawa's centralizing attitude did not go very far, and the 1920s were characterized by the weakening of the federal government. As a result of the war effort and the bankruptcy of federally-backed railways, the public debt increased sevenfold between 1913 and 1920. The government wanted to return to an orthodox financial policy — debt reduction, lower taxes, a balanced budget — and the only major social measure of the period was the introduction of old-age pensions in 1927. Ottawa committed itself to paying 50 per cent of the cost of pensions paid to old people in provinces participating in the agreement. Provinces that rejected this intrusion into an area under their jurisdiction were victims of a clear injustice, as their citizens paid taxes for a service they did not receive, but it was a singularly effective way of forcing the provinces to bend to priorities determined by Ottawa. Quebec was the last province to yield, in 1936. This kind of arrangement, however, was an exceptional case in the pre-1930 period.

Meanwhile, development of industries based on natural resources and the growing importance of the automobile made it possible for the provinces to play a major role in the economy. Not only did they have to invest more in infrastructure, but they also had to assume responsibilities in areas such as health and education that were now beyond the scope of municipal action. As a result, the provinces had to find new sources of revenue. The yield of the major direct taxes increased with prosperity, especially since the federal government's demands in this area were quite moderate. Liquor sales and automobile licences were notable revenue producers. In addition, taxes on consumption became part of the provinces' array of fiscal instruments — amusement tax, gasoline tax, tobacco tax, sales tax.

All in all, it can be said that the twenties were the golden age of provincial autonomy. While the central government had accounted for sixty-four per cent of all public expenditures in 1874, this figure had dropped to forty-six per cent in 1930. Provincial revenues increased by more than 800 per cent between 1896 and 1921, from $11 million to $90 million, and they doubled again between 1921 and 1930, reaching $183.4 million. The provinces also became financially less dependent on the federal government; whereas Ottawa had financed 57.7 per cent of provincial expenditures through statutory subsidies in 1874, the comparable figure for 1930 was 10.3 per cent. At the same time, the provinces replaced the municipalities in the area of social policy.

However, this kind of development led to problems of regional inequality. The

Maritimes and the prairie provinces were not in a position to benefit from industrialization in the same way as Quebec, Ontario and British Columbia, as became clear during the federal-provincial conferences of 1918, 1926 and 1927. The federal government had to come to the assistance of the disadvantaged regions. After the Royal Commission on Maritime Claims (Duncan Commission) issued its report in 1926, it increased subsidies to the Maritimes and gave grants to the railways to lower transportation costs. In 1930, the federal government finally turned administration of natural resources in the prairie provinces over to the provincial governments and compensated them financially for the lack of revenue during the preceding decades. Quebec and Ontario did not resist arrangements of this sort and did not demand subsidies, but British Columbia thought it was being unfairly treated in being classified as one of the more favoured regions.

On the whole, the federal system functioned fairly harmoniously during these years of prosperity. In the 1930s, however, the depression caused the problems of regional and social inequality inherent in Canadian federalism to show up clearly, and brought about a challenge to the fundamental elements of the type of federalism that had developed since 1896.

Quebec's Struggle for Autonomy

To evaluate Quebec's position in the general process described above, two additional questions must be raised: the influence of Quebec leaders on federal political developments and the impact of ethnic conflicts. During the first three decades of the twentieth century, Quebec played a much more active role than it had previously in defending provincial autonomy. Early in the period it stuck to its traditional position, which consisted essentially of demanding more money from Ottawa in the form of statutory subsidies. Thus, in 1899, Premier Marchand brought this subject up with his colleagues in the other provinces. The premier of Ontario showed little enthusiasm for his initiative, preferring that the provinces get their revenue from direct taxes, a very logical attitude for the richest province. Marchand's proposal for a conference on the matter was stalled by his death in 1900, but the idea was taken up again by his successor, S.-N. Parent. The new Ontario government expressed sympathy with Quebec's point of view, and the other provinces were in agreement with it as well, but as noted above it was not until 1907 that the federal government agreed to new financial arrangements. As a result of these new arrangements, Quebec's subsidy was increased from $1,086,000 to $1,686,000 per year.

With the war came a change in strategy. Instead of demanding increases in the federal subsidy, Quebec, like Ontario, now struggled to maintain its share of direct taxes and its financial autonomy. Premier Gouin's threat not to respect the federal regulation that sought to block Quebec from borrowing outside Canada was very significant in this context.

Quebec had to bear federal centralization during the war, but Premier Taschereau vigorously denounced its aftereffects once peace had been restored. He recalled that in 1867 federal subsidies to the provinces represented twenty per cent of Ottawa's revenues, while by 1920 that figure was only two per cent. Instead of giving money to the provinces, Taschereau said, Ottawa was interfering in areas of provincial jurisdiction such as roads, education and agriculture. He added: "Ottawa taxes our income, taxes profits, taxes commercial corporations, taxes sales, taxes everything. If our own revenue is insufficient, we have no alternative left but to raise all these same taxes, which are already quite high. Ottawa has unceremoniously taken for itself our own sources of revenue."

But the situation straightened itself out during the 1920s. Quebec defended its autonomy more vigorously and, in concert with Ontario, carefully made use of its own tax fields instead of demanding subsidies. Taschereau attacked the federal government's attempts to interfere in the natural resource sector and challenged its authority in the new area of broadcasting. It was also in the name of provincial autonomy that he resisted all proposals for a St. Lawrence seaway and rejected the federal old-age pension plan. Meanwhile, he succeeded in obtaining full jurisdiction in the area of fisheries and did not hesitate to resort to the sales tax, despite opposition arguments that it was an indirect tax and therefore reserved for Ottawa. In short, during the 1920s Premier Taschereau was a vigilant defender of provincial autonomy.

The party allegiances of political leaders and the links between them sometimes affected the course of federal-provincial relations. Thus, early in the period being discussed, Laurier's prestige was such that it tended to blur the lines of demarcation between the two levels of government and place Quebec's leaders in a state of dependency with respect to Ottawa. F.-G. Marchand, who took power in Quebec in the wake of Laurier's victory, had to consult the federal leader before forming his cabinet. That the Marchand government was forced to withdraw its proposal to establish a Department of Public Instruction was a notably unfortunate consequence of this dependence. As mentioned earlier, S.-N. Parent, who became premier in 1900, was a loyal servant of Laurier and close relations prevailed between the federal and provincial wings of the Liberal party. However, the situation changed somewhat with Lomer Gouin, who came to power on his own.

When the Conservatives were in power in Ottawa, Gouin came increasingly to be regarded as the spokesman for Quebec. This role was inherited by Taschereau who, while maintaining close links between the two wings of the Liberal party, was nevertheless quick to take up the cause of provincial autonomy. This mediation of federal-provincial relations through the Liberal party was undoubtedly one reason for the degree of harmony that prevailed during the period.

But Canadian federalism is also based on the co-existence of French and English Canadians within the same political structure. This period was marked by ethnic conflicts over minority schools and the conscription crisis. Despite the seriousness of these conflicts, they were not a challenge to federalism; they were, however, a major threat to the Conservative party, as the federal Liberals were able to turn the situation to their full advantage.

As a result of Henri Bourassa's influence, the attention of the Quebec nationalists was turned more towards Ottawa than towards Quebec City. They were in favour of provincial autonomy, but they were interested primarily in federal politics. They continued to hope that by maintaining a strong presence in Ottawa they would be able to correct the injustices perpetrated against French minorities outside Quebec and persuade a majority of Canadians not to allow themselves to be led into imperial wars.

After the extremely disappointing experiences with Regulation 17 and conscription, nationalist attention in the 1920s turned more towards Quebec. The inspiration this time came from the Action Française group and its leading figure, Abbé Groulx. The nationalists of the Action Française toyed with the idea of independence for a time but eventually moderated their stand, advocating respect for the Confederation "compact" and reiterating traditional nationalist demands —justice for the French minorities outside Quebec, respect for bilingualism in Ottawa and within Quebec, more French Canadians in the federal civil service, a degree of Quebec control over immigration policy. In essence, they supported Taschereau's policy of upholding Quebec's autonomy with regard to Ottawa, although they attacked his economic policy through which Quebec's wealth was given away to foreigners.

French Canadians and the Federal Government

While Quebec continued to have sixty-five seats in the House of Commons in Ottawa, its relative power tended to decline as the population of Canada increased. In 1896, Quebec MPs occupied thirty per cent of the seats in the House, while in 1926 this figure was only 26.4 per cent. Throughout this period, a large majority of Quebec's MPs were Liberals, and this affected the extent to which Quebec was represented in the cabinet. In a cabinet consisting of about twenty members, between four and six were from Quebec, one or two of these being English Quebecers. As before, Quebecers were generally given secondary portfolios and were often put in charge of departments notable for their patronage potential. Of course, this general model varied according to circumstances and according to which party was in power.

Between 1896 and 1911 Quebec had five ministers, two of them English-speaking, and Quebecers gained satisfaction primarily from the fact that one of their number was the leader of the country. In a climate of good relations between provincial and federal Liberals and economic prosperity, Quebec received its share of patronage and public investment. But it must not be forgotten that Ontario was the centre of power, and Laurier was surrounded by influential Ontario ministers. He also had to accept compromise on questions of minority rights and relations between Britain and Canada. Quebec nationalists reacted to these disappointments and ultimately rebelled against the French-Canadian leader, joining ranks with the Conservatives in 1911. On that occasion, Quebecers elected enough Conservatives and nationalists to participate actively in the

Conservative government of Robert Laird Borden. The new prime minister, however, had enough support in the other provinces to govern without Quebec, and the Quebec caucus was internally divided and included very few men of stature. Quebec had about five cabinet positions, two of which went to English-speaking ministers, but between 1911 and 1917 the Quebec ministers had little prestige in their own province and little influence in Ottawa.

In 1917, in an effort to win acceptance for their conscription policy, the Conservatives invited the Liberals to join them in a coalition and establish a Union government. French-speaking MPs and some of their English-speaking colleagues, united behind Laurier, refused the invitation, while a majority of English-speaking Liberals agreed to join the Conservatives. Between 1917 and 1921, under the Union government, Quebec's influence was almost nonexistent. Once the government had imposed conscription, the few French Canadians who collaborated with it were denounced as traitors. There were two English Quebecers in the Union cabinet and only one French Canadian, P.-E. Blondin, who had not been elected and had to be appointed to the Senate. When Arthur Meighen succeeded Borden in 1920, he named a few French Canadians to the cabinet. In 1921, Quebec responded by electing sixty-five Liberals and no Conservatives.

Under the leadership of William Lyon Mackenzie King, chosen as Laurier's successor in 1919, the Liberals held power from 1921 to 1930 except for a brief interruption of a few months in 1926. King's opposition to conscription had led to his defeat in the 1917 election but had won him faithful support among Quebecers. He did not speak French and did not pretend to understand Quebec. As a result, he left the province in the hands of the Liberal organization and considered it important to have a French-Canadian lieutenant; from 1924 on, this position was held by Ernest Lapointe.

Quebec continued to have between four and six ministers in the traditional portfolios. Provincial and federal Liberals maintained good relations and the King-Lapointe tandem tried not to have too many run-ins with Taschereau. This did not prevent the federal government from offering only a very weak defence of Quebec's interests in the Labrador affair or from bringing in the Old-Age Pensions Act, despite Taschereau's objection, to attract the support of the western Progressives. Where Quebecers had felt isolated during the 1910s, they had the impression of enjoying an honest degree of influence during the 1920s, with the further satisfaction, repeated at each election, of taking revenge for conscription by wiping out the Conservatives. The nationalists, however, complained that French Canadians were not fairly represented in the civil service and that French was not really recognized in Ottawa. The Liberals tried to soothe them without upsetting the rest of Canada by bringing in harmless measures such as bilingual postage stamps.

The Liberals' formula appeared to work well in Quebec which, with the exception of 1911, gave them massive support throughout the thirty-year period. In some elections, the bloc Liberal vote in Quebec was a determining factor. Thus, in 1896, Laurier's thirty-seat majority was primarily due to his forty-nine seats in

TABLE 53
Distribution between the Two Major Parties of Quebec Seats in the House of Commons 1896-1926

	Liberals		*Conservatives*	
Election	*Seats*	*Vote %*	*Seats*	*Vote %*
1896	49	53.5	16	45.8
1900	57	55.9	8	43.5
1904	53	56.4	11	41.7
1908	54	56.7	11	40.8
1911	38	50.2	27[1]	48.1
1917	62	72.7	3	24.7
1921	65	70.2	0	18.4
1925	59	59.3	4	33.7
1926	60	62.3	4	34.1

[1]This figure includes 10 Conservatives and 17 Conservative Nationalists.

Source: J.M. Beck, *Pendulum of Power.*

Quebec. In 1921, Mackenzie King won 116 seats in Canada as a whole, and Quebec provided sixty-five of these. In 1925, although the Conservatives won 116 seats, the Liberals managed to stay in power with ninety-nine seats, fifty-nine of them from Quebec (Table 53).

The negative side of this situation was that when the Conservatives came to power, Quebecers were poorly represented and had little influence. The Conservative-nationalist alliance of 1911 was based on a misunderstanding and was short-lived. What the nationalists did, in effect, was to express their opposition to Laurier's imperialism by voting for an even more imperialist party. As a result of Bourassa's refusal to provide leadership to the nationalist caucus, within a year most of the nationalists had become orthodox Conservatives, although this did not lead to any change in the balance of forces within the cabinet. Whatever ambivalence remained in Quebecers' minds was removed by conscription and the formation of the Union government in 1917; they were now overwhelmingly opposed to everything *bleu* (Conservative). Not only were they not concerned about being isolated, they were proud of it. Whenever any French-speaking politician who had agreed to collaborate with the Borden or Meighen government dared to face the French-Canadian electorate of Quebec, he could be certain of a resounding defeat. Never had French-Canadian voters been so unanimous as they were during this crisis.

The Conscription Crisis

From the time of the Boer War in 1899, the nationalist movement attacked English imperialism and predicted that sooner or later Canada would be drawn

During the First World War, a variety of propaganda techniques were used to persuade French Canadians to enlist. The poster on the left says, "CANADIANS — IT'S TIME TO ACT — DON'T WAIT TILL THE JERRIES COME SPREAD FIRE AND BLOOD IN CANADA." In the poster on the right, Canadians are urged to "Follow the example of Dollard des Ormeaux — Don't wait by the fireside for the enemy, but go confront him."

into additional and even more murderous imperial wars. The nationalists preached loyalty to Canada and declared themselves eternally ready to fight for the defence of Canadian soil, but they were vehemently opposed to any attempt to require them to defend Britain or any other country, including France. When war broke out in 1914 they did not oppose Canadian participation, but they demanded that this participation be voluntary and kept at a reasonable level. They also argued that if it was appropriate to defend civilization and justice on European soil, perhaps it was equally appropriate to re-establish French-language rights in Canada, and especially in Ontario where the battle over Regulation 17 was raging. A fair place for French-speaking Canadians and respect for French culture and language in the army was a further nationalist demand.

While French Canadians supported the war effort, they were in no hurry to

An anticonscription demonstration in Montreal, 1917.

enlist. For that matter, English-speaking Canadians born in Canada did not answer the call with heedless enthusiasm either, and most of the early recruits were people from Britain living in Canada. In any case, it is clear that French Canadians showed little interest in fighting in Europe. But as the war dragged on, Canada's war effort became more intense. With a population of eight million, Canada had set itself a quota of 500,000 men. Despite the fierce propaganda campaign that was unleashed, it was not possible to reach this figure through voluntary enlistment, especially since the troops were being decimated in the murderous battles taking place in Europe.

In English Canada, Quebec was openly accused of not doing its share, and Prime Minister Borden, responding to the will of the English-speaking majority, brought in a bill to make military service compulsory. There was a vehement

MONTREAL, MARDI 2 AVRIL 1918

CALENDRIER

DERNIÈRE HEURE

LE DEVOIR

Toutes les nouvelles par nos rédacteurs, nos correspondants et les services de dépêches du monde entier

DEMAIN

LE SANG COULE A QUEBEC--5 CITOYENS PAISIBLES TUES

PLUS FORT QU'EN 1916

LES SALAIRES INSUFFISANTS

LE JUGE MARÉCHAL STATUANT DANS UNE CAUSE D'EXEMPTION, FUSTIGE LES PATRONS QUI NE DONNENT PAS LES EMOLUMENTS VOULUS A DES EMPLOYÉS EXPERTS.

LES SOLDATS DE TORONTO FONT FEU SUR LA FOULE

Les émeutiers ayant les premiers tiré sur les troupes, au dire des autorités militaires, les mitrailleuses sont mises en jeu au parc Langelier hier soir, et des innocents, y compris un ouvrier revenant de son travail, tombent sous les balles — Le domicile d'un médecin qui secourt les blessés est bombardé

SOIXANTE-DEUX ARRESTATIONS SONT OPEREES

LES MORTS

(tous des civils)

LES BLESSES

LA MAISON D'UN MEDECIN ATTEINTE PAR LA MITRAILLE

Le maire Lavigueur demande des libérations

UNE AVANCE DES ALLIÉS

Au cours de la nuit, les troupes françaises et anglaises ont progressé entre la Somme et Demuin — Les Tommies capturent une cinquantaine de prisonniers et s'emparent de 13 mitrailleuses.

LA FIN DES OPÉRATIONS D'INFANTERIE

LES ANGLAIS FONT DES PRISONNIERS

PARIS EST ENCORE

The conscription riot in Quebec City in April 1918 was the culmination of anticonscription sentiment in Quebec. The headline in *Le Devoir* reads: "BLOOD FLOWS IN QUEBEC CITY—5 PEACEFUL CITIZENS KILLED. SOLDIERS FROM TORONTO FIRE ON THE CROWD. After rioters had first fired on troops, according to military authorities, machine guns were used in Langelier Park last night, and innocent people, including a worker returning from work, fell under the bullets—The home of a doctor who was tending to the wounded was bombarded. SIXTY-TWO ARRESTS MADE."

reaction in Quebec, and the French-language press, with the exception of the Conservative newspapers *La Patrie* and *L'Événement*, attacked the bill. Anti-conscription leagues were organized, there were many protest meetings, and the summer home of the owner of the *Montreal Star* was dynamited. When the bill was signed by the governor general at the end of August 1917, virtual riots broke out in Montreal—broken windows, street fights, shooting. Archbishop Bruchési, who had demonstrated his unswerving loyalty on the question of Canadian participation, wrote to Borden on August 31: "The people are aroused. They are liable to commit excesses of all kinds. There is one brawl after another. Killings are to be feared in our cities. In the countryside, the people will not yield. They seem determined to go all the way. And there is no one who can calm them down. The life of everyone who has been in favour of the bill or voted for it is in danger."

During the December 1917 election campaign, the population was so angry that the Unionists were unable to hold public meetings. The only Conservatives elected were three English-speaking members, while the Liberals won sixty-two seats. Canada was divided into two blocs, and French Canadians had to submit to the law of the majority. They resisted as best they could under the constraint of the War Measures Act. Many conscripts fled to the woods or hid in lofts; others sought exemptions. The police looked for the missing youths as people's anger smouldered. In late March 1918, a riot broke out in Quebec City. The army intervened, martial law was declared, and soldiers fired on the crowd — five civilians were killed and dozens were injured.

Conscription was a failure; only 19,050 Quebecers were successfully conscripted while 18,827 others refused to submit. Canada came out of the war deeply divided, and the experience had a profound effect on French-Canadian nationalism in the 1920s.

CULTURE AND IDEOLOGY

The socio-economic changes that marked Quebec society at the beginning of the twentieth century were also reflected at the level of ideas. A strong liberal current, centred on themes of modernization, progress and individual effort, provided the ideological support for the changes that Quebec was experiencing. The liberal current was a strong one, but adherence to it was far from unanimous. Intellectuals and clerical spokesmen saw in these changes a threat to French-Canadian culture and advocated a return to traditional values.

This traditionalism was reflected in the literature of the period, which except for the poetry of the École Littéraire de Montréal, continued to be based on traditional models and scarcely reflected Quebec's socio-economic evolution. In contrast, painters were more open to outside influences and found new inspirations and styles.

Thus in the world of ideas and of art there were both new modes of expression and resistance to change.

CHAPTER 35
IDEOLOGIES

The process of developing new ideological themes that had been undertaken in the late nineteenth century appeared to be all but complete by the beginning of the twentieth. From that time on, Quebecers had two major social programs to choose from. First, there was the unshakeably optimistic liberal ideology, with its emphasis on economic development and individual advancement, through which it was believed the progress of society could be accomplished. The clerical-nationalist ideology, on the other hand, had a pessimistic view of economic change, to which its adherents attributed negative social effects; they proposed a strategy of retrenchment, based on the conservation of traditional values and structures. The differences between these two programs led to lively debates about what Quebec society was to become. There were also other ideological currents, which tried to express a working-class conception of society, but they remained relatively marginal.

The Triumph of Liberalism

Liberal ideology is the ideology of the bourgeoisie, and was expressed by businessmen, political leaders and the mass-circulation press. The motive force of this ideology is the belief in the positive nature of material progress, which is achieved through economic development. The periods of rapid growth that Quebec experienced between 1896 and 1929 provided an opportunity for many paeans to the glory of industrialization and progress. As early as 1894, the author of the *Montreal Illustrated* burst with pride in describing his city:

> Suffice it to say in these few preliminary remarks that Montreal is essentially and distinctively a modern city, though the early recollections of its discovery teem with romance and original tradition. Today, however, from whatever point approached, and from any standpoint viewed, it presents all the aspects of metropolitan end-of-the-century life. On every hand are to be seen unmistakable evidence of material wealth and prosperity, irrefutable indications of comfort and luxury, of taste, culture and refinement, while on the principal shopping thoroughfares, lined with mammoth and truly magnificent mercantile establishments, all the features of the metropolis are still more noticeable.

Growth even became synonymous with beauty. In 1908, *La Presse* showed the steel structures of the new sheds on Montreal harbour under the heading "The Wonders of a Major Port."

Political leaders were quick to emphasize that prosperity was a result of their openness to progress. The mayor of the industrial town of Maisonneuve declared in 1912: "This is a prosperity unequalled in the history of the country. It is due to a policy of progress, to which the leaders of the municipality of Maisonneuve have always demonstrated their commitment." In 1916, Premier Lomer Gouin defended his policy of building dams in the following terms: "With the Saint-Maurice dam, we will create the largest artificial reservoir in the world, more than double the size of the Aswan reservoir on the Nile, the largest existing today. Gentlemen, I invite you to meet me here in five years to take stock of the amount of energy, development, progress and wealth that this gigantic project will produce for our country."

While in the nineteenth century railway projects were presented as symbols of growth, in the early twentieth century two new themes were used towards the same end: urban promotion and industrialization based on natural resources. "We want these industrial centres that spread progress and wealth to proliferate over the territory of our province," said Gouin in 1919. In the souvenir program published on the occasion of the Eucharistic Congress held in Montreal in 1910, the following passage appears: "Constant and uninterrupted progress in Maisonneuve. The considerable development of the most industrious town in the Province of Quebec means that the Capitalists, Industrialists, Builders, Workers and Young People of initiative who invest their capital, savings and labour there will gain a *quick and solid* fortune." In this context, it is only natural that the advantages of foreign capital would be proclaimed; this was especially true under the Taschereau government, as Yves Roby has shown. Premier Taschereau took satisfaction in the beneficial effects of American capital and hoped that still more would come.

Related to this faith in progress was another phenomenon — the high value placed on private enterprise and individual effort. The myth that anyone could become rich and that effort was rewarded with success was propagated with unprecedented intensity, and "success stories" proliferated in the mass-circulation press. Biographical dictionaries contained paeans to businessmen whose

Vous tous qui cherchez le succes
et la fortune, venez visiter

MAISONNEUVE

Et y prendre votre part de la
grande prosperite qui y regne.

Progress, enrichment and equality of opportunity for all were the major themes of liberal ideology. This ad reads: "Everyone who is looking for success and fortune, come visit MAISONNEUVE and take your share of the great prosperity that reigns there."

work and energy had brought them success and who through the corporations they established had become benefactors of the people and "great Canadians." Even more clearly than before, education in the early twentieth century was presented as the road to advancement for French Canadians. It was by expanding education and, most important, better adapting it to economic conditions that members of society would be given the opportunity to improve their lot and rise to positions of power. This is a recurring theme in the liberal rhetoric of the early years of the century.

To reach this goal, it was essential to modernize the school system and adapt it to the new requirements of the economy, and hence it was important to establish a network of specialized schools aimed at training technicians and managers. Vocational training became a key dimension of the social programs developed by the Gouin and Taschereau governments. "We want to add to all that we have already done for the great cause of education," said Lomer Gouin in 1919, "and especially to make it possible for the parents of every child to send him to a vocational school where his natural qualities and aptitudes can be developed." Three years later, the Taschereau government could say: "To help meet the needs of industry, commerce and agriculture, it is desirable to encourage the establishment and development of vocational courses aimed at the immediate training of skilled workers and competent employees, for which the industrialists, merchants and farmers of the province have an ever greater demand."

There also continued to be a more radical current of opinion that favoured greater changes in the school system, changes that would have wider political implications and challenge the dominance of the Catholic church. Its spokesmen demanded that education be compulsory and secular. Quebec's political leaders, however, had to reckon with the clergy, and put the demands of this group — which was, in any case, a minority — on the shelf.

Imbued with the idea of progress, believers in liberal ideology championed certain social reforms, especially in the area of public health. Praise for scientific, technological and medical accomplishments was an integral part of their rhetoric. Illness and a high death rate were, in a sense, challenges to reason and progress. A society that wanted to be modern had to be healthy. As many reformers and hygienists emphasized, when some people were sick they could endanger the health of all. Statements, lectures and articles about the need for government intervention towards such ends as improving health and sanitary conditions and making dwellings more wholesome proliferated in the early part of the century. This reform current represented an adaptation of one aspect of liberal ideology to the new conditions created by industrialization and urbanization.

While liberals continued to emphasize individual responsibility, the ideology also evolved to the point where its representatives could propose government intervention in areas such as poor relief, where social problems had reached new levels. This, however, was a change that occurred very slowly in Quebec, as it ran up against the deep social conservatism of the bourgeoisie.

Rationalization of the government apparatus was also part of the liberal program. Government was supposed to function according to rules of rationality and efficiency. The importance of the expert and the technocrat was emphasized. Another aim of rationalization was to counter the effects of a democracy that was now more open and therefore more difficult to control. Montreal businessmen, for example, demanded that their city be administered by experts rather than by elected representatives.

Nevertheless, respect for tradition occupied a large place in the liberal program as presented to Quebecers, and liberal rhetoric continued to praise French-Canadian culture and rural life. This was because the political and economic establishment continued to have to reckon with the religious establishment and take the power of the clergy into account. The clergy was an important ally for the bourgeoisie, a guarantor of social stability. It should also be remembered that the French-speaking portion of the bourgeoisie was trained in the classical colleges and came under clerical influence there. Another factor to take into account was that the major political leaders were lawyers, and because of their training often saw social relations in legal terms and had a relatively static view of social structures. The emphasis on the importance of agriculture by political leaders can also be explained by the fact that the electoral map gave considerably more weight to rural than to urban voters.

While nationalism was in no sense the main theme of liberal ideology, there was nevertheless room for it in liberal rhetoric. There was a high degree of consensus among both French- and English-speaking representatives of the bourgeoisie in favour of putting aside the national question and preaching good relations among the "races" (a word that was used at the time as a synonym for nation or people). The strategy consisted of avoiding confrontation by practising tolerance and allowing each major ethnic group to control its own educational and charitable institutions. French-speaking leaders made clear their attachment to French-Canadian traditions while expressing the belief that the ties binding Canada to Britain were beneficial. Spokesmen for English-speaking Quebec were ardent in their imperialism but respected French-Canadian particularity. This same compromise did not apply in the other provinces, however, where French Canadians lost the right to education in their own language as a result of the intemperate zeal of their English-speaking compatriots.

Even in Quebec, the compromise was shaken somewhat by the First World War. The imperialist fervour of Montreal's powerful English-speaking businessmen was extraordinary, and it won them royal decorations and sumptuous war contracts. French-Canadian leaders could not allow themselves the same excesses of zeal for fear of losing all popular support; while they endorsed the war effort, their approval was much more restrained and they accompanied it with a defence of French-Canadian interests.

The task of propagating the liberal vision of material progress was carried out in different ways in the two major language communities. There was no problem on the English-speaking side, where the network of institutions was secular and under the undisputed control of the bourgeoisie. On the French-speaking side, it was difficult to disseminate the liberal program through the clerically-dominated school system. Instead, the mass-circulation press, with its large headlines, sensational articles and advertising, was used to this effect, and did valuable propaganda work. Political speeches were also a good instrument for praising the wonders of progress, the benefits of industry, private enterprise and foreign capital, and the limitless opportunities to which education provided access. What was the response of Quebecers to this appeal? The electoral majorities with which they endowed the Liberal party, the speed with which they became an urban people, their interest in the sensational press and a number of other indicators are all evidence that they were not deaf to it and increasingly accepted the values it contained.

The Clerical-Nationalist Resistance

The clerical-nationalist social program was very different. This ideology was expressed by members of the clergy and, still more forcefully, by nationalist groups; its most cogent formulation can be found in editorials in *Le Devoir* and articles in *L'Action Française*.

In the last three decades, a number of historians and sociologists have studied this clerical-nationalist ideology, or ideology of conservation, to the point where it was the only thing they could see on the Quebec ideological landscape. From there, it was only one step to regarding it as the "dominant ideology," and this step was quickly taken. Because it was formulated by clerics and intellectuals, there was an internal coherence to its written expression, in editorials and published speeches, that made it easier to analyse.

The major themes of its rhetoric can be summarized briefly. The clerical-nationalist program was systematically oriented towards the past. Its main characteristics were a rejection of new values and constant recourse to French-Canadian and Catholic tradition. Its spokesmen were convinced that these traditional values were a precious heritage, and that French Canadians had to conserve and cling to them in order to survive as a people. Abbé Lionel Groulx wrote in 1921: "The more we retain our French and Catholic virtues, stay faithful to our history and traditions, and continue to love this land as our only country, the less the American spirit will be able to penetrate us and the more we will remain the most steadfast representatives of order and stability."

The family was presented as the fundamental social unit; its members were considered to have a sense of solidarity and responsibility towards one another. The high value placed on the family was a basic element in Catholic social thinking, in Quebec as elsewhere. The family, in which the husband has authority over his wife, and children must obey their parents, teaches respect for hierarchical structures and acts as a guarantee of social stability. The family must have control over its members' education, and is responsible for coming to their assistance when they are ill or in need. The Roman Catholic church regarded itself as the agent of the family in the areas of education, health and welfare. Any attempt by the government to intervene in these areas was considered an attack on the family and a threat to the social order.

The second key element in the ideology of conservation was religion. It regarded religion not as being limited to worship but rather as including a set of values which the church had transmitted through the centuries and which was to infuse all aspects of a Christian's life. Thus, education had to be Catholic, charity had to be Catholic, employer-employee relations had to be based on Christian principles. This conception led to the attempt by the clergy to place the main activities of life in a Catholic context and organize every social grouping in church-related associations.

From the primacy of religion came the demand that a determining role in society be accorded to the church and its official spokesmen, the priests and bishops. The leap from the idea of the clergy as guide to the faithful to the idea of the clergy as authority was quickly made, and thought control and censorship could then be used in good conscience. Jean Hamelin and André Beaulieu have aptly summed up the ideological consequences of the clergy's omnipresence: "Regarding itself as the bearer of a gospel that it had embodied in an ideology once and for all, and more concerned with the formulation of its message than with its content, the church fell into the trap to which ideologues through the ages have been subject — it became dogmatic, intolerant, and suspicious of newness and compromise. On the basis of this attitude, it criticized any innovation that might jeopardize the social outcome it intended to achieve."

The third key element in the social model proposed by the clerical-nationalist ideology, after the family and religion, was agriculture and rural life. In a pamphlet entitled *Les avantages de l'agriculture* (The Advantages of Agriculture) published in 1916, the Jesuit Alexandre Dugré offered a good synthesis of agrarian thought in Quebec. In the pamphlet, he listed the major advantages of agriculture over urban life. Some of these were economic in nature. For example, the farmer had much greater protection from fluctuations in the economy than the city-dweller, as people always need food products. In addition, while the farmer's expenses were less than those of the city-dweller, his income was increasing as a result of improvements in techniques and equipment. In discussing the economic aspects of agriculture, Father Dugré also pinpointed some of the obstacles to its advancement. One of these was the farmer's attachment to habit, but others included the lack of concern on the part of political leaders and an educational system in which too much emphasis was placed on business.

Father Dugré also pointed out the physical advantages of agriculture. Life in the open air strengthened the body, and country people were in better health than city-dwellers. In addition, city-dwellers longed for the countryside, and never missed an opportunity to escape the city for a sojourn in the country.

Finally, Father Dugré listed the moral advantages of agriculture which he regarded as the most important — the "nobility of agriculture," the only truly creative activity; the Christian character of the countryside; the farmer's freedom in not being subject to the factory whistle; the countryside as the "shield of tradition" and of the race; the stability of the rural family; the strength of parish life. All these advantages were preferable, in his view, to the instability of urban life and the difficulties that arose there.

The city was used as a foil against which a social ideal was defined. According to Jean Hamelin and André Beaulieu:

> In the clerical-nationalist ideology, the city was seen in a number of ways — sometimes as a polluted place to live, often as a dangerous way of life, and most often as a system of values and behaviours that reduced man to the level of a beast. To speak of the city was to raise the spectre of the foundations of people's beliefs and customs destroyed by the press, the sabbath desecrated, piety held up to ridicule, the family ruined by marital infidelity and drunkenness, youth corrupted by the immorality of fashions, dances and shows. The city was the home of the plague and would mean death for Catholicism in Quebec. It had no place in the ideal society.

Thus, agriculture was valued both as an economic activity and as a way of life, and some writers went so far as to discredit other sectors of the economy and regard them as foreign to the essence of French-Canadian nationality. Mgr Paquet of Quebec City said in a famous speech in 1902: "Our mission is less to manage capital than to propagate ideas. It will be fulfilled not so much in lighting factory fires as in fueling the fire of religion and thought and letting its brilliant light radiate to distant lands."

Nationalist thinkers were interested in economic development, but saw agriculture and colonization as its central elements. They devoted many articles and publications to rural problems. The 1928 annual meeting of the Semaines Sociales du Canada even took as its theme "The Economic Problem Considered Primarily from an Agricultural Point of View." The view taken of industry was not a wholly disapproving one, and *curés* and bishops vied with each other to bless new factories; in 1902, Mgr Labrecque thanked "the good capitalists" who had built the mill at Val-Jalbert. But the industries the nationalists wanted were ones that were closely integrated into rural life. The ideal factory should be small in size, be established in an agricultural region, use one or more commodities produced by the farmer as raw materials, and run only during the winter, when agricultural manpower was available. Thus, the nationalists wanted to establish an economy in which industrial production would be subordinated to the higher interests of agriculture.

Needless to say, Quebec society was in reality organized quite differently, to the great regret of those thinkers who wanted to hold back the changes that were taking place. While clerical-nationalist ideology could to a certain extent accommodate itself to industry, it rejected the socio-economic process of industrialization that was endangering the rural society it idealized. This resistance to change became increasingly open in the early twentieth century. The extent of new industrial investment led to cries of protest in the nationalist press. The nationalists demanded a drastic change of course by the government to give a new impetus to agriculture and colonization so as to slow the exodus of rural Quebecers to the cities. They saw the situation as being all the more serious in that industrialization was being accomplished by foreign capital, which brought its values in with it and led to the decline of Catholic and French civilization.

Nevertheless, within the nationalist group, there were some who accepted the need for a degree of industrialization and did not want French Canadians limited to a subordinate role in it. Starting in 1901, Errol Bouchette proposed that to the traditional motto of "Emparons-nous du sol" ("Let us take possession of the land"), a new one be added — "Emparons-nous de l'industrie" ("Let us take possession of industry"). The journalist Olivar Asselin, the economist Édouard Montpetit and the financier Joseph Versailles were among the more notable representatives of this current of thought, which borrowed much from economic liberalism but coloured it with nationalist statements.

Nationalism was a dominant characteristic of the ideology of conservation. According to the ideology, the nation was defined as much by its Catholicism and rural origins as by its ethnic and linguistic properties. The national dimension of the clerical-nationalist program changed over the course of the period, however, and its evolution can be seen by looking at two major thinkers who contributed to it in turn — Henri Bourassa and Lionel Groulx.

Bourassa was the first to come on the scene. As noted in chapter 32, he reacted against the imperialist form of English-Canadian nationalism strongly in evidence at the turn of the century. He believed that Canadians' primary attachment should be to their own country rather than to Britain. Thus, he advocated development of a true Canadian nationalism in which the specific characteristics of the two language groups would be respected. Replying in 1904 to the journalist Jules-Paul Tardivel, who favoured a strictly French-Canadian nationalism, Bourassa defined his thinking in the following terms:

> Our nationalism is Canadian nationalism, based on the duality of the races and the particular traditions involved in this duality. We are working for the development of Canadian patriotism, which we regard as the best guarantee that the two races will continue to exist and pay the mutual respect they owe each other. Like M. Tardivel, we regard the French-Canadian people as our own people. But English Canadians are not foreigners to us, and we regard any English Canadian who respects us and joins us in desiring the full maintenance of Canadian autonomy as an ally. We consider our fatherland to be Canada as a whole, that is a federation of distinct races and autonomous provinces. The nation we would like to see develop is the Canadian nation, composed of French Canadians and English Canadians, two elements separated by language and religion and by the legal arrangements needed to maintain their respective traditions, but united in their attachment to brotherhood and their common attachment to their common country.

Bourassa's nationalism, then, was Canadian nationalism, but with a bi-ethnic, bilingual and bicultural character. Bourassa demanded respect for minority rights everywhere in Canada. As there was no threat to Quebec's English-speaking minority, Bourassa became the champion of the cause of French-speaking minorities outside Quebec. The kind of nationalism he advocated had little success in English Canada, which wanted to assimilate all its minority groups, including the French minorities. This was manifested most notably in an attack on French-Canadian educational rights, which were reduced in most of the provinces and territories between 1896 and 1929. Bourassa's campaigns against this situation and against participation in British wars were veritable crusades, but he had little success on either front, and the main result of his campaign was to stimulate French-Canadian nationalism in Quebec.

The 1914-18 war led to a virtual break between English and French Canadians and confirmed that the kind of nationalism advocated by Bourassa had failed. His disciples increasingly veered towards a purely Quebec nationalism. Meanwhile, Bourassa underwent a personal evolution in the twenties as a result of which he put aside his nationalism and instead emphasized the supremacy of religion and the church.

His position as leader was taken up by a priest and historian, Lionel Groulx, who made the journal *L'Action Française* the focal point for a group of young intellectuals who gave new impetus and a new direction to nationalist ideology. This group emphasized linguistic and cultural questions and took an interest in

Lionel Groulx (1878-1967), in his office at *L'Action Française* in 1925.

economic nationalism. In 1922, it even went through a brief phase in which it was sympathetic to Quebec independence. As a result of the recognition of the principle of nationalities at the 1919 Versailles negotiations and the political tensions within Canada, it believed that the country would soon explode. In a major study entitled *Notre avenir politique* (Our Political Future), contributors examined the viability of a separate French Canada. They didn't demand independence, but it appeared inevitable to them. As their apprehensions proved unfounded, they quickly forgot their fleeting vision of independence.

While the *L'Action Française* group did not subsequently challenge the basis of the federal link, it did develop a nationalism centred primarily on Quebec. Lionel Groulx endeavoured first of all to establish an awareness of the historical roots of nationalism. He was very interested in New France, which he idealized and made into the symbol of ancestral virtues and Catholic and French roots. He went so far as to make a cult figure of one of its heroes, Dollard des Ormeaux. He was equally interested in the history of the constitutional battles that French Canadians had had to fight since the Conquest.

Groulx was a teacher, first at the classical college and later at the university level, and as a result of his concern with education, training youth in nationalism with a view towards moulding what he regarded as tomorrow's élite was an especially cherished goal. He and his disciples were also strong defenders of the French language and culture. The French language was in a very unfortunate state in Quebec, even though it was the language of the majority. In many utilities, stores and companies, English was the only language of communication, and a citizen who wished to correspond with the department of the provincial treasurer could do so only in English. Americanization was a further cause of concern. French culture thus appeared to be seriously threatened, especially in the cities.

Also threatened was French-Canadians' presence in the economy. With the growth of monopolies and the invasion of foreign capital, the share of the French-Canadian bourgeoisie was reduced to a minimum. In response to this situation, a form of economic nationalism was developed in which a return to rural life and small business was regarded as desirable and massive industrialization with foreign backing was rejected. Even if the ideas of *L'Action Française* were not fully shared by all clerics and nationalists, they were an increasingly significant element in clerical-nationalist ideology and were disseminated within the petty bourgeoisie.

The support group for clerical-nationalist ideology comprised a large part of the petty bourgeoisie and the clergy. Its social program was opposed to the liberal program on a number of levels. As with liberal ideology, the degree of penetration of clerical-nationalist ideology is difficult to measure. The clergy was able to disseminate its message through its control of education and the religious apparatus as well as through the organizations it established or took control of and gave a denominational character. Notable among these organizations were the Association Catholique de la Jeunesse Canadienne-française (ACJC), the École Sociale Populaire (ESP) and the Catholic unions.

Clerical-nationalist ideology was also disseminated through a network of newspapers called the "Catholic press" or "bonne presse" ("good press"). The best-known of these newspapers was undoubtedly *Le Devoir* of Montreal, founded in 1910 by Henri Bourassa; others included *L'Action Catholique* in Quebec City, *Le Droit* in Ottawa, *Le Bien Public* in Trois-Rivières and *Le Progrès du Saguenay*. These newspapers did not have the resources or circulation of *La Presse*, *La Patrie*, the *Montreal Star* or *Le Soleil*, and their influence was felt most directly by members of the clergy and Catholic intellectuals.

There is no doubt that the clerical-nationalist ideology had considerable influence in Quebec, but it met resistance from the political and economic establishments, and did not succeed in winning complete acceptance for its social model.

However, it would be wrong to conclude that the liberal and clerical-nationalist ideologies were totally incompatible or that the leading groups in society were divided into two irremediably opposed blocs. Power relations led to compromises between businessmen and politicians on the one hand and the clergy on the other. There was a degree of osmosis between the two ideologies. Lay French-Canadian leaders were trained in the classical colleges and came under clerical influence. The bourgeoisie was conservative enough to agree with some of the positions taken by the clerical-nationalist ideology, as for example on the status of women in society, while there were divisions within both groups on the national question. In addition, as a result of political constraints, what some leaders said out loud was the reverse of what they really believed. Meanwhile, in this overview of major currents, a third, more egalitarian one must also be considered.

Ideology in the Working Class

In the early twentieth century, ideologies were also developed and disseminated by working-class groups. Their content varied from group to group; the most significant one, represented by the Parti Ouvrier (see chapter 32) and Quebec leaders of international unions, did not fundamentally challenge the capitalist system but rather attacked the abuses and the exploitation of the working class to which it led. According to this labour ideology, the wrongs caused by the system could be redressed and exploitation eliminated by making sure the game was played according to more egalitarian rules. Thus, part of its program was aimed at improving the lot of the worker and another part at limiting the power of the capitalists.

Supporters of the labour ideology believed that the advancement of the worker would be achieved through education, and hence there were demands to make access to education easier — free and compulsory education, a ban on child labour, creation of a department of education and establishment of a network of public libraries. The program also advocated protective measures to make workers safe from excessive exploitation — limitation of working hours, abolition of garnisheeing of wages and seizure of property, and legislation against loans at usurious rates. Other suggestions to improve the lot of the workers included easier access to mortgage loans and to the courts. Finally, the irregular income of most workers did not allow them to accumulate savings for their retirement or for use in case of illness; the program proposed to correct this situation by bringing in health insurance and old-age pensions.

The section of the labour program dealing with the power of the capitalists was directed primarily against monopolies, especially in the utility sector; it demanded that these be brought under public ownership. In the financial sector, it demanded that a government-owned bank be established and private banks abolished. But that was as far as the supporters of this ideology went. They did not advocate a general program of nationalization, which was a clear difference between them and the socialists. Another recommendation aimed at the power of the capitalists was recognition of employers' responsibility for work accidents.

These objectives could be realized only if workers had a say in political decisions. To achieve this, the right to vote had to be extended and exercising it had to be made easier, through such measures as universal suffrage, compulsory voting, a guaranteed holiday on election day, "one man, one vote" and proportional representation. But measures of this sort were not enough, and the desire to encourage a working-class presence in decisionmaking bodies led to repeated attempts, starting in the 1880s, at working-class political activity. As workers began to take an interest in municipal politics in the early part of the century, their leaders demanded abolition of the property qualification for electoral candidates, which was an unfair handicap. The goal of increasing the political power of the working class was also behind populist demands such as election of judges by the people and adoption of the referendum principle.

However, direct political action did not have unanimous support among proponents of the labour ideology. Because labour candidates achieved such limited electoral success, many international union leaders believed, especially after 1914, that political action should instead take the form of trade union pressure-group activity.

The other notable working-class ideological current was socialism, but it remained fairly marginal in Quebec and does not appear to have been supported by more than a few hundred people. The march in Montreal organized by the Socialist party to celebrate May Day in 1906 attracted between five and six hundred people and caused a flutter in the clergy, among political leaders and even within the Parti Ouvrier, but there was little follow-up to this impressive demonstration. The leader of the French-Canadian socialists was Albert Saint-Martin, while an English-speaking lawyer, W.U. Cotton, had a degree of influence through his socialist publication, *Cotton's Weekly*. The arrival of a large number of European immigrants in the early part of the century created a favourable environment for the dissemination of socialism. At present, however, the degree of penetration achieved by the various socialist groups that developed in Quebec is difficult to measure. The founding of the Université Ouvrière in Montreal in 1926 was an important step in the dissemination of socialist ideas. At the very end of the period the Communist party of Canada, founded in the early 1920s, began to do organizing work in Quebec; in 1928, there were only some sixty party activists in Quebec, of whom about ten were French Canadians. On the whole, socialist and communist groups remained on the margins of the Quebec political scene before 1930, but in the depression that followed conditions were more favourable to their growth.

In the case of the Catholic unions, the ideological underpinning, at least at the beginning, was not a working-class ideology, but rather the clerical-nationalist ideology with additional attention paid to the place of workers within it. The Catholic unions did not present a social program constructed from a working-class point of view, and many of the major documents that outlined their official thinking were written by members of the clergy.

Thus, from the beginning of the twentieth century, a labour ideology was developed and disseminated through the trade unions. It did not have the benefit of the means of distribution which the other two major ideologies had at their disposal, and this seriously limited its penetration and confined it primarily to Montreal. The socialist and communist ideological currents faced even greater problems of dissemination, and their influence appears to have been limited to small groups.

CHAPTER 36
CULTURE

As for the preceding period, Quebec culture in the early twentieth century will be analysed primarily with reference to literature and painting. Cultural output continued to reflect the effects of external influences, but it also remained closely linked to the developments that determined the course of Quebec society's economic and ideological life. The literature of the era cannot be understood without relating it to the profound changes that industrialization and urbanization were bringing to Quebec. Painting, dependent for its existence on commissions by institutions and wealthy collectors, was also affected by social change, and its history is marked by tensions and time-lags between artists and their patrons.

Literature*

At the end of the nineteenth century, Quebec literature was clearly lagging, behind the reality of its own socio-economic environment in terms of content and behind esthetic developments in Europe in terms of form. By recalling the glorious deeds of the past, taking refuge in adventure or idealizing peasant life, it sought to deny the real conditions under which Quebecers lived. It was a literature of escape and compensation, bearing the stamp of a conquered and dominated people. When it did not exaggerate the negative aspects of rapid industrialization, natural resource development and urbanization, it had nothing at all to say about them. It was also the literature of an élite and saw the people only in the roles of peasant and soldier. As the faithful transmitter of an ideology of retrenchment, it tried to raise the contingencies of a reality pervaded by mediocrity to the level of absolute cultural values.

---

*This section was written by Sylvain Simard.

In the last years of the nineteenth century, however, a group of poets appeared whose desire for change stands out clearly against the grey background of pre-1945 Quebec literary history. The problem of interpreting the appearance of this movement, and its continued existence for a number of years, has not yet been resolved. Young Montreal poets, organized in tiny literary clubs and around underground avant-garde reviews, formed the École Littéraire de Montréal, a group whose structural model was the literary academy and whose aim was a virtual revolution in literature. The revolution it sought was, in the first instance, esthetic, as it chose symbolism and the Parnassian school as models in place of the established paradigms of romanticism and classicism, but it was also a thematic revolution, in which the obligatory defence of the higher interest of the nation and expression of the soul of the race gave way to a poetry dealing with man, death and love.

The movement's most illustrious representative was Émile Nelligan, whose poetic output between 1896 and 1898 outshone that of all his predecessors. But Nelligan was a shooting star who quickly became lost "in Dream's abyss," and he left few heirs. One by one, Montreal's young bohemians were swallowed up by the exigencies of a society that had no interest in "literary" and "gratuitous" poetry. At the end of the First World War, the review *Le Nigog* became the focal point for a group of talented poets who had returned from Europe and again looked to France for the tools of artistic creation. But these were cultured esthetes whose work had very little influence on their countrymen.

The main characteristic of literature between 1896 and 1930 was continuity with the nineteenth century. Poems and novels continued to be written under the literary banners of the *terroir* school and regionalism. Literature cut itself off from the rest of the world and took refuge in traditional values so that it appeared to be a negation of the outside world. Even the essay was almost exclusively a vehicle of conservative nationalism. With the exception of a few landmark works, the novel was uniformly weak; it was held captive by outdated esthetic principles, paralysed by rigid moral canons and limited by the narrow requirements of historical and peasant themes. Milked to excess, this genre finally came to produce works whose realism was a sign that the mythic deception that had prevailed for so long was coming to an end. After the outstanding and deserved success of Louis Hémon's *Maria Chapdelaine*, Albert Laberge's novel *La Scouine* described the misery of peasant life for the first time; it presaged Ringuet's *Thirty Acres* and the end of a vision that sought to mystify the world.

According to Pierre de Grandpré, literature during this period was an obstacle course for its creators. Some obstacles they faced were historical, resulting from accumulated defeats and the abdication of French Canada's élites. Others were geographical, the product of living in a natural environment over which little mastery had been attained and with which little integration had been achieved. Thus, through force of inertia the environment was able to impose the fatalistic conception of a tragic destiny, which was then confirmed by the vagaries of history. There were also sociological obstacles, despite the apparently unanimous adherence of French-Canadian writers to an ideology that was totally out of step with the new social and industrial realities shaped by the forces of economic determinism and the rise of an urban proletariat. And finally, there were constraints relating to the psychology of the creator, which flowed inevitably from the other constraints and not only prevented writers from attaining originality but, even more important, made them incapable of envisaging any possibility of change.

Poetry and the École de Montréal

The history of poetry during the period consists almost completely, except for the *Le Nigog* episode, of the fortunes and different directions taken by the École Littéraire de Montréal. This movement was a product of meetings of the group of *six éponges* (six sponges), which included Jean Charbonneau and Louvigny de Montigny, held in the Café Ayotte on Sainte-Catherine Street about 1890. Its founding meeting, to which most revolutionary young poets of their generation as well as a few older ones were invited, took place on November 7, 1895. Initially it met in the homes of some of its leading members — its president, Germain Beaulieu, was the first host, followed by the secretary, Louvigny de Montigny — but starting in 1898 it held public sessions in the Château de Ramezay. The group survived through many vicissitudes until the early 1930s.

Paul Wyczynski has identified three major stages in the life of the École de Montréal. Its initial period of exuberance, between 1895 and 1900, was characterized primarily by a desire to achieve a renewal in the area of form, on the model of the Parnassians and symbolists; this energy waned after 1900 and the period of quiescence that followed lasted until 1907. Between 1907 and 1913, a new focus for the École de Montréal's poetic forces developed in the form of the review *Le Terroir*; under the banner of regionalism, these forces were directed towards a search for "the soul of the people in the Canadian countryside." After a second period of quiescence, the École de Montréal regained its vigour during the 1920s, when the dominant eclecticism made it possible for poets with different esthetic and thematic orientations to live together without really influencing one another.

But it was in the creative exuberance of the early years that the most interesting works were produced; this was the real École Littéraire de Montréal. In particular, the poems of Émile Nelligan put Quebec poetry into the historical mainstream. Not only was his art fed by the works of Baudelaire and Rimbaud, but he was also the first Quebec poet to assimilate the works of Maurice Rollinat, Paul Verlaine and Georges Rodenbach and make them an essential part of his life. He used his still uncontrolled creative forces and his authentic personal inspiration to breathe new life into the art of writing. After Louis Dantin published Nelligan's work in 1904, he became surrounded by a myth in which he was cast as the child-poet, the genius with a tragic destiny. But the myth aside, Nelligan's sense of image and the depth and life of the themes he touched made him Quebec's first modern poet. Panegyrics to the race, the legendary or heroic past and pastoral elegies were not his material. Instead, he concentrated entirely on the realities that obsessed him, at the centre of which were death, motherhood, love and the city. Montreal's cultivated bourgeoisie criticized Nelligan's poetry although his concerns were a million miles away from their own; Nelligan's escape from this closed world was writing:

*Ah comme la neige a neigé!**
Ma vitre est un jardin de givre
Ah comme la neige a neigé
Qu'est-ce que le spasme de vivre
Ah la douleur que j'ai, que j'ai!
(Soirs d'hiver)

He also flees from an unintelligible world through wonder at the eyes of language:

*Elle a des yeux pareils à d'étranges flambeaux,***
Et ses cheveux d'or faux sur ses maigres épaules,
Dans des subtiles frissons de feuillages de saules,
L'habillent comme font les cyprès des tombeaux!
(La Vierge noire)

This rejection of reality can lead only to refuge in the troubled waters of the unconscious, in a call — a desire — for madness:

*Ce fut un Vaisseau d'or dont les flancs diaphanes****
Révélaient des trésors que les marins profanes,
Dégoût, Haine et Névrose, entre eux ont disputé.

Que reste-t-il de lui dans la tempête brève?
Qu'est devenu mon coeur déserté?
Hélas, il a sombré dans l'abîme du Rêve!
(Le Vaisseau d'Or)

---

*Ah! how the snow has snowed!
My glass is a garden of frost.
Ah! how the snow has snowed!
What is life's brief outburst
To the grief that I know, I know?
(Winter Evening)

**Her eyes are like strange torches: golden hair,
Whose gold is counterfeit, falls down to dress
Thin shoulders with the subtle restlessness
Of willow leaves: So tombs their cypress wear.
(The Dark Maiden)

Émile Nelligan (1879-1941).

Nelligan's work was an integral part of the literary efforts of Montreal's *fin-de-siècle* bohemian underground. The voices of Paul Verlaine, Arthur Rimbaud and Stéphane Mallarmé exercised a fascination for these "sons of merchants and wealthy farmers," the first marginal intellectuals in a French Canada that was rapidly becoming an industrial society. Grouped around ephemeral avant-garde reviews, they were attacked by some of the older intellectuals, among them Adjutor Rivard and Arthur Buies, and encouraged by others, including the venerable national poet, Louis Fréchette. For a few years, they made the École Littéraire de Montréal a scene of intense creative activity. During this period, Jean Charbonneau, Louvigny de Montigny, Henry Desjardins, Arthur de Bussières, Paul de Martigny and others jolted the conformism and mediocrity of Montreal's intellectual life. The high point of the movement came in 1898 when Nelligan, surrounded by his friends, gave two triumphal public readings of some of his poems at the Château de Ramezay.

But what happened to this generation? The disastrous state of the troops of

---

***She was a golden ship: but there showed through
Translucent sides treasures the blasphemous crew,
Hatred, Disgust and Madness, fought to share.

How much survives after the storm's brief race?
Where is my heart, that empty ship, oh where?
Alas, in Dream's abyss sunk without trace.
(The Golden Ship) —Nelligan translations by P.F. Widdows

1900 has been catalogued by Wyczynski — Nelligan had *sombré dans l'abîme du rêve* (in Dream's abyss sunk without trace); a similar fate threatened Hector Demers; Alfred Desloges died in August 1899, followed soon afterwards by Denys Lanctôt; Henry Desjardins was suffering from tuberculosis and labouring as a notary in Hull; helpless in the face of reality, Antonio Pelletier and Arthur de Bussières lived from day to day; while the others stagnated in a state not far removed from inertia.

Although there is no evidence of a call to order by the conservative forces or of any actual censorship, the generation of the 1890s vanished as quickly as it had appeared. It was an avant-garde whose only public was itself. In part, its existence was attributable to the fascination that new French artistic values held for a cultivated segment of Montreal's French-speaking bourgeoisie. At the same time, it was a function of the emergence of new groups for whom industrial society provided such occupational niches as journalism, the civil service, teaching, art and bookselling, and the access of these groups to intellectual life.

The appearance of these poets at the end of the nineteenth century was also an indication of the difficulty that clerical and conservative forces would henceforth face in trying to control all sectors of intellectual activity. The clergy could still refuse the Carnegie Foundation's offers of assistance and instead establish its own "public" library (see chapter 30). But for a while, a few sheep — poets — escaped from the authority of the clerical shepherd, although the flock was soon reassembled within the national fold.

After a period of almost total eclipse (1900-7), the École Littéraire de Montréal came to life again; the focus of this new activity was a review whose program was summed up in its name — *Le Terroir*. Reiterating all the regionalist clichés that had been current in the École Littéraire de Québec fifty years earlier, Charles Gill, Albert Ferland, Jean Charbonneau, Germain Beaulieu and their friends set out in search of "the soul of the people." In their outdated return to romanticism and their self-imposed isolation from every literary movement in Europe and the United States, they often confused good will and purity of national feeling with poetic inspiration, and left no works that are worthy of attention. Charles Gill's *Cap Éternité*, Albert Ferland's *Canada chanté* and Blanche Lamontagne's *Visions gaspésiennes* are not entirely without merit, but today they are of essentially historical interest. They are a good indication of the isolation in which the dominant élite tried to keep Quebecers. Quebec's clerics were incensed at the "atrocities" of the secular French republic; encouraged along their reactionary course by the French religious who were driven to immigrate to Quebec by the policies of the anticlerical prime minister Émile Combes, they tried to close the province to destructive cultural influences coming from France. In the early twentieth century, the only French poetry with which Quebecers were familiar consisted of the songs of the famous Catholic Breton bard, Théodore Botrel.

Some Quebecers, however, escaped from this reductionist view of culture. These were the scions of wealthy bourgeois families who had only one dream — to visit Paris and, if possible, to live there. From the late nineteenth century until the First World War, there were dozens of young Quebecers in the City of Light, entranced by its artistic and cultural effervescence. Some were medical students, while others took courses from fashionable artists at the Louvre, enrolled at the École des Beaux-Arts or even studied at the École Normale Supérieure on the rue d'Ulm. More typically, they immersed themselves in the daily life of the Parisian cultural underground. But in all cases, they underwent an experience that affected them deeply. They frequented the Gardenia, a theatrical and cultural circle founded by Paul Fabre, where they came in contact with artists from all corners of the world. Some of them, such as Paul Morin and René Chopin, published collections of poetry in Paris. The rate of exchange between the Canadian dollar and the French franc was favourable, and many of these young expatriates wanted to live in Paris forever, but the war forced them to return to Canada.

These cultivated youths, who had come to grips with the rich cultural scene of cosmopolitan Paris, had nothing in common with the *terroir* bards of the École Littéraire de Montréal, phase two. In 1918, after meeting for a few years in the salons of the architect Fernand Préfontaine, they founded *Le Nigog*, a literary and artistic review based on the credo "art must innovate." Writers such as Jean-Aubert Loranger, Marcel Dugas and Robert de Roquebrune, the musician Léo-Pol Morin, the sculptor Henri Hébert, the painters Adrien Hébert and Ozias Leduc, the scientist Louis Bourgoin, the art critic Jean Chauvin, the journalist Eustache Letellier de Saint-Just and the architect Fernand Préfontaine set out to upset the outworn esthetic conceptions of their countrymen and confront the upholders of regionalism. In the final months of the war, *Le Nigog* closed the gap between Quebec and France and opened some minds to the most advanced literary and artistic conceptions current in Europe.

This primacy of estheticism over the promotion and illustration of local subjects shows up clearly in the work of Paul Morin who, endowed with a considerable fortune, had frequented the smartest salons in Paris. A remarkably skilled writer of highly refined verse, Morin took refuge in ultra-Parnassian writing, so perfect and cold as to be slightly boring. René Chopin also wrote within the Parnassian and symbolist framework, but his poetry is more original; its outstanding beauty can be seen in the following verses from the poem "Je contemple mon rêve," included in the collection *Le coeur en exil:*

*Je contemple mon rêve ainsi qu'une ruine**
Où pierre à pierre coule un somptueux palais
Chaque jour, sur le mur qui plus vétuste incline
Par touffes rampe et croît le lichen, plus épais.

La porte se lézarde où de l'ombre est entrée,
Le plâtre s'en effrite et le marbre y noircit;
Une fenêtre à jour et de lierre encadrée
Dans une vieille tour se fronce, haut sourcil

Au château de mon rêve, invasion brutale
À leurs points lourds portent la pique et le flambeau
Ils ont passé le coeur aigri, de salle en salle;
De chaque sanctuaire ils ont fait un tombeau

Guy Delahaye went to Paris to do medical research and ended up doing advanced experimentation with poetic form. The poetry of André Bourassa even shows clear similarities with the futurist endeavours of Filippo Tommaso Marinetti and is marked by Dadaist influences — enigmatic writing, savage humour, "vers ordonnances." Delahaye soon abandoned avant-garde poetry for psychiatric research and the certainties of religion.

Marcel Dugas, like René Chopin and Guy Delahaye a member of the literary club Le Soc, also spent some time in France and wrote very beautiful prose poems. An active member of the *Le Nigog* group and an ardent admirer of things Parisian, Jean-Aubert Loranger was a symbolist before adopting the unanimism of Jules Romains. It is interesting that Loranger, like the young Victor Barbeau, became reconciled with the by now less sectarian regionalists of the École Littéraire de Montréal, phase three. No significant work emerged from this joining of forces, and by 1930 the École Littéraire was only a memory.

The novel

The genre of historical novels that had developed in the last third of the nineteenth century (see chapter 17) remained popular, and reached a peak with the work of Laure Conan. She used subtle analytical techniques to etch her uplifting portraits of the religious and national past, most effectively in *À l'oeuvre et à l'épreuve* (1891) and *L'Oublié* (1900). Robert de Roquebrune and Léo-Paul Desrosiers were also good novelists who took their inspiration from New France and produced works of high quality by freeing themselves from the need to simplify to prove a point.

---

*I contemplate my dream, and I see
A ruined castle, once splendid, now in slow decay,
Where each day, thickening clumps of lichen crawl
Higher up the crooked, crumbling wall.

The door admits shadows through a crack,
The plaster grows brittle and the marble black;
In an old tower, a window
In an ivy frame wrinkles its brow.

Brutally have the pike and the flame
Invaded the castle of my dreams;
Hard-hearted, they pass from room to room
And turn every sanctuary into a tomb.

On the other hand, the desire to convince was paramount in the two patriotic novels written by the historian Lionel Groulx under the pseudonym of Alonié de Lestre. *L'Appel de la Race* and *Le Cap Blomidon* were literary fabrications in which the historian used the novel to illustrate the great nationalist lessons he had drawn from the past.

However, even more than the historical novel, the peasant novel was the truly characteristic genre of the period. Most of the peasant novelists made it their primary task to idealize country life and present it as a model to emulate. Craftsmen rather than artists, the authors of these many typical scenes of traditional Quebec life patiently chiselled their simple, robust works as if they were pieces of old French-Canadian furniture. They remained outside all the major literary currents and philosophical movements and wrote hymns to a Quebec that wanted to remain rural. Thus, the novels of Ernest Choquette, Damase Potvin, Harry Bernard and Adélard Dugré, to name only a few, all aimed at uplifting the reader by describing a simple, ideal world.

The great literary success of the period, and the only novel that can still be read and reread with pleasure, was written by a Frenchman, Louis Hémon. In *Maria Chapdelaine*, for the first time, nature in Quebec was not reduced to the role of decorative background. While the novel's characters are simple, they have an intense inner life, and live in complete symbiosis with the primal forces of the forest, lakes and rivers. The Chapdelaines, although close to being carried away by the temptation of the city, are totally rooted in the land. They regard their life as determined by historical continuity: "We came here three hundred years ago and we stayed."

Hémon was an attentive and faithful observer of the reality of rural life, and the necessity of remaining true to his subject requires him to reproduce the major themes that had inspired the tradition of the Quebec novel before him. As with previous novelists, his characters represent specific choices — François Paradis is the free man, the *coureur de bois*; Lorenzo Surprenant incarnates the seductions of the city; while Eutrope Gagnon is the champion of continuity on the land. Maria is enchanted by the escape that each of her first two suitors offers her in turn; then, deeply distressed by the deaths of François Paradis and Laura Chapdelaine, she rises to the stature of an epic figure as she comes to accept the hard necessity of national continuity.

But that is not all there is to Hémon's work. Unlike his predecessors, he is able to fit his traditional theme comfortably into an esthetic framework in which the narrative and the lyric are combined. He used the classical methods of the Balzac novel to achieve something that had escaped all previous Quebec novelists; he brought believable characters to life within a story that, while simple, had the ring of truth. Hémon showed tenderness in situating his characters in their world of space and time, and respect for the rhythm of seasonal change and the arduousness of peasant labour. He was the first to give his characters a real sense of nature. By observing his models closely and sympathetically but nevertheless remaining at a distance from them, he was able to give his book a tone and local colour far removed from facile exoticism. *Maria Chapdelaine* remains a classic of French literature, and early Quebec critics attributed its huge success to the strangeness of its milieu and its local flavour, but this is unfair. Nothing of comparable quality was produced until Félix-Antoine Savard's *Menaud, maître-draveur* and Germaine Guèvremont's *Le Survenant.*

In the meantime, a number of novels presaged the end of the illegitimate reign of the rural myth. Early on, Rodolphe Girard in *Marie Calumet*, and especially Albert Laberge in *La Scouine*, strayed from the straight and narrow path of treating rural life as an idyll. These works marked a clear departure from the "sentimental song of the land" and "the ode in prose to the happy, peaceful peasant who dispenses our daily bread, protects his family traditions and works for . . . the survival of the race." While Girard's countryside is a place where salaciousness and sensual pleasure are significant elements, *La Scouine* offered a naturalistic vision of the intellectual mediocrity and physical misery of Quebec rural life. Laberge's book came out when the novel of the *terroir* school was at its zenith, but it stood outside the literary trend of the time. It was another twenty years before Ringuet's *Thirty Acres* appeared and brought the rural myth in the Quebec novel to an end.

The essay

The arrival of hundreds of thousands of European immigrants in the Canadian West made French Canadians a permanent minority in Canada and ended their great dream of one day becoming the majority. While England was trying to tighten the bonds — military, economic and political — linking the colonies of its empire, nationalist sentiment developed in Quebec. This sentiment, pro-Canadian at first and later favourable to Quebec autonomy, was exacerbated by the legislative harassment of French-speaking people in Manitoba, New Brunswick and Ontario. These were the main themes developed by Quebec essayists in the early twentieth century.

The work of Edmond de Nevers, now almost completely forgotten, is among the most original in French-Canadian literature. In his first essay, "L'avenir du peuple canadien-français" (The Future of the French-Canadian People), de Nevers urges the reader to accept an idealistic vision in harmony with clerical-nationalist ideology. It is the duty of French Canadians to carry an original message to America; assuming the role played by France in Europe, they are to be the keepers of a distinct culture and civilization. This society is to be based on art and spiritual values, devoted to things of the spirit, and scornful of wealth and economic development. French Canadians are to recapture the heroic and selfless spirit of the settlers of New France, leave behind their sterile partisan struggles, and devote themselves entirely to education, art and agriculture, which the author regards as comparable to one of the fine arts:

> I like to imagine that one day, when science has accomplished part of its mission of mowing down prejudices and opening minds, every farmer will have room

in his life for art, and every field, every prairie will be like a canvas where man in collaboration with the rain and the sun will seek not only to bring forth produce from the earth but also to achieve beauty, the eternal dream of every higher organism. It will be pleasant then to go as a joyous pilgrim through mountains and valleys and along shady roads, as in a museum where everything is arranged to please the viewer and everyone is charmed.

In "L'Âme américaine" (The American Soul), an essay in the tradition of the classic works of Alexis de Tocqueville and James Bryce, de Nevers tries to explain one of the most complex sociological and psychological conjunctions of recent centuries. In a long study in the *Revue des Deux Mondes* devoted to this essay, Ferdinand Brunetière, while disagreeing with its basic thesis, nevertheless recognized it as "one of the most important works on America published in a long time." Although de Nevers uses racial concepts and his defence of the integrity of the race against American influence is sometimes at the expense of rationality, he demonstrates an analytical capacity and a critical intelligence that make this piece one of the best literary essays of the era.

There were very few genuine essayists at the time. But there were a few writers who both were concerned with fundamental cultural questions and paid sufficient attention to literary form so that their work rises above the mediocrity almost universally attributed to their contemporaries. Notable among these were Jules Fournier and Olivar Asselin, journalists and polemicists; Wilfrid Laurier, Henri Bourassa and Armand Lavergne, highly popular political orators; Thomas Chapais and Lionel Groulx, historians committed to particular points of view; and Camille Roy and Louis Dantin, literary critics.

The fight against low standards and vulgarity in behaviour and expression was the highest priority for Asselin and the young Fournier. They were also fervent nationalists and faithful followers of Henri Bourassa, opposed to British imperialism and suspicious of parliamentary institutions. As we have seen, their nationalism was pan-Canadian, although their first commitment was to the survival of the French-Canadian "race"; thus, they adopted the cause of the French-speaking minorities outside Quebec. They also tried to arouse the anger of their readers against governments that allowed foreigners to develop Quebec's great natural resources, and regularly denounced the venality and powerlessness of French-speaking MPs in Ottawa.

Their leader, Bourassa, followed a tortuous path, and according to Fernand Dumont is a good illustration of the ideological uncertainties of Quebec society. He was Papineau's grandson and yet an ultramontane, a friend of Laurier's but an opponent of the empire, a man who tried to reconcile nationalism with Catholicism. Bourassa was a political leader, a charismatic speaker, an influential editorialist and, for generations of French Canadians, the symbol of *survivance* and the prophet admired for his resistance to the English. He electrified crowds with his oratorical gifts, and his articles defined the parameters of political thought within the nationalist élite, although they were often unclear. As a Catholic, Bourassa always subordinated his social and political ideas to a view of man in which spiritual reality was paramount. For many of his contemporaries, while he was a symbol of resistance, he was not always a credible political guide.

The writings of Lionel Groulx — historical works, novels and essays — were a reaction to Thomas Chapais's conciliatory, pro-English interpretation of history. Groulx devoted his entire career to defining a national doctrine through which the well-being of his countrymen could be brought about, and tried through his writings to spark a dynamic territorial nationalism in Quebec. He took his inspiration from the spectrum of nationalist political currents in Europe, and especially from the right wing in France. But while the social doctrines whose advocate he became were to have consequences in Europe with which we are only too familiar, Groulx avoided some of the narrowness of European nationalist thought. He strove to arouse people's consciousness, and was especially concerned with awakening a reaction to the prevailing apathy among Quebec's youth. It is still not possible to appreciate the full significance of the national doctrine he propagated.

This quick panorama of the development of Quebec literature in the early twentieth century is clearly incomplete. The study of this literature is still in an embryonic state. Almost nothing has been done, for example, on the dissemination and content of popular literature; it is to be suspected, however, that popular literature was much closer to the ideological and economic reality of a liberal Quebec than the literature of the élites. Nor has much been done on the development of an interesting English-language literary tradition in Montreal. Very few original studies have been done on writers in this tradition, with the exception of the humorist Stephen Leacock. This rapid survey, however, does show the strengths and weaknesses of Quebec literature, and demonstrates that it was more the afterglow of a traditional world view than the beacon of a world in transformation.

Painting*

The influence of The Hague school

At the end of the nineteenth century, a new enthusiasm developed among the wealthy art collectors of Montreal. They had become bored with the Barbizon school and its Canadian imitators and bestowed all their favour on the painters of The Hague. This Dutch school had developed in the 1870s as a reaction against the dominant academicism. The Hague painters drew from the same sources — Corot, Théodore Rousseau and Millet — as the Impressionists, but the style of painting that resulted was quite different.

Instead of analysing light into its colour components, the painters of The Hague school specialized in the expression of atmospheres. Their paintings are often monochromatic and fairly sombre, if not ominous; they are devoted primarily to

*This section was written by François-Marc Gagnon.

exploring the richness of tonal variation and, in this way, evoking the various moods that atmospheres can suggest. The word "subjective" has been used to describe their painting. This style of painting held a very strong attraction for the Anglo-Saxon bourgeoisie of Montreal — stronger, in any case, than the vividly coloured canvases of French Impressionism. One measure of the significance of these Dutch painters for the Montreal collectors is the fact that the first art books published in Canada were works by E.B. Greenshields in 1906 and 1914 dealing with The Hague school and especially with one of its members, Jan Hendrik Weissenbruch, a painter who is now all but forgotten.

Another indication of the extent to which The Hague school was in fashion is that during his first stay in Europe, the young James Wilson Morrice (1865-1924) spent part of a summer in the small Dutch town of Dordrecht. He had always dreamed of painting this picturesque location because he had seen it represented in many of the canvases collected by his father, David Morrice, and their neighbour on Redpath Street in Montreal, Sir William Van Horne.

The collectors who bought the paintings of Homer Watson and Horatio Walker (see chapter 17) became interested in works by Canadian artists who painted in the style of The Hague school, such as the Ontario painter Edmund Morris (1871-1913) and, to a lesser degree, Curtis Williamson, whose popularity was more limited to Toronto.

What was the reason for this new vogue? Can it be identified purely and simply with the widespread taste for landscapes? The landscapes of the Canadian painters influenced by The Hague school are quite different from those of Lucius R. O'Brien and John Arthur Fraser (see chapter 17) in that they do not resort at all to the idea of the picturesque. In fact, this idea is quite foreign to a painting such as Edmund M. Morris's *The St. Lawrence near Quebec* (c. 1905). The martello tower on the right — the only thing that might attract the viewer's eye to these low, grey banks — tends to disappear into the background. The main element in the canvas is the grey sky, with a kind of opening in the clouds in the centre. What is essential here is the oppressive feeling expressed by the sky hanging over Quebec. Morris's painting is a work of feeling, of mood, and can justly be described as "subjective" since what the painter feels takes precedence over rendering appearances. Ultimately, this idea of making a subjective mark on space is where the angle of vision of the artist who created such a painting coincided with that of the businessman who bought one. Businessmen, after all, were engaged in a task that followed similar lines — to transform raw nature as a function of a subjective (if not collective) vision.

In any case, by becoming attached to this new trend, the Montreal collectors opened the door to forms of art in which subjectivity played an even greater role. James Wilson Morrice would soon offer them a form of painting close to that of the Fauves, and especially Matisse. In sum, the importance of the style of painting based on The Hague school in the development of artistic taste in Montreal in the late nineteenth and early twentieth centuries is worth noting. It would later be attacked, notably by A.Y. Jackson in the 1920s, but it should not be forgotten that

Edmund M. Morris (1871-1913), *The St. Lawrence near Quebec*, 1905.

this style of painting was the channel through which "subjectivism" came to occupy its rightful place in the development of modern art in Quebec. In opposing it in the name of a kind of "nationalist objectivism," the Group of Seven showed its at least partly retrograde character.

Ozias Leduc

A significant part of the career of Ozias Leduc (1864-1955) coincided with the development described above. Leduc has been associated with his near-contemporary Homer Watson, nine years his senior. There is a persistent myth that he was a kind of recluse, the "hermit of Saint-Hyacinthe." According to this myth, because Leduc was a French Canadian, he never won the fame he deserved and was "marginalized" in his own society. The myth grew up in the early 1930s when Leduc, over sixty years old and feeling the repercussions of the depression, might have given the impression of not being a very active person. To Arthur Lemay, Jean Chauvin and René Bergeron, who visited him in this period, he seemed an old sage, dispensing aphorisms in the calm of his studio or the shade of his apple trees.

This, however, was a forced idleness, imposed by the difficulties of the time. When more attention is paid to the active years of Leduc's career, an entirely different impression emerges. The dominant element in his career consisted of major contracts for religious decoration. Laurier Lacroix has drawn up an impressive list of these contracts; between 1893 and 1927, Leduc fulfilled no fewer than twenty-three. In other words, he was far from being a recluse! In fact, he was one of the most important church decorators of his time, as well as one of the major contractors in this field. His work slackened only during the 1930s. Even during this difficult period, he managed to get contracts in Lachine and Rougemont.

The context of church sponsorship in which Leduc worked required him to carry out a well-defined iconographic program, which at first glance appears to bear little relationship to the themes explored by the painters of the period. However, even within the iconographic tradition that was imposed on him, Leduc often showed a great capacity for original work. And the aspects of church decoration that were less dependent on iconography gave him ample opportunity to demonstrate his great mastery of the decorative principles of Art Nouveau.

Another part of the myth is that Leduc never exhibited his paintings, and so as a result had no buyers for them. Again, the truth is quite different, as Jean-René Ostiguy has shown in his catalogue *Ozias Leduc: Peinture symbolique et religieuse*. In 1890, Leduc exhibited at the Salle Cavallo on Saint-Dominique Street in Montreal. The next year, he began his regular participation in the Art Association of Montreal's Spring Salon, where he exhibited fourteen times between 1891 and 1922; in the same period, his works were shown eleven times at the Royal Canadian Academy. It was only at the Canadian National Exhibition that he was not represented so frequently — three times between 1914 and 1917.

When the Saint-Sulpice Library gave him the opportunity to show forty of his works in 1916, it was putting its stamp of approval on an already recognized talent. In other words, given the state of the distribution network at the time, Leduc's works were shown neither more nor less than those of most of his fellow artists. In addition, his participation in exhibitions won him prizes (as for his *Still Life*, at the 1895 Salon) and led to sales (his canvas *The Green Apples* was acquired by the National Gallery after it was shown at the 1915 Salon). There were also many portrait commissions, which occupied his attention sporadically during the same period. In sum, the picture of a Leduc who never knew success and never became part of the artistic scene of his time does not stand up to the facts.

This is not the place to undertake a detailed analysis of Leduc's work. As Ostiguy has amply shown, it can be placed under the heading of symbolism and shows evidence of Leduc's considerable openness to the *fin-de-siècle* sensibility. His still life paintings always contain some hidden messages; his *Phrenology*,

Ozias Leduc (1864-1955), *Pommes vertes* (Green Apples), 1914-15.

painted in 1892, is actually a sort of allegory of painting, while the preparatory sketch for his *Child with Bread* (1892-99), bears the Latin motto *multum in parvo* (much in something small). The landscapes on which he worked in 1913 (the year of the *Blue Cumulus*) and 1921 (the year of *The Mauve Hour*) all explored various forms of atmospheric lighting suggesting the passage from light to shadow, from life to death.

If The Hague school helped introduce Quebec painters to a form of subjectivism in painting, it can be said that Leduc's symbolist sources performed a similar function. Here too, appearances are subordinated to a subjective interpretation of reality. In following this style, Leduc was in harmony with the taste of his immediate entourage, and especially the group associated with the review *Le Nigog*.

French-Canadian artists

Considerable attention has been devoted here to Ozias Leduc because his career followed a pattern typical of many French-Canadian artists of his time. Not only did their ethnic origin not harm their careers, but it often opened doors to them that were closed to their English-speaking colleagues. Nor was religious decora-

Ozias Leduc, *L'enfant au pain* (Child with Bread), 1892.

tion the only area that was reserved to French-Canadian artists. As noted in chapter 17, the vogue for historical monuments had been initiated in the preceding period by Louis-Philippe Hébert; this genre continued to flourish between 1896 and 1929. In the meantime, however, styles had changed, and sculptors adopted the *fin-de-siècle* sensibility, with its vogue for symbolism and Art Nouveau. The most characteristic sculptor of this tendency was Alfred Laliberté (1878-1953). In his well-known monument to Dollard des Ormeaux (1920) in Lafontaine Park in Montreal, a symbolic figure stands over the "hero" of Long Sault. Laliberté studied in Paris in 1898 under Thomas and Injalbert, and the Salons of the Société des Artistes Français showed some of his works in 1905 and

Alfred Laliberté (1878-1953), monument to Dollard des Ormeaux in Lafontaine Park in Montreal.

1912. He attracted notice for his sculpture representing *Young Indians Hunting*. Back in Canada, he pursued a twofold career, working as an official sculptor while at the same time doing personal work that was often much more daring.

The major architectural projects of the period created openings for French-Canadian painters and sculptors. Probably the best example of this is the decoration program for the parliament building in Quebec City, begun in 1883 and still incomplete at the end of the First World War. As Robert Derome has aptly shown, every French-Canadian artist of any consequence at the time was affected in one way or another by this project. The nationalist architect Eugène-Étienne Taché — to whom Quebec's motto "Je me souviens" (I remember) has been attributed — designed the building and, as noted in chapter 17, its façade was decorated with ten sculptures by Louis-Philippe Hébert. Interior decoration of the building presented greater problems. Practically every painter of any significance submitted a proposal. Napoléon Bourassa (1827-1916) made an unsuccessful attempt to palm off his enormous *Apotheosis of Christopher Columbus*. Others in the running were Joseph Arthur; Eugène Hamel (1845-1932); Marc-Aurèle de Foy Suzor-Coté (1869-1937); Henri Beau (1863-1949); Joseph Saint-Charles (1868-1956); and Charles Huot (1855-1930), who finally won the contract in 1910 with a proposal for three murals.

The three elements in Huot's successful proposal were two large canvases and a ceiling decoration. His interpretation of *The Sovereign Council* (1926-31) can still be seen in the former legislative council chamber, as can his *Debate on Language: Session of the Legislative Assembly of Lower Canada, January 21, 1793* (1910-13) in the national assembly (formerly legislative assembly) chamber. Mounted on the ceiling of the assembly chamber is a large canvas illustrating the partiotic theme *Je me souviens* (1914-20). In carrying out this commission, Huot had to conform to the nationalist ideology of his sponsors, and in this respect he was in a similar position to a painter who worked for the church during the same period. He too was subject to a specific iconographic program, and had access to large surfaces where he could exercise his talent.

The reasons why some of the rival proposals were rejected have been noted by Derome, and they provide a good indication of how the ideological pressure on the painter operated. Bourassa's *Apotheosis of Christopher Columbus* was considered too general and, "in the final analysis, not very nationalist." A proposal by Charles Alexander Smith, *The Assembly of the Six Counties* (1890) was rejected because the new premier who took office in 1891, Charles Boucher de Boucherville, considered it "too revolutionary." The subjects Huot dealt with represented the golden mean, neither too far to the right nor too far to the left, and corresponded most closely to the conservative thinking of the politicians of the time.

It is necessary to take these commissions for religious and historical paintings into consideration if one is to get a reasonable picture of how French-Canadian artists fared during the period. It is now customary to look down on academic art of this sort, but that is to apply today's standards to work that was viewed very differently at the time. Indeed, a major commission was regarded as an opportunity for an artist to exercise his talent to the fullest.

James Wilson Morrice

Just after 1900, a significant change occurred in Quebec painting. Interest in landscapes and paintings inspired by the Barbizon and Hague schools waned, and there was a new openness to modern forms of inspiration. The great painter of the period was James Wilson Morrice, but Morrice would not have been what he was without an audience in Canada. It was shown earlier how mythical is the persistent belief that Ozias Leduc was denied the success he deserved because he was French Canadian. There is an equally persistent myth about Morrice, according to which he was unappreciated in his own country and gained success only on the international scene. In truth, his international success has been greatly exaggerated, and as a result the support he received in his own country has gone almost unnoticed. Morrice owed his success to an institution that made its appearance soon after the turn of the century — the Canadian Art Club, founded in 1907. It is far from coincidental that the idea for the club was due to two Canadian disciples of The Hague school, Edmund M. Morris and Curtis Williamson. Founded to encourage artists with "subjective" tendencies and initially recruiting its members from among Toronto artists and collectors, including the banker D.R. Wilkie, the club became the champion of avant-garde painting, and it was here that Morrice's artistic audacity was most sympathetically received.

At first, the club was almost exclusively a Toronto institution, and its first president was none other than Homer Watson. But neither Morris nor Williamson was satisfied with this state of affairs, and they were eager for Montreal to be represented as well. William Brymner (1855-1925) was approached, and he turned out to be one of the club's most valuable recruits. It was he who provided it with a strong representation from Montreal; a friend of Brymner's, Maurice Cullen (1866-1934), and two of his former students, Clarence Gagnon (1881-1942) and W.H. Clapp (1879-1954), were admitted on his recommendation. Participation in the Canadian Art Club gave these Quebec painters access to the Toronto market and undoubtedly contributed to their success.

In return, the entry of Montreal painters into the Canadian Art Club made Canadian collectors more open to a different form of painting, less dependent on The Hague school and closer to Impressionism and Fauvism. Suzor-Coté participated in one of the club's exhibitions in 1913. Like Maurice Cullen, Suzor-Coté had been attracted to Impressionism while in France and had applied its formulas to Canadian subjects, as in his *Winter Landscape* (1909). In the foreground of this painting is a small river, the Nicolet in Arthabaska county, soon after spring thaw. The arches of a bridge and a few houses at the edge of the woods are visible in the background. Painted in white, pale blue and gold, the canvas is a hymn to the triumph of the forces of life over the forces of frost and death. Thus, Suzor-Coté

Aurèle de Foy Suzor-Coté (1869-1937), *Winter Landscape,* 1909.

added a symbolic dimension that would not be expected in the Impressionist models that inspired him.

But the Montreal painter most highly esteemed by the members of the Canadian Art Club was James Wilson Morrice. Morrice was a friend of Cullen, Brymner, Williamson and Morris and became the idol of younger painters such as Clarence Gagnon, A.Y. Jackson (1882-1974) and Lawren S. Harris (1885-1970) and even John G. Lyman (1886-1970) and Paul-Émile Borduas (1905-60). His career shows evidence of a continuing desire to assimilate the new currents that grew up in French painting during his time. After a disappointing stay in the academies of Paris — he left the Académie Jullian after a few weeks in 1891 — Morrice sought advice from Henri Harpignies (1819-1916) in nearby Bois-le-Roi. In other words, he went where the taste of his Montreal patrons led him, as Harpignies was still part of the Barbizon school. It was a judicious choice.

At the time, the English "esthetic movement" — Oscar Wilde, James Whistler,

James Wilson Morrice (1865-1924), *Landscape, Tangiers*, c. 1911-12.

Aubrey Beardsley — was all the rage in Paris. Morrice eventually understood this and became infatuated with Whistler. This new enthusiasm led him to Venice, which he visited in 1896 along with Maurice Cullen. Then, the two friends together came under the influence of Impressionism. They both began to use brighter colours and, painting on the north bank of the St. Lawrence east of Quebec City during the winter of 1896-97, attempted to depict Quebec winter scenes in these bold colours. *On Shipboard*, which dates from 1900-3, shows how far Morrice had moved from the misty atmospheres favoured by Whistler towards the brilliant colours of Impressionism.

In 1900, Morrice settled at 45 Quai des Grands-Augustins in Paris, and this was the beginning of one of his most fruitful periods. He alternated between Parisian and Canadian subjects, and demonstrated an increasingly profound understanding of pure painting. The painting of Matisse had a great impact on him and led to a new and final period in his work. Morrice may have met Matisse in 1908, but he was familiar with Matisse's work before that date. It was of such great interest to him that he decided to follow the master to Tangier and may have spent the winter of 1911-12 — or 1912-13, or both — at his side. *Landscape, Tangiers* (c. 1911-12) shows the influence of Matisse's painting on him. In this landscape, perspective is distorted to achieve a decorative organization of the surface. Colour is applied in broad strokes, rather than in light touches as in the works of the previous period, when Impressionist influence was most strongly felt. From that time on, Morrice continued to develop in the same direction, until his death in Tunis in 1924.

This quick summary of Morrice's development gives only a very sketchy idea of his influence on painting in Quebec. But it can be said that Quebec artists owed their familiarity with the language of modern painting to Morrice. For the first time, painting itself became its own object, and the subject treated became secondary. When the Group of Seven came into fashion, this new commitment would be obscured, but this was a development that did not affect the Quebec art scene as directly. John Lyman devoted a small book to Morrice in the *L'Art vivant* (Living Art) collection edited by Maurice Gagnon, and restored him to his rightful place as the forerunner of modern art in Quebec.

GENERAL BIBLIOGRAPHY

Specialized works covering particular topics are listed by chapters. However, there are also some general works of fundamental importance, a few of which are listed below.

Research tools

Both the Quebec and the federal government publish annual collections of statistical data covering a very wide range of subjects. These collections — the *Quebec Yearbook*, published since 1914, and the *Canada Year Book*, published since 1885 — are valuable research tools. The results of the decennial *Census of Canada*, published in book form every ten years since 1851, are another major source on Canada's population, economy and society. There is also a collection in which significant statistical series are presented in historical perspective:

Urquhart, M.C. and K.A.H. Buckley, eds. *Historical Statistics of Canada*. Toronto: Macmillan, 1965. 672 pp.

Three guides to the literature are useful supplements for the period under consideration. The first two cover Canadian history as a whole, while the third deals more specifically with post-Confederation Quebec:

Beaulieu, André, Jean Hamelin, and Benoît Bernier. *Guide d'histoire du Canada*. Quebec City: Presses de l'Université Laval, 1969. 540 pp.

Thibault, Claude. *Bibliographia Canadiana*. Don Mills, Ont.: Longmans, 1973. 795 pp.

Durocher, René and Paul-André Linteau. *Histoire du Québec: Bibliographie sélective (1867-1970)*. Montreal: Boréal Express, 1970. 189 pp.

Finally, a historical atlas is worth noting:

Kerr, D.G.G. *A Historical Atlas of Canada*. Don Mills, Ont.: Nelson, 1966. 120 pp.

General works

The first work that must be mentioned here is Robert Rumilly's monumental *Histoire de la province de Québec* in forty-one volumes (Montreal: different publishers, 1940-69). This sprawling narrative deals primarily with Quebec's political life, but touches on many other topics as well. The period under consideration is covered in the first thirty volumes.

The geographer Raoul Blanchard conducted a vast inquiry into Quebec's human geography, with considerable emphasis on historical aspects. His work was published in five volumes, each covering a portion of Quebec's territory. Familiarity with this work is essential for anyone who wishes to study modern Quebec history:

Blanchard, Raoul. *L'est du Canada français*. 2 vols. Montreal: Beauchemin, 1935.

———. *Le centre du Canada français*. Montreal: Beauchemin, 1948. 577 pp.

———. *L'Ouest du Canada français. Montréal et sa région*. Montreal: Beauchemin, 1953. 399 pp.

———. *L'ouest du Canada français. Les pays de l'Ottawa. L'Abitibi-Temiscamingue*. Montreal: Beauchemin, 1954. 334 pp.

Readers wishing to put Quebec history in its Canadian context would do best to consult the Canadian Centenary series. Three volumes in this series deal with the years between 1867 and 1929:

Morton, W.L. *The Critical Years: The Union of British North America 1857-1873*. Toronto: McClelland and Stewart, 1964. 322 pp.

Waite, P.B. *Canada 1874-1896: Arduous Destiny*. Toronto: McClelland and Stewart, 1971. 340 pp.

Brown, Robert Craig and Ramsay Cook. *Canada 1896-1921: A Nation Transformed*. Toronto: McClelland and Stewart, 1974. 412 pp.

Finally, there are, in French, a number of major syntheses of Quebec and Canadian history. Among them are the following three works:

Vaugeois, Denis and Jacques Lacoursière, eds. *Canada-Québec: Synthèse historique*. Montreal: Renouveau pédagogique, 1969. 615 pp.

Robert, Jean-Claude. *Du Canada français au Québec libre: Histoire d'un mouvement indépendantiste*. Paris and Montreal: Flammarion, 1975. 323 pp.

Hamelin, Jean, ed. *Histoire du Québec*. Toulouse: Privat, 1976. 538 pp.

BIBLIOGRAPHIES BY CHAPTER

Chapter 1

Blanchard, Raoul. *Le Canada français*. Montreal: Librairie Arthème Fayard (Canada) Ltée, 1960. 314 pp.

Gourou, Pierre, Fernard Grenier, and Louis-Edmond Hamelin, *Atlas du monde contemporain*. Montreal: Éditions du Renouveau pédagogique, 1967.

Quebec. Department of Communications. *Le Québec tel quel*. Quebec City, 1973. 254 pp.

Chapter 2

Bouvier, Léon F. "La stratification sociale du groupe ethnique canadien-français aux États-Unis." *Recherches sociographiques*, vol. 5, no. 3 (Sept.-Dec. 1964), pp. 371-79.

Charbonneau, Hubert. *La population du Québec: études rétrospectives*. Montreal: Boréal Express, 1973. 110 pp.

Copp, Terry. *The Anatomy of Poverty: The Condition of the Working Class in Montreal 1897-1929*. Toronto: McClelland and Stewart, 1974. 192 pp.

Faucher, Albert. "L'émigration des Canadiens français au XIXe siècle: position du problème et perspectives." *Recherches sociographiques*, vol. 5, no. 3 (Sept.-Dec. 1964), pp. 277-318.

Groulx, Adélard. "La mortalité maternelle et la mortalité infantile à Montréal." *Union Médicale du Canada*, Dec. 1943, pp. 1415-17.

Hamelin, Jean. "Quebec and the Outside World 1867-1967." *Quebec Yearbook 1968-1969*, pp. 37-60. Quebec City: Éditeur Officiel du Québec, 1969.

——— and Yves Roby. *Histoire économique du Québec, 1851-1896*. Montreal: Fides, 1971. Part 1, chapter 2.

Henripin, Jacques. *Le coût de la croissance démographique*. Montreal: Presses de l'Université de Montréal, 1968. 43 pp.

———. "Population et main-d'oeuvre." In *Croissance et structure économiques de la province de Québec*, edited by André Raynauld, pp. 247-67. Quebec City: Department of Industry and Commerce, 1961.

———. "Quebec and the Demographic Dilemma of French-Canadian Society." In *Quebec Society and Politics*, edited by Dale C. Thomson, pp. 155-66. Toronto: McClelland and Stewart, 1973.

———. *Trends and Factors of Fertility in Canada*. Ottawa: Statistics Canada, 1972. 421 pp.

——— and Yves Péron. "The Demographic Transition of the Province of Quebec." In *Population and Social Change*, edited by D.V. Glass and Roger Revelle, pp. 213-31. London: Edward Arnold, 1972.

Langlois, Georges. *Histoire de la population canadienne-française*. Montreal: Éditions Albert Lévesque, 1935. 309 pp.

Morin, Rosaire. *L'immigration au Canada*. Montreal: Action nationale, 1966. 172 pp.

Silver, Arthur I. "French Canada and the Prairie Frontier, 1870-1890." *Canadian Historical Review*, vol. 50, no. 1 (March 1969), pp. 11-36.

Télé-Université. *Histoire du Québec d'aujourd'hui: Population et société*.

Chapter 3

Arès, Richard. *Les positions ethniques, linguistiques et religieuses des Canadiens français à la suite du recensement de 1971*. Montreal: Bellarmin, 1975. 210 pp.

Brunet, Michel. *Québec/Canada anglais: Deux itinéraires, un affrontement*. Montreal: HMH, 1968. Pp. 185-204.

Charbonneau, Hubert, ed. *La Population du Québec: études rétrospectives*. Montreal: Boréal Express, 1973. 110 pp.

——— and Robert Maheu. *Les aspects démographiques de la question linguistique*. Synthesis (S 3) prepared for the Commission of Inquiry on the position of the French language and on language rights in Quebec. Quebec City: Éditeur Officiel du Québec, 1973. 438 pp.

Sellar, Robert. *The Tragedy of Quebec: The Expulsion of Its Protestant Farmers*. 1916. Toronto: University of Toronto Press, 1974. 374 pp.

Chapter 4

Angers, François-Albert. "L'évolution économique du Canada et du Québec depuis la Confédération." *Revue d'histoire de l'Amérique française*, Vol. 21, no. 3a (1967), pp. 637-55.

Bertram, Gordon W. "Economic Growth in Canadian Industry, 1870-1915: The Staple Model." In *Approaches to Canadian Economic History*, edited by W.T. Easterbrook and M.H. Watkins, pp. 74-98. Toronto: McClelland and Stewart, 1967.

Canada. Royal Commission on Dominion-Provincial Relations (Rowell-Sirois Commission). *Report*. Vol. 1: *Canada: 1867-1939*. Ottawa, 1940. 259 pp.

Caves, Richard F. and Richard H. Holton. *The Canadian Economy: Prospect and Retrospect*. Cambridge, Mass.: Harvard University Press, 1961. 676 pp.

Creighton, Donald G. *The Empire of the St. Lawrence*. Toronto: Macmillan of Canada, 1956. Originally published as *The Commercial Empire of the St. Lawrence, 1760-1850*. Toronto: Ryerson Press, 1937. 441 pp.

Dales, J.H. *The Protective Tariff in Canada's Development*. Toronto: University of Toronto Press, 1966. 168 pp.

Dubuc, Alfred. "Développement économique et politique de développement: Canada 1900-1940." In *Économie québécoise*, edited by Robert Comeau, pp. 175-217. Montreal: Presses de l'Université du Québec, 1969.

Easterbrook, W.T. and Hugh G.J. Aitken. *Canadian Economic History*. Toronto: Macmillan of Canada, 1967. 606 pp.

Faucher, Albert. *Histoire économique et unité canadienne*. Montreal: Fides, 1970. 296 pp.

———. *Québec en Amérique au XIXe siècle: Essai sur les caractères économiques de la Laurentie*. Montreal: Fides, 1973. 247 pp.

——— and Maurice Lamontagne. "History of Industrial Development." In *French-Canadian Society*, 2 vols., edited by Marcel Rioux and Yves Martin, vol. 1, pp. 257-71. Toronto: McClelland and Stewart, Carleton Library. 1968.

Gervais, Gaétan. "L'expansion du réseau ferroviaire québécois (1875-1895)." Ph.D. thesis (history), University of Ottawa, Ottawa, 1978. 538 pp.

Grimal, Henri. *De l'empire britannique au Commonwealth*. Paris: Armand Colin, 1971. 416 pp.

Hamelin, Jean and Yves Roby. *Histoire économique du Québec, 1851-1896*. Montreal: Fides, 1971. 436 pp.

Hobsbawm, Eric J. *Industry and Empire*. London: Weidenfeld and Nicolson, 1968. 336 pp.

Mackintosh, W.A. *The Economic Background of Dominion-Provincial Relations*. Study prepared for the Royal Commission on Dominion-Provincial Relations. Ottawa: King's Printer, 1939.

Rivard, Jean-Yves. "La politique nationale et le développement industriel du Québec, 1870-1910." MA thesis (economics), University of Montreal, Montreal, 1960. 108 pp.

Chapter 5

Gagnon, Rodolphe, "Le chemin de fer de Québec au Lac Saint-Jean (1854-1900)." D.E.S. thesis (history), Laval University, Quebec City, 1968. 219 pp.

Gervais, Gaétan. "L'expansion du réseau ferroviaire québécois (1875-1895)." Ph.D. thesis (history), University of Ottawa, Ottawa, 1978. 538 pp.

Glazebrook, G.P. de T. *A History of Transportation in Canada*. Toronto: Ryerson Press, 1938. Paperback edition, 2 vols. Toronto: McClelland and Stewart, Carleton Library, 1964.

Hamelin, Jean and Yves Roby. *Histoire économique du Québec, 1851-1896*. Montreal: Fides, 1971. 436 pp.

Hamelin, Marcel. *Les premières années du parlementarisme québécois (1867-1878)*. Quebec City: Presses de l'Université Laval, 1974. 386 pp.

Naylor, Tom. *The History of Canadian Business 1867-1914*. 2 vols. Toronto: James Lorimer and Co., 1975.

Provost, Honorius. *Sainte-Marie de la Nouvelle-Beauce: Histoire civile*. Quebec City: Éditions de la Nouvelle-Beauce, 1970. Chapters 31 and 32.

Séguin, Normand. *La conquête du sol au 19e siècle*. Montreal: Boréal Express, 1977. 295 pp.

Stevens, G.R. *Canadian National Railways*. 2 vols. Toronto: Clarke Irwin, 1960-62.

Rudin, Ronald. "The Development of Four Quebec Towns, 1840-1914: A Study of Urban and Economic Growth in Quebec." Ph.D. thesis, York University, Toronto, 1977.

Young, Brian J. *Promoters and Politicians: The North-Shore Railways in the History of Quebec, 1854-85*. Toronto: University of Toronto Press, 1978. 193 pp.

Chapter 6

De Montigny, Benjamin-Antoine-Testard. *La colonisation.* Montreal: C.O. Beauchemin & Fils, 1895. 350 pp.

Hamelin, Jean and Yves Roby. *Histoire économique du Québec 1851-1896.* Montreal: Fides, 1971. Part 3, chapters 1-3.

Létourneau, Firmin. *Histoire de l'agriculture.* N.p., 1968. 398 pp.

Minville, Esdras, ed. *L'agriculture.* Montreal: Fides, 1943. 555 pp.

———, ed. *La forêt.* Montreal: Fides, 1944. 414 pp.

Séguin, Normand. *La conquête du sol au 19e siècle.* Montreal: Boréal Express, 1977. 295 pp.

Taché, Joseph-Charles. *Report of the Special Committee on the State of Agriculture in Lower Canada.* Province of Canada. Legislative Assembly. *Journals,* vol. 9. Appendix 1850.

Chapter 7

Acheson, T.W. "The Social Origins of Canadian Industrialism: A Study in the Structure of Entrepreneurship." Ph.D. thesis (history) University of Toronto, Toronto, 1971.

Angers, François-Albert and Roland Parenteau. *Statistiques manufacturières du Québec.* Montreal: École des Hautes Études commerciales, 1966. 166 pp.

Blanchard, Raoul. *L'Est du Canada français.* 2 vols. Montreal: Beauchemin, 1935.

———. *L'Ouest du Canada français: Montréal et sa région.* Montreal: Beauchemin, 1953. 399 pp.

Cooper, John Irwin. *Montreal: A Brief History.* 1942. Montreal: McGill-Queen's University Press, 1969. 217 pp.

Faucher, Albert. *Québec en Amérique au XIXe siècle: Essai sur les caractères économiques de la Laurentie.* Montreal: Fides, 1973. 247 pp.

Hamelin, Jean and Yves Roby. *Histoire économique du Québec, 1851-1896.* Montreal: Fides, 1971. Part 4, chapters 2 and 3.

Harvey, Fernand. *Révolution industrielle et travailleurs.* Montreal: Boréal Express, 1978. 347 pp.

Kilbourn, William. *The Elements Combined: A History of the Steel Company of Canada.* Toronto: Clarke Irwin, 1960. 335 pp.

Linteau, Paul-André. *Maisonneuve ou Comment des promoteurs fabriquent une ville (1883-1918)*. Montreal: Boréal Express, 1981. 280 pp.

Rouillard, Jacques. *Les travailleurs du coton au Québec, 1900-1915*. Montreal: Presses de l'Université du Québec, 1974. 152 pp.

Stone, Leroy O. *Urban Development in Canada*. Ottawa: Dominion Bureau of Statistics, 1967. 293 pp.

Trotier, Louis. "Caractères de l'organisation urbaine de la province de Québec." *Revue de Géographie de Montréal*, vol. 18, no. 2 (1964), pp. 279-85.

———. "La genèse du réseau urbain du Québec." *Recherches sociographiques*, vol. 9, nos. 1-2 (Jan.-Aug. 1968), pp. 23-32.

Chapter 8

Bouchard, Gérard. "Introduction à l'étude de la société saguenayenne aux XIXe et XXe siècles." *Revue d'histoire de l'Amérique française*, vol. 31, no. 1 (June 1977), pp. 3-27.

Bourque, Gilles and Nicole Laurin-Frenette. "Social Classes and Nationalist Ideologies in Quebec, 1760-1970." Translated by P. Resnick and P. Renyi. In *Capitalism and the National Question in Canada*, edited by Gary Teeple, pp. 185-210. Toronto: University of Toronto Press, 1972.

Hamelin, Jean and Yves Roby. *Histoire économique du Québec, 1851-1896*. Montreal: Fides, 1971. 436 pp.

Harvey, Fernand. *Révolution industrielle et travailleurs*. Montreal: Boréal Express, 1978. 347 pp.

Létourneau, Firmin. *Histoire de l'agriculture*. N.p., 1968. 398 pp.

Linteau, Paul-André. "Quelques réflexions autour de la bourgeoisie québécoise, 1850-1914." *Revue d'histoire de l'Amérique française*, vol. 30, no. 1 (June 1976), pp. 55-66.

Macdonald, L.R. "Merchants against Industry: An Idea and Its Origins." *Canadian Historical Review*, vol. 56, no. 3 (Sept. 1975), pp. 263-81.

Naylor, R.T. "The Rise and Fall of the Third Commercial Empire of the St. Lawrence." In *Capitalism and the National Question in Canada*, edited by Gary Teeple, pp. 1-41. Toronto: University of Toronto Press, 1972.

Rioux, Marcel and Yves Martin, eds. *French-Canadian Society*. 2 vols. Toronto: McClelland and Stewart Carleton Library, 1968. 405 pp.

Séguin, Normand. *La conquête du sol au 19e siècle*. Montreal: Boréal Express, 1977. 295 pp.

Chapter 9

Ames, Herbert Brown. *The City below the Hill*. 1897. Toronto: University of Toronto Press, 1972. 116 pp.

De Bonville, Jean. *Jean-Baptiste Gagnepetit: Les travailleurs montréalais à la fin du XIXe siècle*. Montreal: L'Aurore, 1975. 253 pp.

De Montigny, Benjamin-Antoine-Testard. *La colonisation*. Montreal: C.O. Beauchemin & Fils, 1895. 350 pp.

Gérin, Léon. "L'habitant de Saint-Justin." *Proceedings of the Royal Society of Canada*, 2d ser., no. 4 (May 1898), pp. 139-216.

Harvey, Fernand. *Révolution industrielle et travailleurs*. Montreal: Boréal Express, 1978. 347 pp.

Létourneau, Firmin. *Histoire de l'agriculture*. N.p., 1968. 398 pp.

Savard, Pierre, ed. *Paysans et ouvriers québécois d'autrefois*. Quebec City: Presses de l'Université Laval, 1968. 153 pp.

Séguin, Normand. *La conquête du sol au 19e siècle*. Montreal: Boréal Express, 1977. 295 pp.

Taché, Joseph-Charles. *Report of the Special Committee on the State of Agriculture in Lower Canada*. Province of Canada. Legislative Assembly. *Journals*, vol. 9. Appendix. 1850.

Chapter 10

Burgess, Joanne. "L'industrie de la chaussure à Montréal: 1840-1870 — le passage de l'artisanat à la fabrique." *Revue d'histoire de l'Amérique française*, vol. 31, no. 2 (Sept. 1977), pp. 187-210.

De Bonville, Jean. *Jean-Baptiste Gagnepetit: Les travailleurs montréalais à la fin du XIXe siècle*. Montreal: L'Aurore, 1975. 253 pp.

Hamelin, Jean, ed. *Les travailleurs québécois, 1851-1896*. Montreal: Presses de l'Université du Québec, 1973. 221 pp.

———, Paul Larocque, and Jacques Rouillard. *Répertoire des grèves dans la province de Québec au XIXe siècle*. Montreal: Les Presses de l'École des Hautes Études Commerciales, 1970. 168 pp.

Harvey, Fernand. "Les Chevaliers du Travail, les États-Unis et la société québécoise (1882-1902)." In *Aspects historiques du mouvement ouvrier au Québec*, pp. 33-118. Montreal: Boréal Express, 1973.

——. *Révolution industrielle et travailleurs*. Montreal: Boréal Express, 1978. 347 pp.

Héroux, Denis and Richard Desrosiers. *Le travailleur québécois et le syndicalisme*. Montreal: Les Éditions de Sainte-Marie, n.d. 120 pp.

Histoire du mouvement ouvrier au Québec (1825-1976). CNTU-CEQ, 1979. 235 pp.

Chapter 11

Boucher, Jacques. "L'histoire de la condition juridique et sociale de la femme au Canada français." In *Livre du centenaire du Code civil*, 2 vols., compiled by Jacques Boucher and André Morel, vol. 1, pp. 155-67. Montreal: Presses de l'Université de Montréal, 1970.

Jean, Michèle. *Québécoises du 20e siècle*. Montreal: Éditions du Jour, 1974. 303 pp.

Johnson, Micheline Dumont. "History of the Status of Women in the Province of Quebec." In *Cultural Tradition and Political History of Women in Canada*. Studies of the Royal Commission on the Status of Women in Canada, no. 8. Ottawa: Information Canada, 1971. 55 pp.

Labarrère-Paulé, André. *Les instituteurs laïques au Canada français 1836-1900*. Quebec City: Presses de l'Université Laval, 1965. 471 pp.

Lavigne, Marie and Yoland Pinard, eds. *Les femmes dans la société québécoise*. Montreal: Boréal Express, 1977. 214 pp.

Chapter 12

Aubert, R. *Le pontificat de Pie IX (1846-1878)*. Paris: Bloud et Gay, n.d. 592 pp.

Audet, Louis-Philippe. *Histoire de l'enseignement au Québec*, 2 vols. Montreal: Holt, Rinehart & Winston, 1971. Vol. 2. 496 pp.

——. *Histoire du Conseil de l'instruction publique de la province de Québec, 1856-1964*. Montreal: Leméac, 1964. 346 pp.

——. "La fondation de l'école polytechnique de Montréal." *Cahier des dix*, no. 30 (1965), pp. 149-76.

Boucher de la Bruère, M. *Le Conseil de l'instruction publique et le Comité catholique*. Montreal: Le Devoir, 1918. 270 pp.

Denault, Bernard and Benoît Lévesque. *Éléments pour une sociologie des communautés religieuses au Québec*. Montreal: Presses de l'Université de Montréal; Sherbrooke: Université de Sherbrooke, 1975. 220 pp.

Hamelin, Louis-Edmond. "Évolution numérique séculaire du clergé catholique dans le Québec." *Recherches sociographiques*, vol. 2, no. 2 (April-June 1961), pp. 189-242.

Labarrère-Paulé, André. *Les instituteurs laïques au Canada français 1836-1900*. Quebec City: Presses de l'Université Laval, 1965. 471 pp.

Lajeunesse, Marcel, ed. *L'éducation au Québec, 19e-20e siècles*. Montreal: Boréal Express, 1971. 145 pp.

Voisine, Nive, ed. *Histoire de l'église catholique au Québec, 1608-1970*. Montreal: Fides, 1971. 112 pp.

Wade, Mason. *The French Canadians 1760-1967*. 2 vols. Rev. ed. Toronto: Macmillan of Canada, 1968. Vol. 1, 1760-1911. 607 pp.

Walsh, H.H. *The Christian Church in Canada*. Toronto: Ryerson Press, 1968.

Chapter 13

Arès, Richard, *Dossier sur le pacte fédératif de 1867*. Montreal: Bellarmin, 1967. 264 pp.

Canada. Constitution. *British North America Act and Selected Statutes, 1867-1962*. Prepared and annotated by Maurice Ollivier. Ottawa: Queen's Printer, 1962. 662 pp.

Cook, Ramsay. *Provincial Autonomy, Minority Rights and the Compact Theory, 1867-1921*. Study No. 4 of the Royal Commission on Bilingualism and Biculturalism. Ottawa: Queen's Printer, 1969. 81 pp.

Desrosiers, Richard, ed. *Le personnel politique québécois*. Montreal: Boréal Express, 1972. 142 pp.

Hamelin, Marcel. *Les premières années du parlementarisme québécois (1867-1878)*. Quebec City: Presses de l'Université Laval, 1974. 386 pp.

Quebec. Royal Commission of Inquiry on Constitutional Problems (Tremblay Commission). *Report*. 4 vols. Quebec City, 1956.

Wheare, K.C. *Federal Government*. 4th ed. London: Oxford University Press, 1963. 266 pp.

Chapter 14

Bernard, Jean-Paul, *Les Rouges: libéralisme, nationalisme et anticléricalisme au milieu du XIXe siècle*. Montreal: Presses de l'Université du Québec, 1971. 394 pp.

Caya, Marcel. "Aperçu sur les élections provinciales du Québec de 1867 à 1886." *Revue d'histoire de l'Amérique française*, vol. 29, no. 2 (September 1975), pp. 191-208.

Desilets, André. "La succession de Cartier, 1873-1891," Canadian Historical Association, *Historical Papers* (1968), pp. 49-64.

Hamelin, Jean et al. *Aperçu de la politique canadienne au XIXe siècle*. Quebec City: Culture, 1965. 154 pp.

———. *Les première années du parlementarisme québécois (1867-1878)*. Quebec City: Presses de l'Université Laval, 1974. 386 pp.

——— et al. "Les élections provinciales dans le Québec." *Cahiers de Géographie de Québec*, vol. 4, no. 7 (special issue, October 1959-March 1960), pp. 5-207.

——— and Marcel Hamelin. *Les moeurs électorales dans le Québec de 1791 à nos jours*. Montreal: Éditions du Jour, 1962. 125 pp.

Laforte, Denis and André Bernard. *La législation électorale au Québec, 1790-1967*. Montreal: Éditions Sainte-Marie, 1969. 197 pp.

Neatby, H. Blair and John T. Saywell. "Chapleau and the Conservative Party in Quebec," *Canadian Historical Review*, vol. 37, no. 1 (March 1956), pp. 1-22.

Chapter 15

Bonenfant, Jean-Charles. *La naissance de la Confédération*. Montreal: Leméac, 1969. 155 pp.

Brunet, Michel. *Québec/Canada anglais: Deux itinéraires, un affrontement*, pp. 231-86. Montreal: HMH, 1968.

Canada. Royal Commission on Dominion-Provincial Relations (Rowell-Sirois Commission). *Report*. Vol. 1: *Canada: 1867-1939*. Ottawa, 1940. 259 pp.

Cook, Ramsay. *Provincial Autonomy, Minority Rights and the Compact Theory, 1867-1921*. Study No. 4 of the Royal Commission on Bilingualism and Biculturalism. Ottawa: Queen's Printer, 1969. 81 pp.

Dominion-Provincial and Interprovincial Conferences from 1887 to 1926. Ottawa: King's Printer, 1951. 114 pp.

Gibson, Frederick W., ed. *Cabinet Formation and Bicultural Relations: Seven Case Studies*. Study No. 6 of the Royal Commission on Bilingualism and Biculturalism. Ottawa: Queen's Printer, 1970. 190 pp.

Hamelin, Marcel. *Les premières années du parlementarisme québécois (1867-1878)*. Quebec City: Presses de l'Université Laval, 1974. 386 pp.

Lamontagne, Maurice. *Le fédéralisme canadien*. Quebec City: Presses de l'Université Laval, 1954. 298 pp.

Moore, A. Milton et al. *The Financing of Canadian Federation: The First Hundred Years*. Toronto: Canadian Tax Foundation, 1966.

Morison, J.C. "Oliver Mowat and the Development of Provincial Rights in Ontario: A Study in Dominion-Provincial Relations, 1867-1896." *Three History Theses*. Toronto: Ontario Department of Public Records and Archives, 1961. 308 pp.

Quebec. Royal Commission of Inquiry on Constitutional Problems (Tremblay Commission). *Report*. 4 vols. Quebec City, 1956.

Smiley, Donald V. *The Canadian Political Nationality*. Toronto: Methuen, 1967. 142 pp.

Chapter 16

Berger, Carl. *Imperialism and Nationalism, 1884-1914: A Conflict in Canadian Thought*. Toronto: Copp Clark, 1969. 119 pp.

———. *The Sense of Power: Studies in the Ideas of Canadian Imperialism 1867-1914*. Toronto: University of Toronto Press, 1970. 277 pp.

Bernard, Jean-Paul, ed. *Les idéologies québécoises au 19e siècle*. Montreal: Boréal Express, 1973. 149 pp.

———. *Les Rouges: libéralisme, nationalisme et anticléricalisme au milieu du XIXe siècle*. Montreal: Presses de l'Université du Québec, 1971. 394 pp.

Bonenfant, Jean-Charles. *Thomas Chapais*. Montreal: Fides, 1957. 95 pp.

Brunet, Michel. "Trois dominantes de la pensée canadienne-française: l'agriculturalisme, l'anti-étatisme et le messianisme." In *La présence anglaise et les Canadiens: Études sur l'histoire et la pensée des deux Canadas*, pp. 113-66. Montreal: Beauchemin, 1958.

Dumont, Fernand et al. *Idéologies au Canada français, 1850-1900*. Quebec City: Presses de l'Université Laval, 1971.

Eid, Nadia F. *Le clergé et le pouvoir politique au Québec: Une analyse de l'idéologie ultramontane au milieu du XIXe siècle*. Montreal: Hurtubise HMH, 1978. 318 pp.

Hamelin, Marcel. *Les premières années du parlementarisme québécois (1867-1878)*. Quebec City: Presses de l'Université Laval, 1974. 386 pp.

Monière, Denis. *Ideologies in Quebec: The Historical Development*. Toronto: University of Toronto Press, 1981. 328 pp.

Morton, W.L. *The Critical Years: The Union of British North America, 1857-1873*. Toronto: McClelland and Stewart, 1964. 322 pp.

Parliamentary Debates on the Subject of the Confederation of the British North American Provinces. Quebec City: Hunter, Rose and Lemieux, parliamentary printers, 1865. 1,027 pp.

Rioux, Marcel. "Sur l'évolution des idéologies au Québec." *Revue de l'Institut de sociologie* (Brussels), vol. 1 (1968), pp. 95-124.

Saint-Germain, Yves. "The Genesis of the French Language Business Press and Journalists in Quebec, 1871-1914." Ph.D. thesis (history), University of Delaware, Newark, Del., 1974.

Wade, Mason. *The French Canadians 1760-1967*. 2 vols. Rev. ed. Toronto: Macmillan of Canada, 1968. Vol. 1, 1760-1911. 607 pp.

Waite, Peter B. *Canada 1874-1896: Arduous Destiny*. Toronto: McClelland and Stewart, 1971. 340 pp.

Chapter 17

De Grandpré, Pierre. *Histoire de la littérature française au Québec*. Montreal: Beauchemin, 1967-. Vols. 1-2.

Harper, J. Russell. *Painting in Canada: A History*. Toronto: University of Toronto Press, 1966. 2nd ed. 1970. 443 pp.

Mailhot, Laurent. *La littérature québécoise*. Que Sais-je? no. 1579. Paris: Presses Universitaires de France, 1974. 127 pp.

Ostiguy, J.R. *Un siècle de peinture canadienne (1870-1970)*. Quebec City: Presses de l'Université Laval, 1971. 206 pp.

Reid, Dennis. *A Concise History of Canadian Painting*. Toronto: Oxford University Press, 1973. 319 pp.

Robert, Guy. *La peinture au Québec depuis ses origines*. Ottawa: Iconia, 1978. 221 pp.

Simard, Sylvain. "L'image du Canada en France 1850-1914." Doctoral thesis (letters), University of Bordeaux III, Bordeaux, 1975. 726 pp.

Chapter 18

Dales, John H. *Hydroelectricity and Industrial Development: Quebec 1898-1940*. Cambridge, Mass.: Harvard University Press, 1957. 269 pp.

Faucher, Albert. "Le caractère continental de l'industrialisation au Québec." In *Histoire économique et unité canadienne*, pp. 161-78. Montreal: Fides, 1970.

Gérin-Lajoie, Jean. "Financial History of the Asbestos Industry." In *The Asbestos Strike*, edited by Pierre Elliott Trudeau, translated by James Boake, pp. 83-106. Toronto: James Lewis and Samuel, 1974.

Guthrie, John A. *The Newsprint Paper Industry: An Economic Analysis*. Cambridge, Mass.: Harvard University Press, 1941. 274 pp.

Lebourdais, D.M. *Metals and Men: The Story of Canadian Mining*. Toronto: McClelland and Stewart, 1957. 416 pp.

Niosi, Jorge. "La Laurentide (1887-1928): pionnière du papier journal au Canada." *Revue d'histoire de l'Amérique française*, vol. 29, no. 3 (December 1975), pp. 375-415.

Piédalue, Gilles. "Les groupes financiers et la guerre du papier au Canada, 1920-1930." *Revue d'histoire de l'Amérique française*, vol. 30, no. 2 (September 1976), pp. 223-58.

Ryan, William. *The Clergy and Economic Growth in Quebec (1896-1914)*. Quebec City: Presses de l'Université Laval, 1966. 348 pp.

Chapter 19

Angers, François-Albert and Roland Parenteau. *Statistiques manufacturières du Québec*. Montreal: École des Hautes Études Commerciales, 1966. 166 pp.

Durocher, René and Paul-André Linteau, eds. *Le retard du Québec et l'infériorité économique des Canadiens français*. Montreal: Boréal Express, 1971. 127 pp.

Raynauld, André. *Croissance et structure économiques de la province de Québec*. Quebec City: Department of Industry and Commerce, 1961. 657 pp.

Vallières, Marc. "Les industries manufacturières du Québec 1900-1959: Essai de normalisation des données statistiques en dix-sept groupes industriels et étude sommaire de la croissance de ces groupes." MA thesis (history), Laval University, Quebec City, 1973. 234 pp.

Chapter 20

Bonin, Bernard. *L'investissement étranger à long terme au Canada: Ses caractères et ses effets sur l'économie canadienne*. Montreal: École des Hautes Études Commerciales, 1967. 462 pp.

Clement, Wallace. *The Canadian Corporate Elite: An Analysis of Economic Power*. Toronto: McClelland and Stewart, 1975. Chapter 2.

———. *Continental Corporate Power: Economic Linkages between Canada and the United States*. Toronto: McClelland and Stewart, 1977. 408 pp.

Dales, John H. *Hydroelectricity and Industrial Development: Quebec 1898-1940*. Cambridge, Mass.: Harvard University Press, 1957. 269 pp.

Levitt, Kari. *Silent Surrender: The Multinational Corporation in Canada*. Toronto: Macmillan of Canada, 1970. 185 pp.

Marshall, Herbert, Frank Southard, Jr., and Kenneth W. Taylor. *Canadian-American Industry: A Study in International Investment*. 1936. Toronto: McClelland and Stewart, 1976. 360 pp.

Naylor, Tom. *The History of Canadian Business 1867-1914*. 2 vols. Toronto: James Lorimer and Co., 1975.

Niosi, Jorge. *The Economy of Canada: A Study of Ownership and Control*. Translated by Penelope Williams. Montreal: Black Rose Books, 1978. 179 pp.

Piédalue, Gilles. "Les groupes financiers du Canada 1900-1930: Étude préliminaire." *Revue d'histoire de l'Amérique française*, vol. 30, no. 1 (June 1976), pp. 3-34.

Roby, Yves. *Les Québécois et les investissements américains (1918-1929)*. Quebec City: Presses de l'Université Laval, 1976. 250 pp.

Weldon, J.C. *Consolidation in Canadian Industry 1900-1948*. Ottawa: Combines Investigation Commission, 1948. 65 pp.

Chapter 21

Angers, François-Albert. "Les institutions économiques." In *Notre Milieu*, edited by Esdras Minville, pp. 367-421. Montreal: Fides; École des Hautes Études Commerciales, 1946.

Beaulieu, André and Jean Hamelin. "Aperçu du journalisme québécois d'expression française." *Recherches sociographiques*, vol. 7, no. 3 (Sept.-Dec. 1966), pp. 305-48.

Easterbrook, W.T. and Hugh Aitken. *Canadian Economic History*. Toronto: Macmillan, 1967. Chapter 18.

Glazebrook, G.P. de T. *A History of Transportation in Canada*. 1938. Paperback edition, 2 vols. Toronto: McClelland and Stewart, 1967.

Guillet, Edwin C. *The Story of Canadian Roads*. Toronto: University of Toronto Press, 1966. 246 pp.

Linteau, Paul-André. "Le développement du port de Montréal au début du 20e siècle." Canadian Historical Association, *Historical Papers* (1972), pp. 181-205.

Murray, Gilles. "Le commerce." In *Montréal économique*, edited by Esdras

Minville, pp. 243-72. Montreal: Fides; École des Hautes Études Commerciales, 1943.

Regehr, T.D. *The Canadian Northern Railway*. Toronto: Macmillan of Canada, 1976. 543 pp.

Roby, Yves. *Alphonse Desjardins et les caisses populaires 1854-1920*. Montreal: Fides, 1964. 149 pp.

Rudin, Ronald. "The Development of Four Quebec Towns, 1840-1914: A Study of Urban and Economic Growth in Quebec." Ph.D. thesis, York University, Toronto, 1977.

Chapter 22

Blanchard, Raoul. *L'Ouest du Canada français: Montréal et sa région*. Montreal: Beauchemin, 1953. 399 pp.

Cooper, John Irwin. *Montreal: A Brief History*. 1942. Montreal: McGill-Queen's University Press, 1969. 217 pp.

Linteau, Paul-André. *Maisonneuve ou Comment des promoteurs fabriquent une ville (1883-1918)*. Montreal: Boréal Express, 1981. 280 pp.

Minville, Esdras, ed. *Montréal économique*. Montreal: Fides; École des Hautes Études Commerciales, 1943. 430 pp.

Stone, Leroy O. *Urban Development in Canada*. Ottawa: Dominion Bureau of Statistics, 1967. 293 pp.

Chapter 23

Filion, Gérard. "L'agriculture." In *Notre Milieu*, edited by Esdras Minville, pp. 133-51. Montreal: Fides, 1942.

Haythorne, G.V. and L.C. Marsh, *Land and Labour*. Toronto: Oxford University Press, 1941. 568 pp.

Jean, Bruno. *Les idéologies éducatives agricoles (1860-1891) et l'origine de l'agronomie québécoise*. Quebec City: Université Laval, Cahiers de l'ISSH, 1977. 237 pp.

Létourneau, Firmin. *Histoire de l'agriculture*. N.p., 1968. 398 pp.

———. *L'U.C.C.* Oka, 1949. 246 pp.

Migner, Robert-Maurice. "Le monde agricole québécois et les premières années de l'Union catholique des cultivateurs (1918-1930)." Ph.D. thesis (history), University of Montreal, Montreal, 1975. 424 pp.

Minville, Esdras, ed. *L'agriculture*. Montreal: Fides, 1943. 555 pp.

———, ed. *La forêt*. Montreal: Fides, 1944. 414 pp.

Monette, René. "Essai sur le mode de mise en valeur des exploitations agricoles québécoises." *Agriculture*, vol. 2, no. 3 (September 1945), pp. 227-44; vol. 2, no. 4 (December 1945), pp. 357-74; vol. 3, no. 3 (September 1946), pp. 247-63.

Perron, Normand. "Genèse des activités laitières au Québec, 1850-1960." In *Agriculture et colonisation*, edited by Normand Séguin, pp. 113-40. Montreal: Boréal Express, 1981.

Raynauld, André. *Croissance et structure économiques de la province de Québec*. Quebec City: Department of Industry and Commerce, 1961. 657 pp.

Chapter 24

Levitt, Joseph. *Henri Bourassa and the Golden Calf: The Social Program of the Nationalists of Quebec, 1900-1914*. Ottawa: Éditions de l'Université d'Ottawa, 1969. 178 pp.

Roby, Yves. *Les Québécois et les investissements américains (1918-1929)*. Quebec City: Presses de l'Université Laval, 1976. 250 pp.

Roy, Jean-Louis. *Les programmes électoraux du Québec*. 2 vols. Montreal: Leméac, 1970. Vol. 1. 236 pp.

Chapter 25

Barbeau, Victor. *Mesure de notre taille*. Montreal: Le Devoir, 1936. 243 pp.

Bédard, Roger-J., ed. *L'essor économique du Québec*. Montreal: Beauchemin, 1969. 524 pp.

Clement, Wallace. *The Canadian Corporate Elite: An Analysis of Economic Power*. Toronto: McClelland and Stewart, 1975. 479 pp.

Linteau, Paul-André. "Quelques réflexions autour de la bourgeoisie québécoise, 1850-1914." *Revue d'histoire de l'Amérique française*, vol. 30, no. 1 (June 1976), pp. 55-66.

Piédalue, Gilles. "La bourgeoisie canadienne et la réalisation du profit au Canada, 1900-1930." Ph.D. thesis (history), University of Montreal, Montreal, 1976. 401 pp.

———. "Les groupes financiers au Canada, 1900-1930: Étude préliminaire." *Revue d'histoire de l'Amérique française*, vol. 30, no. 1 (June 1976), pp. 3-34.

Rudin, Ronald. "The Development of Four Quebec Towns, 1840-1914: A Study of Urban and Economic Growth in Quebec." Ph.D. thesis (history), York University, Toronto, 1977.

Saint-Germain, Yves. "The Genesis of the French Language Business Press and Journalists in Quebec, 1871-1914." Ph.D. thesis (history), University of Delaware, Newark, Del., 1974.

Chapter 26

Copp, Terry. *The Anatomy of Poverty: The Condition of the Working Class in Montreal 1897-1929*. Toronto: McClelland and Stewart, 1974. 192 pp.

Gagné, Jean H. and Gérard Trudel. *La législation du travail dans la province de Québec, 1900-1953*. Annex 6 to the Report of the Royal Commission of Inquiry on Constitutional Problems (Tremblay Commission). Quebec City, 1955. 81 pp.

Harvey, Fernand, ed. *Aspects historiques du mouvement ouvrier au Québec*. Montreal: Boréal Express, 1973. 226 pp.

Histoire du mouvement ouvrier au Québec (1825-1976). CNTU-CEQ, 1979. 235 pp.

Minville, Esdras. *Labour Legislation and Social Services in the Province of Quebec*. A study prepared for the Royal Commission on Dominion-Provincial Relations. Ottawa: King's Printer, 1939. 97 pp.

Pelletier, Michel and Yves Vaillancourt. *Les politiques sociales et les travailleurs*. Vol. 1: *Les années 1900 à 1929*. Montreal, 1974. 132 pp.

Rouillard, Jacques. "L'action politique ouvrière, 1899-1915." In *Idéologies au Canada français 1900-1929*, edited by Fernand Dumont et al., pp. 267-312. Quebec City: Presses de l'Université Laval, 1974.

———. *Les syndicats nationaux au Québec de 1900 à 1930*. Quebec City: Presses de l'Université Laval, 1979. 342 pp.

———. *Les travailleurs du coton au Québec, 1900-1915*. Montreal: Presses de l'Université du Québec, 1974. 152 pp.

Saint-Pierre, Arthur. *L'organisation ouvrière dans la province de Québec*. Montreal: École Sociale Populaire, 1911.

Chapter 27

Faucher, Albert. *Histoire économique et unité canadienne*. Montreal: Fides, 1970. 296 pp. Part 1, chapters 5 and 6; part 2, chapter 5.

Hamelin, Jean and Yves Roby. "Québec 1896-1929: une deuxième phase d'industrialisation." In *Idéologies au Canada français 1900-1929*, edited by Fernand Dumont et al., pp. 15-28. Quebec City: Presses de l'Université Laval, 1974.

Haythorne, G.V. and L.C. Marsh. *Land and Labour*. Toronto: Oxford University Press, 1941. 568 pp.

Létourneau, Firmin. *Histoire de l'agriculture*. N.p., 1968. 398 pp.

Migner, Robert-Maurice. "Le monde agricole québécois et les premières années de l'Union catholique des cultivateurs (1918-1930)." Ph.D. thesis (history), University of Montreal, Montreal, 1975. 424 pp.

Chapter 28

Abbott, Maude E. "Medicine and Surgery in the Province of Quebec." In *The Storied Province of Quebec: Past and Present*, edited by W. Wood, vol. 2, pp. 1066-1150. Toronto: Dominion Publishing Co., 1931.

Copp, Terry. *The Anatomy of Poverty: The Condition of the Working Class in Montreal 1897-1929*. Toronto: McClelland and Stewart, 1974. 192 pp.

Dugré, Adélard. *La campagne canadienne: Croquis et leçons*. Montreal: Imprimerie du Messager, 1925. 235 pp.

Dupont, Antonin. "Louis-Alexandre Taschereau et la législation sociale au Québec, 1920-1936." *Revue d'histoire de l'Amérique française*, vol. 26, no. 3 (December 1972), pp. 397-426.

Haythorne, G.V. and L.C. Marsh. *Land and Labour*. Toronto: Oxford University Press, 1941. 568 pp.

Minville, Esdras. *Labour Legislation and Social Services in the Province of Quebec*. A study prepared for the Royal Commission on Dominion-Provincial Relations (Rowell-Sirois Commission). Ottawa: King's Printer, 1939. 97 pp.

Pelletier, Michel and Yves Vaillancourt. *Les politiques sociales et les travailleurs*. Vol. 1: *Les années 1900 à 1929*. Montreal, 1974. 132 pp.

Poulin, Gonzalve. *L'assistance sociale dans la province de Québec, 1608-1951*. Annex 2 to the Report of the Royal Commission of Inquiry on Constitutional Problems (Tremblay Commission). Quebec City, 1955. 201 pp.

Chapter 29

Cleverdon, Catherine L. *The Woman Suffrage Movement in Canada: The Start of Liberation 1900-20*. 2nd edition. Toronto: University of Toronto Press, 1974. 324 pp.

Jean, Michèle. *Québécoises du 20e siècle*. Montreal: Éditions du Jour, 1974. 303 pp.

Johnson, Micheline Dumont. "History of the Status of Women in the Province of Quebec." In *Cultural Tradition and Political History of Women in Canada*. Studies of the Royal Commission on the Status of Women in Canada, no. 8. Ottawa: Information Canada, 1971. 55 pp.

Lavigne, Marie and Yolande Pinard, eds. *Les femmes dans la société québécoise*. Montreal: Boréal Express, 1977. 214 pp.

——— and Jennifer Stoddart. "Analyse du travail féminin à Montreal entre les deux guerres." MA thesis (history), University of Quebec at Montreal, 1974. 268 pp.

Pinard, Yolande. "Le féminisme à Montréal au commencement du XXe siècle (1893-1920)." MA thesis (history), University of Quebec at Montreal, 1976. 246 pp.

Stoddart, Jennifer. "The Woman Suffrage Bill in Quebec." In *Women in Canada*, edited by Marylee Stephenson, pp. 90-106. Toronto: New Press, 1973.

Trifiro, Luigi. "Une intervention à Rome dans la lutte pour le suffrage féminin au Québec." *Revue d'histoire de l'Amérique française*, vol. 32, no. 2 (June 1978), pp. 3-18.

Chapter 30

Audet, Louis-Philippe. *Histoire de l'enseignement au Québec*. 2 vols. Montreal: Holt, Rinehart and Winston, 1971. Vol. 2. 496 pp.

———. *Histoire du Conseil de l'instruction publique de la province de Québec, 1856-1964*. Montreal: Leméac, 1964. 346 pp.

———. "La querelle de l'instruction obligatoire." *Cahiers des dix*, no. 24 (1959), pp. 132-50.

Beaulieu, André and Jean Hamelin. "Une Église triomphaliste (1896-1940)." In *Histoire de l'église catholique au Québec 1608-1970*, edited by Nive Voisine, pp. 55-72. Montreal: Fides, 1971.

Canada. Royal Commission on Industrial Training and Technical Education. *Report of the Commissioners*. Ottawa: King's Printer, 1913. Part 4, pp. 1838-93.

Denault, Bernard and Benoît Levesque. *Éléments pour une sociologie des communautés religieuses au Québec*. Montreal: Presses de l'Université de Montreal; Sherbrooke: Université de Sherbrooke, 1975. 220 pp.

Duchesne, Raymond. *La science et le pouvoir au Québec, 1920-1965*. Quebec City: Éditeur officiel du Québec, 1978. 126 pp.

Galarneau, Claude. *Les collèges classiques au Canada français, 1620-1970*. Montreal: Fides, 1978. 287 pp.

Grant, John Webster. *The Church in the Canadian Era: The First Century of Confederation*. Toronto: McGraw-Hill Ryerson, 1972.

Hamelin, Louis-Edmond. "Évolution numérique séculaire du clergé catholique dans le Québec." *Recherches sociographiques*, vol. 2, no. 2 (April-June 1961), pp. 189-242.

Lajeunesse, Marcel, ed. *L'éducation au Québec, 19e et 20e siècles*. Montreal: Boréal Express, 1971. 145 pp.

Percival, Walter P. *Across the Years: A Century of Education in the Province of Quebec*. Montreal: Gazette Printing Company, 1946. 195 pp.

Rumilly, Robert. *Histoire de l'École des Hautes Études Commerciales de Montréal*. Montreal: Beauchemin, 1966. 214 pp.

Vigod, Bernard V. "Qu'on ne craigne pas l'encombrement des compétences: le gouvernement Taschereau et l'éducation, 1920-1929." *Revue d'histoire de l'Amérique française*, vol. 28, no. 2 (September 1974), pp. 209-44.

Walsh, H.H. *The Christian Church in Canada*. Toronto: Ryerson Press, 1968.

Chapter 31

Desrosiers, Richard, ed. *Le personnel politique québécois*. Montreal: Boréal Express, 1972. 142 pp.

Chapter 32

Durocher, René. "Un journaliste catholique au XXe siècle: Henri Bourassa." In *Le laïc dans l'église canadienne-française de 1830 à nos jours*, edited by Pierre Hurtubise, pp. 185-213. Montreal: Fides, 1972.

Gauvin, Michael. "The Municipal Reform Movement in Montreal 1896-1914." MA thesis (history), University of Ottawa, Ottawa, 1972.

Hamelin, Marcel, ed. *Les mémoires du sénateur Raoul Dandurand (1861-1942)*. Quebec City: Presses de l'Université Laval, 1967. 372 pp.

L'action politique des ouvriers québécois (fin du XIXe siècle à 1919): Recueil de documents. Montreal: Presses de l'Université du Québec, 1976. 176 pp.

Laforte, Denis and André Bernard. *La législation électorale au Québec, 1790-1967*. Montreal: Éditions Sainte-Marie, 1969. 197 pp.

Rouillard, Jacques. "L'action politique ouvrière, 1899-1915." In *Idéologies au Canada français 1900-1929*, edited by Fernand Dumont et al., pp. 267-312. Quebec City: Presses de l'Université Laval, 1974.

Rumilly, Robert. *Henri Bourassa: La vie politique d'un grand canadien*. Montreal: Chantecler, 1953. 791 pp.

Russell, Daniel. "H.B. Ames and Municipal Reform." MA thesis (history), McGill University, Montreal, 1971.

Wade, Mason. *The French Canadians 1760-1967*. 2 vols. Rev. ed. Toronto: Macmillan of Canada, 1968.

Chapter 33

Angell, Harold M. "Quebec Provincial Politics in the 1920's." MA thesis (political science), McGill University, Montreal, 1960.

Beck, J. Murray. *Pendulum of Power: Canada's Federal Elections*. Scarborough, Ont.: Prentice-Hall, 1968. 442 pp.

Bonenfant, Jean-Charles. "La vie politique du Québec de 1910 à 1935." In *Aux sources du présent*, edited by Léon Lortie and Adrien Plouffe, pp. 25-33. Toronto: University of Toronto Press, 1960.

Dupont, Antonin. *Les relations entre l'Église et l'État sous Louis-Alexandre Taschereau 1920-1936*. Montreal: Guérin, 1972. 366 pp.

Hamelin, Jean et al. "Les élections provinciales dans le Québec." *Cahiers de Géographie de Québec*, vol. 4, no. 7 (special issue, Oct. 1959-March 1960), pp. 5-207.

Lovink, J. Anton. "The Politics of Quebec: Provincial Political Parties, 1897-1936." Ph.D. thesis, Duke University, Durham, N.C., 1967. 397 pp.

Neatby, H. Blair. *Laurier and a Liberal Quebec*. Toronto: McClelland and Stewart, 1973. 244 pp.

Orban, Edmond. *Le Conseil législatif au Québec, 1867-1967*. Montreal: Bellarmin, 1967. 355 pp.

Roby, Yves. *Les Québécois et les investissements américains (1918-1929)*. Quebec City: Presses de l'Université Laval, 1976. 247 pp.

Weilbrenner, Bernard. "Les idées politiques de Lomer Gouin." Canadian Historical Association, *Report* (1965), pp. 46-57.

Chapter 34

Beck, J. Murray. *Pendulum of Power: Canada's Federal Elections*. Scarborough, Ont.: Prentice-Hall, 1968. 442 pp.

Brunet, Michel. *Quebec/Canada anglais: Deux itinéraires, un affrontement*. Montreal: HMH, 1968. Pp. 231-86.

Cook, Ramsay. *Provincial Autonomy, Minority Rights and the Compact Theory, 1867-1921*. Study No. 4 of the Royal Commission on Bilingualism and Biculturalism. Ottawa: Queen's Printer, 1969. 81 pp.

Dominion-Provincial and Interprovincial Conferences from 1887 to 1926. Ottawa: King's Printer, 1951. 114 pp.

Dominion-Provincial Conference, November 3-10, 1927. Ottawa: King's Printer, 1951.

Durocher, René. "Henri Bourassa, les évêques et la guerre de 1914-1918." Canadian Historical Association, *Historical Papers* (1971), pp. 248-75.

Gibson, Frederick W., ed. *Cabinet Formation and Bicultural Relations: Seven Case Studies*. Study No. 6 of the Royal Commission on Bilingualism and Biculturalism. Ottawa: Queen's Printer, 1970. 190 pp.

Lamontagne, Maurice. *Le fédéralisme canadien*. Quebec City: Presses de l'Université Laval, 1954. 298 pp.

Moore, A. Milton et al. *The Financing of Canadian Federation: The First Hundred Years*. Toronto: Canadian Tax Foundation, 1966.

Provencher, Jean. *Québec sous la loi des mesures de guerre*. Montreal: Boréal Express, 1971. 148 pp.

Wade, Mason. *The French Canadians 1760-1967*. 2 vols. Rev. ed. Toronto: Macmillan of Canada, 1968. Vol. 2.

Chapter 35

Angers, François-Albert, ed. *La pensée de Henri Bourassa*. Montreal: Action Nationale, 1954. 244 pp.

Bourque, Gilles and Nicole Laurin-Frenette. "Social Classes and Nationalist Ideologies in Quebec, 1760-1970." Translated by P. Resnick and P. Renyi. In *Capitalism and the National Question in Canada*, edited by Gary Teeple, pp. 185-210. Toronto: University of Toronto Press, 1972.

Brunet, Michel. "Trois dominantes de la pensée canadienne-française: l'agriculturalisme, l'anti-étatisme, et le messianisme." In *La présence anglaise et les Canadiens: Études sur l'histoire et la pensée des deux Canadas*, pp. 113-66. Montreal: Beauchemin, 1958.

Fournier, Marcel. "Histoire et idéologie du groupe canadien-français du parti communiste (1925-1945)." *Socialisme 69*, 16 (Jan.-Mar. 1969), pp. 63-78.

Hamelin, Jean and André Beaulieu. "Une église triomphaliste." In *Histoire de l'église catholique au Québec (1608-1970)*, edited by Nive Voisine, pp. 55-72. Montreal: Fides, 1971.

Levitt, Joseph. *Henri Bourassa and the Golden Calf: The Social Program of the Nationalists of Quebec, 1900-1914*. Ottawa: Éditions de l'Université d'Ottawa, 1969. 178 pp.

Linteau, Paul-André. *Maisonneuve ou Comment des promoteurs fabriquent une ville (1883-1918)*. Montreal: Boréal Express, 1981. 280 pp.

Monière, Denis. *Ideologies in Quebec: The Historical Development*. Toronto: University of Toronto Press, 1981. 328 pp.

Rioux, Marcel. "Sur l'évolution des idéologies au Québec." *Revue de l'Institut de sociologie* (Brussels), 1 (1968), pp. 95-124.

Roby, Yves. *Les Québécois et les investissements américains (1918-1929)*. Quebec City: Presses de l'Université Laval, 1976. 250 pp.

Rouillard, Jacques. "L'action politique ouvrière, 1899-1915." In *Idéologies au Canada français 1900-1929*, edited by Fernand Dumont et al., pp. 267-312. Quebec City: Presses de l'Université Laval, 1974.

Roy, Jean-Louis. *Les programmes électoraux du Québec*. 2 vols. Montreal: Leméac, 1970. Vol. 1. 236 pp.

Rutherford, Paul. "Tomorrow's Metropolis: The Urban Reform Movement in Canada, 1880-1920." Canadian Historical Association, *Historical Papers* (1971), pp. 203-24.

Ryan, William F. *The Clergy and Economic Growth in Quebec (1896-1914)*. Quebec City: Presses de l'Université Laval, 1966. 348 pp.

Trofimenkoff, Susan Mann. *L'Action Française: French-Canadian Nationalism in the Twenties*. Toronto: University of Toronto Press, 1975. 157 pp.

Wade, Mason. *The French Canadians 1760-1967*. Rev. ed. 2 vols. Toronto: Macmillan of Canada, 1968.

Chapter 36

De Grandpré, Pierre. *Histoire de la littérature française au Québec*. Montreal: Beauchemin, 1967-. Vols. 1-2.

Harper, J. Russell. *Painting in Canada: A History*. Toronto: University of Toronto Press, 1966. 2nd ed. 1970. 443 pp.

Mailhot, Laurent. *La littérature québécoise*. Que Sais-je? no. 1579. Paris: Presses Universitaires de France, 1974. 127 pp.

Ostiguy, J.R. *Un siècle de peinture canadienne (1870-1970)*. Quebec City: Presses de l'Université Laval, 1971. 206 pp.

Reid, Dennis. *A Concise History of Canadian Painting*. Toronto: Oxford University Press, 1973. 319 pp.

Robert, Guy. *La peinture au Québec depuis ses origines*. Ottawa: Iconia, 1978. 221 pp.

Simard, Sylvain. "L'image du Canada en France 1850-1914." Doctoral thesis (letters), University of Bordeaux III, Bordeaux, 1975. 726 pp.

ILLUSTRATION CREDITS

Public Archives of Canada: 35 (PA10270), 66 (C3693), 84 (C11223), 111 (C6073), 118 (PA59231), 131 (C82840), 137 (C36616), 143 (C26820), 146 (PA25541 left, C3841 right), 160 (C80420), 171 (C11041), 232 right (C14246), 237 (C1879), 238 (C21088), 242 (C26721 left, C33234 right), 243 (C33234), 245 (PA26577), 248 left (PA25540), 249 (PA25376 left, C21904 right), 250 (C3844), 259 (C78864), 262 (C11583), 311 (PA15576), 316 (PA15582), 317 (PA24468), 318 (C38069), 319 (PA13702), 320 (PA13834), 323 (C36956), 328 (PA24510), 330 (PA23476), 342 (C55787), 345 (PA44433), 361 (PA44338), 372 (PA10413), 374 (PA19964), 378 (PA9736), 379 (PA11677), 381 bottom (PA70056), 383 (C31469), 385 (PA10324), 386 (C31467), 396 (PA24437), 413 (PA24447), 418 (PA86586), 442 (PA24436), 490 (C4956), 503 (C16748), 524 (C6859). **National Archives of Quebec:** 45 (N675-6), 99 (N1173-131), 105 (GH770-19), 107 (N174-37), 109 (N1173-79), 201 (N774-39), 203 (GH370-86), 222 (N1073-85), 224 (N77-11-1-5), 248 right (GH1172-24), 253 (GH370-90), 271 (N377-201), 287 (GH570-38), 290 (GH1070-84), 293 (GH473-20), 294 (N177-28), 368 (GH1070-89), 384 (N1175-27), 387 (Wurtele Collection, F-80), 388 (N1175-3), 426 (P456), 428 (GH1072-33), 455 (N77-5-11-10), 469 (N78-4-40-11), 482 (GH871-6), 489 (GH571-9), 504 right (N974-39), 505 (GH370-99), 545 (N277-77). **Éditeur officiel du Québec:** 10, 504 left (6941196), 512 (283-61H). **Fonds Dubuc:** 404 right. **Quebec Department of Lands and Forests, Cartography Service:** 14. **Canadian National Railways Archives:** 343, 411, 429. **Annual Report of the Harbour Commissioners on Montreal, 1928:** 348. **Alex Girard, La province de Québec:** 21, 315. **La Presse:** 338, 366, 416, 510. **Archives of the Sisters of Providence:** 437, 445. **Walker Collection,**

McCord Museum: 24, 117, 167. **Notman Archives, McCord Museum:** 91, 119, 135, 157, 173, 190, 191, 193, 232 right, 334, 400, 401, 404 left, 435, 444, 471. **Archives of the City of Montreal:** 43 (38-406), 64 (38-1791), 165, 229, 347, 351, 353, 365, 381 top, 439, 460. **L'Opinion publique:** 81, 86, 125, 179, 204, 296. **Canadian Illustrated News:** 89, 92, 94, 100, 114, 123, 151, 152, 161, 163, 168, 175, 177, 196, 247. **Montreal Herald:** 159. **Inventaire des oeuvres d'art, Quebec City:** 164. **Le Canada d'hier:** 170. **Le diocèse de Montréal à la fin du XIXe siècle:** 199. **Archives of the University of Quebec at Montreal:** 208, 211, 212. **Archives of the Montreal Urban Community Transit Commission:** 312, 364. **National Gallery of Canada:** 298 (113), 299 (1398), 300 (6454), 554 (3656), 556 (1154), 557 (15793), 561 (4575), 562 (6108). **Montreal Museum of Fine Arts:** 302. **Archives of the Institut d'Histoire de l'Amérique Française:** 537. **Archives of the Sisters of Our Lady of Good Counsel:** 448. **Hormisdas Magnan, Monographies paroissiales, 1913:** 457.

INDEX

Abitibi and Temiscamingue regions, 6, 10, 15, 17, 49, 75, 104, 318, 320, 341, 357, 375, 387, 395

Action Française, 53, 357, 392, 495, 520, 532, 536-38

Agricultural circles, 102, 253, 421

Agricultural credit, 385, 426

Agricultural societies, 102, 385

Agriculturalism, 96-97, 172, 266-67, 301-2, 534-35

Agriculture, 12-13, 15, 29-30, 43, 45, 57, 61, 69-74, 93, 95-104, 106-7, 110, 115, 119, 136, 141, 153-55, 170-71, 210, 218, 223, 225, 241-42, 251, 253, 265-67, 283, 288-89, 306-7, 322, 329, 372-80, 382-86, 388, 396, 421-28, 492, 507-8, 511, 517, 531, 534-35, 550-51

Agriculture and Colonization, Department of, 102, 105, 223, 227, 251, 391, 505

Agro-forest economy, 15, 57, 106-7, 109-10, 115, 136, 155, 320, 388

Alcan, 310, 316

Allan, Hugh, 79-80, 145, 400

Allan, Montagu, 400

Aluminum, 308-11, 315-16, 350

American Federation of Labor, 180-81, 267, 274, 277, 408-9, 412

Appalachian Highlands, 4-5, 8, 13, 104, 387

Art Association of Montreal, 295-96, 555

Arvida, 316

Asbestos, 137, 318-19, 321, 350

Asbestos Corporation, 319-20

Association Catholique de la Jeunesse Canadienne-française (ACJC), 53, 456, 459, 494, 538

Atlantic provinces, 62-63, 70, 74, 78, 82, 257-58, 297, 340, 342, 515-16, 518

Automobiles, 329, 339-40, 345-46, 360, 362, 377, 382, 384, 392, 398, 427, 507, 517

Aviation, 340, 347-48

Baie des Chaleurs Railway, 82-83, 108, 237, 251-52

Bank of Montreal, 66, 80, 88-89, 132, 145, 147, 252, 313, 333, 351-52, 355, 361, 399, 402, 463

Banks, 67, 72, 87-90, 142, 144, 147, 217, 309, 333, 335, 339, 351-52, 354-55, 361, 367, 399, 403, 405, 495, 539

Banque Canadienne Nationale, 90, 351-52, 393, 403-4

Banque d'Hochelaga, 89-90, 147, 351, 393, 403

Banque Jacques-Cartier, 72, 89, 145-47, 351
Banque Nationale, 90, 147, 351, 354, 367, 393
Barré, Laurent, 425-26
Beauce region, 11-12, 82, 101, 136
Beaugrand, Honoré, 284
Bégin, Louis-Nazaire, 411-12
Béïque, Caroline, 446
Béïque, Frédéric-Liguori, 403
Bilingualism, 51-52, 54, 219, 495, 520-21, 536
Birth rates, 20, 26, 28, 38, 331
Bishops, *see* Roman Catholic Church
Board of Health, *see* Montreal Board of Health, Provincial Board of Health
Board of Trade, 265, 405-6, 483, 497
Bois-Francs region, 12, 75, 358, 369
Borders, 6, 8, 17, 347
Bouchard, T.-D., 425, 464, 487
Boucherville, Charles-Boucher de, *see* De Boucherville, Charles-Boucher
Bourassa, Henri, 34, 54, 392, 437, 447-49, 458, 488-95, 505, 508-9, 512, 520, 522, 535-36, 551
Bourassa, Napoléon, 290, 294-95, 559
Bourgeoisie, 43, 46, 61-62, 64, 67, 70, 80-81, 88, 90, 117, 132, 136, 141-49, 153, 157-58, 174, 176, 216-17, 228-29, 232, 265-68, 270, 278-80, 296-99, 301-2, 305-6, 309, 339, 367, 392-93, 398-400, 402-6, 413, 432, 482-84, 486, 497, 528, 531-32, 538, 544, 546, 552-53
Bourget, Ignace, 200, 202-4, 211, 271-72
Britain, 18, 33-34, 40-42, 46, 59-62, 70, 87, 98-99, 110-11, 114, 116, 118, 123, 134, 142, 146-47, 150, 191, 196, 217, 243, 268, 275, 279-80, 305-6, 309, 314, 336-39, 350, 362, 378, 380, 395, 404, 422, 447, 451, 489, 491-92, 494, 509, 520, 523-24, 532, 550
British Empire, 57, 59-61, 217, 258, 277, 279, 489, 491-92, 550-51
British North America Act, *see* Constitution
Bruchési, Paul, 446-47, 459, 461-62, 464, 525
Buies, Arthur, 53, 149, 210, 284, 291, 545
Bulletin des Agriculteurs, 424-25

Cabinet, 227-28, 252, 255-56, 391, 484, 506, 520-22
Caisses populaires, 352, 354, 458
Canada Power and Paper, 314, 335
Canadian and Catholic Confederation of Labour, *see* Catholic unions
Canadian International Paper, *see* International Paper
Canadian National Railways, 344, 360
Canadian Northern Railway, 340-44, 360, 367
Canadian Pacific Railway, 66, 73, 78, 80-82, 87, 125, 132, 145, 246, 297, 313, 340, 344, 367, 400, 403, 463
Canadian Shield, 4-5, 8, 10, 15, 30, 341, 387
Canadian unions, 409, 414
Canals, 42, 63, 69, 85-86, 118, 130, 142
Capitalism, 16, 59-61, 116-17, 123, 140, 142-51, 165-66, 172, 178, 182, 204, 265, 267, 284, 307, 332-39, 399-400, 402-5
Caron, J.-E., 424-25, 511
Cartier, George-Étienne, 231, 233-35, 241-42, 254-55, 257, 260, 291
Casgrain, Thérèse, 481
Catholic church, *see* Roman Catholic church
Catholic Program, 200, 233, 242, 271
Catholic unions, 408-9, 411-14, 419, 456, 459, 538, 540
Cauchon, Joseph, 206, 240-41
Chambers of Commerce, 147, 405-6, 483, 497
Chapais, Thomas, 271, 291, 462-63, 552
Chapleau, J.-Adolphe, 80, 90, 209, 233-34, 240, 246-48, 255, 461-62
Charity, 43, 139, 156, 169, 172, 174-77, 192, 194, 197, 203, 223-25, 269-70, 417, 434-37, 439, 447, 453-56, 459-60, 509, 532-33
Chauveau, P.-J.-O., 205-7, 210, 212, 240-42, 255-56, 287
Chemical industry, 308, 311, 315-17, 326, 357

Chicoutimi, 121, 201, 251, 314, 371, 412
Children, 22, 166-67, 171, 184-86, 415, 417-19, 440, 443, 445, 455, 464-67, 470, 478, 496, 539. *See also* Infant mortality
Classes, social, 24, 43, 139, 141-51, 153-58, 160, 165, 189, 228, 264, 279, 398-400, 402-8, 413, 415, 417-20, 430, 432, 434-35, 456, 459, 477, 539
Classical colleges, 42, 200, 205, 210, 284, 449, 456, 467, 471-74, 494, 531, 537-38
Clerical-nationalist ideology, 105, 264, 266-72, 276, 279-80, 283-84, 287, 291, 295, 447, 458, 528, 532-38, 540, 542, 550
Clothing industry, 47, 120-22, 124, 129, 166-68, 189, 326-27, 339, 360, 367, 403, 410, 415, 443
Colonization, 30, 32, 57, 78-79, 82, 84, 93, 95-96, 102-10, 115, 154, 169, 171-72, 199, 223-25, 241-42, 251, 266, 288, 308, 320, 341, 375, 386-91, 395, 426, 481, 491-92, 499, 505, 507-8, 511, 535
Colonization, Department of, *see* Agriculture and Colonization, Department of
Commerce, 47, 57, 59-64, 68-69, 71-72, 74-75, 84, 86-87, 93, 100-12, 114, 119, 126-27, 142, 144-45, 148, 153, 217, 265, 307, 349-50, 361, 395, 403, 407, 507
Communications, 57, 63, 75, 86-87, 99, 106, 126, 134, 307, 345, 348-49, 395, 427
Communism, 267, 415, 463, 465, 540
Compulsory education, 208, 273, 418, 461, 464, 466, 495, 508, 531, 539
Conan, Laure, 290, 548
Confederation, 6, 17-18, 30, 34, 37, 46, 57, 62-63, 65, 69, 73, 80, 97, 110, 129, 132, 136, 142, 172, 197-98, 200, 205-6, 218-19, 221-22, 231-32, 234, 239, 250, 253-58, 260, 275-77, 279, 400, 452, 478, 501, 509, 520
Conscription, 412, 414, 425, 447, 488, 495, 509, 511-12, 520-26
Conservatism, 141, 144, 185, 226, 233, 250, 268-72, 276-77, 279, 283, 291, 293, 439, 531, 538
Conservative party, 80, 146-47, 205, 207-9, 215, 230-38, 241-43, 245-50, 252-54, 256, 258, 260-61, 276, 392, 395, 462-63, 485-89, 493-94, 499-502, 504-5, 508-9, 511-14, 517, 519-22, 525-26
Constitution, 34, 37, 46, 198, 205-6, 217-21, 226-27, 254, 257-58, 275, 419, 439, 449, 465, 515-16, 537
Construction, 42, 45, 112, 143, 150-51, 158, 166, 178, 318, 321, 329, 395, 409-10, 430, 435, 480
Cooperatives, 183, 253, 421-26, 458
Copper, 320-21, 350
Corporate concentration, 67, 123-24, 305, 314, 319, 323, 332-35, 361, 367, 398-400, 402-4, 477
Council of Public Instruction, 207-9, 214, 225, 461, 464-66, 468, 474, 508
Cousineau, Philémon, 488, 511
Crédit Foncier Franco-Canadien, 90-91, 149, 246
Customs duty, *see* Tariff, customs

Dandurand, Josephine, 446
De Boucherville, Charles-Boucher, 206-7, 228, 235, 244-46, 252-53, 559
De Nevers, Edmond, 53, 550-51
Death, causes of, 23-26, 431-32
Death rates, 23, 26, 28, 134, 160, 430-31, 477, 531
Department of Agriculture and Colonization, *see* Agriculture and Colonization, Department of
Department of Labour, *see* Labour, Department of
Department of Public Instruction, *see* Public Instruction, Department of
Desjardins, Alphonse (caisses populaires), 352, 354
Desjardins, Alphonse (senator), 89, 145-47
Devoir, Le, 357, 437, 447, 458, 492-94, 532, 538
Dorion Commission on women's rights, 449-50

Dubuc, J.-E.-A., 314, 404, 412

Eastern Townships, 12, 32, 40-41, 46, 49, 82, 98, 100-1, 120-21, 127, 137-38, 226, 310, 318-19, 357-58, 369, 375
École Littéraire de Montréal, 542-48
École Sociale Populaire, 456, 538
Economic cycles, 21, 72-73, 306-7, 443
Economic policy (Quebec), 57, 91, 93, 95, 223, 225, 232, 241-44, 246, 251, 253, 390-94, 491, 504-5, 507, 520
Edson, Allan A., 297
Education, 26, 31, 37, 192, 194-95, 197-99, 205-14, 216-17, 219-20, 223, 225-26, 235, 241, 243-44, 250-51, 265, 268-70, 273-74, 277-78, 280, 288, 386, 398, 418, 426, 447, 454-55, 459-75, 481, 487-88, 491, 495, 501-3, 508-9, 511, 517, 530-33, 536-39, 550
Elections, 200, 215, 235-45, 248-49, 251, 253-54, 274, 424, 486-89, 492-94, 497-502, 504-5, 508-9, 511-14, 521-22, 526
Electricity, *see* Hydroelectricity
Emigration, 18, 20, 29-33, 65, 76, 104, 109, 126, 128-29, 141, 154-55, 241, 265-66, 277, 362, 389, 391, 511, 513
Energy, 71, 118, 124, 308, 310-11, 315-16, 323, 384, 393-94, 529
English Canadians, 34, 37-38, 140, 219-20, 236, 250-51, 255, 258, 261, 272, 276-79, 309, 352, 409, 488-90, 494, 509, 519, 524, 532, 535-36, 556
English Quebecers, 15, 18-19, 22-23, 37, 39-43, 46-54, 133-34, 136, 141, 145, 147, 151, 176, 192, 206-7, 209-11, 219, 226-29, 231-32, 240-41, 250, 252, 255-56, 265, 268-70, 272, 292, 357, 366, 402, 407, 411, 436, 446-47, 464-69, 472-73, 475, 484, 486, 497, 512-13, 520-21, 526, 531-32, 536, 540, 552-53
Epidemics, 23, 26, 172
Essays, 291, 550-52
Exports, 57, 59-62, 64, 68-69, 87, 98-99, 100-1, 110-14, 134, 142, 308, 313-14, 319, 344-45, 349-50, 360, 378, 380, 394, 404, 505, 513
External affairs, 217, 251, 516

Fabre, Hector, 283, 291
Fabre, Mgr, 180, 201, 272, 285
Families, 22, 28, 97, 103, 140, 153, 169, 171, 270, 379, 421, 437, 448, 477, 533-34
Farm machinery, 102, 138, 170, 382-85
Faucher, Albert, 6, 30-31, 67, 70-71, 309, 330
Federal-provincial relations, 215, 217-19, 222-23, 250, 254-62, 396-97, 419, 438-39, 476, 491, 494, 503, 511, 515-21
Fédération Nationale Saint-Jean-Baptiste, 445-47
Fertility rates, 20-22, 26
Finance capital, 333
First World War, 25, 51, 306-7, 310, 316, 318, 320, 322, 324, 336, 338, 341, 343-44, 349, 358, 360, 364, 373, 376, 380, 382, 390, 394-97, 408-9, 412, 414, 421, 423, 425, 431, 440-41, 452-53, 470, 479, 488, 495-96, 508-9, 516, 518, 523-26, 532, 536, 542
Fisheries, 41, 44-45, 103, 155, 372, 388, 428, 519
Flynn, Edmund James, 240, 253, 488, 505
Food industry, 113, 119-22, 129, 326, 335, 339
Foreign investment, 61, 65, 306, 309, 315, 319, 333, 335-39, 393-95, 513, 529, 535, 538
Forest industry, 15, 42, 57, 61, 93, 96, 101, 103, 106-15, 119, 121, 129, 134, 136-37, 154, 171-72, 221, 241, 244, 251, 308-9, 313-14, 325, 329, 349-50, 372, 386-89, 392-93, 428, 491, 505, 507
Forget, Louis-Joseph, 145, 334, 402-3
Francoeur, J.-N., 509
Fraser, John Arthur, 297, 553
Fréchette, Louis Honoré, 284-87, 545
French Canadians, 8, 15, 18-19, 22-23, 28, 31-32, 34-39, 42-43, 46-47, 49-54, 71, 104-5, 134, 136, 140-41, 143, 145, 147-48, 151, 161, 181, 192, 197,

219-20, 226, 229, 231-32, 234, 236-37, 250, 254-56, 258, 260-62, 265-66, 268, 270, 272, 275-78, 291, 309, 331, 352, 355, 357, 361, 366, 392-93, 402-7, 414, 436, 447, 449, 458, 468-69, 472, 486, 488, 490, 494-95, 497, 501, 504, 509, 514, 519-20, 522-26, 530-33, 535-38, 540, 542-43, 546, 550-51, 554, 556-59

Galt, A.T., 206, 232
Gaspé, 4, 10-11, 32, 41, 45, 78, 83, 155, 357, 367, 375, 387, 454
Gérin-Lajoie, Antoine, 288-89
Gérin-Lajoie, Marie, 446-49
German Quebecers, 41, 43, 46, 51
Gold, 320-21
Gouin, Lomer, 394, 396, 402, 406, 464, 467-68, 475, 486-87, 492, 494, 498, 506-9, 511, 518-19, 529-30
Gouttes de lait, 25, 434, 438, 447, 455
Grand-Mère, 137, 313-14, 369
Grand Trunk Railway, 76, 79-80, 87, 118, 125, 127, 132, 135, 137, 231, 340-41, 343-44, 360
Grande Association, 181, 183
Great Northern Railway of Canada, 83, 342
Groulx, Lionel, 392, 407, 495, 520, 533, 535-37, 549, 551-52
Guibord, Joseph, 203-4

Harbours, 42, 85-86, 132, 134-36, 151, 157, 344-45, 349, 360, 367, 404, 435, 529
Health, 23-26, 31, 134, 157-58, 160-61, 169-70, 174, 176-77, 217, 220, 225, 407, 428-30, 434, 436, 438, 447, 455, 460, 477, 495, 531, 533
Hébert, Louis-Philippe, 295, 557, 559
Hébert, Nicolas-Tolentin, 105
Helbronner, Jules, 183
Hémon, Louis, 387, 542, 549-50
Historiographic debates, 6, 57, 65-71, 73
Holt, Herbert, 314, 334, 400
Hospitals, 174-75, 192, 269, 359, 361, 434, 436-37, 447, 454
Houde, Camillien, 489, 513
House of Commons, 54, 146, 255-56, 267, 274, 352, 490, 492, 496, 501, 516, 520
Housing, 31, 158-60, 169-70, 398, 430, 432, 439-40
Hull, 79, 121, 136, 358, 414, 467, 546
Huot, Charles, 559
Hydroelectricity, 71, 124, 136, 161, 163-65, 226, 305, 308, 310-11, 315, 316-17, 323, 326, 334, 365, 371, 391-92, 394, 398, 481, 504, 507, 513
Hygiene, *see* Health

Ideologies, 233, 263-80, 283, 292-93, 527-41, 551
Ideology of conservation, *see* Clerical nationalist ideology
Immigration, 18, 20, 33-36, 38-44, 46-47, 51, 63, 65, 70, 72, 118, 120, 124, 134, 150, 179, 196, 218, 279, 322, 337, 362, 366, 394-95, 398, 410, 451, 520, 540, 550
Imperialism, 59-61, 278, 488-94, 508, 522-23, 532, 535, 551
Imports, 59-62, 69, 87, 142, 350
Indians, native, *see* Native Indians
Industrialization, 16, 26, 28, 30, 48, 57-58, 66-67, 71, 73-74, 95, 110, 116-22, 126-29, 139-42, 144, 149-50, 156-57, 165-66, 169, 176, 178-79, 189, 220, 241, 246, 266-67, 287, 306, 309, 318, 322, 330-31, 390-91, 394-95, 408, 415, 420, 441, 456, 458, 477, 499, 507, 511, 513-15, 517, 518, 528-29, 531, 535, 538, 541
Infant mortality, 24-26, 45, 160-61, 429, 431-32, 447
Institut Canadien, 203-4
Insurance, 90, 146, 184, 355, 361-62, 399, 457
Intercolonial Railway, 78, 344
Internal migration, 31-32, 41, 48, 109, 128-29, 265-66, 362, 372-75, 389, 398, 477, 511, 535
International Paper, 314-15, 391
Inuit, 44, 46, 62
Irish Quebecers, 41-43, 49, 51, 129, 136,

141, 147, 151, 192, 197, 227, 400
Iron and steel, 59, 71, 119, 124-25, 129, 138, 150, 158, 328-30, 335, 339, 360
Italian Quebecers, 43, 47, 51, 366, 395

Jewish Quebecers, 43, 46-47, 49, 51, 124, 151, 209, 366, 395, 407, 411, 440, 451, 453, 461, 465-66
Joliette, 76, 101, 137-38, 342, 369, 380, 454, 458
Joly, Henri, 235, 240, 244-46, 502, 515

Kirby, William, 292
Knights of Labor, 168, 180-82, 184, 201, 238, 267, 273-74, 277, 279, 408-10, 495

La Patrie, see Patrie, La
La Presse, see Presse, La
Labelle, Antoine, 28, 32, 35, 79, 105, 112, 149, 223, 251
Labour ideology, 267, 273-74, 539-40
Labour, Department of, 419, 481
Labrador, 6, 8, 521
Lachine, 360, 362, 467, 555
Laflèche, Louis-François, 271, 276, 291
Laliberté, Alfred, 557-58
Lanctôt, Médéric, 181, 238
Language, 37-38, 42-43, 49-54, 219, 274-75, 277-78, 488, 490, 509, 523, 536, 538
Lapointe, Ernest, 488, 521
Lapointe, Eugène, 444
Laurentian Highlands, 8, 13, 104, 112, 383, 387
Laurentian thesis, 6, 67-70
Laurentide Pulp and Paper, 313-14
Laurier, Wilfrid, 234-37, 253, 261, 306, 340, 395, 463-64, 487-93, 501-5, 508-9, 512-13, 518-22, 551
Lavergne, Armand, 34, 54, 490, 492-93, 508-9, 512, 551
Le Devoir, see Devoir, Le
Le Nationaliste, see Nationaliste, Le
Le Nigog, see Nigog, Le
Leblanc, Évariste, 488
Leduc, Ozias, 294, 547, 554-56, 560
Legislative Assembly, 29, 54, 226-28, 238, 241, 244, 246, 249, 252, 256, 449, 464, 484, 488, 499-500, 502, 504-6, 511, 513
Legislative Council, 226-27, 246, 252, 273, 462-63
Leman, Beaudry, 403-4
Lépine, Alphonse Télésphore, 238, 267, 274
Letellier de Saint-Just, Luc, 227, 235, 244, 256, 261
Lévis and Kennebec Railway, 82, 136
Liberal party, 54, 80, 214-15, 230, 233-38, 240, 244-50, 251-52, 258-61, 272-73, 276, 390-95, 425, 461, 476, 478, 480, 484-90, 492, 494, 496, 498-509, 511-15, 519-22, 526, 532
Liberalism, 91, 172, 177, 198, 203-4, 215-17, 220-21, 232-33, 236, 265-67, 271, 276, 279-80, 283, 286, 291, 295, 301-2, 477, 487, 507, 529-32, 535, 538
Lieutenant Governor, Office of the, 218, 227, 259
Ligue Nationaliste Canadienne, 53, 490-91
Lower Laurentian Railway, 83, 342
Lower St. Lawrence, 32, 41, 78, 121, 154, 375, 387, 423

Macdonald, Sir John A., 8, 80, 180, 218, 232, 236, 253, 255-57, 260, 291
Maisonneuve, 132, 146-47, 323, 344, 360, 362-64, 405-6, 410, 432, 496, 529
Marchand, Félix-Gabriel, 214, 253, 459, 461-63, 475, 486, 502-3, 518-19
Marie-Victorin, Brother, 474
Martin, Médéric, 497
Mercier, Honoré, 35, 83, 105, 208-9, 223, 227, 234-37, 247-52, 260-61, 276, 486, 502, 506
Métis, 44, 62, 236, 249, 257
Milk, 25-26, 432. *See also* Dairy industry
Minimum wage, 419, 444-45, 481
Mining, 17, 103, 137, 308, 317-21, 337, 348, 369, 388, 395, 481
Montreal, 3, 16, 23-26, 31-32, 41-42,

44-49, 52, 58, 63, 67-70, 76, 78-82, 84-87, 95, 112, 118-20, 122-27, 129-30, 132-38, 143, 145-47, 150-51, 157-58, 160-62, 164-65, 174-75, 181-82, 188-90, 192, 194, 197, 200, 202, 211, 220, 223, 227, 229, 234, 239, 244, 252, 254, 267, 271-73, 283, 285, 292, 295-302, 308-10, 313, 323, 333-34, 340, 342-43, 347, 349-52, 357-67, 369, 380, 392, 395, 400, 402, 404, 406, 409-10, 414, 419, 423, 430-32, 434-36, 439, 441, 451, 453-56, 458-59, 461, 464, 467-70, 481-84, 486-87, 489, 495-99, 506, 511-13, 525, 529, 532, 538, 540, 542-46, 552-53, 555, 557, 560

Montreal Board of Health, 25-26, 432

Montreal Light, Heat and Power, 310, 334, 365, 392

Montreal Local Council of Women, 194, 446-47

Montreal region, 32, 41, 43, 46, 49, 58, 101, 120-21, 126-27, 137-38, 147, 154, 308, 357-59, 375, 380, 383, 395

Montreal Star, 348, 403, 486, 525, 538

Morrice, James Wilson, 553, 560-63

Morris, Edmund, 553, 560

Mousseau, J.-Alfred, 208, 240, 248

Municipalities, 95, 127, 132-33, 161, 163-64, 176, 188, 217, 220, 223-26, 228-29, 244, 306, 346, 362-64, 392, 403, 428, 436-38, 440, 476, 478, 480-81, 507, 517

National Council of Women, 194, 446-47

National policy, 63-67, 73, 279, 394-95

National Transcontinental Railway, 320, 341, 343-44, 367, 387, 395

Nationalism, 22, 26, 34, 39, 70, 249-50, 261-62, 264, 274-79, 458-59, 490-91, 494-95, 531-32, 534-39, 542, 550-52, 559

Nationaliste, Le, 491, 493, 508

Nationalists, 34, 53-54, 391-94, 413, 476, 485-86, 488-95, 500, 507-9, 512, 514, 520-23, 532

Native Indians, 43-46, 62, 155, 217, 236, 257, 498

Natural resources, 68-71, 221, 225, 265, 305, 307-11, 313-14, 316-22, 330, 337, 339, 349, 358, 371, 393-94, 478, 491-92, 494, 502-3, 505, 507, 513, 515, 517-19, 529, 541

Nelligan, Émile, 542-46

New Quebec (Ungava), 6, 32, 44, 46

Newspapers, 31, 43, 146, 203, 209, 239, 265, 272-73, 280, 283-84, 313, 348-49, 386, 406, 458, 486, 491-94, 502, 509, 512-13, 525, 528, 532, 538

Nicolet, 201, 423

Nigog, Le, 542-43, 547-48, 556

Noranda Mines, 320

Normal schools, 192, 194, 210, 212, 214, 468, 471-73

Novels, 282-85, 287-90, 292, 542, 548-50, 552

O'Brien, Lucius R., 297, 553

Ontario, 15, 20-21, 23, 32, 36, 38, 42, 45-46, 54, 62-63, 66-67, 71, 76, 85, 88, 95, 101, 128, 185, 196, 222, 233, 236, 251, 255, 258, 260-62, 272, 278, 296-97, 306, 314, 320, 325, 328-31, 333, 335, 339-42, 356-57, 374, 380, 385, 391-92, 394-96, 402, 422, 441, 488, 495, 507-9, 515-16, 518, 520, 523, 550, 553

Ottawa Valley, *see* Outaouais

Ouimet, Gédéon, 207-8, 210, 240, 242-43

Outaouais, 16-17, 32, 41, 49, 110, 115, 121, 226, 310, 375, 387

Painting, 263, 281, 292-302, 527, 541, 552-57, 559-63

Papal zouaves, *see* Zouaves, papal

Parent, S.-N., 391, 486-88, 498, 503-6, 518-19

Parishes, 11, 31, 42, 47, 102-3, 105, 148-49, 153, 176, 199-200, 220, 269, 380, 426, 454, 534

Parti National, 235, 237, 249

Parti Ouvrier, 408, 410, 495-96, 539
Parties, political, *see* Political parties
Patrie, La, 273, 283, 349, 486, 525, 538
Patronage, 223-25, 239, 260, 405, 483, 485-86, 499, 507, 514, 520
Petty bourgeoisie, 141, 148-49, 153-54, 228, 267, 279, 398, 406-7, 484, 538
Poetry, 283-87, 542-48
Political parties, 215-16, 230-40, 276, 403, 476, 484-89, 491-96, 514, 519-22
Politicians, 215, 227-28, 240-53, 484, 501-9, 511-14, 538
Ponton, J.-N., 424-26
Population, 3, 18-22, 26, 28-29, 31-34, 36, 38-40, 50-51, 74-75, 104, 129, 220, 226, 331, 356-58, 373, 421, 499
Poverty, 172, 176, 429-32, 434-37
Presse, La, 183, 283, 348-49, 486, 505, 529, 538
Price Brothers, 115, 228, 310, 314-15
Privy Council, 6, 8, 257-59, 419, 449, 465, 516
Protestant churches, 172, 174-75, 195-97, 199, 269, 272, 451-53, 459, 473, 478. *See also* English Quebecers
Provincial Bank of Canada, 351-52
Provincial Board of Health, 25, 161, 438
Public administration, 223-26, 240-41, 243, 476-85, 507, 531
Public assistance, *see* Social security
Public finance, 209-10, 218, 220-24, 240, 242-44, 246, 251-52, 260-61, 338, 391, 397, 438-39, 478-81, 502-3, 505, 507, 516-19
Public Instruction, Department of, 207, 227, 241, 244, 461-64, 466, 503, 519
Public transportation, *see* Transportation, public
Pulp and paper industry, 112, 122, 136, 143-45, 308-9, 311, 313-15, 325-26, 335, 337, 339, 349-50, 357, 369, 371, 391, 394, 404, 412, 440, 478, 505, 507

Quebec and Lake St. John Railway, 82, 108, 136, 251, 342, 367
Quebec Central Railway, 82, 367
Quebec City, 15-16, 32, 42-44, 48, 69, 79-85, 87, 95, 101, 111, 114, 120, 125-27, 129, 134-36, 147, 150, 157-58, 162, 165, 178, 181-82, 189, 192, 220, 227, 231, 234, 239-40, 244, 246, 249-50, 255-57, 260-61, 283, 285, 292-93, 295, 310, 340-43, 345, 351, 357-59, 367, 369, 375, 390, 395, 409, 411, 414, 419, 425, 449, 453, 456, 458, 461, 467, 484, 486-87, 491, 499, 502-5, 509, 512, 520, 526, 534, 538, 562
Quebec, Montreal, Ottawa and Occidental Railway (QMO&O), 78-80, 223, 244, 246, 248, 256, 260

Radicalism, 230, 233-35, 237, 250, 264, 268, 270, 272-73, 279-80, 291, 464, 487, 508, 530-31
Radio, 349, 427, 459, 493, 519
Railway rolling stock, 120, 124-25, 129, 328-29
Railways, 30, 34, 42, 54, 57, 63-65, 67, 69, 75-76, 78-83, 86-87, 93, 95, 108, 111, 118-19, 125, 127, 132, 135, 142, 144, 169, 223-25, 228, 241-44, 246, 251, 306, 308, 336-37, 340-44, 346, 349, 360, 367, 390-92, 394-95, 397, 403, 419, 427, 480, 491, 518, 529
Range system, 13, 15, 102, 153
Reciprocity Treaty (1854), 62, 99
Reform ideology and movements, 272-73, 279, 497
Religious communities, 149, 174, 176, 186, 189, 192, 194, 199-202, 213-14, 250, 437-38, 443, 449, 454-55, 458, 473, 478
Rerum Novarum, 198, 453, 455-56, 458
Riel, Louis, 236-37, 249, 257, 261, 276-78
Right to vote, *see* Vote, right to
Rimouski, 78, 201, 372
Rivière-du-Loup, 76, 78, 127
Roads, 29, 83-84, 86, 101, 108, 220, 226, 251, 340, 346-47, 360, 388, 392, 427-28, 480-81, 485, 507, 511
Robidoux, J.-E., 462-64, 503

Rolland, Jean-Baptiste, 144-45, 446
Roman Catholic church, 26, 41-42, 47, 104-6, 109, 141, 148-49, 172, 174, 177, 180, 186, 194-95, 197-204, 207-11, 213, 216, 220, 235-36, 244, 250-51, 264, 266, 268-73, 275-77, 279-80, 291, 354, 388, 391, 408, 411-14, 418, 421, 425-26, 436, 438, 440, 446, 448-49, 451, 453-67, 472-75, 478, 494, 501-3, 530-33, 535-38, 540, 546, 551, 555
Ross, John Jones, 227, 248-49
Rouyn, 320
Royal Bank of Canada, 314-15, 333, 351-52, 355, 361, 399-400
Royal Commission on the Relations of Labour and Capital, 166, 184-85, 268, 274, 415
Rural Quebecers, 97, 102-4, 140-41, 148-50, 153-55, 168-70, 172, 226, 267, 301, 352, 372-74, 379, 421-29, 438, 454, 499-500, 511-12, 514, 531, 534-35

Saguenay/Lake St. John region, 10-11, 15, 32, 49, 75, 82, 90-91, 104-5, 107, 115, 121, 136, 155, 310, 314, 316, 341, 357-58, 371, 375, 387, 404, 412
Saint-Hyacinthe, 76, 120, 127, 137, 147, 201, 239, 253, 351, 369, 425, 464, 554
Saint-Jean, 76, 120, 137, 147, 351, 369, 502
Saint-Jean, Idola, 441, 449
Saint-Jérôme, 28, 79, 105, 137, 143-44, 342, 369, 425, 464
St. Lawrence Lowlands, 5-6, 8, 12-13, 63, 75, 97, 104, 288, 308, 375
Saint-Martin, Albert, 540
St. Maurice Valley, 32, 101, 104, 121, 309, 311, 313-14, 342, 357-58, 369, 371
St. Vincent de Paul societies, 166, 172, 174, 436, 455
Sauvé, Arthur, 488-89, 512-13
Sawmills, 111, 114-15, 121-22, 137, 389, 403
School commissions, 188-89, 205, 210, 213, 226, 465-66, 470, 475, 481, 508-9
Scottish Quebecers, 41-43, 143, 145, 147, 151, 313
Sculpture, 281, 292-93, 295, 557-59
Sénécal, Louis-Adélard, 80, 228, 234, 246, 248
Shawinigan, 53, 137, 310, 314, 316-17, 342, 369, 393, 467
Shawinigan Water and Power, 310-11, 316, 369, 404
Sherbrooke, 10, 12, 52-53, 76, 82, 120, 127, 136-37, 147, 201, 358, 369, 392, 424, 467, 512
Shipbuilding, 111, 114, 125, 134
Shoe industry, 113, 118-19, 121-23, 129, 136, 166, 182, 189, 307, 325-26, 339, 360, 367, 403, 405, 409-11, 413
Smith, Donald (Lord Strathcona), 132, 143, 145-47, 175, 297, 300, 463
Social classes, *see* Classes, social
Social legislation, 184-85, 225, 415, 417-20, 436-40, 443-45, 477-78, 511-12, 517
Social security, 172, 176-77, 217, 430, 436-39, 477-78, 495, 517, 531, 533, 539
Socialism, 198, 265, 267, 273, 413, 456, 463, 539-40
Sorel, 120, 137, 345, 369, 375, 405
Strathcona, Lord, *see* Smith, Donald
Suffrage, *see* Vote, right to
Suzor-Coté, Marc-Aurel de Foy, 559-60

Taillon, Louis-Olivier, 240, 249, 252-53
Tardivel, Jules-Paul, 53, 272, 277, 285, 291, 536
Tariff, customs, 62-66, 72-73, 93, 110, 119, 221, 246, 278-79, 314, 395-95, 397
Taschereau, Cardinal Elzéar, 180, 201, 209, 236, 511
Taschereau, Louis-Alexandre, 30, 391, 393-94, 424, 436-39, 449, 465, 475, 478, 480, 486, 511-13, 518-21, 529-30

Teachers, 192, 199, 205, 211-14, 407, 443, 445, 460-61, 464, 469-71, 473, 475, 508
Technical and vocational education, 210-11, 460, 467-68, 471-74, 508, 517, 530
Telegraphs, 345, 349
Tellier, Mathias, 488
Textile industry, 59, 118, 120, 122-24, 129, 145, 166, 189, 307, 326-27, 334-35, 339, 350, 360, 369, 409-10, 443
Tobacco, 101, 120, 125, 129, 166, 326-27, 360, 367, 380, 410, 443
Trade, *see* Commerce
Trade union movement, 47, 139, 150, 169, 178-85, 216, 265, 277, 279-80, 395, 408-15, 417-20, 445, 456, 495-96, 540
Trades and Labour Congress of Canada, 181-83, 409, 412, 414-15, 496
Transportation, 63-64, 66, 68-71, 74-76, 78-87, 108, 111, 130, 132, 135, 142, 151, 178, 308, 318, 340-48, 360, 367, 427, 491, 518
Transportation, public, 161-65, 359, 362-63, 365
Trois-Rivières, 32, 76, 78, 120, 136-37, 201, 239, 271-72, 314, 345, 358, 369, 412, 458, 467, 538
Tuberculosis, 24, 26, 429, 432, 434, 438, 546

Ultramontanes, 146, 208, 230, 233-34, 236, 242, 247-49, 264, 270-72, 276-77, 279-80, 551
Unemployment, 166, 190, 306, 415, 417, 435-36, 477, 495-96
Ungava, *see* New Quebec
Union Catholique des Cultivateurs, 385, 423-26, 456
United Farmers, 423-26
United States, 18, 28, 30-35, 37, 40-42, 45-46, 60-63, 65, 68-69, 71-73, 76, 85, 87, 98-100, 104, 108-12, 114, 118, 122-24, 128, 134, 140-41, 147, 154-55, 158, 180-81, 195-96, 241, 266, 268, 277-80, 284-85, 301, 305-6, 309-10, 313-15, 319, 336-39, 348-50, 362, 380, 389, 391, 393-95, 422, 430, 447, 499, 511, 513, 529, 546
Universities, 194, 201, 205, 210-11, 251, 359, 361, 407, 468-69, 472-75, 508, 537
Urban reform, 273, 482-84, 497, 531
Urbanization, 11, 16, 26, 32, 75, 99, 107, 109-10, 116-17, 126-30, 132-41, 156, 176, 220, 226, 265-66, 287, 305, 307, 322, 356-59, 369, 372, 389, 398, 407, 429, 439, 441, 454, 477, 499, 531, 541
Utilities, 54, 163-64, 310, 334, 362, 365, 392, 477, 495, 539

Valleyfield, 120, 123-24, 136-37, 201, 369, 410
Verville, Alphonse, 410, 496
Villages, 87, 97, 126-27, 137, 148, 153-54, 220, 373, 421, 427
Vote, right to, 188, 240, 447-48, 496, 498-99, 539

Walker, Horatio, 301-2, 553
Water, 25, 160, 161, 163-64, 220, 226, 365, 428-29, 432
Water transport, 63-64, 69, 71, 85-86, 111, 132, 142, 166, 340, 344-45, 349, 360, 367, 519
Watson, Homer, 299-302, 553-54, 560
Welfare, *see* Social security
Western Canada, 31-32, 38, 46, 54, 63-64, 67, 71, 73-74, 80-81, 85, 121, 147, 233, 236, 249, 251, 257-58, 272, 278, 297, 306, 337, 340-42, 349, 360, 382, 385, 394-95, 412-13, 423, 451, 463, 469, 501, 515, 518, 521
Westmount, 164, 305, 362, 392, 432
Women, 22, 122, 139, 150-51, 166-68, 174, 184-94, 200, 212-14, 216, 240, 398, 415, 417-19, 434, 441, 443-50, 455, 471, 473, 481, 498, 538

Working class, 24, 42, 117, 120, 141, 148-51, 157-58, 161, 176, 178-85, 189-92, 228, 238, 265, 267, 273-74, 277, 279, 306, 352, 398, 408-15, 417-20, 430, 432, 435, 453, 456, 458, 496-97, 528, 539-40, 543

Working conditions, 139, 150-51, 161, 166-69, 171-72, 182, 184-85, 189, 212, 225, 274, 410, 415, 417-18, 427-28, 443-44, 496, 539

Zouaves, papal, 204, 284